The Iliad of Homer by Homer

Translated by Alexander Pope

Alexander Pope was born on May 21st, 1688 in London into a Catholic family.

His education was affected by the recent Test Acts, upholding the status of the Church of England and banning Catholics from teaching. In effect this meant his formal education was over by the age of 12 and Pope was to now immerse himself in classical literature and languages and to, in effect, educate himself.

From this age too he also suffered from numerous health problems including a type of tuberculosis (Pott's disease) which resulted in a stunted, deformed body. Only to grow to a height of 4' 6", with a severe hunchback and complicated further by respiratory difficulties, high fevers, inflamed eyes and abdominal pain all of which served to further isolate him, initially, from society.

However his talent was evident to all. Best known for his satirical verse, his translations of Homer and the use of the heroic couplet, he is the second-most frequently quoted writer in The Oxford Dictionary of Quotations, after Shakespeare.

With the publication of Pastorals in 1709 followed by An Essay on Criticism (1711) and his most famous work The Rape of the Lock (1712; revised and enlarged in 1714) Pope became not only famous but wealthy.

His translations of the Iliad and the Odyssey further enhanced both reputation and purse. His engagement to produce an opulent new edition of Shakespeare met with a mixed reception. Pope attempted to "regularise" Shakespeare's metre and rewrote some of his verse and cut 1500 lines, that Pope considered to be beneath the Bard's standard, to mere footnotes.

Alexander Pope died on May 30th, 1744 at his villa at Twickenham (where he created his famous grotto and gardens) and was buried in the nave of the nearby Church of England Church of St Mary the Virgin.

Over the years and centuries since his death Pope's work has been in and out of favour but with this distance he is now truly recognised as one of England's greatest poets.

Index of Contents
INTRODUCTION
ALEXANDER POPE'S PREFACE TO THE ILIAD OF HOMER
BOOK I - ARGUMENT - THE CONTENTION OF ACHILLES AND AGAMEMNON
BOOK II - ARGUMENT - THE TRIAL OF THE ARMY, AND CATALOGUE OF THE FORCES
BOOK III - ARGUMENT - THE DUEL OF MENELAUS AND PARIS
BOOK IV - ARGUMENT - THE BREACH OF THE TRUCE, AND THE FIRST BATTLE
BOOK V - ARGUMENT - THE ACTS OF DIOMED

BOOK VI - ARGUMENT - THE EPISODES OF GLAUCUS AND DIOMED, AND OF HECTOR AND ANDROMACHE
BOOK VII - ARGUMENT - THE SINGLE COMBAT OF HECTOR AND AJAX
BOOK VIII - ARGUMENT - THE SECOND BATTLE, AND THE DISTRESS OF THE GREEKS
BOOK IX - ARGUMENT - THE EMBASSY TO ACHILLES
BOOK X - ARGUMENT - THE NIGHT-ADVENTURE OF DIOMED AND ULYSSES
BOOK XI - ARGUMENT - THE THIRD BATTLE, AND THE ACTS OF AGAMEMNON
BOOK XII - ARGUMENT - THE BATTLE AT THE GRECIAN WALL
BOOK XIII - ARGUMENT - THE FOURTH BATTLE CONTINUED, IN WHICH NEPTUNE ASSISTS THE GREEKS: THE ACTS OF IDOMENEUS
BOOK XIV - ARGUMENT - JUNO DECEIVES JUPITER BY THE GIRDLE OF VENUS
BOOK XV - ARGUMENT - THE FIFTH BATTLE AT THE SHIPS; AND THE ACTS OF AJAX
BOOK XVI - ARGUMENT - THE SIXTH BATTLE, THE ACTS AND DEATH OF PATROCLUS
BOOK XVII - ARGUMENT - THE SEVENTH BATTLE, FOR THE BODY OF PATROCLUS—THE ACTS OF MENELAUS
BOOK XVIII - ARGUMENT - THE GRIEF OF ACHILLES, AND NEW ARMOUR MADE HIM BY VULCAN
BOOK XIX - ARGUMENT - THE RECONCILIATION OF ACHILLES AND AGAMEMNON
BOOK XX - ARGUMENT - THE BATTLE OF THE GODS, AND THE ACTS OF ACHILLES
BOOK XXI - ARGUMENT - THE BATTLE IN THE RIVER SCAMANDER
BOOK XXII - ARGUMENT - THE DEATH OF HECTOR
BOOK XXIII - ARGUMENT - FUNERAL GAMES IN HONOUR OF PATROCLUS
BOOK XXIV - ARGUMENT - THE REDEMPTION OF THE BODY OF HECTOR
CONCLUDING NOTE
ALEXANDER POPE – A SHORT BIOGRAPHY
ALEXANDER POPE – A CONCISE BIBLIOGRAPHY: THE MAJOR WORKS

INTRODUCTION

Scepticism is as much the result of knowledge, as knowledge is of scepticism. To be content with what we at present know, is, for the most part, to shut our ears against conviction; since, from the very gradual character of our education, we must continually forget, and emancipate ourselves from, knowledge previously acquired; we must set aside old notions and embrace fresh ones; and, as we learn, we must be daily unlearning something which it has cost us no small labour and anxiety to acquire.

And this difficulty attaches itself more closely to an age in which progress has gained a strong ascendency over prejudice, and in which persons and things are, day by day, finding their real level, in lieu of their conventional value. The same principles which have swept away traditional abuses, and which are making rapid havoc among the revenues of sinecurists, and stripping the thin, tawdry veil from attractive superstitions, are working as actively in literature as in society. The credulity of one writer, or the partiality of another, finds as powerful a touchstone and as wholesome a chastisement in the healthy scepticism of a temperate class of antagonists, as the dreams of conservatism, or the impostures of pluralist sinecures in the Church. History and tradition, whether of ancient or comparatively recent times, are subjected to very different handling from that which the indulgence or credulity of former ages could allow. Mere statements are jealously watched, and the motives of the writer form as important an ingredient in the analysis of his history, as the facts he records. Probability is a powerful and troublesome test; and it is by this troublesome standard that a large portion of historical evidence is sifted. Consistency is no less pertinacious and exacting in its demands. In brief, to write a history, we must know more than mere facts. Human nature, viewed under an induction of extended experience, is the best help to the criticism of human history. Historical characters can only be estimated by the standard which human experience, whether actual or traditionary, has furnished. To form correct views of individuals we must regard them as forming parts of a great whole—we must measure them by their relation to the mass of beings by whom they are surrounded, and, in contemplating the incidents in their lives or condition which tradition has handed down to us, we must rather consider the general bearing of the whole narrative, than the respective probability of its details.

It is unfortunate for us, that, of some of the greatest men, we know least, and talk most. Homer, Socrates, and Shakespere have, perhaps, contributed more to the intellectual enlightenment of mankind than any other three writers who could be named, and yet the history of all three has given rise to a boundless ocean of discussion, which has left us little save the option of choosing which theory or theories we will follow. The personality of Shakespere is, perhaps, the only thing in which critics will allow us to believe without controversy; but upon everything else, even down to the authorship of plays, there is more or less of doubt and uncertainty. Of Socrates we know as little as the contradictions of Plato and Xenophon will allow us to know. He was one of the dramatis personae in two dramas as unlike in principles as in style. He appears as the enunciator of opinions as different in their tone as those of the writers who have handed them down. When we have read Plato or Xenophon, we think we know something of Socrates; when we have fairly read and examined both, we feel convinced that we are something worse than ignorant.

It has been an easy, and a popular expedient, of late years, to deny the personal or real existence of men and things whose life and condition were too much for our belief. This system—which has often comforted the religious sceptic, and substituted the consolations of Strauss for those of the New Testament—has been of incalculable value to the historical theorists of the last and present centuries. To question the existence of Alexander the Great, would be a more excusable act, than to believe in that of Romulus. To deny a fact related in Herodotus, because it is inconsistent with a theory developed from an Assyrian inscription which no two scholars read in the same way, is more pardonable, than to believe in the good-natured old king whom the elegant pen of Florian has idealized—Numa Pompilius.

Scepticism has attained its culminating point with respect to Homer, and the state of our Homeric knowledge may be described as a free permission to believe any theory, provided we throw overboard all written tradition, concerning the author or authors of the Iliad and Odyssey. What few authorities exist on the subject, are summarily dismissed, although the arguments appear to run in a circle. "This cannot be true, because it is not true; and, that is not true, because it cannot be true." Such seems to be the style, in which testimony upon testimony, statement upon statement, is consigned to denial and oblivion.

It is, however, unfortunate that the professed biographies of Homer are partly forgeries, partly freaks of ingenuity and imagination, in which truth is the requisite most wanting. Before taking a brief review of the Homeric theory in its present conditions, some notice must be taken of the treatise on the Life of Homer which has been attributed to Herodotus.

According to this document, the city of Cumae in Ćolia, was, at an early period, the seat of frequent immigrations from various parts of Greece. Among the immigrants was Menapolus, the son of Ithagenes. Although poor, he married, and the result of the union was a girl named Critheis. The girl was left an orphan at an early age, under the guardianship of Cleanax, of Argos. It is to the indiscretion of this maiden that we "are indebted for so much happiness." Homer was the first fruit of her juvenile frailty, and received the name of Melesigenes, from having been born near the river Meles, in Boeotia, whither Critheis had been transported in order to save her reputation.

"At this time," continues our narrative, "there lived at Smyrna a man named Phemius, a teacher of literature and music, who, not being married, engaged Critheis to manage his household, and spin the flax he received as the price of his scholastic labours. So satisfactory was her performance of this task, and so modest her conduct, that he made proposals of marriage, declaring himself, as a further inducement, willing to adopt her son, who, he asserted, would become a clever man, if he were carefully brought up."

They were married; careful cultivation ripened the talents which nature had bestowed, and Melesigenes soon surpassed his schoolfellows in every attainment, and, when older, rivalled his preceptor in wisdom. Phemius died, leaving him sole heir to his property, and his mother soon followed. Melesigenes carried on his adopted father's school with great success, exciting the admiration not only of the inhabitants of Smyrna, but also of the strangers whom the trade carried on there, especially in the exportation of corn, attracted to that city. Among these visitors, one Mentes, from Leucadia, the modern Santa Maura, who evinced a knowledge and intelligence rarely found in those times, persuaded Melesigenes to close his school, and accompany him on his travels. He promised not only to pay his expenses, but to furnish him with a further stipend, urging, that, "While he was yet young, it was fitting that he should see with his own eyes the countries and cities which might hereafter be the subjects of his discourses." Melesigenes consented, and set out with his patron, "examining all the curiosities of the countries they visited, and informing himself of everything by interrogating those whom he met." We may also suppose, that he wrote memoirs of all that he deemed worthy of preservation. Having set sail from Tyrrhenia and Iberia, they reached Ithaca. Here Melesigenes, who had already suffered in his eyes, became much worse, and Mentes, who was about to leave for Leucadia, left him to the medical superintendence of a friend of his, named Mentor, the son of Alcinor. Under his hospitable and intelligent host, Melesigenes rapidly became acquainted with the legends respecting Ulysses, which afterwards formed the subject of the Odyssey. The inhabitants of Ithaca assert, that it was here that Melesigenes became blind, but the Colophomans make their city the seat of that misfortune. He then returned to Smyrna, where he applied himself to the study of poetry.

But poverty soon drove him to Cumae. Having passed over the Hermaean plain, he arrived at Neon Teichos, the New Wall, a colony of Cumae. Here his misfortunes and poetical talent gained him the friendship of one Tychias, an armourer. "And up to my time," continued the author, "the inhabitants showed the place where he used to sit when giving a recitation of his verses, and they greatly honoured the spot. Here also a poplar grew, which they said had sprung up ever since Melesigenes arrived".

But poverty still drove him on, and he went by way of Larissa, as being the most convenient road. Here, the Cumans say, he composed an epitaph on Gordius, king of Phrygia, which has however, and with greater probability, been attributed to Cleobulus of Lindus.

Arrived at Cumae, he frequented the converzationes of the old men, and delighted all by the charms of his poetry. Encouraged by this favourable reception, he declared that, if they would allow him a public maintenance, he would render their city most gloriously renowned. They avowed their willingness to support him in the measure he proposed, and procured him an audience in the council. Having made the speech, with the purport of which our author has forgotten to acquaint us, he retired, and left them to debate respecting the answer to be given to his proposal. The greater part of the assembly seemed favourable to the poet's demand, but one man observed that "if they were to feed Homers, they would be encumbered with a multitude of useless people." "From this circumstance," says the writer, "Melesigenes acquired the name of Homer, for the Cumans call blind men Homers." With a love of economy, which shows how similar the world has always been in its treatment of literary men, the pension was denied, and the poet vented his disappointment in a wish that Cumoea might never produce a poet capable of giving it renown and glory.

At Phocoea, Homer was destined to experience another literary distress. One Thestorides, who aimed at the reputation of poetical genius, kept Homer in his own house, and allowed him a pittance, on condition of the verses of the poet passing in his name. Having collected sufficient poetry to be profitable, Thestorides, like some would-be-literary publishers, neglected the man whose brains he had sucked, and left him. At his departure, Homer is said to have observed: "O Thestorides, of the many things hidden from the knowledge of man, nothing is more unintelligible than the human heart."

Homer continued his career of difficulty and distress, until some Chian merchants, struck by the similarity of the verses they heard him recite, acquainted him with the fact that Thestorides was pursuing a profitable livelihood by the recital of the very same poems. This at once determined him to set out for Chios. No vessel happened then to be setting sail thither, but he found one ready to Start for Erythrae, a town of Ionia, which faces that island, and he prevailed upon the seamen to allow him to accompany them. Having embarked, he invoked a favourable wind, and prayed that he might be able to expose the imposture of Thestorides, who, by his breach of hospitality, had drawn down the wrath of Jove the Hospitable.

At Erythrae, Homer fortunately met with a person who had known him in Phocoea, by whose assistance he at length, after some difficulty, reached the little hamlet of Pithys. Here he met with an adventure, which we will continue in the words of our author. "Having set out from Pithys, Homer went on, attracted by the cries of some goats that were pasturing. The dogs barked on his approach, and he cried out. Glaucus (for that was the name of the goat-herd) heard his voice, ran up quickly, called off his dogs, and drove them away from Homer. For or some time he stood wondering how a blind man should have reached such a place alone, and what could be his design in coming. He then went up to him, and inquired who he was, and how he had come to desolate places and untrodden spots, and of what he stood in need. Homer, by recounting to him the whole history of his misfortunes, moved him with compassion; and he took him, and led him to his cot, and having lit a fire, bade him sup.

"The dogs, instead of eating, kept barking at the stranger, according to their usual habit. Whereupon Homer addressed Glaucus thus: O Glaucus, my friend, prythee attend to my behest. First give the dogs their supper at the doors of the hut: for so it is better, since, whilst they watch, nor thief nor wild beast will approach the fold.

Glaucus was pleased with the advice, and marvelled at its author. Having finished supper, they banqueted afresh on conversation, Homer narrating his wanderings, and telling of the cities he had visited.

At length they retired to rest; but on the following morning, Glaucus resolved to go to his master, and acquaint him with his meeting with Homer. Having left the goats in charge of a fellow-servant, he left Homer at home, promising to return quickly. Having arrived at Bolissus, a place near the farm, and finding his mate, he told him the whole story respecting Homer and his journey. He paid little attention to what he said, and blamed Glaucus for his stupidity in taking in and feeding maimed and enfeebled persons. However, he bade him bring the stranger to him.

Glaucus told Homer what had taken place, and bade him follow him, assuring him that good fortune would be the result. Conversation soon showed that the stranger was a man of much cleverness and general knowledge, and the Chian persuaded him to remain, and to undertake the charge of his children.

Besides the satisfaction of driving the impostor Thestorides from the island, Homer enjoyed considerable success as a teacher. In the town of Chios he established a school where he taught the precepts of poetry. "To this day," says Chandler, "the most curious remain is that which has been named, without reason, the School of Homer. It is on the coast, at some distance from the city, northward, and appears to have been an open temple of Cybele, formed on the top of a rock. The shape is oval, and in the centre is the image of the goddess, the head and an arm wanting. She is represented, as usual, sitting. The chair has a lion carved on each side, and on the back. The area is bounded by a low rim, or seat, and about five yards over. The whole is hewn out of the mountain, is rude, indistinct, and probably of the most remote antiquity."

So successful was this school, that Homer realised a considerable fortune. He married, and had two daughters, one of whom died single, the other married a Chian.

The following passage betrays the same tendency to connect the personages of the poems with the history of the poet, which has already been mentioned:—

"In his poetical compositions Homer displays great gratitude towards Mentor of Ithaca, in the Odyssey, whose name he has inserted in his poem as the companion of Ulysses, in return for the care taken of him when afflicted with blindness. He also testifies his gratitude to Phemius, who had given him both sustenance and instruction."

His celebrity continued to increase, and many persons advised him to visit Greece, whither his reputation had now extended. Having, it is said, made some additions to his poems calculated to please the vanity of the Athenians, of whose city he had hitherto made no mention, he sent out for Samos. Here being recognized by a Samian, who had met with him in Chios, he was handsomely received, and invited to join in celebrating the Apaturian festival. He recited some verses, which gave great satisfaction, and by singing the Eiresione at the New Moon festivals, he earned a subsistence, visiting the houses of the rich, with whose children he was very popular.

In the spring he sailed for Athens, and arrived at the island of Ios, now Ino, where he fell extremely ill, and died. It is said that his death arose from vexation, at not having been able to unravel an enigma proposed by some fishermen's children.

Such is, in brief, the substance of the earliest life of Homer we possess, and so broad are the evidences of its historical worthlessness, that it is scarcely necessary to point them out in detail. Let us now consider some of the opinions to which a persevering, patient, and learned—but by no means consistent—series of investigations has led. In doing so, I profess to bring forward statements, not to vouch for their reasonableness or probability.

"Homer appeared. The history of this poet and his works is lost in doubtful obscurity, as is the history of many of the first minds who have done honour to humanity, because they rose amidst darkness. The majestic stream of his song, blessing and fertilizing, flows like the Nile, through many lands and nations; and, like the sources of the Nile, its fountains will ever remain concealed."

Such are the words in which one of the most judicious German critics has eloquently described the uncertainty in which the whole of the Homeric question is involved. With no less truth and feeling he proceeds:—

"It seems here of chief importance to expect no more than the nature of things makes possible. If the period of tradition in history is the region of twilight, we should not expect in it perfect light. The creations of genius always seem like miracles, because they are, for the most part, created far out of the reach of observation. If we were in possession of all the historical testimonies, we never could wholly explain the origin of the Iliad and the Odyssey; for their origin, in all essential points, must have remained the secret of the poet."

From this criticism, which shows as much insight into the depths of human nature as into the minute wire-drawings of scholastic investigation, let us pass on to the main question at issue. Was Homer an individual? or were the Iliad and Odyssey the result of an ingenious arrangement of fragments by earlier poets?

Well has Landor remarked: "Some tell us there were twenty Homers; some deny that there was ever one. It were idle and foolish to shake the contents of a vase, in order to let them settle at last. We are perpetually labouring to destroy our delights, our composure, our devotion to superior power. Of all the animals on earth we least know what is good for us. My opinion is, that what is best for us is our admiration of good. No man living venerates Homer more than I do."

But, greatly as we admire the generous enthusiasm which rests contented with the poetry on which its best impulses had been nurtured and fostered, without seeking to destroy the vividness of first impressions by minute analysis—our editorial office compels us to give some attention to the doubts and difficulties with which the Homeric question is beset, and to entreat our reader, for a brief period, to prefer his judgment to his imagination, and to condescend to dry details.

Before, however, entering into particulars respecting the question of this unity of the Homeric poems, (at least of the Iliad,) I must express my sympathy with the sentiments expressed in the following remarks:—

"We cannot but think the universal admiration of its unity by the better, the poetic age of Greece, almost conclusive testimony to its original composition. It was not till the age of the grammarians that its primitive integrity was called in question; nor is it injustice to assert, that the minute and analytical spirit of a grammarian is not the best qualification for the profound feeling, the comprehensive conception of an harmonious whole. The most exquisite anatomist may be no judge of the symmetry of the human frame: and we would take the opinion of Chantrey or Westmacott on the proportions and general beauty of a form, rather than that of Mr. Brodie or Sir Astley Cooper.

"There is some truth, though some malicious exaggeration, in the lines of Pope.—

"'The critic eye—that microscope of wit

Sees hairs and pores, examines bit by bit,
How parts relate to parts, or they to whole
The body's harmony, the beaming soul,
Are things which Kuster, Burmann, Wasse, shall see,
When man's whole frame is obvious to a flea.'"

Long was the time which elapsed before any one dreamt of questioning the unity of the authorship of the Homeric poems. The grave and cautious Thucydides quoted without hesitation the Hymn to Apollo, the authenticity of which has been already disclaimed by modern critics. Longinus, in an oft quoted passage, merely expressed an opinion touching the comparative inferiority of the Odyssey to the Iliad, and, among a mass of ancient authors, whose very names it would be tedious to detail, no suspicion of the personal non-existence of Homer ever arose. So far, the voice of antiquity seems to be in favour of our early ideas on the subject; let us now see what are the discoveries to which more modern investigations lay claim.

At the end of the seventeenth century, doubts had begun to awaken on the subject, and we find Bentley remarking that "Homer wrote a sequel of songs and rhapsodies, to be sung by himself, for small comings and good cheer, at festivals and other days of merriment. These loose songs were not collected together, in the form of an epic poem, till about Peisistratus' time, about five hundred years after."

Two French writers—Hedelin and Perrault—avowed a similar scepticism on the subject; but it is in the "Scienza Nuova" of Battista Vico, that we first meet with the germ of the theory, subsequently defended by Wolf with so much learning and acuteness. Indeed, it is with the Wolfian theory that we have chiefly to deal, and with the following bold hypothesis, which we will detail in the words of Grote—

"Half a century ago, the acute and valuable Prolegomena of F. A. Wolf, turning to account the Venetian Scholia, which had then been recently published, first opened philosophical discussion as to the history of the Homeric text. A considerable part of that dissertation (though by no means the whole) is employed in vindicating the position, previously announced by Bentley, amongst others, that the separate constituent portions of the Iliad and Odyssey had not been cemented together into any compact body and unchangeable order, until the days of Peisistratus, in the sixth century before Christ. As a step towards that conclusion, Wolf maintained that no written copies of either poem could be shown to have existed during the earlier times, to which their composition is referred; and that without writing, neither the perfect symmetry of so complicated a work could have been originally conceived by any poet, nor, if realized by him, transmitted with assurance to posterity. The absence of easy and convenient writing, such as must be indispensably supposed for long manuscripts, among the early Greeks, was thus one of the points in Wolf's case against the primitive integrity of the Iliad and Odyssey. By Nitzsch, and other leading opponents of Wolf, the connection of the one with the other seems to have been accepted as he originally put it; and it has been considered incumbent on those who defended the ancient aggregate character of the Iliad and Odyssey, to maintain that they were written poems from the beginning.

"To me it appears, that the architectonic functions ascribed by Wolf to Peisistratus and his associates, in reference to the Homeric poems, are nowise admissible. But much would undoubtedly be gained towards that view of the question, if it could be shown, that, in order to controvert it, we were driven to the necessity of admitting long written poems, in the ninth century before the Christian aera. Few things, in my opinion, can be more improbable; and Mr. Payne Knight, opposed as he is to the Wolfian hypothesis, admits this no less than Wolf himself. The traces of writing in Greece, even in the seventh century before the Christian aera, are exceedingly trifling. We have no remaining inscription earlier than the fortieth Olympiad, and the early inscriptions are rude and unskilfully executed; nor can we even assure ourselves whether Archilochus, Simonides of Amorgus, Kallinus, Tyrtaeus, Xanthus, and the other early elegiac and lyric poets, committed their compositions to writing, or at what time the practice of doing so became familiar. The first positive ground which authorizes us to presume the existence of a manuscript of Homer, is in the famous ordinance of Solon, with regard to the rhapsodies at the Panathenaea: but for what length of time previously manuscripts had existed, we are unable to say.

"Those who maintain the Homeric poems to have been written from the beginning, rest their case, not upon positive proofs, nor yet upon the existing habits of society with regard to poetry—for they admit generally that the Iliad and Odyssey were not read, but recited and heard,—but upon the supposed necessity that there must have been manuscripts to ensure the preservation of the poems—the unassisted memory of reciters being neither sufficient nor trustworthy. But here we only escape a smaller difficulty by running into a greater; for the existence of trained bards, gifted with extraordinary memory, is far less astonishing than that of long manuscripts, in an age essentially non-reading and non-writing, and when even suitable instruments and materials for the process are not obvious. Moreover, there is a strong positive reason for believing that the bard was under no necessity of refreshing his memory by consulting a manuscript; for if such had been the fact, blindness would have been a disqualification for the profession, which we know that it was not, as well from the example of Demodokus, in the Odyssey, as from that of the blind bard of Chios, in the Hymn to the Delian Apollo, whom Thucydides, as well as the general tenor of Grecian legend, identifies with Homer himself. The author of that hymn, be he who he may, could never have described a blind man as attaining the utmost perfection in his art, if he had been conscious that the memory of the bard was only maintained by constant reference to the manuscript in his chest."

The loss of the digamma, that crux of critics, that quicksand upon which even the acumen of Bentley was shipwrecked, seems to prove beyond a doubt, that the pronunciation of the Greek language had undergone a considerable change. Now it is certainly difficult to suppose that the Homeric poems could have suffered by this change, had written copies been preserved. If Chaucer's poetry, for instance, had not been written, it could only have come down to us in a softened form, more like the effeminate version of Dryden, than the rough, quaint, noble original.

"At what period," continues Grote, "these poems, or indeed any other Greek poems, first began to be written, must be matter of conjecture, though there is ground for assurance that it was before the time of Solon. If, in the absence of evidence, we may venture upon naming any more determinate period, the question a once suggests itself, What were the purposes which, in that state of society, a manuscript at its first commencement must have been intended to answer? For whom was a written Iliad necessary? Not for the rhapsodes; for with them it was not only planted in the memory, but also interwoven with the feelings, and conceived in conjunction with all those flexions and intonations of voice, pauses, and other oral artifices which were required for emphatic delivery, and which the naked manuscript could never reproduce. Not for the general public—they were accustomed to receive it with its rhapsodic delivery, and with its accompaniments of a solemn and crowded festival. The only persons for whom the written Iliad would be suitable would be a select few; studious and curious men; a class of readers capable of analyzing the complicated emotions which they had experienced as hearers in the crowd, and who would, on perusing the written words, realize in their imaginations a sensible portion of the impression communicated by the reciter. Incredible as the statement may seem in an age like the present, there is in all early societies, and there was in early Greece, a time when no such reading class existed. If we could discover at what time such a class first began to be formed, we should be able to make a guess at the time when the old epic poems were first committed to writing. Now the period which may with the greatest probability be fixed upon as having first witnessed the formation even of the narrowest reading class in Greece, is the middle of the seventh century before the Christian aera (B.C. 660 to B.C. 630), the age of Terpander, Kallinus, Archilochus, Simonides of Amorgus, &c. I ground this supposition on the change then operated in the character and tendencies of Grecian poetry and music—the elegiac and the iambic measures having been introduced as rivals to the primitive hexameter, and poetical compositions having been transferred from the epical past to the affairs of present and real life. Such a change was important at a time when poetry was the only known mode of publication (to use a modern phrase not altogether suitable, yet the nearest approaching to the sense). It argued a new way of looking at the old epical treasures of the people as well as a thirst for new poetical effect; and the men who stood forward in it, may well be considered as desirous to study, and competent to criticize, from their own individual point of view, the written words of the Homeric rhapsodies, just as we are told that Kallinus both noticed and eulogized the Thebais as the production of Homer. There seems, therefore, ground for conjecturing that (for the use of this newly-formed and important, but very narrow class), manuscripts of the Homeric poems and other old epics,—the Thebais and the Cypria, as well as the Iliad and the Odyssey,—began to be compiled towards the middle of the seventh century (B.C. 1); and the opening of Egypt to Grecian commerce, which took place about the same period, would furnish increased facilities for obtaining the requisite papyrus to write upon. A reading class, when once formed, would doubtless slowly increase, and the number of manuscripts along with it; so that before the time of Solon, fifty years afterwards, both readers and manuscripts, though still comparatively few, might have attained a certain recognized authority, and formed a tribunal of reference against the carelessness of individual rhapsodes."

But even Peisistratus has not been suffered to remain in possession of the credit, and we cannot help feeling the force of the following observations—

"There are several incidental circumstances which, in our opinion, throw some suspicion over the whole history of the Peisistratid compilation, at least over the theory, that the Iliad was cast into its present stately and harmonious form by the directions of the Athenian ruler. If the great poets, who flourished at the bright period of Grecian song, of which, alas! we have inherited little more than the fame, and the faint echo, if Stesichorus, Anacreon, and Simonides were employed in the noble task of compiling the Iliad and Odyssey, so much must have been done to arrange, to connect, to harmonize, that it is almost incredible, that stronger marks of Athenian manufacture should not remain. Whatever occasional anomalies may be detected, anomalies which no doubt arise out of our own ignorance of the language of the Homeric age, however the irregular use of the digamma may have perplexed our Bentleys, to whom the name of Helen is said to have caused as much disquiet and distress as the fair one herself among the heroes of her age, however Mr. Knight may have failed in reducing the Homeric language to its primitive form; however, finally, the Attic dialect may not have assumed all its more marked and distinguishing characteristics—still it is difficult to suppose that the language, particularly in the joinings and transitions, and connecting parts, should not more clearly betray the incongruity between the more ancient and modern forms of expression. It is not quite in character with such a period to imitate an antique style, in order to piece out an imperfect poem in the character of the original, as Sir Walter Scott has done in his continuation of Sir Tristram.

"If, however, not even such faint and indistinct traces of Athenian compilation are discoverable in the language of the poems, the total absence of Athenian national feeling is perhaps no less worthy of observation. In later, and it may fairly be suspected in earlier times, the Athenians were more than ordinarily jealous of the fame of their ancestors. But, amid all the traditions of the glories of early

Greece embodied in the Iliad, the Athenians play a most subordinate and insignificant part. Even the few passages which relate to their ancestors, Mr. Knight suspects to be interpolations. It is possible, indeed, that in its leading outline, the Iliad may be true to historic fact, that in the great maritime expedition of western Greece against the rival and half-kindred empire of the Laomedontiadae, the chieftain of Thessaly, from his valour and the number of his forces, may have been the most important ally of the Peloponnesian sovereign; the preeminent value of the ancient poetry on the Trojan war may thus have forced the national feeling of the Athenians to yield to their taste. The songs which spoke of their own great ancestor were, no doubt, of far inferior sublimity and popularity, or, at first sight, a Theseid would have been much more likely to have emanated from an Athenian synod of compilers of ancient song, than an Achilleid or an Olysseid. Could France have given birth to a Tasso, Tancred would have been the hero of the Jerusalem. If, however, the Homeric ballads, as they are sometimes called, which related the wrath of Achilles, with all its direful consequences, were so far superior to the rest of the poetic cycle, as to admit no rivalry,—it is still surprising, that throughout the whole poem the callida junctura should never betray the workmanship of an Athenian hand, and that the national spirit of a race, who have at a later period not inaptly been compared to our self admiring neighbours, the French, should submit with lofty self denial to the almost total exclusion of their own ancestors—or, at least, to the questionable dignity of only having produced a leader tolerably skilled in the military tactics of his age."

To return to the Wolfian theory. While it is to be confessed, that Wolf's objections to the primitive integrity of the Iliad and Odyssey have never been wholly got over, we cannot help discovering that they have failed to enlighten us as to any substantial point, and that the difficulties with which the whole subject is beset, are rather augmented than otherwise, if we admit his hypothesis. Nor is Lachmann's modification of his theory any better. He divides the first twenty-two books of the Iliad into sixteen different songs, and treats as ridiculous the belief that their amalgamation into one regular poem belongs to a period earlier than the age of Peisistratus. This, as Grote observes, "explains the gaps and contradictions in the narrative, but it explains nothing else." Moreover, we find no contradictions warranting this belief, and the so-called sixteen poets concur in getting rid of the following leading men in the first battle after the secession of Achilles: Elphenor, chief of the Euboeans; Tlepolemus, of the Rhodians; Pandarus, of the Lycians; Odius, of the Halizonians; Pirous and Acamas, of the Thracians. None of these heroes again make their appearance, and we can but agree with Colonel Mure, that "it seems strange that any number of independent poets should have so harmoniously dispensed with the services of all six in the sequel." The discrepancy, by which Pylaemenes, who is represented as dead in the fifth book, weeps at his son's funeral in the thirteenth, can only be regarded as the result of an interpolation.

Grote, although not very distinct in stating his own opinions on the subject, has done much to clearly show the incongruity of the Wolfian theory, and of Lachmann's modifications with the character of Peisistratus. But he has also shown, and we think with equal success, that the two questions relative to the primitive unity of these poems, or, supposing that impossible, the unison of these parts by Peisistratus, and not before his time, are essentially distinct. In short, "a man may believe the Iliad to have been put together out of pre-existing songs, without recognising the age of Peisistratus as the period of its first compilation." The friends or literary employes of Peisistratus must have found an Iliad that was already ancient, and the silence of the Alexandrine critics respecting the Peisistratic "recension," goes far to prove, that, among the numerous manuscripts they examined, this was either wanting, or thought unworthy of attention.

"Moreover," he continues, "the whole tenor of the poems themselves confirms what is here remarked. There is nothing, either in the Iliad or Odyssey, which savours of modernism, applying that term to the age of Peisistratus—nothing which brings to our view the alterations brought about by two centuries, in the Greek language, the coined money, the habits of writing and reading, the despotisms and republican governments, the close military array, the improved construction of ships, the Amphiktyonic convocations, the mutual frequentation of religious festivals, the Oriental and Egyptian veins of religion, &c., familiar to the latter epoch. These alterations Onomakritus, and the other literary friends of Peisistratus, could hardly have failed to notice, even without design, had they then, for the first time, undertaken the task of piecing together many self existent epics into one large aggregate. Everything in the two great Homeric poems, both in substance and in language, belongs to an age two or three centuries earlier than Peisistratus. Indeed, even the interpolations (or those passages which, on the best grounds, are pronounced to be such) betray no trace of the sixth century before Christ, and may well have been heard by Archilochus and Kallinus—in some cases even by Arktinus and Hesiod—as genuine Homeric matter. As far as the evidences on the case, as well internal as external, enable us to judge, we seem warranted in believing that the Iliad and Odyssey were recited substantially as they now stand (always allowing for paitial divergences of text and interpolations) in 776 B.C., our first trustworthy mark of Grecian time; and this ancient date, let it be added, as it is the best-authenticated fact, so it is also the most important attribute of the Homeric poems, considered in reference to Grecian history; for they thus afford us an insight into the anti-historical character of the Greeks, enabling us to trace the subsequent forward march of the nation, and to seize instructive contrasts between their former and their later condition."

On the whole, I am inclined to believe, that the labours of Peisistratus were wholly of an editorial character, although, I must confess, that I can lay down nothing respecting the extent of his labours. At the same time, so far from believing that the composition or primary arrangement of these poems, in their present form, was the work of Peisistratus, I am rather persuaded that the fine taste and elegant mind of that Athenian would lead him to preserve an ancient and traditional order of the poems, rather than to patch and re-construct them according to a fanciful hypothesis. I will not repeat the many discussions respecting whether the poems were written or not, or whether the art of writing was known in the time of their reputed author. Suffice it to say, that the more we read, the less satisfied we are upon either subject.

I cannot, however, help thinking, that the story which attributes the preservation of these poems to Lycurgus, is little else than a version of the same story as that of Peisistratus, while its historical probability must be measured by that of many others relating to the Spartan Confucius.

I will conclude this sketch of the Homeric theories, with an attempt, made by an ingenious friend, to unite them into something like consistency. It is as follows:—

"No doubt the common soldiers of that age had, like the common sailors of some fifty years ago, some one qualified to 'discourse in excellent music' among them. Many of these, like those of the negroes in the United States, were extemporaneous, and allusive to events passing around them. But what was passing around them? The grand events of a spirit-stirring war; occurrences likely to impress themselves, as the mystical legends of former times had done, upon their memory; besides which, a retentive memory was deemed a virtue of the first water, and was cultivated accordingly in those ancient times. Ballads at first, and down to the beginning of the war with Troy, were merely recitations, with an intonation. Then followed a species of recitative, probably with an intoned burden. Tune next followed, as it aided the memory considerably.

"It was at this period, about four hundred years after the war, that a poet flourished of the name of Melesigenes, or Moeonides, but most probably the former. He saw that these ballads might be made of great utility to his purpose of writing a poem on the social position of Hellas, and, as a collection, he published these lays, connecting them by a tale of his own. This poem now exists, under the title of the 'Odyssea.' The author, however, did not affix his own name to the poem, which, in fact, was, great part of it, remodelled from the archaic dialect of Crete, in which tongue the ballads were found by him. He therefore called it the poem of Homeros, or the Collector; but this is rather a proof of his modesty and talent, than of his mere drudging arrangement of other people's ideas; for, as Grote has finely observed, arguing for the unity of authorship, 'a great poet might have re-cast pre-existing separate songs into one comprehensive whole; but no mere arrangers or compilers would be competent to do so.'

"While employed on the wild legend of Odysseus, he met with a ballad, recording the quarrel of Achilles and Agamemnon. His noble mind seized the hint that there presented itself, and the Achilleis grew under his hand. Unity of design, however, caused him to publish the poem under the same pseudonyme as his former work: and the disjointed lays of the ancient bards were joined together, like those relating to the Cid, into a chronicle history, named the Iliad. Melesigenes knew that the poem was destined to be a lasting one, and so it has proved; but, first, the poems were destined to undergo many vicissitudes and corruptions, by the people who took to singing them in the streets, assemblies, and agoras. However, Solon first, and then Peisistratus, and afterwards Aristoteles and others, revised the poems, and restored the works of Melesigenes Homeros to their original integrity in a great measure."

Having thus given some general notion of the strange theories which have developed themselves respecting this most interesting subject, I must still express my conviction as to the unity of the authorship of the Homeric poems. To deny that many corruptions and interpolations disfigure them, and that the intrusive hand of the poetasters may here and there have inflicted a wound more serious than the negligence of the copyist, would be an absurd and captious assumption, but it is to a higher criticism that we must appeal, if we would either understand or enjoy these poems. In maintaining the authenticity and personality of their one author, be he Homer or Melesigenes, quocunque nomine vocari eum jus fasque sit, I feel conscious that, while the whole weight of historical evidence is against the hypothesis which would assign these great works to a plurality of authors, the most powerful internal evidence, and that which springs from the deepest and most immediate impulse of the soul, also speaks eloquently to the contrary.

The minutiae of verbal criticism I am far from seeking to despise. Indeed, considering the character of some of my own books, such an attempt would be gross inconsistency. But, while I appreciate its importance in a philological view, I am inclined to set little store on its aesthetic value, especially in poetry. Three parts of the emendations made upon poets are mere alterations, some of which, had they been suggested to the author by his Maecenas or Africanus, he would probably have adopted. Moreover, those who are most exact in laying down rules of verbal criticism and interpretation, are often least competent to carry out their own precepts. Grammarians are not poets by profession, but may be so per accidens. I do not at this moment remember two emendations on Homer, calculated to substantially improve the poetry of a passage, although a mass of remarks, from Herodotus down to Loewe, have given us the history of a thousand minute points, without which our Greek knowledge would be gloomy and jejune.

But it is not on words only that grammarians, mere grammarians, will exercise their elaborate and often tiresome ingenuity. Binding down an heroic or dramatic poet to the block upon which they have previously dissected his words and sentences, they proceed to use the axe and the pruning knife by wholesale, and inconsistent in everything but their wish to make out a case of unlawful affiliation, they cut out book after book, passage after passage, till the author is reduced to a collection of fragments, or till those, who fancied they possessed the works of some great man, find that they have been put off with a vile counterfeit got up at second hand. If we compare the theories of Knight, Wolf, Lachmann, and others, we shall feel better satisfied of the utter uncertainty of criticism than of the apocryphal position of Homer. One rejects what another considers the turning-point of his theory. One cuts a supposed knot by expunging what another would explain by omitting something else.

Nor is this morbid species of sagacity by any means to be looked upon as a literary novelty. Justus Lipsius, a scholar of no ordinary skill, seems to revel in the imaginary discovery, that the tragedies attributed to Seneca are by four different authors. Now, I will venture to assert, that these tragedies are so uniform, not only in their borrowed phraseology—a phraseology with which writers like Boethius and Saxo Grammaticus were more charmed than ourselves—in their freedom from real poetry, and last, but not least, in an ultra-refined and consistent abandonment of good taste, that few writers of the present day would question the capabilities of the same gentleman, be he Seneca or not, to produce not only these, but a great many more equally bad. With equal sagacity, Father Hardouin astonished the world with the startling announcement that the Ćneid of Virgil, and the satires of Horace, were literary deceptions. Now, without wishing to say one word of disrespect against the industry and learning—nay, the refined acuteness—which scholars, like Wolf, have bestowed upon this subject, I must express my fears, that many of our modern Homeric theories will become matter for the surprise and entertainment, rather than the instruction, of posterity. Nor can I help thinking, that the literary history of more recent times will account for many points of difficulty in the transmission of the Iliad and Odyssey to a period so remote from that of their first creation.

I have already expressed my belief that the labours of Peisistratus were of a purely editorial character; and there seems no more reason why corrupt and imperfect editions of Homer may not have been abroad in his day, than that the poems of Valerius Flaccus and Tibullus should have given so much trouble to Poggio, Scaliger, and others. But, after all, the main fault in all the Homeric theories is, that they demand too great a sacrifice of those feelings to which poetry most powerfully appeals, and which are its most fitting judges. The ingenuity which has sought to rob us of the name and existence of Homer, does too much violence to that inward emotion, which makes our whole soul yearn with love and admiration for the blind bard of Chios. To believe the author of the Iliad a mere compiler, is to degrade the powers of human invention; to elevate analytical judgment at the expense of the most ennobling impulses of the soul; and to forget the ocean in the contemplation of a polypus. There is a catholicity, so to speak, in the very name of Homer. Our faith in the author of the Iliad may be a mistaken one, but as yet nobody has taught us a better.

While, however, I look upon the belief in Homer as one that has nature herself for its mainspring; while I can join with old Ennius in believing in Homer as the ghost, who, like some patron saint, hovers round the bed of the poet, and even bestows rare gifts from that wealth of imagination which a host of imitators could not exhaust,—still I am far from wishing to deny that the author of these great poems found a rich fund of tradition, a well-stocked mythical storehouse from whence he might derive both subject and embellishment. But it is one thing to use existing romances in the embellishment of a poem, another to patch up the poem itself from such materials. What consistency of style and execution can be hoped for from such an attempt? or, rather, what bad taste and tedium will not be the infallible result?

A blending of popular legends, and a free use of the songs of other bards, are features perfectly consistent with poetical originality. In fact, the most original writer is still drawing upon outward impressions—nay, even his own thoughts are a kind of secondary agents which support and feed the impulses of imagination. But unless there be some grand pervading principle—some invisible, yet most distinctly stamped archetypus of the great whole, a poem like the Iliad can never come to the birth. Traditions the most picturesque, episodes the most pathetic, local associations teeming with the thoughts of gods and great men, may crowd in one mighty vision, or reveal themselves in more substantial forms to the mind of the poet; but, except the power to create a grand whole, to which these shall be but as details and embellishments, be present, we shall have nought but a scrap-book, a parterre filled with flowers and weeds strangling each other in their wild redundancy: we shall have a cento of rags and tatters, which will require little acuteness to detect.

Sensible as I am of the difficulty of disproving a negative, and aware as I must be of the weighty grounds there are for opposing my belief, it still seems to me that the Homeric question is one that is reserved for a higher criticism than it has often obtained. We are not by nature intended to know all things; still less, to compass the powers by which the greatest blessings of life have been placed at our disposal. Were faith no virtue, then we might indeed wonder why God willed our ignorance on any matter. But we are too well taught the contrary lesson; and it seems as though our faith should be especially tried touching the men and the events which have wrought most influence upon the condition of humanity. And there is a kind of sacredness attached to the memory of the great and the good, which seems to bid us repulse the scepticism which would allegorize their existence into a pleasing apologue, and measure the giants of intellect by an homeopathic dynameter.

Long and habitual reading of Homer appears to familiarize our thoughts even to his incongruities; or rather, if we read in a right spirit and with a heartfelt appreciation, we are too much dazzled, too deeply wrapped in admiration of the whole, to dwell upon the minute spots which mere analysis can discover. In reading an heroic poem we must transform ourselves into heroes of the time being, we in imagination must fight over the same battles, woo the same loves, burn with the same sense of injury, as an Achilles or a Hector. And if we can but attain this degree of enthusiasm (and less enthusiasm will scarcely suffice for the reading of Homer), we shall feel that the poems of Homer are not only the work of one writer, but of the greatest writer that ever touched the hearts of men by the power of song.

And it was this supposed unity of authorship which gave these poems their powerful influence over the minds of the men of old. Heeren, who is evidently little disposed in favour of modern theories, finely observes:—

"It was Homer who formed the character of the Greek nation. No poet has ever, as a poet, exercised a similar influence over his countrymen. Prophets, lawgivers, and sages have formed the character of other nations; it was reserved to a poet to form that of the Greeks. This is a feature in their character which was not wholly erased even in the period of their degeneracy. When lawgivers and sages appeared in Greece, the work of the poet had already been accomplished; and they paid homage to his superior genius. He held up before his nation the mirror, in which they were to behold the world of gods and heroes no less than of feeble mortals, and to behold them reflected with purity and truth. His poems are founded on the first feeling of human nature; on the love of children, wife, and country; on that passion which outweighs all others, the love of glory. His songs were poured forth from a breast which sympathized with all the feelings of man; and therefore they enter, and will continue to enter, every breast which cherishes the same sympathies. If it is granted to his immortal spirit, from another heaven than any of which he dreamed on earth, to look down on his race, to see the nations from the fields of Asia to the forests of Hercynia, performing pilgrimages to the fountain which his magic wand caused to flow; if it is permitted to him to view the vast assemblage of grand, of elevated, of glorious productions, which had been called into being by means of his songs; wherever his immortal spirit may reside, this alone would suffice to complete his happiness."

Can we contemplate that ancient monument, on which the "Apotheosis of Homer" is depictured, and not feel how much of pleasing association, how much that appeals most forcibly and most distinctly to our minds, is lost by the admittance of any theory but our old tradition? The more we read, and the more we think—think as becomes the readers of Homer,—the more rooted becomes the conviction that the Father of Poetry gave us this rich inheritance, whole and entire. Whatever were the means of its preservation, let us rather be thankful for the treasury of taste and eloquence thus laid open to our use, than seek to make it a mere centre around which to drive a series of theories, whose wildness is only equalled by their inconsistency with each other.

As the hymns, and some other poems usually ascribed to Homer, are not included in Pope's translation, I will content myself with a brief account of the Battle of the Frogs and Mice, from the pen of a writer who has done it full justice:—

"This poem," says Coleridge, "is a short mock-heroic of ancient date. The text varies in different editions, and is obviously disturbed and corrupt to a great degree; it is commonly said to have been a juvenile essay of Homer's genius; others have attributed it to the same Pigrees, mentioned above, and whose reputation for humour seems to have invited the appropriation of any piece of ancient wit, the author of which was uncertain; so little did the Greeks, before the age of the Ptolemies, know or care about that department of criticism employed in determining the genuineness of ancient writings. As to this little poem being a youthful prolusion of Homer, it seems sufficient to say that from the beginning to the end it is a plain and palpable parody, not only of the general spirit, but of the numerous passages of the Iliad itself; and even, if no such intention to parody were discernible in it, the objection would still remain, that to suppose a work of mere burlesque to be the primary effort of poetry in a simple age, seems to reverse that order in the development of national taste, which the history of every other people in Europe, and of many in Asia, has almost ascertained to be a law of the human mind; it is in a state of society much more refined and permanent than that described in the Iliad, that any popularity would attend such a ridicule of war and the gods as is contained in this poem; and the fact of there having existed three other poems of the same kind attributed, for aught we can see, with as much reason to Homer, is a strong inducement to believe that none of them were of the Homeric age. Knight infers from the usage of the word deltos, "writing tablet," instead of diphthera, "skin," which, according to Herod. 5, 58, was the material employed by the Asiatic Greeks for that purpose, that this poem was another offspring of Attic ingenuity; and generally that the familiar mention of the cock (v. 191) is a strong argument against so ancient a date for its composition."

Having thus given a brief account of the poems comprised in Pope's design, I will now proceed to make a few remarks on his translation, and on my own purpose in the present edition.

Pope was not a Grecian. His whole education had been irregular, and his earliest acquaintance with the poet was through the version of Ogilby. It is not too much to say that his whole work bears the impress of a disposition to be satisfied with the general sense, rather than to dive deeply into the minute and delicate features of language. Hence his whole work is to be looked upon rather as an elegant paraphrase than a translation. There are, to be sure, certain conventional anecdotes, which prove that Pope consulted various friends, whose classical attainments were sounder than his own, during the undertaking; but it is probable that these examinations were the result rather of the contradictory versions already existing, than of a desire to make a perfect transcript of the original. And in those days, what is called literal translation was less cultivated than at present. If something like the general sense could be decorated with the easy gracefulness of a practised poet; if the charms of metrical cadence and a pleasing fluency could be made consistent with a fair interpretation of the poet's meaning, his words were less jealously sought for, and those who could read so good a poem as Pope's Iliad had fair reason to be satisfied.

It would be absurd, therefore, to test Pope's translation by our own advancing knowledge of the original text. We must be content to look at it as a most delightful work in itself,—a work which is as much a part of English literature as Homer himself is of Greek. We must not be torn from our kindly associations with the old Iliad, that once was our most cherished companion, or our most looked-for prize, merely because Buttmann, Loewe, and Liddell have made us so much more accurate as to amphikupellon being an adjective, and not a substantive. Far be it from us to defend the faults of Pope, especially when we think of Chapman's fine, bold, rough old English;—far be it from, us to hold up his translation as what a translation of Homer might be. But we can still dismiss Pope's Iliad to the hands of our readers, with the consciousness that they must have read a very great number of books before they have read its fellow.

As to the Notes accompanying the present volume, they are drawn up without pretension, and mainly with the view of helping the general reader. Having some little time since translated all the works of Homer for another publisher, I might have brought a large amount of accumulated matter, sometimes of a critical character, to bear upon the text. But Pope's version was no field for such a display; and my purpose was to touch briefly on antiquarian or mythological allusions, to notice occasionally some departures from the original, and to give a few parallel passages from our English Homer, Milton. In the latter task I cannot pretend to novelty, but I trust that my other annotations, while utterly disclaiming high scholastic views, will be found to convey as much as is wanted; at least, as far as the necessary limits of these volumes could be expected to admit. To write a commentary on Homer is not my present aim; but if I have made Pope's translation a little more entertaining and instructive to a mass of miscellaneous readers, I shall consider my wishes satisfactorily accomplished.

THEODORE ALOIS BUCKLEY
Christ Church.

ALEXANDER POPE'S PREFACE TO THE ILIAD OF HOMER

Homer is universally allowed to have had the greatest invention of any writer whatever. The praise of judgment Virgil has justly contested with him, and others may have their pretensions as to particular excellences; but his invention remains yet unrivalled. Nor is it a wonder if he has ever been acknowledged the greatest of poets, who most excelled in that which is the very foundation of poetry. It is the invention that, in different degrees, distinguishes all great geniuses: the utmost stretch of human study, learning, and industry, which masters everything besides, can never attain to this. It furnishes art with all her materials, and without it judgment itself can at best but "steal wisely:" for art is only like a prudent steward that lives on managing the riches of nature. Whatever praises may be given to works of judgment, there is not even a single beauty in them to which the invention must not contribute: as in the most regular gardens, art can only reduce beauties of nature to more regularity, and such a figure, which the common eye may better take in, and is, therefore, more entertained with. And, perhaps, the reason why common critics are inclined to prefer a judicious and methodical genius to a great and fruitful one, is, because they find it easier for themselves to pursue their observations through a uniform and bounded walk of art, than to comprehend the vast and various extent of nature.

Our author's work is a wild paradise, where, if we cannot see all the beauties so distinctly as in an ordered garden, it is only because the number of them is infinitely greater. It is like a copious nursery, which contains the seeds and first productions of every kind, out of which those who followed him have but selected some particular plants, each according to his fancy, to cultivate and beautify. If some things are too luxuriant it is owing to the richness of the soil; and if others are not arrived to perfection or maturity, it is only because they are overrun and oppressed by those of a stronger nature.

It is to the strength of this amazing invention we are to attribute that unequalled fire and rapture which is so forcible in Homer, that no man of a true poetical spirit is master of himself while he reads him. What he writes is of the most animated nature imaginable; every thing moves, every thing lives, and is put in action. If a council be called, or a battle fought, you are not coldly informed of what was said or done as from a third person; the reader is hurried out of himself by the force of the poet's imagination, and turns in one place to a hearer, in another to a spectator. The course of his verses resembles that of the army he describes,

Hoid' ar' isan hosei te puri chthon pasa nemoito.

"They pour along like a fire that sweeps the whole earth before it." It is, however, remarkable, that his fancy, which is everywhere vigorous, is not discovered immediately at the beginning of his poem in its fullest splendour: it grows in the progress both upon himself and others, and becomes on fire, like a chariot-wheel, by its own rapidity. Exact disposition, just thought, correct elocution, polished numbers, may have been found in a thousand; but this poetic fire, this "vivida vis animi," in a very few. Even in works where all those are imperfect or neglected, this can overpower criticism, and make us admire even while we disapprove. Nay, where this appears, though attended with absurdities, it brightens all the rubbish about it, till we see nothing but its own splendour. This fire is discerned in Virgil, but discerned as through a glass, reflected from Homer, more shining than fierce, but everywhere equal and constant: in Lucan and Statius it bursts out in sudden, short, and interrupted flashes: In Milton it glows like a furnace kept up to an uncommon ardour by the force of art: in Shakspeare it strikes before we are aware, like an accidental fire from heaven: but in Homer, and in him only, it burns everywhere clearly and everywhere irresistibly.

I shall here endeavour to show how this vast invention exerts itself in a manner superior to that of any poet through all the main constituent parts of his work: as it is the great and peculiar characteristic which distinguishes him from all other authors.

This strong and ruling faculty was like a powerful star, which, in the violence of its course, drew all things within its vortex. It seemed not enough to have taken in the whole circle of arts, and the whole compass of nature, to supply his maxims and reflections; all the inward passions and affections of mankind, to furnish his characters: and all the outward forms and images of things for his descriptions: but wanting yet an ampler sphere to expatiate in, he opened a new and boundless walk for his imagination, and created a world for himself in the invention of fable. That which Aristotle calls "the soul of poetry," was first breathed into it by Homer, I shall begin with considering him in his part, as it is naturally the first; and I speak of it both as it means the design of a poem, and as it is taken for fiction.

Fable may be divided into the probable, the allegorical, and the marvellous. The probable fable is the recital of such actions as, though they did not happen, yet might, in the common course of nature; or of such as, though they did, became fables by the additional episodes and manner of telling them. Of this sort is the main story of an epic poem, "The return of Ulysses, the settlement of the Trojans in Italy," or the like. That of the Iliad is the "anger of Achilles," the most short and single subject that ever was chosen by any poet. Yet this he has supplied with a vaster variety of incidents and events, and crowded with a greater number of councils, speeches, battles, and episodes of all kinds, than are to be found even in those poems whose schemes are of the utmost latitude and irregularity. The action is hurried on with the most vehement spirit, and its whole duration employs not so much as fifty days. Virgil, for want of so warm a genius, aided himself by taking in a more extensive subject, as well as a greater length of time, and contracting the design of both Homer's poems into one, which is yet but a fourth part as large as his. The other epic poets have used the same practice, but generally carried it so far as to superinduce a multiplicity of fables, destroy the unity of action, and lose their readers in an unreasonable length of time. Nor is it only in the main design that they have been unable to add to his invention, but they have followed him in every episode and part of story. If he has given a regular catalogue of an army, they all draw up their forces in the same order. If he has funeral games for Patroclus, Virgil has the same for Anchises, and Statius (rather than omit them) destroys the unity of his actions for those of Archemorus. If Ulysses visit the shades, the Ćneas of Virgil and Scipio of Silius are sent after him. If he be detained from his return by the allurements of Calypso, so is Ćneas by Dido, and Rinaldo by Armida. If Achilles be absent from the army on the score of a quarrel through half the poem, Rinaldo must absent himself just as long on the like account. If he gives his hero a suit of celestial armour, Virgil and Tasso make the same present to theirs. Virgil has not only observed this close imitation of Homer, but, where he had not led the way, supplied the want from other Greek authors. Thus the story of Sinon, and the taking of Troy, was copied (says Macrobius) almost word for word from Pisander, as the loves of Dido and Ćneas are taken from those of Medea and Jason in Apollonius, and several others in the same manner.

To proceed to the allegorical fable—If we reflect upon those innumerable knowledges, those secrets of nature and physical philosophy which Homer is generally supposed to have wrapped up in his allegories, what a new and ample scene of wonder may this consideration afford us! How fertile will that imagination appear, which as able to clothe all the properties of elements, the qualifications of the mind, the virtues and vices, in forms and persons, and to introduce them into actions agreeable to the nature of the things they shadowed! This is a field in which no succeeding poets could dispute with Homer, and whatever commendations have been allowed them on this head, are by no means for their invention in having enlarged his circle, but for their judgment in having contracted it. For when the mode of learning changed in the following ages, and science was delivered in a plainer manner, it then became as reasonable in the more modern poets to lay it aside, as it was in Homer to make use of it. And perhaps it was no unhappy circumstance for Virgil, that there was not in his time that demand upon him of so great an invention as might be capable of furnishing all those allegorical parts of a poem.

The marvellous fable includes whatever is supernatural, and especially the machines of the gods. If Homer was not the first who introduced the deities (as Herodotus imagines) into the religion of Greece, he seems the first who brought them into a system of machinery for poetry, and such a one as makes its greatest importance and dignity: for we find those authors who have been offended at the literal notion of the gods, constantly laying their accusation against Homer as the chief support of it. But whatever cause there might be to blame his machines in a philosophical or religious view, they are so perfect in the poetic, that mankind have been ever since contented to follow them: none have been able to enlarge the sphere of poetry beyond the limits he has set: every attempt of this nature has proved unsuccessful; and after all the various changes of times and religions, his gods continue to this day the gods of poetry.

We come now to the characters of his persons; and here we shall find no author has ever drawn so many, with so visible and surprising a variety, or given us such lively and affecting impressions of them.

Every one has something so singularly his own, that no painter could have distinguished them more by their features, than the poet has by their manners. Nothing can be more exact than the distinctions he has observed in the different degrees of virtues and vices. The single quality of courage is wonderfully diversified in the several characters of the Iliad. That of Achilles is furious and intractable; that of Diomede forward, yet listening to advice, and subject to command; that of Ajax is heavy and self-confiding; of Hector, active and vigilant: the courage of Agamemnon is inspirited by love of empire and ambition; that of Menelaus mixed with softness and tenderness for his people: we find in Idomeneus a plain direct soldier; in Sarpedon a gallant and generous one. Nor is this judicious and astonishing diversity to be found only in the principal quality which constitutes the main of each character, but even in the under parts of it, to which he takes care to give a tincture of that principal one. For example: the main characters of Ulysses and Nestor consist in wisdom; and they are distinct in this, that the wisdom of one is artificial and various, of the other natural, open, and regular. But they have, besides, characters of courage; and this quality also takes a different turn in each from the difference of his prudence; for one in the war depends still upon caution, the other upon experience. It would be endless to produce instances of these kinds. The characters of Virgil are far from striking us in this open manner; they lie, in a great degree, hidden and undistinguished; and, where they are marked most evidently affect us not in proportion to those of Homer. His characters of valour are much alike; even that of Turnus seems no way peculiar, but, as it is, in a superior degree; and we see nothing that differences the courage of Mnestheus from that of Sergestus, Cloanthus, or the rest, In like manner it may be remarked of Statius's heroes, that an air of impetuosity runs through them all; the same horrid and savage courage appears in his Capaneus, Tydeus, Hippomedon, &c. They have a parity of character, which makes them seem brothers of one family. I believe when the reader is led into this tract of reflection, if he will pursue it through the epic and tragic writers, he will be convinced how infinitely superior, in this point, the invention of Homer was to that of all others.

The speeches are to be considered as they flow from the characters; being perfect or defective as they agree or disagree with the manners, of those who utter them. As there is more variety of characters in the Iliad, so there is of speeches, than in any other poem. "Everything in it has manner" (as Aristotle expresses it), that is, everything is acted or spoken. It is hardly credible, in a work of such length, how small a number of lines are employed in narration. In Virgil the dramatic part is less in proportion to the narrative, and the speeches often consist of general reflections or thoughts, which might be equally just in any person's mouth upon the same occasion. As many of his persons have no apparent characters, so many of his speeches escape being applied and judged by the rule of propriety. We oftener think of the author himself when we read Virgil, than when we are engaged in Homer, all which are the effects of a colder invention, that interests us less in the action described. Homer makes us hearers, and Virgil leaves us readers.

If, in the next place, we take a view of the sentiments, the same presiding faculty is eminent in the sublimity and spirit of his thoughts. Longinus has given his opinion, that it was in this part Homer principally excelled. What were alone sufficient to prove the grandeur and excellence of his sentiments in general, is, that they have so remarkable a parity with those of the Scripture. Duport, in his Gnomologia Homerica, has collected innumerable instances of this sort. And it is with justice an excellent modern writer allows, that if Virgil has not so many thoughts that are low and vulgar, he has not so many that are sublime and noble; and that the Roman author seldom rises into very astonishing sentiments where he is not fired by the Iliad.

If we observe his descriptions, images, and similes, we shall find the invention still predominant. To what else can we ascribe that vast comprehension of images of every sort, where we see each circumstance of art, and individual of nature, summoned together by the extent and fecundity of his imagination to which all things, in their various views presented themselves in an instant, and had their impressions taken off to perfection at a heat? Nay, he not only gives us the full prospects of things, but several unexpected peculiarities and side views, unobserved by any painter but Homer. Nothing is so surprising as the descriptions of his battles, which take up no less than half the Iliad, and are supplied with so vast a variety of incidents, that no one bears a likeness to another; such different kinds of deaths, that no two heroes are wounded in the same manner, and such a profusion of noble ideas, that every battle rises above the last in greatness, horror, and confusion. It is certain there is not near that number of images and descriptions in any epic poet, though every one has assisted himself with a great quantity out of him; and it is evident of Virgil especially, that he has scarce any comparisons which are not drawn from his master.

If we descend from hence to the expression, we see the bright imagination of Homer shining out in the most enlivened forms of it. We acknowledge him the father of poetical diction; the first who taught that "language of the gods" to men. His expression is like the colouring of some great masters, which discovers itself to be laid on boldly, and executed with rapidity. It is, indeed, the strongest and most glowing imaginable, and touched with the greatest spirit. Aristotle had reason to say, he was the only poet who had found out "living words;" there are in him more daring figures and metaphors than in any good author whatever. An arrow is "impatient" to be on the wing, a weapon "thirsts" to drink the blood of an enemy, and the like, yet his expression is never too big for the sense, but justly great in proportion to it. It is the sentiment that swells and fills out the diction, which rises with it, and forms itself about it, for in the same degree that a thought is warmer, an expression will be brighter, as that is more strong, this will become more perspicuous; like glass in the furnace, which grows to a greater magnitude, and refines to a greater clearness, only as the breath within is more powerful, and the heat more intense.

To throw his language more out of prose, Homer seems to have affected the compound epithets. This was a sort of composition peculiarly proper to poetry, not only as it heightened the diction, but as it assisted and filled the numbers with greater sound and pomp, and likewise conduced in some measure to thicken the images. On this last consideration I cannot but attribute these also to the fruitfulness of his invention, since (as he has managed them) they are a sort of supernumerary pictures of the persons or things to which they were joined. We see the motion of Hector's plumes in the epithet Korythaiolos, the landscape of Mount Neritus in that of Einosiphyllos, and so of others, which particular images could not have been insisted upon so long as to express them in a description (though but of a single line) without diverting the reader too much from the principal action or figure. As a metaphor is a short simile, one of these epithets is a short description.

Lastly, if we consider his versification, we shall be sensible what a share of praise is due to his invention in that also. He was not satisfied with his language as he found it settled in any one part of Greece, but searched through its different dialects with this particular view, to beautify and perfect his numbers he considered these as they had a greater mixture of vowels or consonants, and accordingly employed them as the verse required either a greater smoothness or strength. What he most affected was the Ionic, which has a peculiar sweetness, from its never using contractions, and from its custom of resolving the diphthongs into two syllables, so as to make the words open themselves with a more spreading and sonorous fluency. With this he mingled the Attic contractions, the broader Doric, and the feebler Ćolic, which often rejects its aspirate, or takes off its accent, and completed this variety by altering some letters with the licence of poetry. Thus his measures, instead of being fetters to his sense, were always in readiness to run along with the warmth of his rapture, and even to give a further representation of his notions, in the correspondence of their sounds to what they signified. Out of all these he has derived that harmony which makes us confess he had not only the richest head, but the finest ear in the world. This is so great a truth, that whoever will but consult the tune of his verses, even without understanding them (with the same sort of diligence as we daily see practised in the case of Italian operas), will find more sweetness, variety, and majesty of sound, than in any other language of poetry. The beauty of his numbers is allowed by the critics to be copied but faintly by Virgil himself, though they are so just as to ascribe it to the nature of the Latin tongue: indeed the Greek has some advantages both from the natural sound of its words, and the turn and cadence of its verse, which agree with the genius of no other language. Virgil was very sensible of this, and used the utmost diligence in working up a more intractable language to whatsoever graces it was capable of, and, in particular, never failed to bring the sound of his line to a beautiful agreement with its sense. If the Grecian poet has not been so frequently celebrated on this account as the Roman, the only reason is, that fewer critics have understood one language than the other. Dionysius of Halicarnassus has pointed out many of our author's beauties in this kind, in his treatise of the Composition of Words. It suffices at present to observe of his numbers, that they flow with so much ease, as to make one imagine Homer had no other care than to transcribe as fast as the Muses dictated, and, at the same time, with so much force and inspiriting vigour, that they awaken and raise us like the sound of a trumpet. They roll along as a plentiful river, always in motion, and always full; while we are borne away by a tide of verse, the most rapid, and yet the most smooth imaginable.

Thus on whatever side we contemplate Homer, what principally strikes us is his invention. It is that which forms the character of each part of his work; and accordingly we find it to have made his fable more extensive and copious than any other, his manners more lively and strongly marked, his speeches more affecting and transported, his sentiments more warm and sublime, his images and descriptions more full and animated, his expression more raised and daring, and his numbers more rapid and various. I hope, in what has been said of Virgil, with regard to any of these heads, I have no way derogated from his character. Nothing is more absurd or endless, than the common method of comparing eminent writers by an opposition of particular passages in them, and forming a judgment from thence of their merit upon the whole. We ought to have a certain knowledge of the principal character and distinguishing excellence of each: it is in that we are to consider him, and in proportion to his degree in that we are to admire him. No author or man ever excelled all the world in more than one faculty; and as Homer has done this in invention, Virgil has in judgment. Not that we are to think that Homer wanted judgment, because Virgil had it in a more eminent degree; or that Virgil wanted invention, because Homer possessed a larger share of it; each of these great authors had more of both than perhaps any man besides, and are only said to have less in comparison with one another. Homer was the greater genius, Virgil the better artist. In one we most admire the man, in the other the work. Homer hurries and transports us with a commanding impetuosity; Virgil leads us with an attractive majesty; Homer scatters with a generous profusion; Virgil bestows with a careful magnificence; Homer, like the Nile, pours out his riches with a boundless overflow; Virgil, like a river in its banks, with a gentle and constant stream. When we behold their battles, methinks the two poets resemble the heroes they celebrate. Homer, boundless and resistless as Achilles, bears all before him, and shines more and more as the tumult increases; Virgil, calmly daring, like Ćneas, appears undisturbed in the midst of the action; disposes all about him, and conquers with tranquillity. And when we look upon their machines, Homer seems like his own Jupiter in his terrors, shaking Olympus, scattering the lightnings, and firing the heavens: Virgil, like the same power in his benevolence, counselling with the gods, laying plans for empires, and regularly ordering his whole creation.

But after all, it is with great parts, as with great virtues, they naturally border on some imperfection; and it is often hard to distinguish exactly where the virtue ends, or the fault begins. As prudence may sometimes sink to suspicion, so may a great judgment decline to coldness; and as magnanimity may run up to profusion or extravagance, so may a great invention to redundancy or wildness. If we look upon Homer in this view, we shall perceive the chief objections against him to proceed from so noble a cause as the excess of this faculty.

Among these we may reckon some of his marvellous fictions, upon which so much criticism has been spent, as surpassing all the bounds of probability. Perhaps it may be with great and superior souls, as with gigantic bodies, which, exerting themselves with unusual strength, exceed what is commonly thought the due proportion of parts, to become miracles in the whole; and, like the old heroes of that make, commit something near extravagance, amidst a series of glorious and inimitable performances. Thus Homer has his "speaking horses;" and Virgil his "myrtles distilling blood;" where the latter has not so much as contrived the easy intervention of a deity to save the probability.

It is owing to the same vast invention, that his similes have been thought too exuberant and full of circumstances. The force of this faculty is seen in nothing more, than in its inability to confine itself to that single circumstance upon which the comparison is grounded: it runs out into embellishments of additional images, which, however, are so managed as not to overpower the main one. His similes are like pictures, where the principal figure has not only its proportion given agreeable to the original, but is also set off with occasional ornaments and prospects. The same will account for his manner of heaping a number of comparisons together in one breath, when his fancy suggested to him at once so many various and correspondent images. The reader will easily extend this observation to more objections of the same kind.

If there are others which seem rather to charge him with a defect or narrowness of genius, than an excess of it, those seeming defects will be found upon examination to proceed wholly from the nature of the times he lived in. Such are his grosser representations of the gods; and the vicious and imperfect manners of his heroes; but I must here speak a word of the latter, as it is a point generally carried into extremes, both by the censurers and defenders of Homer. It must be a strange partiality to antiquity, to think with Madame Dacier, "that those times and manners are so much the more excellent, as they are more contrary to ours." Who can be so prejudiced in their favour as to magnify the felicity of those ages, when a spirit of revenge and cruelty, joined with the practice of rapine and robbery, reigned through the world: when no mercy was shown but for the sake of lucre; when the greatest princes were put to the sword, and their wives and daughters made slaves and concubines? On the other side, I would not be so delicate as those modern critics, who are shocked at the servile offices and mean employments in which we sometimes see the heroes of Homer engaged. There is a pleasure in taking a view of that simplicity, in opposition to the luxury of succeeding ages: in beholding monarchs without their guards; princes tending their flocks, and princesses drawing water from the springs. When we read Homer, we ought to reflect that we are reading the most ancient author in the heathen world; and those who consider him in this light, will double their pleasure in the perusal of him. Let them think they are growing acquainted with nations and people that are now no more; that they are stepping almost three thousand years back into the remotest antiquity, and entertaining themselves with a clear and surprising vision of things nowhere else to be found, the only true mirror of that ancient world. By this means alone their greatest obstacles will vanish; and what usually creates their dislike, will become a satisfaction.

This consideration may further serve to answer for the constant use of the same epithets to his gods and heroes; such as the "far-darting Phoebus," the "blue-eyed Pallas," the "swift-footed Achilles," &c., which some have censured as impertinent, and tediously repeated. Those of the gods depended upon the powers and offices then believed to belong to them; and had contracted a weight and veneration from the rites and solemn devotions in which they were used: they were a sort of attributes with which it was a matter of religion to salute them on all occasions, and which it was an irreverence to omit. As for the epithets of great men, Mons. Boileau is of opinion, that they were in the nature of surnames, and repeated as such; for the Greeks having no names derived from their fathers, were obliged to add some other distinction of each person; either naming his parents expressly, or his place of birth, profession, or the like: as Alexander the son of Philip, Herodotus of Halicarnassus, Diogenes the Cynic, &c. Homer, therefore, complying with the custom of his country, used such distinctive additions as better agreed with poetry. And, indeed, we have something parallel to these in modern times, such as the names of Harold Harefoot, Edmund Ironside, Edward Longshanks, Edward the Black Prince, &c. If yet this be thought to account better for the propriety than for the repetition, I shall add a further conjecture. Hesiod, dividing the world into its different ages, has placed a fourth age, between the brazen and the iron one, of "heroes distinct from other men; a divine race who fought at Thebes and Troy, are called demi-gods, and live by the care of Jupiter in the islands of the blessed." Now among the divine honours which were paid them, they might have this also in common with the gods, not to be mentioned without the solemnity of an epithet, and such as might be acceptable to them by celebrating their families, actions or qualities.

What other cavils have been raised against Homer, are such as hardly deserve a reply, but will yet be taken notice of as they occur in the course of the work. Many have been occasioned by an injudicious endeavour to exalt Virgil; which is much the same, as if one should think to raise the superstructure by undermining the foundation: one would imagine, by the whole course of their parallels, that these critics never so much as heard of Homer's having written first; a consideration which whoever compares these two poets ought to have always in his eye. Some accuse him for the same things which they overlook or praise in the other; as when they prefer the fable and moral of the Ćneis to those of the Iliad, for the same reasons which might set the Odyssey above the Ćneis; as that the hero is a wiser man, and the action of the one more beneficial to his country than that of the other; or else they blame him for not doing what he never designed; as because Achilles is not as good and perfect a prince as Ćneas, when the very moral of his poem required a contrary character: it is thus that Rapin judges in his comparison of Homer and Virgil. Others select those particular passages of Homer which are not so laboured as some that Virgil drew out of them: this is the whole management of Scaliger in his Poetics. Others quarrel with what they take for low and mean expressions, sometimes through a false delicacy and refinement, oftener from an ignorance of the graces of the original, and then triumph in the awkwardness of their own translations: this is the conduct of Perrault in his Parallels. Lastly, there are others, who, pretending to a fairer proceeding, distinguish between the personal merit of Homer, and that of his work; but when they come to assign the causes of the great reputation of the Iliad, they found it upon the ignorance of his times, and the prejudice of those that followed: and in pursuance of this principle, they make those accidents (such as the contention of the cities, &c.) to be the causes of his fame, which were in reality the consequences of his merit. The same might as well be said of Virgil, or any great author whose general character will infallibly raise many casual additions to their reputation. This is the method of Mons. de la Mott; who yet confesses upon the whole that in whatever age Homer had lived, he must have been the greatest poet of his nation, and that he may be said in his sense to be the master even of those who surpassed him.

In all these objections we see nothing that contradicts his title to the honour of the chief invention: and as long as this (which is indeed the characteristic of poetry itself) remains unequalled by his followers, he still continues superior to them. A cooler judgment may commit fewer faults, and be more approved in the eyes of one sort of critics: but that warmth of fancy will carry the loudest and most universal applauses which holds the heart of a reader under the strongest enchantment. Homer not only appears the inventor of poetry, but excels all the inventors of other arts, in this, that he has swallowed up the honour of those who succeeded him. What he has done admitted no increase, it only left room for contraction or regulation. He showed all the stretch of fancy at once; and if he has failed in some of his flights, it was but because he attempted everything. A work of this kind seems like a mighty tree, which rises from the most vigorous seed, is improved with industry, flourishes, and produces the finest fruit: nature and art conspire to raise it; pleasure and profit join to make it valuable: and they who find the justest faults, have only said that a few branches which run luxuriant through a richness of nature, might be lopped into form to give it a more regular appearance.

Having now spoken of the beauties and defects of the original, it remains to treat of the translation, with the same view to the chief characteristic. As far as that is seen in the main parts of the poem, such as the fable, manners, and sentiments, no translator can prejudice it but by wilful omissions or contractions. As it also breaks out in every particular image, description, and simile, whoever lessens or too much softens those, takes off from this chief character. It is the first grand duty of an interpreter to give his author entire and unmaimed; and for the rest, the diction and versification only are his proper province, since these must be his own, but the others he is to take as he finds them.

It should then be considered what methods may afford some equivalent in our language for the graces of these in the Greek. It is certain no literal translation can be just to an excellent original in a superior language: but it is a great mistake to imagine (as many have done) that a rash paraphrase can make amends for this general defect; which is no less in danger to lose the spirit of an ancient, by deviating into the modern manners of expression. If there be sometimes a darkness, there is often a light in antiquity, which nothing better preserves than a version almost literal. I know no liberties one ought to take, but those which are necessary to transfusing the spirit of the original, and supporting the poetical style of the translation: and I will venture to say, there have not been more men misled in former times by a servile, dull adherence to the letter, than have been deluded in ours by a chimerical, insolent hope of raising and improving their author. It is not to be doubted, that the fire of the poem is what a translator should principally regard, as it is most likely to expire in his managing: however, it is his safest way to be content with preserving this to his utmost in the whole, without endeavouring to be more than he finds his author is, in any particular place. It is a great secret in writing, to know when to be plain, and when poetical and figurative; and it is what Homer will teach us, if we will but follow modestly in his footsteps. Where his diction is bold and lofty, let us raise ours as high as we can; but where his is plain and humble, we ought not to be deterred from imitating him by the fear of incurring the censure of a mere English critic. Nothing that belongs to Homer seems to have been more commonly mistaken than the just pitch of his style: some of his translators having swelled into fustian in a proud confidence of the sublime; others sunk into flatness, in a cold and timorous notion of simplicity. Methinks I see these different followers of Homer, some sweating and straining after him by violent leaps and bounds (the certain signs of false mettle), others slowly and servilely creeping in his train, while the poet himself is all the time proceeding with an unaffected and equal majesty before them. However, of the two extremes one could sooner pardon frenzy than frigidity; no author is to be envied for such commendations, as he may gain by that character of style, which his friends must agree together to call simplicity, and the rest of the world will call dulness. There is a graceful and dignified simplicity, as well as a bold and sordid one; which differ as much from each other as the air of a plain man from that of a sloven: it is one thing to be tricked up, and another not to be dressed at all. Simplicity is the mean between ostentation and rusticity.

This pure and noble simplicity is nowhere in such perfection as in the Scripture and our author. One may affirm, with all respect to the inspired writings, that the Divine Spirit made use of no other words but what were intelligible and common to men at that time, and in that part of the world; and, as Homer is the author nearest to those, his style must of course bear a greater resemblance to the sacred books than that of any other writer. This consideration (together with what has been observed of the parity of some of his thoughts) may, methinks, induce a translator, on the one hand, to give in to several of those general phrases and manners of expression, which have attained a veneration even in our language from being used in the Old Testament; as, on the other, to avoid those which have been appropriated to the Divinity, and in a manner consigned to mystery and religion.

For a further preservation of this air of simplicity, a particular care should be taken to express with all plainness those moral sentences and proverbial speeches which are so numerous in this poet. They have something venerable, and as I may say, oracular, in that unadorned gravity and shortness with which they are delivered: a grace which would be utterly lost by endeavouring to give them what we call a more ingenious (that is, a more modern) turn in the paraphrase.

Perhaps the mixture of some Graecisms and old words after the manner of Milton, if done without too much affectation, might not have an ill effect in a version of this particular work, which most of any other seems to require a venerable, antique cast. But certainly the use of modern terms of war and government, such as "platoon, campaign, junto," or the like, (into which some of his translators have fallen) cannot be allowable; those only excepted without which it is impossible to treat the subjects in any living language.

There are two peculiarities in Homer's diction, which are a sort of marks or moles by which every common eye distinguishes him at first sight; those who are not his greatest admirers look upon them as defects, and those who are, seemed pleased with them as beauties. I speak of his compound epithets, and of his repetitions. Many of the former cannot be done literally into English without destroying the purity of our language. I believe such should be retained as slide easily of themselves into an English compound, without violence to the ear or to the received rules of composition, as well as those which have received a sanction from the authority of our best poets, and are become familiar through their use of them; such as "the cloud-compelling Jove," &c. As for the rest, whenever any can be as fully and significantly expressed in a single word as in a compounded one, the course to be taken is obvious.

Some that cannot be so turned, as to preserve their full image by one or two words, may have justice done them by circumlocution; as the epithet einosiphyllos to a mountain, would appear little or ridiculous translated literally "leaf-shaking," but affords a majestic idea in the periphrasis: "the lofty mountain shakes his waving woods." Others that admit of different significations, may receive an advantage from a judicious variation, according to the occasions on which they are introduced. For example, the epithet of Apollo, hekaebolos or "far-shooting," is capable of two explications; one literal, in respect of the darts and bow, the ensigns of that god; the other allegorical, with regard to the rays of the sun; therefore, in such places where Apollo is represented as a god in person, I would use the former interpretation; and where the effects of the sun are described, I would make choice of the latter. Upon the whole, it will be necessary to avoid that perpetual repetition of the same epithets which we find in Homer, and which, though it might be accommodated (as has been already shown) to the ear of those times, is by no means so to ours: but one may wait for opportunities of placing them, where they derive an additional beauty from the occasions on which they are employed; and in doing this properly, a translator may at once show his fancy and his judgment.

As for Homer's repetitions, we may divide them into three sorts: of whole narrations and speeches, of single sentences, and of one verse or hemistitch. I hope it is not impossible to have such a regard to these, as neither to lose so known a mark of the author on the one hand, nor to offend the reader too much on the other. The repetition is not ungraceful in those speeches, where the dignity of the speaker renders it a sort of insolence to alter his words; as in the messages from gods to men, or from higher powers to inferiors in concerns of state, or where the ceremonial of religion seems to require it, in the solemn forms of prayers, oaths, or the like. In other cases, I believe the best rule is, to be guided by the nearness, or distance, at which the repetitions are placed in the original: when they follow too close, one may vary the expression; but it is a question, whether a professed translator be authorized to omit any: if they be tedious, the author is to answer for it.

It only remains to speak of the versification. Homer (as has been said) is perpetually applying the sound to the sense, and varying it on every new subject. This is indeed one of the most exquisite beauties of poetry, and attainable by very few: I only know of Homer eminent for it in the Greek, and Virgil in the Latin. I am sensible it is what may sometimes happen by chance, when a writer is warm, and fully possessed of his image: however, it may reasonably be believed they designed this, in whose verse it so manifestly appears in a superior degree to all others. Few readers have the ear to be judges of it: but those who have, will see I have endeavoured at this beauty.

Upon the whole, I must confess myself utterly incapable of doing justice to Homer. I attempt him in no other hope but that which one may entertain without much vanity, of giving a more tolerable copy of him than any entire translation in verse has yet done. We have only those of Chapman, Hobbes, and Ogilby. Chapman has taken the advantage of an immeasurable length of verse, notwithstanding which, there is scarce any paraphrase more loose and rambling than his. He has frequent interpolations of four or six lines; and I remember one in the thirteenth book of the Odyssey, ver. 312, where he has spun twenty verses out of two. He is often mistaken in so bold a manner, that one might think he deviated on purpose, if he did not in other places of his notes insist so much upon verbal trifles. He appears to have had a strong affectation of extracting new meanings out of his author; insomuch as to promise, in his rhyming preface, a poem of the mysteries he had revealed in Homer; and perhaps he endeavoured to strain the obvious sense to this end. His expression is involved in fustian; a fault for which he was remarkable in his original writings, as in the tragedy of Bussy d'Amboise, &c. In a word, the nature of the man may account for his whole performance; for he appears, from his preface and remarks, to have been of an arrogant turn, and an enthusiast in poetry. His own boast, of having finished half the Iliad in less than fifteen weeks, shows with what negligence his version was performed. But that which is to be allowed him, and which very much contributed to cover his defects, is a daring fiery spirit that animates his translation, which is something like what one might imagine Homer himself would have writ before he arrived at years of discretion.

Hobbes has given us a correct explanation of the sense in general; but for particulars and circumstances he continually lops them, and often omits the most beautiful. As for its being esteemed a close translation, I doubt not many have been led into that error by the shortness of it, which proceeds not from his following the original line by line, but from the contractions above mentioned. He sometimes omits whole similes and sentences; and is now and then guilty of mistakes, into which no writer of his learning could have fallen, but through carelessness. His poetry, as well as Ogilby's, is too mean for criticism.

It is a great loss to the poetical world that Mr. Dryden did not live to translate the Iliad. He has left us only the first book, and a small part of the sixth; in which if he has in some places not truly interpreted the sense, or preserved the antiquities, it ought to be excused on account of the haste he was obliged to write in. He seems to have had too much regard to Chapman, whose words he sometimes copies, and has unhappily followed him in passages where he wanders from the original. However, had he translated the whole work, I would no more have attempted Homer after him than Virgil: his version of whom (notwithstanding some human errors) is the most noble and spirited translation I know in any language. But the fate of great geniuses is like that of great ministers: though they are confessedly the first in the commonwealth of letters, they must be envied and calumniated only for being at the head of it.

That which, in my opinion, ought to be the endeavour of any one who translates Homer, is above all things to keep alive that spirit and fire which makes his chief character: in particular places, where the sense can bear any doubt, to follow the strongest and most poetical, as most agreeing with that character; to copy him in all the variations of his style, and the different modulations of his numbers; to preserve, in the more active or descriptive parts, a warmth and elevation; in the more sedate or narrative, a plainness and solemnity; in the speeches, a fulness and perspicuity; in the sentences, a shortness and gravity; not to neglect even the little figures and turns on the words, nor sometimes the very cast of the periods; neither to omit nor confound any rites or customs of antiquity: perhaps too he ought to include the whole in a shorter compass than has hitherto been done by any translator who has tolerably preserved either the sense or poetry. What I would further recommend to him is, to study his author rather from his own text, than from any commentaries, how learned soever, or whatever figure they may make in the estimation of the world; to consider him attentively in comparison with Virgil above all the ancients, and with Milton above all the moderns. Next these, the Archbishop of Cambray's Telemachus may give him the truest idea of the spirit and turn of our author; and Bossu's admirable Treatise of the Epic Poem the justest notion of his design and conduct. But after all, with whatever judgment and study a man may proceed, or with whatever happiness he may perform such a work, he must hope to please but a few; those only who have at once a taste of poetry, and competent learning. For to satisfy such a want either, is not in the nature of this undertaking; since a mere modern wit can like nothing that is not modern, and a pedant nothing that is not Greek.

What I have done is submitted to the public; from whose opinions I am prepared to learn; though I fear no judges so little as our best poets, who are most sensible of the weight of this task. As for the worst, whatever they shall please to say, they may give me some concern as they are unhappy men, but none as they are malignant writers. I was guided in this translation by judgments very different from theirs, and by persons for whom they can have no kindness, if an old observation be true, that the strongest antipathy in the world is that of fools to men of wit. Mr. Addison was the first whose advice determined me to undertake this task; who was pleased to write to me upon that occasion in such terms as I cannot repeat without vanity. I was obliged to Sir Richard Steele for a very early recommendation of my undertaking to the public. Dr. Swift promoted my interest with that warmth with which he always serves his friend. The humanity and frankness of Sir Samuel Garth are what I never knew wanting on any occasion. I must also acknowledge, with infinite pleasure, the many friendly offices, as well as sincere criticisms, of Mr. Congreve, who had led me the way in translating some parts of Homer. I must add the names of Mr. Rowe, and Dr. Parnell, though I shall take a further opportunity of doing justice to the last, whose good nature (to give it a great panegyric), is no less extensive than his learning. The favour of these gentlemen is not entirely undeserved by one who bears them so true an affection. But what can I say of the honour so many of the great have done me; while the first names of the age appear as my subscribers, and the most distinguished patrons and ornaments of learning as my chief encouragers? Among these it is a particular pleasure to me to find, that my highest obligations are to such who have done most honour to the name of poet: that his grace the Duke of Buckingham was not displeased I should undertake the author to whom he has given (in his excellent Essay), so complete a praise:

"Read Homer once, and you can read no more;
For all books else appear so mean, so poor,
Verse will seem prose: but still persist to read,
And Homer will be all the books you need."

That the Earl of Halifax was one of the first to favour me; of whom it is hard to say whether the advancement of the polite arts is more owing to his generosity or his example: that such a genius as my Lord Bolingbroke, not more distinguished in the great scenes of business, than in all the useful and entertaining parts of learning, has not refused to be the critic of these sheets, and the patron of their writer: and that the noble author of the tragedy of "Heroic Love" has continued his partiality to me, from my writing pastorals to my attempting the Iliad. I cannot deny myself the pride of confessing, that I have had the advantage not only of their advice for the conduct in general, but their correction of several particulars of this translation.

I could say a great deal of the pleasure of being distinguished by the Earl of Carnarvon; but it is almost absurd to particularize any one generous action in a person whose whole life is a continued series of them. Mr. Stanhope, the present secretary of state, will pardon my desire of having it known that he was pleased to promote this affair. The particular zeal of Mr. Harcourt (the son of the late Lord Chancellor) gave me a proof how much I am honoured in a share of his friendship. I must attribute to the same motive that of several others of my friends: to whom all acknowledgments are rendered unnecessary by the privileges of a familiar correspondence; and I am satisfied I can no way better oblige men of their turn than by my silence.

In short, I have found more patrons than ever Homer wanted. He would have thought himself happy to have met the same favour at Athens that has been shown me by its learned rival, the University of Oxford. And I can hardly envy him those pompous honours he received after death, when I reflect on the enjoyment of so many agreeable obligations, and easy friendships, which make the satisfaction of life. This distinction is the more to be acknowledged, as it is shown to one whose pen has never gratified the prejudices of particular parties, or the vanities of particular men. Whatever the success may prove, I shall never repent of an undertaking in which I have experienced the candour and friendship of so many persons of merit; and in which I hope to pass some of those years of youth that are generally lost in a circle of follies, after a manner neither wholly unuseful to others, nor disagreeable to myself.

—

THE ILIAD

BOOK I

ARGUMENT

THE CONTENTION OF ACHILLES AND AGAMEMNON

In the war of Troy, the Greeks having sacked some of the neighbouring towns, and taken from thence two beautiful captives, Chryseis and Briseis, allotted the first to Agamemnon, and the last to Achilles. Chryses, the father of Chryseis, and priest of Apollo, comes to the Grecian camp to ransom her; with which the action of the poem opens, in the tenth year of the siege. The priest being refused, and insolently dismissed by Agamemnon, entreats for vengeance from his god; who inflicts a pestilence on the Greeks. Achilles calls a council, and encourages Chalcas to declare the cause of it; who attributes it to the refusal of Chryseis. The king, being obliged to send back his captive, enters into a furious contest with Achilles, which Nestor pacifies; however, as he had the absolute command of the army, he seizes on Briseis in revenge. Achilles in discontent withdraws himself and his forces from the rest of the Greeks; and complaining to Thetis, she supplicates Jupiter to render them sensible of the wrong done to her son, by giving victory to the Trojans. Jupiter, granting her suit, incenses Juno: between whom the debate runs high, till they are reconciled by the address of Vulcan.

The time of two-and-twenty days is taken up in this book: nine during the plague, one in the council and quarrel of the princes, and twelve for Jupiter's stay with the Ćthiopians, at whose return Thetis prefers her petition. The scene lies in the Grecian camp, then changes to Chrysa, and lastly to Olympus.

Achilles' wrath, to Greece the direful spring
Of woes unnumber'd, heavenly goddess, sing!
That wrath which hurl'd to Pluto's gloomy reign
The souls of mighty chiefs untimely slain;
Whose limbs unburied on the naked shore,
Devouring dogs and hungry vultures tore.
Since great Achilles and Atrides strove,
Such was the sovereign doom, and such the will of Jove!

Declare, O Muse! in what ill-fated hour
Sprung the fierce strife, from what offended power
Latona's son a dire contagion spread,
And heap'd the camp with mountains of the dead;
The king of men his reverent priest defied,
And for the king's offence the people died.

For Chryses sought with costly gifts to gain
His captive daughter from the victor's chain.
Suppliant the venerable father stands;
Apollo's awful ensigns grace his hands
By these he begs; and lowly bending down,
Extends the sceptre and the laurel crown
He sued to all, but chief implored for grace
The brother-kings, of Atreus' royal race

"Ye kings and warriors! may your vows be crown'd,
And Troy's proud walls lie level with the ground.
May Jove restore you when your toils are o'er
Safe to the pleasures of your native shore.
But, oh! relieve a wretched parent's pain,
And give Chryseis to these arms again;
If mercy fail, yet let my presents move,
And dread avenging Phoebus, son of Jove."

The Greeks in shouts their joint assent declare,
The priest to reverence, and release the fair.

Not so Atrides; he, with kingly pride,
Repulsed the sacred sire, and thus replied:

"Hence on thy life, and fly these hostile plains,
Nor ask, presumptuous, what the king detains
Hence, with thy laurel crown, and golden rod,
Nor trust too far those ensigns of thy god.
Mine is thy daughter, priest, and shall remain;
And prayers, and tears, and bribes, shall plead in vain;
Till time shall rifle every youthful grace,
And age dismiss her from my cold embrace,
In daily labours of the loom employ'd,
Or doom'd to deck the bed she once enjoy'd
Hence then; to Argos shall the maid retire,
Far from her native soil and weeping sire."

The trembling priest along the shore return'd,
And in the anguish of a father mourn'd.
Disconsolate, not daring to complain,
Silent he wander'd by the sounding main;
Till, safe at distance, to his god he prays,
The god who darts around the world his rays.

"O Smintheus! sprung from fair Latona's line,
Thou guardian power of Cilla the divine,
Thou source of light! whom Tenedos adores,
And whose bright presence gilds thy Chrysa's shores.
If e'er with wreaths I hung thy sacred fane,
Or fed the flames with fat of oxen slain;
God of the silver bow! thy shafts employ,
Avenge thy servant, and the Greeks destroy."

Thus Chryses pray'd.—the favouring power attends,
And from Olympus' lofty tops descends.
Bent was his bow, the Grecian hearts to wound;
Fierce as he moved, his silver shafts resound.
Breathing revenge, a sudden night he spread,
And gloomy darkness roll'd about his head.
The fleet in view, he twang'd his deadly bow,
And hissing fly the feather'd fates below.
On mules and dogs the infection first began;
And last, the vengeful arrows fix'd in man.
For nine long nights, through all the dusky air,
The pyres, thick-flaming, shot a dismal glare.
But ere the tenth revolving day was run,
Inspired by Juno, Thetis' godlike son
Convened to council all the Grecian train;
For much the goddess mourn'd her heroes slain.

The assembly seated, rising o'er the rest,
Achilles thus the king of men address'd:

"Why leave we not the fatal Trojan shore,
And measure back the seas we cross'd before?
The plague destroying whom the sword would spare,
'Tis time to save the few remains of war.
But let some prophet, or some sacred sage,
Explore the cause of great Apollo's rage;
Or learn the wasteful vengeance to remove
By mystic dreams, for dreams descend from Jove.
If broken vows this heavy curse have laid,
Let altars smoke, and hecatombs be paid.
So Heaven, atoned, shall dying Greece restore,
And Phoebus dart his burning shafts no more."

He said, and sat: when Chalcas thus replied;
Chalcas the wise, the Grecian priest and guide,
That sacred seer, whose comprehensive view,
The past, the present, and the future knew:
Uprising slow, the venerable sage
Thus spoke the prudence and the fears of age:

"Beloved of Jove, Achilles! would'st thou know
Why angry Phoebus bends his fatal bow?
First give thy faith, and plight a prince's word
Of sure protection, by thy power and sword:
For I must speak what wisdom would conceal,
And truths, invidious to the great, reveal,
Bold is the task, when subjects, grown too wise,
Instruct a monarch where his error lies;
For though we deem the short-lived fury past,
'Tis sure the mighty will revenge at last."
To whom Pelides:—"From thy inmost soul
Speak what thou know'st, and speak without control.
E'en by that god I swear who rules the day,
To whom thy hands the vows of Greece convey.
And whose bless'd oracles thy lips declare;
Long as Achilles breathes this vital air,
No daring Greek, of all the numerous band,
Against his priest shall lift an impious hand;
Not e'en the chief by whom our hosts are led,
The king of kings, shall touch that sacred head."

Encouraged thus, the blameless man replies:
"Nor vows unpaid, nor slighted sacrifice,
But he, our chief, provoked the raging pest,
Apollo's vengeance for his injured priest.

Nor will the god's awaken'd fury cease,
But plagues shall spread, and funeral fires increase,
Till the great king, without a ransom paid,
To her own Chrysa send the black-eyed maid.
Perhaps, with added sacrifice and prayer,
The priest may pardon, and the god may spare."

The prophet spoke: when with a gloomy frown
The monarch started from his shining throne;
Black choler fill'd his breast that boil'd with ire,
And from his eye-balls flash'd the living fire:
"Augur accursed! denouncing mischief still,
Prophet of plagues, for ever boding ill!
Still must that tongue some wounding message bring,
And still thy priestly pride provoke thy king?
For this are Phoebus' oracles explored,
To teach the Greeks to murmur at their lord?
For this with falsehood is my honour stain'd,
Is heaven offended, and a priest profaned;
Because my prize, my beauteous maid, I hold,
And heavenly charms prefer to proffer'd gold?
A maid, unmatch'd in manners as in face,
Skill'd in each art, and crown'd with every grace;
Not half so dear were Clytaemnestra's charms,
When first her blooming beauties bless'd my arms.
Yet, if the gods demand her, let her sail;
Our cares are only for the public weal:
Let me be deem'd the hateful cause of all,
And suffer, rather than my people fall.
The prize, the beauteous prize, I will resign,
So dearly valued, and so justly mine.
But since for common good I yield the fair,
My private loss let grateful Greece repair;
Nor unrewarded let your prince complain,
That he alone has fought and bled in vain."
"Insatiate king (Achilles thus replies),
Fond of the power, but fonder of the prize!
Would'st thou the Greeks their lawful prey should yield,
The due reward of many a well-fought field?

The spoils of cities razed and warriors slain,
We share with justice, as with toil we gain;
But to resume whate'er thy avarice craves
(That trick of tyrants) may be borne by slaves.
Yet if our chief for plunder only fight,
The spoils of Ilion shall thy loss requite,
Whene'er, by Jove's decree, our conquering powers
Shall humble to the dust her lofty towers."

Then thus the king: "Shall I my prize resign
With tame content, and thou possess'd of thine?
Great as thou art, and like a god in fight,
Think not to rob me of a soldier's right.
At thy demand shall I restore the maid?
First let the just equivalent be paid;
Such as a king might ask; and let it be
A treasure worthy her, and worthy me.
Or grant me this, or with a monarch's claim
This hand shall seize some other captive dame.
The mighty Ajax shall his prize resign;
Ulysses' spoils, or even thy own, be mine.
The man who suffers, loudly may complain;
And rage he may, but he shall rage in vain.
But this when time requires.—It now remains
We launch a bark to plough the watery plains,
And waft the sacrifice to Chrysa's shores,
With chosen pilots, and with labouring oars.
Soon shall the fair the sable ship ascend,
And some deputed prince the charge attend:
This Creta's king, or Ajax shall fulfil,
Or wise Ulysses see perform'd our will;
Or, if our royal pleasure shall ordain,
Achilles' self conduct her o'er the main;
Let fierce Achilles, dreadful in his rage,
The god propitiate, and the pest assuage."

At this, Pelides, frowning stern, replied:
"O tyrant, arm'd with insolence and pride!
Inglorious slave to interest, ever join'd
With fraud, unworthy of a royal mind!
What generous Greek, obedient to thy word,
Shall form an ambush, or shall lift the sword?
What cause have I to war at thy decree?
The distant Trojans never injured me;
To Phthia's realms no hostile troops they led:
Safe in her vales my warlike coursers fed;
Far hence removed, the hoarse-resounding main,
And walls of rocks, secure my native reign,
Whose fruitful soil luxuriant harvests grace,
Rich in her fruits, and in her martial race.
Hither we sail'd, a voluntary throng,
To avenge a private, not a public wrong:
What else to Troy the assembled nations draws,
But thine, ungrateful, and thy brother's cause?
Is this the pay our blood and toils deserve;
Disgraced and injured by the man we serve?

And darest thou threat to snatch my prize away,
Due to the deeds of many a dreadful day?
A prize as small, O tyrant! match'd with thine,
As thy own actions if compared to mine.
Thine in each conquest is the wealthy prey,
Though mine the sweat and danger of the day.
Some trivial present to my ships I bear:
Or barren praises pay the wounds of war.
But know, proud monarch, I'm thy slave no more;
My fleet shall waft me to Thessalia's shore:
Left by Achilles on the Trojan plain,
What spoils, what conquests, shall Atrides gain?"

To this the king: "Fly, mighty warrior! fly;
Thy aid we need not, and thy threats defy.
There want not chiefs in such a cause to fight,
And Jove himself shall guard a monarch's right.
Of all the kings (the god's distinguish'd care)
To power superior none such hatred bear:
Strife and debate thy restless soul employ,
And wars and horrors are thy savage joy,
If thou hast strength, 'twas Heaven that strength bestow'd;
For know, vain man! thy valour is from God.
Haste, launch thy vessels, fly with speed away;
Rule thy own realms with arbitrary sway;
I heed thee not, but prize at equal rate
Thy short-lived friendship, and thy groundless hate.
Go, threat thy earth-born Myrmidons:—but here
'Tis mine to threaten, prince, and thine to fear.
Know, if the god the beauteous dame demand,
My bark shall waft her to her native land;
But then prepare, imperious prince! prepare,
Fierce as thou art, to yield thy captive fair:
Even in thy tent I'll seize the blooming prize,
Thy loved Briseis with the radiant eyes.
Hence shalt thou prove my might, and curse the hour
Thou stood'st a rival of imperial power;
And hence, to all our hosts it shall be known,
That kings are subject to the gods alone."

Achilles heard, with grief and rage oppress'd,
His heart swell'd high, and labour'd in his breast;
Distracting thoughts by turns his bosom ruled;
Now fired by wrath, and now by reason cool'd:
That prompts his hand to draw the deadly sword,
Force through the Greeks, and pierce their haughty lord;
This whispers soft his vengeance to control,
And calm the rising tempest of his soul.

Just as in anguish of suspense he stay'd,
While half unsheathed appear'd the glittering blade,
Minerva swift descended from above,
Sent by the sister and the wife of Jove
(For both the princes claim'd her equal care);
Behind she stood, and by the golden hair
Achilles seized; to him alone confess'd;
A sable cloud conceal'd her from the rest.
He sees, and sudden to the goddess cries,
Known by the flames that sparkle from her eyes:

"Descends Minerva, in her guardian care,
A heavenly witness of the wrongs I bear
From Atreus' son?—Then let those eyes that view
The daring crime, behold the vengeance too."

"Forbear (the progeny of Jove replies)
To calm thy fury I forsake the skies:
Let great Achilles, to the gods resign'd,
To reason yield the empire o'er his mind.
By awful Juno this command is given;
The king and you are both the care of heaven.
The force of keen reproaches let him feel;
But sheathe, obedient, thy revenging steel.
For I pronounce (and trust a heavenly power)
Thy injured honour has its fated hour,
When the proud monarch shall thy arms implores
And bribe thy friendship with a boundless store.
Then let revenge no longer bear the sway;
Command thy passions, and the gods obey."

To her Pelides:—"With regardful ear,
'Tis just, O goddess! I thy dictates hear.
Hard as it is, my vengeance I suppress:
Those who revere the gods the gods will bless."
He said, observant of the blue-eyed maid;
Then in the sheath return'd the shining blade.
The goddess swift to high Olympus flies,
And joins the sacred senate of the skies.

Nor yet the rage his boiling breast forsook,
Which thus redoubling on Atrides broke:
"O monster! mix'd of insolence and fear,
Thou dog in forehead, but in heart a deer!
When wert thou known in ambush'd fights to dare,
Or nobly face the horrid front of war?
'Tis ours, the chance of fighting fields to try;
Thine to look on, and bid the valiant die:

So much 'tis safer through the camp to go,
And rob a subject, than despoil a foe.
Scourge of thy people, violent and base!
Sent in Jove's anger on a slavish race;
Who, lost to sense of generous freedom past,
Are tamed to wrongs;—or this had been thy last.
Now by this sacred sceptre hear me swear,
Which never more shall leaves or blossoms bear,
Which sever'd from the trunk (as I from thee)
On the bare mountains left its parent tree;
This sceptre, form'd by temper'd steel to prove
An ensign of the delegates of Jove,
From whom the power of laws and justice springs
(Tremendous oath! inviolate to kings);
By this I swear:—when bleeding Greece again
Shall call Achilles, she shall call in vain.
When, flush'd with slaughter, Hector comes to spread
The purpled shore with mountains of the dead,
Then shall thou mourn the affront thy madness gave,
Forced to deplore when impotent to save:
Then rage in bitterness of soul to know
This act has made the bravest Greek thy foe."

He spoke; and furious hurl'd against the ground
His sceptre starr'd with golden studs around:
Then sternly silent sat. With like disdain
The raging king return'd his frowns again.

To calm their passion with the words of age,
Slow from his seat arose the Pylian sage,
Experienced Nestor, in persuasion skill'd;
Words, sweet as honey, from his lips distill'd:
Two generations now had pass'd away,
Wise by his rules, and happy by his sway;
Two ages o'er his native realm he reign'd,
And now the example of the third remain'd.
All view'd with awe the venerable man;
Who thus with mild benevolence began:—

"What shame, what woe is this to Greece! what joy
To Troy's proud monarch, and the friends of Troy!
That adverse gods commit to stern debate
The best, the bravest, of the Grecian state.
Young as ye are, this youthful heat restrain,
Nor think your Nestor's years and wisdom vain.
A godlike race of heroes once I knew,
Such as no more these aged eyes shall view!
Lives there a chief to match Pirithous' fame,

Dryas the bold, or Ceneus' deathless name;
Theseus, endued with more than mortal might,
Or Polyphemus, like the gods in fight?
With these of old, to toils of battle bred,
In early youth my hardy days I led;
Fired with the thirst which virtuous envy breeds,
And smit with love of honourable deeds,
Strongest of men, they pierced the mountain boar,
Ranged the wild deserts red with monsters' gore,
And from their hills the shaggy Centaurs tore:
Yet these with soft persuasive arts I sway'd;
When Nestor spoke, they listen'd and obey'd.
If in my youth, even these esteem'd me wise;
Do you, young warriors, hear my age advise.
Atrides, seize not on the beauteous slave;
That prize the Greeks by common suffrage gave:
Nor thou, Achilles, treat our prince with pride;
Let kings be just, and sovereign power preside.
Thee, the first honours of the war adorn,
Like gods in strength, and of a goddess born;
Him, awful majesty exalts above
The powers of earth, and sceptred sons of Jove.
Let both unite with well-consenting mind,
So shall authority with strength be join'd.
Leave me, O king! to calm Achilles' rage;
Rule thou thyself, as more advanced in age.
Forbid it, gods! Achilles should be lost,
The pride of Greece, and bulwark of our host."

This said, he ceased. The king of men replies:
"Thy years are awful, and thy words are wise.
But that imperious, that unconquer'd soul,
No laws can limit, no respect control.
Before his pride must his superiors fall;
His word the law, and he the lord of all?
Him must our hosts, our chiefs, ourself obey?
What king can bear a rival in his sway?
Grant that the gods his matchless force have given;
Has foul reproach a privilege from heaven?"

Here on the monarch's speech Achilles broke,
And furious, thus, and interrupting spoke:
"Tyrant, I well deserved thy galling chain,
To live thy slave, and still to serve in vain,
Should I submit to each unjust decree:—
Command thy vassals, but command not me.
Seize on Briseis, whom the Grecians doom'd
My prize of war, yet tamely see resumed;

And seize secure; no more Achilles draws
His conquering sword in any woman's cause.
The gods command me to forgive the past:
But let this first invasion be the last:
For know, thy blood, when next thou darest invade,
Shall stream in vengeance on my reeking blade."

At this they ceased: the stern debate expired:
The chiefs in sullen majesty retired.

Achilles with Patroclus took his way
Where near his tents his hollow vessels lay.
Meantime Atrides launch'd with numerous oars
A well-rigg'd ship for Chrysa's sacred shores:
High on the deck was fair Chryseis placed,
And sage Ulysses with the conduct graced:
Safe in her sides the hecatomb they stow'd,
Then swiftly sailing, cut the liquid road.

The host to expiate next the king prepares,
With pure lustrations, and with solemn prayers.
Wash'd by the briny wave, the pious train
Are cleansed; and cast the ablutions in the main.
Along the shore whole hecatombs were laid,
And bulls and goats to Phoebus' altars paid;
The sable fumes in curling spires arise,
And waft their grateful odours to the skies.

The army thus in sacred rites engaged,
Atrides still with deep resentment raged.
To wait his will two sacred heralds stood,
Talthybius and Eurybates the good.
"Haste to the fierce Achilles' tent (he cries),
Thence bear Briseis as our royal prize:
Submit he must; or if they will not part,
Ourself in arms shall tear her from his heart."

The unwilling heralds act their lord's commands;
Pensive they walk along the barren sands:
Arrived, the hero in his tent they find,
With gloomy aspect on his arm reclined.
At awful distance long they silent stand,
Loth to advance, and speak their hard command;
Decent confusion! This the godlike man
Perceived, and thus with accent mild began:

"With leave and honour enter our abodes,
Ye sacred ministers of men and gods!

I know your message; by constraint you came;
Not you, but your imperious lord I blame.
Patroclus, haste, the fair Briseis bring;
Conduct my captive to the haughty king.
But witness, heralds, and proclaim my vow,
Witness to gods above, and men below!
But first, and loudest, to your prince declare
(That lawless tyrant whose commands you bear),
Unmoved as death Achilles shall remain,
Though prostrate Greece shall bleed at every vein:
The raging chief in frantic passion lost,
Blind to himself, and useless to his host,
Unskill'd to judge the future by the past,
In blood and slaughter shall repent at last."

Patroclus now the unwilling beauty brought;
She, in soft sorrows, and in pensive thought,
Pass'd silent, as the heralds held her hand,
And of look'd back, slow-moving o'er the strand.
Not so his loss the fierce Achilles bore;
But sad, retiring to the sounding shore,
O'er the wild margin of the deep he hung,
That kindred deep from whence his mother sprung:
There bathed in tears of anger and disdain,
Thus loud lamented to the stormy main:

"O parent goddess! since in early bloom
Thy son must fall, by too severe a doom;
Sure to so short a race of glory born,
Great Jove in justice should this span adorn:
Honour and fame at least the thunderer owed;
And ill he pays the promise of a god,
If yon proud monarch thus thy son defies,
Obscures my glories, and resumes my prize."

Far from the deep recesses of the main,
Where aged Ocean holds his watery reign,
The goddess-mother heard. The waves divide;
And like a mist she rose above the tide;
Beheld him mourning on the naked shores,
And thus the sorrows of his soul explores.
"Why grieves my son? Thy anguish let me share;
Reveal the cause, and trust a parent's care."

He deeply sighing said: "To tell my woe
Is but to mention what too well you know.
From Thebe, sacred to Apollo's name
(Aetion's realm), our conquering army came,

With treasure loaded and triumphant spoils,
Whose just division crown'd the soldier's toils;
But bright Chryseis, heavenly prize! was led,
By vote selected, to the general's bed.
The priest of Phoebus sought by gifts to gain
His beauteous daughter from the victor's chain;
The fleet he reach'd, and, lowly bending down,
Held forth the sceptre and the laurel crown,
Intreating all; but chief implored for grace
The brother-kings of Atreus' royal race:
The generous Greeks their joint consent declare,
The priest to reverence, and release the fair;
Not so Atrides: he, with wonted pride,
The sire insulted, and his gifts denied:
The insulted sire (his god's peculiar care)
To Phoebus pray'd, and Phoebus heard the prayer:
A dreadful plague ensues: the avenging darts
Incessant fly, and pierce the Grecian hearts.
A prophet then, inspired by heaven, arose,
And points the crime, and thence derives the woes:
Myself the first the assembled chiefs incline
To avert the vengeance of the power divine;
Then rising in his wrath, the monarch storm'd;
Incensed he threaten'd, and his threats perform'd:
The fair Chryseis to her sire was sent,
With offer'd gifts to make the god relent;
But now he seized Briseis' heavenly charms,
And of my valour's prize defrauds my arms,
Defrauds the votes of all the Grecian train;
And service, faith, and justice, plead in vain.
But, goddess! thou thy suppliant son attend.
To high Olympus' shining court ascend,
Urge all the ties to former service owed,
And sue for vengeance to the thundering god.
Oft hast thou triumph'd in the glorious boast,
That thou stood'st forth of all the ethereal host,
When bold rebellion shook the realms above,
The undaunted guard of cloud-compelling Jove:
When the bright partner of his awful reign,
The warlike maid, and monarch of the main,
The traitor-gods, by mad ambition driven,
Durst threat with chains the omnipotence of Heaven.
Then, call'd by thee, the monster Titan came
(Whom gods Briareus, men Ćgeon name),
Through wondering skies enormous stalk'd along;
Not he that shakes the solid earth so strong:
With giant-pride at Jove's high throne he stands,
And brandish'd round him all his hundred hands:

The affrighted gods confess'd their awful lord,
They dropp'd the fetters, trembled, and adored.
This, goddess, this to his remembrance call,
Embrace his knees, at his tribunal fall;
Conjure him far to drive the Grecian train,
To hurl them headlong to their fleet and main,
To heap the shores with copious death, and bring
The Greeks to know the curse of such a king.
Let Agamemnon lift his haughty head
O'er all his wide dominion of the dead,
And mourn in blood that e'er he durst disgrace
The boldest warrior of the Grecian race."

"Unhappy son! (fair Thetis thus replies,
While tears celestial trickle from her eyes)
Why have I borne thee with a mother's throes,
To Fates averse, and nursed for future woes?
So short a space the light of heaven to view!
So short a space! and fill'd with sorrow too!
O might a parent's careful wish prevail,
Far, far from Ilion should thy vessels sail,
And thou, from camps remote, the danger shun
Which now, alas! too nearly threats my son.
Yet (what I can) to move thy suit I'll go
To great Olympus crown'd with fleecy snow.
Meantime, secure within thy ships, from far
Behold the field, not mingle in the war.
The sire of gods and all the ethereal train,
On the warm limits of the farthest main,
Now mix with mortals, nor disdain to grace
The feasts of Ćthiopia's blameless race,
Twelve days the powers indulge the genial rite,
Returning with the twelfth revolving light.
Then will I mount the brazen dome, and move
The high tribunal of immortal Jove."

The goddess spoke: the rolling waves unclose;
Then down the steep she plunged from whence she rose,
And left him sorrowing on the lonely coast,
In wild resentment for the fair he lost.

In Chrysa's port now sage Ulysses rode;
Beneath the deck the destined victims stow'd:
The sails they furl'd, they lash the mast aside,
And dropp'd their anchors, and the pinnace tied.
Next on the shore their hecatomb they land;
Chryseis last descending on the strand.
Her, thus returning from the furrow'd main,

Ulysses led to Phoebus' sacred fane;
Where at his solemn altar, as the maid
He gave to Chryses, thus the hero said:

"Hail, reverend priest! to Phoebus' awful dome
A suppliant I from great Atrides come:
Unransom'd, here receive the spotless fair;
Accept the hecatomb the Greeks prepare;
And may thy god who scatters darts around,
Atoned by sacrifice, desist to wound."

At this, the sire embraced the maid again,
So sadly lost, so lately sought in vain.
Then near the altar of the darting king,
Disposed in rank their hecatomb they bring;
With water purify their hands, and take
The sacred offering of the salted cake;
While thus with arms devoutly raised in air,
And solemn voice, the priest directs his prayer:

"God of the silver bow, thy ear incline,
Whose power incircles Cilla the divine;
Whose sacred eye thy Tenedos surveys,
And gilds fair Chrysa with distinguish'd rays!
If, fired to vengeance at thy priest's request,
Thy direful darts inflict the raging pest:
Once more attend! avert the wasteful woe,
And smile propitious, and unbend thy bow."

So Chryses pray'd. Apollo heard his prayer:
And now the Greeks their hecatomb prepare;
Between their horns the salted barley threw,
And, with their heads to heaven, the victims slew:
The limbs they sever from the inclosing hide;
The thighs, selected to the gods, divide:
On these, in double cauls involved with art,
The choicest morsels lay from every part.
The priest himself before his altar stands,
And burns the offering with his holy hands.
Pours the black wine, and sees the flames aspire;
The youth with instruments surround the fire:
The thighs thus sacrificed, and entrails dress'd,
The assistants part, transfix, and roast the rest:
Then spread the tables, the repast prepare;
Each takes his seat, and each receives his share.
When now the rage of hunger was repress'd,
With pure libations they conclude the feast;
The youths with wine the copious goblets crown'd,

And, pleased, dispense the flowing bowls around;
With hymns divine the joyous banquet ends,
The paeans lengthen'd till the sun descends:
The Greeks, restored, the grateful notes prolong;
Apollo listens, and approves the song.

'Twas night; the chiefs beside their vessel lie,
Till rosy morn had purpled o'er the sky:
Then launch, and hoist the mast: indulgent gales,
Supplied by Phoebus, fill the swelling sails;
The milk-white canvas bellying as they blow,
The parted ocean foams and roars below:
Above the bounding billows swift they flew,
Till now the Grecian camp appear'd in view.
Far on the beach they haul their bark to land,
(The crooked keel divides the yellow sand,)
Then part, where stretch'd along the winding bay,
The ships and tents in mingled prospect lay.

But raging still, amidst his navy sat
The stern Achilles, stedfast in his hate;
Nor mix'd in combat, nor in council join'd;
But wasting cares lay heavy on his mind:
In his black thoughts revenge and slaughter roll,
And scenes of blood rise dreadful in his soul.

Twelve days were past, and now the dawning light
The gods had summon'd to the Olympian height:
Jove, first ascending from the watery bowers,
Leads the long order of ethereal powers.
When, like the morning-mist in early day,
Rose from the flood the daughter of the sea:
And to the seats divine her flight address'd.
There, far apart, and high above the rest,
The thunderer sat; where old Olympus shrouds
His hundred heads in heaven, and props the clouds.
Suppliant the goddess stood: one hand she placed
Beneath his beard, and one his knees embraced.
"If e'er, O father of the gods! (she said)
My words could please thee, or my actions aid,
Some marks of honour on my son bestow,
And pay in glory what in life you owe.
Fame is at least by heavenly promise due
To life so short, and now dishonour'd too.
Avenge this wrong, O ever just and wise!
Let Greece be humbled, and the Trojans rise;
Till the proud king and all the Achaian race
Shall heap with honours him they now disgrace."

Thus Thetis spoke; but Jove in silence held
The sacred counsels of his breast conceal'd.
Not so repulsed, the goddess closer press'd,
Still grasp'd his knees, and urged the dear request.
"O sire of gods and men! thy suppliant hear;
Refuse, or grant; for what has Jove to fear?
Or oh! declare, of all the powers above,
Is wretched Thetis least the care of Jove?"

She said; and, sighing, thus the god replies,
Who rolls the thunder o'er the vaulted skies:

"What hast thou ask'd? ah, why should Jove engage
In foreign contests and domestic rage,
The gods' complaints, and Juno's fierce alarms,
While I, too partial, aid the Trojan arms?
Go, lest the haughty partner of my sway
With jealous eyes thy close access survey;
But part in peace, secure thy prayer is sped:
Witness the sacred honours of our head,
The nod that ratifies the will divine,
The faithful, fix'd, irrevocable sign;
This seals thy suit, and this fulfils thy vows—"
He spoke, and awful bends his sable brows,
Shakes his ambrosial curls, and gives the nod,
The stamp of fate and sanction of the god:
High heaven with trembling the dread signal took,
And all Olympus to the centre shook.

Swift to the seas profound the goddess flies,
Jove to his starry mansions in the skies.
The shining synod of the immortals wait
The coming god, and from their thrones of state
Arising silent, wrapp'd in holy fear,
Before the majesty of heaven appear.
Trembling they stand, while Jove assumes the throne,
All, but the god's imperious queen alone:
Late had she view'd the silver-footed dame,
And all her passions kindled into flame.
"Say, artful manager of heaven (she cries),
Who now partakes the secrets of the skies?
Thy Juno knows not the decrees of fate,
In vain the partner of imperial state.
What favourite goddess then those cares divides,
Which Jove in prudence from his consort hides?"

To this the thunderer: "Seek not thou to find

The sacred counsels of almighty mind:
Involved in darkness likes the great decree,
Nor can the depths of fate be pierced by thee.
What fits thy knowledge, thou the first shalt know;
The first of gods above, and men below;
But thou, nor they, shall search the thoughts that roll
Deep in the close recesses of my soul."

Full on the sire the goddess of the skies
Roll'd the large orbs of her majestic eyes,
And thus return'd:—"Austere Saturnius, say,
From whence this wrath, or who controls thy sway?
Thy boundless will, for me, remains in force,
And all thy counsels take the destined course.
But 'tis for Greece I fear: for late was seen,
In close consult, the silver-footed queen.
Jove to his Thetis nothing could deny,
Nor was the signal vain that shook the sky.
What fatal favour has the goddess won,
To grace her fierce, inexorable son?
Perhaps in Grecian blood to drench the plain,
And glut his vengeance with my people slain."

Then thus the god: "O restless fate of pride,
That strives to learn what heaven resolves to hide;
Vain is the search, presumptuous and abhorr'd,
Anxious to thee, and odious to thy lord.
Let this suffice: the immutable decree
No force can shake: what is, that ought to be.
Goddess, submit; nor dare our will withstand,
But dread the power of this avenging hand:
The united strength of all the gods above
In vain resists the omnipotence of Jove."

The thunderer spoke, nor durst the queen reply;
A reverent horror silenced all the sky.
The feast disturb'd, with sorrow Vulcan saw
His mother menaced, and the gods in awe;
Peace at his heart, and pleasure his design,
Thus interposed the architect divine:
"The wretched quarrels of the mortal state
Are far unworthy, gods! of your debate:
Let men their days in senseless strife employ,
We, in eternal peace and constant joy.
Thou, goddess-mother, with our sire comply,
Nor break the sacred union of the sky:
Lest, roused to rage, he shake the bless'd abodes,
Launch the red lightning, and dethrone the gods.

If you submit, the thunderer stands appeased;
The gracious power is willing to be pleased."

Thus Vulcan spoke: and rising with a bound,
The double bowl with sparkling nectar crown'd,
Which held to Juno in a cheerful way,
"Goddess (he cried), be patient and obey.
Dear as you are, if Jove his arm extend,
I can but grieve, unable to defend
What god so daring in your aid to move,
Or lift his hand against the force of Jove?
Once in your cause I felt his matchless might,
Hurl'd headlong down from the ethereal height;
Toss'd all the day in rapid circles round,
Nor till the sun descended touch'd the ground.
Breathless I fell, in giddy motion lost;
The Sinthians raised me on the Lemnian coast;

He said, and to her hands the goblet heaved,
Which, with a smile, the white-arm'd queen received
Then, to the rest he fill'd; and in his turn,
Each to his lips applied the nectar'd urn,
Vulcan with awkward grace his office plies,
And unextinguish'd laughter shakes the skies.

Thus the blest gods the genial day prolong,
In feasts ambrosial, and celestial song.
Apollo tuned the lyre; the Muses round
With voice alternate aid the silver sound.
Meantime the radiant sun to mortal sight
Descending swift, roll'd down the rapid light:
Then to their starry domes the gods depart,
The shining monuments of Vulcan's art:
Jove on his couch reclined his awful head,
And Juno slumber'd on the golden bed.

BOOK II

ARGUMENT

THE TRIAL OF THE ARMY, AND CATALOGUE OF THE FORCES

Jupiter, in pursuance of the request of Thetis, sends a deceitful vision to Agamemnon, persuading him to lead the army to battle, in order to make the Greeks sensible of their want of Achilles. The general, who is deluded with the hopes of taking Troy without his assistance, but fears the army was discouraged by his absence, and the late plague, as well as by the length of time, contrives to make trial of their

disposition by a stratagem. He first communicates his design to the princes in council, that he would
propose a return to the soldiers, and that they should put a stop to them if the proposal was embraced.
Then he assembles the whole host, and upon moving for a return to Greece, they unanimously agree to
it, and run to prepare the ships. They are detained by the management of Ulysses, who chastises the
insolence of Thersites. The assembly is recalled, several speeches made on the occasion, and at length
the advice of Nestor followed, which was to make a general muster of the troops, and to divide them
into their several nations, before they proceeded to battle. This gives occasion to the poet to enumerate
all the forces of the Greeks and Trojans, and in a large catalogue.

The time employed in this book consists not entirely of one day. The scene lies in the Grecian camp, and
upon the sea-shore; towards the end it removes to Troy.

Now pleasing sleep had seal'd each mortal eye,
Stretch'd in the tents the Grecian leaders lie:
The immortals slumber'd on their thrones above;
All, but the ever-wakeful eyes of Jove.
To honour Thetis' son he bends his care,
And plunge the Greeks in all the woes of war:
Then bids an empty phantom rise to sight,
And thus commands the vision of the night.

"Fly hence, deluding Dream! and light as air,
To Agamemnon's ample tent repair.
Bid him in arms draw forth the embattled train,
Lead all his Grecians to the dusty plain.
Declare, e'en now 'tis given him to destroy
The lofty towers of wide-extended Troy.
For now no more the gods with fate contend,
At Juno's suit the heavenly factions end.
Destruction hangs o'er yon devoted wall,
And nodding Ilion waits the impending fall."

Swift as the word the vain illusion fled,
Descends, and hovers o'er Atrides' head;
Clothed in the figure of the Pylian sage,
Renown'd for wisdom, and revered for age:
Around his temples spreads his golden wing,
And thus the flattering dream deceives the king.

"Canst thou, with all a monarch's cares oppress'd,
O Atreus' son! canst thou indulge the rest?
Ill fits a chief who mighty nations guides,
Directs in council, and in war presides,
To whom its safety a whole people owes,
To waste long nights in indolent repose.
Monarch, awake! 'tis Jove's command I bear;
Thou, and thy glory, claim his heavenly care.
In just array draw forth the embattled train,

Lead all thy Grecians to the dusty plain;
E'en now, O king! 'tis given thee to destroy
The lofty towers of wide-extended Troy.
For now no more the gods with fate contend,
At Juno's suit the heavenly factions end.
Destruction hangs o'er yon devoted wall,
And nodding Ilion waits the impending fall.
Awake, but waking this advice approve,
And trust the vision that descends from Jove."

The phantom said; then vanish'd from his sight,
Resolves to air, and mixes with the night.
A thousand schemes the monarch's mind employ;
Elate in thought he sacks untaken Troy:
Vain as he was, and to the future blind,
Nor saw what Jove and secret fate design'd,
What mighty toils to either host remain,
What scenes of grief, and numbers of the slain!
Eager he rises, and in fancy hears
The voice celestial murmuring in his ears.
First on his limbs a slender vest he drew,
Around him next the regal mantle threw,
The embroider'd sandals on his feet were tied;
The starry falchion glitter'd at his side;
And last, his arm the massy sceptre loads,
Unstain'd, immortal, and the gift of gods.

Now rosy Morn ascends the court of Jove,
Lifts up her light, and opens day above.
The king despatch'd his heralds with commands
To range the camp and summon all the bands:
The gathering hosts the monarch's word obey;
While to the fleet Atrides bends his way.
In his black ship the Pylian prince he found;
There calls a senate of the peers around:
The assembly placed, the king of men express'd
The counsels labouring in his artful breast.

"Friends and confederates! with attentive ear
Receive my words, and credit what you hear.
Late as I slumber'd in the shades of night,
A dream divine appear'd before my sight;
Whose visionary form like Nestor came,
The same in habit, and in mien the same.
The heavenly phantom hover'd o'er my head,
'And, dost thou sleep, O Atreus' son? (he said)
Ill fits a chief who mighty nations guides,
Directs in council, and in war presides;

To whom its safety a whole people owes,
To waste long nights in indolent repose.
Monarch, awake! 'tis Jove's command I bear,
Thou and thy glory claim his heavenly care.
In just array draw forth the embattled train,
And lead the Grecians to the dusty plain;
E'en now, O king! 'tis given thee to destroy
The lofty towers of wide-extended Troy.
For now no more the gods with fate contend,
At Juno's suit the heavenly factions end.
Destruction hangs o'er yon devoted wall,
And nodding Ilion waits the impending fall.

This hear observant, and the gods obey!'
The vision spoke, and pass'd in air away.
Now, valiant chiefs! since heaven itself alarms,
Unite, and rouse the sons of Greece to arms.
But first, with caution, try what yet they dare,
Worn with nine years of unsuccessful war.
To move the troops to measure back the main,
Be mine; and yours the province to detain."

He spoke, and sat: when Nestor, rising said,
(Nestor, whom Pylos' sandy realms obey'd,)
"Princes of Greece, your faithful ears incline,
Nor doubt the vision of the powers divine;
Sent by great Jove to him who rules the host,
Forbid it, heaven! this warning should be lost!
Then let us haste, obey the god's alarms,
And join to rouse the sons of Greece to arms."

Thus spoke the sage: the kings without delay
Dissolve the council, and their chief obey:
The sceptred rulers lead; the following host,
Pour'd forth by thousands, darkens all the coast.
As from some rocky cleft the shepherd sees
Clustering in heaps on heaps the driving bees,
Rolling and blackening, swarms succeeding swarms,
With deeper murmurs and more hoarse alarms;
Dusky they spread, a close embodied crowd,
And o'er the vale descends the living cloud.
So, from the tents and ships, a lengthen'd train
Spreads all the beach, and wide o'ershades the plain:
Along the region runs a deafening sound;
Beneath their footsteps groans the trembling ground.
Fame flies before the messenger of Jove,
And shining soars, and claps her wings above.
Nine sacred heralds now, proclaiming loud

The monarch's will, suspend the listening crowd.
Soon as the throngs in order ranged appear,
And fainter murmurs died upon the ear,
The king of kings his awful figure raised:
High in his hand the golden sceptre blazed;
The golden sceptre, of celestial flame,
By Vulcan form'd, from Jove to Hermes came.
To Pelops he the immortal gift resign'd;
The immortal gift great Pelops left behind,
In Atreus' hand, which not with Atreus ends,
To rich Thyestes next the prize descends;
And now the mark of Agamemnon's reign,
Subjects all Argos, and controls the main.

On this bright sceptre now the king reclined,
And artful thus pronounced the speech design'd:
"Ye sons of Mars, partake your leader's care,
Heroes of Greece, and brothers of the war!
Of partial Jove with justice I complain,
And heavenly oracles believed in vain
A safe return was promised to our toils,
Renown'd, triumphant, and enrich'd with spoils.
Now shameful flight alone can save the host,
Our blood, our treasure, and our glory lost.
So Jove decrees, resistless lord of all!
At whose command whole empires rise or fall:
He shakes the feeble props of human trust,
And towns and armies humbles to the dust
What shame to Greece a fruitful war to wage,
Oh, lasting shame in every future age!
Once great in arms, the common scorn we grow,
Repulsed and baffled by a feeble foe.
So small their number, that if wars were ceased,
And Greece triumphant held a general feast,
All rank'd by tens, whole decades when they dine
Must want a Trojan slave to pour the wine.
But other forces have our hopes o'erthrown,
And Troy prevails by armies not her own.
Now nine long years of mighty Jove are run,
Since first the labours of this war begun:
Our cordage torn, decay'd our vessels lie,
And scarce insure the wretched power to fly.
Haste, then, for ever leave the Trojan wall!
Our weeping wives, our tender children call:
Love, duty, safety, summon us away,
'Tis nature's voice, and nature we obey,
Our shatter'd barks may yet transport us o'er,
Safe and inglorious, to our native shore.

Fly, Grecians, fly, your sails and oars employ,
And dream no more of heaven-defended Troy."

His deep design unknown, the hosts approve
Atrides' speech. The mighty numbers move.
So roll the billows to the Icarian shore,
From east and south when winds begin to roar,
Burst their dark mansions in the clouds, and sweep
The whitening surface of the ruffled deep.
And as on corn when western gusts descend,
Before the blast the lofty harvests bend:
Thus o'er the field the moving host appears,
With nodding plumes and groves of waving spears.
The gathering murmur spreads, their trampling feet
Beat the loose sands, and thicken to the fleet;
With long-resounding cries they urge the train
To fit the ships, and launch into the main.
They toil, they sweat, thick clouds of dust arise,
The doubling clamours echo to the skies.
E'en then the Greeks had left the hostile plain,
And fate decreed the fall of Troy in vain;
But Jove's imperial queen their flight survey'd,
And sighing thus bespoke the blue-eyed maid:

"Shall then the Grecians fly! O dire disgrace!
And leave unpunish'd this perfidious race?
Shall Troy, shall Priam, and the adulterous spouse,
In peace enjoy the fruits of broken vows?
And bravest chiefs, in Helen's quarrel slain,
Lie unrevenged on yon detested plain?
No: let my Greeks, unmoved by vain alarms,
Once more refulgent shine in brazen arms.
Haste, goddess, haste! the flying host detain,
Nor let one sail be hoisted on the main."

Pallas obeys, and from Olympus' height
Swift to the ships precipitates her flight.
Ulysses, first in public cares, she found,
For prudent counsel like the gods renown'd:
Oppress'd with generous grief the hero stood,
Nor drew his sable vessels to the flood.
"And is it thus, divine Laertes' son,
Thus fly the Greeks (the martial maid begun),
Thus to their country bear their own disgrace,
And fame eternal leave to Priam's race?
Shall beauteous Helen still remain unfreed,
Still unrevenged, a thousand heroes bleed!
Haste, generous Ithacus! prevent the shame,

Recall your armies, and your chiefs reclaim.
Your own resistless eloquence employ,
And to the immortals trust the fall of Troy."

The voice divine confess'd the warlike maid,
Ulysses heard, nor uninspired obey'd:
Then meeting first Atrides, from his hand
Received the imperial sceptre of command.
Thus graced, attention and respect to gain,
He runs, he flies through all the Grecian train;
Each prince of name, or chief in arms approved,
He fired with praise, or with persuasion moved.

"Warriors like you, with strength and wisdom bless'd,
By brave examples should confirm the rest.
The monarch's will not yet reveal'd appears;
He tries our courage, but resents our fears.
The unwary Greeks his fury may provoke;
Not thus the king in secret council spoke.
Jove loves our chief, from Jove his honour springs,
Beware! for dreadful is the wrath of kings."

But if a clamorous vile plebeian rose,
Him with reproof he check'd or tamed with blows.
"Be still, thou slave, and to thy betters yield;
Unknown alike in council and in field!
Ye gods, what dastards would our host command!
Swept to the war, the lumber of a land.
Be silent, wretch, and think not here allow'd
That worst of tyrants, an usurping crowd.
To one sole monarch Jove commits the sway;
His are the laws, and him let all obey."

With words like these the troops Ulysses ruled,
The loudest silenced, and the fiercest cool'd.
Back to the assembly roll the thronging train,
Desert the ships, and pour upon the plain.
Murmuring they move, as when old ocean roars,
And heaves huge surges to the trembling shores;
The groaning banks are burst with bellowing sound,
The rocks remurmur and the deeps rebound.
At length the tumult sinks, the noises cease,
And a still silence lulls the camp to peace.
Thersites only clamour'd in the throng,
Loquacious, loud, and turbulent of tongue:
Awed by no shame, by no respect controll'd,
In scandal busy, in reproaches bold:
With witty malice studious to defame,

Scorn all his joy, and laughter all his aim:—
But chief he gloried with licentious style
To lash the great, and monarchs to revile.
His figure such as might his soul proclaim;
One eye was blinking, and one leg was lame:
His mountain shoulders half his breast o'erspread,
Thin hairs bestrew'd his long misshapen head.
Spleen to mankind his envious heart possess'd,
And much he hated all, but most the best:
Ulysses or Achilles still his theme;
But royal scandal his delight supreme,
Long had he lived the scorn of every Greek,
Vex'd when he spoke, yet still they heard him speak.
Sharp was his voice; which in the shrillest tone,
Thus with injurious taunts attack'd the throne.

"Amidst the glories of so bright a reign,
What moves the great Atrides to complain?
'Tis thine whate'er the warrior's breast inflames,
The golden spoil, and thine the lovely dames.
With all the wealth our wars and blood bestow,
Thy tents are crowded and thy chests o'erflow.
Thus at full ease in heaps of riches roll'd,
What grieves the monarch? Is it thirst of gold?
Say, shall we march with our unconquer'd powers
(The Greeks and I) to Ilion's hostile towers,
And bring the race of royal bastards here,
For Troy to ransom at a price too dear?
But safer plunder thy own host supplies;
Say, wouldst thou seize some valiant leader's prize?
Or, if thy heart to generous love be led,
Some captive fair, to bless thy kingly bed?
Whate'er our master craves submit we must,
Plagued with his pride, or punish'd for his lust.
Oh women of Achaia; men no more!
Hence let us fly, and let him waste his store
In loves and pleasures on the Phrygian shore.
We may be wanted on some busy day,
When Hector comes: so great Achilles may:
From him he forced the prize we jointly gave,
From him, the fierce, the fearless, and the brave:
And durst he, as he ought, resent that wrong,
This mighty tyrant were no tyrant long."

Fierce from his seat at this Ulysses springs,
In generous vengeance of the king of kings.
With indignation sparkling in his eyes,
He views the wretch, and sternly thus replies:

"Peace, factious monster, born to vex the state,
With wrangling talents form'd for foul debate:
Curb that impetuous tongue, nor rashly vain,
And singly mad, asperse the sovereign reign.
Have we not known thee, slave! of all our host,
The man who acts the least, upbraids the most?
Think not the Greeks to shameful flight to bring,
Nor let those lips profane the name of king.
For our return we trust the heavenly powers;
Be that their care; to fight like men be ours.
But grant the host with wealth the general load,
Except detraction, what hast thou bestow'd?
Suppose some hero should his spoils resign,
Art thou that hero, could those spoils be thine?
Gods! let me perish on this hateful shore,
And let these eyes behold my son no more;
If, on thy next offence, this hand forbear
To strip those arms thou ill deserv'st to wear,
Expel the council where our princes meet,
And send thee scourged and howling through the fleet."

He said, and cowering as the dastard bends,
The weighty sceptre on his bank descends.
On the round bunch the bloody tumours rise:
The tears spring starting from his haggard eyes;
Trembling he sat, and shrunk in abject fears,
From his vile visage wiped the scalding tears;
While to his neighbour each express'd his thought:

"Ye gods! what wonders has Ulysses wrought!
What fruits his conduct and his courage yield!
Great in the council, glorious in the field.
Generous he rises in the crown's defence,
To curb the factious tongue of insolence,
Such just examples on offenders shown,
Sedition silence, and assert the throne."

'Twas thus the general voice the hero praised,
Who, rising, high the imperial sceptre raised:
The blue-eyed Pallas, his celestial friend,
(In form a herald,) bade the crowds attend.
The expecting crowds in still attention hung,
To hear the wisdom of his heavenly tongue.
Then deeply thoughtful, pausing ere he spoke,
His silence thus the prudent hero broke:

"Unhappy monarch! whom the Grecian race

With shame deserting, heap with vile disgrace.
Not such at Argos was their generous vow:
Once all their voice, but ah! forgotten now:
Ne'er to return, was then the common cry,
Till Troy's proud structures should in ashes lie.
Behold them weeping for their native shore;
What could their wives or helpless children more?
What heart but melts to leave the tender train,
And, one short month, endure the wintry main?
Few leagues removed, we wish our peaceful seat,
When the ship tosses, and the tempests beat:
Then well may this long stay provoke their tears,
The tedious length of nine revolving years.
Not for their grief the Grecian host I blame;
But vanquish'd! baffled! oh, eternal shame!
Expect the time to Troy's destruction given.
And try the faith of Chalcas and of heaven.
What pass'd at Aulis, Greece can witness bear,
And all who live to breathe this Phrygian air.
Beside a fountain's sacred brink we raised
Our verdant altars, and the victims blazed:
'Twas where the plane-tree spread its shades around,
The altars heaved; and from the crumbling ground
A mighty dragon shot, of dire portent;
From Jove himself the dreadful sign was sent.
Straight to the tree his sanguine spires he roll'd,
And curl'd around in many a winding fold;
The topmost branch a mother-bird possess'd;
Eight callow infants fill'd the mossy nest;
Herself the ninth; the serpent, as he hung,
Stretch'd his black jaws and crush'd the crying young;
While hovering near, with miserable moan,
The drooping mother wail'd her children gone.
The mother last, as round the nest she flew,
Seized by the beating wing, the monster slew;
Nor long survived: to marble turn'd, he stands
A lasting prodigy on Aulis' sands.
Such was the will of Jove; and hence we dare
Trust in his omen, and support the war.
For while around we gazed with wondering eyes,
And trembling sought the powers with sacrifice,
Full of his god, the reverend Chalcas cried,
'Ye Grecian warriors! lay your fears aside.
This wondrous signal Jove himself displays,
Of long, long labours, but eternal praise.
As many birds as by the snake were slain,
So many years the toils of Greece remain;
But wait the tenth, for Ilion's fall decreed:'

Thus spoke the prophet, thus the Fates succeed.
Obey, ye Grecians! with submission wait,
Nor let your flight avert the Trojan fate."
He said: the shores with loud applauses sound,
The hollow ships each deafening shout rebound.
Then Nestor thus—"These vain debates forbear,
Ye talk like children, not like heroes dare.
Where now are all your high resolves at last?
Your leagues concluded, your engagements past?
Vow'd with libations and with victims then,
Now vanish'd like their smoke: the faith of men!
While useless words consume the unactive hours,
No wonder Troy so long resists our powers.
Rise, great Atrides! and with courage sway;
We march to war, if thou direct the way.
But leave the few that dare resist thy laws,
The mean deserters of the Grecian cause,
To grudge the conquests mighty Jove prepares,
And view with envy our successful wars.
On that great day, when first the martial train,
Big with the fate of Ilion, plough'd the main,
Jove, on the right, a prosperous signal sent,
And thunder rolling shook the firmament.
Encouraged hence, maintain the glorious strife,
Till every soldier grasp a Phrygian wife,
Till Helen's woes at full revenged appear,
And Troy's proud matrons render tear for tear.
Before that day, if any Greek invite
His country's troops to base, inglorious flight,
Stand forth that Greek! and hoist his sail to fly,
And die the dastard first, who dreads to die.
But now, O monarch! all thy chiefs advise:
Nor what they offer, thou thyself despise.
Among those counsels, let not mine be vain;
In tribes and nations to divide thy train:
His separate troops let every leader call,
Each strengthen each, and all encourage all.
What chief, or soldier, of the numerous band,
Or bravely fights, or ill obeys command,
When thus distinct they war, shall soon be known
And what the cause of Ilion not o'erthrown;
If fate resists, or if our arms are slow,
If gods above prevent, or men below."

To him the king: "How much thy years excel
In arts of counsel, and in speaking well!
O would the gods, in love to Greece, decree
But ten such sages as they grant in thee;

Such wisdom soon should Priam's force destroy,
And soon should fall the haughty towers of Troy!
But Jove forbids, who plunges those he hates
In fierce contention and in vain debates:
Now great Achilles from our aid withdraws,
By me provoked; a captive maid the cause:
If e'er as friends we join, the Trojan wall
Must shake, and heavy will the vengeance fall!
But now, ye warriors, take a short repast;
And, well refresh'd, to bloody conflict haste.
His sharpen'd spear let every Grecian wield,
And every Grecian fix his brazen shield,
Let all excite the fiery steeds of war,
And all for combat fit the rattling car.
This day, this dreadful day, let each contend;
No rest, no respite, till the shades descend;
Till darkness, or till death, shall cover all:
Let the war bleed, and let the mighty fall;
Till bathed in sweat be every manly breast,
With the huge shield each brawny arm depress'd,
Each aching nerve refuse the lance to throw,
And each spent courser at the chariot blow.
Who dares, inglorious, in his ships to stay,
Who dares to tremble on this signal day;
That wretch, too mean to fall by martial power,
The birds shall mangle, and the dogs devour."

The monarch spoke; and straight a murmur rose,
Loud as the surges when the tempest blows,
That dash'd on broken rocks tumultuous roar,
And foam and thunder on the stony shore.
Straight to the tents the troops dispersing bend,
The fires are kindled, and the smokes ascend;
With hasty feasts they sacrifice, and pray,
To avert the dangers of the doubtful day.
A steer of five years' age, large limb'd, and fed,
To Jove's high altars Agamemnon led:
There bade the noblest of the Grecian peers;
And Nestor first, as most advanced in years.
Next came Idomeneus, and Tydeus' son,
Ajax the less, and Ajax Telamon;
Then wise Ulysses in his rank was placed;
And Menelaus came, unbid, the last.
The chiefs surround the destined beast, and take
The sacred offering of the salted cake:
When thus the king prefers his solemn prayer;
"O thou! whose thunder rends the clouded air,
Who in the heaven of heavens hast fixed thy throne,

Supreme of gods! unbounded, and alone!
Hear! and before the burning sun descends,
Before the night her gloomy veil extends,
Low in the dust be laid yon hostile spires,
Be Priam's palace sunk in Grecian fires.
In Hector's breast be plunged this shining sword,
And slaughter'd heroes groan around their lord!"

Thus prayed the chief: his unavailing prayer
Great Jove refused, and toss'd in empty air:
The God averse, while yet the fumes arose,
Prepared new toils, and doubled woes on woes.
Their prayers perform'd the chiefs the rite pursue,
The barley sprinkled, and the victim slew.
The limbs they sever from the inclosing hide,
The thighs, selected to the gods, divide.
On these, in double cauls involved with art,
The choicest morsels lie from every part,
From the cleft wood the crackling flames aspire
While the fat victims feed the sacred fire.
The thighs thus sacrificed, and entrails dress'd
The assistants part, transfix, and roast the rest;
Then spread the tables, the repast prepare,
Each takes his seat, and each receives his share.
Soon as the rage of hunger was suppress'd,
The generous Nestor thus the prince address'd.

"Now bid thy heralds sound the loud alarms,
And call the squadrons sheathed in brazen arms;
Now seize the occasion, now the troops survey,
And lead to war when heaven directs the way."

He said; the monarch issued his commands;
Straight the loud heralds call the gathering bands
The chiefs inclose their king; the hosts divide,
In tribes and nations rank'd on either side.
High in the midst the blue-eyed virgin flies;
From rank to rank she darts her ardent eyes;
The dreadful aegis, Jove's immortal shield,
Blazed on her arm, and lighten'd all the field:
Round the vast orb a hundred serpents roll'd,
Form'd the bright fringe, and seem'd to burn in gold,
With this each Grecian's manly breast she warms,
Swells their bold hearts, and strings their nervous arms,
No more they sigh, inglorious, to return,
But breathe revenge, and for the combat burn.

As on some mountain, through the lofty grove,

The crackling flames ascend, and blaze above;
The fires expanding, as the winds arise,
Shoot their long beams, and kindle half the skies:
So from the polish'd arms, and brazen shields,
A gleamy splendour flash'd along the fields.
Not less their number than the embodied cranes,
Or milk-white swans in Asius' watery plains.
That, o'er the windings of Cayster's springs,
Stretch their long necks, and clap their rustling wings,
Now tower aloft, and course in airy rounds,
Now light with noise; with noise the field resounds.
Thus numerous and confused, extending wide,
The legions crowd Scamander's flowery side;
With rushing troops the plains are cover'd o'er,
And thundering footsteps shake the sounding shore.
Along the river's level meads they stand,
Thick as in spring the flowers adorn the land,
Or leaves the trees; or thick as insects play,
The wandering nation of a summer's day:
That, drawn by milky steams, at evening hours,
In gather'd swarms surround the rural bowers;
From pail to pail with busy murmur run
The gilded legions, glittering in the sun.
So throng'd, so close, the Grecian squadrons stood
In radiant arms, and thirst for Trojan blood.
Each leader now his scatter'd force conjoins
In close array, and forms the deepening lines.
Not with more ease the skilful shepherd-swain
Collects his flocks from thousands on the plain.
The king of kings, majestically tall,
Towers o'er his armies, and outshines them all;
Like some proud bull, that round the pastures leads
His subject herds, the monarch of the meads,
Great as the gods, the exalted chief was seen,
His strength like Neptune, and like Mars his mien;
Jove o'er his eyes celestial glories spread,
And dawning conquest played around his head.

Say, virgins, seated round the throne divine,
All-knowing goddesses! immortal nine!
Since earth's wide regions, heaven's umneasur'd height,
And hell's abyss, hide nothing from your sight,
(We, wretched mortals! lost in doubts below,
But guess by rumour, and but boast we know,)
O say what heroes, fired by thirst of fame,
Or urged by wrongs, to Troy's destruction came.
To count them all, demands a thousand tongues,
A throat of brass, and adamantine lungs.

Daughters of Jove, assist! inspired by you
The mighty labour dauntless I pursue;
What crowded armies, from what climes they bring,
Their names, their numbers, and their chiefs I sing.

The hardy warriors whom Boeotia bred,
Penelius, Leitus, Prothoenor, led:
With these Arcesilaus and Clonius stand,
Equal in arms, and equal in command.
These head the troops that rocky Aulis yields,
And Eteon's hills, and Hyrie's watery fields,
And Schoenos, Scholos, Graea near the main,
And Mycalessia's ample piny plain;
Those who in Peteon or Ilesion dwell,
Or Harma where Apollo's prophet fell;
Heleon and Hyle, which the springs o'erflow;
And Medeon lofty, and Ocalea low;
Or in the meads of Haliartus stray,
Or Thespia sacred to the god of day:
Onchestus, Neptune's celebrated groves;
Copae, and Thisbe, famed for silver doves;
For flocks Erythrae, Glissa for the vine;
Platea green, and Nysa the divine;
And they whom Thebe's well-built walls inclose,
Where Myde, Eutresis, Corone, rose;
And Arne rich, with purple harvests crown'd;
And Anthedon, Boeotia's utmost bound.
Full fifty ships they send, and each conveys
Twice sixty warriors through the foaming seas.

To these succeed Aspledon's martial train,
Who plough the spacious Orchomenian plain.
Two valiant brothers rule the undaunted throng,
Ialmen and Ascalaphus the strong:
Sons of Astyoche, the heavenly fair,
Whose virgin charms subdued the god of war:
(In Actor's court as she retired to rest,
The strength of Mars the blushing maid compress'd)
Their troops in thirty sable vessels sweep,
With equal oars, the hoarse-resounding deep.

The Phocians next in forty barks repair;
Epistrophus and Schedius head the war:
From those rich regions where Cephisus leads
His silver current through the flowery meads;
From Panopea, Chrysa the divine,
Where Anemoria's stately turrets shine,
Where Pytho, Daulis, Cyparissus stood,

And fair Lilaea views the rising flood.
These, ranged in order on the floating tide,
Close, on the left, the bold Boeotians' side.

Fierce Ajax led the Locrian squadrons on,
Ajax the less, Oileus' valiant son;
Skill'd to direct the flying dart aright;
Swift in pursuit, and active in the fight.
Him, as their chief, the chosen troops attend,
Which Bessa, Thronus, and rich Cynos send;
Opus, Calliarus, and Scarphe's bands;
And those who dwell where pleasing Augia stands,
And where Boagrius floats the lowly lands,
Or in fair Tarphe's sylvan seats reside:
In forty vessels cut the yielding tide.

Euboea next her martial sons prepares,
And sends the brave Abantes to the wars:
Breathing revenge, in arms they take their way
From Chalcis' walls, and strong Eretria;
The Isteian fields for generous vines renown'd,
The fair Caristos, and the Styrian ground;
Where Dios from her towers o'erlooks the plain,
And high Cerinthus views the neighbouring main.
Down their broad shoulders falls a length of hair;
Their hands dismiss not the long lance in air;
But with protended spears in fighting fields
Pierce the tough corslets and the brazen shields.
Twice twenty ships transport the warlike bands,
Which bold Elphenor, fierce in arms, commands.

Full fifty more from Athens stem the main,
Led by Menestheus through the liquid plain.
(Athens the fair, where great Erectheus sway'd,
That owed his nurture to the blue-eyed maid,
But from the teeming furrow took his birth,
The mighty offspring of the foodful earth.
Him Pallas placed amidst her wealthy fane,
Adored with sacrifice and oxen slain;
Where, as the years revolve, her altars blaze,
And all the tribes resound the goddess' praise.)
No chief like thee, Menestheus! Greece could yield,
To marshal armies in the dusty field,
The extended wings of battle to display,
Or close the embodied host in firm array.
Nestor alone, improved by length of days,
For martial conduct bore an equal praise.

With these appear the Salaminian bands,
Whom the gigantic Telamon commands;
In twelve black ships to Troy they steer their course,
And with the great Athenians join their force.

Next move to war the generous Argive train,
From high Troezene, and Maseta's plain,
And fair Ćgina circled by the main:
Whom strong Tyrinthe's lofty walls surround,
And Epidaure with viny harvests crown'd:
And where fair Asinen and Hermoin show
Their cliffs above, and ample bay below.
These by the brave Euryalus were led,
Great Sthenelus, and greater Diomed;
But chief Tydides bore the sovereign sway:
In fourscore barks they plough the watery way.

The proud Mycene arms her martial powers,
Cleone, Corinth, with imperial towers,
Fair Araethyrea, Ornia's fruitful plain,
And Ćgion, and Adrastus' ancient reign;
And those who dwell along the sandy shore,
And where Pellene yields her fleecy store,
Where Helice and Hyperesia lie,
And Gonoessa's spires salute the sky.
Great Agamemnon rules the numerous band,
A hundred vessels in long order stand,
And crowded nations wait his dread command.
High on the deck the king of men appears,
And his refulgent arms in triumph wears;
Proud of his host, unrivall'd in his reign,
In silent pomp he moves along the main.

His brother follows, and to vengeance warms
The hardy Spartans, exercised in arms:
Phares and Brysia's valiant troops, and those
Whom Lacedaemon's lofty hills inclose;
Or Messe's towers for silver doves renown'd,
Amyclae, Laas, Augia's happy ground,
And those whom OEtylos' low walls contain,
And Helos, on the margin of the main:
These, o'er the bending ocean, Helen's cause,
In sixty ships with Menelaus draws:
Eager and loud from man to man he flies,
Revenge and fury flaming in his eyes;
While vainly fond, in fancy oft he hears
The fair one's grief, and sees her falling tears.

In ninety sail, from Pylos' sandy coast,
Nestor the sage conducts his chosen host:
From Amphigenia's ever-fruitful land,
Where Ćpy high, and little Pteleon stand;
Where beauteous Arene her structures shows,
And Thryon's walls Alpheus' streams inclose:
And Dorion, famed for Thamyris' disgrace,
Superior once of all the tuneful race,
Till, vain of mortals' empty praise, he strove
To match the seed of cloud-compelling Jove!
Too daring bard! whose unsuccessful pride
The immortal Muses in their art defied.
The avenging Muses of the light of day
Deprived his eyes, and snatch'd his voice away;
No more his heavenly voice was heard to sing,
His hand no more awaked the silver string.

Where under high Cyllene, crown'd with wood,
The shaded tomb of old Ćpytus stood;
From Ripe, Stratie, Tegea's bordering towns,
The Phenean fields, and Orchomenian downs,
Where the fat herds in plenteous pasture rove;
And Stymphelus with her surrounding grove;
Parrhasia, on her snowy cliffs reclined,
And high Enispe shook by wintry wind,
And fair Mantinea's ever-pleasing site;
In sixty sail the Arcadian bands unite.
Bold Agapenor, glorious at their head,
(Ancaeus' son) the mighty squadron led.
Their ships, supplied by Agamemnon's care,
Through roaring seas the wondering warriors bear;
The first to battle on the appointed plain,
But new to all the dangers of the main.

Those, where fair Elis and Buprasium join;
Whom Hyrmin, here, and Myrsinus confine,
And bounded there, where o'er the valleys rose
The Olenian rock; and where Alisium flows;
Beneath four chiefs (a numerous army) came:
The strength and glory of the Epean name.
In separate squadrons these their train divide,
Each leads ten vessels through the yielding tide.
One was Amphimachus, and Thalpius one;
(Eurytus' this, and that Teatus' son;)
Diores sprung from Amarynceus' line;
And great Polyxenus, of force divine.

But those who view fair Elis o'er the seas

From the blest islands of the Echinades,
In forty vessels under Meges move,
Begot by Phyleus, the beloved of Jove:
To strong Dulichium from his sire he fled,
And thence to Troy his hardy warriors led.

Ulysses follow'd through the watery road,
A chief, in wisdom equal to a god.
With those whom Cephalenia's line inclosed,
Or till their fields along the coast opposed;
Or where fair Ithaca o'erlooks the floods,
Where high Neritos shakes his waving woods,
Where Ćgilipa's rugged sides are seen,
Crocylia rocky, and Zacynthus green.
These in twelve galleys with vermilion prores,
Beneath his conduct sought the Phrygian shores.

Thoas came next, Andraemon's valiant son,
From Pleuron's walls, and chalky Calydon,
And rough Pylene, and the Olenian steep,
And Chalcis, beaten by the rolling deep.
He led the warriors from the Ćtolian shore,
For now the sons of OEneus were no more!
The glories of the mighty race were fled!
OEneus himself, and Meleager dead!
To Thoas' care now trust the martial train,
His forty vessels follow through the main.

Next, eighty barks the Cretan king commands,
Of Gnossus, Lyctus, and Gortyna's bands;
And those who dwell where Rhytion's domes arise,
Or white Lycastus glitters to the skies,
Or where by Phaestus silver Jardan runs;
Crete's hundred cities pour forth all her sons.
These march'd, Idomeneus, beneath thy care,
And Merion, dreadful as the god of war.

Tlepolemus, the sun of Hercules,
Led nine swift vessels through the foamy seas,
From Rhodes, with everlasting sunshine bright,
Jalyssus, Lindus, and Camirus white.
His captive mother fierce Alcides bore
From Ephyr's walls and Selle's winding shore,
Where mighty towns in ruins spread the plain,
And saw their blooming warriors early slain.
The hero, when to manly years he grew,
Alcides' uncle, old Licymnius, slew;
For this, constrain'd to quit his native place,

And shun the vengeance of the Herculean race,
A fleet he built, and with a numerous train
Of willing exiles wander'd o'er the main;
Where, many seas and many sufferings past,
On happy Rhodes the chief arrived at last:
There in three tribes divides his native band,
And rules them peaceful in a foreign land;
Increased and prosper'd in their new abodes
By mighty Jove, the sire of men and gods;
With joy they saw the growing empire rise,
And showers of wealth descending from the skies.

Three ships with Nireus sought the Trojan shore,
Nireus, whom Aglae to Charopus bore,
Nireus, in faultless shape and blooming grace,
The loveliest youth of all the Grecian race;
Pelides only match'd his early charms;
But few his troops, and small his strength in arms.

Next thirty galleys cleave the liquid plain,
Of those Calydnae's sea-girt isles contain;
With them the youth of Nisyrus repair,
Casus the strong, and Crapathus the fair;
Cos, where Eurypylus possess'd the sway,
Till great Alcides made the realms obey:
These Antiphus and bold Phidippus bring,
Sprung from the god by Thessalus the king.

Now, Muse, recount Pelasgic Argos' powers,
From Alos, Alope, and Trechin's towers:
From Phthia's spacious vales; and Hella, bless'd
With female beauty far beyond the rest.
Full fifty ships beneath Achilles' care,
The Achaians, Myrmidons, Hellenians bear;
Thessalians all, though various in their name;
The same their nation, and their chief the same.
But now inglorious, stretch'd along the shore,
They hear the brazen voice of war no more;
No more the foe they face in dire array:
Close in his fleet the angry leader lay;
Since fair Briseis from his arms was torn,
The noblest spoil from sack'd Lyrnessus borne,
Then, when the chief the Theban walls o'erthrew,
And the bold sons of great Evenus slew.
There mourn'd Achilles, plunged in depth of care,
But soon to rise in slaughter, blood, and war.

To these the youth of Phylace succeed,

Itona, famous for her fleecy breed,
And grassy Pteleon deck'd with cheerful greens,
The bowers of Ceres, and the sylvan scenes.
Sweet Pyrrhasus, with blooming flowerets crown'd,
And Antron's watery dens, and cavern'd ground.
These own'd, as chief, Protesilas the brave,
Who now lay silent in the gloomy grave:
The first who boldly touch'd the Trojan shore,
And dyed a Phrygian lance with Grecian gore;
There lies, far distant from his native plain;
Unfinish'd his proud palaces remain,
And his sad consort beats her breast in vain.
His troops in forty ships Podarces led,
Iphiclus' son, and brother to the dead;
Nor he unworthy to command the host;
Yet still they mourn'd their ancient leader lost.

The men who Glaphyra's fair soil partake,
Where hills incircle Boebe's lowly lake,
Where Phaere hears the neighbouring waters fall,
Or proud Iolcus lifts her airy wall,
In ten black ships embark'd for Ilion's shore,
With bold Eumelus, whom Alceste bore:
All Pelias' race Alceste far outshined,
The grace and glory of the beauteous kind,

The troops Methone or Thaumacia yields,
Olizon's rocks, or Meliboea's fields,
With Philoctetes sail'd whose matchless art
From the tough bow directs the feather'd dart.
Seven were his ships; each vessel fifty row,
Skill'd in his science of the dart and bow.
But he lay raging on the Lemnian ground,
A poisonous hydra gave the burning wound;
There groan'd the chief in agonizing pain,
Whom Greece at length shall wish, nor wish in vain.
His forces Medon led from Lemnos' shore,
Oileus' son, whom beauteous Rhena bore.

The OEchalian race, in those high towers contain'd
Where once Eurytus in proud triumph reign'd,
Or where her humbler turrets Tricca rears,
Or where Ithome, rough with rocks, appears,
In thirty sail the sparkling waves divide,
Which Podalirius and Machaon guide.
To these his skill their parent-god imparts,
Divine professors of the healing arts.

The bold Ormenian and Asterian bands
In forty barks Eurypylus commands.
Where Titan hides his hoary head in snow,
And where Hyperia's silver fountains flow.
Thy troops, Argissa, Polypoetes leads,
And Eleon, shelter'd by Olympus' shades,
Gyrtone's warriors; and where Orthe lies,
And Oloosson's chalky cliffs arise.
Sprung from Pirithous of immortal race,
The fruit of fair Hippodame's embrace,
(That day, when hurl'd from Pelion's cloudy head,
To distant dens the shaggy Centaurs fled)
With Polypoetes join'd in equal sway
Leonteus leads, and forty ships obey.

In twenty sail the bold Perrhaebians came
From Cyphus, Guneus was their leader's name.
With these the Enians join'd, and those who freeze
Where cold Dodona lifts her holy trees;
Or where the pleasing Titaresius glides,
And into Peneus rolls his easy tides;
Yet o'er the silvery surface pure they flow,
The sacred stream unmix'd with streams below,
Sacred and awful! from the dark abodes
Styx pours them forth, the dreadful oath of gods!

Last, under Prothous the Magnesians stood,
(Prothous the swift, of old Tenthredon's blood;)
Who dwell where Pelion, crown'd with piny boughs,
Obscures the glade, and nods his shaggy brows;
Or where through flowery Tempe Peneus stray'd:
(The region stretch'd beneath his mighty shade:)
In forty sable barks they stemm'd the main;
Such were the chiefs, and such the Grecian train.

Say next, O Muse! of all Achaia breeds,
Who bravest fought, or rein'd the noblest steeds?
Eumelus' mares were foremost in the chase,
As eagles fleet, and of Pheretian race;
Bred where Pieria's fruitful fountains flow,
And train'd by him who bears the silver bow.
Fierce in the fight their nostrils breathed a flame,
Their height, their colour, and their age the same;
O'er fields of death they whirl the rapid car,
And break the ranks, and thunder through the war.
Ajax in arms the first renown acquired,
While stern Achilles in his wrath retired:
(His was the strength that mortal might exceeds,

And his the unrivall'd race of heavenly steeds:)
But Thetis' son now shines in arms no more;
His troops, neglected on the sandy shore.
In empty air their sportive javelins throw,
Or whirl the disk, or bend an idle bow:
Unstain'd with blood his cover'd chariots stand;
The immortal coursers graze along the strand;
But the brave chiefs the inglorious life deplored,
And, wandering o'er the camp, required their lord.

Now, like a deluge, covering all around,
The shining armies sweep along the ground;
Swift as a flood of fire, when storms arise,
Floats the wild field, and blazes to the skies.
Earth groan'd beneath them; as when angry Jove
Hurls down the forky lightning from above,
On Arime when he the thunder throws,
And fires Typhoeus with redoubled blows,
Where Typhon, press'd beneath the burning load,
Still feels the fury of the avenging god.

But various Iris, Jove's commands to bear,
Speeds on the wings of winds through liquid air;
In Priam's porch the Trojan chiefs she found,
The old consulting, and the youths around.
Polites' shape, the monarch's son, she chose,
Who from Ćsetes' tomb observed the foes,
High on the mound; from whence in prospect lay
The fields, the tents, the navy, and the bay.
In this dissembled form, she hastes to bring
The unwelcome message to the Phrygian king.

"Cease to consult, the time for action calls;
War, horrid war, approaches to your walls!
Assembled armies oft have I beheld;
But ne'er till now such numbers charged a field:
Thick as autumnal leaves or driving sand,
The moving squadrons blacken all the strand.
Thou, godlike Hector! all thy force employ,
Assemble all the united bands of Troy;
In just array let every leader call
The foreign troops: this day demands them all!"

The voice divine the mighty chief alarms;
The council breaks, the warriors rush to arms.
The gates unfolding pour forth all their train,
Nations on nations fill the dusky plain,
Men, steeds, and chariots, shake the trembling ground:

The tumult thickens, and the skies resound.

Amidst the plain, in sight of Ilion, stands
A rising mount, the work of human hands;
(This for Myrinne's tomb the immortals know,
Though call'd Bateia in the world below;)
Beneath their chiefs in martial order here,
The auxiliar troops and Trojan hosts appear.

The godlike Hector, high above the rest,
Shakes his huge spear, and nods his plumy crest:
In throngs around his native bands repair,
And groves of lances glitter in the air.

Divine Ćneas brings the Dardan race,
Anchises' son, by Venus' stolen embrace,
Born in the shades of Ida's secret grove;
(A mortal mixing with the queen of love;)
Archilochus and Acamas divide
The warrior's toils, and combat by his side.

Who fair Zeleia's wealthy valleys till,
Fast by the foot of Ida's sacred hill,
Or drink, Ćsepus, of thy sable flood,
Were led by Pandarus, of royal blood;
To whom his art Apollo deign'd to show,
Graced with the presents of his shafts and bow.

From rich Apaesus and Adrestia's towers,
High Teree's summits, and Pityea's bowers;
From these the congregated troops obey
Young Amphius and Adrastus' equal sway;
Old Merops' sons; whom, skill'd in fates to come,
The sire forewarn'd, and prophesied their doom:
Fate urged them on! the sire forewarn'd in vain,
They rush'd to war, and perish'd on the plain.

From Practius' stream, Percote's pasture lands,
And Sestos and Abydos' neighbouring strands,
From great Arisba's walls and Selle's coast,
Asius Hyrtacides conducts his host:
High on his car he shakes the flowing reins,
His fiery coursers thunder o'er the plains.

The fierce Pelasgi next, in war renown'd,
March from Larissa's ever-fertile ground:
In equal arms their brother leaders shine,
Hippothous bold, and Pyleus the divine.

Next Acamas and Pyrous lead their hosts,
In dread array, from Thracia's wintry coasts;
Round the bleak realms where Hellespontus roars,
And Boreas beats the hoarse-resounding shores.

With great Euphemus the Ciconians move,
Sprung from Troezenian Ceus, loved by Jove.

Pyraechmes the Paeonian troops attend,
Skill'd in the fight their crooked bows to bend;
From Axius' ample bed he leads them on,
Axius, that laves the distant Amydon,
Axius, that swells with all his neighbouring rills,
And wide around the floating region fills.

The Paphlagonians Pylaemenes rules,
Where rich Henetia breeds her savage mules,
Where Erythinus' rising cliffs are seen,
Thy groves of box, Cytorus! ever green,
And where Ćgialus and Cromna lie,
And lofty Sesamus invades the sky,
And where Parthenius, roll'd through banks of flowers,
Reflects her bordering palaces and bowers.

Here march'd in arms the Halizonian band,
Whom Odius and Epistrophus command,
From those far regions where the sun refines
The ripening silver in Alybean mines.

There mighty Chromis led the Mysian train,
And augur Ennomus, inspired in vain;
For stern Achilles lopp'd his sacred head,
Roll'd down Scamander with the vulgar dead.

Phorcys and brave Ascanius here unite
The Ascanian Phrygians, eager for the fight.

Of those who round Maeonia's realms reside,
Or whom the vales in shades of Tmolus hide,
Mestles and Antiphus the charge partake,
Born on the banks of Gyges' silent lake.
There, from the fields where wild Maeander flows,
High Mycale, and Latmos' shady brows,
And proud Miletus, came the Carian throngs,
With mingled clamours and with barbarous tongues.
Amphimachus and Naustes guide the train,
Naustes the bold, Amphimachus the vain,

Who, trick'd with gold, and glittering on his car,
Rode like a woman to the field of war.
Fool that he was! by fierce Achilles slain,
The river swept him to the briny main:
There whelm'd with waves the gaudy warrior lies
The valiant victor seized the golden prize.

The forces last in fair array succeed,
Which blameless Glaucus and Sarpedon lead
The warlike bands that distant Lycia yields,
Where gulfy Xanthus foams along the fields.

BOOK III

ARGUMENT

THE DUEL OF MENELAUS AND PARIS

The armies being ready to engage, a single combat is agreed upon between Menelaus and Paris (by the intervention of Hector) for the determination of the war. Iris is sent to call Helen to behold the fight. She leads her to the walls of Troy, where Priam sat with his counsellors observing the Grecian leaders on the plain below, to whom Helen gives an account of the chief of them. The kings on either part take the solemn oath for the conditions of the combat. The duel ensues; wherein Paris being overcome, he is snatched away in a cloud by Venus, and transported to his apartment. She then calls Helen from the walls, and brings the lovers together. Agamemnon, on the part of the Grecians, demands the restoration of Helen, and the performance of the articles.

The three-and-twentieth day still continues throughout this book. The scene is sometimes in the fields before Troy, and sometimes in Troy itself.

Thus by their leaders' care each martial band
Moves into ranks, and stretches o'er the land.
With shouts the Trojans, rushing from afar,
Proclaim their motions, and provoke the war
So when inclement winters vex the plain
With piercing frosts, or thick-descending rain,
To warmer seas the cranes embodied fly,
With noise, and order, through the midway sky;
To pigmy nations wounds and death they bring,
And all the war descends upon the wing,
But silent, breathing rage, resolved and skill'd
By mutual aids to fix a doubtful field,
Swift march the Greeks: the rapid dust around
Darkening arises from the labour'd ground.
Thus from his flaggy wings when Notus sheds
A night of vapours round the mountain heads,

Swift-gliding mists the dusky fields invade,
To thieves more grateful than the midnight shade;
While scarce the swains their feeding flocks survey,
Lost and confused amidst the thicken'd day:
So wrapp'd in gathering dust, the Grecian train,
A moving cloud, swept on, and hid the plain.

Now front to front the hostile armies stand,
Eager of fight, and only wait command;
When, to the van, before the sons of fame
Whom Troy sent forth, the beauteous Paris came:
In form a god! the panther's speckled hide
Flow'd o'er his armour with an easy pride:
His bended bow across his shoulders flung,
His sword beside him negligently hung;
Two pointed spears he shook with gallant grace,
And dared the bravest of the Grecian race.

As thus, with glorious air and proud disdain,
He boldly stalk'd, the foremost on the plain,
Him Menelaus, loved of Mars, espies,
With heart elated, and with joyful eyes:
So joys a lion, if the branching deer,
Or mountain goat, his bulky prize, appear;
Eager he seizes and devours the slain,
Press'd by bold youths and baying dogs in vain.
Thus fond of vengeance, with a furious bound,
In clanging arms he leaps upon the ground
From his high chariot: him, approaching near,
The beauteous champion views with marks of fear,
Smit with a conscious sense, retires behind,
And shuns the fate he well deserved to find.
As when some shepherd, from the rustling trees
Shot forth to view, a scaly serpent sees,
Trembling and pale, he starts with wild affright
And all confused precipitates his flight:
So from the king the shining warrior flies,
And plunged amid the thickest Trojans lies.

As godlike Hector sees the prince retreat,
He thus upbraids him with a generous heat:
"Unhappy Paris! but to women brave!
So fairly form'd, and only to deceive!
Oh, hadst thou died when first thou saw'st the light,
Or died at least before thy nuptial rite!
A better fate than vainly thus to boast,
And fly, the scandal of thy Trojan host.
Gods! how the scornful Greeks exult to see

Their fears of danger undeceived in thee!
Thy figure promised with a martial air,
But ill thy soul supplies a form so fair.
In former days, in all thy gallant pride,
When thy tall ships triumphant stemm'd the tide,
When Greece beheld thy painted canvas flow,
And crowds stood wondering at the passing show,
Say, was it thus, with such a baffled mien,
You met the approaches of the Spartan queen,
Thus from her realm convey'd the beauteous prize,
And both her warlike lords outshined in Helen's eyes?
This deed, thy foes' delight, thy own disgrace,
Thy father's grief, and ruin of thy race;
This deed recalls thee to the proffer'd fight;
Or hast thou injured whom thou dar'st not right?
Soon to thy cost the field would make thee know
Thou keep'st the consort of a braver foe.
Thy graceful form instilling soft desire,
Thy curling tresses, and thy silver lyre,
Beauty and youth; in vain to these you trust,
When youth and beauty shall be laid in dust:
Troy yet may wake, and one avenging blow
Crush the dire author of his country's woe."

His silence here, with blushes, Paris breaks:
"'Tis just, my brother, what your anger speaks:
But who like thee can boast a soul sedate,
So firmly proof to all the shocks of fate?
Thy force, like steel, a temper'd hardness shows,
Still edged to wound, and still untired with blows,
Like steel, uplifted by some strenuous swain,
With falling woods to strew the wasted plain.
Thy gifts I praise; nor thou despise the charms
With which a lover golden Venus arms;
Soft moving speech, and pleasing outward show,
No wish can gain them, but the gods bestow.
Yet, would'st thou have the proffer'd combat stand,
The Greeks and Trojans seat on either hand;
Then let a midway space our hosts divide,
And, on that stage of war, the cause be tried:
By Paris there the Spartan king be fought,
For beauteous Helen and the wealth she brought;
And who his rival can in arms subdue,
His be the fair, and his the treasure too.
Thus with a lasting league your toils may cease,
And Troy possess her fertile fields in peace;
Thus may the Greeks review their native shore,
Much famed for generous steeds, for beauty more."

He said. The challenge Hector heard with joy,
Then with his spear restrain'd the youth of Troy,
Held by the midst, athwart; and near the foe
Advanced with steps majestically slow:
While round his dauntless head the Grecians pour
Their stones and arrows in a mingled shower.

Then thus the monarch, great Atrides, cried:
"Forbear, ye warriors! lay the darts aside:
A parley Hector asks, a message bears;
We know him by the various plume he wears."
Awed by his high command the Greeks attend,
The tumult silence, and the fight suspend.

While from the centre Hector rolls his eyes
On either host, and thus to both applies:
"Hear, all ye Trojan, all ye Grecian bands,
What Paris, author of the war, demands.
Your shining swords within the sheath restrain,
And pitch your lances in the yielding plain.
Here in the midst, in either army's sight,
He dares the Spartan king to single fight;
And wills that Helen and the ravish'd spoil,
That caused the contest, shall reward the toil.
Let these the brave triumphant victor grace,
And different nations part in leagues of peace."

He spoke: in still suspense on either side
Each army stood: the Spartan chief replied:

"Me too, ye warriors, hear, whose fatal right
A world engages in the toils of fight.
To me the labour of the field resign;
Me Paris injured; all the war be mine.
Fall he that must, beneath his rival's arms;
And live the rest, secure of future harms.
Two lambs, devoted by your country's rite,
To earth a sable, to the sun a white,
Prepare, ye Trojans! while a third we bring
Select to Jove, the inviolable king.
Let reverend Priam in the truce engage,
And add the sanction of considerate age;
His sons are faithless, headlong in debate,
And youth itself an empty wavering state;
Cool age advances, venerably wise,
Turns on all hands its deep-discerning eyes;
Sees what befell, and what may yet befall,

Concludes from both, and best provides for all.

The nations hear with rising hopes possess'd,
And peaceful prospects dawn in every breast.
Within the lines they drew their steeds around,
And from their chariots issued on the ground;
Next, all unbuckling the rich mail they wore,
Laid their bright arms along the sable shore.
On either side the meeting hosts are seen
With lances fix'd, and close the space between.
Two heralds now, despatch'd to Troy, invite
The Phrygian monarch to the peaceful rite.

Talthybius hastens to the fleet, to bring
The lamb for Jove, the inviolable king.

Meantime to beauteous Helen, from the skies
The various goddess of the rainbow flies:
(Like fair Laodice in form and face,
The loveliest nymph of Priam's royal race:)
Her in the palace, at her loom she found;
The golden web her own sad story crown'd,
The Trojan wars she weaved (herself the prize)
And the dire triumphs of her fatal eyes.
To whom the goddess of the painted bow:
"Approach, and view the wondrous scene below!
Each hardy Greek, and valiant Trojan knight,
So dreadful late, and furious for the fight,
Now rest their spears, or lean upon their shields;
Ceased is the war, and silent all the fields.
Paris alone and Sparta's king advance,
In single fight to toss the beamy lance;
Each met in arms, the fate of combat tries,
Thy love the motive, and thy charms the prize."

This said, the many-coloured maid inspires
Her husband's love, and wakes her former fires;
Her country, parents, all that once were dear,
Rush to her thought, and force a tender tear,
O'er her fair face a snowy veil she threw,
And, softly sighing, from the loom withdrew.
Her handmaids, Clymene and Æthra, wait
Her silent footsteps to the Scaean gate.

There sat the seniors of the Trojan race:
(Old Priam's chiefs, and most in Priam's grace,)
The king the first; Thymoetes at his side;
Lampus and Clytius, long in council tried;

Panthus, and Hicetaon, once the strong;
And next, the wisest of the reverend throng,
Antenor grave, and sage Ucalegon,
Lean'd on the walls and bask'd before the sun:
Chiefs, who no more in bloody fights engage,
But wise through time, and narrative with age,
In summer days, like grasshoppers rejoice,
A bloodless race, that send a feeble voice.
These, when the Spartan queen approach'd the tower,
In secret own'd resistless beauty's power:
They cried, "No wonder such celestial charms
For nine long years have set the world in arms;
What winning graces! what majestic mien!
She moves a goddess, and she looks a queen!
Yet hence, O Heaven, convey that fatal face,
And from destruction save the Trojan race."

The good old Priam welcomed her, and cried,
"Approach, my child, and grace thy father's side.
See on the plain thy Grecian spouse appears,
The friends and kindred of thy former years.
No crime of thine our present sufferings draws,
Not thou, but Heaven's disposing will, the cause
The gods these armies and this force employ,
The hostile gods conspire the fate of Troy.
But lift thy eyes, and say, what Greek is he
(Far as from hence these aged orbs can see)
Around whose brow such martial graces shine,
So tall, so awful, and almost divine!
Though some of larger stature tread the green,
None match his grandeur and exalted mien:
He seems a monarch, and his country's pride."
Thus ceased the king, and thus the fair replied:

"Before thy presence, father, I appear,
With conscious shame and reverential fear.
Ah! had I died, ere to these walk I fled,
False to my country, and my nuptial bed;
My brothers, friends, and daughter left behind,
False to them all, to Paris only kind!
For this I mourn, till grief or dire disease
Shall waste the form whose fault it was to please!
The king of kings, Atrides, you survey,
Great in the war, and great in arts of sway:
My brother once, before my days of shame!
And oh! that still he bore a brother's name!"

With wonder Priam view'd the godlike man,

Extoll'd the happy prince, and thus began:
"O bless'd Atrides! born to prosperous fate,
Successful monarch of a mighty state!
How vast thy empire! Of your matchless train
What numbers lost, what numbers yet remain!
In Phrygia once were gallant armies known,
In ancient time, when Otreus fill'd the throne,
When godlike Mygdon led their troops of horse,
And I, to join them, raised the Trojan force:
Against the manlike Amazons we stood,
And Sangar's stream ran purple with their blood.
But far inferior those, in martial grace,
And strength of numbers, to this Grecian race."

This said, once more he view'd the warrior train;
"What's he, whose arms lie scatter'd on the plain?
Broad is his breast, his shoulders larger spread,
Though great Atrides overtops his head.
Nor yet appear his care and conduct small;
From rank to rank he moves, and orders all.
The stately ram thus measures o'er the ground,
And, master of the flock, surveys them round."

Then Helen thus: "Whom your discerning eyes
Have singled out, is Ithacus the wise;
A barren island boasts his glorious birth;
His fame for wisdom fills the spacious earth."

Antenor took the word, and thus began:
"Myself, O king! have seen that wondrous man
When, trusting Jove and hospitable laws,
To Troy he came, to plead the Grecian cause;
(Great Menelaus urged the same request;)
My house was honour'd with each royal guest:
I knew their persons, and admired their parts,
Both brave in arms, and both approved in arts.
Erect, the Spartan most engaged our view;
Ulysses seated, greater reverence drew.
When Atreus' son harangued the listening train,
Just was his sense, and his expression plain,
His words succinct, yet full, without a fault;
He spoke no more than just the thing he ought.
But when Ulysses rose, in thought profound,
His modest eyes he fix'd upon the ground;
As one unskill'd or dumb, he seem'd to stand,
Nor raised his head, nor stretch'd his sceptred hand;
But, when he speaks, what elocution flows!
Soft as the fleeces of descending snows,

The copious accents fall, with easy art;
Melting they fall, and sink into the heart!
Wondering we hear, and fix'd in deep surprise,
Our ears refute the censure of our eyes."

The king then ask'd (as yet the camp he view'd)
"What chief is that, with giant strength endued,
Whose brawny shoulders, and whose swelling chest,
And lofty stature, far exceed the rest?
"Ajax the great, (the beauteous queen replied,)
Himself a host: the Grecian strength and pride.
See! bold Idomeneus superior towers
Amid yon circle of his Cretan powers,
Great as a god! I saw him once before,
With Menelaus on the Spartan shore.
The rest I know, and could in order name;
All valiant chiefs, and men of mighty fame.
Yet two are wanting of the numerous train,
Whom long my eyes have sought, but sought in vain:
Castor and Pollux, first in martial force,
One bold on foot, and one renown'd for horse.
My brothers these; the same our native shore,
One house contain'd us, as one mother bore.
Perhaps the chiefs, from warlike toils at ease,
For distant Troy refused to sail the seas;
Perhaps their swords some nobler quarrel draws,
Ashamed to combat in their sister's cause."

So spoke the fair, nor knew her brothers' doom;
Wrapt in the cold embraces of the tomb;
Adorn'd with honours in their native shore,
Silent they slept, and heard of wars no more.

Meantime the heralds, through the crowded town.
Bring the rich wine and destined victims down.
Idaeus' arms the golden goblets press'd,
Who thus the venerable king address'd:
"Arise, O father of the Trojan state!
The nations call, thy joyful people wait
To seal the truce, and end the dire debate.
Paris, thy son, and Sparta's king advance,
In measured lists to toss the weighty lance;
And who his rival shall in arms subdue,
His be the dame, and his the treasure too.
Thus with a lasting league our toils may cease,
And Troy possess her fertile fields in peace:
So shall the Greeks review their native shore,
Much famed for generous steeds, for beauty more."

With grief he heard, and bade the chiefs prepare
To join his milk-white coursers to the car;
He mounts the seat, Antenor at his side;
The gentle steeds through Scaea's gates they guide:
Next from the car descending on the plain,
Amid the Grecian host and Trojan train,
Slow they proceed: the sage Ulysses then
Arose, and with him rose the king of men.
On either side a sacred herald stands,
The wine they mix, and on each monarch's hands
Pour the full urn; then draws the Grecian lord
His cutlass sheathed beside his ponderous sword;
From the sign'd victims crops the curling hair;
The heralds part it, and the princes share;
Then loudly thus before the attentive bands
He calls the gods, and spreads his lifted hands:

"O first and greatest power! whom all obey,
Who high on Ida's holy mountain sway,
Eternal Jove! and you bright orb that roll
From east to west, and view from pole to pole!
Thou mother Earth! and all ye living floods!
Infernal furies, and Tartarean gods,
Who rule the dead, and horrid woes prepare
For perjured kings, and all who falsely swear!
Hear, and be witness. If, by Paris slain,
Great Menelaus press the fatal plain;
The dame and treasures let the Trojan keep,
And Greece returning plough the watery deep.
If by my brother's lance the Trojan bleed,
Be his the wealth and beauteous dame decreed:
The appointed fine let Ilion justly pay,
And every age record the signal day.
This if the Phrygians shall refuse to yield,
Arms must revenge, and Mars decide the field."

With that the chief the tender victims slew,
And in the dust their bleeding bodies threw;
The vital spirit issued at the wound,
And left the members quivering on the ground.
From the same urn they drink the mingled wine,
And add libations to the powers divine.
While thus their prayers united mount the sky,
"Hear, mighty Jove! and hear, ye gods on high!
And may their blood, who first the league confound,
Shed like this wine, disdain the thirsty ground;
May all their consorts serve promiscuous lust,

And all their lust be scatter'd as the dust!"
Thus either host their imprecations join'd,
Which Jove refused, and mingled with the wind.

The rites now finish'd, reverend Priam rose,
And thus express'd a heart o'ercharged with woes:
"Ye Greeks and Trojans, let the chiefs engage,
But spare the weakness of my feeble age:
In yonder walls that object let me shun,
Nor view the danger of so dear a son.
Whose arms shall conquer and what prince shall fall,
Heaven only knows; for heaven disposes all."

This said, the hoary king no longer stay'd,
But on his car the slaughter'd victims laid:
Then seized the reins his gentle steeds to guide,
And drove to Troy, Antenor at his side.

Bold Hector and Ulysses now dispose
The lists of combat, and the ground inclose:
Next to decide, by sacred lots prepare,
Who first shall launch his pointed spear in air.
The people pray with elevated hands,
And words like these are heard through all the bands:
"Immortal Jove, high Heaven's superior lord,
On lofty Ida's holy mount adored!
Whoe'er involved us in this dire debate,
O give that author of the war to fate
And shades eternal! let division cease,
And joyful nations join in leagues of peace."

With eyes averted Hector hastes to turn
The lots of fight and shakes the brazen urn.
Then, Paris, thine leap'd forth; by fatal chance
Ordain'd the first to whirl the weighty lance.
Both armies sat the combat to survey.
Beside each chief his azure armour lay,
And round the lists the generous coursers neigh.
The beauteous warrior now arrays for fight,
In gilded arms magnificently bright:
The purple cuishes clasp his thighs around,
With flowers adorn'd, with silver buckles bound:
Lycaon's corslet his fair body dress'd,
Braced in and fitted to his softer breast;
A radiant baldric, o'er his shoulder tied,
Sustain'd the sword that glitter'd at his side:
His youthful face a polish'd helm o'erspread;
The waving horse-hair nodded on his head:

His figured shield, a shining orb, he takes,
And in his hand a pointed javelin shakes.
With equal speed and fired by equal charms,
The Spartan hero sheathes his limbs in arms.

Now round the lists the admiring armies stand,
With javelins fix'd, the Greek and Trojan band.
Amidst the dreadful vale, the chiefs advance,
All pale with rage, and shake the threatening lance.
The Trojan first his shining javelin threw;
Full on Atrides' ringing shield it flew,
Nor pierced the brazen orb, but with a bound
Leap'd from the buckler, blunted, on the ground.
Atrides then his massy lance prepares,
In act to throw, but first prefers his prayers:

"Give me, great Jove! to punish lawless lust,
And lay the Trojan gasping in the dust:
Destroy the aggressor, aid my righteous cause,
Avenge the breach of hospitable laws!
Let this example future times reclaim,
And guard from wrong fair friendship's holy name."
Be said, and poised in air the javelin sent,
Through Paris' shield the forceful weapon went,
His corslet pierces, and his garment rends,
And glancing downward, near his flank descends.
The wary Trojan, bending from the blow,
Eludes the death, and disappoints his foe:
But fierce Atrides waved his sword, and strook
Full on his casque: the crested helmet shook;
The brittle steel, unfaithful to his hand,
Broke short: the fragments glitter'd on the sand.
The raging warrior to the spacious skies
Raised his upbraiding voice and angry eyes:
"Then is it vain in Jove himself to trust?
And is it thus the gods assist the just?
When crimes provoke us, Heaven success denies;
The dart falls harmless, and the falchion flies."
Furious he said, and towards the Grecian crew
(Seized by the crest) the unhappy warrior drew;
Struggling he followed, while the embroider'd thong
That tied his helmet, dragg'd the chief along.
Then had his ruin crown'd Atrides' joy,
But Venus trembled for the prince of Troy:
Unseen she came, and burst the golden band;
And left an empty helmet in his hand.
The casque, enraged, amidst the Greeks he threw;
The Greeks with smiles the polish'd trophy view.

Then, as once more he lifts the deadly dart,
In thirst of vengeance, at his rival's heart;
The queen of love her favour'd champion shrouds
(For gods can all things) in a veil of clouds.
Raised from the field the panting youth she led,
And gently laid him on the bridal bed,
With pleasing sweets his fainting sense renews,
And all the dome perfumes with heavenly dews.
Meantime the brightest of the female kind,
The matchless Helen, o'er the walls reclined;
To her, beset with Trojan beauties, came,
In borrow'd form, the laughter-loving dame.
(She seem'd an ancient maid, well-skill'd to cull
The snowy fleece, and wind the twisted wool.)
The goddess softly shook her silken vest,
That shed perfumes, and whispering thus address'd:

"Haste, happy nymph! for thee thy Paris calls,
Safe from the fight, in yonder lofty walls,
Fair as a god; with odours round him spread,
He lies, and waits thee on the well-known bed;
Not like a warrior parted from the foe,
But some gay dancer in the public show."

She spoke, and Helen's secret soul was moved;
She scorn'd the champion, but the man she loved.
Fair Venus' neck, her eyes that sparkled fire,
And breast, reveal'd the queen of soft desire.
Struck with her presence, straight the lively red
Forsook her cheek; and trembling, thus she said:
"Then is it still thy pleasure to deceive?
And woman's frailty always to believe!
Say, to new nations must I cross the main,
Or carry wars to some soft Asian plain?
For whom must Helen break her second vow?
What other Paris is thy darling now?
Left to Atrides, (victor in the strife,)
An odious conquest and a captive wife,
Hence let me sail; and if thy Paris bear
My absence ill, let Venus ease his care.
A handmaid goddess at his side to wait,
Renounce the glories of thy heavenly state,
Be fix'd for ever to the Trojan shore,
His spouse, or slave; and mount the skies no more.
For me, to lawless love no longer led,
I scorn the coward, and detest his bed;
Else should I merit everlasting shame,
And keen reproach, from every Phrygian dame:

Ill suits it now the joys of love to know,
Too deep my anguish, and too wild my woe."

Then thus incensed, the Paphian queen replies:
"Obey the power from whom thy glories rise:
Should Venus leave thee, every charm must fly,
Fade from thy cheek, and languish in thy eye.
Cease to provoke me, lest I make thee more
The world's aversion, than their love before;
Now the bright prize for which mankind engage,
Than, the sad victim, of the public rage."

At this, the fairest of her sex obey'd,
And veil'd her blushes in a silken shade;
Unseen, and silent, from the train she moves,
Led by the goddess of the Smiles and Loves.
Arrived, and enter'd at the palace gate,
The maids officious round their mistress wait;
Then, all dispersing, various tasks attend;
The queen and goddess to the prince ascend.
Full in her Paris' sight, the queen of love
Had placed the beauteous progeny of Jove;
Where, as he view'd her charms, she turn'd away
Her glowing eyes, and thus began to say:

"Is this the chief, who, lost to sense of shame,
Late fled the field, and yet survives his fame?
O hadst thou died beneath the righteous sword
Of that brave man whom once I call'd my lord!
The boaster Paris oft desired the day
With Sparta's king to meet in single fray:
Go now, once more thy rival's rage excite,
Provoke Atrides, and renew the fight:
Yet Helen bids thee stay, lest thou unskill'd
Shouldst fall an easy conquest on the field."

The prince replies: "Ah cease, divinely fair,
Nor add reproaches to the wounds I bear;
This day the foe prevail'd by Pallas' power:
We yet may vanquish in a happier hour:
There want not gods to favour us above;
But let the business of our life be love:
These softer moments let delights employ,
And kind embraces snatch the hasty joy.
Not thus I loved thee, when from Sparta's shore
My forced, my willing heavenly prize I bore,
When first entranced in Cranae's isle I lay,
Mix'd with thy soul, and all dissolved away!"

Thus having spoke, the enamour'd Phrygian boy
Rush'd to the bed, impatient for the joy.
Him Helen follow'd slow with bashful charms,
And clasp'd the blooming hero in her arms.

While these to love's delicious rapture yield,
The stern Atrides rages round the field:
So some fell lion whom the woods obey,
Roars through the desert, and demands his prey.
Paris he seeks, impatient to destroy,
But seeks in vain along the troops of Troy;
Even those had yielded to a foe so brave
The recreant warrior, hateful as the grave.
Then speaking thus, the king of kings arose,
"Ye Trojans, Dardans, all our generous foes!
Hear and attest! from Heaven with conquest crown'd,
Our brother's arms the just success have found:
Be therefore now the Spartan wealth restor'd,
Let Argive Helen own her lawful lord;
The appointed fine let Ilion justly pay,
And age to age record this signal day."

He ceased; his army's loud applauses rise,
And the long shout runs echoing through the skies.

BOOK IV

ARGUMENT

THE BREACH OF THE TRUCE, AND THE FIRST BATTLE

The gods deliberate in council concerning the Trojan war: they agree upon the continuation of it, and Jupiter sends down Minerva to break the truce. She persuades Pandarus to aim an arrow at Menelaus, who is wounded, but cured by Machaon. In the meantime some of the Trojan troops attack the Greeks. Agamemnon is distinguished in all the parts of a good general; he reviews the troops, and exhorts the leaders, some by praises and others by reproof. Nestor is particularly celebrated for his military discipline. The battle joins, and great numbers are slain on both sides.

The same day continues through this as through the last book (as it does also through the two following, and almost to the end of the seventh book). The scene is wholly in the field before Troy.

And now Olympus' shining gates unfold;
The gods, with Jove, assume their thrones of gold:
Immortal Hebe, fresh with bloom divine,
The golden goblet crowns with purple wine:

While the full bowls flow round, the powers employ
Their careful eyes on long-contended Troy.

When Jove, disposed to tempt Saturnia's spleen,
Thus waked the fury of his partial queen,
"Two powers divine the son of Atreus aid,
Imperial Juno, and the martial maid;
But high in heaven they sit, and gaze from far,
The tame spectators of his deeds of war.
Not thus fair Venus helps her favour'd knight,
The queen of pleasures shares the toils of fight,
Each danger wards, and constant in her care,
Saves in the moment of the last despair.
Her act has rescued Paris' forfeit life,
Though great Atrides gain'd the glorious strife.
Then say, ye powers! what signal issue waits
To crown this deed, and finish all the fates!
Shall Heaven by peace the bleeding kingdoms spare,
Or rouse the furies, and awake the war?
Yet, would the gods for human good provide,
Atrides soon might gain his beauteous bride,
Still Priam's walls in peaceful honours grow,
And through his gates the crowding nations flow."

Thus while he spoke, the queen of heaven, enraged,
And queen of war, in close consult engaged:
Apart they sit, their deep designs employ,
And meditate the future woes of Troy.
Though secret anger swell'd Minerva's breast,
The prudent goddess yet her wrath suppress'd;
But Juno, impotent of passion, broke
Her sullen silence, and with fury spoke:

"Shall then, O tyrant of the ethereal reign!
My schemes, my labours, and my hopes be vain?
Have I, for this, shook Ilion with alarms,
Assembled nations, set two worlds in arms?
To spread the war, I flew from shore to shore;
The immortal coursers scarce the labour bore.
At length ripe vengeance o'er their heads impends,
But Jove himself the faithless race defends.
Loth as thou art to punish lawless lust,
Not all the gods are partial and unjust."

The sire whose thunder shakes the cloudy skies,
Sighs from his inmost soul, and thus replies:
"Oh lasting rancour! oh insatiate hate
To Phrygia's monarch, and the Phrygian state!

What high offence has fired the wife of Jove?
Can wretched mortals harm the powers above,
That Troy, and Troy's whole race thou wouldst confound,
And yon fair structures level with the ground!
Haste, leave the skies, fulfil thy stern desire,
Burst all her gates, and wrap her walls in fire!
Let Priam bleed! if yet you thirst for more,
Bleed all his sons, and Ilion float with gore:
To boundless vengeance the wide realm be given,
Till vast destruction glut the queen of heaven!
So let it be, and Jove his peace enjoy,
When heaven no longer hears the name of Troy.
But should this arm prepare to wreak our hate
On thy loved realms, whose guilt demands their fate;
Presume not thou the lifted bolt to stay,
Remember Troy, and give the vengeance way.
For know, of all the numerous towns that rise
Beneath the rolling sun and starry skies,
Which gods have raised, or earth-born men enjoy,
None stands so dear to Jove as sacred Troy.
No mortals merit more distinguish'd grace
Than godlike Priam, or than Priam's race.
Still to our name their hecatombs expire,
And altars blaze with unextinguish'd fire."

At this the goddess rolled her radiant eyes,
Then on the Thunderer fix'd them, and replies:
"Three towns are Juno's on the Grecian plains,
More dear than all the extended earth contains,
Mycenae, Argos, and the Spartan wall;

These thou mayst raze, nor I forbid their fall:
'Tis not in me the vengeance to remove;
The crime's sufficient that they share my love.
Of power superior why should I complain?
Resent I may, but must resent in vain.
Yet some distinction Juno might require,
Sprung with thyself from one celestial sire,
A goddess born, to share the realms above,
And styled the consort of the thundering Jove;
Nor thou a wife and sister's right deny;
Let both consent, and both by terms comply;
So shall the gods our joint decrees obey,
And heaven shall act as we direct the way.
See ready Pallas waits thy high commands
To raise in arms the Greek and Phrygian bands;
Their sudden friendship by her arts may cease,
And the proud Trojans first infringe the peace."

The sire of men and monarch of the sky
The advice approved, and bade Minerva fly,
Dissolve the league, and all her arts employ
To make the breach the faithless act of Troy.
Fired with the charge, she headlong urged her flight,
And shot like lightning from Olympus' height.
As the red comet, from Saturnius sent
To fright the nations with a dire portent,
(A fatal sign to armies on the plain,
Or trembling sailors on the wintry main,)
With sweeping glories glides along in air,
And shakes the sparkles from its blazing hair:
Between both armies thus, in open sight
Shot the bright goddess in a trail of light,
With eyes erect the gazing hosts admire
The power descending, and the heavens on fire!
"The gods (they cried), the gods this signal sent,
And fate now labours with some vast event:
Jove seals the league, or bloodier scenes prepares;
Jove, the great arbiter of peace and wars."

They said, while Pallas through the Trojan throng,
(In shape a mortal,) pass'd disguised along.
Like bold Laodocus, her course she bent,
Who from Antenor traced his high descent.
Amidst the ranks Lycaon's son she found,
The warlike Pandarus, for strength renown'd;
Whose squadrons, led from black Ćsepus' flood,
With flaming shields in martial circle stood.
To him the goddess: "Phrygian! canst thou hear
A well-timed counsel with a willing ear?
What praise were thine, couldst thou direct thy dart,
Amidst his triumph, to the Spartan's heart?
What gifts from Troy, from Paris wouldst thou gain,
Thy country's foe, the Grecian glory slain?
Then seize the occasion, dare the mighty deed,
Aim at his breast, and may that aim succeed!
But first, to speed the shaft, address thy vow
To Lycian Phoebus with the silver bow,
And swear the firstlings of thy flock to pay,
On Zelia's altars, to the god of day."

He heard, and madly at the motion pleased,
His polish'd bow with hasty rashness seized.
'Twas form'd of horn, and smooth'd with artful toil:
A mountain goat resign'd the shining spoil.
Who pierced long since beneath his arrows bled;

The stately quarry on the cliffs lay dead,
And sixteen palms his brow's large honours spread:
The workmen join'd, and shaped the bended horns,
And beaten gold each taper point adorns.
This, by the Greeks unseen, the warrior bends,
Screen'd by the shields of his surrounding friends:
There meditates the mark; and couching low,
Fits the sharp arrow to the well-strung bow.
One from a hundred feather'd deaths he chose,
Fated to wound, and cause of future woes;
Then offers vows with hecatombs to crown
Apollo's altars in his native town.

Now with full force the yielding horn he bends,
Drawn to an arch, and joins the doubling ends;
Close to his breast he strains the nerve below,
Till the barb'd points approach the circling bow;
The impatient weapon whizzes on the wing;
Sounds the tough horn, and twangs the quivering string.

But thee, Atrides! in that dangerous hour
The gods forget not, nor thy guardian power,
Pallas assists, and (weakened in its force)
Diverts the weapon from its destined course:
So from her babe, when slumber seals his eye,
The watchful mother wafts the envenom'd fly.
Just where his belt with golden buckles join'd,
Where linen folds the double corslet lined,
She turn'd the shaft, which, hissing from above,
Pass'd the broad belt, and through the corslet drove;
The folds it pierced, the plaited linen tore,
And razed the skin, and drew the purple gore.
As when some stately trappings are decreed
To grace a monarch on his bounding steed,
A nymph in Caria or Maeonia bred,
Stains the pure ivory with a lively red;
With equal lustre various colours vie,
The shining whiteness, and the Tyrian dye:
So great Atrides! show'd thy sacred blood,
As down thy snowy thigh distill'd the streaming flood.
With horror seized, the king of men descried
The shaft infix'd, and saw the gushing tide:
Nor less the Spartan fear'd, before he found
The shining barb appear above the wound,
Then, with a sigh, that heaved his manly breast,
The royal brother thus his grief express'd,
And grasp'd his hand; while all the Greeks around
With answering sighs return'd the plaintive sound.

"Oh, dear as life! did I for this agree
The solemn truce, a fatal truce to thee!
Wert thou exposed to all the hostile train,
To fight for Greece, and conquer, to be slain!
The race of Trojans in thy ruin join,
And faith is scorn'd by all the perjured line.
Not thus our vows, confirm'd with wine and gore,
Those hands we plighted, and those oaths we swore,
Shall all be vain: when Heaven's revenge is slow,
Jove but prepares to strike the fiercer blow.
The day shall come, that great avenging day,
When Troy's proud glories in the dust shall lay,
When Priam's powers and Priam's self shall fall,
And one prodigious ruin swallow all.
I see the god, already, from the pole
Bare his red arm, and bid the thunder roll;
I see the Eternal all his fury shed,
And shake his aegis o'er their guilty head.
Such mighty woes on perjured princes wait;
But thou, alas! deserv'st a happier fate.
Still must I mourn the period of thy days,
And only mourn, without my share of praise?
Deprived of thee, the heartless Greeks no more
Shall dream of conquests on the hostile shore;
Troy seized of Helen, and our glory lost,
Thy bones shall moulder on a foreign coast;
While some proud Trojan thus insulting cries,
(And spurns the dust where Menelaus lies,)
'Such are the trophies Greece from Ilion brings,
And such the conquest of her king of kings!
Lo his proud vessels scatter'd o'er the main,
And unrevenged, his mighty brother slain.'
Oh! ere that dire disgrace shall blast my fame,
O'erwhelm me, earth! and hide a monarch's shame."

He said: a leader's and a brother's fears
Possess his soul, which thus the Spartan cheers:
"Let not thy words the warmth of Greece abate;
The feeble dart is guiltless of my fate:
Stiff with the rich embroider'd work around,
My varied belt repell'd the flying wound."

To whom the king: "My brother and my friend,
Thus, always thus, may Heaven thy life defend!
Now seek some skilful hand, whose powerful art
May stanch the effusion, and extract the dart.
Herald, be swift, and bid Machaon bring

His speedy succour to the Spartan king;
Pierced with a winged shaft (the deed of Troy),
The Grecian's sorrow, and the Dardan's joy."

With hasty zeal the swift Talthybius flies;
Through the thick files he darts his searching eyes,
And finds Machaon, where sublime he stands
In arms incircled with his native bands.
Then thus: "Machaon, to the king repair,
His wounded brother claims thy timely care;
Pierced by some Lycian or Dardanian bow,
A grief to us, a triumph to the foe."

The heavy tidings grieved the godlike man
Swift to his succour through the ranks he ran.
The dauntless king yet standing firm he found,
And all the chiefs in deep concern around.
Where to the steely point the reed was join'd,
The shaft he drew, but left the head behind.
Straight the broad belt with gay embroidery graced,
He loosed; the corslet from his breast unbraced;
Then suck'd the blood, and sovereign balm infused,
Which Chiron gave, and Ćsculapius used.

While round the prince the Greeks employ their care,
The Trojans rush tumultuous to the war;
Once more they glitter in refulgent arms,
Once more the fields are fill'd with dire alarms.
Nor had you seen the king of men appear
Confused, unactive, or surprised with fear;
But fond of glory, with severe delight,
His beating bosom claim'd the rising fight.
No longer with his warlike steeds he stay'd,
Or press'd the car with polish'd brass inlaid
But left Eurymedon the reins to guide;
The fiery coursers snorted at his side.
On foot through all the martial ranks he moves
And these encourages, and those reproves.
"Brave men!" he cries, (to such who boldly dare
Urge their swift steeds to face the coming war),
"Your ancient valour on the foes approve;
Jove is with Greece, and let us trust in Jove.
'Tis not for us, but guilty Troy, to dread,
Whose crimes sit heavy on her perjured head;
Her sons and matrons Greece shall lead in chains,
And her dead warriors strew the mournful plains."

Thus with new ardour he the brave inspires;

Or thus the fearful with reproaches fires:
"Shame to your country, scandal of your kind;
Born to the fate ye well deserve to find!
Why stand ye gazing round the dreadful plain,
Prepared for flight, but doom'd to fly in vain?
Confused and panting thus, the hunted deer
Falls as he flies, a victim to his fear.
Still must ye wait the foes, and still retire,
Till yon tall vessels blaze with Trojan fire?
Or trust ye, Jove a valiant foe shall chase,
To save a trembling, heartless, dastard race?"

This said, he stalk'd with ample strides along,
To Crete's brave monarch and his martial throng;
High at their head he saw the chief appear,
And bold Meriones excite the rear.
At this the king his generous joy express'd,
And clasp'd the warrior to his armed breast.
"Divine Idomeneus! what thanks we owe
To worth like thine! what praise shall we bestow?
To thee the foremost honours are decreed,
First in the fight and every graceful deed.
For this, in banquets, when the generous bowls
Restore our blood, and raise the warriors' souls,
Though all the rest with stated rules we bound,
Unmix'd, unmeasured, are thy goblets crown'd.
Be still thyself, in arms a mighty name;
Maintain thy honours, and enlarge thy fame."
To whom the Cretan thus his speech address'd:
"Secure of me, O king! exhort the rest.
Fix'd to thy side, in every toil I share,
Thy firm associate in the day of war.
But let the signal be this moment given;
To mix in fight is all I ask of Heaven.
The field shall prove how perjuries succeed,
And chains or death avenge the impious deed."

Charm'd with this heat, the king his course pursues,
And next the troops of either Ajax views:
In one firm orb the bands were ranged around,
A cloud of heroes blacken'd all the ground.
Thus from the lofty promontory's brow
A swain surveys the gathering storm below;
Slow from the main the heavy vapours rise,
Spread in dim streams, and sail along the skies,
Till black as night the swelling tempest shows,
The cloud condensing as the west-wind blows:
He dreads the impending storm, and drives his flock

To the close covert of an arching rock.

Such, and so thick, the embattled squadrons stood,
With spears erect, a moving iron wood:
A shady light was shot from glimmering shields,
And their brown arms obscured the dusky fields.

"O heroes! worthy such a dauntless train,
Whose godlike virtue we but urge in vain,
(Exclaim'd the king), who raise your eager bands
With great examples, more than loud commands.
Ah! would the gods but breathe in all the rest
Such souls as burn in your exalted breast,
Soon should our arms with just success be crown'd,
And Troy's proud walls lie smoking on the ground."

Then to the next the general bends his course;
(His heart exults, and glories in his force);
There reverend Nestor ranks his Pylian bands,
And with inspiring eloquence commands;
With strictest order sets his train in arms,
The chiefs advises, and the soldiers warms.
Alastor, Chromius, Haemon, round him wait,
Bias the good, and Pelagon the great.
The horse and chariots to the front assign'd,
The foot (the strength of war) he ranged behind;
The middle space suspected troops supply,
Inclosed by both, nor left the power to fly;
He gives command to "curb the fiery steed,
Nor cause confusion, nor the ranks exceed:
Before the rest let none too rashly ride;
No strength nor skill, but just in time, be tried:
The charge once made, no warrior turn the rein,
But fight, or fall; a firm embodied train.
He whom the fortune of the field shall cast
From forth his chariot, mount the next in haste;
Nor seek unpractised to direct the car,
Content with javelins to provoke the war.
Our great forefathers held this prudent course,
Thus ruled their ardour, thus preserved their force;
By laws like these immortal conquests made,
And earth's proud tyrants low in ashes laid."

So spoke the master of the martial art,
And touch'd with transport great Atrides' heart.
"Oh! hadst thou strength to match thy brave desires,
And nerves to second what thy soul inspires!
But wasting years, that wither human race,

Exhaust thy spirits, and thy arms unbrace.
What once thou wert, oh ever mightst thou be!
And age the lot of any chief but thee."

Thus to the experienced prince Atrides cried;
He shook his hoary locks, and thus replied:
"Well might I wish, could mortal wish renew
That strength which once in boiling youth I knew;
Such as I was, when Ereuthalion, slain
Beneath this arm, fell prostrate on the plain.
But heaven its gifts not all at once bestows,
These years with wisdom crowns, with action those:
The field of combat fits the young and bold,
The solemn council best becomes the old:
To you the glorious conflict I resign,
Let sage advice, the palm of age, be mine."

He said. With joy the monarch march'd before,
And found Menestheus on the dusty shore,
With whom the firm Athenian phalanx stands;
And next Ulysses, with his subject bands.
Remote their forces lay, nor knew so far
The peace infringed, nor heard the sounds of war;
The tumult late begun, they stood intent
To watch the motion, dubious of the event.
The king, who saw their squadrons yet unmoved,
With hasty ardour thus the chiefs reproved:

"Can Peleus' son forget a warrior's part.
And fears Ulysses, skill'd in every art?
Why stand you distant, and the rest expect
To mix in combat which yourselves neglect?
From you 'twas hoped among the first to dare
The shock of armies, and commence the war;
For this your names are call'd before the rest,
To share the pleasures of the genial feast:
And can you, chiefs! without a blush survey
Whole troops before you labouring in the fray?
Say, is it thus those honours you requite?
The first in banquets, but the last in fight."

Ulysses heard: the hero's warmth o'erspread
His cheek with blushes: and severe, he said:
"Take back the unjust reproach! Behold we stand
Sheathed in bright arms, and but expect command.
If glorious deeds afford thy soul delight,
Behold me plunging in the thickest fight.
Then give thy warrior-chief a warrior's due,

Who dares to act whate'er thou dar'st to view."
Struck with his generous wrath, the king replies:

"O great in action, and in council wise!
With ours, thy care and ardour are the same,
Nor need I to commend, nor aught to blame.
Sage as thou art, and learn'd in human kind,
Forgive the transport of a martial mind.
Haste to the fight, secure of just amends;
The gods that make, shall keep the worthy, friends."

He said, and pass'd where great Tydides lay,
His steeds and chariots wedged in firm array;
(The warlike Sthenelus attends his side;)
To whom with stern reproach the monarch cried:
"O son of Tydeus! (he, whose strength could tame
The bounding steed, in arms a mighty name)
Canst thou, remote, the mingling hosts descry,
With hands unactive, and a careless eye?
Not thus thy sire the fierce encounter fear'd;
Still first in front the matchless prince appear'd:
What glorious toils, what wonders they recite,
Who view'd him labouring through the ranks of fight?
I saw him once, when gathering martial powers,
A peaceful guest, he sought Mycenae's towers;
Armies he ask'd, and armies had been given,
Not we denied, but Jove forbade from heaven;
While dreadful comets glaring from afar,
Forewarn'd the horrors of the Theban war.
Next, sent by Greece from where Asopus flows,
A fearless envoy, he approach'd the foes;
Thebes' hostile walls unguarded and alone,
Dauntless he enters, and demands the throne.
The tyrant feasting with his chiefs he found,
And dared to combat all those chiefs around:
Dared, and subdued before their haughty lord;
For Pallas strung his arm and edged his sword.
Stung with the shame, within the winding way,
To bar his passage fifty warriors lay;
Two heroes led the secret squadron on,
Mason the fierce, and hardy Lycophon;
Those fifty slaughter'd in the gloomy vale.
He spared but one to bear the dreadful tale,
Such Tydeus was, and such his martial fire;
Gods! how the son degenerates from the sire!"

No words the godlike Diomed return'd,
But heard respectful, and in secret burn'd:

Not so fierce Capaneus' undaunted son;
Stern as his sire, the boaster thus begun:

"What needs, O monarch! this invidious praise,
Ourselves to lessen, while our sire you raise?
Dare to be just, Atrides! and confess
Our value equal, though our fury less.
With fewer troops we storm'd the Theban wall,
And happier saw the sevenfold city fall,
In impious acts the guilty father died;
The sons subdued, for Heaven was on their side.
Far more than heirs of all our parents' fame,
Our glories darken their diminish'd name."

To him Tydides thus: "My friend, forbear;
Suppress thy passion, and the king revere:
His high concern may well excuse this rage,
Whose cause we follow, and whose war we wage:
His the first praise, were Ilion's towers o'erthrown,
And, if we fail, the chief disgrace his own.
Let him the Greeks to hardy toils excite,
'Tis ours to labour in the glorious fight."

He spoke, and ardent, on the trembling ground
Sprung from his car: his ringing arms resound.
Dire was the clang, and dreadful from afar,
Of arm'd Tydides rushing to the war.
As when the winds, ascending by degrees,
First move the whitening surface of the seas,
The billows float in order to the shore,
The wave behind rolls on the wave before;
Till, with the growing storm, the deeps arise,
Foam o'er the rocks, and thunder to the skies.
So to the fight the thick battalions throng,
Shields urged on shields, and men drove men along
Sedate and silent move the numerous bands;
No sound, no whisper, but the chief's commands,
Those only heard; with awe the rest obey,
As if some god had snatch'd their voice away.
Not so the Trojans; from their host ascends
A general shout that all the region rends.
As when the fleecy flocks unnumber'd stand
In wealthy folds, and wait the milker's hand,
The hollow vales incessant bleating fills,
The lambs reply from all the neighbouring hills:
Such clamours rose from various nations round,
Mix'd was the murmur, and confused the sound.
Each host now joins, and each a god inspires,

These Mars incites, and those Minerva fires,
Pale flight around, and dreadful terror reign;
And discord raging bathes the purple plain;
Discord! dire sister of the slaughtering power,
Small at her birth, but rising every hour,
While scarce the skies her horrid head can bound,
She stalks on earth, and shakes the world around;
The nations bleed, where'er her steps she turns,
The groan still deepens, and the combat burns.

Now shield with shield, with helmet helmet closed,
To armour armour, lance to lance opposed,
Host against host with shadowy squadrons drew,
The sounding darts in iron tempests flew,
Victors and vanquish'd join'd promiscuous cries,
And shrilling shouts and dying groans arise;
With streaming blood the slippery fields are dyed,
And slaughter'd heroes swell the dreadful tide.

As torrents roll, increased by numerous rills,
With rage impetuous, down their echoing hills
Rush to the vales, and pour'd along the plain.
Roar through a thousand channels to the main:
The distant shepherd trembling hears the sound;
So mix both hosts, and so their cries rebound.

The bold Antilochus the slaughter led,
The first who struck a valiant Trojan dead:
At great Echepolus the lance arrives,
Razed his high crest, and through his helmet drives;
Warm'd in the brain the brazen weapon lies,
And shades eternal settle o'er his eyes.
So sinks a tower, that long assaults had stood
Of force and fire, its walls besmear'd with blood.
Him, the bold leader of the Abantian throng,
Seized to despoil, and dragg'd the corpse along:
But while he strove to tug the inserted dart,
Agenor's javelin reach'd the hero's heart.
His flank, unguarded by his ample shield,
Admits the lance: he falls, and spurns the field;
The nerves, unbraced, support his limbs no more;
The soul comes floating in a tide of gore.
Trojans and Greeks now gather round the slain;
The war renews, the warriors bleed again:
As o'er their prey rapacious wolves engage,
Man dies on man, and all is blood and rage.

In blooming youth fair Simoisius fell,

Sent by great Ajax to the shades of hell;
Fair Simoisius, whom his mother bore
Amid the flocks on silver Simois' shore:
The nymph descending from the hills of Ide,
To seek her parents on his flowery side,
Brought forth the babe, their common care and joy,
And thence from Simois named the lovely boy.
Short was his date! by dreadful Ajax slain,
He falls, and renders all their cares in vain!
So falls a poplar, that in watery ground
Raised high the head, with stately branches crown'd,
(Fell'd by some artist with his shining steel,
To shape the circle of the bending wheel,)
Cut down it lies, tall, smooth, and largely spread,
With all its beauteous honours on its head
There, left a subject to the wind and rain,
And scorch'd by suns, it withers on the plain
Thus pierced by Ajax, Simoisius lies
Stretch'd on the shore, and thus neglected dies.

At Ajax, Antiphus his javelin threw;
The pointed lance with erring fury flew,
And Leucus, loved by wise Ulysses, slew.
He drops the corpse of Simoisius slain,
And sinks a breathless carcase on the plain.
This saw Ulysses, and with grief enraged,
Strode where the foremost of the foes engaged;
Arm'd with his spear, he meditates the wound,
In act to throw; but cautious look'd around,
Struck at his sight the Trojans backward drew,
And trembling heard the javelin as it flew.
A chief stood nigh, who from Abydos came,
Old Priam's son, Democoon was his name.
The weapon entered close above his ear,
Cold through his temples glides the whizzing spear;
With piercing shrieks the youth resigns his breath,
His eye-balls darken with the shades of death;
Ponderous he falls; his clanging arms resound,
And his broad buckler rings against the ground.

Seized with affright the boldest foes appear;
E'en godlike Hector seems himself to fear;
Slow he gave way, the rest tumultuous fled;
The Greeks with shouts press on, and spoil the dead:
But Phoebus now from Ilion's towering height
Shines forth reveal'd, and animates the fight.
"Trojans, be bold, and force with force oppose;
Your foaming steeds urge headlong on the foes!

Nor are their bodies rocks, nor ribb'd with steel;
Your weapons enter, and your strokes they feel.
Have ye forgot what seem'd your dread before?
The great, the fierce Achilles fights no more."

Apollo thus from Ilion's lofty towers,
Array'd in terrors, roused the Trojan powers:
While war's fierce goddess fires the Grecian foe,
And shouts and thunders in the fields below.
Then great Diores fell, by doom divine,
In vain his valour and illustrious line.
A broken rock the force of Pyrus threw,
(Who from cold Ćnus led the Thracian crew,)
Full on his ankle dropp'd the ponderous stone,
Burst the strong nerves, and crash'd the solid bone.
Supine he tumbles on the crimson sands,
Before his helpless friends, and native bands,
And spreads for aid his unavailing hands.
The foe rush'd furious as he pants for breath,
And through his navel drove the pointed death:
His gushing entrails smoked upon the ground,
And the warm life came issuing from the wound.

His lance bold Thoas at the conqueror sent,
Deep in his breast above the pap it went,
Amid the lungs was fix'd the winged wood,
And quivering in his heaving bosom stood:
Till from the dying chief, approaching near,
The Ćtolian warrior tugg'd his weighty spear:
Then sudden waved his flaming falchion round,
And gash'd his belly with a ghastly wound;
The corpse now breathless on the bloody plain,
To spoil his arms the victor strove in vain;
The Thracian bands against the victor press'd,
A grove of lances glitter'd at his breast.
Stern Thoas, glaring with revengeful eyes,
In sullen fury slowly quits the prize.

Thus fell two heroes; one the pride of Thrace,
And one the leader of the Epeian race;
Death's sable shade at once o'ercast their eyes,
In dust the vanquish'd and the victor lies.
With copious slaughter all the fields are red,
And heap'd with growing mountains of the dead.

Had some brave chief this martial scene beheld,
By Pallas guarded through the dreadful field;
Might darts be bid to turn their points away,

And swords around him innocently play;
The war's whole art with wonder had he seen,
And counted heroes where he counted men.

So fought each host, with thirst of glory fired,
And crowds on crowds triumphantly expired.

BOOK V

ARGUMENT

THE ACTS OF DIOMED

Diomed, assisted by Pallas, performs wonders in this day's battle. Pandarus wounds him with an arrow, but the goddess cures him, enables him to discern gods from mortals, and prohibits him from contending with any of the former, excepting Venus. Ćneas joins Pandarus to oppose him; Pandarus is killed, and Ćneas in great danger but for the assistance of Venus; who, as she is removing her son from the fight, is wounded on the hand by Diomed. Apollo seconds her in his rescue, and at length carries off Ćneas to Troy, where he is healed in the temple of Pergamus. Mars rallies the Trojans, and assists Hector to make a stand. In the meantime Ćneas is restored to the field, and they overthrow several of the Greeks; among the rest Tlepolemus is slain by Sarpedon. Juno and Minerva descend to resist Mars; the latter incites Diomed to go against that god; he wounds him, and sends him groaning to heaven.

The first battle continues through this book. The scene is the same as in the former.

But Pallas now Tydides' soul inspires,
Fills with her force, and warms with all her fires,
Above the Greeks his deathless fame to raise,
And crown her hero with distinguish'd praise.
High on his helm celestial lightnings play,
His beamy shield emits a living ray;
The unwearied blaze incessant streams supplies,
Like the red star that fires the autumnal skies,
When fresh he rears his radiant orb to sight,
And, bathed in ocean, shoots a keener light.
Such glories Pallas on the chief bestow'd,
Such, from his arms, the fierce effulgence flow'd:
Onward she drives him, furious to engage,
Where the fight burns, and where the thickest rage.

The sons of Dares first the combat sought,
A wealthy priest, but rich without a fault;
In Vulcan's fane the father's days were led,
The sons to toils of glorious battle bred;
These singled from their troops the fight maintain,

These, from their steeds, Tydides on the plain.
Fierce for renown the brother-chiefs draw near,
And first bold Phegeus cast his sounding spear,
Which o'er the warrior's shoulder took its course,
And spent in empty air its erring force.
Not so, Tydides, flew thy lance in vain,
But pierced his breast, and stretch'd him on the plain.
Seized with unusual fear, Idaeus fled,
Left the rich chariot, and his brother dead.
And had not Vulcan lent celestial aid,
He too had sunk to death's eternal shade;
But in a smoky cloud the god of fire
Preserved the son, in pity to the sire.
The steeds and chariot, to the navy led,
Increased the spoils of gallant Diomed.

Struck with amaze and shame, the Trojan crew,
Or slain, or fled, the sons of Dares view;
When by the blood-stain'd hand Minerva press'd
The god of battles, and this speech address'd:

"Stern power of war! by whom the mighty fall,
Who bathe in blood, and shake the lofty wall!
Let the brave chiefs their glorious toils divide;
And whose the conquest, mighty Jove decide:
While we from interdicted fields retire,
Nor tempt the wrath of heaven's avenging sire."

Her words allay the impetuous warrior's heat,
The god of arms and martial maid retreat;
Removed from fight, on Xanthus' flowery bounds
They sat, and listen'd to the dying sounds.

Meantime, the Greeks the Trojan race pursue,
And some bold chieftain every leader slew:
First Odius falls, and bites the bloody sand,
His death ennobled by Atrides' hand:

As he to flight his wheeling car address'd,
The speedy javelin drove from back to breast.
In dust the mighty Halizonian lay,
His arms resound, the spirit wings its way.

Thy fate was next, O Phaestus! doom'd to feel
The great Idomeneus' protended steel;
Whom Borus sent (his son and only joy)
From fruitful Tarne to the fields of Troy.
The Cretan javelin reach'd him from afar,

And pierced his shoulder as he mounts his car;
Back from the car he tumbles to the ground,
And everlasting shades his eyes surround.

Then died Scamandrius, expert in the chase,
In woods and wilds to wound the savage race;
Diana taught him all her sylvan arts,
To bend the bow, and aim unerring darts:
But vainly here Diana's arts he tries,
The fatal lance arrests him as he flies;
From Menelaus' arm the weapon sent,
Through his broad back and heaving bosom went:
Down sinks the warrior with a thundering sound,
His brazen armour rings against the ground.

Next artful Phereclus untimely fell;
Bold Merion sent him to the realms of hell.
Thy father's skill, O Phereclus! was thine,
The graceful fabric and the fair design;
For loved by Pallas, Pallas did impart
To him the shipwright's and the builder's art.
Beneath his hand the fleet of Paris rose,
The fatal cause of all his country's woes;
But he, the mystic will of heaven unknown,
Nor saw his country's peril, nor his own.
The hapless artist, while confused he fled,
The spear of Merion mingled with the dead.
Through his right hip, with forceful fury cast,
Between the bladder and the bone it pass'd;
Prone on his knees he falls with fruitless cries,
And death in lasting slumber seals his eyes.

From Meges' force the swift Pedaeus fled,
Antenor's offspring from a foreign bed,
Whose generous spouse, Theanor, heavenly fair,
Nursed the young stranger with a mother's care.
How vain those cares! when Meges in the rear
Full in his nape infix'd the fatal spear;
Swift through his crackling jaws the weapon glides,
And the cold tongue and grinning teeth divides.

Then died Hypsenor, generous and divine,
Sprung from the brave Dolopion's mighty line,
Who near adored Scamander made abode,
Priest of the stream, and honoured as a god.
On him, amidst the flying numbers found,
Eurypylus inflicts a deadly wound;
On his broad shoulders fell the forceful brand,

Thence glancing downwards, lopp'd his holy hand,
Which stain'd with sacred blood the blushing sand.
Down sunk the priest: the purple hand of death
Closed his dim eye, and fate suppress'd his breath.

Thus toil'd the chiefs, in different parts engaged.
In every quarter fierce Tydides raged;
Amid the Greek, amid the Trojan train,
Rapt through the ranks he thunders o'er the plain;
Now here, now there, he darts from place to place,
Pours on the rear, or lightens in their face.
Thus from high hills the torrents swift and strong
Deluge whole fields, and sweep the trees along,
Through ruin'd moles the rushing wave resounds,
O'erwhelm's the bridge, and bursts the lofty bounds;
The yellow harvests of the ripen'd year,
And flatted vineyards, one sad waste appear!
While Jove descends in sluicy sheets of rain,
And all the labours of mankind are vain.

So raged Tydides, boundless in his ire,
Drove armies back, and made all Troy retire.
With grief the leader of the Lycian band
Saw the wide waste of his destructive hand:
His bended bow against the chief he drew;
Swift to the mark the thirsty arrow flew,
Whose forky point the hollow breastplate tore,
Deep in his shoulder pierced, and drank the gore:
The rushing stream his brazen armour dyed,
While the proud archer thus exulting cried:

"Hither, ye Trojans, hither drive your steeds!
Lo! by our hand the bravest Grecian bleeds,
Not long the deathful dart he can sustain;
Or Phoebus urged me to these fields in vain."
So spoke he, boastful: but the winged dart
Stopp'd short of life, and mock'd the shooter's art.
The wounded chief, behind his car retired,
The helping hand of Sthenelus required;
Swift from his seat he leap'd upon the ground,
And tugg'd the weapon from the gushing wound;
When thus the king his guardian power address'd,
The purple current wandering o'er his vest:

"O progeny of Jove! unconquer'd maid!
If e'er my godlike sire deserved thy aid,
If e'er I felt thee in the fighting field;
Now, goddess, now, thy sacred succour yield.

O give my lance to reach the Trojan knight,
Whose arrow wounds the chief thou guard'st in fight;
And lay the boaster grovelling on the shore,
That vaunts these eyes shall view the light no more."

Thus pray'd Tydides, and Minerva heard,
His nerves confirm'd, his languid spirits cheer'd;
He feels each limb with wonted vigour light;
His beating bosom claim'd the promised fight.
"Be bold, (she cried), in every combat shine,
War be thy province, thy protection mine;
Rush to the fight, and every foe control;
Wake each paternal virtue in thy soul:
Strength swells thy boiling breast, infused by me,
And all thy godlike father breathes in thee;
Yet more, from mortal mists I purge thy eyes,
And set to view the warring deities.
These see thou shun, through all the embattled plain;
Nor rashly strive where human force is vain.
If Venus mingle in the martial band,
Her shalt thou wound: so Pallas gives command."

With that, the blue-eyed virgin wing'd her flight;
The hero rush'd impetuous to the fight;
With tenfold ardour now invades the plain,
Wild with delay, and more enraged by pain.
As on the fleecy flocks when hunger calls,
Amidst the field a brindled lion falls;
If chance some shepherd with a distant dart
The savage wound, he rouses at the smart,
He foams, he roars; the shepherd dares not stay,
But trembling leaves the scattering flocks a prey;
Heaps fall on heaps; he bathes with blood the ground,
Then leaps victorious o'er the lofty mound.
Not with less fury stern Tydides flew;
And two brave leaders at an instant slew;
Astynous breathless fell, and by his side,
His people's pastor, good Hypenor, died;
Astynous' breast the deadly lance receives,
Hypenor's shoulder his broad falchion cleaves.
Those slain he left, and sprung with noble rage
Abas and Polyidus to engage;
Sons of Eurydamus, who, wise and old,
Could fate foresee, and mystic dreams unfold;
The youths return'd not from the doubtful plain,
And the sad father tried his arts in vain;
No mystic dream could make their fates appear,
Though now determined by Tydides' spear.

Young Xanthus next, and Thoon felt his rage;
The joy and hope of Phaenops' feeble age:
Vast was his wealth, and these the only heirs
Of all his labours and a life of cares.
Cold death o'ertakes them in their blooming years,
And leaves the father unavailing tears:
To strangers now descends his heapy store,
The race forgotten, and the name no more.

Two sons of Priam in one chariot ride,
Glittering in arms, and combat side by side.
As when the lordly lion seeks his food
Where grazing heifers range the lonely wood,
He leaps amidst them with a furious bound,
Bends their strong necks, and tears them to the ground:
So from their seats the brother chiefs are torn,
Their steeds and chariot to the navy borne.

With deep concern divine Ćneas view'd
The foe prevailing, and his friends pursued;
Through the thick storm of singing spears he flies,
Exploring Pandarus with careful eyes.
At length he found Lycaon's mighty son;
To whom the chief of Venus' race begun:

"Where, Pandarus, are all thy honours now,
Thy winged arrows and unerring bow,
Thy matchless skill, thy yet unrivall'd fame,
And boasted glory of the Lycian name?
O pierce that mortal! if we mortal call
That wondrous force by which whole armies fall;
Or god incensed, who quits the distant skies
To punish Troy for slighted sacrifice;
(Which, oh avert from our unhappy state!
For what so dreadful as celestial hate)?
Whoe'er he be, propitiate Jove with prayer;
If man, destroy; if god, entreat to spare."

To him the Lycian: "Whom your eyes behold,
If right I judge, is Diomed the bold:
Such coursers whirl him o'er the dusty field,
So towers his helmet, and so flames his shield.
If 'tis a god, he wears that chief's disguise:
Or if that chief, some guardian of the skies,
Involved in clouds, protects him in the fray,
And turns unseen the frustrate dart away.
I wing'd an arrow, which not idly fell,

The stroke had fix'd him to the gates of hell;
And, but some god, some angry god withstands,
His fate was due to these unerring hands.
Skill'd in the bow, on foot I sought the war,
Nor join'd swift horses to the rapid car.
Ten polish'd chariots I possess'd at home,
And still they grace Lycaon's princely dome:
There veil'd in spacious coverlets they stand;
And twice ten coursers wait their lord's command.
The good old warrior bade me trust to these,
When first for Troy I sail'd the sacred seas;
In fields, aloft, the whirling car to guide,
And through the ranks of death triumphant ride.
But vain with youth, and yet to thrift inclined,
I heard his counsels with unheedful mind,
And thought the steeds (your large supplies unknown)
Might fail of forage in the straiten'd town;
So took my bow and pointed darts in hand
And left the chariots in my native land.

"Too late, O friend! my rashness I deplore;
These shafts, once fatal, carry death no more.
Tydeus' and Atreus' sons their points have found,
And undissembled gore pursued the wound.
In vain they bleed: this unavailing bow
Serves, not to slaughter, but provoke the foe.
In evil hour these bended horns I strung,
And seized the quiver where it idly hung.
Cursed be the fate that sent me to the field
Without a warrior's arms, the spear and shield!
If e'er with life I quit the Trojan plain,
If e'er I see my spouse and sire again,
This bow, unfaithful to my glorious aims,
Broke by my hand, shall feed the blazing flames."

To whom the leader of the Dardan race:
"Be calm, nor Phoebus' honour'd gift disgrace.
The distant dart be praised, though here we need
The rushing chariot and the bounding steed.
Against yon hero let us bend our course,
And, hand to hand, encounter force with force.
Now mount my seat, and from the chariot's height
Observe my father's steeds, renown'd in fight;
Practised alike to turn, to stop, to chase,
To dare the shock, or urge the rapid race;
Secure with these, through fighting fields we go;
Or safe to Troy, if Jove assist the foe.
Haste, seize the whip, and snatch the guiding rein;

The warrior's fury let this arm sustain;
Or, if to combat thy bold heart incline,
Take thou the spear, the chariot's care be mine."

"O prince! (Lycaon's valiant son replied)
As thine the steeds, be thine the task to guide.
The horses, practised to their lord's command,
Shall bear the rein, and answer to thy hand;
But, if, unhappy, we desert the fight,
Thy voice alone can animate their flight;
Else shall our fates be number'd with the dead,
And these, the victor's prize, in triumph led.
Thine be the guidance, then: with spear and shield
Myself will charge this terror of the field."

And now both heroes mount the glittering car;
The bounding coursers rush amidst the war;
Their fierce approach bold Sthenelus espied,
Who thus, alarm'd, to great Tydides cried:

"O friend! two chiefs of force immense I see,
Dreadful they come, and bend their rage on thee:
Lo the brave heir of old Lycaon's line,
And great Æneas, sprung from race divine!
Enough is given to fame. Ascend thy car!
And save a life, the bulwark of our war."

At this the hero cast a gloomy look,
Fix'd on the chief with scorn; and thus he spoke:

"Me dost thou bid to shun the coming fight?
Me wouldst thou move to base, inglorious flight?
Know, 'tis not honest in my soul to fear,
Nor was Tydides born to tremble here.
I hate the cumbrous chariot's slow advance,
And the long distance of the flying lance;
But while my nerves are strong, my force entire,
Thus front the foe, and emulate my sire.
Nor shall yon steeds, that fierce to fight convey
Those threatening heroes, bear them both away;
One chief at least beneath this arm shall die;
So Pallas tells me, and forbids to fly.
But if she dooms, and if no god withstand,
That both shall fall by one victorious hand,
Then heed my words: my horses here detain,
Fix'd to the chariot by the straiten'd rein;
Swift to Æneas' empty seat proceed,
And seize the coursers of ethereal breed;

The race of those, which once the thundering god
For ravish'd Ganymede on Tros bestow'd,
The best that e'er on earth's broad surface run,
Beneath the rising or the setting sun.
Hence great Anchises stole a breed unknown,
By mortal mares, from fierce Laomedon:
Four of this race his ample stalls contain,
And two transport Œneas o'er the plain.
These, were the rich immortal prize our own,
Through the wide world should make our glory known."

Thus while they spoke, the foe came furious on,
And stern Lycaon's warlike race begun:

"Prince, thou art met. Though late in vain assail'd,
The spear may enter where the arrow fail'd."

He said, then shook the ponderous lance, and flung;
On his broad shield the sounding weapon rung,
Pierced the tough orb, and in his cuirass hung,
"He bleeds! the pride of Greece! (the boaster cries,)
Our triumph now, the mighty warrior lies!"
"Mistaken vaunter! (Diomed replied;)
Thy dart has erred, and now my spear be tried;
Ye 'scape not both; one, headlong from his car,
With hostile blood shall glut the god of war."

He spoke, and rising hurl'd his forceful dart,
Which, driven by Pallas, pierced a vital part;
Full in his face it enter'd, and betwixt
The nose and eye-ball the proud Lycian fix'd;
Crash'd all his jaws, and cleft the tongue within,
Till the bright point look'd out beneath the chin.
Headlong he falls, his helmet knocks the ground:
Earth groans beneath him, and his arms resound;
The starting coursers tremble with affright;
The soul indignant seeks the realms of night.

To guard his slaughter'd friend, Œneas flies,
His spear extending where the carcase lies;
Watchful he wheels, protects it every way,
As the grim lion stalks around his prey.
O'er the fall'n trunk his ample shield display'd,
He hides the hero with his mighty shade,
And threats aloud! the Greeks with longing eyes
Behold at distance, but forbear the prize.
Then fierce Tydides stoops; and from the fields
Heaved with vast force, a rocky fragment wields.

Not two strong men the enormous weight could raise,
Such men as live in these degenerate days:
He swung it round; and, gathering strength to throw,
Discharged the ponderous ruin at the foe.
Where to the hip the inserted thigh unites,
Full on the bone the pointed marble lights;
Through both the tendons broke the rugged stone,
And stripp'd the skin, and crack'd the solid bone.
Sunk on his knees, and staggering with his pains,
His falling bulk his bended arm sustains;
Lost in a dizzy mist the warrior lies;
A sudden cloud comes swimming o'er his eyes.
There the brave chief, who mighty numbers sway'd,
Oppress'd had sunk to death's eternal shade,
But heavenly Venus, mindful of the love
She bore Anchises in the Idaean grove,
His danger views with anguish and despair,
And guards her offspring with a mother's care.
About her much-loved son her arms she throws,
Her arms whose whiteness match the falling snows.
Screen'd from the foe behind her shining veil,
The swords wave harmless, and the javelins fail;
Safe through the rushing horse, and feather'd flight
Of sounding shafts, she bears him from the fight.

Nor Sthenelus, with unassisting hands,
Remain'd unheedful of his lord's commands:
His panting steeds, removed from out the war,
He fix'd with straiten'd traces to the car,
Next, rushing to the Dardan spoil, detains
The heavenly coursers with the flowing manes:
These in proud triumph to the fleet convey'd,
No longer now a Trojan lord obey'd.
That charge to bold Deipylus he gave,
(Whom most he loved, as brave men love the brave,)
Then mounting on his car, resumed the rein,
And follow'd where Tydides swept the plain.

Meanwhile (his conquest ravished from his eyes)
The raging chief in chase of Venus flies:
No goddess she, commission'd to the field,
Like Pallas dreadful with her sable shield,
Or fierce Bellona thundering at the wall,
While flames ascend, and mighty ruins fall;
He knew soft combats suit the tender dame,
New to the field, and still a foe to fame.
Through breaking ranks his furious course he bends,
And at the goddess his broad lance extends;

Through her bright veil the daring weapon drove,
The ambrosial veil which all the Graces wove;
Her snowy hand the razing steel profaned,
And the transparent skin with crimson stain'd,
From the clear vein a stream immortal flow'd,
Such stream as issues from a wounded god;
Pure emanation! uncorrupted flood!
Unlike our gross, diseased, terrestrial blood:
(For not the bread of man their life sustains,
Nor wine's inflaming juice supplies their veins:)
With tender shrieks the goddess fill'd the place,
And dropp'd her offspring from her weak embrace.
Him Phoebus took: he casts a cloud around
The fainting chief, and wards the mortal wound.

Then with a voice that shook the vaulted skies,
The king insults the goddess as she flies:
"Ill with Jove's daughter bloody fights agree,
The field of combat is no scene for thee:
Go, let thy own soft sex employ thy care,
Go, lull the coward, or delude the fair.
Taught by this stroke renounce the war's alarms,
And learn to tremble at the name of arms."

Tydides thus. The goddess, seized with dread,
Confused, distracted, from the conflict fled.
To aid her, swift the winged Iris flew,
Wrapt in a mist above the warring crew.
The queen of love with faded charms she found.
Pale was her cheek, and livid look'd the wound.
To Mars, who sat remote, they bent their way:
Far, on the left, with clouds involved he lay;
Beside him stood his lance, distain'd with gore,
And, rein'd with gold, his foaming steeds before.
Low at his knee, she begg'd with streaming eyes
Her brother's car, to mount the distant skies,
And show'd the wound by fierce Tydides given,
A mortal man, who dares encounter heaven.
Stern Mars attentive hears the queen complain,
And to her hand commits the golden rein;
She mounts the seat, oppress'd with silent woe,
Driven by the goddess of the painted bow.
The lash resounds, the rapid chariot flies,
And in a moment scales the lofty skies:
They stopp'd the car, and there the coursers stood,
Fed by fair Iris with ambrosial food;
Before her mother, love's bright queen appears,
O'erwhelmed with anguish, and dissolved in tears:

She raised her in her arms, beheld her bleed,
And ask'd what god had wrought this guilty deed?

Then she: "This insult from no god I found,
An impious mortal gave the daring wound!
Behold the deed of haughty Diomed!
'Twas in the son's defence the mother bled.
The war with Troy no more the Grecians wage;
But with the gods (the immortal gods) engage."

Dione then: "Thy wrongs with patience bear,
And share those griefs inferior powers must share:
Unnumber'd woes mankind from us sustain,
And men with woes afflict the gods again.
The mighty Mars in mortal fetters bound,
And lodged in brazen dungeons underground,
Full thirteen moons imprison'd roar'd in vain;
Otus and Ephialtes held the chain:
Perhaps had perish'd had not Hermes' care
Restored the groaning god to upper air.
Great Juno's self has borne her weight of pain,
The imperial partner of the heavenly reign;
Amphitryon's son infix'd the deadly dart,
And fill'd with anguish her immortal heart.
E'en hell's grim king Alcides' power confess'd,
The shaft found entrance in his iron breast;
To Jove's high palace for a cure he fled,
Pierced in his own dominions of the dead;
Where Paeon, sprinkling heavenly balm around,
Assuaged the glowing pangs, and closed the wound.
Rash, impious man! to stain the bless'd abodes,
And drench his arrows in the blood of gods!

"But thou (though Pallas urged thy frantic deed),
Whose spear ill-fated makes a goddess bleed,
Know thou, whoe'er with heavenly power contends,
Short is his date, and soon his glory ends;
From fields of death when late he shall retire,
No infant on his knees shall call him sire.
Strong as thou art, some god may yet be found,
To stretch thee pale and gasping on the ground;
Thy distant wife, Ćgiale the fair,
Starting from sleep with a distracted air,
Shall rouse thy slaves, and her lost lord deplore,
The brave, the great, the glorious now no more!"

This said, she wiped from Venus' wounded palm
The sacred ichor, and infused the balm.

Juno and Pallas with a smile survey'd,
And thus to Jove began the blue-eyed maid:

"Permit thy daughter, gracious Jove! to tell
How this mischance the Cyprian queen befell,
As late she tried with passion to inflame
The tender bosom of a Grecian dame;
Allured the fair, with moving thoughts of joy,
To quit her country for some youth of Troy;
The clasping zone, with golden buckles bound,
Razed her soft hand with this lamented wound."

The sire of gods and men superior smiled,
And, calling Venus, thus address'd his child:
"Not these, O daughter are thy proper cares,
Thee milder arts befit, and softer wars;
Sweet smiles are thine, and kind endearing charms;
To Mars and Pallas leave the deeds of arms."

Thus they in heaven: while on the plain below
The fierce Tydides charged his Dardan foe,
Flush'd with celestial blood pursued his way,
And fearless dared the threatening god of day;
Already in his hopes he saw him kill'd,
Though screen'd behind Apollo's mighty shield.
Thrice rushing furious, at the chief he strook;
His blazing buckler thrice Apollo shook:
He tried the fourth: when, breaking from the cloud,
A more than mortal voice was heard aloud.

"O son of Tydeus, cease! be wise and see
How vast the difference of the gods and thee;
Distance immense! between the powers that shine
Above, eternal, deathless, and divine,
And mortal man! a wretch of humble birth,
A short-lived reptile in the dust of earth."

So spoke the god who darts celestial fires:
He dreads his fury, and some steps retires.
Then Phoebus bore the chief of Venus' race
To Troy's high fane, and to his holy place;
Latona there and Phoebe heal'd the wound,
With vigour arm'd him, and with glory crown'd.
This done, the patron of the silver bow
A phantom raised, the same in shape and show
With great Ćneas; such the form he bore,
And such in fight the radiant arms he wore.
Around the spectre bloody wars are waged,

And Greece and Troy with clashing shields engaged.
Meantime on Ilion's tower Apollo stood,
And calling Mars, thus urged the raging god:

"Stern power of arms, by whom the mighty fall;
Who bathest in blood, and shakest the embattled wall,
Rise in thy wrath! to hell's abhorr'd abodes
Despatch yon Greek, and vindicate the gods.
First rosy Venus felt his brutal rage;
Me next he charged, and dares all heaven engage:
The wretch would brave high heaven's immortal sire,
His triple thunder, and his bolts of fire."

The god of battle issues on the plain,
Stirs all the ranks, and fires the Trojan train;
In form like Acamas, the Thracian guide,
Enraged to Troy's retiring chiefs he cried:

"How long, ye sons of Priam! will ye fly,
And unrevenged see Priam's people die?
Still unresisted shall the foe destroy,
And stretch the slaughter to the gates of Troy?
Lo, brave Ćneas sinks beneath his wound,
Not godlike Hector more in arms renown'd:
Haste all, and take the generous warrior's part.
He said;—new courage swell'd each hero's heart.
Sarpedon first his ardent soul express'd,
And, turn'd to Hector, these bold words address'd:

"Say, chief, is all thy ancient valour lost?
Where are thy threats, and where thy glorious boast,
That propp'd alone by Priam's race should stand
Troy's sacred walls, nor need a foreign hand?
Now, now thy country calls her wonted friends,
And the proud vaunt in just derision ends.
Remote they stand while alien troops engage,
Like trembling hounds before the lion's rage.
Far distant hence I held my wide command,
Where foaming Xanthus laves the Lycian land;
With ample wealth (the wish of mortals) bless'd,
A beauteous wife, and infant at her breast;
With those I left whatever dear could be:
Greece, if she conquers, nothing wins from me;
Yet first in fight my Lycian bands I cheer,
And long to meet this mighty man ye fear;
While Hector idle stands, nor bids the brave
Their wives, their infants, and their altars save.
Haste, warrior, haste! preserve thy threaten'd state,

Or one vast burst of all-involving fate
Full o'er your towers shall fall, and sweep away
Sons, sires, and wives, an undistinguish'd prey.
Rouse all thy Trojans, urge thy aids to fight;
These claim thy thoughts by day, thy watch by night;
With force incessant the brave Greeks oppose;
Such cares thy friends deserve, and such thy foes."

Stung to the heart the generous Hector hears,
But just reproof with decent silence bears.
From his proud car the prince impetuous springs,
On earth he leaps, his brazen armour rings.
Two shining spears are brandish'd in his hands;
Thus arm'd, he animates his drooping bands,
Revives their ardour, turns their steps from flight,
And wakes anew the dying flames of fight.
They turn, they stand; the Greeks their fury dare,
Condense their powers, and wait the growing war.

As when, on Ceres' sacred floor, the swain
Spreads the wide fan to clear the golden grain,
And the light chaff, before the breezes borne,
Ascends in clouds from off the heapy corn;
The grey dust, rising with collected winds,
Drives o'er the barn, and whitens all the hinds:
So white with dust the Grecian host appears.
From trampling steeds, and thundering charioteers;
The dusky clouds from labour'd earth arise,
And roll in smoking volumes to the skies.
Mars hovers o'er them with his sable shield,
And adds new horrors to the darken'd field:
Pleased with his charge, and ardent to fulfil,
In Troy's defence, Apollo's heavenly will:
Soon as from fight the blue-eyed maid retires,
Each Trojan bosom with new warmth he fires.
And now the god, from forth his sacred fane,
Produced Ćneas to the shouting train;
Alive, unharm'd, with all his peers around,
Erect he stood, and vigorous from his wound:
Inquiries none they made; the dreadful day
No pause of words admits, no dull delay;
Fierce Discord storms, Apollo loud exclaims,
Fame calls, Mars thunders, and the field's in flames.

Stern Diomed with either Ajax stood,
And great Ulysses, bathed in hostile blood.
Embodied close, the labouring Grecian train
The fiercest shock of charging hosts sustain.

Unmoved and silent, the whole war they wait
Serenely dreadful, and as fix'd as fate.
So when the embattled clouds in dark array,
Along the skies their gloomy lines display;
When now the North his boisterous rage has spent,
And peaceful sleeps the liquid element:
The low-hung vapours, motionless and still,
Rest on the summits of the shaded hill;
Till the mass scatters as the winds arise,
Dispersed and broken through the ruffled skies.

Nor was the general wanting to his train;
From troop to troop he toils through all the plain,
"Ye Greeks, be men! the charge of battle bear;
Your brave associates and yourselves revere!
Let glorious acts more glorious acts inspire,
And catch from breast to breast the noble fire!
On valour's side the odds of combat lie,
The brave live glorious, or lamented die;
The wretch who trembles in the field of fame,
Meets death, and worse than death, eternal shame!"

These words he seconds with his flying lance,
To meet whose point was strong Deicoon's chance:
Ćneas' friend, and in his native place
Honour'd and loved like Priam's royal race:
Long had he fought the foremost in the field,
But now the monarch's lance transpierced his shield:
His shield too weak the furious dart to stay,
Through his broad belt the weapon forced its way:
The grisly wound dismiss'd his soul to hell,
His arms around him rattled as he fell.

Then fierce Ćneas, brandishing his blade,
In dust Orsilochus and Crethon laid,
Whose sire Diocleus, wealthy, brave and great,
In well-built Pherae held his lofty seat:
Sprung from Alpheus' plenteous stream, that yields
Increase of harvests to the Pylian fields.
He got Orsilochus, Diocleus he,
And these descended in the third degree.
Too early expert in the martial toil,
In sable ships they left their native soil,
To avenge Atrides: now, untimely slain,
They fell with glory on the Phrygian plain.
So two young mountain lions, nursed with blood
In deep recesses of the gloomy wood,
Rush fearless to the plains, and uncontroll'd

Depopulate the stalls and waste the fold:
Till pierced at distance from their native den,
O'erpowered they fall beneath the force of men.
Prostrate on earth their beauteous bodies lay,
Like mountain firs, as tall and straight as they.
Great Menelaus views with pitying eyes,
Lifts his bright lance, and at the victor flies;
Mars urged him on; yet, ruthless in his hate,
The god but urged him to provoke his fate.
He thus advancing, Nestor's valiant son
Shakes for his danger, and neglects his own;
Struck with the thought, should Helen's lord be slain,
And all his country's glorious labours vain.
Already met, the threatening heroes stand;
The spears already tremble in their hand:
In rush'd Antilochus, his aid to bring,
And fall or conquer by the Spartan king.
These seen, the Dardan backward turn'd his course,
Brave as he was, and shunn'd unequal force.
The breathless bodies to the Greeks they drew,
Then mix in combat, and their toils renew.

First, Pylaemenes, great in battle, bled,
Who sheathed in brass the Paphlagonians led.
Atrides mark'd him where sublime he stood;
Fix'd in his throat the javelin drank his blood.
The faithful Mydon, as he turn'd from fight
His flying coursers, sunk to endless night;
A broken rock by Nestor's son was thrown:
His bended arm received the falling stone;
From his numb'd hand the ivory-studded reins,
Dropp'd in the dust, are trail'd along the plains:
Meanwhile his temples feel a deadly wound;
He groans in death, and ponderous sinks to ground:
Deep drove his helmet in the sands, and there
The head stood fix'd, the quivering legs in air,
Till trampled flat beneath the coursers' feet:
The youthful victor mounts his empty seat,
And bears the prize in triumph to the fleet.

Great Hector saw, and, raging at the view,
Pours on the Greeks: the Trojan troops pursue:
He fires his host with animating cries,
And brings along the furies of the skies,
Mars, stern destroyer! and Bellona dread,
Flame in the front, and thunder at their head:
This swells the tumult and the rage of fight;
That shakes a spear that casts a dreadful light.

Where Hector march'd, the god of battles shined,
Now storm'd before him, and now raged behind.

Tydides paused amidst his full career;
Then first the hero's manly breast knew fear.
As when some simple swain his cot forsakes,
And wide through fens an unknown journey takes:
If chance a swelling brook his passage stay,
And foam impervious 'cross the wanderer's way,
Confused he stops, a length of country pass'd,
Eyes the rough waves, and tired, returns at last.
Amazed no less the great Tydides stands:
He stay'd, and turning thus address'd his bands:

"No wonder, Greeks! that all to Hector yield;
Secure of favouring gods, he takes the field;
His strokes they second, and avert our spears.
Behold where Mars in mortal arms appears!
Retire then, warriors, but sedate and slow;
Retire, but with your faces to the foe.
Trust not too much your unavailing might;
'Tis not with Troy, but with the gods ye fight."

Now near the Greeks the black battalions drew;
And first two leaders valiant Hector slew:
His force Anchialus and Mnesthes found,
In every art of glorious war renown'd;
In the same car the chiefs to combat ride,
And fought united, and united died.
Struck at the sight, the mighty Ajax glows
With thirst of vengeance, and assaults the foes.
His massy spear with matchless fury sent,
Through Amphius' belt and heaving belly went;
Amphius Apaesus' happy soil possess'd,
With herds abounding, and with treasure bless'd;
But fate resistless from his country led
The chief, to perish at his people's head.
Shook with his fall his brazen armour rung,
And fierce, to seize it, conquering Ajax sprung;
Around his head an iron tempest rain'd;
A wood of spears his ample shield sustain'd:
Beneath one foot the yet warm corpse he press'd,
And drew his javelin from the bleeding breast:
He could no more; the showering darts denied
To spoil his glittering arms, and plumy pride.
Now foes on foes came pouring on the fields,
With bristling lances, and compacted shields;
Till in the steely circle straiten'd round,

Forced he gives way, and sternly quits the ground.

While thus they strive, Tlepolemus the great,
Urged by the force of unresisted fate,
Burns with desire Sarpedon's strength to prove;
Alcides' offspring meets the son of Jove.
Sheathed in bright arms each adverse chief came on.
Jove's great descendant, and his greater son.
Prepared for combat, ere the lance he toss'd,
The daring Rhodian vents his haughty boast:

"What brings this Lycian counsellor so far,
To tremble at our arms, not mix in war!
Know thy vain self, nor let their flattery move,
Who style thee son of cloud-compelling Jove.
How far unlike those chiefs of race divine,
How vast the difference of their deeds and thine!
Jove got such heroes as my sire, whose soul
No fear could daunt, nor earth nor hell control.
Troy felt his arm, and yon proud ramparts stand
Raised on the ruins of his vengeful hand:
With six small ships, and but a slender train,
He left the town a wide-deserted plain.
But what art thou, who deedless look'st around,
While unrevenged thy Lycians bite the ground!
Small aid to Troy thy feeble force can be;
But wert thou greater, thou must yield to me.
Pierced by my spear, to endless darkness go!
I make this present to the shades below."

The son of Hercules, the Rhodian guide,
Thus haughty spoke. The Lycian king replied:

"Thy sire, O prince! o'erturn'd the Trojan state,
Whose perjured monarch well deserved his fate;
Those heavenly steeds the hero sought so far,
False he detain'd, the just reward of war.
Nor so content, the generous chief defied,
With base reproaches and unmanly pride.
But you, unworthy the high race you boast,
Shall raise my glory when thy own is lost:
Now meet thy fate, and by Sarpedon slain,
Add one more ghost to Pluto's gloomy reign."

He said: both javelins at an instant flew;
Both struck, both wounded, but Sarpedon's slew:
Full in the boaster's neck the weapon stood,
Transfix'd his throat, and drank the vital blood;

The soul disdainful seeks the caves of night,
And his seal'd eyes for ever lose the light.

Yet not in vain, Tlepolemus, was thrown
Thy angry lance; which piercing to the bone
Sarpedon's thigh, had robb'd the chief of breath;
But Jove was present, and forbade the death.
Borne from the conflict by his Lycian throng,
The wounded hero dragg'd the lance along.
(His friends, each busied in his several part,
Through haste, or danger, had not drawn the dart.)
The Greeks with slain Tlepolemus retired;
Whose fall Ulysses view'd, with fury fired;
Doubtful if Jove's great son he should pursue,
Or pour his vengeance on the Lycian crew.
But heaven and fate the first design withstand,
Nor this great death must grace Ulysses' hand.
Minerva drives him on the Lycian train;
Alastor, Cronius, Halius, strew'd the plain,
Alcander, Prytanis, Noemon fell:
And numbers more his sword had sent to hell,
But Hector saw; and, furious at the sight,
Rush'd terrible amidst the ranks of fight.
With joy Sarpedon view'd the wish'd relief,
And, faint, lamenting, thus implored the chief:

"O suffer not the foe to bear away
My helpless corpse, an unassisted prey;
If I, unbless'd, must see my son no more,
My much-loved consort, and my native shore,
Yet let me die in Ilion's sacred wall;
Troy, in whose cause I fell, shall mourn my fall."

He said, nor Hector to the chief replies,
But shakes his plume, and fierce to combat flies;
Swift as a whirlwind, drives the scattering foes;
And dyes the ground with purple as he goes.

Beneath a beech, Jove's consecrated shade,
His mournful friends divine Sarpedon laid:
Brave Pelagon, his favourite chief, was nigh,
Who wrench'd the javelin from his sinewy thigh.
The fainting soul stood ready wing'd for flight,
And o'er his eye-balls swam the shades of night;
But Boreas rising fresh, with gentle breath,
Recall'd his spirit from the gates of death.

The generous Greeks recede with tardy pace,

Though Mars and Hector thunder in their face;
None turn their backs to mean ignoble flight,
Slow they retreat, and even retreating fight.
Who first, who last, by Mars' and Hector's hand,
Stretch'd in their blood, lay gasping on the sand?
Tenthras the great, Orestes the renown'd
For managed steeds, and Trechus press'd the ground;,
Next OEnomaus and OEnops' offspring died;
Oresbius last fell groaning at their side:
Oresbius, in his painted mitre gay,
In fat Boeotia held his wealthy sway,
Where lakes surround low Hyle's watery plain;
A prince and people studious of their gain.

The carnage Juno from the skies survey'd,
And touch'd with grief bespoke the blue-eyed maid:
"Oh, sight accursed! Shall faithless Troy prevail,
And shall our promise to our people fail?
How vain the word to Menelaus given
By Jove's great daughter and the queen of heaven,
Beneath his arms that Priam's towers should fall,
If warring gods for ever guard the wall!
Mars, red with slaughter, aids our hated foes:
Haste, let us arm, and force with force oppose!"

She spoke; Minerva burns to meet the war:
And now heaven's empress calls her blazing car.
At her command rush forth the steeds divine;
Rich with immortal gold their trappings shine.
Bright Hebe waits; by Hebe, ever young,
The whirling wheels are to the chariot hung.
On the bright axle turns the bidden wheel
Of sounding brass; the polished axle steel.
Eight brazen spokes in radiant order flame;
The circles gold, of uncorrupted frame,
Such as the heavens produce: and round the gold
Two brazen rings of work divine were roll'd.
The bossy naves of sold silver shone;
Braces of gold suspend the moving throne:
The car, behind, an arching figure bore;
The bending concave form'd an arch before.
Silver the beam, the extended yoke was gold,
And golden reins the immortal coursers hold.
Herself, impatient, to the ready car,
The coursers joins, and breathes revenge and war.

Pallas disrobes; her radiant veil untied,
With flowers adorn'd, with art diversified,

(The laboured veil her heavenly fingers wove,)
Flows on the pavement of the court of Jove.
Now heaven's dread arms her mighty limbs invest,
Jove's cuirass blazes on her ample breast;
Deck'd in sad triumph for the mournful field,
O'er her broad shoulders hangs his horrid shield,
Dire, black, tremendous! Round the margin roll'd,
A fringe of serpents hissing guards the gold:
Here all the terrors of grim War appear,
Here rages Force, here tremble Flight and Fear,
Here storm'd Contention, and here Fury frown'd,
And the dire orb portentous Gorgon crown'd.
The massy golden helm she next assumes,
That dreadful nods with four o'ershading plumes;
So vast, the broad circumference contains
A hundred armies on a hundred plains.
The goddess thus the imperial car ascends;
Shook by her arm the mighty javelin bends,
Ponderous and huge; that when her fury burns,
Proud tyrants humbles, and whole hosts o'erturns.

Swift at the scourge the ethereal coursers fly,
While the smooth chariot cuts the liquid sky.
Heaven's gates spontaneous open to the powers,
Heaven's golden gates, kept by the winged Hours;
Commission'd in alternate watch they stand,
The sun's bright portals and the skies command,
Involve in clouds the eternal gates of day,
Or the dark barrier roll with ease away.
The sounding hinges ring on either side
The gloomy volumes, pierced with light, divide.
The chariot mounts, where deep in ambient skies,
Confused, Olympus' hundred heads arise;
Where far apart the Thunderer fills his throne,
O'er all the gods superior and alone.
There with her snowy hand the queen restrains
The fiery steeds, and thus to Jove complains:

"O sire! can no resentment touch thy soul?
Can Mars rebel, and does no thunder roll?
What lawless rage on yon forbidden plain,
What rash destruction! and what heroes slain!
Venus, and Phoebus with the dreadful bow,
Smile on the slaughter, and enjoy my woe.
Mad, furious power! whose unrelenting mind
No god can govern, and no justice bind.
Say, mighty father! shall we scourge this pride,
And drive from fight the impetuous homicide?"

To whom assenting, thus the Thunderer said:
"Go! and the great Minerva be thy aid.
To tame the monster-god Minerva knows,
And oft afflicts his brutal breast with woes."

He said; Saturnia, ardent to obey,
Lash'd her white steeds along the aerial way
Swift down the steep of heaven the chariot rolls,
Between the expanded earth and starry poles
Far as a shepherd, from some point on high,
O'er the wide main extends his boundless eye,
Through such a space of air, with thundering sound,
At every leap the immortal coursers bound
Troy now they reach'd and touch'd those banks divine,
Where silver Simois and Scamander join
There Juno stopp'd, and (her fair steeds unloosed)
Of air condensed a vapour circumfused
For these, impregnate with celestial dew,
On Simois, brink ambrosial herbage grew.
Thence to relieve the fainting Argive throng,
Smooth as the sailing doves they glide along.

The best and bravest of the Grecian band
(A warlike circle) round Tydides stand.
Such was their look as lions bathed in blood,
Or foaming boars, the terror of the wood
Heaven's empress mingles with the mortal crowd,
And shouts, in Stentor's sounding voice, aloud;
Stentor the strong, endued with brazen lungs,
Whose throats surpass'd the force of fifty tongues.

"Inglorious Argives! to your race a shame,
And only men in figure and in name!
Once from the walls your timorous foes engaged,
While fierce in war divine Achilles raged;
Now issuing fearless they possess the plain,
Now win the shores, and scarce the seas remain."

Her speech new fury to their hearts convey'd;
While near Tydides stood the Athenian maid;
The king beside his panting steeds she found,
O'erspent with toil reposing on the ground;
To cool his glowing wound he sat apart,
(The wound inflicted by the Lycian dart.)
Large drops of sweat from all his limbs descend,
Beneath his ponderous shield his sinews bend,
Whose ample belt, that o'er his shoulder lay,

He eased; and wash'd the clotted gore away.
The goddess leaning o'er the bending yoke,
Beside his coursers, thus her silence broke:

"Degenerate prince! and not of Tydeus' kind,
Whose little body lodged a mighty mind;
Foremost he press'd in glorious toils to share,
And scarce refrain'd when I forbade the war.
Alone, unguarded, once he dared to go,
And feast, incircled by the Theban foe;
There braved, and vanquish'd, many a hardy knight;
Such nerves I gave him, and such force in fight.
Thou too no less hast been my constant care;
Thy hands I arm'd, and sent thee forth to war:
But thee or fear deters, or sloth detains;
No drop of all thy father warms thy veins."

The chief thus answered mild: "Immortal maid!
I own thy presence, and confess thy aid.
Not fear, thou know'st, withholds me from the plains,
Nor sloth hath seized me, but thy word restrains:
From warring gods thou bad'st me turn my spear,
And Venus only found resistance here.
Hence, goddess! heedful of thy high commands,
Loth I gave way, and warn'd our Argive bands:
For Mars, the homicide, these eyes beheld,
With slaughter red, and raging round the field."

Then thus Minerva:—"Brave Tydides, hear!
Not Mars himself, nor aught immortal, fear.
Full on the god impel thy foaming horse:
Pallas commands, and Pallas lends thee force.
Rash, furious, blind, from these to those he flies,
And every side of wavering combat tries;
Large promise makes, and breaks the promise made:
Now gives the Grecians, now the Trojans aid."

She said, and to the steeds approaching near,
Drew from his seat the martial charioteer.
The vigorous power the trembling car ascends,
Fierce for revenge; and Diomed attends:
The groaning axle bent beneath the load;
So great a hero, and so great a god.
She snatch'd the reins, she lash'd with all her force,
And full on Mars impelled the foaming horse:
But first, to hide her heavenly visage, spread
Black Orcus' helmet o'er her radiant head.

Just then gigantic Periphas lay slain,
The strongest warrior of the Ćtolian train;
The god, who slew him, leaves his prostrate prize
Stretch'd where he fell, and at Tydides flies.
Now rushing fierce, in equal arms appear
The daring Greek, the dreadful god of war!
Full at the chief, above his courser's head,
From Mars's arm the enormous weapon fled:
Pallas opposed her hand, and caused to glance
Far from the car the strong immortal lance.
Then threw the force of Tydeus' warlike son;
The javelin hiss'd; the goddess urged it on:
Where the broad cincture girt his armour round,
It pierced the god: his groin received the wound.
From the rent skin the warrior tugs again
The smoking steel. Mars bellows with the pain:
Loud as the roar encountering armies yield,
When shouting millions shake the thundering field.
Both armies start, and trembling gaze around;
And earth and heaven re-bellow to the sound.
As vapours blown by Auster's sultry breath,
Pregnant with plagues, and shedding seeds of death,
Beneath the rage of burning Sirius rise,
Choke the parch'd earth, and blacken all the skies;
In such a cloud the god from combat driven,
High o'er the dusky whirlwind scales the heaven.
Wild with his pain, he sought the bright abodes,
There sullen sat beneath the sire of gods,
Show'd the celestial blood, and with a groan
Thus pour'd his plaints before the immortal throne:

"Can Jove, supine, flagitious facts survey,
And brook the furies of this daring day?
For mortal men celestial powers engage,
And gods on gods exert eternal rage:
From thee, O father! all these ills we bear,
And thy fell daughter with the shield and spear;
Thou gavest that fury to the realms of light,
Pernicious, wild, regardless of the right.
All heaven beside reveres thy sovereign sway,
Thy voice we hear, and thy behests obey:
'Tis hers to offend, and even offending share
Thy breast, thy counsels, thy distinguish'd care:
So boundless she, and thou so partial grown,
Well may we deem the wondrous birth thy own.
Now frantic Diomed, at her command,
Against the immortals lifts his raging hand:
The heavenly Venus first his fury found,

Me next encountering, me he dared to wound;
Vanquish'd I fled; even I, the god of fight,
From mortal madness scarce was saved by flight.
Else hadst thou seen me sink on yonder plain,
Heap'd round, and heaving under loads of slain!
Or pierced with Grecian darts, for ages lie,
Condemn'd to pain, though fated not to die."

Him thus upbraiding, with a wrathful look
The lord of thunders view'd, and stern bespoke:
"To me, perfidious! this lamenting strain?
Of lawless force shall lawless Mars complain?
Of all the gods who tread the spangled skies,
Thou most unjust, most odious in our eyes!
Inhuman discord is thy dire delight,
The waste of slaughter, and the rage of fight.
No bounds, no law, thy fiery temper quells,
And all thy mother in thy soul rebels.
In vain our threats, in vain our power we use;
She gives the example, and her son pursues.
Yet long the inflicted pangs thou shall not mourn,
Sprung since thou art from Jove, and heavenly-born.
Else, singed with lightning, hadst thou hence been thrown,
Where chain'd on burning rocks the Titans groan."

Thus he who shakes Olympus with his nod;
Then gave to Paeon's care the bleeding god.
With gentle hand the balm he pour'd around,
And heal'd the immortal flesh, and closed the wound.
As when the fig's press'd juice, infused in cream,
To curds coagulates the liquid stream,
Sudden the fluids fix the parts combined;
Such, and so soon, the ethereal texture join'd.
Cleansed from the dust and gore, fair Hebe dress'd
His mighty limbs in an immortal vest.
Glorious he sat, in majesty restored,
Fast by the throne of heaven's superior lord.
Juno and Pallas mount the bless'd abodes,
Their task perform'd, and mix among the gods.

BOOK VI

ARGUMENT

THE EPISODES OF GLAUCUS AND DIOMED, AND OF HECTOR AND ANDROMACHE

The gods having left the field, the Grecians prevail. Helenus, the chief augur of Troy, commands Hector to return to the city, in order to appoint a solemn procession of the queen and the Trojan matrons to the temple of Minerva, to entreat her to remove Diomed from the fight. The battle relaxing during the absence of Hector, Glaucus and Diomed have an interview between the two armies; where, coming to the knowledge, of the friendship and hospitality passed between their ancestors, they make exchange of their arms. Hector, having performed the orders of Helenus, prevails upon Paris to return to the battle, and, taking a tender leave of his wife Andromache, hastens again to the field.

The scene is first in the field of battle, between the rivers Simois and Scamander, and then changes to Troy.

Now heaven forsakes the fight: the immortals yield
To human force and human skill the field:
Dark showers of javelins fly from foes to foes;
Now here, now there, the tide of combat flows;
While Troy's famed streams, that bound the deathful plain
On either side, run purple to the main.

Great Ajax first to conquest led the way,
Broke the thick ranks, and turn'd the doubtful day.
The Thracian Acamas his falchion found,
And hew'd the enormous giant to the ground;
His thundering arm a deadly stroke impress'd
Where the black horse-hair nodded o'er his crest;
Fix'd in his front the brazen weapon lies,
And seals in endless shades his swimming eyes.
Next Teuthras' son distain'd the sands with blood,
Axylus, hospitable, rich, and good:
In fair Arisbe's walls (his native place)
He held his seat! a friend to human race.
Fast by the road, his ever-open door
Obliged the wealthy, and relieved the poor.
To stern Tydides now he falls a prey,
No friend to guard him in the dreadful day!
Breathless the good man fell, and by his side
His faithful servant, old Calesius died.

By great Euryalus was Dresus slain,
And next he laid Opheltius on the plain.
Two twins were near, bold, beautiful, and young,
From a fair naiad and Bucolion sprung:
(Laomedon's white flocks Bucolion fed,
That monarch's first-born by a foreign bed;
In secret woods he won the naiad's grace,
And two fair infants crown'd his strong embrace:)
Here dead they lay in all their youthful charms;
The ruthless victor stripp'd their shining arms.

Astyalus by Polypoetes fell;
Ulysses' spear Pidytes sent to hell;
By Teucer's shaft brave Aretaon bled,
And Nestor's son laid stern Ablerus dead;
Great Agamemnon, leader of the brave,
The mortal wound of rich Elatus gave,
Who held in Pedasus his proud abode,
And till'd the banks where silver Satnio flow'd.
Melanthius by Eurypylus was slain;
And Phylacus from Leitus flies in vain.

Unbless'd Adrastus next at mercy lies
Beneath the Spartan spear, a living prize.
Scared with the din and tumult of the fight,
His headlong steeds, precipitate in flight,
Rush'd on a tamarisk's strong trunk, and broke
The shatter'd chariot from the crooked yoke;
Wide o'er the field, resistless as the wind,
For Troy they fly, and leave their lord behind.
Prone on his face he sinks beside the wheel:
Atrides o'er him shakes his vengeful steel;
The fallen chief in suppliant posture press'd
The victor's knees, and thus his prayer address'd:

"O spare my youth, and for the life I owe
Large gifts of price my father shall bestow.
When fame shall tell, that, not in battle slain,
Thy hollow ships his captive son detain:
Rich heaps of brass shall in thy tent be told,
And steel well-temper'd, and persuasive gold."

He said: compassion touch'd the hero's heart
He stood, suspended with the lifted dart:
As pity pleaded for his vanquish'd prize,
Stern Agamemnon swift to vengeance flies,
And, furious, thus: "Oh impotent of mind!
Shall these, shall these Atrides' mercy find?
Well hast thou known proud Troy's perfidious land,
And well her natives merit at thy hand!
Not one of all the race, nor sex, nor age,
Shall save a Trojan from our boundless rage:
Ilion shall perish whole, and bury all;
Her babes, her infants at the breast, shall fall;
A dreadful lesson of exampled fate,
To warn the nations, and to curb the great!"

The monarch spoke; the words, with warmth address'd,

To rigid justice steel'd his brother's breast
Fierce from his knees the hapless chief he thrust;
The monarch's javelin stretch'd him in the dust,
Then pressing with his foot his panting heart,
Forth from the slain he tugg'd the reeking dart.
Old Nestor saw, and roused the warrior's rage;
"Thus, heroes! thus the vigorous combat wage;
No son of Mars descend, for servile gains,
To touch the booty, while a foe remains.
Behold yon glittering host, your future spoil!
First gain the conquest, then reward the toil."

And now had Greece eternal fame acquired,
And frighted Troy within her walls, retired,
Had not sage Helenus her state redress'd,
Taught by the gods that moved his sacred breast.
Where Hector stood, with great Ćneas join'd,
The seer reveal'd the counsels of his mind:

"Ye generous chiefs! on whom the immortals lay
The cares and glories of this doubtful day;
On whom your aids, your country's hopes depend;
Wise to consult, and active to defend!
Here, at our gates, your brave efforts unite,
Turn back the routed, and forbid the flight,
Ere yet their wives' soft arms the cowards gain,
The sport and insult of the hostile train.
When your commands have hearten'd every band,
Ourselves, here fix'd, will make the dangerous stand;
Press'd as we are, and sore of former fight,
These straits demand our last remains of might.
Meanwhile thou, Hector, to the town retire,
And teach our mother what the gods require:
Direct the queen to lead the assembled train
Of Troy's chief matrons to Minerva's fane;
Unbar the sacred gates, and seek the power,
With offer'd vows, in Ilion's topmost tower.
The largest mantle her rich wardrobes hold,
Most prized for art, and labour'd o'er with gold,
Before the goddess' honour'd knees be spread,
And twelve young heifers to her altars led:
If so the power, atoned by fervent prayer,
Our wives, our infants, and our city spare,
And far avert Tydides' wasteful ire,
That mows whole troops, and makes all Troy retire;
Not thus Achilles taught our hosts to dread,
Sprung though he was from more than mortal bed;
Not thus resistless ruled the stream of fight,

In rage unbounded, and unmatch'd in might."

Hector obedient heard: and, with a bound,
Leap'd from his trembling chariot to the ground;
Through all his host inspiring force he flies,
And bids the thunder of the battle rise.
With rage recruited the bold Trojans glow,
And turn the tide of conflict on the foe:
Fierce in the front he shakes two dazzling spears;
All Greece recedes, and 'midst her triumphs fears;
Some god, they thought, who ruled the fate of wars,
Shot down avenging from the vault of stars.

Then thus aloud: "Ye dauntless Dardans, hear!
And you whom distant nations send to war!
Be mindful of the strength your fathers bore;
Be still yourselves, and Hector asks no more.
One hour demands me in the Trojan wall,
To bid our altars flame, and victims fall:
Nor shall, I trust, the matrons' holy train,
And reverend elders, seek the gods in vain."

This said, with ample strides the hero pass'd;
The shield's large orb behind his shoulder cast,
His neck o'ershading, to his ankle hung;
And as he march'd the brazen buckler rung.

Now paused the battle (godlike Hector gone),
Where daring Glaucus and great Tydeus' son
Between both armies met: the chiefs from far
Observed each other, and had mark'd for war.
Near as they drew, Tydides thus began:

"What art thou, boldest of the race of man?
Our eyes till now that aspect ne'er beheld,
Where fame is reap'd amid the embattled field;
Yet far before the troops thou dar'st appear,
And meet a lance the fiercest heroes fear.
Unhappy they, and born of luckless sires,
Who tempt our fury when Minerva fires!
But if from heaven, celestial, thou descend,
Know with immortals we no more contend.
Not long Lycurgus view'd the golden light,
That daring man who mix'd with gods in fight.
Bacchus, and Bacchus' votaries, he drove,
With brandish'd steel, from Nyssa's sacred grove:
Their consecrated spears lay scatter'd round,
With curling vines and twisted ivy bound;

While Bacchus headlong sought the briny flood,
And Thetis' arms received the trembling god.
Nor fail'd the crime the immortals' wrath to move;
(The immortals bless'd with endless ease above;)
Deprived of sight by their avenging doom,
Cheerless he breathed, and wander'd in the gloom,
Then sunk unpitied to the dire abodes,
A wretch accursed, and hated by the gods!
I brave not heaven: but if the fruits of earth
Sustain thy life, and human be thy birth,
Bold as thou art, too prodigal of breath,
Approach, and enter the dark gates of death."

"What, or from whence I am, or who my sire,
(Replied the chief,) can Tydeus' son inquire?
Like leaves on trees the race of man is found,
Now green in youth, now withering on the ground;
Another race the following spring supplies;
They fall successive, and successive rise:
So generations in their course decay;
So flourish these, when those are pass'd away.
But if thou still persist to search my birth,
Then hear a tale that fills the spacious earth.

"A city stands on Argos' utmost bound,
(Argos the fair, for warlike steeds renown'd,)
Aeolian Sisyphus, with wisdom bless'd,
In ancient time the happy wall possess'd,
Then call'd Ephyre: Glaucus was his son;
Great Glaucus, father of Bellerophon,
Who o'er the sons of men in beauty shined,
Loved for that valour which preserves mankind.
Then mighty Praetus Argos' sceptre sway'd,
Whose hard commands Bellerophon obey'd.
With direful jealousy the monarch raged,
And the brave prince in numerous toils engaged.
For him Antaea burn'd with lawless flame,
And strove to tempt him from the paths of fame:
In vain she tempted the relentless youth,
Endued with wisdom, sacred fear, and truth.
Fired at his scorn the queen to Praetus fled,
And begg'd revenge for her insulted bed:
Incensed he heard, resolving on his fate;
But hospitable laws restrain'd his hate:
To Lycia the devoted youth he sent,
With tablets seal'd, that told his dire intent.
Now bless'd by every power who guards the good,
The chief arrived at Xanthus' silver flood:

There Lycia's monarch paid him honours due,
Nine days he feasted, and nine bulls he slew.
But when the tenth bright morning orient glow'd,
The faithful youth his monarch's mandate show'd:
The fatal tablets, till that instant seal'd,
The deathful secret to the king reveal'd.
First, dire Chimaera's conquest was enjoin'd;
A mingled monster of no mortal kind!
Behind, a dragon's fiery tail was spread;
A goat's rough body bore a lion's head;
Her pitchy nostrils flaky flames expire;
Her gaping throat emits infernal fire.

"This pest he slaughter'd, (for he read the skies,
And trusted heaven's informing prodigies,)
Then met in arms the Solymaean crew,
(Fiercest of men,) and those the warrior slew;
Next the bold Amazons' whole force defied;
And conquer'd still, for heaven was on his side.

"Nor ended here his toils: his Lycian foes,
At his return, a treacherous ambush rose,
With levell'd spears along the winding shore:
There fell they breathless, and return'd no more.

"At length the monarch, with repentant grief,
Confess'd the gods, and god-descended chief;
His daughter gave, the stranger to detain,
With half the honours of his ample reign:
The Lycians grant a chosen space of ground,
With woods, with vineyards, and with harvests crown'd.
There long the chief his happy lot possess'd,
With two brave sons and one fair daughter bless'd;
(Fair e'en in heavenly eyes: her fruitful love
Crown'd with Sarpedon's birth the embrace of Jove;)
But when at last, distracted in his mind,
Forsook by heaven, forsaking humankind,
Wide o'er the Aleian field he chose to stray,
A long, forlorn, uncomfortable way!
Woes heap'd on woes consumed his wasted heart:
His beauteous daughter fell by Phoebe's dart;
His eldest born by raging Mars was slain,
In combat on the Solymaean plain.
Hippolochus survived: from him I came,
The honour'd author of my birth and name;
By his decree I sought the Trojan town;
By his instructions learn to win renown,
To stand the first in worth as in command,

To add new honours to my native land,
Before my eyes my mighty sires to place,
And emulate the glories of our race."

He spoke, and transport fill'd Tydides' heart;
In earth the generous warrior fix'd his dart,
Then friendly, thus the Lycian prince address'd:
"Welcome, my brave hereditary guest!
Thus ever let us meet, with kind embrace,
Nor stain the sacred friendship of our race.
Know, chief, our grandsires have been guests of old;
OEneus the strong, Bellerophon the bold:
Our ancient seat his honour'd presence graced,
Where twenty days in genial rites he pass'd.
The parting heroes mutual presents left;
A golden goblet was thy grandsire's gift;
OEneus a belt of matchless work bestowed,
That rich with Tyrian dye refulgent glow'd.
(This from his pledge I learn'd, which, safely stored
Among my treasures, still adorns my board:
For Tydeus left me young, when Thebe's wall
Beheld the sons of Greece untimely fall.)
Mindful of this, in friendship let us join;
If heaven our steps to foreign lands incline,
My guest in Argos thou, and I in Lycia thine.
Enough of Trojans to this lance shall yield,
In the full harvest of yon ample field;
Enough of Greeks shall dye thy spear with gore;
But thou and Diomed be foes no more.
Now change we arms, and prove to either host
We guard the friendship of the line we boast."

Thus having said, the gallant chiefs alight,
Their hands they join, their mutual faith they plight;
Brave Glaucus then each narrow thought resign'd,
(Jove warm'd his bosom, and enlarged his mind,)
For Diomed's brass arms, of mean device,
For which nine oxen paid, (a vulgar price,)
He gave his own, of gold divinely wrought,
A hundred beeves the shining purchase bought.

Meantime the guardian of the Trojan state,
Great Hector, enter'd at the Scaean gate.
Beneath the beech-tree's consecrated shades,
The Trojan matrons and the Trojan maids
Around him flock'd, all press'd with pious care
For husbands, brothers, sons, engaged in war.
He bids the train in long procession go,

And seek the gods, to avert the impending woe.
And now to Priam's stately courts he came,
Rais'd on arch'd columns of stupendous frame;
O'er these a range of marble structure runs,
The rich pavilions of his fifty sons,
In fifty chambers lodged: and rooms of state,
Opposed to those, where Priam's daughters sate.
Twelve domes for them and their loved spouses shone,
Of equal beauty, and of polish'd stone.
Hither great Hector pass'd, nor pass'd unseen
Of royal Hecuba, his mother-queen.
(With her Laodice, whose beauteous face
Surpass'd the nymphs of Troy's illustrious race.)
Long in a strict embrace she held her son,
And press'd his hand, and tender thus begun:

"O Hector! say, what great occasion calls
My son from fight, when Greece surrounds our walls;
Com'st thou to supplicate the almighty power
With lifted hands, from Ilion's lofty tower?
Stay, till I bring the cup with Bacchus crown'd,
In Jove's high name, to sprinkle on the ground,
And pay due vows to all the gods around.
Then with a plenteous draught refresh thy soul,
And draw new spirits from the generous bowl;
Spent as thou art with long laborious fight,
The brave defender of thy country's right."

"Far hence be Bacchus' gifts; (the chief rejoin'd;)
Inflaming wine, pernicious to mankind,
Unnerves the limbs, and dulls the noble mind.
Let chiefs abstain, and spare the sacred juice
To sprinkle to the gods, its better use.
By me that holy office were profaned;
Ill fits it me, with human gore distain'd,
To the pure skies these horrid hands to raise,
Or offer heaven's great Sire polluted praise.
You, with your matrons, go! a spotless train,
And burn rich odours in Minerva's fane.
The largest mantle your full wardrobes hold,
Most prized for art, and labour'd o'er with gold,
Before the goddess' honour'd knees be spread,
And twelve young heifers to her altar led.
So may the power, atoned by fervent prayer,
Our wives, our infants, and our city spare;
And far avert Tydides' wasteful ire,
Who mows whole troops, and makes all Troy retire.
Be this, O mother, your religious care:

I go to rouse soft Paris to the war;
If yet not lost to all the sense of shame,
The recreant warrior hear the voice of fame.
Oh, would kind earth the hateful wretch embrace,
That pest of Troy, that ruin of our race!
Deep to the dark abyss might he descend,
Troy yet should flourish, and my sorrows end."

This heard, she gave command: and summon'd came
Each noble matron and illustrious dame.
The Phrygian queen to her rich wardrobe went,
Where treasured odours breathed a costly scent.
There lay the vestures of no vulgar art,
Sidonian maids embroider'd every part,
Whom from soft Sidon youthful Paris bore,
With Helen touching on the Tyrian shore.
Here, as the queen revolved with careful eyes
The various textures and the various dyes,
She chose a veil that shone superior far,
And glow'd refulgent as the morning star.
Herself with this the long procession leads;
The train majestically slow proceeds.
Soon as to Ilion's topmost tower they come,
And awful reach the high Palladian dome,
Antenor's consort, fair Theano, waits
As Pallas' priestess, and unbars the gates.
With hands uplifted and imploring eyes,
They fill the dome with supplicating cries.
The priestess then the shining veil displays,
Placed on Minerva's knees, and thus she prays:

"Oh awful goddess! ever-dreadful maid,
Troy's strong defence, unconquer'd Pallas, aid!
Break thou Tydides' spear, and let him fall
Prone on the dust before the Trojan wall!
So twelve young heifers, guiltless of the yoke,
Shall fill thy temple with a grateful smoke.
But thou, atoned by penitence and prayer,
Ourselves, our infants, and our city spare!"
So pray'd the priestess in her holy fane;
So vow'd the matrons, but they vow'd in vain.

While these appear before the power with prayers,
Hector to Paris' lofty dome repairs.
Himself the mansion raised, from every part
Assembling architects of matchless art.
Near Priam's court and Hector's palace stands
The pompous structure, and the town commands.

A spear the hero bore of wondrous strength,
Of full ten cubits was the lance's length,
The steely point with golden ringlets join'd,
Before him brandish'd, at each motion shined
Thus entering, in the glittering rooms he found
His brother-chief, whose useless arms lay round,
His eyes delighting with their splendid show,
Brightening the shield, and polishing the bow.
Beside him Helen with her virgins stands,
Guides their rich labours, and instructs their hands.

Him thus inactive, with an ardent look
The prince beheld, and high-resenting spoke.
"Thy hate to Troy, is this the time to show?
(O wretch ill-fated, and thy country's foe!)
Paris and Greece against us both conspire,
Thy close resentment, and their vengeful ire.
For thee great Ilion's guardian heroes fall,
Till heaps of dead alone defend her wall,
For thee the soldier bleeds, the matron mourns,
And wasteful war in all its fury burns.
Ungrateful man! deserves not this thy care,
Our troops to hearten, and our toils to share?
Rise, or behold the conquering flames ascend,
And all the Phrygian glories at an end."

"Brother, 'tis just, (replied the beauteous youth,)
Thy free remonstrance proves thy worth and truth:
Yet charge my absence less, O generous chief!
On hate to Troy, than conscious shame and grief:
Here, hid from human eyes, thy brother sate,
And mourn'd, in secret, his and Ilion's fate.
'Tis now enough; now glory spreads her charms,
And beauteous Helen calls her chief to arms.
Conquest to-day my happier sword may bless,
'Tis man's to fight, but heaven's to give success.
But while I arm, contain thy ardent mind;
Or go, and Paris shall not lag behind."

He said, nor answer'd Priam's warlike son;
When Helen thus with lowly grace begun:

"Oh, generous brother! (if the guilty dame
That caused these woes deserve a sister's name!)
Would heaven, ere all these dreadful deeds were done,
The day that show'd me to the golden sun
Had seen my death! why did not whirlwinds bear
The fatal infant to the fowls of air?

Why sunk I not beneath the whelming tide,
And midst the roarings of the waters died?
Heaven fill'd up all my ills, and I accursed
Bore all, and Paris of those ills the worst.
Helen at least a braver spouse might claim,
Warm'd with some virtue, some regard of fame!
Now tired with toils, thy fainting limbs recline,
With toils, sustain'd for Paris' sake and mine
The gods have link'd our miserable doom,
Our present woe, and infamy to come:
Wide shall it spread, and last through ages long,
Example sad! and theme of future song."

The chief replied: "This time forbids to rest;
The Trojan bands, by hostile fury press'd,
Demand their Hector, and his arm require;
The combat urges, and my soul's on fire.
Urge thou thy knight to march where glory calls,
And timely join me, ere I leave the walls.
Ere yet I mingle in the direful fray,
My wife, my infant, claim a moment's stay;
This day (perhaps the last that sees me here)
Demands a parting word, a tender tear:
This day, some god who hates our Trojan land
May vanquish Hector by a Grecian hand."

He said, and pass'd with sad presaging heart
To seek his spouse, his soul's far dearer part;
At home he sought her, but he sought in vain;
She, with one maid of all her menial train,
Had hence retired; and with her second joy,
The young Astyanax, the hope of Troy,
Pensive she stood on Ilion's towery height,
Beheld the war, and sicken'd at the sight;
There her sad eyes in vain her lord explore,
Or weep the wounds her bleeding country bore.

But he who found not whom his soul desired,
Whose virtue charm'd him as her beauty fired,
Stood in the gates, and ask'd "what way she bent
Her parting step? If to the fane she went,
Where late the mourning matrons made resort;
Or sought her sisters in the Trojan court?"
"Not to the court, (replied the attendant train,)
Nor mix'd with matrons to Minerva's fane:
To Ilion's steepy tower she bent her way,
To mark the fortunes of the doubtful day.
Troy fled, she heard, before the Grecian sword;

She heard, and trembled for her absent lord:
Distracted with surprise, she seem'd to fly,
Fear on her cheek, and sorrow m her eye.
The nurse attended with her infant boy,
The young Astyanax, the hope of Troy."

Hector this heard, return'd without delay;
Swift through the town he trod his former way,
Through streets of palaces, and walks of state;
And met the mourner at the Scaean gate.
With haste to meet him sprung the joyful fair.
His blameless wife, Aetion's wealthy heir:
(Cilician Thebe great Aetion sway'd,
And Hippoplacus' wide extended shade:)
The nurse stood near, in whose embraces press'd,
His only hope hung smiling at her breast,
Whom each soft charm and early grace adorn,
Fair as the new-born star that gilds the morn.
To this loved infant Hector gave the name
Scamandrius, from Scamander's honour'd stream;
Astyanax the Trojans call'd the boy,
From his great father, the defence of Troy.
Silent the warrior smiled, and pleased resign'd
To tender passions all his mighty mind;
His beauteous princess cast a mournful look,
Hung on his hand, and then dejected spoke;
Her bosom laboured with a boding sigh,
And the big tear stood trembling in her eye.

"Too daring prince! ah, whither dost thou run?
Ah, too forgetful of thy wife and son!
And think'st thou not how wretched we shall be,
A widow I, a helpless orphan he?
For sure such courage length of life denies,
And thou must fall, thy virtue's sacrifice.
Greece in her single heroes strove in vain;
Now hosts oppose thee, and thou must be slain.
O grant me, gods, ere Hector meets his doom,
All I can ask of heaven, an early tomb!
So shall my days in one sad tenor run,
And end with sorrows as they first begun.
No parent now remains my griefs to share,
No father's aid, no mother's tender care.
The fierce Achilles wrapt our walls in fire,
Laid Thebe waste, and slew my warlike sire!
His fate compassion in the victor bred;
Stern as he was, he yet revered the dead,
His radiant arms preserved from hostile spoil,

And laid him decent on the funeral pile;
Then raised a mountain where his bones were burn'd,
The mountain-nymphs the rural tomb adorn'd,
Jove's sylvan daughters bade their elms bestow
A barren shade, and in his honour grow.

"By the same arm my seven brave brothers fell;
In one sad day beheld the gates of hell;
While the fat herds and snowy flocks they fed,
Amid their fields the hapless heroes bled!
My mother lived to wear the victor's bands,
The queen of Hippoplacia's sylvan lands:
Redeem'd too late, she scarce beheld again
Her pleasing empire and her native plain,
When ah! oppress'd by life-consuming woe,
She fell a victim to Diana's bow.

"Yet while my Hector still survives, I see
My father, mother, brethren, all, in thee:
Alas! my parents, brothers, kindred, all
Once more will perish, if my Hector fall,
Thy wife, thy infant, in thy danger share:
Oh, prove a husband's and a father's care!
That quarter most the skilful Greeks annoy,
Where yon wild fig-trees join the wall of Troy;
Thou, from this tower defend the important post;
There Agamemnon points his dreadful host,
That pass Tydides, Ajax, strive to gain,
And there the vengeful Spartan fires his train.
Thrice our bold foes the fierce attack have given,
Or led by hopes, or dictated from heaven.
Let others in the field their arms employ,
But stay my Hector here, and guard his Troy."

The chief replied: "That post shall be my care,
Not that alone, but all the works of war.
How would the sons of Troy, in arms renown'd,
And Troy's proud dames, whose garments sweep the ground
Attaint the lustre of my former name,
Should Hector basely quit the field of fame?
My early youth was bred to martial pains,
My soul impels me to the embattled plains!
Let me be foremost to defend the throne,
And guard my father's glories, and my own.

"Yet come it will, the day decreed by fates!
(How my heart trembles while my tongue relates!)
The day when thou, imperial Troy! must bend,

And see thy warriors fall, thy glories end.
And yet no dire presage so wounds my mind,
My mother's death, the ruin of my kind,
Not Priam's hoary hairs defiled with gore,
Not all my brothers gasping on the shore;
As thine, Andromache! Thy griefs I dread:
I see thee trembling, weeping, captive led!
In Argive looms our battles to design,
And woes, of which so large a part was thine!
To bear the victor's hard commands, or bring
The weight of waters from Hyperia's spring.
There while you groan beneath the load of life,
They cry, 'Behold the mighty Hector's wife!'
Some haughty Greek, who lives thy tears to see,
Imbitters all thy woes, by naming me.
The thoughts of glory past, and present shame,
A thousand griefs shall waken at the name!
May I lie cold before that dreadful day,
Press'd with a load of monumental clay!
Thy Hector, wrapt in everlasting sleep,
Shall neither hear thee sigh, nor see thee weep."

Thus having spoke, the illustrious chief of Troy
Stretch'd his fond arms to clasp the lovely boy.
The babe clung crying to his nurse's breast,
Scared at the dazzling helm, and nodding crest.
With secret pleasure each fond parent smiled,
And Hector hasted to relieve his child,
The glittering terrors from his brows unbound,
And placed the beaming helmet on the ground;
Then kiss'd the child, and, lifting high in air,
Thus to the gods preferr'd a father's prayer:

"O thou! whose glory fills the ethereal throne,
And all ye deathless powers! protect my son!
Grant him, like me, to purchase just renown,
To guard the Trojans, to defend the crown,
Against his country's foes the war to wage,
And rise the Hector of the future age!
So when triumphant from successful toils
Of heroes slain he bears the reeking spoils,
Whole hosts may hail him with deserved acclaim,
And say, 'This chief transcends his father's fame:'
While pleased amidst the general shouts of Troy,
His mother's conscious heart o'erflows with joy."

He spoke, and fondly gazing on her charms,
Restored the pleasing burden to her arms;

Soft on her fragrant breast the babe she laid,
Hush'd to repose, and with a smile survey'd.
The troubled pleasure soon chastised by fear,
She mingled with a smile a tender tear.
The soften'd chief with kind compassion view'd,
And dried the falling drops, and thus pursued:

"Andromache! my soul's far better part,
Why with untimely sorrows heaves thy heart?
No hostile hand can antedate my doom,
Till fate condemns me to the silent tomb.
Fix'd is the term to all the race of earth;
And such the hard condition of our birth:
No force can then resist, no flight can save,
All sink alike, the fearful and the brave.
No more—but hasten to thy tasks at home,
There guide the spindle, and direct the loom:
Me glory summons to the martial scene,
The field of combat is the sphere for men.
Where heroes war, the foremost place I claim,
The first in danger as the first in fame."

Thus having said, the glorious chief resumes
His towery helmet, black with shading plumes.
His princess parts with a prophetic sigh,
Unwilling parts, and oft reverts her eye
That stream'd at every look; then, moving slow,
Sought her own palace, and indulged her woe.
There, while her tears deplored the godlike man,
Through all her train the soft infection ran;
The pious maids their mingled sorrows shed,
And mourn the living Hector, as the dead.

But now, no longer deaf to honour's call,
Forth issues Paris from the palace wall.
In brazen arms that cast a gleamy ray,
Swift through the town the warrior bends his way.
The wanton courser thus with reins unbound
Breaks from his stall, and beats the trembling ground;
Pamper'd and proud, he seeks the wonted tides,
And laves, in height of blood his shining sides;
His head now freed, he tosses to the skies;
His mane dishevell'd o'er his shoulders flies;
He snuffs the females in the distant plain,
And springs, exulting, to his fields again.
With equal triumph, sprightly, bold, and gay,
In arms refulgent as the god of day,
The son of Priam, glorying in his might,

Rush'd forth with Hector to the fields of fight.

And now, the warriors passing on the way,
The graceful Paris first excused his stay.
To whom the noble Hector thus replied:
"O chief! in blood, and now in arms, allied!
Thy power in war with justice none contest;
Known is thy courage, and thy strength confess'd.
What pity sloth should seize a soul so brave,
Or godlike Paris live a woman's slave!
My heart weeps blood at what the Trojans say,
And hopes thy deeds shall wipe the stain away.
Haste then, in all their glorious labours share,
For much they suffer, for thy sake, in war.
These ills shall cease, whene'er by Jove's decree
We crown the bowl to heaven and liberty:
While the proud foe his frustrate triumphs mourns,
And Greece indignant through her seas returns."

BOOK VII

ARGUMENT

THE SINGLE COMBAT OF HECTOR AND AJAX

The battle renewing with double ardour upon the return of Hector, Minerva is under apprehensions for the Greeks. Apollo, seeing her descend from Olympus, joins her near the Scaean gate. They agree to put off the general engagement for that day, and incite Hector to challenge the Greeks to a single combat. Nine of the princes accepting the challenge, the lot is cast and falls upon Ajax. These heroes, after several attacks, are parted by the night. The Trojans calling a council, Antenor purposes the delivery of Helen to the Greeks, to which Paris will not consent, but offers to restore them her riches. Priam sends a herald to make this offer, and to demand a truce for burning the dead, the last of which only is agreed to by Agamemnon. When the funerals are performed, the Greeks, pursuant to the advice of Nestor, erect a fortification to protect their fleet and camp, flanked with towers, and defended by a ditch and palisades. Neptune testifies his jealousy at this work, but is pacified by a promise from Jupiter. Both armies pass the night in feasting but Jupiter disheartens the Trojans with thunder, and other signs of his wrath.

The three and twentieth day ends with the duel of Hector and Ajax, the next day the truce is agreed; another is taken up in the funeral rites of the slain and one more in building the fortification before the ships. So that somewhat about three days is employed in this book. The scene lies wholly in the field.

So spoke the guardian of the Trojan state,
Then rush'd impetuous through the Scaean gate.
Him Paris follow'd to the dire alarms;

Both breathing slaughter, both resolved in arms.
As when to sailors labouring through the main,
That long have heaved the weary oar in vain,
Jove bids at length the expected gales arise;
The gales blow grateful, and the vessel flies.
So welcome these to Troy's desiring train,
The bands are cheer'd, the war awakes again.

Bold Paris first the work of death begun
On great Menestheus, Areithous' son,
Sprung from the fair Philomeda's embrace,
The pleasing Arne was his native place.
Then sunk Eioneus to the shades below,
Beneath his steely casque he felt the blow
Full on his neck, from Hector's weighty hand;
And roll'd, with limbs relax'd, along the land.
By Glaucus' spear the bold Iphmous bleeds,
Fix'd in the shoulder as he mounts his steeds;
Headlong he tumbles: his slack nerves unbound,
Drop the cold useless members on the ground.

When now Minerva saw her Argives slain,
From vast Olympus to the gleaming plain
Fierce she descends: Apollo marked her flight,
Nor shot less swift from Ilion's towery height.
Radiant they met, beneath the beechen shade;
When thus Apollo to the blue-eyed maid:

"What cause, O daughter of Almighty Jove!
Thus wings thy progress from the realms above?
Once more impetuous dost thou bend thy way,
To give to Greece the long divided day?
Too much has Troy already felt thy hate,
Now breathe thy rage, and hush the stern debate;
This day, the business of the field suspend;
War soon shall kindle, and great Ilion bend;
Since vengeful goddesses confederate join
To raze her walls, though built by hands divine."

To whom the progeny of Jove replies:
"I left, for this, the council of the skies:
But who shall bid conflicting hosts forbear,
What art shall calm the furious sons of war?"
To her the god: "Great Hector's soul incite
To dare the boldest Greek to single fight,
Till Greece, provoked, from all her numbers show
A warrior worthy to be Hector's foe."

At this agreed, the heavenly powers withdrew;
Sage Helenus their secret counsels knew;
Hector, inspired, he sought: to him address'd,
Thus told the dictates of his sacred breast:
"O son of Priam! let thy faithful ear
Receive my words: thy friend and brother hear!
Go forth persuasive, and a while engage
The warring nations to suspend their rage;
Then dare the boldest of the hostile train
To mortal combat on the listed plain.
For not this day shall end thy glorious date;
The gods have spoke it, and their voice is fate."

He said: the warrior heard the word with joy;
Then with his spear restrain'd the youth of Troy,
Held by the midst athwart. On either hand
The squadrons part; the expecting Trojans stand;
Great Agamemnon bids the Greeks forbear:
They breathe, and hush the tumult of the war.
The Athenian maid, and glorious god of day,
With silent joy the settling hosts survey:
In form of vultures, on the beech's height
They sit conceal'd, and wait the future fight.

The thronging troops obscure the dusky fields,
Horrid with bristling spears, and gleaming shields.
As when a general darkness veils the main,
(Soft Zephyr curling the wide wat'ry plain,)
The waves scarce heave, the face of ocean sleeps,
And a still horror saddens all the deeps;
Thus in thick orders settling wide around,
At length composed they sit, and shade the ground.
Great Hector first amidst both armies broke
The solemn silence, and their powers bespoke:

"Hear, all ye Trojan, all ye Grecian bands,
What my soul prompts, and what some god commands.
Great Jove, averse our warfare to compose,
O'erwhelms the nations with new toils and woes;
War with a fiercer tide once more returns,
Till Ilion falls, or till yon navy burns.
You then, O princes of the Greeks! appear;
'Tis Hector speaks, and calls the gods to hear:
From all your troops select the boldest knight,
And him, the boldest, Hector dares to fight.
Here if I fall, by chance of battle slain,
Be his my spoil, and his these arms remain;
But let my body, to my friends return'd,

By Trojan hands and Trojan flames be burn'd.
And if Apollo, in whose aid I trust,
Shall stretch your daring champion in the dust;
If mine the glory to despoil the foe;
On Phoebus' temple I'll his arms bestow:
The breathless carcase to your navy sent,
Greece on the shore shall raise a monument;
Which when some future mariner surveys,
Wash'd by broad Hellespont's resounding seas,
Thus shall he say, 'A valiant Greek lies there,
By Hector slain, the mighty man of war,'
The stone shall tell your vanquish'd hero's name.
And distant ages learn the victor's fame."

This fierce defiance Greece astonish'd heard,
Blush'd to refuse, and to accept it fear'd.
Stern Menelaus first the silence broke,
And, inly groaning, thus opprobrious spoke:

"Women of Greece! O scandal of your race,
Whose coward souls your manly form disgrace,
How great the shame, when every age shall know
That not a Grecian met this noble foe!
Go then! resolve to earth, from whence ye grew,
A heartless, spiritless, inglorious crew!
Be what ye seem, unanimated clay,
Myself will dare the danger of the day;
'Tis man's bold task the generous strife to try,
But in the hands of God is victory."

These words scarce spoke, with generous ardour press'd,
His manly limbs in azure arms he dress'd.
That day, Atrides! a superior hand
Had stretch'd thee breathless on the hostile strand;
But all at once, thy fury to compose,
The kings of Greece, an awful band, arose;
Even he their chief, great Agamemnon, press'd
Thy daring hand, and this advice address'd:
"Whither, O Menelaus! wouldst thou run,
And tempt a fate which prudence bids thee shun?
Grieved though thou art, forbear the rash design;
Great Hectors arm is mightier far than thine:
Even fierce Achilles learn'd its force to fear,
And trembling met this dreadful son of war.
Sit thou secure, amidst thy social band;
Greece in our cause shall arm some powerful hand.
The mightiest warrior of the Achaian name,
Though bold and burning with desire of fame,

Content the doubtful honour might forego,
So great the danger, and so brave the foe."

He said, and turn'd his brother's vengeful mind;
He stoop'd to reason, and his rage resign'd,
No longer bent to rush on certain harms;
His joyful friends unbrace his azure arms.

He from whose lips divine persuasion flows,
Grave Nestor, then, in graceful act arose;
Thus to the kings he spoke: "What grief, what shame
Attend on Greece, and all the Grecian name!
How shall, alas! her hoary heroes mourn
Their sons degenerate, and their race a scorn!
What tears shall down thy silvery beard be roll'd,
O Peleus, old in arms, in wisdom old!
Once with what joy the generous prince would hear
Of every chief who fought this glorious war,
Participate their fame, and pleased inquire
Each name, each action, and each hero's sire!
Gods! should he see our warriors trembling stand,
And trembling all before one hostile hand;
How would he lift his aged arms on high,
Lament inglorious Greece, and beg to die!
Oh! would to all the immortal powers above,
Minerva, Phoebus, and almighty Jove!
Years might again roll back, my youth renew,
And give this arm the spring which once it knew
When fierce in war, where Jardan's waters fall,
I led my troops to Phea's trembling wall,
And with the Arcadian spears my prowess tried,
Where Celadon rolls down his rapid tide.
There Ereuthalion braved us in the field,
Proud Areithous' dreadful arms to wield;
Great Areithous, known from shore to shore
By the huge, knotted, iron mace he bore;
No lance he shook, nor bent the twanging bow,
But broke, with this, the battle of the foe.
Him not by manly force Lycurgus slew,
Whose guileful javelin from the thicket flew,
Deep in a winding way his breast assailed,
Nor aught the warrior's thundering mace avail'd.
Supine he fell: those arms which Mars before
Had given the vanquish'd, now the victor bore:
But when old age had dimm'd Lycurgus' eyes,
To Ereuthalion he consign'd the prize.
Furious with this he crush'd our levell'd bands,
And dared the trial of the strongest hands;

Nor could the strongest hands his fury stay:
All saw, and fear'd, his huge tempestuous sway
Till I, the youngest of the host, appear'd,
And, youngest, met whom all our army fear'd.
I fought the chief: my arms Minerva crown'd:
Prone fell the giant o'er a length of ground.
What then I was, O were your Nestor now!
Not Hector's self should want an equal foe.
But, warriors, you that youthful vigour boast,
The flower of Greece, the examples of our host,
Sprung from such fathers, who such numbers sway,
Can you stand trembling, and desert the day?"

His warm reproofs the listening kings inflame;
And nine, the noblest of the Grecian name,
Up-started fierce: but far before the rest
The king of men advanced his dauntless breast:
Then bold Tydides, great in arms, appear'd;
And next his bulk gigantic Ajax rear'd;
Oileus follow'd; Idomen was there,
And Merion, dreadful as the god of war:
With these Eurypylus and Thoas stand,
And wise Ulysses closed the daring band.
All these, alike inspired with noble rage,
Demand the fight. To whom the Pylian sage:

"Lest thirst of glory your brave souls divide,
What chief shall combat, let the gods decide.
Whom heaven shall choose, be his the chance to raise
His country's fame, his own immortal praise."

The lots produced, each hero signs his own:
Then in the general's helm the fates are thrown,
The people pray, with lifted eyes and hands,
And vows like these ascend from all the bands:
"Grant, thou Almighty! in whose hand is fate,
A worthy champion for the Grecian state:
This task let Ajax or Tydides prove,
Or he, the king of kings, beloved by Jove."
Old Nestor shook the casque. By heaven inspired,
Leap'd forth the lot, of every Greek desired.
This from the right to left the herald bears,
Held out in order to the Grecian peers;
Each to his rival yields the mark unknown,
Till godlike Ajax finds the lot his own;
Surveys the inscription with rejoicing eyes,
Then casts before him, and with transport cries:

"Warriors! I claim the lot, and arm with joy;
Be mine the conquest of this chief of Troy.
Now while my brightest arms my limbs invest,
To Saturn's son be all your vows address'd:
But pray in secret, lest the foes should hear,
And deem your prayers the mean effect of fear.
Said I in secret? No, your vows declare
In such a voice as fills the earth and air,
Lives there a chief whom Ajax ought to dread?
Ajax, in all the toils of battle bred!
From warlike Salamis I drew my birth,
And, born to combats, fear no force on earth."

He said. The troops with elevated eyes,
Implore the god whose thunder rends the skies:
"O father of mankind, superior lord!
On lofty Ida's holy hill adored:
Who in the highest heaven hast fix'd thy throne,
Supreme of gods! unbounded and alone:
Grant thou, that Telamon may bear away
The praise and conquest of this doubtful day;
Or, if illustrious Hector be thy care,
That both may claim it, and that both may share."

Now Ajax braced his dazzling armour on;
Sheathed in bright steel the giant-warrior shone:
He moves to combat with majestic pace;
So stalks in arms the grisly god of Thrace,
When Jove to punish faithless men prepares,
And gives whole nations to the waste of wars,
Thus march'd the chief, tremendous as a god;
Grimly he smiled; earth trembled as he strode:
His massy javelin quivering in his hand,
He stood, the bulwark of the Grecian band.
Through every Argive heart new transport ran;
All Troy stood trembling at the mighty man:
Even Hector paused; and with new doubt oppress'd,
Felt his great heart suspended in his breast:
'Twas vain to seek retreat, and vain to fear;
Himself had challenged, and the foe drew near.

Stern Telamon behind his ample shield,
As from a brazen tower, o'erlook'd the field.
Huge was its orb, with seven thick folds o'ercast,
Of tough bull-hides; of solid brass the last,
(The work of Tychius, who in Hyle dwell'd
And in all arts of armoury excell'd,)
This Ajax bore before his manly breast,

And, threatening, thus his adverse chief address'd:

"Hector! approach my arm, and singly know
What strength thou hast, and what the Grecian foe.
Achilles shuns the fight; yet some there are,
Not void of soul, and not unskill'd in war:
Let him, unactive on the sea-beat shore,
Indulge his wrath, and aid our arms no more;
Whole troops of heroes Greece has yet to boast,
And sends thee one, a sample of her host,
Such as I am, I come to prove thy might;
No more—be sudden, and begin the fight."

"O son of Telamon, thy country's pride!
(To Ajax thus the Trojan prince replied)
Me, as a boy, or woman, wouldst thou fright,
New to the field, and trembling at the fight?
Thou meet'st a chief deserving of thy arms,
To combat born, and bred amidst alarms:
I know to shift my ground, remount the car,
Turn, charge, and answer every call of war;
To right, to left, the dexterous lance I wield,
And bear thick battle on my sounding shield
But open be our fight, and bold each blow;
I steal no conquest from a noble foe."

He said, and rising, high above the field
Whirl'd the long lance against the sevenfold shield.
Full on the brass descending from above
Through six bull-hides the furious weapon drove,
Till in the seventh it fix'd. Then Ajax threw;
Through Hector's shield the forceful javelin flew,
His corslet enters, and his garment rends,
And glancing downwards, near his flank descends.
The wary Trojan shrinks, and bending low
Beneath his buckler, disappoints the blow.
From their bored shields the chiefs their javelins drew,
Then close impetuous, and the charge renew;
Fierce as the mountain-lions bathed in blood,
Or foaming boars, the terror of the wood.
At Ajax, Hector his long lance extends;
The blunted point against the buckler bends;
But Ajax, watchful as his foe drew near,
Drove through the Trojan targe the knotty spear;
It reach'd his neck, with matchless strength impell'd!
Spouts the black gore, and dims his shining shield.
Yet ceased not Hector thus; but stooping down,
In his strong hand up-heaved a flinty stone,

Black, craggy, vast: to this his force he bends;
Full on the brazen boss the stone descends;
The hollow brass resounded with the shock:
Then Ajax seized the fragment of a rock,
Applied each nerve, and swinging round on high,
With force tempestuous, let the ruin fly;
The huge stone thundering through his buckler broke:
His slacken'd knees received the numbing stroke;
Great Hector falls extended on the field,
His bulk supporting on the shatter'd shield:
Nor wanted heavenly aid: Apollo's might
Confirm'd his sinews, and restored to fight.
And now both heroes their broad falchions drew
In flaming circles round their heads they flew;
But then by heralds' voice the word was given.
The sacred ministers of earth and heaven:
Divine Talthybius, whom the Greeks employ.
And sage Idaeus on the part of Troy,
Between the swords their peaceful sceptres rear'd;
And first Idaeus' awful voice was heard:

"Forbear, my sons! your further force to prove,
Both dear to men, and both beloved of Jove.
To either host your matchless worth is known,
Each sounds your praise, and war is all your own.
But now the Night extends her awful shade;
The goddess parts you; be the night obey'd."

To whom great Ajax his high soul express'd:
"O sage! to Hector be these words address'd.
Let him, who first provoked our chiefs to fight,
Let him demand the sanction of the night;
If first he ask'd it, I content obey,
And cease the strife when Hector shows the way."

"O first of Greeks! (his noble foe rejoin'd)
Whom heaven adorns, superior to thy kind,
With strength of body, and with worth of mind!
Now martial law commands us to forbear;
Hereafter we shall meet in glorious war,
Some future day shall lengthen out the strife,
And let the gods decide of death or life!
Since, then, the night extends her gloomy shade,
And heaven enjoins it, be the night obey'd.
Return, brave Ajax, to thy Grecian friends,
And joy the nations whom thy arm defends;
As I shall glad each chief, and Trojan wife,
Who wearies heaven with vows for Hector's life.

But let us, on this memorable day,
Exchange some gift: that Greece and Troy may say,
'Not hate, but glory, made these chiefs contend;
And each brave foe was in his soul a friend.'"

With that, a sword with stars of silver graced,
The baldric studded, and the sheath enchased,
He gave the Greek. The generous Greek bestow'd
A radiant belt that rich with purple glow'd.
Then with majestic grace they quit the plain;
This seeks the Grecian, that the Phrygian train.

The Trojan bands returning Hector wait,
And hail with joy the Champion of their state;
Escaped great Ajax, they survey him round,
Alive, unarm'd, and vigorous from his wound;
To Troy's high gates the godlike man they bear
Their present triumph, as their late despair.

But Ajax, glorying in his hardy deed,
The well-arm'd Greeks to Agamemnon lead.
A steer for sacrifice the king design'd,
Of full five years, and of the nobler kind.
The victim falls; they strip the smoking hide,
The beast they quarter, and the joints divide;
Then spread the tables, the repast prepare,
Each takes his seat, and each receives his share.
The king himself (an honorary sign)
Before great Ajax placed the mighty chine.
When now the rage of hunger was removed,
Nestor, in each persuasive art approved,
The sage whose counsels long had sway'd the rest,
In words like these his prudent thought express'd:

"How dear, O kings! this fatal day has cost,
What Greeks are perish'd! what a people lost!
What tides of blood have drench'd Scamander's shore!
What crowds of heroes sunk to rise no more!
Then hear me, chief! nor let the morrow's light
Awake thy squadrons to new toils of fight:
Some space at least permit the war to breathe,
While we to flames our slaughter'd friends bequeath,
From the red field their scatter'd bodies bear,
And nigh the fleet a funeral structure rear;
So decent urns their snowy bones may keep,
And pious children o'er their ashes weep.
Here, where on one promiscuous pile they blazed,
High o'er them all a general tomb be raised;

Next, to secure our camp and naval powers,
Raise an embattled wall, with lofty towers;
From space to space be ample gates around,
For passing chariots; and a trench profound.
So Greece to combat shall in safety go,
Nor fear the fierce incursions of the foe."
'Twas thus the sage his wholesome counsel moved;
The sceptred kings of Greece his words approved.

Meanwhile, convened at Priam's palace-gate,
The Trojan peers in nightly council sate;
A senate void of order, as of choice:
Their hearts were fearful, and confused their voice.
Antenor, rising, thus demands their ear:
"Ye Trojans, Dardans, and auxiliars, hear!
'Tis heaven the counsel of my breast inspires,
And I but move what every god requires:
Let Sparta's treasures be this hour restored,
And Argive Helen own her ancient lord.
The ties of faith, the sworn alliance, broke,
Our impious battles the just gods provoke.
As this advice ye practise, or reject,
So hope success, or dread the dire effect."

The senior spoke and sate. To whom replied
The graceful husband of the Spartan bride:
"Cold counsels, Trojan, may become thy years
But sound ungrateful in a warrior's ears:
Old man, if void of fallacy or art,
Thy words express the purpose of thy heart,
Thou, in thy time, more sound advice hast given;
But wisdom has its date, assign'd by heaven.
Then hear me, princes of the Trojan name!
Their treasures I'll restore, but not the dame;
My treasures too, for peace, I will resign;
But be this bright possession ever mine."

'Twas then, the growing discord to compose,
Slow from his seat the reverend Priam rose:
His godlike aspect deep attention drew:
He paused, and these pacific words ensue:

"Ye Trojans, Dardans, and auxiliar bands!
Now take refreshment as the hour demands;
Guard well the walls, relieve the watch of night.
Till the new sun restores the cheerful light.
Then shall our herald, to the Atrides sent,
Before their ships proclaim my son's intent.

Next let a truce be ask'd, that Troy may burn
Her slaughter'd heroes, and their bones inurn;
That done, once more the fate of war be tried,
And whose the conquest, mighty Jove decide!"

The monarch spoke: the warriors snatch'd with haste
(Each at his post in arms) a short repast.
Soon as the rosy morn had waked the day,
To the black ships Idaeus bent his way;
There, to the sons of Mars, in council found,
He raised his voice: the host stood listening round.

"Ye sons of Atreus, and ye Greeks, give ear!
The words of Troy, and Troy's great monarch, hear.
Pleased may ye hear (so heaven succeed my prayers)
What Paris, author of the war, declares.
The spoils and treasures he to Ilion bore
(Oh had he perish'd ere they touch'd our shore!)
He proffers injured Greece: with large increase
Of added Trojan wealth to buy the peace.
But to restore the beauteous bride again,
This Greece demands, and Troy requests in vain.
Next, O ye chiefs! we ask a truce to burn
Our slaughter'd heroes, and their bones inurn.
That done, once more the fate of war be tried,
And whose the conquest, mighty Jove decide!"

The Greeks gave ear, but none the silence broke;
At length Tydides rose, and rising spoke:
"Oh, take not, friends! defrauded of your fame,
Their proffer'd wealth, nor even the Spartan dame.
Let conquest make them ours: fate shakes their wall,
And Troy already totters to her fall."

The admiring chiefs, and all the Grecian name,
With general shouts return'd him loud acclaim.
Then thus the king of kings rejects the peace:
"Herald! in him thou hear'st the voice of Greece
For what remains; let funeral flames be fed
With heroes' corps: I war not with the dead:
Go search your slaughtered chiefs on yonder plain,
And gratify the manes of the slain.
Be witness, Jove, whose thunder rolls on high!"
He said, and rear'd his sceptre to the sky.

To sacred Troy, where all her princes lay
To wait the event, the herald bent his way.
He came, and standing in the midst, explain'd

The peace rejected, but the truce obtain'd.
Straight to their several cares the Trojans move,
Some search the plains, some fell the sounding grove:
Nor less the Greeks, descending on the shore,
Hew'd the green forests, and the bodies bore.
And now from forth the chambers of the main,
To shed his sacred light on earth again,
Arose the golden chariot of the day,
And tipp'd the mountains with a purple ray.
In mingled throngs the Greek and Trojan train
Through heaps of carnage search'd the mournful plain.
Scarce could the friend his slaughter'd friend explore,
With dust dishonour'd, and deformed with gore.
The wounds they wash'd, their pious tears they shed,
And, laid along their cars, deplored the dead.
Sage Priam check'd their grief: with silent haste
The bodies decent on the piles were placed:
With melting hearts the cold remains they burn'd,
And, sadly slow, to sacred Troy return'd.
Nor less the Greeks their pious sorrows shed,
And decent on the pile dispose the dead;
The cold remains consume with equal care;
And slowly, sadly, to their fleet repair.
Now, ere the morn had streak'd with reddening light
The doubtful confines of the day and night,
About the dying flames the Greeks appear'd,
And round the pile a general tomb they rear'd.
Then, to secure the camp and naval powers,
They raised embattled walls with lofty towers:
From space to space were ample gates around,
For passing chariots, and a trench profound
Of large extent; and deep in earth below,
Strong piles infix'd stood adverse to the foe.

So toil'd the Greeks: meanwhile the gods above,
In shining circle round their father Jove,
Amazed beheld the wondrous works of man:
Then he, whose trident shakes the earth, began:

"What mortals henceforth shall our power adore,
Our fanes frequent, our oracles implore,
If the proud Grecians thus successful boast
Their rising bulwarks on the sea-beat coast?
See the long walls extending to the main,
No god consulted, and no victim slain!
Their fame shall fill the world's remotest ends,
Wide as the morn her golden beam extends;
While old Laomedon's divine abodes,

Those radiant structures raised by labouring gods,
Shall, razed and lost, in long oblivion sleep."
Thus spoke the hoary monarch of the deep.

The almighty Thunderer with a frown replies,
That clouds the world, and blackens half the skies:
"Strong god of ocean! thou, whose rage can make
The solid earth's eternal basis shake!
What cause of fear from mortal works could move
The meanest subject of our realms above?
Where'er the sun's refulgent rays are cast,
Thy power is honour'd, and thy fame shall last.
But yon proud work no future age shall view,
No trace remain where once the glory grew.
The sapp'd foundations by thy force shall fall,
And, whelm'd beneath the waves, drop the huge wall:
Vast drifts of sand shall change the former shore:
The ruin vanish'd, and the name no more."

Thus they in heaven: while, o'er the Grecian train,
The rolling sun descending to the main
Beheld the finish'd work. Their bulls they slew;
Back from the tents the savoury vapour flew.
And now the fleet, arrived from Lemnos' strands,
With Bacchus' blessings cheered the generous bands.
Of fragrant wines the rich Eunaeus sent
A thousand measures to the royal tent.
(Eunaeus, whom Hypsipyle of yore
To Jason, shepherd of his people, bore,)
The rest they purchased at their proper cost,
And well the plenteous freight supplied the host:
Each, in exchange, proportion'd treasures gave;
Some, brass or iron; some, an ox, or slave.
All night they feast, the Greek and Trojan powers:
Those on the fields, and these within their towers.
But Jove averse the signs of wrath display'd,
And shot red lightnings through the gloomy shade:
Humbled they stood; pale horror seized on all,
While the deep thunder shook the aerial hall.
Each pour'd to Jove before the bowl was crown'd;
And large libations drench'd the thirsty ground:
Then late, refresh'd with sleep from toils of fight,
Enjoy'd the balmy blessings of the night.

ARGUMENT

THE SECOND BATTLE, AND THE DISTRESS OF THE GREEKS

Jupiter assembles a council of the deities, and threatens them with the pains of Tartarus if they assist either side: Minerva only obtains of him that she may direct the Greeks by her counsels. He balances the fates of both, and affrights the Greeks with his thunders and lightnings. Nestor alone continues in the field in great danger: Diomed relieves him; whose exploits, and those of Hector, are excellently described. Juno endeavours to animate Neptune to the assistance of the Greeks, but in vain. The acts of Teucer, who is at length wounded by Hector, and carried off. Juno and Minerva prepare to aid the Grecians, but are restrained by Iris, sent from Jupiter. The night puts an end to the battle. Hector continues in the field, (the Greeks being driven to their fortifications before the ships,) and gives orders to keep the watch all night in the camp, to prevent the enemy from re-embarking and escaping by flight. They kindle fires through all the fields, and pass the night under arms.

The time of seven and twenty days is employed from the opening of the poem to the end of this book. The scene here (except of the celestial machines) lies in the field towards the seashore.

Aurora now, fair daughter of the dawn,
Sprinkled with rosy light the dewy lawn;
When Jove convened the senate of the skies,
Where high Olympus' cloudy tops arise,
The sire of gods his awful silence broke;
The heavens attentive trembled as he spoke:

"Celestial states! immortal gods! give ear,
Hear our decree, and reverence what ye hear;
The fix'd decree which not all heaven can move;
Thou, fate! fulfil it! and, ye powers, approve!
What god but enters yon forbidden field,
Who yields assistance, or but wills to yield,
Back to the skies with shame he shall be driven,
Gash'd with dishonest wounds, the scorn of heaven;
Or far, oh far, from steep Olympus thrown,
Low in the dark Tartarean gulf shall groan,
With burning chains fix'd to the brazen floors,
And lock'd by hell's inexorable doors;
As deep beneath the infernal centre hurl'd,
As from that centre to the ethereal world.
Let him who tempts me, dread those dire abodes:
And know, the Almighty is the god of gods.
League all your forces, then, ye powers above,
Join all, and try the omnipotence of Jove.
Let down our golden everlasting chain
Whose strong embrace holds heaven, and earth, and main
Strive all, of mortal and immortal birth,
To drag, by this, the Thunderer down to earth

Ye strive in vain! if I but stretch this hand,
I heave the gods, the ocean, and the land;
I fix the chain to great Olympus' height,
And the vast world hangs trembling in my sight!
For such I reign, unbounded and above;
And such are men, and gods, compared to Jove."

The all-mighty spoke, nor durst the powers reply:
A reverend horror silenced all the sky;
Trembling they stood before their sovereign's look;
At length his best-beloved, the power of wisdom, spoke:

"O first and greatest! God, by gods adored
We own thy might, our father and our lord!
But, ah! permit to pity human state:
If not to help, at least lament their fate.
From fields forbidden we submiss refrain,
With arms unaiding mourn our Argives slain;
Yet grant my counsels still their breasts may move,
Or all must perish in the wrath of Jove."

The cloud-compelling god her suit approved,
And smiled superior on his best beloved;
Then call'd his coursers, and his chariot took;
The stedfast firmament beneath them shook:
Rapt by the ethereal steeds the chariot roll'd;
Brass were their hoofs, their curling manes of gold:
Of heaven's undrossy gold the gods array,
Refulgent, flash'd intolerable day.
High on the throne he shines: his coursers fly
Between the extended earth and starry sky.
But when to Ida's topmost height he came,
(Fair nurse of fountains, and of savage game,)
Where o'er her pointed summits proudly raised,
His fane breathed odours, and his altar blazed:
There, from his radiant car, the sacred sire
Of gods and men released the steeds of fire:
Blue ambient mists the immortal steeds embraced;
High on the cloudy point his seat he placed;
Thence his broad eye the subject world surveys,
The town, and tents, and navigable seas.

Now had the Grecians snatch'd a short repast,
And buckled on their shining arms with haste.
Troy roused as soon; for on this dreadful day
The fate of fathers, wives, and infants lay.
The gates unfolding pour forth all their train;
Squadrons on squadrons cloud the dusky plain:

Men, steeds, and chariots shake the trembling ground,
The tumult thickens, and the skies resound;
And now with shouts the shocking armies closed,
To lances lances, shields to shields opposed,
Host against host with shadowy legends drew,
The sounding darts in iron tempests flew;
Victors and vanquish'd join promiscuous cries,
Triumphant shouts and dying groans arise;
With streaming blood the slippery fields are dyed,
And slaughter'd heroes swell the dreadful tide.
Long as the morning beams, increasing bright,
O'er heaven's clear azure spread the sacred light,
Commutual death the fate of war confounds,
Each adverse battle gored with equal wounds.
But when the sun the height of heaven ascends,
The sire of gods his golden scales suspends,
With equal hand: in these explored the fate
Of Greece and Troy, and poised the mighty weight:
Press'd with its load, the Grecian balance lies
Low sunk on earth, the Trojan strikes the skies.
Then Jove from Ida's top his horrors spreads;
The clouds burst dreadful o'er the Grecian heads;
Thick lightnings flash; the muttering thunder rolls;
Their strength he withers, and unmans their souls.
Before his wrath the trembling hosts retire;
The gods in terrors, and the skies on fire.
Nor great Idomeneus that sight could bear,
Nor each stern Ajax, thunderbolts of war:
Nor he, the king of war, the alarm sustain'd
Nestor alone, amidst the storm remain'd.
Unwilling he remain'd, for Paris' dart
Had pierced his courser in a mortal part;
Fix'd in the forehead, where the springing man
Curl'd o'er the brow, it stung him to the brain;
Mad with his anguish, he begins to rear,
Paw with his hoofs aloft, and lash the air.
Scarce had his falchion cut the reins, and freed
The encumber'd chariot from the dying steed,
When dreadful Hector, thundering through the war,
Pour'd to the tumult on his whirling car.
That day had stretch'd beneath his matchless hand
The hoary monarch of the Pylian band,
But Diomed beheld; from forth the crowd
He rush'd, and on Ulysses call'd aloud:

"Whither, oh whither does Ulysses run?
Oh, flight unworthy great Laertes' son!
Mix'd with the vulgar shall thy fate be found,

Pierced in the back, a vile, dishonest wound?
Oh turn and save from Hector's direful rage
The glory of the Greeks, the Pylian sage."
His fruitless words are lost unheard in air,
Ulysses seeks the ships, and shelters there.
But bold Tydides to the rescue goes,
A single warrior midst a host of foes;
Before the coursers with a sudden spring
He leap'd, and anxious thus bespoke the king:

"Great perils, father! wait the unequal fight;
These younger champions will oppress thy might.
Thy veins no more with ancient vigour glow,
Weak is thy servant, and thy coursers slow.
Then haste, ascend my seat, and from the car
Observe the steeds of Tros, renown'd in war.
Practised alike to turn, to stop, to chase,
To dare the fight, or urge the rapid race:
These late obey'd Ćneas' guiding rein;
Leave thou thy chariot to our faithful train;
With these against yon Trojans will we go,
Nor shall great Hector want an equal foe;
Fierce as he is, even he may learn to fear
The thirsty fury of my flying spear."

Thus said the chief; and Nestor, skill'd in war,
Approves his counsel, and ascends the car:
The steeds he left, their trusty servants hold;
Eurymedon, and Sthenelus the bold:
The reverend charioteer directs the course,
And strains his aged arm to lash the horse.
Hector they face; unknowing how to fear,
Fierce he drove on; Tydides whirl'd his spear.
The spear with erring haste mistook its way,
But plunged in Eniopeus' bosom lay.
His opening hand in death forsakes the rein;
The steeds fly back: he falls, and spurns the plain.
Great Hector sorrows for his servant kill'd,
Yet unrevenged permits to press the field;
Till, to supply his place and rule the car,
Rose Archeptolemus, the fierce in war.
And now had death and horror cover'd all;
Like timorous flocks the Trojans in their wall
Inclosed had bled: but Jove with awful sound
Roll'd the big thunder o'er the vast profound:
Full in Tydides' face the lightning flew;
The ground before him flamed with sulphur blue;
The quivering steeds fell prostrate at the sight;

And Nestor's trembling hand confess'd his fright:
He dropp'd the reins: and, shook with sacred dread,
Thus, turning, warn'd the intrepid Diomed:

"O chief! too daring in thy friend's defence
Retire advised, and urge the chariot hence.
This day, averse, the sovereign of the skies
Assists great Hector, and our palm denies.
Some other sun may see the happier hour,
When Greece shall conquer by his heavenly power.
'Tis not in man his fix'd decree to move:
The great will glory to submit to Jove."

"O reverend prince! (Tydides thus replies)
Thy years are awful, and thy words are wise.
But ah, what grief! should haughty Hector boast
I fled inglorious to the guarded coast.
Before that dire disgrace shall blast my fame,
O'erwhelm me, earth; and hide a warrior's shame!"
To whom Gerenian Nestor thus replied:
"Gods! can thy courage fear the Phrygian's pride?
Hector may vaunt, but who shall heed the boast?
Not those who felt thy arm, the Dardan host,
Nor Troy, yet bleeding in her heroes lost;
Not even a Phrygian dame, who dreads the sword
That laid in dust her loved, lamented lord."
He said, and, hasty, o'er the gasping throng
Drives the swift steeds: the chariot smokes along;
The shouts of Trojans thicken in the wind;
The storm of hissing javelins pours behind.
Then with a voice that shakes the solid skies,
Pleased, Hector braves the warrior as he flies.
"Go, mighty hero! graced above the rest
In seats of council and the sumptuous feast:
Now hope no more those honours from thy train;
Go less than woman, in the form of man!
To scale our walls, to wrap our towers in flames,
To lead in exile the fair Phrygian dames,
Thy once proud hopes, presumptuous prince! are fled;
This arm shall reach thy heart, and stretch thee dead."

Now fears dissuade him, and now hopes invite.
To stop his coursers, and to stand the fight;
Thrice turn'd the chief, and thrice imperial Jove
On Ida's summits thunder'd from above.
Great Hector heard; he saw the flashing light,
(The sign of conquest,) and thus urged the fight:

"Hear, every Trojan, Lycian, Dardan band,
All famed in war, and dreadful hand to hand.
Be mindful of the wreaths your arms have won,
Your great forefathers' glories, and your own.
Heard ye the voice of Jove? Success and fame
Await on Troy, on Greece eternal shame.
In vain they skulk behind their boasted wall,
Weak bulwarks; destined by this arm to fall.
High o'er their slighted trench our steeds shall bound,
And pass victorious o'er the levell'd mound.
Soon as before yon hollow ships we stand,
Fight each with flames, and toss the blazing brand;
Till, their proud navy wrapt in smoke and fires,
All Greece, encompass'd, in one blaze expires."

Furious he said; then bending o'er the yoke,
Encouraged his proud steeds, while thus he spoke:

"Now, Xanthus, Ćthon, Lampus, urge the chase,
And thou, Podargus! prove thy generous race;
Be fleet, be fearless, this important day,
And all your master's well-spent care repay.
For this, high-fed, in plenteous stalls ye stand,
Served with pure wheat, and by a princess' hand;
For this my spouse, of great Aetion's line,
So oft has steep'd the strengthening grain in wine.
Now swift pursue, now thunder uncontroll'd;
Give me to seize rich Nestor's shield of gold;
From Tydeus' shoulders strip the costly load,
Vulcanian arms, the labour of a god:
These if we gain, then victory, ye powers!
This night, this glorious night, the fleet is ours!"

That heard, deep anguish stung Saturnia's soul;
She shook her throne, that shook the starry pole:
And thus to Neptune: "Thou, whose force can make
The stedfast earth from her foundations shake,
Seest thou the Greeks by fates unjust oppress'd,
Nor swells thy heart in that immortal breast?
Yet Ćgae, Helice, thy power obey,
And gifts unceasing on thine altars lay.
Would all the deities of Greece combine,
In vain the gloomy Thunderer might repine:
Sole should he sit, with scarce a god to friend,
And see his Trojans to the shades descend:
Such be the scene from his Idaean bower;
Ungrateful prospect to the sullen power!"

Neptune with wrath rejects the rash design:
"What rage, what madness, furious queen! is thine?
I war not with the highest. All above
Submit and tremble at the hand of Jove."

Now godlike Hector, to whose matchless might
Jove gave the glory of the destined fight,
Squadrons on squadrons drives, and fills the fields
With close-ranged chariots, and with thicken'd shields.
Where the deep trench in length extended lay,
Compacted troops stand wedged in firm array,
A dreadful front! they shake the brands, and threat
With long-destroying flames the hostile fleet.
The king of men, by Juno's self inspired,
Toil'd through the tents, and all his army fired.
Swift as he moved, he lifted in his hand
His purple robe, bright ensign of command.
High on the midmost bark the king appear'd:
There, from Ulysses' deck, his voice was heard:
To Ajax and Achilles reach'd the sound,
Whose distant ships the guarded navy bound.
"O Argives! shame of human race! (he cried:
The hollow vessels to his voice replied,)
Where now are all your glorious boasts of yore,
Your hasty triumphs on the Lemnian shore?
Each fearless hero dares a hundred foes,
While the feast lasts, and while the goblet flows;
But who to meet one martial man is found,
When the fight rages, and the flames surround?
O mighty Jove! O sire of the distress'd!
Was ever king like me, like me oppress'd?
With power immense, with justice arm'd in vain;
My glory ravish'd, and my people slain!
To thee my vows were breathed from every shore;
What altar smoked not with our victims' gore?
With fat of bulls I fed the constant flame,
And ask'd destruction to the Trojan name.
Now, gracious god! far humbler our demand;
Give these at least to 'scape from Hector's hand,
And save the relics of the Grecian land!"

Thus pray'd the king, and heaven's great father heard
His vows, in bitterness of soul preferr'd:
The wrath appeased, by happy signs declares,
And gives the people to their monarch's prayers.
His eagle, sacred bird of heaven! he sent,
A fawn his talons truss'd, (divine portent!)
High o'er the wondering hosts he soar'd above,

Who paid their vows to Panomphaean Jove;
Then let the prey before his altar fall;
The Greeks beheld, and transport seized on all:
Encouraged by the sign, the troops revive,
And fierce on Troy with doubled fury drive.
Tydides first, of all the Grecian force,
O'er the broad ditch impell'd his foaming horse,
Pierced the deep ranks, their strongest battle tore,
And dyed his javelin red with Trojan gore.
Young Agelaus (Phradmon was his sire)
With flying coursers shunn'd his dreadful ire;
Struck through the back, the Phrygian fell oppress'd;
The dart drove on, and issued at his breast:
Headlong he quits the car: his arms resound;
His ponderous buckler thunders on the ground.
Forth rush a tide of Greeks, the passage freed;
The Atridae first, the Ajaces next succeed:
Meriones, like Mars in arms renown'd,
And godlike Idomen, now passed the mound;
Evaemon's son next issues to the foe,
And last young Teucer with his bended bow.
Secure behind the Telamonian shield
The skilful archer wide survey'd the field,
With every shaft some hostile victim slew,
Then close beneath the sevenfold orb withdrew:
The conscious infant so, when fear alarms,
Retires for safety to the mother's arms.
Thus Ajax guards his brother in the field,
Moves as he moves, and turns the shining shield.
Who first by Teucer's mortal arrows bled?
Orsilochus; then fell Ormenus dead:
The godlike Lycophon next press'd the plain,
With Chromius, Daetor, Ophelestes slain:
Bold Hamopaon breathless sunk to ground;
The bloody pile great Melanippus crown'd.
Heaps fell on heaps, sad trophies of his art,
A Trojan ghost attending every dart.
Great Agamemnon views with joyful eye
The ranks grow thinner as his arrows fly:
"O youth forever dear! (the monarch cried)
Thus, always thus, thy early worth be tried;
Thy brave example shall retrieve our host,
Thy country's saviour, and thy father's boast!
Sprung from an alien's bed thy sire to grace,
The vigorous offspring of a stolen embrace:
Proud of his boy, he own'd the generous flame,
And the brave son repays his cares with fame.
Now hear a monarch's vow: If heaven's high powers

Give me to raze Troy's long-defended towers;
Whatever treasures Greece for me design,
The next rich honorary gift be thine:
Some golden tripod, or distinguished car,
With coursers dreadful in the ranks of war:
Or some fair captive, whom thy eyes approve,
Shall recompense the warrior's toils with love."

To this the chief: "With praise the rest inspire,
Nor urge a soul already fill'd with fire.
What strength I have, be now in battle tried,
Till every shaft in Phrygian blood be dyed.
Since rallying from our wall we forced the foe,
Still aim'd at Hector have I bent my bow:
Eight forky arrows from this hand have fled,
And eight bold heroes by their points lie dead:
But sure some god denies me to destroy
This fury of the field, this dog of Troy."

He said, and twang'd the string. The weapon flies
At Hector's breast, and sings along the skies:
He miss'd the mark; but pierced Gorgythio's heart,
And drench'd in royal blood the thirsty dart.
(Fair Castianira, nymph of form divine,
This offspring added to king Priam's line.)
As full-blown poppies, overcharged with rain,
Decline the head, and drooping kiss the plain;
So sinks the youth: his beauteous head, depress'd
Beneath his helmet, drops upon his breast.
Another shaft the raging archer drew,
That other shaft with erring fury flew,
(From Hector, Phoebus turn'd the flying wound,)
Yet fell not dry or guiltless to the ground:
Thy breast, brave Archeptolemus! it tore,
And dipp'd its feathers in no vulgar gore.
Headlong he falls: his sudden fall alarms
The steeds, that startle at his sounding arms.
Hector with grief his charioteer beheld
All pale and breathless on the sanguine field:
Then bids Cebriones direct the rein,
Quits his bright car, and issues on the plain.
Dreadful he shouts: from earth a stone he took,
And rush'd on Teucer with the lifted rock.
The youth already strain'd the forceful yew;
The shaft already to his shoulder drew;
The feather in his hand, just wing'd for flight,
Touch'd where the neck and hollow chest unite;
There, where the juncture knits the channel bone,

The furious chief discharged the craggy stone:
The bow-string burst beneath the ponderous blow,
And his numb'd hand dismiss'd his useless bow.
He fell: but Ajax his broad shield display'd,
And screen'd his brother with the mighty shade;
Till great Alaster, and Mecistheus, bore
The batter'd archer groaning to the shore.

Troy yet found grace before the Olympian sire,
He arm'd their hands, and fill'd their breasts with fire.
The Greeks repulsed, retreat behind their wall,
Or in the trench on heaps confusedly fall.
First of the foe, great Hector march'd along,
With terror clothed, and more than mortal strong.
As the bold hound, that gives the lion chase,
With beating bosom, and with eager pace,
Hangs on his haunch, or fastens on his heels,
Guards as he turns, and circles as he wheels;
Thus oft the Grecians turn'd, but still they flew;
Thus following, Hector still the hindmost slew.
When flying they had pass'd the trench profound,
And many a chief lay gasping on the ground;
Before the ships a desperate stand they made,
And fired the troops, and called the gods to aid.
Fierce on his rattling chariot Hector came:
His eyes like Gorgon shot a sanguine flame
That wither'd all their host: like Mars he stood:
Dire as the monster, dreadful as the god!
Their strong distress the wife of Jove survey'd;
Then pensive thus, to war's triumphant maid:

"O daughter of that god, whose arm can wield
The avenging bolt, and shake the sable shield!
Now, in this moment of her last despair,
Shall wretched Greece no more confess our care,
Condemn'd to suffer the full force of fate,
And drain the dregs of heaven's relentless hate?
Gods! shall one raging hand thus level all?
What numbers fell! what numbers yet shall fall!
What power divine shall Hector's wrath assuage?
Still swells the slaughter, and still grows the rage!"

So spake the imperial regent of the skies;
To whom the goddess with the azure eyes:

"Long since had Hector stain'd these fields with gore,
Stretch'd by some Argive on his native shore:
But he above, the sire of heaven, withstands,

Mocks our attempts, and slights our just demands;
The stubborn god, inflexible and hard,
Forgets my service and deserved reward:
Saved I, for this, his favourite son distress'd,
By stern Eurystheus with long labours press'd?
He begg'd, with tears he begg'd, in deep dismay;
I shot from heaven, and gave his arm the day.
Oh had my wisdom known this dire event,
When to grim Pluto's gloomy gates he went;
The triple dog had never felt his chain,
Nor Styx been cross'd, nor hell explored in vain.
Averse to me of all his heaven of gods,
At Thetis' suit the partial Thunderer nods;
To grace her gloomy, fierce, resenting son,
My hopes are frustrate, and my Greeks undone.
Some future day, perhaps, he may be moved
To call his blue-eyed maid his best beloved.
Haste, launch thy chariot, through yon ranks to ride;
Myself will arm, and thunder at thy side.
Then, goddess! say, shall Hector glory then?
(That terror of the Greeks, that man of men)
When Juno's self, and Pallas shall appear,
All dreadful in the crimson walks of war!
What mighty Trojan then, on yonder shore,
Expiring, pale, and terrible no more,
Shall feast the fowls, and glut the dogs with gore?"

She ceased, and Juno rein'd the steeds with care:
(Heaven's awful empress, Saturn's other heir:)
Pallas, meanwhile, her various veil unbound,
With flowers adorn'd, with art immortal crown'd;
The radiant robe her sacred fingers wove
Floats in rich waves, and spreads the court of Jove.
Her father's arms her mighty limbs invest,
His cuirass blazes on her ample breast.
The vigorous power the trembling car ascends:
Shook by her arm, the massy javelin bends:
Huge, ponderous, strong! that when her fury burns
Proud tyrants humbles, and whole hosts o'erturns.

Saturnia lends the lash; the coursers fly;
Smooth glides the chariot through the liquid sky.
Heaven's gates spontaneous open to the powers,
Heaven's golden gates, kept by the winged Hours.
Commission'd in alternate watch they stand,
The sun's bright portals and the skies command;
Close, or unfold, the eternal gates of day
Bar heaven with clouds, or roll those clouds away.

The sounding hinges ring, the clouds divide.
Prone down the steep of heaven their course they guide.
But Jove, incensed, from Ida's top survey'd,
And thus enjoin'd the many-colour'd maid.

"Thaumantia! mount the winds, and stop their car;
Against the highest who shall wage the war?
If furious yet they dare the vain debate,
Thus have I spoke, and what I speak is fate:
Their coursers crush'd beneath the wheels shall lie,
Their car in fragments, scatter'd o'er the sky:
My lightning these rebellious shall confound,
And hurl them flaming, headlong, to the ground,
Condemn'd for ten revolving years to weep
The wounds impress'd by burning thunder deep.
So shall Minerva learn to fear our ire,
Nor dare to combat hers and nature's sire.
For Juno, headstrong and imperious still,
She claims some title to transgress our will."

Swift as the wind, the various-colour'd maid
From Ida's top her golden wings display'd;
To great Olympus' shining gate she flies,
There meets the chariot rushing down the skies,
Restrains their progress from the bright abodes,
And speaks the mandate of the sire of gods.

"What frenzy goddesses! what rage can move
Celestial minds to tempt the wrath of Jove?
Desist, obedient to his high command:
This is his word; and know his word shall stand:
His lightning your rebellion shall confound,
And hurl ye headlong, flaming, to the ground;
Your horses crush'd beneath the wheels shall lie,
Your car in fragments scatter'd o'er the sky;
Yourselves condemn'd ten rolling years to weep
The wounds impress'd by burning thunder deep.
So shall Minerva learn to fear his ire,
Nor dare to combat hers and nature's sire.
For Juno, headstrong and imperious still,
She claims some title to transgress his will:
But thee, what desperate insolence has driven
To lift thy lance against the king of heaven?"

Then, mounting on the pinions of the wind,
She flew; and Juno thus her rage resign'd:

"O daughter of that god, whose arm can wield

The avenging bolt, and shake the dreadful shield
No more let beings of superior birth
Contend with Jove for this low race of earth;
Triumphant now, now miserably slain,
They breathe or perish as the fates ordain:
But Jove's high counsels full effect shall find;
And, ever constant, ever rule mankind."

She spoke, and backward turn'd her steeds of light,
Adorn'd with manes of gold, and heavenly bright.
The Hours unloosed them, panting as they stood,
And heap'd their mangers with ambrosial food.
There tied, they rest in high celestial stalls;
The chariot propp'd against the crystal walls,
The pensive goddesses, abash'd, controll'd,
Mix with the gods, and fill their seats of gold.

And now the Thunderer meditates his flight
From Ida's summits to the Olympian height.
Swifter than thought, the wheels instinctive fly,
Flame through the vast of air, and reach the sky.
'Twas Neptune's charge his coursers to unbrace,
And fix the car on its immortal base;
There stood the chariot, beaming forth its rays,
Till with a snowy veil he screen'd the blaze.
He, whose all-conscious eyes the world behold,
The eternal Thunderer sat, enthroned in gold.
High heaven the footstool of his feet he makes,
And wide beneath him all Olympus shakes.
Trembling afar the offending powers appear'd,
Confused and silent, for his frown they fear'd.
He saw their soul, and thus his word imparts:
"Pallas and Juno! say, why heave your hearts?
Soon was your battle o'er: proud Troy retired
Before your face, and in your wrath expired.
But know, whoe'er almighty power withstand!
Unmatch'd our force, unconquer'd is our hand:
Who shall the sovereign of the skies control?
Not all the gods that crown the starry pole.
Your hearts shall tremble, if our arms we take,
And each immortal nerve with horror shake.
For thus I speak, and what I speak shall stand;
What power soe'er provokes our lifted hand,
On this our hill no more shall hold his place;
Cut off, and exiled from the ethereal race."

Juno and Pallas grieving hear the doom,
But feast their souls on Ilion's woes to come.

Though secret anger swell'd Minerva's breast,
The prudent goddess yet her wrath repress'd;
But Juno, impotent of rage, replies:
"What hast thou said, O tyrant of the skies!
Strength and omnipotence invest thy throne;
'Tis thine to punish; ours to grieve alone.
For Greece we grieve, abandon'd by her fate
To drink the dregs of thy unmeasured hate.
From fields forbidden we submiss refrain,
With arms unaiding see our Argives slain;
Yet grant our counsels still their breasts may move,
Lest all should perish in the rage of Jove."

The goddess thus; and thus the god replies,
Who swells the clouds, and blackens all the skies:

"The morning sun, awaked by loud alarms,
Shall see the almighty Thunderer in arms.
What heaps of Argives then shall load the plain,
Those radiant eyes shall view, and view in vain.
Nor shall great Hector cease the rage of fight,
The navy flaming, and thy Greeks in flight,
Even till the day when certain fates ordain
That stern Achilles (his Patroclus slain)
Shall rise in vengeance, and lay waste the plain.
For such is fate, nor canst thou turn its course
With all thy rage, with all thy rebel force.
Fly, if thy wilt, to earth's remotest bound,
Where on her utmost verge the seas resound;
Where cursed Iapetus and Saturn dwell,
Fast by the brink, within the streams of hell;
No sun e'er gilds the gloomy horrors there;
No cheerful gales refresh the lazy air:
There arm once more the bold Titanian band;
And arm in vain; for what I will, shall stand."

Now deep in ocean sunk the lamp of light,
And drew behind the cloudy veil of night:
The conquering Trojans mourn his beams decay'd;
The Greeks rejoicing bless the friendly shade.

The victors keep the field; and Hector calls
A martial council near the navy walls;
These to Scamander's bank apart he led,
Where thinly scatter'd lay the heaps of dead.
The assembled chiefs, descending on the ground,
Attend his order, and their prince surround.
A massy spear he bore of mighty strength,

Of full ten cubits was the lance's length;
The point was brass, refulgent to behold,
Fix'd to the wood with circling rings of gold:
The noble Hector on his lance reclined,
And, bending forward, thus reveal'd his mind:

"Ye valiant Trojans, with attention hear!
Ye Dardan bands, and generous aids, give ear!
This day, we hoped, would wrap in conquering flame
Greece with her ships, and crown our toils with fame.
But darkness now, to save the cowards, falls,
And guards them trembling in their wooden walls.
Obey the night, and use her peaceful hours
Our steeds to forage, and refresh our powers.
Straight from the town be sheep and oxen sought,
And strengthening bread and generous wine be brought
Wide o'er the field, high blazing to the sky,
Let numerous fires the absent sun supply,
The flaming piles with plenteous fuel raise,
Till the bright morn her purple beam displays;
Lest, in the silence and the shades of night,
Greece on her sable ships attempt her flight.
Not unmolested let the wretches gain
Their lofty decks, or safely cleave the main;
Some hostile wound let every dart bestow,
Some lasting token of the Phrygian foe,
Wounds, that long hence may ask their spouses' care.
And warn their children from a Trojan war.
Now through the circuit of our Ilion wall,
Let sacred heralds sound the solemn call;
To bid the sires with hoary honours crown'd,
And beardless youths, our battlements surround.
Firm be the guard, while distant lie our powers,
And let the matrons hang with lights the towers;
Lest, under covert of the midnight shade,
The insidious foe the naked town invade.
Suffice, to-night, these orders to obey;
A nobler charge shall rouse the dawning day.
The gods, I trust, shall give to Hector's hand
From these detested foes to free the land,
Who plough'd, with fates averse, the watery way:
For Trojan vultures a predestined prey.
Our common safety must be now the care;
But soon as morning paints the fields of air,
Sheathed in bright arms let every troop engage,
And the fired fleet behold the battle rage.
Then, then shall Hector and Tydides prove
Whose fates are heaviest in the scales of Jove.

To-morrow's light (O haste the glorious morn!)
Shall see his bloody spoils in triumph borne,
With this keen javelin shall his breast be gored,
And prostrate heroes bleed around their lord.
Certain as this, oh! might my days endure,
From age inglorious, and black death secure;
So might my life and glory know no bound,
Like Pallas worshipp'd, like the sun renown'd!
As the next dawn, the last they shall enjoy,
Shall crush the Greeks, and end the woes of Troy."

The leader spoke. From all his host around
Shouts of applause along the shores resound.
Each from the yoke the smoking steeds untied,
And fix'd their headstalls to his chariot-side.
Fat sheep and oxen from the town are led,
With generous wine, and all-sustaining bread,
Full hecatombs lay burning on the shore:
The winds to heaven the curling vapours bore.
Ungrateful offering to the immortal powers!
Whose wrath hung heavy o'er the Trojan towers:
Nor Priam nor his sons obtain'd their grace;
Proud Troy they hated, and her guilty race.

The troops exulting sat in order round,
And beaming fires illumined all the ground.
As when the moon, refulgent lamp of night,
O'er heaven's pure azure spreads her sacred light,
When not a breath disturbs the deep serene,
And not a cloud o'ercasts the solemn scene,
Around her throne the vivid planets roll,
And stars unnumber'd gild the glowing pole,
O'er the dark trees a yellower verdure shed,
And tip with silver every mountain's head:
Then shine the vales, the rocks in prospect rise,
A flood of glory bursts from all the skies:
The conscious swains, rejoicing in the sight,
Eye the blue vault, and bless the useful light.
So many flames before proud Ilion blaze,
And lighten glimmering Xanthus with their rays.
The long reflections of the distant fires
Gleam on the walls, and tremble on the spires.
A thousand piles the dusky horrors gild,
And shoot a shady lustre o'er the field.
Full fifty guards each flaming pile attend,
Whose umber'd arms, by fits, thick flashes send,
Loud neigh the coursers o'er their heaps of corn,
And ardent warriors wait the rising morn.

BOOK IX

ARGUMENT

THE EMBASSY TO ACHILLES

Agamemnon, after the last day's defeat, proposes to the Greeks to quit the siege, and return to their country. Diomed opposes this, and Nestor seconds him, praising his wisdom and resolution. He orders the guard to be strengthened, and a council summoned to deliberate what measures are to be followed in this emergency. Agamemnon pursues this advice, and Nestor further prevails upon him to send ambassadors to Achilles, in order to move him to a reconciliation. Ulysses and Ajax are made choice of, who are accompanied by old Phoenix. They make, each of them, very moving and pressing speeches, but are rejected with roughness by Achilles, who notwithstanding retains Phoenix in his tent. The ambassadors return unsuccessfully to the camp, and the troops betake themselves to sleep.

This book, and the next following, take up the space of one night, which is the twenty-seventh from the beginning of the poem. The scene lies on the sea-shore, the station of the Grecian ships.

Thus joyful Troy maintain'd the watch of night;
While fear, pale comrade of inglorious flight,
And heaven-bred horror, on the Grecian part,
Sat on each face, and sadden'd every heart.
As from its cloudy dungeon issuing forth,
A double tempest of the west and north
Swells o'er the sea, from Thracia's frozen shore,
Heaps waves on waves, and bids the Ægean roar:
This way and that the boiling deeps are toss'd:
Such various passions urged the troubled host,
Great Agamemnon grieved above the rest;
Superior sorrows swell'd his royal breast;
Himself his orders to the heralds bears,
To bid to council all the Grecian peers,
But bid in whispers: these surround their chief,
In solemn sadness and majestic grief.
The king amidst the mournful circle rose:
Down his wan cheek a briny torrent flows.
So silent fountains, from a rock's tall head,
In sable streams soft-trickling waters shed.
With more than vulgar grief he stood oppress'd;
Words, mix'd with sighs, thus bursting from his breast:

"Ye sons of Greece! partake your leader's care;
Fellows in arms and princes of the war!
Of partial Jove too justly we complain,

And heavenly oracles believed in vain.
A safe return was promised to our toils,
With conquest honour'd and enrich'd with spoils:
Now shameful flight alone can save the host;
Our wealth, our people, and our glory lost.
So Jove decrees, almighty lord of all!
Jove, at whose nod whole empires rise or fall,
Who shakes the feeble props of human trust,
And towers and armies humbles to the dust.
Haste then, for ever quit these fatal fields,
Haste to the joys our native country yields;
Spread all your canvas, all your oars employ,
Nor hope the fall of heaven-defended Troy."

He said: deep silence held the Grecian band;
Silent, unmov'd in dire dismay they stand;
A pensive scene! till Tydeus' warlike son
Roll'd on the king his eyes, and thus begun:
"When kings advise us to renounce our fame,
First let him speak who first has suffer'd shame.
If I oppose thee, prince! thy wrath withhold,
The laws of council bid my tongue be bold.
Thou first, and thou alone, in fields of fight,
Durst brand my courage, and defame my might:
Nor from a friend the unkind reproach appear'd,
The Greeks stood witness, all our army heard.
The gods, O chief! from whom our honours spring,
The gods have made thee but by halves a king:
They gave thee sceptres, and a wide command;
They gave dominion o'er the seas and land;
The noblest power that might the world control
They gave thee not—a brave and virtuous soul.
Is this a general's voice, that would suggest
Fears like his own to every Grecian breast?
Confiding in our want of worth, he stands;
And if we fly, 'tis what our king commands.
Go thou, inglorious! from the embattled plain;
Ships thou hast store, and nearest to the main;
A noble care the Grecians shall employ,
To combat, conquer, and extirpate Troy.
Here Greece shall stay; or, if all Greece retire,
Myself shall stay, till Troy or I expire;
Myself, and Sthenelus, will fight for fame;
God bade us fight, and 'twas with God we came."

He ceased; the Greeks loud acclamations raise,
And voice to voice resounds Tydides' praise.
Wise Nestor then his reverend figure rear'd;

He spoke: the host in still attention heard:

"O truly great! in whom the gods have join'd
Such strength of body with such force of mind:
In conduct, as in courage, you excel,
Still first to act what you advise so well.
These wholesome counsels which thy wisdom moves,
Applauding Greece with common voice approves.
Kings thou canst blame; a bold but prudent youth:
And blame even kings with praise, because with truth.
And yet those years that since thy birth have run
Would hardly style thee Nestor's youngest son.
Then let me add what yet remains behind,
A thought unfinish'd in that generous mind;
Age bids me speak! nor shall the advice I bring
Distaste the people, or offend the king:

"Cursed is the man, and void of law and right,
Unworthy property, unworthy light,
Unfit for public rule, or private care,
That wretch, that monster, who delights in war;
Whose lust is murder, and whose horrid joy,
To tear his country, and his kind destroy!
This night, refresh and fortify thy train;
Between the trench and wall let guards remain:
Be that the duty of the young and bold;
But thou, O king, to council call the old;
Great is thy sway, and weighty are thy cares;
Thy high commands must spirit all our wars.
With Thracian wines recruit thy honour'd guests,
For happy counsels flow from sober feasts.
Wise, weighty counsels aid a state distress'd,
And such a monarch as can choose the best.
See what a blaze from hostile tents aspires,
How near our fleet approach the Trojan fires!
Who can, unmoved, behold the dreadful light?
What eye beholds them, and can close to-night?
This dreadful interval determines all;
To-morrow, Troy must flame, or Greece must fall."

Thus spoke the hoary sage: the rest obey;
Swift through the gates the guards direct their way.
His son was first to pass the lofty mound,
The generous Thrasymed, in arms renown'd:
Next him, Ascalaphus, Ialmen, stood,
The double offspring of the warrior-god:
Deipyrus, Aphareus, Merion join,
And Lycomed of Creon's noble line.

Seven were the leaders of the nightly bands,
And each bold chief a hundred spears commands.
The fires they light, to short repasts they fall,
Some line the trench, and others man the wall.

The king of men, on public counsels bent,
Convened the princes in his ample tent,
Each seized a portion of the kingly feast,
But stay'd his hand when thirst and hunger ceased.
Then Nestor spoke, for wisdom long approved,
And slowly rising, thus the council moved.

"Monarch of nations! whose superior sway
Assembled states, and lords of earth obey,
The laws and sceptres to thy hand are given,
And millions own the care of thee and Heaven.
O king! the counsels of my age attend;
With thee my cares begin, with thee must end.
Thee, prince! it fits alike to speak and hear,
Pronounce with judgment, with regard give ear,
To see no wholesome motion be withstood,
And ratify the best for public good.
Nor, though a meaner give advice, repine,
But follow it, and make the wisdom thine.
Hear then a thought, not now conceived in haste,
At once my present judgment and my past.
When from Pelides' tent you forced the maid,
I first opposed, and faithful, durst dissuade;
But bold of soul, when headlong fury fired,
You wronged the man, by men and gods admired:
Now seek some means his fatal wrath to end,
With prayers to move him, or with gifts to bend."

To whom the king. "With justice hast thou shown
A prince's faults, and I with reason own.
That happy man, whom Jove still honours most,
Is more than armies, and himself a host.
Bless'd in his love, this wondrous hero stands;
Heaven fights his war, and humbles all our bands.
Fain would my heart, which err'd through frantic rage,
The wrathful chief and angry gods assuage.
If gifts immense his mighty soul can bow,
Hear, all ye Greeks, and witness what I vow.
Ten weighty talents of the purest gold,
And twice ten vases of refulgent mould:
Seven sacred tripods, whose unsullied frame
Yet knows no office, nor has felt the flame;
Twelve steeds unmatch'd in fleetness and in force,

And still victorious in the dusty course;
(Rich were the man whose ample stores exceed
The prizes purchased by their winged speed;)
Seven lovely captives of the Lesbian line,
Skill'd in each art, unmatch'd in form divine,
The same I chose for more than vulgar charms,
When Lesbos sank beneath the hero's arms:
All these, to buy his friendship, shall be paid,
And join'd with these the long-contested maid;
With all her charms, Briseis I resign,
And solemn swear those charms were never mine;
Untouch'd she stay'd, uninjured she removes,
Pure from my arms, and guiltless of my loves,
These instant shall be his; and if the powers
Give to our arms proud Ilion's hostile towers,
Then shall he store (when Greece the spoil divides)
With gold and brass his loaded navy's sides:
Besides, full twenty nymphs of Trojan race
With copious love shall crown his warm embrace,
Such as himself will choose; who yield to none,
Or yield to Helen's heavenly charms alone.
Yet hear me further: when our wars are o'er,
If safe we land on Argos' fruitful shore,
There shall he live my son, our honours share,
And with Orestes' self divide my care.
Yet more—three daughters in my court are bred,
And each well worthy of a royal bed;
Laodice and Iphigenia fair,
And bright Chrysothemis with golden hair;
Her let him choose whom most his eyes approve,
I ask no presents, no reward for love:
Myself will give the dower; so vast a store
As never father gave a child before.
Seven ample cities shall confess his sway,
Him Enope, and Pherae him obey,
Cardamyle with ample turrets crown'd,
And sacred Pedasus for vines renown'd;
Épea fair, the pastures Hira yields,
And rich Antheia with her flowery fields:
The whole extent to Pylos' sandy plain,
Along the verdant margin of the main
There heifers graze, and labouring oxen toil;
Bold are the men, and generous is the soil;
There shall he reign, with power and justice crown'd,
And rule the tributary realms around.
All this I give, his vengeance to control,
And sure all this may move his mighty soul.
Pluto, the grisly god, who never spares,

Who feels no mercy, and who hears no prayers,
Lives dark and dreadful in deep hell's abodes,
And mortals hate him, as the worst of gods
Great though he be, it fits him to obey,
Since more than his my years, and more my sway."

The monarch thus. The reverend Nestor then:
"Great Agamemnon! glorious king of men!
Such are thy offers as a prince may take,
And such as fits a generous king to make.
Let chosen delegates this hour be sent
(Myself will name them) to Pelides' tent.
Let Phoenix lead, revered for hoary age,
Great Ajax next, and Ithacus the sage.
Yet more to sanctify the word you send,
Let Hodius and Eurybates attend.
Now pray to Jove to grant what Greece demands;
Pray in deep silence, and with purest hands."

He said; and all approved. The heralds bring
The cleansing water from the living spring.
The youth with wine the sacred goblets crown'd,
And large libations drench'd the sands around.
The rite perform'd, the chiefs their thirst allay,
Then from the royal tent they take their way;
Wise Nestor turns on each his careful eye,
Forbids to offend, instructs them to apply;
Much he advised them all, Ulysses most,
To deprecate the chief, and save the host.
Through the still night they march, and hear the roar
Of murmuring billows on the sounding shore.
To Neptune, ruler of the seas profound,
Whose liquid arms the mighty globe surround,
They pour forth vows, their embassy to bless,
And calm the rage of stern Ċacides.
And now, arrived, where on the sandy bay
The Myrmidonian tents and vessels lay;
Amused at ease, the godlike man they found,
Pleased with the solemn harp's harmonious sound.
(The well wrought harp from conquered Thebae came;
Of polish'd silver was its costly frame.)
With this he soothes his angry soul, and sings
The immortal deeds of heroes and of kings.
Patroclus only of the royal train,
Placed in his tent, attends the lofty strain:
Full opposite he sat, and listen'd long,
In silence waiting till he ceased the song.
Unseen the Grecian embassy proceeds

To his high tent; the great Ulysses leads.
Achilles starting, as the chiefs he spied,
Leap'd from his seat, and laid the harp aside.
With like surprise arose Menoetius' son:
Pelides grasp'd their hands, and thus begun:

"Princes, all hail! whatever brought you here.
Or strong necessity, or urgent fear;
Welcome, though Greeks! for not as foes ye came;
To me more dear than all that bear the name."

With that, the chiefs beneath his roof he led,
And placed in seats with purple carpets spread.
Then thus—"Patroclus, crown a larger bowl,
Mix purer wine, and open every soul.
Of all the warriors yonder host can send,
Thy friend most honours these, and these thy friend."

He said: Patroclus o'er the blazing fire
Heaps in a brazen vase three chines entire:
The brazen vase Automedon sustains,
Which flesh of porker, sheep, and goat contains.
Achilles at the genial feast presides,
The parts transfixes, and with skill divides.
Meanwhile Patroclus sweats, the fire to raise;
The tent is brighten'd with the rising blaze:
Then, when the languid flames at length subside,
He strows a bed of glowing embers wide,
Above the coals the smoking fragments turns
And sprinkles sacred salt from lifted urns;
With bread the glittering canisters they load,
Which round the board Menoetius' son bestow'd;
Himself, opposed to Ulysses full in sight,
Each portion parts, and orders every rite.
The first fat offering to the immortals due,
Amidst the greedy flames Patroclus threw;
Then each, indulging in the social feast,
His thirst and hunger soberly repress'd.
That done, to Phoenix Ajax gave the sign:
Not unperceived; Ulysses crown'd with wine
The foaming bowl, and instant thus began,
His speech addressing to the godlike man.

"Health to Achilles! happy are thy guests!
Not those more honour'd whom Atrides feasts:
Though generous plenty crown thy loaded boards,
That, Agamemnon's regal tent affords;
But greater cares sit heavy on our souls,

Nor eased by banquets or by flowing bowls.
What scenes of slaughter in yon fields appear!
The dead we mourn, and for the living fear;
Greece on the brink of fate all doubtful stands,
And owns no help but from thy saving hands:
Troy and her aids for ready vengeance call;
Their threatening tents already shade our wall:
Hear how with shouts their conquest they proclaim,
And point at every ship their vengeful flame!
For them the father of the gods declares,
Theirs are his omens, and his thunder theirs.
See, full of Jove, avenging Hector rise!
See! heaven and earth the raging chief defies;
What fury in his breast, what lightning in his eyes!
He waits but for the morn, to sink in flame
The ships, the Greeks, and all the Grecian name.
Heavens! how my country's woes distract my mind,
Lest Fate accomplish all his rage design'd!
And must we, gods! our heads inglorious lay
In Trojan dust, and this the fatal day?
Return, Achilles: oh return, though late,
To save thy Greeks, and stop the course of Fate;
If in that heart or grief or courage lies,
Rise to redeem; ah, yet to conquer, rise!
The day may come, when, all our warriors slain,
That heart shall melt, that courage rise in vain:
Regard in time, O prince divinely brave!
Those wholesome counsels which thy father gave.
When Peleus in his aged arms embraced
His parting son, these accents were his last:

"'My child! with strength, with glory, and success,
Thy arms may Juno and Minerva bless!
Trust that to Heaven: but thou, thy cares engage
To calm thy passions, and subdue thy rage:
From gentler manners let thy glory grow,
And shun contention, the sure source of woe;
That young and old may in thy praise combine,
The virtues of humanity be thine—'
This now-despised advice thy father gave;
Ah! check thy anger; and be truly brave.
If thou wilt yield to great Atrides' prayers,
Gifts worthy thee his royal hand prepares;
If not—but hear me, while I number o'er
The proffer'd presents, an exhaustless store.
Ten weighty talents of the purest gold,
And twice ten vases of refulgent mould;
Seven sacred tripods, whose unsullied frame

Yet knows no office, nor has felt the flame;
Twelve steeds unmatched in fleetness and in force,
And still victorious in the dusty course;
(Rich were the man, whose ample stores exceed
The prizes purchased by their winged speed;)
Seven lovely captives of the Lesbian line,
Skill'd in each art, unmatch'd in form divine,
The same he chose for more than vulgar charms,
When Lesbos sank beneath thy conquering arms.
All these, to buy thy friendship shall be paid,
And, join'd with these, the long-contested maid;
With all her charms, Briseis he'll resign,
And solemn swear those charms were only thine;
Untouch'd she stay'd, uninjured she removes,
Pure from his arms, and guiltless of his loves.
These instant shall be thine; and if the powers
Give to our arms proud Ilion's hostile towers,
Then shalt thou store (when Greece the spoil divides)
With gold and brass thy loaded navy's sides.
Besides, full twenty nymphs of Trojan race
With copious love shall crown thy warm embrace;
Such as thyself shall chose; who yield to none,
Or yield to Helen's heavenly charms alone.
Yet hear me further: when our wars are o'er,
If safe we land on Argos' fruitful shore,
There shalt thou live his son, his honour share,
And with Orestes' self divide his care.
Yet more—three daughters in his court are bred,
And each well worthy of a royal bed:
Laodice and Iphigenia fair,
And bright Chrysothemis with golden hair:
Her shalt thou wed whom most thy eyes approve;
He asks no presents, no reward for love:
Himself will give the dower; so vast a store
As never father gave a child before.
Seven ample cities shall confess thy sway,
The Enope and Pherae thee obey,
Cardamyle with ample turrets crown'd,
And sacred Pedasus, for vines renown'd:
Ćpea fair, the pastures Hira yields,
And rich Antheia with her flowery fields;
The whole extent to Pylos' sandy plain,
Along the verdant margin of the main.
There heifers graze, and labouring oxen toil;
Bold are the men, and generous is the soil.
There shalt thou reign, with power and justice crown'd,
And rule the tributary realms around.
Such are the proffers which this day we bring,

Such the repentance of a suppliant king.
But if all this, relentless, thou disdain,
If honour and if interest plead in vain,
Yet some redress to suppliant Greece afford,
And be, amongst her guardian gods, adored.
If no regard thy suffering country claim,
Hear thy own glory, and the voice of fame:
For now that chief, whose unresisted ire
Made nations tremble, and whole hosts retire,
Proud Hector, now, the unequal fight demands,
And only triumphs to deserve thy hands."

Then thus the goddess-born: "Ulysses, hear
A faithful speech, that knows nor art nor fear;
What in my secret soul is understood,
My tongue shall utter, and my deeds make good.
Let Greece then know, my purpose I retain:
Nor with new treaties vex my peace in vain.
Who dares think one thing, and another tell,
My heart detests him as the gates of hell.

"Then thus in short my fix'd resolves attend,
Which nor Atrides nor his Greeks can bend;
Long toils, long perils in their cause I bore,
But now the unfruitful glories charm no more.
Fight or not fight, a like reward we claim,
The wretch and hero find their prize the same.
Alike regretted in the dust he lies,
Who yields ignobly, or who bravely dies.
Of all my dangers, all my glorious pains,
A life of labours, lo! what fruit remains?
As the bold bird her helpless young attends,
From danger guards them, and from want defends;
In search of prey she wings the spacious air,
And with the untasted food supplies her care:
For thankless Greece such hardships have I braved,
Her wives, her infants, by my labours saved;
Long sleepless nights in heavy arms I stood,
And sweat laborious days in dust and blood.
I sack'd twelve ample cities on the main,
And twelve lay smoking on the Trojan plain:
Then at Atrides' haughty feet were laid
The wealth I gathered, and the spoils I made.
Your mighty monarch these in peace possess'd;
Some few my soldiers had, himself the rest.
Some present, too, to every prince was paid;
And every prince enjoys the gift he made:
I only must refund, of all his train;

See what pre-eminence our merits gain!
My spoil alone his greedy soul delights:
My spouse alone must bless his lustful nights:
The woman, let him (as he may) enjoy;
But what's the quarrel, then, of Greece to Troy?
What to these shores the assembled nations draws,
What calls for vengeance but a woman's cause?
Are fair endowments and a beauteous face
Beloved by none but those of Atreus' race?
The wife whom choice and passion doth approve,
Sure every wise and worthy man will love.
Nor did my fair one less distinction claim;
Slave as she was, my soul adored the dame.
Wrong'd in my love, all proffers I disdain;
Deceived for once, I trust not kings again.
Ye have my answer—what remains to do,
Your king, Ulysses, may consult with you.
What needs he the defence this arm can make?
Has he not walls no human force can shake?
Has he not fenced his guarded navy round
With piles, with ramparts, and a trench profound?
And will not these (the wonders he has done)
Repel the rage of Priam's single son?
There was a time ('twas when for Greece I fought)
When Hector's prowess no such wonders wrought;
He kept the verge of Troy, nor dared to wait
Achilles' fury at the Scaean gate;
He tried it once, and scarce was saved by fate.
But now those ancient enmities are o'er;
To-morrow we the favouring gods implore;
Then shall you see our parting vessels crown'd,
And hear with oars the Hellespont resound.
The third day hence shall Pthia greet our sails,
If mighty Neptune send propitious gales;
Pthia to her Achilles shall restore
The wealth he left for this detested shore:
Thither the spoils of this long war shall pass,
The ruddy gold, the steel, and shining brass:
My beauteous captives thither I'll convey,
And all that rests of my unravish'd prey.
One only valued gift your tyrant gave,
And that resumed—the fair Lyrnessian slave.
Then tell him: loud, that all the Greeks may hear,
And learn to scorn the wretch they basely fear;
(For arm'd in impudence, mankind he braves,
And meditates new cheats on all his slaves;
Though shameless as he is, to face these eyes
Is what he dares not: if he dares he dies;)

Tell him, all terms, all commerce I decline,
Nor share his council, nor his battle join;
For once deceiv'd, was his; but twice were mine,
No—let the stupid prince, whom Jove deprives
Of sense and justice, run where frenzy drives;
His gifts are hateful: kings of such a kind
Stand but as slaves before a noble mind,
Not though he proffer'd all himself possess'd,
And all his rapine could from others wrest:
Not all the golden tides of wealth that crown
The many-peopled Orchomenian town;
Not all proud Thebes' unrivall'd walls contain,
The world's great empress on the Egyptian plain
(That spreads her conquests o'er a thousand states,
And pours her heroes through a hundred gates,
Two hundred horsemen and two hundred cars
From each wide portal issuing to the wars);
Though bribes were heap'd on bribes, in number more
Than dust in fields, or sands along the shore;
Should all these offers for my friendship call,
'Tis he that offers, and I scorn them all.
Atrides' daughter never shall be led
(An ill-match'd consort) to Achilles' bed;
Like golden Venus though she charm'd the heart,
And vied with Pallas in the works of art;
Some greater Greek let those high nuptials grace,
I hate alliance with a tyrant's race.
If heaven restore me to my realms with life,
The reverend Peleus shall elect my wife;
Thessalian nymphs there are of form divine,
And kings that sue to mix their blood with mine.
Bless'd in kind love, my years shall glide away,
Content with just hereditary sway;
There, deaf for ever to the martial strife,
Enjoy the dear prerogative of life.
Life is not to be bought with heaps of gold.
Not all Apollo's Pythian treasures hold,
Or Troy once held, in peace and pride of sway,
Can bribe the poor possession of a day!
Lost herds and treasures we by arms regain,
And steeds unrivall'd on the dusty plain:
But from our lips the vital spirit fled,
Returns no more to wake the silent dead.
My fates long since by Thetis were disclosed,
And each alternate, life or fame, proposed;
Here, if I stay, before the Trojan town,
Short is my date, but deathless my renown:
If I return, I quit immortal praise

For years on years, and long-extended days.
Convinced, though late, I find my fond mistake,
And warn the Greeks the wiser choice to make;
To quit these shores, their native seats enjoy,
Nor hope the fall of heaven-defended Troy.
Jove's arm display'd asserts her from the skies!
Her hearts are strengthen'd, and her glories rise.
Go then to Greece, report our fix'd design;
Bid all your counsels, all your armies join,
Let all your forces, all your arts conspire,
To save the ships, the troops, the chiefs, from fire.
One stratagem has fail'd, and others will:
Ye find, Achilles is unconquer'd still.
Go then—digest my message as ye may—
But here this night let reverend Phoenix stay:
His tedious toils and hoary hairs demand
A peaceful death in Pthia's friendly land.
But whether he remain or sail with me,
His age be sacred, and his will be free."

The son of Peleus ceased: the chiefs around
In silence wrapt, in consternation drown'd,
Attend the stern reply. Then Phoenix rose;
(Down his white beard a stream of sorrow flows;)
And while the fate of suffering Greece he mourn'd,
With accent weak these tender words return'd.

"Divine Achilles! wilt thou then retire,
And leave our hosts in blood, our fleets on fire?
If wrath so dreadful fill thy ruthless mind,
How shall thy friend, thy Phoenix, stay behind?
The royal Peleus, when from Pthia's coast
He sent thee early to the Achaian host;
Thy youth as then in sage debates unskill'd,
And new to perils of the direful field:
He bade me teach thee all the ways of war,
To shine in councils, and in camps to dare.
Never, ah, never let me leave thy side!
No time shall part us, and no fate divide,
Not though the god, that breathed my life, restore
The bloom I boasted, and the port I bore,
When Greece of old beheld my youthful flames
(Delightful Greece, the land of lovely dames),
My father faithless to my mother's arms,
Old as he was, adored a stranger's charms.
I tried what youth could do (at her desire)
To win the damsel, and prevent my sire.
My sire with curses loads my hated head,

And cries, 'Ye furies! barren be his bed.'
Infernal Jove, the vengeful fiends below,
And ruthless Proserpine, confirm'd his vow.
Despair and grief distract my labouring mind!
Gods! what a crime my impious heart design'd!
I thought (but some kind god that thought suppress'd)
To plunge the poniard in my father's breast;
Then meditate my flight: my friends in vain
With prayers entreat me, and with force detain.
On fat of rams, black bulls, and brawny swine,
They daily feast, with draughts of fragrant wine;
Strong guards they placed, and watch'd nine nights entire;
The roofs and porches flamed with constant fire.
The tenth, I forced the gates, unseen of all:
And, favour'd by the night, o'erleap'd the wall,
My travels thence through spacious Greece extend;
In Phthia's court at last my labours end.
Your sire received me, as his son caress'd,
With gifts enrich'd, and with possessions bless'd.
The strong Dolopians thenceforth own'd my reign,
And all the coast that runs along the main.
By love to thee his bounties I repaid,
And early wisdom to thy soul convey'd:
Great as thou art, my lessons made thee brave:
A child I took thee, but a hero gave.
Thy infant breast a like affection show'd;
Still in my arms (an ever-pleasing load)
Or at my knee, by Phoenix wouldst thou stand;
No food was grateful but from Phoenix' hand.
I pass my watchings o'er thy helpless years,
The tender labours, the compliant cares,
The gods (I thought) reversed their hard decree,
And Phoenix felt a father's joys in thee:
Thy growing virtues justified my cares,
And promised comfort to my silver hairs.
Now be thy rage, thy fatal rage, resign'd;
A cruel heart ill suits a manly mind:
The gods (the only great, and only wise)
Are moved by offerings, vows, and sacrifice;
Offending man their high compassion wins,
And daily prayers atone for daily sins.
Prayers are Jove's daughters, of celestial race,
Lame are their feet, and wrinkled is their face;
With humble mien, and with dejected eyes,
Constant they follow, where injustice flies.
Injustice swift, erect, and unconfined,
Sweeps the wide earth, and tramples o'er mankind,
While Prayers, to heal her wrongs, move slow behind.

Who hears these daughters of almighty Jove,
For him they mediate to the throne above
When man rejects the humble suit they make,
The sire revenges for the daughters' sake;
From Jove commission'd, fierce injustice then
Descends to punish unrelenting men.
O let not headlong passion bear the sway
These reconciling goddesses obey
Due honours to the seed of Jove belong,
Due honours calm the fierce, and bend the strong.
Were these not paid thee by the terms we bring,
Were rage still harbour'd in the haughty king;
Nor Greece nor all her fortunes should engage
Thy friend to plead against so just a rage.
But since what honour asks the general sends,
And sends by those whom most thy heart commends;
The best and noblest of the Grecian train;
Permit not these to sue, and sue in vain!
Let me (my son) an ancient fact unfold,
A great example drawn from times of old;
Hear what our fathers were, and what their praise,
Who conquer'd their revenge in former days.

"Where Calydon on rocky mountains stands
Once fought the Ćtolian and Curetian bands;
To guard it those; to conquer, these advance;
And mutual deaths were dealt with mutual chance.
The silver Cynthia bade contention rise,
In vengeance of neglected sacrifice;
On OEneus fields she sent a monstrous boar,
That levell'd harvests, and whole forests tore:
This beast (when many a chief his tusks had slain)
Great Meleager stretch'd along the plain,
Then, for his spoils, a new debate arose,
The neighbour nations thence commencing foes.
Strong as they were, the bold Curetes fail'd,
While Meleager's thundering arm prevail'd:
Till rage at length inflamed his lofty breast
(For rage invades the wisest and the best).

"Cursed by Althaea, to his wrath he yields,
And in his wife's embrace forgets the fields.
(She from Marpessa sprung, divinely fair,
And matchless Idas, more than man in war:
The god of day adored the mother's charms;
Against the god the father bent his arms:
The afflicted pair, their sorrows to proclaim,
From Cleopatra changed their daughter's name,

And call'd Alcyone; a name to show
The father's grief, the mourning mother's woe.)
To her the chief retired from stern debate,
But found no peace from fierce Althaea's hate:
Althaea's hate the unhappy warrior drew,
Whose luckless hand his royal uncle slew;
She beat the ground, and call'd the powers beneath
On her own son to wreak her brother's death;
Hell heard her curses from the realms profound,
And the red fiends that walk the nightly round.
In vain Ćtolia her deliverer waits,
War shakes her walls, and thunders at her gates.
She sent ambassadors, a chosen band,
Priests of the gods, and elders of the land;
Besought the chief to save the sinking state:
Their prayers were urgent, and their proffers great:
(Full fifty acres of the richest ground,
Half pasture green, and half with vineyards crown'd:)
His suppliant father, aged OEneus, came;
His sisters follow'd; even the vengeful dame,
Althaea, sues; his friends before him fall:
He stands relentless, and rejects them all.
Meanwhile the victor's shouts ascend the skies;
The walls are scaled; the rolling flames arise;
At length his wife (a form divine) appears,
With piercing cries, and supplicating tears;
She paints the horrors of a conquer'd town,
The heroes slain, the palaces o'erthrown,
The matrons ravish'd, the whole race enslaved:
The warrior heard, he vanquish'd, and he saved.
The Ćtolians, long disdain'd, now took their turn,
And left the chief their broken faith to mourn.
Learn hence, betimes to curb pernicious ire,
Nor stay till yonder fleets ascend in fire;
Accept the presents; draw thy conquering sword;
And be amongst our guardian gods adored."

Thus he: the stern Achilles thus replied:
"My second father, and my reverend guide:
Thy friend, believe me, no such gifts demands,
And asks no honours from a mortal's hands;
Jove honours me, and favours my designs;
His pleasure guides me, and his will confines;
And here I stay (if such his high behest)
While life's warm spirit beats within my breast.
Yet hear one word, and lodge it in thy heart:
No more molest me on Atrides' part:
Is it for him these tears are taught to flow,

For him these sorrows? for my mortal foe?
A generous friendship no cold medium knows,
Burns with one love, with one resentment glows;
One should our interests and our passions be;
My friend must hate the man that injures me.
Do this, my Phoenix, 'tis a generous part;
And share my realms, my honours, and my heart.
Let these return: our voyage, or our stay,
Rest undetermined till the dawning day."

He ceased; then order'd for the sage's bed
A warmer couch with numerous carpets spread.
With that, stern Ajax his long silence broke,
And thus, impatient, to Ulysses spoke:

"Hence let us go—why waste we time in vain?
See what effect our low submissions gain!
Liked or not liked, his words we must relate,
The Greeks expect them, and our heroes wait.
Proud as he is, that iron heart retains
Its stubborn purpose, and his friends disdains.
Stern and unpitying! if a brother bleed,
On just atonement, we remit the deed;
A sire the slaughter of his son forgives;
The price of blood discharged, the murderer lives:
The haughtiest hearts at length their rage resign,
And gifts can conquer every soul but thine.
The gods that unrelenting breast have steel'd,
And cursed thee with a mind that cannot yield.
One woman-slave was ravish'd from thy arms:
Lo, seven are offer'd, and of equal charms.
Then hear, Achilles! be of better mind;
Revere thy roof, and to thy guests be kind;
And know the men of all the Grecian host,
Who honour worth, and prize thy valour most."

"O soul of battles, and thy people's guide!
(To Ajax thus the first of Greeks replied)
Well hast thou spoke; but at the tyrant's name
My rage rekindles, and my soul's on flame:
'Tis just resentment, and becomes the brave:
Disgraced, dishonour'd, like the vilest slave!
Return, then, heroes! and our answer bear,
The glorious combat is no more my care;
Not till, amidst yon sinking navy slain,
The blood of Greeks shall dye the sable main;
Not till the flames, by Hector's fury thrown,
Consume your vessels, and approach my own;

Just there, the impetuous homicide shall stand,
There cease his battle, and there feel our hand."

This said, each prince a double goblet crown'd,
And cast a large libation on the ground;
Then to their vessels, through the gloomy shades,
The chiefs return; divine Ulysses leads.
Meantime Achilles' slaves prepared a bed,
With fleeces, carpets, and soft linen spread:
There, till the sacred morn restored the day,
In slumber sweet the reverend Phoenix lay.
But in his inner tent, an ampler space,
Achilles slept; and in his warm embrace
Fair Diomede of the Lesbian race.
Last, for Patroclus was the couch prepared,
Whose nightly joys the beauteous Iphis shared;
Achilles to his friend consign'd her charms
When Scyros fell before his conquering arms.

And now the elected chiefs whom Greece had sent,
Pass'd through the hosts, and reach'd the royal tent.
Then rising all, with goblets in their hands,
The peers and leaders of the Achaian bands
Hail'd their return: Atrides first begun:

"Say what success? divine Laertes' son!
Achilles' high resolves declare to all:
"Returns the chief, or must our navy fall?"

"Great king of nations! (Ithacus replied)
Fix'd is his wrath, unconquer'd is his pride;
He slights thy friendship, thy proposals scorns,
And, thus implored, with fiercer fury burns.
To save our army, and our fleets to free,
Is not his care; but left to Greece and thee.
Your eyes shall view, when morning paints the sky,
Beneath his oars the whitening billows fly;
Us too he bids our oars and sails employ,
Nor hope the fall of heaven-protected Troy;
For Jove o'ershades her with his arm divine,
Inspires her war, and bids her glory shine.
Such was his word: what further he declared,
These sacred heralds and great Ajax heard.
But Phoenix in his tent the chief retains,
Safe to transport him to his native plains
When morning dawns; if other he decree,
His age is sacred, and his choice is free."

Ulysses ceased: the great Achaian host,
With sorrow seized, in consternation lost,
Attend the stern reply. Tydides broke
The general silence, and undaunted spoke.
"Why should we gifts to proud Achilles send,
Or strive with prayers his haughty soul to bend?
His country's woes he glories to deride,
And prayers will burst that swelling heart with pride.
Be the fierce impulse of his rage obey'd,
Our battles let him or desert or aid;
Then let him arm when Jove or he think fit:
That, to his madness, or to Heaven commit:
What for ourselves we can, is always ours;
This night, let due repast refresh our powers;
(For strength consists in spirits and in blood,
And those are owed to generous wine and food;)
But when the rosy messenger of day
Strikes the blue mountains with her golden ray,
Ranged at the ships, let all our squadrons shine
In flaming arms, a long-extended line:
In the dread front let great Atrides stand,
The first in danger, as in high command."

Shouts of acclaim the listening heroes raise,
Then each to Heaven the due libations pays;
Till sleep, descending o'er the tents, bestows
The grateful blessings of desired repose."

BOOK X

ARGUMENT

THE NIGHT-ADVENTURE OF DIOMED AND ULYSSES

Upon the refusal of Achilles to return to the army, the distress of Agamemnon is described in the most lively manner. He takes no rest that night, but passes through the camp, awaking the leaders, and contriving all possible methods for the public safety. Menelaus, Nestor, Ulysses, and Diomed are employed in raising the rest of the captains. They call a council of war, and determine to send scouts into the enemies' camp, to learn their posture, and discover their intentions. Diomed undertakes this hazardous enterprise, and makes choice of Ulysses for his companion. In their passage they surprise Dolon, whom Hector had sent on a like design to the camp of the Grecians. From him they are informed of the situation of the Trojan and auxiliary forces, and particularly of Rhesus, and the Thracians who were lately arrived. They pass on with success; kill Rhesus, with several of his officers, and seize the famous horses of that prince, with which they return in triumph to the camp.

The same night continues; the scene lies in the two camps.

All night the chiefs before their vessels lay,
And lost in sleep the labours of the day:
All but the king: with various thoughts oppress'd,
His country's cares lay rolling in his breast.
As when by lightnings Jove's ethereal power
Foretels the rattling hail, or weighty shower,
Or sends soft snows to whiten all the shore,
Or bids the brazen throat of war to roar;
By fits one flash succeeds as one expires,
And heaven flames thick with momentary fires:
So bursting frequent from Atrides' breast,
Sighs following sighs his inward fears confess'd.
Now o'er the fields, dejected, he surveys
From thousand Trojan fires the mounting blaze;
Hears in the passing wind their music blow,
And marks distinct the voices of the foe.
Now looking backwards to the fleet and coast,
Anxious he sorrows for the endangered host.
He rends his hair, in sacrifice to Jove,
And sues to him that ever lives above:
Inly he groans; while glory and despair
Divide his heart, and wage a double war.

A thousand cares his labouring breast revolves;
To seek sage Nestor now the chief resolves,
With him, in wholesome counsels, to debate
What yet remains to save the afflicted state.
He rose, and first he cast his mantle round,
Next on his feet the shining sandals bound;
A lion's yellow spoils his back conceal'd;
His warlike hand a pointed javelin held.
Meanwhile his brother, press'd with equal woes,
Alike denied the gifts of soft repose,
Laments for Greece, that in his cause before
So much had suffer'd and must suffer more.
A leopard's spotted hide his shoulders spread:
A brazen helmet glitter'd on his head:
Thus (with a javelin in his hand) he went
To wake Atrides in the royal tent.
Already waked, Atrides he descried,
His armour buckling at his vessel's side.
Joyful they met; the Spartan thus begun:
"Why puts my brother his bright armour on?
Sends he some spy, amidst these silent hours,
To try yon camp, and watch the Trojan powers?
But say, what hero shall sustain that task?

Such bold exploits uncommon courage ask;
Guideless, alone, through night's dark shade to go,
And midst a hostile camp explore the foe."

To whom the king: "In such distress we stand,
No vulgar counsel our affairs demand;
Greece to preserve, is now no easy part,
But asks high wisdom, deep design, and art.
For Jove, averse, our humble prayer denies,
And bows his head to Hector's sacrifice.
What eye has witness'd, or what ear believed,
In one great day, by one great arm achieved,
Such wondrous deeds as Hector's hand has done,
And we beheld, the last revolving sun
What honours the beloved of Jove adorn!
Sprung from no god, and of no goddess born;
Yet such his acts, as Greeks unborn shall tell,
And curse the battle where their fathers fell.

"Now speed thy hasty course along the fleet,
There call great Ajax, and the prince of Crete;
Ourself to hoary Nestor will repair;
To keep the guards on duty be his care,
(For Nestor's influence best that quarter guides,
Whose son with Merion, o'er the watch presides.")
To whom the Spartan: "These thy orders borne,
Say, shall I stay, or with despatch return?"
"There shalt thou stay, (the king of men replied,)
Else may we miss to meet, without a guide,
The paths so many, and the camp so wide.
Still, with your voice the slothful soldiers raise,
Urge by their fathers' fame their future praise.
Forget we now our state and lofty birth;
Not titles here, but works, must prove our worth.
To labour is the lot of man below;
And when Jove gave us life, he gave us woe."

This said, each parted to his several cares:
The king to Nestor's sable ship repairs;
The sage protector of the Greeks he found
Stretch'd in his bed with all his arms around
The various-colour'd scarf, the shield he rears,
The shining helmet, and the pointed spears;
The dreadful weapons of the warrior's rage,
That, old in arms, disdain'd the peace of age.
Then, leaning on his hand his watchful head,
The hoary monarch raised his eyes and said:

"What art thou, speak, that on designs unknown,
While others sleep, thus range the camp alone;
Seek'st thou some friend or nightly sentinel?
Stand off, approach not, but thy purpose tell."

"O son of Neleus, (thus the king rejoin'd,)
Pride of the Greeks, and glory of thy kind!
Lo, here the wretched Agamemnon stands,
The unhappy general of the Grecian bands,
Whom Jove decrees with daily cares to bend,
And woes, that only with his life shall end!
Scarce can my knees these trembling limbs sustain,
And scarce my heart support its load of pain.
No taste of sleep these heavy eyes have known,
Confused, and sad, I wander thus alone,
With fears distracted, with no fix'd design;
And all my people's miseries are mine.
If aught of use thy waking thoughts suggest,
(Since cares, like mine, deprive thy soul of rest,)
Impart thy counsel, and assist thy friend;
Now let us jointly to the trench descend,
At every gate the fainting guard excite,
Tired with the toils of day and watch of night;
Else may the sudden foe our works invade,
So near, and favour'd by the gloomy shade."

To him thus Nestor: "Trust the powers above,
Nor think proud Hector's hopes confirm'd by Jove:
How ill agree the views of vain mankind,
And the wise counsels of the eternal mind!
Audacious Hector, if the gods ordain
That great Achilles rise and rage again,
What toils attend thee, and what woes remain!
Lo, faithful Nestor thy command obeys;
The care is next our other chiefs to raise:
Ulysses, Diomed, we chiefly need;
Meges for strength, Oileus famed for speed.
Some other be despatch'd of nimbler feet,
To those tall ships, remotest of the fleet,
Where lie great Ajax and the king of Crete.
To rouse the Spartan I myself decree;
Dear as he is to us, and dear to thee,
Yet must I tax his sloth, that claims no share
With his great brother in his martial care:
Him it behoved to every chief to sue,
Preventing every part perform'd by you;
For strong necessity our toils demands,
Claims all our hearts, and urges all our hands."

To whom the king: "With reverence we allow
Thy just rebukes, yet learn to spare them now:
My generous brother is of gentle kind,
He seems remiss, but bears a valiant mind;
Through too much deference to our sovereign sway,
Content to follow when we lead the way:
But now, our ills industrious to prevent,
Long ere the rest he rose, and sought my tent.
The chiefs you named, already at his call,
Prepare to meet us near the navy-wall;
Assembling there, between the trench and gates,
Near the night-guards, our chosen council waits."

"Then none (said Nestor) shall his rule withstand,
For great examples justify command."
With that, the venerable warrior rose;
The shining greaves his manly legs enclose;
His purple mantle golden buckles join'd,
Warm with the softest wool, and doubly lined.
Then rushing from his tent, he snatch'd in haste
His steely lance, that lighten'd as he pass'd.
The camp he traversed through the sleeping crowd,
Stopp'd at Ulysses' tent, and call'd aloud.
Ulysses, sudden as the voice was sent,
Awakes, starts up, and issues from his tent.
"What new distress, what sudden cause of fright,
Thus leads you wandering in the silent night?"
"O prudent chief! (the Pylian sage replied)
Wise as thou art, be now thy wisdom tried:
Whatever means of safety can be sought,
Whatever counsels can inspire our thought,
Whatever methods, or to fly or fight;
All, all depend on this important night!"
He heard, return'd, and took his painted shield;
Then join'd the chiefs, and follow'd through the field.
Without his tent, bold Diomed they found,
All sheathed in arms, his brave companions round:
Each sunk in sleep, extended on the field,
His head reclining on his bossy shield.
A wood of spears stood by, that, fix'd upright,
Shot from their flashing points a quivering light.
A bull's black hide composed the hero's bed;
A splendid carpet roll'd beneath his head.
Then, with his foot, old Nestor gently shakes
The slumbering chief, and in these words awakes:

"Rise, son of Tydeus! to the brave and strong

Rest seems inglorious, and the night too long.
But sleep'st thou now, when from yon hill the foe
Hangs o'er the fleet, and shades our walls below?"

At this, soft slumber from his eyelids fled;
The warrior saw the hoary chief, and said:
"Wondrous old man! whose soul no respite knows,
Though years and honours bid thee seek repose,
Let younger Greeks our sleeping warriors wake;
Ill fits thy age these toils to undertake."
"My friend, (he answered,) generous is thy care;
These toils, my subjects and my sons might bear;
Their loyal thoughts and pious love conspire
To ease a sovereign and relieve a sire:
But now the last despair surrounds our host;
No hour must pass, no moment must be lost;
Each single Greek, in this conclusive strife,
Stands on the sharpest edge of death or life:
Yet, if my years thy kind regard engage,
Employ thy youth as I employ my age;
Succeed to these my cares, and rouse the rest;
He serves me most, who serves his country best."

This said, the hero o'er his shoulders flung
A lion's spoils, that to his ankles hung;
Then seized his ponderous lance, and strode along.
Meges the bold, with Ajax famed for speed,
The warrior roused, and to the entrenchments lead.

And now the chiefs approach the nightly guard;
A wakeful squadron, each in arms prepared:
The unwearied watch their listening leaders keep,
And, couching close, repel invading sleep.
So faithful dogs their fleecy charge maintain,
With toil protected from the prowling train;
When the gaunt lioness, with hunger bold,
Springs from the mountains toward the guarded fold:
Through breaking woods her rustling course they hear;
Loud, and more loud, the clamours strike their ear
Of hounds and men: they start, they gaze around,
Watch every side, and turn to every sound.
Thus watch'd the Grecians, cautious of surprise,
Each voice, each motion, drew their ears and eyes:
Each step of passing feet increased the affright;
And hostile Troy was ever full in sight.
Nestor with joy the wakeful band survey'd,
And thus accosted through the gloomy shade.
"'Tis well, my sons! your nightly cares employ;

Else must our host become the scorn of Troy.
Watch thus, and Greece shall live." The hero said;
Then o'er the trench the following chieftains led.
His son, and godlike Merion, march'd behind
(For these the princes to their council join'd).
The trenches pass'd, the assembled kings around
In silent state the consistory crown'd.
A place there was, yet undefiled with gore,
The spot where Hector stopp'd his rage before;
When night descending, from his vengeful hand
Reprieved the relics of the Grecian band:
(The plain beside with mangled corps was spread,
And all his progress mark'd by heaps of dead:)
There sat the mournful kings: when Neleus' son,
The council opening, in these words begun:

"Is there (said he) a chief so greatly brave,
His life to hazard, and his country save?
Lives there a man, who singly dares to go
To yonder camp, or seize some straggling foe?
Or favour'd by the night approach so near,
Their speech, their counsels, and designs to hear?
If to besiege our navies they prepare,
Or Troy once more must be the seat of war?
This could he learn, and to our peers recite,
And pass unharm'd the dangers of the night;
What fame were his through all succeeding days,
While Phoebus shines, or men have tongues to praise!
What gifts his grateful country would bestow!
What must not Greece to her deliverer owe?
A sable ewe each leader should provide,
With each a sable lambkin by her side;
At every rite his share should be increased,
And his the foremost honours of the feast."

Fear held them mute: alone, untaught to fear,
Tydides spoke—"The man you seek is here.
Through yon black camps to bend my dangerous way,
Some god within commands, and I obey.
But let some other chosen warrior join,
To raise my hopes, and second my design.
By mutual confidence and mutual aid,
Great deeds are done, and great discoveries made;
The wise new prudence from the wise acquire,
And one brave hero fans another's fire."

Contending leaders at the word arose;
Each generous breast with emulation glows;

So brave a task each Ajax strove to share,
Bold Merion strove, and Nestor's valiant heir;
The Spartan wish'd the second place to gain,
And great Ulysses wish'd, nor wish'd in vain.
Then thus the king of men the contest ends:
"Thou first of warriors, and thou best of friends,
Undaunted Diomed! what chief to join
In this great enterprise, is only thine.
Just be thy choice, without affection made;
To birth, or office, no respect be paid;
Let worth determine here." The monarch spake,
And inly trembled for his brother's sake.

"Then thus (the godlike Diomed rejoin'd)
My choice declares the impulse of my mind.
How can I doubt, while great Ulysses stands
To lend his counsels and assist our hands?
A chief, whose safety is Minerva's care;
So famed, so dreadful, in the works of war:
Bless'd in his conduct, I no aid require;
Wisdom like his might pass through flames of fire."

"It fits thee not, before these chiefs of fame,
(Replied the sage,) to praise me, or to blame:
Praise from a friend, or censure from a foe,
Are lost on hearers that our merits know.
But let us haste—Night rolls the hours away,
The reddening orient shows the coming day,
The stars shine fainter on the ethereal plains,
And of night's empire but a third remains."

Thus having spoke, with generous ardour press'd,
In arms terrific their huge limbs they dress'd.
A two-edged falchion Thrasymed the brave,
And ample buckler, to Tydides gave:
Then in a leathern helm he cased his head,
Short of its crest, and with no plume o'erspread:
(Such as by youths unused to arms are worn:)
No spoils enrich it, and no studs adorn.
Next him Ulysses took a shining sword,
A bow and quiver, with bright arrows stored:
A well-proved casque, with leather braces bound,
(Thy gift, Meriones,) his temples crown'd;
Soft wool within; without, in order spread,
A boar's white teeth grinn'd horrid o'er his head.
This from Amyntor, rich Ormenus' son,
Autolycus by fraudful rapine won,
And gave Amphidamas; from him the prize

Molus received, the pledge of social ties;
The helmet next by Merion was possess'd,
And now Ulysses' thoughtful temples press'd.
Thus sheathed in arms, the council they forsake,
And dark through paths oblique their progress take.
Just then, in sign she favour'd their intent,
A long-wing'd heron great Minerva sent:
This, though surrounding shades obscured their view.
By the shrill clang and whistling wings they knew.
As from the right she soar'd, Ulysses pray'd,
Hail'd the glad omen, and address'd the maid:

"O daughter of that god whose arm can wield
The avenging bolt, and shake the dreadful shield!
O thou! for ever present in my way,
Who all my motions, all my toils survey!
Safe may we pass beneath the gloomy shade,
Safe by thy succour to our ships convey'd,
And let some deed this signal night adorn,
To claim the tears of Trojans yet unborn."

Then godlike Diomed preferr'd his prayer:
"Daughter of Jove, unconquer'd Pallas! hear.
Great queen of arms, whose favour Tydeus won,
As thou defend'st the sire, defend the son.
When on Ćsopus' banks the banded powers
Of Greece he left, and sought the Theban towers,
Peace was his charge; received with peaceful show,
He went a legate, but return'd a foe:
Then help'd by thee, and cover'd by thy shield,
He fought with numbers, and made numbers yield.
So now be present, O celestial maid!
So still continue to the race thine aid!
A youthful steer shall fall beneath the stroke,
Untamed, unconscious of the galling yoke,
With ample forehead, and with spreading horns,
Whose taper tops refulgent gold adorns."
The heroes pray'd, and Pallas from the skies
Accords their vow, succeeds their enterprise.
Now, like two lions panting for the prey,
With dreadful thoughts they trace the dreary way,
Through the black horrors of the ensanguined plain,
Through dust, through blood, o'er arms, and hills of slain.

Nor less bold Hector, and the sons of Troy,
On high designs the wakeful hours employ;
The assembled peers their lofty chief enclosed;
Who thus the counsels of his breast proposed:

"What glorious man, for high attempts prepared,
Dares greatly venture for a rich reward?
Of yonder fleet a bold discovery make,
What watch they keep, and what resolves they take?
If now subdued they meditate their flight,
And, spent with toil, neglect the watch of night?
His be the chariot that shall please him most,
Of all the plunder of the vanquish'd host;
His the fair steeds that all the rest excel,
And his the glory to have served so well."

A youth there was among the tribes of Troy,
Dolon his name, Eumedes' only boy,
(Five girls beside the reverend herald told.)
Rich was the son in brass, and rich in gold;
Not bless'd by nature with the charms of face,
But swift of foot, and matchless in the race.
"Hector! (he said) my courage bids me meet
This high achievement, and explore the fleet:
But first exalt thy sceptre to the skies,
And swear to grant me the demanded prize;
The immortal coursers, and the glittering car,
That bear Pelides through the ranks of war.
Encouraged thus, no idle scout I go,
Fulfil thy wish, their whole intention know,
Even to the royal tent pursue my way,
And all their counsels, all their aims betray."

The chief then heaved the golden sceptre high,
Attesting thus the monarch of the sky:
"Be witness thou! immortal lord of all!
Whose thunder shakes the dark aerial hall:
By none but Dolon shall this prize be borne,
And him alone the immortal steeds adorn."

Thus Hector swore: the gods were call'd in vain,
But the rash youth prepares to scour the plain:
Across his back the bended bow he flung,
A wolf's grey hide around his shoulders hung,
A ferret's downy fur his helmet lined,
And in his hand a pointed javelin shined.
Then (never to return) he sought the shore,
And trod the path his feet must tread no more.
Scarce had he pass'd the steeds and Trojan throng,
(Still bending forward as he coursed along,)
When, on the hollow way, the approaching tread
Ulysses mark'd, and thus to Diomed;

"O friend! I hear some step of hostile feet,
Moving this way, or hastening to the fleet;
Some spy, perhaps, to lurk beside the main;
Or nightly pillager that strips the slain.
Yet let him pass, and win a little space;
Then rush behind him, and prevent his pace.
But if too swift of foot he flies before,
Confine his course along the fleet and shore,
Betwixt the camp and him our spears employ,
And intercept his hoped return to Troy."

With that they stepp'd aside, and stoop'd their head,
(As Dolon pass'd,) behind a heap of dead:
Along the path the spy unwary flew;
Soft, at just distance, both the chiefs pursue.
So distant they, and such the space between,
As when two teams of mules divide the green,
(To whom the hind like shares of land allows,)
When now new furrows part the approaching ploughs.
Now Dolon, listening, heard them as they pass'd;
Hector (he thought) had sent, and check'd his haste,
Till scarce at distance of a javelin's throw,
No voice succeeding, he perceived the foe.
As when two skilful hounds the leveret wind;
Or chase through woods obscure the trembling hind;
Now lost, now seen, they intercept his way,
And from the herd still turn the flying prey:
So fast, and with such fears, the Trojan flew;
So close, so constant, the bold Greeks pursue.
Now almost on the fleet the dastard falls,
And mingles with the guards that watch the walls;
When brave Tydides stopp'd; a gen'rous thought
(Inspired by Pallas) in his bosom wrought,
Lest on the foe some forward Greek advance,
And snatch the glory from his lifted lance.
Then thus aloud: "Whoe'er thou art, remain;
This javelin else shall fix thee to the plain."
He said, and high in air the weapon cast,
Which wilful err'd, and o'er his shoulder pass'd;
Then fix'd in earth. Against the trembling wood
The wretch stood propp'd, and quiver'd as he stood;
A sudden palsy seized his turning head;
His loose teeth chatter'd, and his colour fled;
The panting warriors seize him as he stands,
And with unmanly tears his life demands.

"O spare my youth, and for the breath I owe,

Large gifts of price my father shall bestow:
Vast heaps of brass shall in your ships be told,
And steel well-temper'd and refulgent gold."

To whom Ulysses made this wise reply:
"Whoe'er thou art, be bold, nor fear to die.
What moves thee, say, when sleep has closed the sight,
To roam the silent fields in dead of night?
Cam'st thou the secrets of our camp to find,
By Hector prompted, or thy daring mind?
Or art some wretch by hopes of plunder led,
Through heaps of carnage, to despoil the dead?"

Then thus pale Dolon, with a fearful look:
(Still, as he spoke, his limbs with horror shook:)
"Hither I came, by Hector's words deceived;
Much did he promise, rashly I believed:
No less a bribe than great Achilles' car,
And those swift steeds that sweep the ranks of war,
Urged me, unwilling, this attempt to make;
To learn what counsels, what resolves you take:
If now subdued, you fix your hopes on flight,
And, tired with toils, neglect the watch of night."

"Bold was thy aim, and glorious was the prize,
(Ulysses, with a scornful smile, replies,)
Far other rulers those proud steeds demand,
And scorn the guidance of a vulgar hand;
Even great Achilles scarce their rage can tame,
Achilles sprung from an immortal dame.
But say, be faithful, and the truth recite!
Where lies encamp'd the Trojan chief to-night?
Where stand his coursers? in what quarter sleep
Their other princes? tell what watch they keep:
Say, since this conquest, what their counsels are;
Or here to combat, from their city far,
Or back to Ilion's walls transfer the war?"

Ulysses thus, and thus Eumedes' son:
"What Dolon knows, his faithful tongue shall own.
Hector, the peers assembling in his tent,
A council holds at Ilus' monument.
No certain guards the nightly watch partake;
Where'er yon fires ascend, the Trojans wake:
Anxious for Troy, the guard the natives keep;
Safe in their cares, the auxiliar forces sleep,
Whose wives and infants, from the danger far,
Discharge their souls of half the fears of war."

"Then sleep those aids among the Trojan train,
(Inquired the chief,) or scattered o'er the plain?"
To whom the spy: "Their powers they thus dispose
The Paeons, dreadful with their bended bows,
The Carians, Caucons, the Pelasgian host,
And Leleges, encamp along the coast.
Not distant far, lie higher on the land
The Lycian, Mysian, and Maeonian band,
And Phrygia's horse, by Thymbras' ancient wall;
The Thracians utmost, and apart from all.
These Troy but lately to her succour won,
Led on by Rhesus, great Eioneus' son:
I saw his coursers in proud triumph go,
Swift as the wind, and white as winter-snow;
Rich silver plates his shining car infold;
His solid arms, refulgent, flame with gold;
No mortal shoulders suit the glorious load,
Celestial panoply, to grace a god!
Let me, unhappy, to your fleet be borne,
Or leave me here, a captive's fate to mourn,
In cruel chains, till your return reveal
The truth or falsehood of the news I tell."

To this Tydides, with a gloomy frown:
"Think not to live, though all the truth be shown:
Shall we dismiss thee, in some future strife
To risk more bravely thy now forfeit life?
Or that again our camps thou may'st explore?
No—once a traitor, thou betray'st no more."

Sternly he spoke, and as the wretch prepared
With humble blandishment to stroke his beard,
Like lightning swift the wrathful falchion flew,
Divides the neck, and cuts the nerves in two;
One instant snatch'd his trembling soul to hell,
The head, yet speaking, mutter'd as it fell.
The furry helmet from his brow they tear,
The wolf's grey hide, the unbended bow and spear;
These great Ulysses lifting to the skies,
To favouring Pallas dedicates the prize:

"Great queen of arms, receive this hostile spoil,
And let the Thracian steeds reward our toil;
Thee, first of all the heavenly host, we praise;
O speed our labours, and direct our ways!"
This said, the spoils, with dropping gore defaced,
High on a spreading tamarisk he placed;

Then heap'd with reeds and gathered boughs the plain,
To guide their footsteps to the place again.

Through the still night they cross the devious fields,
Slippery with blood, o'er arms and heaps of shields,
Arriving where the Thracian squadrons lay,
And eased in sleep the labours of the day.
Ranged in three lines they view the prostrate band:
The horses yoked beside each warrior stand.
Their arms in order on the ground reclined,
Through the brown shade the fulgid weapons shined:
Amidst lay Rhesus, stretch'd in sleep profound,
And the white steeds behind his chariot bound.
The welcome sight Ulysses first descries,
And points to Diomed the tempting prize.
"The man, the coursers, and the car behold!
Described by Dolon, with the arms of gold.
Now, brave Tydides! now thy courage try,
Approach the chariot, and the steeds untie;
Or if thy soul aspire to fiercer deeds,
Urge thou the slaughter, while I seize the steeds."

Pallas (this said) her hero's bosom warms,
Breathed in his heart, and strung his nervous arms;
Where'er he pass'd, a purple stream pursued
His thirsty falchion, fat with hostile blood,
Bathed all his footsteps, dyed the fields with gore,
And a low groan remurmur'd through the shore.
So the grim lion, from his nightly den,
O'erleaps the fences, and invades the pen,
On sheep or goats, resistless in his way,
He falls, and foaming rends the guardless prey;
Nor stopp'd the fury of his vengeful hand,
Till twelve lay breathless of the Thracian band.
Ulysses following, as his partner slew,
Back by the foot each slaughter'd warrior drew;
The milk-white coursers studious to convey
Safe to the ships, he wisely cleared the way:
Lest the fierce steeds, not yet to battles bred,
Should start, and tremble at the heaps of dead.
Now twelve despatch'd, the monarch last they found;
Tydides' falchion fix'd him to the ground.
Just then a deathful dream Minerva sent,
A warlike form appear'd before his tent,
Whose visionary steel his bosom tore:
So dream'd the monarch, and awaked no more.

Ulysses now the snowy steeds detains,

And leads them, fasten'd by the silver reins;
These, with his bow unbent, he lash'd along;
(The scourge forgot, on Rhesus' chariot hung;)
Then gave his friend the signal to retire;
But him, new dangers, new achievements fire;
Doubtful he stood, or with his reeking blade
To send more heroes to the infernal shade,
Drag off the car where Rhesus' armour lay,
Or heave with manly force, and lift away.
While unresolved the son of Tydeus stands,
Pallas appears, and thus her chief commands:

"Enough, my son; from further slaughter cease,
Regard thy safety, and depart in peace;
Haste to the ships, the gotten spoils enjoy,
Nor tempt too far the hostile gods of Troy."

The voice divine confess'd the martial maid;
In haste he mounted, and her word obey'd;
The coursers fly before Ulysses' bow,
Swift as the wind, and white as winter-snow.

Not unobserved they pass'd: the god of light
Had watch'd his Troy, and mark'd Minerva's flight,
Saw Tydeus' son with heavenly succour bless'd,
And vengeful anger fill'd his sacred breast.
Swift to the Trojan camp descends the power,
And wakes Hippocoon in the morning-hour;
(On Rhesus' side accustom'd to attend,
A faithful kinsman, and instructive friend;)
He rose, and saw the field deform'd with blood,
An empty space where late the coursers stood,
The yet-warm Thracians panting on the coast;
For each he wept, but for his Rhesus most:
Now while on Rhesus' name he calls in vain,
The gathering tumult spreads o'er all the plain;
On heaps the Trojans rush, with wild affright,
And wondering view the slaughters of the night.

Meanwhile the chiefs, arriving at the shade
Where late the spoils of Hector's spy were laid,
Ulysses stopp'd; to him Tydides bore
The trophy, dropping yet with Dolon's gore:
Then mounts again; again their nimbler feet
The coursers ply, and thunder towards the fleet.

Old Nestor first perceived the approaching sound,
Bespeaking thus the Grecian peers around:

"Methinks the noise of trampling steeds I hear,
Thickening this way, and gathering on my ear;
Perhaps some horses of the Trojan breed
(So may, ye gods! my pious hopes succeed)
The great Tydides and Ulysses bear,
Return'd triumphant with this prize of war.
Yet much I fear (ah, may that fear be vain!)
The chiefs outnumber'd by the Trojan train;
Perhaps, even now pursued, they seek the shore;
Or, oh! perhaps those heroes are no more."

Scarce had he spoke, when, lo! the chiefs appear,
And spring to earth; the Greeks dismiss their fear:
With words of friendship and extended hands
They greet the kings; and Nestor first demands:

"Say thou, whose praises all our host proclaim,
Thou living glory of the Grecian name!
Say whence these coursers? by what chance bestow'd,
The spoil of foes, or present of a god?
Not those fair steeds, so radiant and so gay,
That draw the burning chariot of the day.
Old as I am, to age I scorn to yield,
And daily mingle in the martial field;
But sure till now no coursers struck my sight
Like these, conspicuous through the ranks of fight.
Some god, I deem, conferred the glorious prize,
Bless'd as ye are, and favourites of the skies;
The care of him who bids the thunder roar,
And her, whose fury bathes the world with gore."

"Father! not so, (sage Ithacus rejoin'd,)
The gifts of heaven are of a nobler kind.
Of Thracian lineage are the steeds ye view,
Whose hostile king the brave Tydides slew;
Sleeping he died, with all his guards around,
And twelve beside lay gasping on the ground.
These other spoils from conquer'd Dolon came,
A wretch, whose swiftness was his only fame;
By Hector sent our forces to explore,
He now lies headless on the sandy shore."

Then o'er the trench the bounding coursers flew;
The joyful Greeks with loud acclaim pursue.
Straight to Tydides' high pavilion borne,
The matchless steeds his ample stalls adorn:
The neighing coursers their new fellows greet,
And the full racks are heap'd with generous wheat.

But Dolon's armour, to his ships convey'd,
High on the painted stern Ulysses laid,
A trophy destin'd to the blue-eyed maid.

Now from nocturnal sweat and sanguine stain
They cleanse their bodies in the neighb'ring main:
Then in the polished bath, refresh'd from toil,
Their joints they supple with dissolving oil,
In due repast indulge the genial hour,
And first to Pallas the libations pour:
They sit, rejoicing in her aid divine,
And the crown'd goblet foams with floods of wine.

BOOK XI

ARGUMENT

THE THIRD BATTLE, AND THE ACTS OF AGAMEMNON

Agamemnon, having armed himself, leads the Grecians to battle; Hector prepares the Trojans to receive them, while Jupiter, Juno, and Minerva give the signals of war. Agamemnon bears all before him and Hector is commanded by Jupiter (who sends Iris for that purpose) to decline the engagement, till the king shall be wounded and retire from the field. He then makes a great slaughter of the enemy. Ulysses and Diomed put a stop to him for a time but the latter, being wounded by Paris, is obliged to desert his companion, who is encompassed by the Trojans, wounded, and in the utmost danger, till Menelaus and Ajax rescue him. Hector comes against Ajax, but that hero alone opposes multitudes, and rallies the Greeks. In the meantime Machaon, in the other wing of the army, is pierced with an arrow by Paris, and carried from the fight in Nestor's chariot. Achilles (who overlooked the action from his ship) sent Patroclus to inquire which of the Greeks was wounded in that manner; Nestor entertains him in his tent with an account of the accidents of the day, and a long recital of some former wars which he remembered, tending to put Patroclus upon persuading Achilles to fight for his countrymen, or at least to permit him to do it, clad in Achilles' armour. Patroclus, on his return, meets Eurypylus also wounded, and assists him in that distress.

This book opens with the eight and-twentieth day of the poem, and the same day, with its various actions and adventures is extended through the twelfth, thirteenth, fourteenth, fifteenth, sixteenth, seventeenth, and part of the eighteenth books. The scene lies in the field near the monument of Ilus.

The saffron morn, with early blushes spread,
Now rose refulgent from Tithonus' bed;
With new-born day to gladden mortal sight,
And gild the courts of heaven with sacred light:
When baleful Eris, sent by Jove's command,
The torch of discord blazing in her hand,
Through the red skies her bloody sign extends,

And, wrapt in tempests, o'er the fleet descends.
High on Ulysses' bark her horrid stand
She took, and thunder'd through the seas and land.

Even Ajax and Achilles heard the sound,
Whose ships, remote, the guarded navy bound,
Thence the black fury through the Grecian throng
With horror sounds the loud Orthian song:
The navy shakes, and at the dire alarms
Each bosom boils, each warrior starts to arms.
No more they sigh, inglorious to return,
But breathe revenge, and for the combat burn.

The king of men his hardy host inspires
With loud command, with great example fires!
Himself first rose, himself before the rest
His mighty limbs in radiant armour dress'd,
And first he cased his manly legs around
In shining greaves with silver buckles bound;
The beaming cuirass next adorn'd his breast,
The same which once king Cinyras possess'd:
(The fame of Greece and her assembled host
Had reach'd that monarch on the Cyprian coast;
'Twas then, the friendship of the chief to gain,
This glorious gift he sent, nor sent in vain:)
Ten rows of azure steel the work infold,
Twice ten of tin, and twelve of ductile gold;
Three glittering dragons to the gorget rise,
Whose imitated scales against the skies
Reflected various light, and arching bow'd,
Like colour'd rainbows o'er a showery cloud
(Jove's wondrous bow, of three celestial dies,
Placed as a sign to man amidst the skies).
A radiant baldric, o'er his shoulder tied,
Sustain'd the sword that glitter'd at his side:
Gold was the hilt, a silver sheath encased
The shining blade, and golden hangers graced.
His buckler's mighty orb was next display'd,
That round the warrior cast a dreadful shade;
Ten zones of brass its ample brim surround,
And twice ten bosses the bright convex crown'd:
Tremendous Gorgon frown'd upon its field,
And circling terrors fill'd the expressive shield:
Within its concave hung a silver thong,
On which a mimic serpent creeps along,
His azure length in easy waves extends,
Till in three heads the embroider'd monster ends.
Last o'er his brows his fourfold helm he placed,

With nodding horse-hair formidably graced;
And in his hands two steely javelins wields,
That blaze to heaven, and lighten all the fields.

That instant Juno, and the martial maid,
In happy thunders promised Greece their aid;
High o'er the chief they clash'd their arms in air,
And, leaning from the clouds, expect the war.

Close to the limits of the trench and mound,
The fiery coursers to their chariots bound
The squires restrain'd: the foot, with those who wield
The lighter arms, rush forward to the field.
To second these, in close array combined,
The squadrons spread their sable wings behind.
Now shouts and tumults wake the tardy sun,
As with the light the warriors' toils begun.
Even Jove, whose thunder spoke his wrath, distill'd
Red drops of blood o'er all the fatal field;
The woes of men unwilling to survey,
And all the slaughters that must stain the day.

Near Ilus' tomb, in order ranged around,
The Trojan lines possess'd the rising ground:
There wise Polydamas and Hector stood;
Æneas, honour'd as a guardian god;
Bold Polybus, Agenor the divine;
The brother-warriors of Antenor's line:
With youthful Acamas, whose beauteous face
And fair proportion match'd the ethereal race.
Great Hector, cover'd with his spacious shield,
Plies all the troops, and orders all the field.
As the red star now shows his sanguine fires
Through the dark clouds, and now in night retires,
Thus through the ranks appear'd the godlike man,
Plunged in the rear, or blazing in the van;
While streamy sparkles, restless as he flies,
Flash from his arms, as lightning from the skies.
As sweating reapers in some wealthy field,
Ranged in two bands, their crooked weapons wield,
Bear down the furrows, till their labours meet;
Thick fall the heapy harvests at their feet:
So Greece and Troy the field of war divide,
And falling ranks are strow'd on every side.
None stoop'd a thought to base inglorious flight;
But horse to horse, and man to man they fight,
Not rabid wolves more fierce contest their prey;
Each wounds, each bleeds, but none resign the day.

Discord with joy the scene of death descries,
And drinks large slaughter at her sanguine eyes:
Discord alone, of all the immortal train,
Swells the red horrors of this direful plain:
The gods in peace their golden mansions fill,
Ranged in bright order on the Olympian hill:
But general murmurs told their griefs above,
And each accused the partial will of Jove.
Meanwhile apart, superior, and alone,
The eternal Monarch, on his awful throne,
Wrapt in the blaze of boundless glory sate;
And fix'd, fulfill'd the just decrees of fate.
On earth he turn'd his all-considering eyes,
And mark'd the spot where Ilion's towers arise;
The sea with ships, the fields with armies spread,
The victor's rage, the dying, and the dead.

Thus while the morning-beams, increasing bright,
O'er heaven's pure azure spread the glowing light,
Commutual death the fate of war confounds,
Each adverse battle gored with equal wounds.
But now (what time in some sequester'd vale
The weary woodman spreads his sparing meal,
When his tired arms refuse the axe to rear,
And claim a respite from the sylvan war;
But not till half the prostrate forests lay
Stretch'd in long ruin, and exposed to day)
Then, nor till then, the Greeks' impulsive might
Pierced the black phalanx, and let in the light.
Great Agamemnon then the slaughter led,
And slew Bienor at his people's head:
Whose squire Oileus, with a sudden spring,
Leap'd from the chariot to revenge his king;
But in his front he felt the fatal wound,
Which pierced his brain, and stretch'd him on the ground.
Atrides spoil'd, and left them on the plain:
Vain was their youth, their glittering armour vain:
Now soil'd with dust, and naked to the sky,
Their snowy limbs and beauteous bodies lie.

Two sons of Priam next to battle move,
The product, one of marriage, one of love:
In the same car the brother-warriors ride;
This took the charge to combat, that to guide:
Far other task, than when they wont to keep,
On Ida's tops, their father's fleecy sheep.
These on the mountains once Achilles found,
And captive led, with pliant osiers bound;

Then to their sire for ample sums restored;
But now to perish by Atrides' sword:
Pierced in the breast the base-born Isus bleeds:
Cleft through the head his brother's fate succeeds,
Swift to the spoil the hasty victor falls,
And, stript, their features to his mind recalls.
The Trojans see the youths untimely die,
But helpless tremble for themselves, and fly.
So when a lion ranging o'er the lawns.
Finds, on some grassy lair, the couching fawns,
Their bones he cracks, their reeking vitals draws,
And grinds the quivering flesh with bloody jaws;
The frighted hind beholds, and dares not stay,
But swift through rustling thickets bursts her way;
All drown'd in sweat, the panting mother flies,
And the big tears roll trickling from her eyes.

Amidst the tumult of the routed train,
The sons of false Antimachus were slain;
He who for bribes his faithless counsels sold,
And voted Helen's stay for Paris' gold.
Atrides mark'd, as these their safety sought,
And slew the children for the father's fault;
Their headstrong horse unable to restrain,
They shook with fear, and dropp'd the silken rein;
Then in the chariot on their knees they fall,
And thus with lifted hands for mercy call:

"O spare our youth, and for the life we owe,
Antimachus shall copious gifts bestow:
Soon as he hears, that, not in battle slain,
The Grecian ships his captive sons detain,
Large heaps of brass in ransom shall be told,
And steel well-tempered, and persuasive gold."

These words, attended with the flood of tears,
The youths address'd to unrelenting ears:
The vengeful monarch gave this stern reply:
"If from Antimachus ye spring, ye die;
The daring wretch who once in council stood
To shed Ulysses' and my brother's blood,
For proffer'd peace! and sues his seed for grace?
No, die, and pay the forfeit of your race."

This said, Pisander from the car he cast,
And pierced his breast: supine he breathed his last.
His brother leap'd to earth; but, as he lay,
The trenchant falchion lopp'd his hands away;

His sever'd head was toss'd among the throng,
And, rolling, drew a bloody train along.
Then, where the thickest fought, the victor flew;
The king's example all his Greeks pursue.
Now by the foot the flying foot were slain,
Horse trod by horse, lay foaming on the plain.
From the dry fields thick clouds of dust arise,
Shade the black host, and intercept the skies.
The brass-hoof'd steeds tumultuous plunge and bound,
And the thick thunder beats the labouring ground,
Still slaughtering on, the king of men proceeds;
The distanced army wonders at his deeds,
As when the winds with raging flames conspire,
And o'er the forests roll the flood of fire,
In blazing heaps the grove's old honours fall,
And one refulgent ruin levels all:
Before Atrides' rage so sinks the foe,
Whole squadrons vanish, and proud heads lie low.
The steeds fly trembling from his waving sword,
And many a car, now lighted of its lord,
Wide o'er the field with guideless fury rolls,
Breaking their ranks, and crushing out their souls;
While his keen falchion drinks the warriors' lives;
More grateful, now, to vultures than their wives!

Perhaps great Hector then had found his fate,
But Jove and destiny prolong'd his date.
Safe from the darts, the care of heaven he stood,
Amidst alarms, and death, and dust, and blood.

Now past the tomb where ancient Ilus lay,
Through the mid field the routed urge their way:
Where the wild figs the adjoining summit crown,
The path they take, and speed to reach the town.
As swift, Atrides with loud shouts pursued,
Hot with his toil, and bathed in hostile blood.
Now near the beech-tree, and the Scaean gates,
The hero halts, and his associates waits.
Meanwhile on every side around the plain,
Dispersed, disorder'd, fly the Trojan train.
So flies a herd of beeves, that hear dismay'd
The lion's roaring through the midnight shade;
On heaps they tumble with successless haste;
The savage seizes, draws, and rends the last.
Not with less fury stern Atrides flew,
Still press'd the rout, and still the hindmost slew;
Hurl'd from their cars the bravest chiefs are kill'd,
And rage, and death, and carnage load the field.

Now storms the victor at the Trojan wall;
Surveys the towers, and meditates their fall.
But Jove descending shook the Idaean hills,
And down their summits pour'd a hundred rills:
The unkindled lightning in his hand he took,
And thus the many-coloured maid bespoke:

"Iris, with haste thy golden wings display,
To godlike Hector this our word convey—
While Agamemnon wastes the ranks around,
Fights in the front, and bathes with blood the ground,
Bid him give way; but issue forth commands,
And trust the war to less important hands:
But when, or wounded by the spear or dart,
That chief shall mount his chariot, and depart,
Then Jove shall string his arm, and fire his breast,
Then to her ships shall flying Greece be press'd,
Till to the main the burning sun descend,
And sacred night her awful shade extend."

He spoke, and Iris at his word obey'd;
On wings of winds descends the various maid.
The chief she found amidst the ranks of war,
Close to the bulwarks, on his glittering car.
The goddess then: "O son of Priam, hear!
From Jove I come, and his high mandate bear.
While Agamemnon wastes the ranks around,
Fights in the front, and bathes with blood the ground,
Abstain from fight; yet issue forth commands,
And trust the war to less important hands:
But when, or wounded by the spear or dart,
The chief shall mount his chariot, and depart,
Then Jove shall string thy arm, and fire thy breast,
Then to her ships shall flying Greece be press'd,
Till to the main the burning sun descend,
And sacred night her awful shade extend."

She said, and vanish'd. Hector, with a bound,
Springs from his chariot on the trembling ground,
In clanging arms: he grasps in either hand
A pointed lance, and speeds from band to band;
Revives their ardour, turns their steps from flight,
And wakes anew the dying flames of fight.
They stand to arms: the Greeks their onset dare,
Condense their powers, and wait the coming war.
New force, new spirit, to each breast returns;
The fight renew'd with fiercer fury burns:

The king leads on: all fix on him their eye,
And learn from him to conquer, or to die.

Ye sacred nine! celestial Muses! tell,
Who faced him first, and by his prowess fell?
The great Iphidamas, the bold and young,
From sage Antenor and Theano sprung;
Whom from his youth his grandsire Cisseus bred,
And nursed in Thrace where snowy flocks are fed.
Scarce did the down his rosy cheeks invest,
And early honour warm his generous breast,
When the kind sire consign'd his daughter's charms
(Theano's sister) to his youthful arms.
But call'd by glory to the wars of Troy,
He leaves untasted the first fruits of joy;
From his loved bride departs with melting eyes,
And swift to aid his dearer country flies.
With twelve black ships he reach'd Percope's strand,
Thence took the long laborious march by land.
Now fierce for fame, before the ranks he springs,
Towering in arms, and braves the king of kings.
Atrides first discharged the missive spear;
The Trojan stoop'd, the javelin pass'd in air.
Then near the corslet, at the monarch's heart,
With all his strength, the youth directs his dart:
But the broad belt, with plates of silver bound,
The point rebated, and repell'd the wound.
Encumber'd with the dart, Atrides stands,
Till, grasp'd with force, he wrench'd it from his hands;
At once his weighty sword discharged a wound
Full on his neck, that fell'd him to the ground.
Stretch'd in the dust the unhappy warrior lies,
And sleep eternal seals his swimming eyes.
Oh worthy better fate! oh early slain!
Thy country's friend; and virtuous, though in vain!
No more the youth shall join his consort's side,
At once a virgin, and at once a bride!
No more with presents her embraces meet,
Or lay the spoils of conquest at her feet,
On whom his passion, lavish of his store,
Bestow'd so much, and vainly promised more!
Unwept, uncover'd, on the plain he lay,
While the proud victor bore his arms away.

Coon, Antenor's eldest hope, was nigh:
Tears, at the sight, came starting from his eye,
While pierced with grief the much-loved youth he view'd,
And the pale features now deform'd with blood.

Then, with his spear, unseen, his time he took,
Aim'd at the king, and near his elbow strook.
The thrilling steel transpierced the brawny part,
And through his arm stood forth the barbed dart.
Surprised the monarch feels, yet void of fear
On Coon rushes with his lifted spear:
His brother's corpse the pious Trojan draws,
And calls his country to assert his cause;
Defends him breathless on the sanguine field,
And o'er the body spreads his ample shield.
Atrides, marking an unguarded part,
Transfix'd the warrior with his brazen dart;
Prone on his brother's bleeding breast he lay,
The monarch's falchion lopp'd his head away:
The social shades the same dark journey go,
And join each other in the realms below.

The vengeful victor rages round the fields,
With every weapon art or fury yields:
By the long lance, the sword, or ponderous stone,
Whole ranks are broken, and whole troops o'erthrown.
This, while yet warm distill'd the purple flood;
But when the wound grew stiff with clotted blood,
Then grinding tortures his strong bosom rend,
Less keen those darts the fierce Ilythiae send:
(The powers that cause the teeming matron's throes,
Sad mothers of unutterable woes!)
Stung with the smart, all-panting with the pain,
He mounts the car, and gives his squire the rein;
Then with a voice which fury made more strong,
And pain augmented, thus exhorts the throng:

"O friends! O Greeks! assert your honours won;
Proceed, and finish what this arm begun:
Lo! angry Jove forbids your chief to stay,
And envies half the glories of the day."

He said: the driver whirls his lengthful thong;
The horses fly; the chariot smokes along.
Clouds from their nostrils the fierce coursers blow,
And from their sides the foam descends in snow;
Shot through the battle in a moment's space,
The wounded monarch at his tent they place.

No sooner Hector saw the king retired,
But thus his Trojans and his aids he fired:
"Hear, all ye Dardan, all ye Lycian race!
Famed in close fight, and dreadful face to face:

Now call to mind your ancient trophies won,
Your great forefathers' virtues, and your own.
Behold, the general flies! deserts his powers!
Lo, Jove himself declares the conquest ours!
Now on yon ranks impel your foaming steeds;
And, sure of glory, dare immortal deeds."

With words like these the fiery chief alarms
His fainting host, and every bosom warms.
As the bold hunter cheers his hounds to tear
The brindled lion, or the tusky bear:
With voice and hand provokes their doubting heart,
And springs the foremost with his lifted dart:
So godlike Hector prompts his troops to dare;
Nor prompts alone, but leads himself the war.
On the black body of the foe he pours;
As from the cloud's deep bosom, swell'd with showers,
A sudden storm the purple ocean sweeps,
Drives the wild waves, and tosses all the deeps.
Say, Muse! when Jove the Trojan's glory crown'd,
Beneath his arm what heroes bit the ground?
Assaeus, Dolops, and Autonous died,
Opites next was added to their side;
Then brave Hipponous, famed in many a fight,
Opheltius, Orus, sunk to endless night;
Ćsymnus, Agelaus; all chiefs of name;
The rest were vulgar deaths unknown to fame.
As when a western whirlwind, charged with storms,
Dispels the gather'd clouds that Notus forms:
The gust continued, violent and strong,
Rolls sable clouds in heaps on heaps along;
Now to the skies the foaming billows rears,
Now breaks the surge, and wide the bottom bares:
Thus, raging Hector, with resistless hands,
O'erturns, confounds, and scatters all their bands.
Now the last ruin the whole host appals;
Now Greece had trembled in her wooden walls;
But wise Ulysses call'd Tydides forth,
His soul rekindled, and awaked his worth.
"And stand we deedless, O eternal shame!
Till Hector's arm involve the ships in flame?
Haste, let us join, and combat side by side."
The warrior thus, and thus the friend replied:

"No martial toil I shun, no danger fear;
Let Hector come; I wait his fury here.
But Jove with conquest crowns the Trojan train:
And, Jove our foe, all human force is vain."

He sigh'd; but, sighing, raised his vengeful steel,
And from his car the proud Thymbraeus fell:
Molion, the charioteer, pursued his lord,
His death ennobled by Ulysses' sword.
There slain, they left them in eternal night,
Then plunged amidst the thickest ranks of fight.
So two wild boars outstrip the following hounds,
Then swift revert, and wounds return for wounds.
Stern Hector's conquests in the middle plain
Stood check'd awhile, and Greece respired again.

The sons of Merops shone amidst the war;
Towering they rode in one refulgent car:
In deep prophetic arts their father skill'd,
Had warn'd his children from the Trojan field.
Fate urged them on: the father warn'd in vain;
They rush'd to fight, and perish'd on the plain;
Their breasts no more the vital spirit warms;
The stern Tydides strips their shining arms.
Hypirochus by great Ulysses dies,
And rich Hippodamus becomes his prize.
Great Jove from Ide with slaughter fills his sight,
And level hangs the doubtful scale of fight.
By Tydeus' lance Agastrophus was slain,
The far-famed hero of Paeonian strain;
Wing'd with his fears, on foot he strove to fly,
His steeds too distant, and the foe too nigh:
Through broken orders, swifter than the wind,
He fled, but flying left his life behind.
This Hector sees, as his experienced eyes
Traverse the files, and to the rescue flies;
Shouts, as he pass'd, the crystal regions rend,
And moving armies on his march attend.
Great Diomed himself was seized with fear,
And thus bespoke his brother of the war:

"Mark how this way yon bending squadrons yield!
The storm rolls on, and Hector rules the field:
Here stand his utmost force."—The warrior said;
Swift at the word his ponderous javelin fled;
Nor miss'd its aim, but where the plumage danced
Razed the smooth cone, and thence obliquely glanced.
Safe in his helm (the gift of Phoebus' hands)
Without a wound the Trojan hero stands;
But yet so stunn'd, that, staggering on the plain.
His arm and knee his sinking bulk sustain;
O'er his dim sight the misty vapours rise,

And a short darkness shades his swimming eyes.
Tydides followed to regain his lance;
While Hector rose, recover'd from the trance,
Remounts his car, and herds amidst the crowd:
The Greek pursues him, and exults aloud:
"Once more thank Phoebus for thy forfeit breath,
Or thank that swiftness which outstrips the death.
Well by Apollo are thy prayers repaid,
And oft that partial power has lent his aid.
Thou shall not long the death deserved withstand,
If any god assist Tydides' hand.
Fly then, inglorious! but thy flight, this day,
Whole hecatombs of Trojan ghosts shall pay,"

Him, while he triumph'd, Paris eyed from far,
(The spouse of Helen, the fair cause of war;)
Around the fields his feather'd shafts he sent,
From ancient Ilus' ruin'd monument:
Behind the column placed, he bent his bow,
And wing'd an arrow at the unwary foe;
Just as he stoop'd, Agastrophus's crest
To seize, and drew the corslet from his breast,
The bowstring twang'd; nor flew the shaft in vain,
But pierced his foot, and nail'd it to the plain.
The laughing Trojan, with a joyful spring.
Leaps from his ambush, and insults the king.

"He bleeds! (he cries) some god has sped my dart!
Would the same god had fix'd it in his heart!
So Troy, relieved from that wide-wasting hand,
Should breathe from slaughter and in combat stand:
Whose sons now tremble at his darted spear,
As scatter'd lambs the rushing lion fear."

He dauntless thus: "Thou conqueror of the fair,
Thou woman-warrior with the curling hair;
Vain archer! trusting to the distant dart,
Unskill'd in arms to act a manly part!
Thou hast but done what boys or women can;
Such hands may wound, but not incense a man.
Nor boast the scratch thy feeble arrow gave,
A coward's weapon never hurts the brave.
Not so this dart, which thou may'st one day feel;
Fate wings its flight, and death is on the steel:
Where this but lights, some noble life expires;
Its touch makes orphans, bathes the cheeks of sires,
Steeps earth in purple, gluts the birds of air,
And leaves such objects as distract the fair."

Ulysses hastens with a trembling heart,
Before him steps, and bending draws the dart:
Forth flows the blood; an eager pang succeeds;
Tydides mounts, and to the navy speeds.

Now on the field Ulysses stands alone,
The Greeks all fled, the Trojans pouring on;
But stands collected in himself, and whole,
And questions thus his own unconquer'd soul:

"What further subterfuge, what hopes remain?
What shame, inglorious if I quit the plain?
What danger, singly if I stand the ground,
My friends all scatter'd, all the foes around?
Yet wherefore doubtful? let this truth suffice,
The brave meets danger, and the coward flies.
To die or conquer, proves a hero's heart;
And, knowing this, I know a soldier's part."

Such thoughts revolving in his careful breast,
Near, and more near, the shady cohorts press'd;
These, in the warrior, their own fate enclose;
And round him deep the steely circle grows.
So fares a boar whom all the troop surrounds
Of shouting huntsmen and of clamorous hounds;
He grinds his ivory tusks; he foams with ire;
His sanguine eye-balls glare with living fire;
By these, by those, on every part is plied;
And the red slaughter spreads on every side.
Pierced through the shoulder, first Deiopis fell;
Next Ennomus and Thoon sank to hell;
Chersidamas, beneath the navel thrust,
Falls prone to earth, and grasps the bloody dust.
Charops, the son of Hippasus, was near;
Ulysses reach'd him with the fatal spear;
But to his aid his brother Socus flies,
Socus the brave, the generous, and the wise.
Near as he drew, the warrior thus began:

"O great Ulysses! much-enduring man!
Not deeper skill'd in every martial sleight,
Than worn to toils, and active in the fight!
This day two brothers shall thy conquest grace,
And end at once the great Hippasian race,
Or thou beneath this lance must press the field."
He said, and forceful pierced his spacious shield:
Through the strong brass the ringing javelin thrown,
Plough'd half his side, and bared it to the bone.

By Pallas' care, the spear, though deep infix'd,
Stopp'd short of life, nor with his entrails mix'd.

The wound not mortal wise Ulysses knew,
Then furious thus (but first some steps withdrew):
"Unhappy man! whose death our hands shall grace,
Fate calls thee hence and finish'd is thy race.
Nor longer check my conquests on the foe;
But, pierced by this, to endless darkness go,
And add one spectre to the realms below!"

He spoke, while Socus, seized with sudden fright,
Trembling gave way, and turn'd his back to flight;
Between his shoulders pierced the following dart,
And held its passage through the panting heart:
Wide in his breast appear'd the grisly wound;
He falls; his armour rings against the ground.
Then thus Ulysses, gazing on the slain:
"Famed son of Hippasus! there press the plain;
There ends thy narrow span assign'd by fate,
Heaven owes Ulysses yet a longer date.
Ah, wretch! no father shall thy corpse compose;
Thy dying eyes no tender mother close;
But hungry birds shall tear those balls away,
And hovering vultures scream around their prey.
Me Greece shall honour, when I meet my doom,
With solemn funerals and a lasting tomb."

Then raging with intolerable smart,
He writhes his body, and extracts the dart.
The dart a tide of spouting gore pursued,
And gladden'd Troy with sight of hostile blood.
Now troops on troops the fainting chief invade,
Forced he recedes, and loudly calls for aid.
Thrice to its pitch his lofty voice he rears;
The well-known voice thrice Menelaus hears:
Alarm'd, to Ajax Telamon he cried,
Who shares his labours, and defends his side:
"O friend! Ulysses' shouts invade my ear;
Distressed he seems, and no assistance near;
Strong as he is, yet one opposed to all,
Oppress'd by multitudes, the best may fall.
Greece robb'd of him must bid her host despair,
And feel a loss not ages can repair."

Then, where the cry directs, his course he bends;
Great Ajax, like the god of war, attends,
The prudent chief in sore distress they found,

With bands of furious Trojans compass'd round.
As when some huntsman, with a flying spear,
From the blind thicket wounds a stately deer;
Down his cleft side, while fresh the blood distils,
He bounds aloft, and scuds from hills to hills,
Till life's warm vapour issuing through the wound,
Wild mountain-wolves the fainting beast surround:
Just as their jaws his prostrate limbs invade,
The lion rushes through the woodland shade,
The wolves, though hungry, scour dispersed away;
The lordly savage vindicates his prey.
Ulysses thus, unconquer'd by his pains,
A single warrior half a host sustains:
But soon as Ajax leaves his tower-like shield,
The scattered crowds fly frighted o'er the field;
Atrides' arm the sinking hero stays,
And, saved from numbers, to his car conveys.

Victorious Ajax plies the routed crew;
And first Doryclus, Priam's son, he slew,
On strong Pandocus next inflicts a wound,
And lays Lysander bleeding on the ground.
As when a torrent, swell'd with wintry rains,
Pours from the mountains o'er the deluged plains,
And pines and oaks, from their foundations torn,
A country's ruins! to the seas are borne:
Fierce Ajax thus o'erwhelms the yielding throng;
Men, steeds, and chariots, roll in heaps along.

But Hector, from this scene of slaughter far,
Raged on the left, and ruled the tide of war:
Loud groans proclaim his progress through the plain,
And deep Scamander swells with heaps of slain.
There Nestor and Idomeneus oppose
The warrior's fury; there the battle glows;
There fierce on foot, or from the chariot's height,
His sword deforms the beauteous ranks of fight.
The spouse of Helen, dealing darts around,
Had pierced Machaon with a distant wound:
In his right shoulder the broad shaft appear'd,
And trembling Greece for her physician fear'd.
To Nestor then Idomeneus begun:
"Glory of Greece, old Neleus' valiant son!
Ascend thy chariot, haste with speed away,
And great Machaon to the ships convey;
A wise physician skill'd our wounds to heal,
Is more than armies to the public weal."
Old Nestor mounts the seat; beside him rode

The wounded offspring of the healing god.
He lends the lash; the steeds with sounding feet
Shake the dry field, and thunder toward the fleet.

But now Cebriones, from Hector's car,
Survey'd the various fortune of the war:
"While here (he cried) the flying Greeks are slain,
Trojans on Trojans yonder load the plain.
Before great Ajax see the mingled throng
Of men and chariots driven in heaps along!
I know him well, distinguish'd o'er the field
By the broad glittering of the sevenfold shield.
Thither, O Hector, thither urge thy steeds,
There danger calls, and there the combat bleeds;
There horse and foot in mingled deaths unite,
And groans of slaughter mix with shouts of fight."

Thus having spoke, the driver's lash resounds;
Swift through the ranks the rapid chariot bounds;
Stung by the stroke, the coursers scour the fields,
O'er heaps of carcases, and hills of shields.
The horses' hoofs are bathed in heroes' gore,
And, dashing, purple all the car before;
The groaning axle sable drops distils,
And mangled carnage clogs the rapid wheels.
Here Hector, plunging through the thickest fight,
Broke the dark phalanx, and let in the light:
(By the long lance, the sword, or ponderous stone.
The ranks he scatter'd and the troops o'erthrown:)
Ajax he shuns, through all the dire debate,
And fears that arm whose force he felt so late.
But partial Jove, espousing Hector's part,
Shot heaven-bred horror through the Grecian's heart;
Confused, unnerved in Hector's presence grown,
Amazed he stood, with terrors not his own.
O'er his broad back his moony shield he threw,
And, glaring round, by tardy steps withdrew.
Thus the grim lion his retreat maintains,
Beset with watchful dogs, and shouting swains;
Repulsed by numbers from the nightly stalls,
Though rage impels him, and though hunger calls,
Long stands the showering darts, and missile fires;
Then sourly slow the indignant beast retires:
So turn'd stern Ajax, by whole hosts repell'd,
While his swoln heart at every step rebell'd.

As the slow beast, with heavy strength endued,
In some wide field by troops of boys pursued,

Though round his sides a wooden tempest rain,
Crops the tall harvest, and lays waste the plain;
Thick on his hide the hollow blows resound,
The patient animal maintains his ground,
Scarce from the field with all their efforts chased,
And stirs but slowly when he stirs at last:
On Ajax thus a weight of Trojans hung,
The strokes redoubled on his buckler rung;
Confiding now in bulky strength he stands,
Now turns, and backward bears the yielding bands;
Now stiff recedes, yet hardly seems to fly,
And threats his followers with retorted eye.
Fix'd as the bar between two warring powers,
While hissing darts descend in iron showers:
In his broad buckler many a weapon stood,
Its surface bristled with a quivering wood;
And many a javelin, guiltless on the plain,
Marks the dry dust, and thirsts for blood in vain.
But bold Eurypylus his aid imparts,
And dauntless springs beneath a cloud of darts;
Whose eager javelin launch'd against the foe,
Great Apisaon felt the fatal blow;
From his torn liver the red current flow'd,
And his slack knees desert their dying load.
The victor rushing to despoil the dead,
From Paris' bow a vengeful arrow fled;
Fix'd in his nervous thigh the weapon stood,
Fix'd was the point, but broken was the wood.
Back to the lines the wounded Greek retired,
Yet thus retreating, his associates fired:

"What god, O Grecians! has your hearts dismay'd?
Oh, turn to arms; 'tis Ajax claims your aid.
This hour he stands the mark of hostile rage,
And this the last brave battle he shall wage:
Haste, join your forces; from the gloomy grave
The warrior rescue, and your country save."
Thus urged the chief: a generous troop appears,
Who spread their bucklers, and advance their spears,
To guard their wounded friend: while thus they stand
With pious care, great Ajax joins the band:
Each takes new courage at the hero's sight;
The hero rallies, and renews the fight.

Thus raged both armies like conflicting fires,
While Nestor's chariot far from fight retires:
His coursers steep'd in sweat, and stain'd with gore,
The Greeks' preserver, great Machaon, bore.

That hour Achilles, from the topmost height
Of his proud fleet, o'erlook'd the fields of fight;
His feasted eyes beheld around the plain
The Grecian rout, the slaying, and the slain.
His friend Machaon singled from the rest,
A transient pity touch'd his vengeful breast.
Straight to Menoetius' much-loved son he sent:
Graceful as Mars, Patroclus quits his tent;
In evil hour! Then fate decreed his doom,
And fix'd the date of all his woes to come.

"Why calls my friend? thy loved injunctions lay;
Whate'er thy will, Patroclus shall obey."

"O first of friends! (Pelides thus replied)
Still at my heart, and ever at my side!
The time is come, when yon despairing host
Shall learn the value of the man they lost:
Now at my knees the Greeks shall pour their moan,
And proud Atrides tremble on his throne.
Go now to Nestor, and from him be taught
What wounded warrior late his chariot brought:
For, seen at distance, and but seen behind,
His form recall'd Machaon to my mind;
Nor could I, through yon cloud, discern his face,
The coursers pass'd me with so swift a pace."

The hero said. His friend obey'd with haste,
Through intermingled ships and tents he pass'd;
The chiefs descending from their car he found:
The panting steeds Eurymedon unbound.
The warriors standing on the breezy shore,
To dry their sweat, and wash away the gore,
Here paused a moment, while the gentle gale
Convey'd that freshness the cool seas exhale;
Then to consult on farther methods went,
And took their seats beneath the shady tent.
The draught prescribed, fair Hecamede prepares,
Arsinous' daughter, graced with golden hairs:
(Whom to his aged arms, a royal slave,
Greece, as the prize of Nestor's wisdom gave:)
A table first with azure feet she placed;
Whose ample orb a brazen charger graced;
Honey new-press'd, the sacred flour of wheat,
And wholesome garlic, crown'd the savoury treat,
Next her white hand an antique goblet brings,
A goblet sacred to the Pylian kings
From eldest times: emboss'd with studs of gold,

Two feet support it, and four handles hold;
On each bright handle, bending o'er the brink,
In sculptured gold, two turtles seem to drink:
A massy weight, yet heaved with ease by him,
When the brisk nectar overlook'd the brim.
Temper'd in this, the nymph of form divine
Pours a large portion of the Pramnian wine;
With goat's-milk cheese a flavourous taste bestows,
And last with flour the smiling surface strows:
This for the wounded prince the dame prepares:
The cordial beverage reverend Nestor shares:
Salubrious draughts the warriors' thirst allay,
And pleasing conference beguiles the day.

Meantime Patroclus, by Achilles sent,
Unheard approached, and stood before the tent.
Old Nestor, rising then, the hero led
To his high seat: the chief refused and said:

"'Tis now no season for these kind delays;
The great Achilles with impatience stays.
To great Achilles this respect I owe;
Who asks, what hero, wounded by the foe,
Was borne from combat by thy foaming steeds?
With grief I see the great Machaon bleeds.
This to report, my hasty course I bend;
Thou know'st the fiery temper of my friend."
"Can then the sons of Greece (the sage rejoin'd)
Excite compassion in Achilles' mind?
Seeks he the sorrows of our host to know?
This is not half the story of our woe.
Tell him, not great Machaon bleeds alone,
Our bravest heroes in the navy groan,
Ulysses, Agamemnon, Diomed,
And stern Eurypylus, already bleed.
But, ah! what flattering hopes I entertain!
Achilles heeds not, but derides our pain:
Even till the flames consume our fleet he stays,
And waits the rising of the fatal blaze.
Chief after chief the raging foe destroys;
Calm he looks on, and every death enjoys.
Now the slow course of all-impairing time
Unstrings my nerves, and ends my manly prime;
Oh! had I still that strength my youth possess'd,
When this bold arm the Epeian powers oppress'd,
The bulls of Elis in glad triumph led,
And stretch'd the great Itymonaeus dead!
Then from my fury fled the trembling swains,

And ours was all the plunder of the plains:
Fifty white flocks, full fifty herds of swine,
As many goats, as many lowing kine:
And thrice the number of unrivall'd steeds,
All teeming females, and of generous breeds.
These, as my first essay of arms, I won;
Old Neleus gloried in his conquering son.
Thus Elis forced, her long arrears restored,
And shares were parted to each Pylian lord.
The state of Pyle was sunk to last despair,
When the proud Elians first commenced the war:
For Neleus' sons Alcides' rage had slain;
Of twelve bold brothers, I alone remain!
Oppress'd, we arm'd; and now this conquest gain'd,
My sire three hundred chosen sheep obtain'd.
(That large reprisal he might justly claim,
For prize defrauded, and insulted fame,
When Elis' monarch, at the public course,
Detain'd his chariot, and victorious horse.)
The rest the people shared; myself survey'd
The just partition, and due victims paid.
Three days were past, when Elis rose to war,
With many a courser, and with many a car;
The sons of Actor at their army's head
(Young as they were) the vengeful squadrons led.
High on the rock fair Thryoessa stands,
Our utmost frontier on the Pylian lands:
Not far the streams of famed Alphaeus flow:
The stream they pass'd, and pitch'd their tents below.
Pallas, descending in the shades of night,
Alarms the Pylians and commands the fight.
Each burns for fame, and swells with martial pride,
Myself the foremost; but my sire denied;
Fear'd for my youth, exposed to stern alarms;
And stopp'd my chariot, and detain'd my arms.
My sire denied in vain: on foot I fled
Amidst our chariots; for the goddess led.

"Along fair Arene's delightful plain
Soft Minyas rolls his waters to the main:
There, horse and foot, the Pylian troops unite,
And sheathed in arms, expect the dawning light.
Thence, ere the sun advanced his noon-day flame,
To great Alphaeus' sacred source we came.
There first to Jove our solemn rites were paid;
An untamed heifer pleased the blue-eyed maid;
A bull, Alphaeus; and a bull was slain
To the blue monarch of the watery main.

In arms we slept, beside the winding flood,
While round the town the fierce Epeians stood.
Soon as the sun, with all-revealing ray,
Flamed in the front of Heaven, and gave the day.
Bright scenes of arms, and works of war appear;
The nations meet; there Pylos, Elis here.
The first who fell, beneath my javelin bled;
King Augias' son, and spouse of Agamede:
(She that all simples' healing virtues knew,
And every herb that drinks the morning dew:)
I seized his car, the van of battle led;
The Epeians saw, they trembled, and they fled.
The foe dispersed, their bravest warrior kill'd,
Fierce as the whirlwind now I swept the field:
Full fifty captive chariots graced my train;
Two chiefs from each fell breathless to the plain.
Then Actor's sons had died, but Neptune shrouds
The youthful heroes in a veil of clouds.
O'er heapy shields, and o'er the prostrate throng,
Collecting spoils, and slaughtering all along,
Through wide Buprasian fields we forced the foes,
Where o'er the vales the Olenian rocks arose;
Till Pallas stopp'd us where Alisium flows.
Even there the hindmost of the rear I slay,
And the same arm that led concludes the day;
Then back to Pyle triumphant take my way.
There to high Jove were public thanks assign'd,
As first of gods; to Nestor, of mankind.
Such then I was, impell'd by youthful blood;
So proved my valour for my country's good.

"Achilles with unactive fury glows,
And gives to passion what to Greece he owes.
How shall he grieve, when to the eternal shade
Her hosts shall sink, nor his the power to aid!
O friend! my memory recalls the day,
When, gathering aids along the Grecian sea,
I, and Ulysses, touch'd at Phthia's port,
And entered Peleus' hospitable court.
A bull to Jove he slew in sacrifice,
And pour'd libations on the flaming thighs.
Thyself, Achilles, and thy reverend sire
Menoetius, turn'd the fragments on the fire.
Achilles sees us, to the feast invites;
Social we sit, and share the genial rites.
We then explained the cause on which we came,
Urged you to arms, and found you fierce for fame.
Your ancient fathers generous precepts gave;

Peleus said only this:—'My son! be brave.'
Menoetius thus: 'Though great Achilles shine
In strength superior, and of race divine,
Yet cooler thoughts thy elder years attend;
Let thy just counsels aid, and rule thy friend.'
Thus spoke your father at Thessalia's court:
Words now forgot, though now of vast import.
Ah! try the utmost that a friend can say:
Such gentle force the fiercest minds obey;
Some favouring god Achilles' heart may move;
Though deaf to glory, he may yield to love.
If some dire oracle his breast alarm,
If aught from Heaven withhold his saving arm,
Some beam of comfort yet on Greece may shine,
If thou but lead the Myrmidonian line;
Clad in Achilles' arms, if thou appear,
Proud Troy may tremble, and desist from war;
Press'd by fresh forces, her o'er-labour'd train
Shall seek their walls, and Greece respire again."

This touch'd his generous heart, and from the tent
Along the shore with hasty strides he went;
Soon as he came, where, on the crowded strand,
The public mart and courts of justice stand,
Where the tall fleet of great Ulysses lies,
And altars to the guardian gods arise;
There, sad, he met the brave Euaemon's son,
Large painful drops from all his members run;
An arrow's head yet rooted in his wound,
The sable blood in circles mark'd the ground.
As faintly reeling he confess'd the smart,
Weak was his pace, but dauntless was his heart.
Divine compassion touch'd Patroclus' breast,
Who, sighing, thus his bleeding friend address'd:

"Ah, hapless leaders of the Grecian host!
Thus must ye perish on a barbarous coast?
Is this your fate, to glut the dogs with gore,
Far from your friends, and from your native shore?
Say, great Eurypylus! shall Greece yet stand?
Resists she yet the raging Hector's hand?
Or are her heroes doom'd to die with shame,
And this the period of our wars and fame?"

Eurypylus replies: "No more, my friend;
Greece is no more! this day her glories end;
Even to the ships victorious Troy pursues,
Her force increasing as her toil renews.

Those chiefs, that used her utmost rage to meet,
Lie pierced with wounds, and bleeding in the fleet.
But, thou, Patroclus! act a friendly part,
Lead to my ships, and draw this deadly dart;
With lukewarm water wash the gore away;
With healing balms the raging smart allay,
Such as sage Chiron, sire of pharmacy,
Once taught Achilles, and Achilles thee.
Of two famed surgeons, Podalirius stands
This hour surrounded by the Trojan bands;
And great Machaon, wounded in his tent,
Now wants that succour which so oft he lent."

To him the chief: "What then remains to do?
The event of things the gods alone can view.
Charged by Achilles' great command I fly,
And bear with haste the Pylian king's reply:
But thy distress this instant claims relief."
He said, and in his arms upheld the chief.
The slaves their master's slow approach survey'd,
And hides of oxen on the floor display'd:
There stretch'd at length the wounded hero lay;
Patroclus cut the forky steel away:
Then in his hands a bitter root he bruised;
The wound he wash'd, the styptic juice infused.
The closing flesh that instant ceased to glow,
The wound to torture, and the blood to flow.

BOOK XII

ARGUMENT

THE BATTLE AT THE GRECIAN WALL

The Greeks having retired into their intrenchments, Hector attempts to force them; but it proving impossible to pass the ditch, Polydamas advises to quit their chariots, and manage the attack on foot. The Trojans follow his counsel; and having divided their army into five bodies of foot, begin the assault. But upon the signal of an eagle with a serpent in his talons, which appeared on the left hand of the Trojans, Polydamas endeavours to withdraw them again. This Hector opposes, and continues the attack; in which, after many actions, Sarpedon makes the first breach in the wall. Hector also, casting a stone of vast size, forces open one of the gates, and enters at the head of his troops, who victoriously pursue the Grecians even to their ships.

While thus the hero's pious cares attend
The cure and safety of his wounded friend,

Trojans and Greeks with clashing shields engage,
And mutual deaths are dealt with mutual rage.
Nor long the trench or lofty walls oppose;
With gods averse the ill-fated works arose;
Their powers neglected, and no victim slain,
The walls were raised, the trenches sunk in vain.

Without the gods, how short a period stands
The proudest monument of mortal hands!
This stood while Hector and Achilles raged.
While sacred Troy the warring hosts engaged;
But when her sons were slain, her city burn'd,
And what survived of Greece to Greece return'd;
Then Neptune and Apollo shook the shore,
Then Ida's summits pour'd their watery store;
Rhesus and Rhodius then unite their rills,
Caresus roaring down the stony hills,
Ćsepus, Granicus, with mingled force,
And Xanthus foaming from his fruitful source;
And gulfy Simois, rolling to the main
Helmets, and shields, and godlike heroes slain:
These, turn'd by Phoebus from their wonted ways,
Deluged the rampire nine continual days;
The weight of waters saps the yielding wall,
And to the sea the floating bulwarks fall.
Incessant cataracts the Thunderer pours,
And half the skies descend in sluicy showers.
The god of ocean, marching stern before,
With his huge trident wounds the trembling shore,
Vast stones and piles from their foundation heaves,
And whelms the smoky ruin in the waves.
Now smooth'd with sand, and levell'd by the flood,
No fragment tells where once the wonder stood;
In their old bounds the rivers roll again,
Shine 'twixt the hills, or wander o'er the plain.

But this the gods in later times perform;
As yet the bulwark stood, and braved the storm;
The strokes yet echoed of contending powers;
War thunder'd at the gates, and blood distain'd the towers.
Smote by the arm of Jove with dire dismay,
Close by their hollow ships the Grecians lay:
Hector's approach in every wind they hear,
And Hector's fury every moment fear.
He, like a whirlwind, toss'd the scattering throng,
Mingled the troops, and drove the field along.
So 'midst the dogs and hunters' daring bands,
Fierce of his might, a boar or lion stands;

Arm'd foes around a dreadful circle form,
And hissing javelins rain an iron storm:
His powers untamed, their bold assault defy,
And where he turns the rout disperse or die:
He foams, he glares, he bounds against them all,
And if he falls, his courage makes him fall.
With equal rage encompass'd Hector glows;
Exhorts his armies, and the trenches shows.
The panting steeds impatient fury breathe,
And snort and tremble at the gulf beneath;
Just at the brink they neigh, and paw the ground,
And the turf trembles, and the skies resound.
Eager they view'd the prospect dark and deep,
Vast was the leap, and headlong hung the steep;
The bottom bare, (a formidable show!)
And bristled thick with sharpen'd stakes below.
The foot alone this strong defence could force,
And try the pass impervious to the horse.
This saw Polydamas; who, wisely brave,
Restrain'd great Hector, and this counsel gave:

"O thou, bold leader of the Trojan bands!
And you, confederate chiefs from foreign lands!
What entrance here can cumbrous chariots find,
The stakes beneath, the Grecian walls behind?
No pass through those, without a thousand wounds,
No space for combat in yon narrow bounds.
Proud of the favours mighty Jove has shown,
On certain dangers we too rashly run:
If 'tis will our haughty foes to tame,
Oh may this instant end the Grecian name!
Here, far from Argos, let their heroes fall,
And one great day destroy and bury all!
But should they turn, and here oppress our train,
What hopes, what methods of retreat remain?
Wedged in the trench, by our own troops confused,
In one promiscuous carnage crush'd and bruised,
All Troy must perish, if their arms prevail,
Nor shall a Trojan live to tell the tale.
Hear then, ye warriors! and obey with speed;
Back from the trenches let your steeds be led;
Then all alighting, wedged in firm array,
Proceed on foot, and Hector lead the way.
So Greece shall stoop before our conquering power,
And this (if Jove consent) her fatal hour."

This counsel pleased: the godlike Hector sprung
Swift from his seat; his clanging armour rung.

The chief's example follow'd by his train,
Each quits his car, and issues on the plain,
By orders strict the charioteers enjoin'd
Compel the coursers to their ranks behind.
The forces part in five distinguish'd bands,
And all obey their several chiefs' commands.
The best and bravest in the first conspire,
Pant for the fight, and threat the fleet with fire:
Great Hector glorious in the van of these,
Polydamas, and brave Cebriones.
Before the next the graceful Paris shines,
And bold Alcathous, and Agenor joins.
The sons of Priam with the third appear,
Deiphobus, and Helenas the seer;
In arms with these the mighty Asius stood,
Who drew from Hyrtacus his noble blood,
And whom Arisba's yellow coursers bore,
The coursers fed on Selle's winding shore.
Antenor's sons the fourth battalion guide,
And great Ćneas, born on fountful Ide.
Divine Sarpedon the last band obey'd,
Whom Glaucus and Asteropaeus aid.
Next him, the bravest, at their army's head,
But he more brave than all the hosts he led.

Now with compacted shields in close array,
The moving legions speed their headlong way:
Already in their hopes they fire the fleet,
And see the Grecians gasping at their feet.

While every Trojan thus, and every aid,
The advice of wise Polydamas obey'd,
Asius alone, confiding in his car,
His vaunted coursers urged to meet the war.
Unhappy hero! and advised in vain;
Those wheels returning ne'er shall mark the plain;
No more those coursers with triumphant joy
Restore their master to the gates of Troy!
Black death attends behind the Grecian wall,
And great Idomeneus shall boast thy fall!
Fierce to the left he drives, where from the plain
The flying Grecians strove their ships to gain;
Swift through the wall their horse and chariots pass'd,
The gates half-open'd to receive the last.
Thither, exulting in his force, he flies:
His following host with clamours rend the skies:
To plunge the Grecians headlong in the main,
Such their proud hopes; but all their hopes were vain!

To guard the gates, two mighty chiefs attend,
Who from the Lapiths' warlike race descend;
This Polypoetes, great Perithous' heir,
And that Leonteus, like the god of war.
As two tall oaks, before the wall they rise;
Their roots in earth, their heads amidst the skies:
Whose spreading arms with leafy honours crown'd,
Forbid the tempest, and protect the ground;
High on the hills appears their stately form,
And their deep roots for ever brave the storm.
So graceful these, and so the shock they stand
Of raging Asius, and his furious band.
Orestes, Acamas, in front appear,
And OEnomaus and Thoon close the rear:
In vain their clamours shake the ambient fields,
In vain around them beat their hollow shields;
The fearless brothers on the Grecians call,
To guard their navies, and defend the wall.
Even when they saw Troy's sable troops impend,
And Greece tumultuous from her towers descend,
Forth from the portals rush'd the intrepid pair,
Opposed their breasts, and stood themselves the war.
So two wild boars spring furious from their den,
Roused with the cries of dogs and voice of men;
On every side the crackling trees they tear,
And root the shrubs, and lay the forest bare;
They gnash their tusks, with fire their eye-balls roll,
Till some wide wound lets out their mighty soul.
Around their heads the whistling javelins sung,
With sounding strokes their brazen targets rung;
Fierce was the fight, while yet the Grecian powers
Maintain'd the walls, and mann'd the lofty towers:
To save their fleet their last efforts they try,
And stones and darts in mingled tempests fly.

As when sharp Boreas blows abroad, and brings
The dreary winter on his frozen wings;
Beneath the low-hung clouds the sheets of snow
Descend, and whiten all the fields below:
So fast the darts on either army pour,
So down the rampires rolls the rocky shower:
Heavy, and thick, resound the batter'd shields,
And the deaf echo rattles round the fields.

With shame repulsed, with grief and fury driven,
The frantic Asius thus accuses Heaven:
"In powers immortal who shall now believe?

Can those too flatter, and can Jove deceive?
What man could doubt but Troy's victorious power
Should humble Greece, and this her fatal hour?
But like when wasps from hollow crannies drive,
To guard the entrance of their common hive,
Darkening the rock, while with unwearied wings
They strike the assailants, and infix their stings;
A race determined, that to death contend:
So fierce these Greeks their last retreats defend.
Gods! shall two warriors only guard their gates,
Repel an army, and defraud the fates?"

These empty accents mingled with the wind,
Nor moved great Jove's unalterable mind;
To godlike Hector and his matchless might
Was owed the glory of the destined fight.
Like deeds of arms through all the forts were tried,
And all the gates sustain'd an equal tide;
Through the long walls the stony showers were heard,
The blaze of flames, the flash of arms appear'd.
The spirit of a god my breast inspire,
To raise each act to life, and sing with fire!
While Greece unconquer'd kept alive the war,
Secure of death, confiding in despair;
And all her guardian gods, in deep dismay,
With unassisting arms deplored the day.

Even yet the dauntless Lapithae maintain
The dreadful pass, and round them heap the slain.
First Damasus, by Polypoetes' steel,
Pierced through his helmet's brazen visor, fell;
The weapon drank the mingled brains and gore!
The warrior sinks, tremendous now no more!
Next Ormenus and Pylon yield their breath:
Nor less Leonteus strews the field with death;
First through the belt Hippomachus he gored,
Then sudden waved his unresisted sword:
Antiphates, as through the ranks he broke,
The falchion struck, and fate pursued the stroke:
Iamenus, Orestes, Menon, bled;
And round him rose a monument of dead.
Meantime, the bravest of the Trojan crew,
Bold Hector and Polydamas, pursue;
Fierce with impatience on the works to fall,
And wrap in rolling flames the fleet and wall.
These on the farther bank now stood and gazed,
By Heaven alarm'd, by prodigies amazed:
A signal omen stopp'd the passing host,

Their martial fury in their wonder lost.
Jove's bird on sounding pinions beat the skies;
A bleeding serpent of enormous size,
His talons truss'd; alive, and curling round,
He stung the bird, whose throat received the wound:
Mad with the smart, he drops the fatal prey,
In airy circles wings his painful way,
Floats on the winds, and rends the heaven with cries:
Amidst the host the fallen serpent lies.
They, pale with terror, mark its spires unroll'd,
And Jove's portent with beating hearts behold.
Then first Polydamas the silence broke,
Long weigh'd the signal, and to Hector spoke:

"How oft, my brother, thy reproach I bear,
For words well meant, and sentiments sincere?
True to those counsels which I judge the best,
I tell the faithful dictates of my breast.
To speak his thoughts is every freeman's right,
In peace, in war, in council, and in fight;
And all I move, deferring to thy sway,
But tends to raise that power which I obey.
Then hear my words, nor may my words be vain!
Seek not this day the Grecian ships to gain;
For sure, to warn us, Jove his omen sent,
And thus my mind explains its clear event:
The victor eagle, whose sinister flight
Retards our host, and fills our hearts with fright,
Dismiss'd his conquest in the middle skies,
Allow'd to seize, but not possess the prize;
Thus, though we gird with fires the Grecian fleet,
Though these proud bulwarks tumble at our feet,
Toils unforeseen, and fiercer, are decreed;
More woes shall follow, and more heroes bleed.
So bodes my soul, and bids me thus advise;
For thus a skilful seer would read the skies."

To him then Hector with disdain return'd:
(Fierce as he spoke, his eyes with fury burn'd:)
"Are these the faithful counsels of thy tongue?
Thy will is partial, not thy reason wrong:
Or if the purpose of thy heart thou vent,
Sure heaven resumes the little sense it lent.
What coward counsels would thy madness move
Against the word, the will reveal'd of Jove?
The leading sign, the irrevocable nod,
And happy thunders of the favouring god,
These shall I slight, and guide my wavering mind

By wandering birds that flit with every wind?
Ye vagrants of the sky! your wings extend,
Or where the suns arise, or where descend;
To right, to left, unheeded take your way,
While I the dictates of high heaven obey.
Without a sign his sword the brave man draws,
And asks no omen but his country's cause.
But why should'st thou suspect the war's success?
None fears it more, as none promotes it less:
Though all our chiefs amidst yon ships expire,
Trust thy own cowardice to escape their fire.
Troy and her sons may find a general grave,
But thou canst live, for thou canst be a slave.
Yet should the fears that wary mind suggests
Spread their cold poison through our soldiers' breasts,
My javelin can revenge so base a part,
And free the soul that quivers in thy heart."

Furious he spoke, and, rushing to the wall,
Calls on his host; his host obey the call;
With ardour follow where their leader flies:
Redoubling clamours thunder in the skies.
Jove breathes a whirlwind from the hills of Ide,
And drifts of dust the clouded navy hide;
He fills the Greeks with terror and dismay,
And gives great Hector the predestined day.
Strong in themselves, but stronger in his aid,
Close to the works their rigid siege they laid.
In vain the mounds and massy beams defend,
While these they undermine, and those they rend;
Upheaved the piles that prop the solid wall;
And heaps on heaps the smoky ruins fall.
Greece on her ramparts stands the fierce alarms;
The crowded bulwarks blaze with waving arms,
Shield touching shield, a long refulgent row;
Whence hissing darts, incessant, rain below.
The bold Ajaces fly from tower to tower,
And rouse, with flame divine, the Grecian power.
The generous impulse every Greek obeys;
Threats urge the fearful; and the valiant, praise.

"Fellows in arms! whose deeds are known to fame,
And you, whose ardour hopes an equal name!
Since not alike endued with force or art;
Behold a day when each may act his part!
A day to fire the brave, and warm the cold,
To gain new glories, or augment the old.
Urge those who stand, and those who faint, excite;

Drown Hector's vaunts in loud exhorts of fight;
Conquest, not safety, fill the thoughts of all;
Seek not your fleet, but sally from the wall;
So Jove once more may drive their routed train,
And Troy lie trembling in her walls again."

Their ardour kindles all the Grecian powers;
And now the stones descend in heavier showers.
As when high Jove his sharp artillery forms,
And opes his cloudy magazine of storms;
In winter's bleak un comfortable reign,
A snowy inundation hides the plain;
He stills the winds, and bids the skies to sleep;
Then pours the silent tempest thick and deep;
And first the mountain-tops are cover'd o'er,
Then the green fields, and then the sandy shore;
Bent with the weight, the nodding woods are seen,
And one bright waste hides all the works of men:
The circling seas, alone absorbing all,
Drink the dissolving fleeces as they fall:
So from each side increased the stony rain,
And the white ruin rises o'er the plain.

Thus godlike Hector and his troops contend
To force the ramparts, and the gates to rend:
Nor Troy could conquer, nor the Greeks would yield,
Till great Sarpedon tower'd amid the field;
For mighty Jove inspired with martial flame
His matchless son, and urged him on to fame.
In arms he shines, conspicuous from afar,
And bears aloft his ample shield in air;
Within whose orb the thick bull-hides were roll'd,
Ponderous with brass, and bound with ductile gold:
And while two pointed javelins arm his hands,
Majestic moves along, and leads his Lycian bands.

So press'd with hunger, from the mountain's brow
Descends a lion on the flocks below;
So stalks the lordly savage o'er the plain,
In sullen majesty, and stern disdain:
In vain loud mastiffs bay him from afar,
And shepherds gall him with an iron war;
Regardless, furious, he pursues his way;
He foams, he roars, he rends the panting prey.

Resolved alike, divine Sarpedon glows
With generous rage that drives him on the foes.
He views the towers, and meditates their fall,

To sure destruction dooms the aspiring wall;
Then casting on his friend an ardent look,
Fired with the thirst of glory, thus he spoke:

"Why boast we, Glaucus! our extended reign,
Where Xanthus' streams enrich the Lycian plain,
Our numerous herds that range the fruitful field,
And hills where vines their purple harvest yield,
Our foaming bowls with purer nectar crown'd,
Our feasts enhanced with music's sprightly sound?
Why on those shores are we with joy survey'd,
Admired as heroes, and as gods obey'd,
Unless great acts superior merit prove,
And vindicate the bounteous powers above?
'Tis ours, the dignity they give to grace;
The first in valour, as the first in place;
That when with wondering eyes our martial bands
Behold our deeds transcending our commands,
Such, they may cry, deserve the sovereign state,
Whom those that envy dare not imitate!
Could all our care elude the gloomy grave,
Which claims no less the fearful and the brave,
For lust of fame I should not vainly dare
In fighting fields, nor urge thy soul to war.
But since, alas! ignoble age must come,
Disease, and death's inexorable doom
The life, which others pay, let us bestow,
And give to fame what we to nature owe;
Brave though we fall, and honour'd if we live,
Or let us glory gain, or glory give!"

He said; his words the listening chief inspire
With equal warmth, and rouse the warrior's fire;
The troops pursue their leaders with delight,
Rush to the foe, and claim the promised fight.
Menestheus from on high the storm beheld
Threatening the fort, and blackening in the field:
Around the walls he gazed, to view from far
What aid appear'd to avert the approaching war,
And saw where Teucer with the Ajaces stood,
Of fight insatiate, prodigal of blood.
In vain he calls; the din of helms and shields
Rings to the skies, and echoes through the fields,
The brazen hinges fly, the walls resound,
Heaven trembles, roar the mountains, thunders all the ground
Then thus to Thoos: "Hence with speed (he said),
And urge the bold Ajaces to our aid;
Their strength, united, best may help to bear

The bloody labours of the doubtful war:
Hither the Lycian princes bend their course,
The best and bravest of the hostile force.
But if too fiercely there the foes contend,
Let Telamon, at least, our towers defend,
And Teucer haste with his unerring bow
To share the danger, and repel the foe."

Swift, at the word, the herald speeds along
The lofty ramparts, through the martial throng,
And finds the heroes bathed in sweat and gore,
Opposed in combat on the dusty shore.
"Ye valiant leaders of our warlike bands!
Your aid (said Thoos) Peteus' son demands;
Your strength, united, best may help to bear
The bloody labours of the doubtful war:
Thither the Lycian princes bend their course,
The best and bravest of the hostile force.
But if too fiercely, here, the foes contend,
At least, let Telamon those towers defend,
And Teucer haste with his unerring bow
To share the danger, and repel the foe."

Straight to the fort great Ajax turn'd his care,
And thus bespoke his brothers of the war:
"Now, valiant Lycomede! exert your might,
And, brave Oileus, prove your force in fight;
To you I trust the fortune of the field,
Till by this arm the foe shall be repell'd:
That done, expect me to complete the day
Then with his sevenfold shield he strode away.
With equal steps bold Teucer press'd the shore,
Whose fatal bow the strong Pandion bore.

High on the walls appear'd the Lycian powers,
Like some black tempest gathering round the towers:
The Greeks, oppress'd, their utmost force unite,
Prepared to labour in the unequal fight:
The war renews, mix'd shouts and groans arise;
Tumultuous clamour mounts, and thickens in the skies.
Fierce Ajax first the advancing host invades,
And sends the brave Epicles to the shades,
Sarpedon's friend. Across the warrior's way,
Rent from the walls, a rocky fragment lay;
In modern ages not the strongest swain
Could heave the unwieldy burden from the plain:
He poised, and swung it round; then toss'd on high,
It flew with force, and labour'd up the sky;

Full on the Lycian's helmet thundering down,
The ponderous ruin crush'd his batter'd crown.
As skilful divers from some airy steep
Headlong descend, and shoot into the deep,
So falls Epicles; then in groans expires,
And murmuring to the shades the soul retires.

While to the ramparts daring Glaucus drew,
From Teucer's hand a winged arrow flew;
The bearded shaft the destined passage found,
And on his naked arm inflicts a wound.
The chief, who fear'd some foe's insulting boast
Might stop the progress of his warlike host,
Conceal'd the wound, and, leaping from his height
Retired reluctant from the unfinish'd fight.
Divine Sarpedon with regret beheld
Disabled Glaucus slowly quit the field;
His beating breast with generous ardour glows,
He springs to fight, and flies upon the foes.
Alcmaon first was doom'd his force to feel;
Deep in his breast he plunged the pointed steel;
Then from the yawning wound with fury tore
The spear, pursued by gushing streams of gore:
Down sinks the warrior with a thundering sound,
His brazen armour rings against the ground.

Swift to the battlement the victor flies,
Tugs with full force, and every nerve applies:
It shakes; the ponderous stones disjointed yield;
The rolling ruins smoke along the field.
A mighty breach appears; the walls lie bare;
And, like a deluge, rushes in the war.
At once bold Teucer draws the twanging bow,
And Ajax sends his javelin at the foe;
Fix'd in his belt the feather'd weapon stood,
And through his buckler drove the trembling wood;
But Jove was present in the dire debate,
To shield his offspring, and avert his fate.
The prince gave back, not meditating flight,
But urging vengeance, and severer fight;
Then raised with hope, and fired with glory's charms,
His fainting squadrons to new fury warms.
"O where, ye Lycians, is the strength you boast?
Your former fame and ancient virtue lost!
The breach lies open, but your chief in vain
Attempts alone the guarded pass to gain:
Unite, and soon that hostile fleet shall fall:
The force of powerful union conquers all."

This just rebuke inflamed the Lycian crew;
They join, they thicken, and the assault renew:
Unmoved the embodied Greeks their fury dare,
And fix'd support the weight of all the war;
Nor could the Greeks repel the Lycian powers,
Nor the bold Lycians force the Grecian towers.
As on the confines of adjoining grounds,
Two stubborn swains with blows dispute their bounds;
They tug, they sweat; but neither gain, nor yield,
One foot, one inch, of the contended field;
Thus obstinate to death, they fight, they fall;
Nor these can keep, nor those can win the wall.
Their manly breasts are pierced with many a wound,
Loud strokes are heard, and rattling arms resound;
The copious slaughter covers all the shore,
And the high ramparts drip with human gore.

As when two scales are charged with doubtful loads,
From side to side the trembling balance nods,
(While some laborious matron, just and poor,
With nice exactness weighs her woolly store,)
Till poised aloft, the resting beam suspends
Each equal weight; nor this, nor that, descends:
So stood the war, till Hector's matchless might,
With fates prevailing, turn'd the scale of fight.
Fierce as a whirlwind up the walls he flies,
And fires his host with loud repeated cries.
"Advance, ye Trojans! lend your valiant hands,
Haste to the fleet, and toss the blazing brands!"
They hear, they run; and, gathering at his call,
Raise scaling engines, and ascend the wall:
Around the works a wood of glittering spears
Shoots up, and all the rising host appears.
A ponderous stone bold Hector heaved to throw,
Pointed above, and rough and gross below:
Not two strong men the enormous weight could raise,
Such men as live in these degenerate days:
Yet this, as easy as a swain could bear
The snowy fleece, he toss'd, and shook in air;
For Jove upheld, and lighten'd of its load
The unwieldy rock, the labour of a god.
Thus arm'd, before the folded gates he came,
Of massy substance, and stupendous frame;
With iron bars and brazen hinges strong,
On lofty beams of solid timber hung:
Then thundering through the planks with forceful sway,
Drives the sharp rock; the solid beams give way,

The folds are shatter'd; from the crackling door
Leap the resounding bars, the flying hinges roar.
Now rushing in, the furious chief appears,
Gloomy as night! and shakes two shining spears:
A dreadful gleam from his bright armour came,
And from his eye-balls flash'd the living flame.
He moves a god, resistless in his course,
And seems a match for more than mortal force.
Then pouring after, through the gaping space,
A tide of Trojans flows, and fills the place;
The Greeks behold, they tremble, and they fly;
The shore is heap'd with death, and tumult rends the sky.

BOOK XIII

ARGUMENT

THE FOURTH BATTLE CONTINUED, IN WHICH NEPTUNE ASSISTS THE GREEKS: THE ACTS OF IDOMENEUS

Neptune, concerned for the loss of the Grecians, upon seeing the fortification forced by Hector, (who had entered the gate near the station of the Ajaces,) assumes the shape of Calchas, and inspires those heroes to oppose him: then, in the form of one of the generals, encourages the other Greeks who had retired to their vessels. The Ajaces form their troops in a close phalanx, and put a stop to Hector and the Trojans. Several deeds of valour are performed; Meriones, losing his spear in the encounter, repairs to seek another at the tent of Idomeneus: this occasions a conversation between those two warriors, who return together to the battle. Idomeneus signalizes his courage above the rest; he kills Othryoneus, Asius, and Alcathous: Deiphobus and Ćneas march against him, and at length Idomeneus retires. Menelaus wounds Helenus, and kills Pisander. The Trojans are repulsed on the left wing; Hector still keeps his ground against the Ajaces, till, being galled by the Locrian slingers and archers, Polydamas advises to call a council of war: Hector approves of his advice, but goes first to rally the Trojans; upbraids Paris, rejoins Polydamas, meets Ajax again, and renews the attack. The eight-and-twentieth day still continues. The scene is between the Grecian wall and the sea-shore.

When now the Thunderer on the sea-beat coast
Had fix'd great Hector and his conquering host,
He left them to the fates, in bloody fray
To toil and struggle through the well-fought day.
Then turn'd to Thracia from the field of fight
Those eyes that shed insufferable light,
To where the Mysians prove their martial force,
And hardy Thracians tame the savage horse;
And where the far-famed Hippomolgian strays,
Renown'd for justice and for length of days;
Thrice happy race! that, innocent of blood,

From milk, innoxious, seek their simple food:
Jove sees delighted; and avoids the scene
Of guilty Troy, of arms, and dying men:
No aid, he deems, to either host is given,
While his high law suspends the powers of Heaven.

Meantime the monarch of the watery main
Observed the Thunderer, nor observed in vain.
In Samothracia, on a mountain's brow,
Whose waving woods o'erhung the deeps below,
He sat; and round him cast his azure eyes
Where Ida's misty tops confusedly rise;
Below, fair Ilion's glittering spires were seen;
The crowded ships and sable seas between.
There, from the crystal chambers of the main
Emerged, he sat, and mourn'd his Argives slain.
At Jove incensed, with grief and fury stung,
Prone down the rocky steep he rush'd along;
Fierce as he pass'd, the lofty mountains nod,
The forest shakes; earth trembled as he trod,
And felt the footsteps of the immortal god.
From realm to realm three ample strides he took,
And, at the fourth, the distant Ćgae shook.

Far in the bay his shining palace stands,
Eternal frame! not raised by mortal hands:
This having reach'd, his brass-hoof'd steeds he reins,
Fleet as the winds, and deck'd with golden manes.
Refulgent arms his mighty limbs infold,
Immortal arms of adamant and gold.
He mounts the car, the golden scourge applies,
He sits superior, and the chariot flies:
His whirling wheels the glassy surface sweep;
The enormous monsters rolling o'er the deep
Gambol around him on the watery way,
And heavy whales in awkward measures play;
The sea subsiding spreads a level plain,
Exults, and owns the monarch of the main;
The parting waves before his coursers fly;
The wondering waters leave his axle dry.

Deep in the liquid regions lies a cave,
Between where Tenedos the surges lave,
And rocky Imbrus breaks the rolling wave:
There the great ruler of the azure round
Stopp'd his swift chariot, and his steeds unbound,
Fed with ambrosial herbage from his hand,
And link'd their fetlocks with a golden band,

Infrangible, immortal: there they stay:
The father of the floods pursues his way:
Where, like a tempest, darkening heaven around,
Or fiery deluge that devours the ground,
The impatient Trojans, in a gloomy throng,
Embattled roll'd, as Hector rush'd along:
To the loud tumult and the barbarous cry
The heavens re-echo, and the shores reply:
They vow destruction to the Grecian name,
And in their hopes the fleets already flame.

But Neptune, rising from the seas profound,
The god whose earthquakes rock the solid ground,
Now wears a mortal form; like Calchas seen,
Such his loud voice, and such his manly mien;
His shouts incessant every Greek inspire,
But most the Ajaces, adding fire to fire.

"'Tis yours, O warriors, all our hopes to raise:
Oh recollect your ancient worth and praise!
'Tis yours to save us, if you cease to fear;
Flight, more than shameful, is destructive here.
On other works though Troy with fury fall,
And pour her armies o'er our batter'd wall:
There Greece has strength: but this, this part o'erthrown,
Her strength were vain; I dread for you alone:
Here Hector rages like the force of fire,
Vaunts of his gods, and calls high Jove his sire:
If yet some heavenly power your breast excite,
Breathe in your hearts, and string your arms to fight,
Greece yet may live, her threaten'd fleet maintain:
And Hector's force, and Jove's own aid, be vain."

Then with his sceptre, that the deep controls,
He touch'd the chiefs, and steel'd their manly souls:
Strength, not their own, the touch divine imparts,
Prompts their light limbs, and swells their daring hearts.
Then, as a falcon from the rocky height,
Her quarry seen, impetuous at the sight,
Forth-springing instant, darts herself from high,
Shoots on the wing, and skims along the sky:
Such, and so swift, the power of ocean flew;
The wide horizon shut him from their view.

The inspiring god Oileus' active son
Perceived the first, and thus to Telamon:

"Some god, my friend, some god in human form

Favouring descends, and wills to stand the storm.
Not Calchas this, the venerable seer;
Short as he turned, I saw the power appear:
I mark'd his parting, and the steps he trod;
His own bright evidence reveals a god.
Even now some energy divine I share,
And seem to walk on wings, and tread in air!"

"With equal ardour (Telamon returns)
My soul is kindled, and my bosom burns;
New rising spirits all my force alarm,
Lift each impatient limb, and brace my arm.
This ready arm, unthinking, shakes the dart;
The blood pours back, and fortifies my heart:
Singly, methinks, yon towering chief I meet,
And stretch the dreadful Hector at my feet."

Full of the god that urged their burning breast,
The heroes thus their mutual warmth express'd.
Neptune meanwhile the routed Greeks inspired;
Who, breathless, pale, with length of labours tired,
Pant in the ships; while Troy to conquest calls,
And swarms victorious o'er their yielding walls:
Trembling before the impending storm they lie,
While tears of rage stand burning in their eye.
Greece sunk they thought, and this their fatal hour;
But breathe new courage as they feel the power.
Teucer and Leitus first his words excite;
Then stern Peneleus rises to the fight;
Thoas, Deipyrus, in arms renown'd,
And Merion next, the impulsive fury found;
Last Nestor's son the same bold ardour takes,
While thus the god the martial fire awakes:

"Oh lasting infamy, oh dire disgrace
To chiefs of vigorous youth, and manly race!
I trusted in the gods, and you, to see
Brave Greece victorious, and her navy free:
Ah, no—the glorious combat you disclaim,
And one black day clouds all her former fame.
Heavens! what a prodigy these eyes survey,
Unseen, unthought, till this amazing day!
Fly we at length from Troy's oft-conquer'd bands?
And falls our fleet by such inglorious hands?
A rout undisciplined, a straggling train,
Not born to glories of the dusty plain;
Like frighted fawns from hill to hill pursued,
A prey to every savage of the wood:

Shall these, so late who trembled at your name,
Invade your camps, involve your ships in flame?
A change so shameful, say, what cause has wrought?
The soldiers' baseness, or the general's fault?
Fools! will ye perish for your leader's vice;
The purchase infamy, and life the price?
'Tis not your cause, Achilles' injured fame:
Another's is the crime, but yours the shame.
Grant that our chief offend through rage or lust,
Must you be cowards, if your king's unjust?
Prevent this evil, and your country save:
Small thought retrieves the spirits of the brave.
Think, and subdue! on dastards dead to fame
I waste no anger, for they feel no shame:
But you, the pride, the flower of all our host,
My heart weeps blood to see your glory lost!
Nor deem this day, this battle, all you lose;
A day more black, a fate more vile, ensues.
Let each reflect, who prizes fame or breath,
On endless infamy, on instant death:
For, lo! the fated time, the appointed shore:
Hark! the gates burst, the brazen barriers roar!
Impetuous Hector thunders at the wall;
The hour, the spot, to conquer, or to fall."

These words the Grecians' fainting hearts inspire,
And listening armies catch the godlike fire.
Fix'd at his post was each bold Ajax found,
With well-ranged squadrons strongly circled round:
So close their order, so disposed their fight,
As Pallas' self might view with fix'd delight;
Or had the god of war inclined his eyes,
The god of war had own'd a just surprise.
A chosen phalanx, firm, resolved as fate,
Descending Hector and his battle wait.
An iron scene gleams dreadful o'er the fields,
Armour in armour lock'd, and shields in shields,
Spears lean on spears, on targets targets throng,
Helms stuck to helms, and man drove man along.
The floating plumes unnumber'd wave above,
As when an earthquake stirs the nodding grove;
And levell'd at the skies with pointing rays,
Their brandish'd lances at each motion blaze.

Thus breathing death, in terrible array,
The close compacted legions urged their way:
Fierce they drove on, impatient to destroy;
Troy charged the first, and Hector first of Troy.

As from some mountain's craggy forehead torn,
A rock's round fragment flies, with fury borne,
(Which from the stubborn stone a torrent rends,)
Precipitate the ponderous mass descends:
From steep to steep the rolling ruin bounds;
At every shock the crackling wood resounds;
Still gathering force, it smokes; and urged amain,
Whirls, leaps, and thunders down, impetuous to the plain:
There stops—so Hector. Their whole force he proved,
Resistless when he raged, and, when he stopp'd, unmoved.

On him the war is bent, the darts are shed,
And all their falchions wave around his head:
Repulsed he stands, nor from his stand retires;
But with repeated shouts his army fires.
"Trojans! be firm; this arm shall make your way
Through yon square body, and that black array:
Stand, and my spear shall rout their scattering power,
Strong as they seem, embattled like a tower;
For he that Juno's heavenly bosom warms,
The first of gods, this day inspires our arms."

He said; and roused the soul in every breast:
Urged with desire of fame, beyond the rest,
Forth march'd Deiphobus; but, marching, held
Before his wary steps his ample shield.
Bold Merion aim'd a stroke (nor aim'd it wide);
The glittering javelin pierced the tough bull-hide;
But pierced not through: unfaithful to his hand,
The point broke short, and sparkled in the sand.
The Trojan warrior, touch'd with timely fear,
On the raised orb to distance bore the spear.
The Greek, retreating, mourn'd his frustrate blow,
And cursed the treacherous lance that spared a foe;
Then to the ships with surly speed he went,
To seek a surer javelin in his tent.

Meanwhile with rising rage the battle glows,
The tumult thickens, and the clamour grows.
By Teucer's arm the warlike Imbrius bleeds,
The son of Mentor, rich in generous steeds.
Ere yet to Troy the sons of Greece were led,
In fair Pedaeus' verdant pastures bred,
The youth had dwelt, remote from war's alarms,
And blest in bright Medesicaste's arms:
(This nymph, the fruit of Priam's ravish'd joy,
Allied the warrior to the house of Troy:)
To Troy, when glory call'd his arms, he came,

And match'd the bravest of her chiefs in fame:
With Priam's sons, a guardian of the throne,
He lived, beloved and honour'd as his own.
Him Teucer pierced between the throat and ear:
He groans beneath the Telamonian spear.
As from some far-seen mountain's airy crown,
Subdued by steel, a tall ash tumbles down,
And soils its verdant tresses on the ground;
So falls the youth; his arms the fall resound.
Then Teucer rushing to despoil the dead,
From Hector's hand a shining javelin fled:
He saw, and shunn'd the death; the forceful dart
Sung on, and pierced Amphimachus's heart,
Cteatus' son, of Neptune's forceful line;
Vain was his courage, and his race divine!
Prostrate he falls; his clanging arms resound,
And his broad buckler thunders on the ground.
To seize his beamy helm the victor flies,
And just had fastened on the dazzling prize,
When Ajax' manly arm a javelin flung;
Full on the shield's round boss the weapon rung;
He felt the shock, nor more was doom'd to feel,
Secure in mail, and sheath'd in shining steel.
Repulsed he yields; the victor Greeks obtain
The spoils contested, and bear off the slain.
Between the leaders of the Athenian line,
(Stichius the brave, Menestheus the divine,)
Deplored Amphimachus, sad object! lies;
Imbrius remains the fierce Ajaces' prize.
As two grim lions bear across the lawn,
Snatch'd from devouring hounds, a slaughter'd fawn.
In their fell jaws high-lifting through the wood,
And sprinkling all the shrubs with drops of blood;
So these, the chief: great Ajax from the dead
Strips his bright arms; Oileus lops his head:
Toss'd like a ball, and whirl'd in air away,
At Hector's feet the gory visage lay.

The god of ocean, fired with stern disdain,
And pierced with sorrow for his grandson slain,
Inspires the Grecian hearts, confirms their hands,
And breathes destruction on the Trojan bands.
Swift as a whirlwind rushing to the fleet,
He finds the lance-famed Idomen of Crete,
His pensive brow the generous care express'd
With which a wounded soldier touch'd his breast,
Whom in the chance of war a javelin tore,
And his sad comrades from the battle bore;

Him to the surgeons of the camp he sent:
That office paid, he issued from his tent
Fierce for the fight: to whom the god begun,
In Thoas' voice, Andraemon's valiant son,
Who ruled where Calydon's white rocks arise,
And Pleuron's chalky cliffs emblaze the skies:

"Where's now the imperious vaunt, the daring boast,
Of Greece victorious, and proud Ilion lost?"

To whom the king: "On Greece no blame be thrown;
Arms are her trade, and war is all her own.
Her hardy heroes from the well-fought plains
Nor fear withholds, nor shameful sloth detains:
'Tis heaven, alas! and Jove's all-powerful doom,
That far, far distant from our native home
Wills us to fall inglorious! Oh, my friend!
Once foremost in the fight, still prone to lend
Or arms or counsels, now perform thy best,
And what thou canst not singly, urge the rest."

Thus he: and thus the god whose force can make
The solid globe's eternal basis shake:
"Ah! never may he see his native land,
But feed the vultures on this hateful strand,
Who seeks ignobly in his ships to stay,
Nor dares to combat on this signal day!
For this, behold! in horrid arms I shine,
And urge thy soul to rival acts with mine.
Together let us battle on the plain;
Two, not the worst; nor even this succour vain:
Not vain the weakest, if their force unite;
But ours, the bravest have confess'd in fight."

This said, he rushes where the combat burns;
Swift to his tent the Cretan king returns:
From thence, two javelins glittering in his hand,
And clad in arms that lighten'd all the strand,
Fierce on the foe the impetuous hero drove,
Like lightning bursting from the arm of Jove,
Which to pale man the wrath of heaven declares,
Or terrifies the offending world with wars;
In streamy sparkles, kindling all the skies,
From pole to pole the trail of glory flies:
Thus his bright armour o'er the dazzled throng
Gleam'd dreadful, as the monarch flash'd along.

Him, near his tent, Meriones attends;

Whom thus he questions: "Ever best of friends!
O say, in every art of battle skill'd,
What holds thy courage from so brave a field?
On some important message art thou bound,
Or bleeds my friend by some unhappy wound?
Inglorious here, my soul abhors to stay,
And glows with prospects of th' approaching day."

"O prince! (Meriones replies) whose care
Leads forth the embattled sons of Crete to war;
This speaks my grief: this headless lance I wield;
The rest lies rooted in a Trojan shield."

To whom the Cretan: "Enter, and receive
The wonted weapons; those my tent can give;
Spears I have store, (and Trojan lances all,)
That shed a lustre round the illumined wall,
Though I, disdainful of the distant war,
Nor trust the dart, nor aim the uncertain spear,
Yet hand to hand I fight, and spoil the slain;
And thence these trophies, and these arms I gain.
Enter, and see on heaps the helmets roll'd,
And high-hung spears, and shields that flame with gold."

"Nor vain (said Merion) are our martial toils;
We too can boast of no ignoble spoils:
But those my ship contains; whence distant far,
I fight conspicuous in the van of war,
What need I more? If any Greek there be
Who knows not Merion, I appeal to thee."

To this, Idomeneus: "The fields of fight
Have proved thy valour, and unconquer'd might:
And were some ambush for the foes design'd,
Even there thy courage would not lag behind:
In that sharp service, singled from the rest,
The fear of each, or valour, stands confess'd.
No force, no firmness, the pale coward shows;
He shifts his place: his colour comes and goes:
A dropping sweat creeps cold on every part;
Against his bosom beats his quivering heart;
Terror and death in his wild eye-balls stare;
With chattering teeth he stands, and stiffening hair,
And looks a bloodless image of despair!
Not so the brave—still dauntless, still the same,
Unchanged his colour, and unmoved his frame:
Composed his thought, determined is his eye,
And fix'd his soul, to conquer or to die:

If aught disturb the tenour of his breast,
'Tis but the wish to strike before the rest.

"In such assays thy blameless worth is known,
And every art of dangerous war thy own.
By chance of fight whatever wounds you bore,
Those wounds were glorious all, and all before;
Such as may teach, 'twas still thy brave delight
T'oppose thy bosom where thy foremost fight.
But why, like infants, cold to honour's charms,
Stand we to talk, when glory calls to arms?
Go—from my conquer'd spears the choicest take,
And to their owners send them nobly back."

Swift at the word bold Merion snatch'd a spear
And, breathing slaughter, follow'd to the war.
So Mars armipotent invades the plain,
(The wide destroyer of the race of man,)
Terror, his best-beloved son, attends his course,
Arm'd with stern boldness, and enormous force;
The pride of haughty warriors to confound,
And lay the strength of tyrants on the ground:
From Thrace they fly, call'd to the dire alarms
Of warring Phlegyans, and Ephyrian arms;
Invoked by both, relentless they dispose,
To these glad conquest, murderous rout to those.
So march'd the leaders of the Cretan train,
And their bright arms shot horror o'er the plain.

Then first spake Merion: "Shall we join the right,
Or combat in the centre of the fight?
Or to the left our wonted succour lend?
Hazard and fame all parts alike attend."

"Not in the centre (Idomen replied:)
Our ablest chieftains the main battle guide;
Each godlike Ajax makes that post his care,
And gallant Teucer deals destruction there,
Skill'd or with shafts to gall the distant field,
Or bear close battle on the sounding shield.
These can the rage of haughty Hector tame:
Safe in their arms, the navy fears no flame,
Till Jove himself descends, his bolts to shed,
And hurl the blazing ruin at our head.
Great must he be, of more than human birth,
Nor feed like mortals on the fruits of earth.
Him neither rocks can crush, nor steel can wound,
Whom Ajax fells not on the ensanguined ground.

In standing fight he mates Achilles' force,
Excell'd alone in swiftness in the course.
Then to the left our ready arms apply,
And live with glory, or with glory die."

He said: and Merion to th' appointed place,
Fierce as the god of battles, urged his pace.
Soon as the foe the shining chiefs beheld
Rush like a fiery torrent o'er the field,
Their force embodied in a tide they pour;
The rising combat sounds along the shore.
As warring winds, in Sirius' sultry reign,
From different quarters sweep the sandy plain;
On every side the dusty whirlwinds rise,
And the dry fields are lifted to the skies:
Thus by despair, hope, rage, together driven,
Met the black hosts, and, meeting, darken'd heaven.
All dreadful glared the iron face of war,
Bristled with upright spears, that flash'd afar;
Dire was the gleam of breastplates, helms, and shields,
And polish'd arms emblazed the flaming fields:
Tremendous scene! that general horror gave,
But touch'd with joy the bosoms of the brave.

Saturn's great sons in fierce contention vied,
And crowds of heroes in their anger died.
The sire of earth and heaven, by Thetis won
To crown with glory Peleus' godlike son,
Will'd not destruction to the Grecian powers,
But spared awhile the destined Trojan towers;
While Neptune, rising from his azure main,
Warr'd on the king of heaven with stern disdain,
And breathed revenge, and fired the Grecian train.
Gods of one source, of one ethereal race,
Alike divine, and heaven their native place;
But Jove the greater; first-born of the skies,
And more than men, or gods, supremely wise.
For this, of Jove's superior might afraid,
Neptune in human form conceal'd his aid.
These powers enfold the Greek and Trojan train
In war and discord's adamantine chain,
Indissolubly strong: the fatal tie
Is stretch'd on both, and close compell'd they die.

Dreadful in arms, and grown in combats grey,
The bold Idomeneus controls the day.
First by his hand Othryoneus was slain,
Swell'd with false hopes, with mad ambition vain;

Call'd by the voice of war to martial fame,
From high Cabesus' distant walls he came;
Cassandra's love he sought, with boasts of power,
And promised conquest was the proffer'd dower.
The king consented, by his vaunts abused;
The king consented, but the fates refused.
Proud of himself, and of the imagined bride,
The field he measured with a larger stride.
Him as he stalk'd, the Cretan javelin found;
Vain was his breastplate to repel the wound:
His dream of glory lost, he plunged to hell;
His arms resounded as the boaster fell.
The great Idomeneus bestrides the dead;
"And thus (he cries) behold thy promise sped!
Such is the help thy arms to Ilion bring,
And such the contract of the Phrygian king!
Our offers now, illustrious prince! receive;
For such an aid what will not Argos give?
To conquer Troy, with ours thy forces join,
And count Atrides' fairest daughter thine.
Meantime, on further methods to advise,
Come, follow to the fleet thy new allies;
There hear what Greece has on her part to say."
He spoke, and dragg'd the gory corse away.
This Asius view'd, unable to contain,
Before his chariot warring on the plain:
(His crowded coursers, to his squire consign'd,
Impatient panted on his neck behind:)
To vengeance rising with a sudden spring,
He hoped the conquest of the Cretan king.
The wary Cretan, as his foe drew near,
Full on his throat discharged the forceful spear:
Beneath the chin the point was seen to glide,
And glitter'd, extant at the further side.
As when the mountain-oak, or poplar tall,
Or pine, fit mast for some great admiral,
Groans to the oft-heaved axe, with many a wound,
Then spreads a length of ruin o'er the ground:
So sunk proud Asius in that dreadful day,
And stretch'd before his much-loved coursers lay.
He grinds the dust distain'd with streaming gore,
And, fierce in death, lies foaming on the shore.
Deprived of motion, stiff with stupid fear,
Stands all aghast his trembling charioteer,
Nor shuns the foe, nor turns the steeds away,
But falls transfix'd, an unresisting prey:
Pierced by Antilochus, he pants beneath
The stately car, and labours out his breath.

Thus Asius' steeds (their mighty master gone)
Remain the prize of Nestor's youthful son.

Stabb'd at the sight, Deiphobus drew nigh,
And made, with force, the vengeful weapon fly.
The Cretan saw; and, stooping, caused to glance
From his slope shield the disappointed lance.
Beneath the spacious targe, (a blazing round,
Thick with bull-hides and brazen orbits bound,
On his raised arm by two strong braces stay'd,)
He lay collected in defensive shade.
O'er his safe head the javelin idly sung,
And on the tinkling verge more faintly rung.
Even then the spear the vigorous arm confess'd,
And pierced, obliquely, king Hypsenor's breast:
Warm'd in his liver, to the ground it bore
The chief, his people's guardian now no more!

"Not unattended (the proud Trojan cries)
Nor unrevenged, lamented Asius lies:
For thee, through hell's black portals stand display'd,
This mate shall joy thy melancholy shade."

Heart-piercing anguish, at the haughty boast,
Touch'd every Greek, but Nestor's son the most.
Grieved as he was, his pious arms attend,
And his broad buckler shields his slaughter'd friend:
Till sad Mecistheus and Alastor bore
His honour'd body to the tented shore.

Nor yet from fight Idomeneus withdraws;
Resolved to perish in his country's cause,
Or find some foe, whom heaven and he shall doom
To wail his fate in death's eternal gloom.
He sees Alcathous in the front aspire:
Great Ćsyetes was the hero's sire;
His spouse Hippodame, divinely fair,
Anchises' eldest hope, and darling care:
Who charm'd her parents' and her husband's heart
With beauty, sense, and every work of art:
He once of Ilion's youth the loveliest boy,
The fairest she of all the fair of Troy.
By Neptune now the hapless hero dies,
Who covers with a cloud those beauteous eyes,
And fetters every limb: yet bent to meet
His fate he stands; nor shuns the lance of Crete.
Fix'd as some column, or deep-rooted oak,
While the winds sleep; his breast received the stroke.

Before the ponderous stroke his corslet yields,
Long used to ward the death in fighting fields.
The riven armour sends a jarring sound;
His labouring heart heaves with so strong a bound,
The long lance shakes, and vibrates in the wound;
Fast flowing from its source, as prone he lay,
Life's purple tide impetuous gush'd away.

Then Idomen, insulting o'er the slain:
"Behold, Deiphobus! nor vaunt in vain:
See! on one Greek three Trojan ghosts attend;
This, my third victim, to the shades I send.
Approaching now thy boasted might approve,
And try the prowess of the seed of Jove.
From Jove, enamour'd of a mortal dame,
Great Minos, guardian of his country, came:
Deucalion, blameless prince, was Minos' heir;
His first-born I, the third from Jupiter:
O'er spacious Crete, and her bold sons, I reign,
And thence my ships transport me through the main:
Lord of a host, o'er all my host I shine,
A scourge to thee, thy father, and thy line."

The Trojan heard; uncertain or to meet,
Alone, with venturous arms the king of Crete,
Or seek auxiliar force; at length decreed
To call some hero to partake the deed,
Forthwith Æneas rises to his thought:
For him in Troy's remotest lines he sought,
Where he, incensed at partial Priam, stands,
And sees superior posts in meaner hands.
To him, ambitious of so great an aid,
The bold Deiphobus approach'd, and said:

"Now, Trojan prince, employ thy pious arms,
If e'er thy bosom felt fair honour's charms.
Alcathous dies, thy brother and thy friend;
Come, and the warrior's loved remains defend.
Beneath his cares thy early youth was train'd,
One table fed you, and one roof contain'd.
This deed to fierce Idomeneus we owe;
Haste, and revenge it on th' insulting foe."

Æneas heard, and for a space resign'd
To tender pity all his manly mind;
Then rising in his rage, he burns to fight:
The Greek awaits him with collected might.
As the fell boar, on some rough mountain's head,

Arm'd with wild terrors, and to slaughter bred,
When the loud rustics rise, and shout from far,
Attends the tumult, and expects the war;
O'er his bent back the bristly horrors rise;
Fires stream in lightning from his sanguine eyes,
His foaming tusks both dogs and men engage;
But most his hunters rouse his mighty rage:
So stood Idomeneus, his javelin shook,
And met the Trojan with a lowering look.
Antilochus, Deipyrus, were near,
The youthful offspring of the god of war,
Merion, and Aphareus, in field renown'd:
To these the warrior sent his voice around.
"Fellows in arms! your timely aid unite;
Lo, great Ćneas rushes to the fight:
Sprung from a god, and more than mortal bold;
He fresh in youth, and I in arms grown old.
Else should this hand, this hour decide the strife,
The great dispute, of glory, or of life."

He spoke, and all, as with one soul, obey'd;
Their lifted bucklers cast a dreadful shade
Around the chief. Ćneas too demands
Th' assisting forces of his native bands;
Paris, Deiphobus, Agenor, join;
(Co-aids and captains of the Trojan line;)
In order follow all th' embodied train,
Like Ida's flocks proceeding o'er the plain;
Before his fleecy care, erect and bold,
Stalks the proud ram, the father of the bold.
With joy the swain surveys them, as he leads
To the cool fountains, through the well-known meads:
So joys Ćneas, as his native band
Moves on in rank, and stretches o'er the land.

Round dread Alcathous now the battle rose;
On every side the steely circle grows;
Now batter'd breast-plates and hack'd helmets ring,
And o'er their heads unheeded javelins sing.
Above the rest, two towering chiefs appear,
There great Idomeneus, Ćneas here.
Like gods of war, dispensing fate, they stood,
And burn'd to drench the ground with mutual blood.
The Trojan weapon whizz'd along in air;
The Cretan saw, and shunn'd the brazen spear:
Sent from an arm so strong, the missive wood
Stuck deep in earth, and quiver'd where it stood.
But OEnomas received the Cretan's stroke;

The forceful spear his hollow corslet broke,
It ripp'd his belly with a ghastly wound,
And roll'd the smoking entrails on the ground.
Stretch'd on the plain, he sobs away his breath,
And, furious, grasps the bloody dust in death.
The victor from his breast the weapon tears;
His spoils he could not, for the shower of spears.
Though now unfit an active war to wage,
Heavy with cumbrous arms, stiff with cold age,
His listless limbs unable for the course,
In standing fight he yet maintains his force;
Till faint with labour, and by foes repell'd,
His tired slow steps he drags from off the field.
Deiphobus beheld him as he pass'd,
And, fired with hate, a parting javelin cast:
The javelin err'd, but held its course along,
And pierced Ascalaphus, the brave and young:
The son of Mars fell gasping on the ground,
And gnash'd the dust, all bloody with his wound.

Nor knew the furious father of his fall;
High-throned amidst the great Olympian hall,
On golden clouds th' immortal synod sate;
Detain'd from bloody war by Jove and Fate.

Now, where in dust the breathless hero lay,
For slain Ascalaphus commenced the fray,
Deiphobus to seize his helmet flies,
And from his temples rends the glittering prize;
Valiant as Mars, Meriones drew near,
And on his loaded arm discharged his spear:
He drops the weight, disabled with the pain;
The hollow helmet rings against the plain.
Swift as a vulture leaping on his prey,
From his torn arm the Grecian rent away
The reeking javelin, and rejoin'd his friends.
His wounded brother good Polites tends;
Around his waist his pious arms he threw,
And from the rage of battle gently drew:
Him his swift coursers, on his splendid car,
Rapt from the lessening thunder of the war;
To Troy they drove him, groaning from the shore,
And sprinkling, as he pass'd, the sands with gore.

Meanwhile fresh slaughter bathes the sanguine ground,
Heaps fall on heaps, and heaven and earth resound.
Bold Aphareus by great Ćneas bled;
As toward the chief he turn'd his daring head,

He pierced his throat; the bending head, depress'd
Beneath his helmet, nods upon his breast;
His shield reversed o'er the fallen warrior lies,
And everlasting slumber seals his eyes.
Antilochus, as Thoon turn'd him round,
Transpierced his back with a dishonest wound:
The hollow vein, that to the neck extends
Along the chine, his eager javelin rends:
Supine he falls, and to his social train
Spreads his imploring arms, but spreads in vain.
Th' exulting victor, leaping where he lay,
From his broad shoulders tore the spoils away;
His time observed; for closed by foes around,
On all sides thick the peals of arms resound.
His shield emboss'd the ringing storm sustains,
But he impervious and untouch'd remains.
(Great Neptune's care preserved from hostile rage
This youth, the joy of Nestor's glorious age.)
In arms intrepid, with the first he fought,
Faced every foe, and every danger sought;
His winged lance, resistless as the wind,
Obeys each motion of the master's mind!
Restless it flies, impatient to be free,
And meditates the distant enemy.
The son of Asius, Adamas, drew near,
And struck his target with the brazen spear
Fierce in his front: but Neptune wards the blow,
And blunts the javelin of th' eluded foe:
In the broad buckler half the weapon stood,
Splinter'd on earth flew half the broken wood.
Disarm'd, he mingled in the Trojan crew;
But Merion's spear o'ertook him as he flew,
Deep in the belly's rim an entrance found,
Where sharp the pang, and mortal is the wound.
Bending he fell, and doubled to the ground,
Lay panting. Thus an ox in fetters tied,
While death's strong pangs distend his labouring side,
His bulk enormous on the field displays;
His heaving heart beats thick as ebbing life decays.
The spear the conqueror from his body drew,
And death's dim shadows swarm before his view.
Next brave Deipyrus in dust was laid:
King Helenus waved high the Thracian blade,
And smote his temples with an arm so strong,
The helm fell off, and roll'd amid the throng:
There for some luckier Greek it rests a prize;
For dark in death the godlike owner lies!
Raging with grief, great Menelaus burns,

And fraught with vengeance, to the victor turns:
That shook the ponderous lance, in act to throw;
And this stood adverse with the bended bow:
Full on his breast the Trojan arrow fell,
But harmless bounded from the plated steel.
As on some ample barn's well harden'd floor,
(The winds collected at each open door,)
While the broad fan with force is whirl'd around,
Light leaps the golden grain, resulting from the ground:
So from the steel that guards Atrides' heart,
Repell'd to distance flies the bounding dart.
Atrides, watchful of the unwary foe,
Pierced with his lance the hand that grasp'd the bow.
And nailed it to the yew: the wounded hand
Trail'd the long lance that mark'd with blood the sand:
But good Agenor gently from the wound
The spear solicits, and the bandage bound;
A sling's soft wool, snatch'd from a soldier's side,
At once the tent and ligature supplied.

Behold! Pisander, urged by fate's decree,
Springs through the ranks to fall, and fall by thee,
Great Menelaus! to enchance thy fame:
High-towering in the front, the warrior came.
First the sharp lance was by Atrides thrown;
The lance far distant by the winds was blown.
Nor pierced Pisander through Atrides' shield:
Pisander's spear fell shiver'd on the field.
Not so discouraged, to the future blind,
Vain dreams of conquest swell his haughty mind;
Dauntless he rushes where the Spartan lord
Like lightning brandish'd his far beaming sword.
His left arm high opposed the shining shield:
His right beneath, the cover'd pole-axe held;
(An olive's cloudy grain the handle made,
Distinct with studs, and brazen was the blade;)
This on the helm discharged a noble blow;
The plume dropp'd nodding to the plain below,
Shorn from the crest. Atrides waved his steel:
Deep through his front the weighty falchion fell;
The crashing bones before its force gave way;
In dust and blood the groaning hero lay:
Forced from their ghastly orbs, and spouting gore,
The clotted eye-balls tumble on the shore.
And fierce Atrides spurn'd him as he bled,
Tore off his arms, and, loud-exulting, said:

"Thus, Trojans, thus, at length be taught to fear;

O race perfidious, who delight in war!
Already noble deeds ye have perform'd;
A princess raped transcends a navy storm'd:
In such bold feats your impious might approve,
Without th' assistance, or the fear of Jove.
The violated rites, the ravish'd dame;
Our heroes slaughter'd and our ships on flame,
Crimes heap'd on crimes, shall bend your glory down,
And whelm in ruins yon flagitious town.
O thou, great father! lord of earth and skies,
Above the thought of man, supremely wise!
If from thy hand the fates of mortals flow,
From whence this favour to an impious foe?
A godless crew, abandon'd and unjust,
Still breathing rapine, violence, and lust?
The best of things, beyond their measure, cloy;
Sleep's balmy blessing, love's endearing joy;
The feast, the dance; whate'er mankind desire,
Even the sweet charms of sacred numbers tire.
But Troy for ever reaps a dire delight
In thirst of slaughter, and in lust of fight."

This said, he seized (while yet the carcase heaved)
The bloody armour, which his train received:
Then sudden mix'd among the warring crew,
And the bold son of Pylaemenes slew.
Harpalion had through Asia travell'd far,
Following his martial father to the war:
Through filial love he left his native shore,
Never, ah, never to behold it more!
His unsuccessful spear he chanced to fling
Against the target of the Spartan king;
Thus of his lance disarm'd, from death he flies,
And turns around his apprehensive eyes.
Him, through the hip transpiercing as he fled,
The shaft of Merion mingled with the dead.
Beneath the bone the glancing point descends,
And, driving down, the swelling bladder rends:
Sunk in his sad companions' arms he lay,
And in short pantings sobb'd his soul away;
(Like some vile worm extended on the ground;)
While life's red torrent gush'd from out the wound.

Him on his car the Paphlagonian train
In slow procession bore from off the plain.
The pensive father, father now no more!
Attends the mournful pomp along the shore;
And unavailing tears profusely shed;

And, unrevenged, deplored his offspring dead.

Paris from far the moving sight beheld,
With pity soften'd and with fury swell'd:
His honour'd host, a youth of matchless grace,
And loved of all the Paphlagonian race!
With his full strength he bent his angry bow,
And wing'd the feather'd vengeance at the foe.
A chief there was, the brave Euchenor named,
For riches much, and more for virtue famed.
Who held his seat in Corinth's stately town;
Polydus' son, a seer of old renown.
Oft had the father told his early doom,
By arms abroad, or slow disease at home:
He climb'd his vessel, prodigal of breath,
And chose the certain glorious path to death.
Beneath his ear the pointed arrow went;
The soul came issuing at the narrow vent:
His limbs, unnerved, drop useless on the ground,
And everlasting darkness shades him round.

Nor knew great Hector how his legions yield,
(Wrapp'd in the cloud and tumult of the field:)
Wide on the left the force of Greece commands,
And conquest hovers o'er th' Achaian bands;
With such a tide superior virtue sway'd,
And he that shakes the solid earth gave aid.
But in the centre Hector fix'd remain'd,
Where first the gates were forced, and bulwarks gain'd;
There, on the margin of the hoary deep,
(Their naval station where the Ajaces keep.
And where low walls confine the beating tides,
Whose humble barrier scarce the foe divides;
Where late in fight both foot and horse engaged,
And all the thunder of the battle raged,)
There join'd, the whole Boeotian strength remains,
The proud Iaonians with their sweeping trains,
Locrians and Phthians, and th' Epaean force;
But join'd, repel not Hector's fiery course.
The flower of Athens, Stichius, Phidas, led;
Bias and great Menestheus at their head:
Meges the strong the Epaean bands controll'd,
And Dracius prudent, and Amphion bold:
The Phthians, Medon, famed for martial might,
And brave Podarces, active in the fight.
This drew from Phylacus his noble line;
Iphiclus' son: and that (Oileus) thine:
(Young Ajax' brother, by a stolen embrace;

He dwelt far distant from his native place,
By his fierce step-dame from his father's reign
Expell'd and exiled for her brother slain:)
These rule the Phthians, and their arms employ,
Mix'd with Boeotians, on the shores of Troy.

Now side by side, with like unwearied care,
Each Ajax laboured through the field of war:
So when two lordly bulls, with equal toil,
Force the bright ploughshare through the fallow soil,
Join'd to one yoke, the stubborn earth they tear,
And trace large furrows with the shining share;
O'er their huge limbs the foam descends in snow,
And streams of sweat down their sour foreheads flow.
A train of heroes followed through the field,
Who bore by turns great Ajax' sevenfold shield;
Whene'er he breathed, remissive of his might,
Tired with the incessant slaughters of the fight.
No following troops his brave associate grace:
In close engagement an unpractised race,
The Locrian squadrons nor the javelin wield,
Nor bear the helm, nor lift the moony shield;
But skill'd from far the flying shaft to wing,
Or whirl the sounding pebble from the sling,
Dexterous with these they aim a certain wound,
Or fell the distant warrior to the ground.
Thus in the van the Telamonian train,
Throng'd in bright arms, a pressing fight maintain:
Far in the rear the Locrian archers lie,
Whose stones and arrows intercept the sky,
The mingled tempest on the foes they pour;
Troy's scattering orders open to the shower.

Now had the Greeks eternal fame acquired,
And the gall'd Ilians to their walls retired;
But sage Polydamas, discreetly brave,
Address'd great Hector, and this counsel gave:

"Though great in all, thou seem'st averse to lend
Impartial audience to a faithful friend;
To gods and men thy matchless worth is known,
And every art of glorious war thy own;
But in cool thought and counsel to excel,
How widely differs this from warring well!
Content with what the bounteous gods have given,
Seek not alone to engross the gifts of Heaven.
To some the powers of bloody war belong,
To some sweet music and the charm of song;

To few, and wondrous few, has Jove assign'd
A wise, extensive, all-considering mind;
Their guardians these, the nations round confess,
And towns and empires for their safety bless.
If Heaven have lodged this virtue in my breast,
Attend, O Hector! what I judge the best,
See, as thou mov'st, on dangers dangers spread,
And war's whole fury burns around thy head.
Behold! distress'd within yon hostile wall,
How many Trojans yield, disperse, or fall!
What troops, out-number'd, scarce the war maintain!
And what brave heroes at the ships lie slain!
Here cease thy fury: and, the chiefs and kings
Convoked to council, weigh the sum of things.
Whether (the gods succeeding our desires)
To yon tall ships to bear the Trojan fires;
Or quit the fleet, and pass unhurt away,
Contented with the conquest of the day.
I fear, I fear, lest Greece, not yet undone,
Pay the large debt of last revolving sun;
Achilles, great Achilles, yet remains
On yonder decks, and yet o'erlooks the plains!"

The counsel pleased; and Hector, with a bound,
Leap'd from his chariot on the trembling ground;
Swift as he leap'd his clanging arms resound.
"To guard this post (he cried) thy art employ,
And here detain the scatter'd youth of Troy;
Where yonder heroes faint, I bend my way,
And hasten back to end the doubtful day."

This said, the towering chief prepares to go,
Shakes his white plumes that to the breezes flow,
And seems a moving mountain topp'd with snow.
Through all his host, inspiring force, he flies,
And bids anew the martial thunder rise.
To Panthus' son, at Hector's high command
Haste the bold leaders of the Trojan band:
But round the battlements, and round the plain,
For many a chief he look'd, but look'd in vain;
Deiphobus, nor Helenus the seer,
Nor Asius' son, nor Asius' self appear:
For these were pierced with many a ghastly wound,
Some cold in death, some groaning on the ground;
Some low in dust, (a mournful object) lay;
High on the wall some breathed their souls away.

Far on the left, amid the throng he found

(Cheering the troops, and dealing deaths around)
The graceful Paris; whom, with fury moved,
Opprobrious thus, th' impatient chief reproved:

"Ill-fated Paris! slave to womankind,
As smooth of face as fraudulent of mind!
Where is Deiphobus, where Asius gone?
The godlike father, and th' intrepid son?
The force of Helenus, dispensing fate;
And great Othryoneus, so fear'd of late?
Black fate hang's o'er thee from th' avenging gods,
Imperial Troy from her foundations nods;
Whelm'd in thy country's ruin shalt thou fall,
And one devouring vengeance swallow all."

When Paris thus: "My brother and my friend,
Thy warm impatience makes thy tongue offend,
In other battles I deserved thy blame,
Though then not deedless, nor unknown to fame:
But since yon rampart by thy arms lay low,
I scatter'd slaughter from my fatal bow.
The chiefs you seek on yonder shore lie slain;
Of all those heroes, two alone remain;
Deiphobus, and Helenus the seer,
Each now disabled by a hostile spear.
Go then, successful, where thy soul inspires:
This heart and hand shall second all thy fires:
What with this arm I can, prepare to know,
Till death for death be paid, and blow for blow.
But 'tis not ours, with forces not our own
To combat: strength is of the gods alone."
These words the hero's angry mind assuage:
Then fierce they mingle where the thickest rage.
Around Polydamas, distain'd with blood,
Cebrion, Phalces, stern Orthaeus stood,
Palmus, with Polypoetes the divine,
And two bold brothers of Hippotion's line
(Who reach'd fair Ilion, from Ascania far,
The former day; the next engaged in war).
As when from gloomy clouds a whirlwind springs,
That bears Jove's thunder on its dreadful wings,
Wide o'er the blasted fields the tempest sweeps;
Then, gather'd, settles on the hoary deeps;
The afflicted deeps tumultuous mix and roar;
The waves behind impel the waves before,
Wide rolling, foaming high, and tumbling to the shore:
Thus rank on rank, the thick battalions throng,
Chief urged on chief, and man drove man along.

Far o'er the plains, in dreadful order bright,
The brazen arms reflect a beamy light:
Full in the blazing van great Hector shined,
Like Mars commission'd to confound mankind.
Before him flaming his enormous shield,
Like the broad sun, illumined all the field;
His nodding helm emits a streamy ray;
His piercing eyes through all the battle stray,
And, while beneath his targe he flash'd along,
Shot terrors round, that wither'd e'en the strong.

Thus stalk'd he, dreadful; death was in his look:
Whole nations fear'd; but not an Argive shook.
The towering Ajax, with an ample stride,
Advanced the first, and thus the chief defied:

"Hector! come on; thy empty threats forbear;
'Tis not thy arm, 'tis thundering Jove we fear:
The skill of war to us not idly given,
Lo! Greece is humbled, not by Troy, but Heaven.
Vain are the hopes that haughty mind imparts,
To force our fleet: the Greeks have hands and hearts.
Long ere in flames our lofty navy fall,
Your boasted city, and your god-built wall,
Shall sink beneath us, smoking on the ground;
And spread a long unmeasured ruin round.
The time shall come, when, chased along the plain,
Even thou shalt call on Jove, and call in vain;
Even thou shalt wish, to aid thy desperate course,
The wings of falcons for thy flying horse;
Shalt run, forgetful of a warrior's fame,
While clouds of friendly dust conceal thy shame."

As thus he spoke, behold, in open view,
On sounding wings a dexter eagle flew.
To Jove's glad omen all the Grecians rise,
And hail, with shouts, his progress through the skies:
Far-echoing clamours bound from side to side;
They ceased; and thus the chief of Troy replied:

"From whence this menace, this insulting strain?
Enormous boaster! doom'd to vaunt in vain.
So may the gods on Hector life bestow,
(Not that short life which mortals lead below,
But such as those of Jove's high lineage born,
The blue-eyed maid, or he that gilds the morn,)
As this decisive day shall end the fame
Of Greece, and Argos be no more a name.

And thou, imperious! if thy madness wait
The lance of Hector, thou shalt meet thy fate:
That giant-corse, extended on the shore,
Shall largely feast the fowls with fat and gore."

He said; and like a lion stalk'd along:
With shouts incessant earth and ocean rung,
Sent from his following host: the Grecian train
With answering thunders fill'd the echoing plain;
A shout that tore heaven's concave, and, above,
Shook the fix'd splendours of the throne of Jove.

BOOK XIV

ARGUMENT

JUNO DECEIVES JUPITER BY THE GIRDLE OF VENUS

Nestor, sitting at the table with Machaon, is alarmed with the increasing clamour of war, and hastens to Agamemnon; on his way he meets that prince with Diomed and Ulysses, whom he informs of the extremity of the danger. Agamemnon proposes to make their escape by night, which Ulysses withstands; to which Diomed adds his advice, that, wounded as they were, they should go forth and encourage the army with their presence, which advice is pursued. Juno, seeing the partiality of Jupiter to the Trojans, forms a design to over-reach him: she sets off her charms with the utmost care, and (the more surely to enchant him) obtains the magic girdle of Venus. She then applies herself to the god of sleep, and, with some difficulty, persuades him to seal the eyes of Jupiter: this done, she goes to mount Ida, where the god, at first sight, is ravished with her beauty, sinks in her embraces, and is laid asleep. Neptune takes advantage of his slumber, and succours the Greeks: Hector is struck to the ground with a prodigious stone by Ajax, and carried off from the battle: several actions succeed, till the Trojans, much distressed, are obliged to give way: the lesser Ajax signalizes himself in a particular manner.

But not the genial feast, nor flowing bowl,
Could charm the cares of Nestor's watchful soul;
His startled ears the increasing cries attend;
Then thus, impatient, to his wounded friend:

"What new alarm, divine Machaon, say,
What mix'd events attend this mighty day?
Hark! how the shouts divide, and how they meet,
And now come full, and thicken to the fleet!
Here with the cordial draught dispel thy care,
Let Hecamede the strengthening bath prepare,
Refresh thy wound, and cleanse the clotted gore;
While I the adventures of the day explore."

He said: and, seizing Thrasymedes' shield,
(His valiant offspring,) hasten'd to the field;
(That day the son his father's buckler bore;)
Then snatch'd a lance, and issued from the door.
Soon as the prospect open'd to his view,
His wounded eyes the scene of sorrow knew;
Dire disarray! the tumult of the fight,
The wall in ruins, and the Greeks in flight.
As when old ocean's silent surface sleeps,
The waves just heaving on the purple deeps:
While yet the expected tempest hangs on high,
Weighs down the cloud, and blackens in the sky,
The mass of waters will no wind obey;
Jove sends one gust, and bids them roll away.
While wavering counsels thus his mind engage,
Fluctuates in doubtful thought the Pylian sage,
To join the host, or to the general haste;
Debating long, he fixes on the last:
Yet, as he moves, the sight his bosom warms,
The field rings dreadful with the clang of arms,
The gleaming falchions flash, the javelins fly;
Blows echo blows, and all or kill or die.

Him, in his march, the wounded princes meet,
By tardy steps ascending from the fleet:
The king of men, Ulysses the divine,
And who to Tydeus owes his noble line.
(Their ships at distance from the battle stand,
In lines advanced along the shelving strand:
Whose bay, the fleet unable to contain
At length; beside the margin of the main,
Rank above rank, the crowded ships they moor:
Who landed first, lay highest on the shore.)
Supported on the spears, they took their way,
Unfit to fight, but anxious for the day.
Nestor's approach alarm'd each Grecian breast,
Whom thus the general of the host address'd:

"O grace and glory of the Achaian name;
What drives thee, Nestor, from the field of fame?
Shall then proud Hector see his boast fulfill'd,
Our fleets in ashes, and our heroes kill'd?
Such was his threat, ah! now too soon made good,
On many a Grecian bosom writ in blood.
Is every heart inflamed with equal rage
Against your king, nor will one chief engage?
And have I lived to see with mournful eyes
In every Greek a new Achilles rise?"

Gerenian Nestor then: "So fate has will'd;
And all-confirming time has fate fulfill'd.
Not he that thunders from the aerial bower,
Not Jove himself, upon the past has power.
The wall, our late inviolable bound,
And best defence, lies smoking on the ground:
Even to the ships their conquering arms extend,
And groans of slaughter'd Greeks to heaven ascend.
On speedy measures then employ your thought
In such distress! if counsel profit aught:
Arms cannot much: though Mars our souls incite,
These gaping wounds withhold us from the fight."

To him the monarch: "That our army bends,
That Troy triumphant our high fleet ascends,
And that the rampart, late our surest trust
And best defence, lies smoking in the dust;
All this from Jove's afflictive hand we bear,
Who, far from Argos, wills our ruin here.
Past are the days when happier Greece was blest,
And all his favour, all his aid confess'd;
Now heaven averse, our hands from battle ties,
And lifts the Trojan glory to the skies.
Cease we at length to waste our blood in vain,
And launch what ships lie nearest to the main;
Leave these at anchor, till the coming night:
Then, if impetuous Troy forbear the fight,
Bring all to sea, and hoist each sail for flight.
Better from evils, well foreseen, to run,
Than perish in the danger we may shun."

Thus he. The sage Ulysses thus replies,
While anger flash'd from his disdainful eyes:
"What shameful words (unkingly as thou art)
Fall from that trembling tongue and timorous heart?
Oh were thy sway the curse of meaner powers,
And thou the shame of any host but ours!
A host, by Jove endued with martial might,
And taught to conquer, or to fall in fight:
Adventurous combats and bold wars to wage,
Employ'd our youth, and yet employs our age.
And wilt thou thus desert the Trojan plain?
And have whole streams of blood been spilt in vain?
In such base sentence if thou couch thy fear,
Speak it in whispers, lest a Greek should hear.
Lives there a man so dead to fame, who dares
To think such meanness, or the thought declares?

And comes it even from him whose sovereign sway
The banded legions of all Greece obey?
Is this a general's voice that calls to flight,
While war hangs doubtful, while his soldiers fight?
What more could Troy? What yet their fate denies
Thou givest the foe: all Greece becomes their prize.
No more the troops (our hoisted sails in view,
Themselves abandon'd) shall the fight pursue;
But thy ships flying, with despair shall see;
And owe destruction to a prince like thee."

"Thy just reproofs (Atrides calm replies)
Like arrows pierce me, for thy words are wise.
Unwilling as I am to lose the host,
I force not Greece to quit this hateful coast;
Glad I submit, whoe'er, or young, or old,
Aught, more conducive to our weal, unfold."

Tydides cut him short, and thus began:
"Such counsel if you seek, behold the man
Who boldly gives it, and what he shall say,
Young though he be, disdain not to obey:
A youth, who from the mighty Tydeus springs,
May speak to councils and assembled kings.
Hear then in me the great OEnides' son,
Whose honoured dust (his race of glory run)
Lies whelm'd in ruins of the Theban wall;
Brave in his life, and glorious in his fall.
With three bold sons was generous Prothous bless'd,
Who Pleuron's walls and Calydon possess'd;
Melas and Agrius, but (who far surpass'd
The rest in courage) OEneus was the last.
From him, my sire. From Calydon expell'd,
He pass'd to Argos, and in exile dwell'd;
The monarch's daughter there (so Jove ordain'd)
He won, and flourish'd where Adrastus reign'd;
There, rich in fortune's gifts, his acres till'd,
Beheld his vines their liquid harvest yield,
And numerous flocks that whiten'd all the field.
Such Tydeus was, the foremost once in fame!
Nor lives in Greece a stranger to his name.
Then, what for common good my thoughts inspire,
Attend, and in the son respect the sire.
Though sore of battle, though with wounds oppress'd,
Let each go forth, and animate the rest,
Advance the glory which he cannot share,
Though not partaker, witness of the war.
But lest new wounds on wounds o'erpower us quite,

Beyond the missile javelin's sounding flight,
Safe let us stand; and, from the tumult far,
Inspire the ranks, and rule the distant war."

He added not: the listening kings obey,
Slow moving on; Atrides leads the way.
The god of ocean (to inflame their rage)
Appears a warrior furrowed o'er with age;
Press'd in his own, the general's hand he took,
And thus the venerable hero spoke:

"Atrides! lo! with what disdainful eye
Achilles sees his country's forces fly;
Blind, impious man! whose anger is his guide,
Who glories in unutterable pride.
So may he perish, so may Jove disclaim
The wretch relentless, and o'erwhelm with shame!
But Heaven forsakes not thee: o'er yonder sands
Soon shall thou view the scattered Trojan bands
Fly diverse; while proud kings, and chiefs renown'd,
Driven heaps on heaps, with clouds involved around
Of rolling dust, their winged wheels employ
To hide their ignominious heads in Troy."

He spoke, then rush'd amid the warrior crew,
And sent his voice before him as he flew,
Loud, as the shout encountering armies yield
When twice ten thousand shake the labouring field;
Such was the voice, and such the thundering sound
Of him whose trident rends the solid ground.
Each Argive bosom beats to meet the fight,
And grisly war appears a pleasing sight.

Meantime Saturnia from Olympus' brow,
High-throned in gold, beheld the fields below;
With joy the glorious conflict she survey'd,
Where her great brother gave the Grecians aid.
But placed aloft, on Ida's shady height
She sees her Jove, and trembles at the sight.
Jove to deceive, what methods shall she try,
What arts, to blind his all-beholding eye?
At length she trusts her power; resolved to prove
The old, yet still successful, cheat of love;
Against his wisdom to oppose her charms,
And lull the lord of thunders in her arms.

Swift to her bright apartment she repairs,
Sacred to dress and beauty's pleasing cares:

With skill divine had Vulcan form'd the bower,
Safe from access of each intruding power.
Touch'd with her secret key, the doors unfold:
Self-closed, behind her shut the valves of gold.
Here first she bathes; and round her body pours
Soft oils of fragrance, and ambrosial showers:
The winds, perfumed, the balmy gale convey
Through heaven, through earth, and all the aerial way:
Spirit divine! whose exhalation greets
The sense of gods with more than mortal sweets.
Thus while she breathed of heaven, with decent pride
Her artful hands the radiant tresses tied;
Part on her head in shining ringlets roll'd,
Part o'er her shoulders waved like melted gold.
Around her next a heavenly mantle flow'd,
That rich with Pallas' labour'd colours glow'd:
Large clasps of gold the foldings gather'd round,
A golden zone her swelling bosom bound.
Far-beaming pendants tremble in her ear,
Each gem illumined with a triple star.
Then o'er her head she cast a veil more white
Than new-fallen snow, and dazzling as the light.
Last her fair feet celestial sandals grace.
Thus issuing radiant with majestic pace,
Forth from the dome the imperial goddess moves,
And calls the mother of the smiles and loves.

"How long (to Venus thus apart she cried)
Shall human strife celestial minds divide?
Ah yet, will Venus aid Saturnia's joy,
And set aside the cause of Greece and Troy?"

"Let heaven's dread empress (Cytheraea said)
Speak her request, and deem her will obey'd."

"Then grant me (said the queen) those conquering charms,
That power, which mortals and immortals warms,
That love, which melts mankind in fierce desires,
And burns the sons of heaven with sacred fires!

"For lo! I haste to those remote abodes,
Where the great parents, (sacred source of gods!)
Ocean and Tethys their old empire keep,
On the last limits of the land and deep.
In their kind arms my tender years were past;
What time old Saturn, from Olympus cast,
Of upper heaven to Jove resign'd the reign,
Whelm'd under the huge mass of earth and main.

For strife, I hear, has made the union cease,
Which held so long that ancient pair in peace.
What honour, and what love, shall I obtain,
If I compose those fatal feuds again;
Once more their minds in mutual ties engage,
And, what my youth has owed, repay their age!"

She said. With awe divine, the queen of love
Obey'd the sister and the wife of Jove;
And from her fragrant breast the zone embraced,
With various skill and high embroidery graced.
In this was every art, and every charm,
To win the wisest, and the coldest warm:
Fond love, the gentle vow, the gay desire,
The kind deceit, the still-reviving fire,
Persuasive speech, and the more persuasive sighs,
Silence that spoke, and eloquence of eyes.
This on her hand the Cyprian Goddess laid:
"Take this, and with it all thy wish;" she said.
With smiles she took the charm; and smiling press'd
The powerful cestus to her snowy breast.

Then Venus to the courts of Jove withdrew;
Whilst from Olympus pleased Saturnia flew.
O'er high Pieria thence her course she bore,
O'er fair Emathia's ever-pleasing shore,
O'er Hemus' hills with snows eternal crown'd;
Nor once her flying foot approach'd the ground.
Then taking wing from Athos' lofty steep,
She speeds to Lemnos o'er the rolling deep,
And seeks the cave of Death's half-brother, Sleep.

"Sweet pleasing Sleep! (Saturnia thus began)
Who spread'st thy empire o'er each god and man;
If e'er obsequious to thy Juno's will,
O power of slumbers! hear, and favour still.
Shed thy soft dews on Jove's immortal eyes,
While sunk in love's entrancing joys he lies.
A splendid footstool, and a throne, that shine
With gold unfading, Somnus, shall be thine;
The work of Vulcan; to indulge thy ease,
When wine and feasts thy golden humours please."

"Imperial dame (the balmy power replies),
Great Saturn's heir, and empress of the skies!
O'er other gods I spread my easy chain;
The sire of all, old Ocean, owns my reign.
And his hush'd waves lie silent on the main.

But how, unbidden, shall I dare to steep
Jove's awful temples in the dew of sleep?
Long since, too venturous, at thy bold command,
On those eternal lids I laid my hand;
What time, deserting Ilion's wasted plain,
His conquering son, Alcides, plough'd the main.
When lo! the deeps arise, the tempests roar,
And drive the hero to the Coan shore:
Great Jove, awaking, shook the blest abodes
With rising wrath, and tumbled gods on gods;
Me chief he sought, and from the realms on high
Had hurl'd indignant to the nether sky,
But gentle Night, to whom I fled for aid,
(The friend of earth and heaven,) her wings display'd;
Impower'd the wrath of gods and men to tame,
Even Jove revered the venerable dame."

"Vain are thy fears (the queen of heaven replies,
And, speaking, rolls her large majestic eyes);
Think'st thou that Troy has Jove's high favour won,
Like great Alcides, his all-conquering son?
Hear, and obey the mistress of the skies,
Nor for the deed expect a vulgar prize;
For know, thy loved-one shall be ever thine,
The youngest Grace, Pasithae the divine."

"Swear then (he said) by those tremendous floods
That roar through hell, and bind the invoking gods:
Let the great parent earth one hand sustain,
And stretch the other o'er the sacred main:
Call the black Titans, that with Chronos dwell,
To hear and witness from the depths of hell;
That she, my loved-one, shall be ever mine,
The youngest Grace, Pasithae the divine."

The queen assents, and from the infernal bowers
Invokes the sable subtartarean powers,
And those who rule the inviolable floods,
Whom mortals name the dread Titanian gods.

Then swift as wind, o'er Lemnos' smoky isle
They wing their way, and Imbrus' sea-beat soil;
Through air, unseen, involved in darkness glide,
And light on Lectos, on the point of Ide:
(Mother of savages, whose echoing hills
Are heard resounding with a hundred rills:)
Fair Ida trembles underneath the god;
Hush'd are her mountains, and her forests nod.

There on a fir, whose spiry branches rise
To join its summit to the neighbouring skies;
Dark in embowering shade, conceal'd from sight,
Sat Sleep, in likeness of the bird of night.
(Chalcis his name by those of heavenly birth,
But call'd Cymindis by the race of earth.)

To Ida's top successful Juno flies;
Great Jove surveys her with desiring eyes:
The god, whose lightning sets the heavens on fire,
Through all his bosom feels the fierce desire;
Fierce as when first by stealth he seized her charms,
Mix'd with her soul, and melted in her arms:
Fix'd on her eyes he fed his eager look,
Then press'd her hand, and thus with transport spoke:

"Why comes my goddess from the ethereal sky,
And not her steeds and flaming chariot nigh?"

Then she—"I haste to those remote abodes
Where the great parents of the deathless gods,
The reverend Ocean and gray Tethys, reign,
On the last limits of the land and main.
I visit these, to whose indulgent cares
I owe the nursing of my tender years:
For strife, I hear, has made that union cease
Which held so long that ancient pair in peace.
The steeds, prepared my chariot to convey
O'er earth and seas, and through the aerial way,
Wait under Ide: of thy superior power
To ask consent, I leave the Olympian bower;
Nor seek, unknown to thee, the sacred cells
Deep under seas, where hoary Ocean dwells."

"For that (said Jove) suffice another day!
But eager love denies the least delay.
Let softer cares the present hour employ,
And be these moments sacred all to joy.
Ne'er did my soul so strong a passion prove,
Or for an earthly, or a heavenly love:
Not when I press'd Ixion's matchless dame,
Whence rose Pirithous like the gods in fame:
Not when fair Danae felt the shower of gold
Stream into life, whence Perseus brave and bold.
Not thus I burn'd for either Theban dame:
(Bacchus from this, from that Alcides came:)
Nor Phoenix' daughter, beautiful and young,
Whence godlike Rhadamanth and Minos sprung.

Not thus I burn'd for fair Latona's face,
Nor comelier Ceres' more majestic grace.
Not thus even for thyself I felt desire,
As now my veins receive the pleasing fire."

He spoke; the goddess with the charming eyes
Glows with celestial red, and thus replies:
"Is this a scene for love? On Ida's height,
Exposed to mortal and immortal sight!
Our joys profaned by each familiar eye;
The sport of heaven, and fable of the sky:
How shall I e'er review the blest abodes,
Or mix among the senate of the gods?
Shall I not think, that, with disorder'd charms,
All heaven beholds me recent from thy arms?
With skill divine has Vulcan form'd thy bower,
Sacred to love and to the genial hour;
If such thy will, to that recess retire,
In secret there indulge thy soft desire."

She ceased; and, smiling with superior love,
Thus answer'd mild the cloud-compelling Jove:
"Nor god nor mortal shall our joys behold,
Shaded with clouds, and circumfused in gold;
Not even the sun, who darts through heaven his rays,
And whose broad eye the extended earth surveys."

Gazing he spoke, and, kindling at the view,
His eager arms around the goddess threw.
Glad Earth perceives, and from her bosom pours
Unbidden herbs and voluntary flowers:
Thick new-born violets a soft carpet spread,
And clustering lotos swell'd the rising bed,
And sudden hyacinths the turf bestrow,
And flamy crocus made the mountain glow
There golden clouds conceal the heavenly pair,
Steep'd in soft joys and circumfused with air;
Celestial dews, descending o'er the ground,
Perfume the mount, and breathe ambrosia round:
At length, with love and sleep's soft power oppress'd,
The panting thunderer nods, and sinks to rest.

Now to the navy borne on silent wings,
To Neptune's ear soft Sleep his message brings;
Beside him sudden, unperceived, he stood,
And thus with gentle words address'd the god:

"Now, Neptune! now, the important hour employ,

To check a while the haughty hopes of Troy:
While Jove yet rests, while yet my vapours shed
The golden vision round his sacred head;
For Juno's love, and Somnus' pleasing ties,
Have closed those awful and eternal eyes."
Thus having said, the power of slumber flew,
On human lids to drop the balmy dew.
Neptune, with zeal increased, renews his care,
And towering in the foremost ranks of war,
Indignant thus—"Oh once of martial fame!
O Greeks! if yet ye can deserve the name!
This half-recover'd day shall Troy obtain?
Shall Hector thunder at your ships again?
Lo! still he vaunts, and threats the fleet with fires,
While stern Achilles in his wrath retires.
One hero's loss too tamely you deplore,
Be still yourselves, and ye shall need no more.
Oh yet, if glory any bosom warms,
Brace on your firmest helms, and stand to arms:
His strongest spear each valiant Grecian wield,
Each valiant Grecian seize his broadest shield;
Let to the weak the lighter arms belong,
The ponderous targe be wielded by the strong.
Thus arm'd, not Hector shall our presence stay;
Myself, ye Greeks! myself will lead the way."

The troops assent; their martial arms they change:
The busy chiefs their banded legions range.
The kings, though wounded, and oppress'd with pain,
With helpful hands themselves assist the train.
The strong and cumbrous arms the valiant wield,
The weaker warrior takes a lighter shield.
Thus sheath'd in shining brass, in bright array
The legions march, and Neptune leads the way:
His brandish'd falchion flames before their eyes,
Like lightning flashing through the frighted skies.
Clad in his might, the earth-shaking power appears;
Pale mortals tremble, and confess their fears.

Troy's great defender stands alone unawed,
Arms his proud host, and dares oppose a god:
And lo! the god, and wondrous man, appear:
The sea's stern ruler there, and Hector here.
The roaring main, at her great master's call,
Rose in huge ranks, and form'd a watery wall
Around the ships: seas hanging o'er the shores,
Both armies join: earth thunders, ocean roars.
Not half so loud the bellowing deeps resound,

When stormy winds disclose the dark profound;
Less loud the winds that from the Éolian hall
Roar through the woods, and make whole forests fall;
Less loud the woods, when flames in torrents pour,
Catch the dry mountain, and its shades devour;
With such a rage the meeting hosts are driven,
And such a clamour shakes the sounding heaven.
The first bold javelin, urged by Hector's force,
Direct at Ajax' bosom winged its course;
But there no pass the crossing belts afford,
(One braced his shield, and one sustain'd his sword.)
Then back the disappointed Trojan drew,
And cursed the lance that unavailing flew:
But 'scaped not Ajax; his tempestuous hand
A ponderous stone upheaving from the sand,
(Where heaps laid loose beneath the warrior's feet,
Or served to ballast, or to prop the fleet,)
Toss'd round and round, the missive marble flings;
On the razed shield the fallen ruin rings,
Full on his breast and throat with force descends;
Nor deaden'd there its giddy fury spends,
But whirling on, with many a fiery round,
Smokes in the dust, and ploughs into the ground.
As when the bolt, red-hissing from above,
Darts on the consecrated plant of Jove,
The mountain-oak in flaming ruin lies,
Black from the blow, and smokes of sulphur rise;
Stiff with amaze the pale beholders stand,
And own the terrors of the almighty hand!
So lies great Hector prostrate on the shore;
His slacken'd hand deserts the lance it bore;
His following shield the fallen chief o'erspread;
Beneath his helmet dropp'd his fainting head;
His load of armour, sinking to the ground,
Clanks on the field, a dead and hollow sound.
Loud shouts of triumph fill the crowded plain;
Greece sees, in hope, Troy's great defender slain:
All spring to seize him; storms of arrows fly,
And thicker javelins intercept the sky.
In vain an iron tempest hisses round;
He lies protected, and without a wound.
Polydamas, Agenor the divine,
The pious warrior of Anchises' line,
And each bold leader of the Lycian band,
With covering shields (a friendly circle) stand,
His mournful followers, with assistant care,
The groaning hero to his chariot bear;
His foaming coursers, swifter than the wind,

Speed to the town, and leave the war behind.

When now they touch'd the mead's enamell'd side,
Where gentle Xanthus rolls his easy tide,
With watery drops the chief they sprinkle round,
Placed on the margin of the flowery ground.
Raised on his knees, he now ejects the gore;
Now faints anew, low-sinking on the shore;
By fits he breathes, half views the fleeting skies,
And seals again, by fits, his swimming eyes.

Soon as the Greeks the chief's retreat beheld,
With double fury each invades the field.
Oilean Ajax first his javelin sped,
Pierced by whose point the son of Enops bled;
(Satnius the brave, whom beauteous Neis bore
Amidst her flocks on Satnio's silver shore;)
Struck through the belly's rim, the warrior lies
Supine, and shades eternal veil his eyes.
An arduous battle rose around the dead;
By turns the Greeks, by turns the Trojans bled.

Fired with revenge, Polydamas drew near,
And at Prothoenor shook the trembling spear;
The driving javelin through his shoulder thrust,
He sinks to earth, and grasps the bloody dust.
"Lo thus (the victor cries) we rule the field,
And thus their arms the race of Panthus wield:
From this unerring hand there flies no dart
But bathes its point within a Grecian heart.
Propp'd on that spear to which thou owest thy fall,
Go, guide thy darksome steps to Pluto's dreary hall."

He said, and sorrow touch'd each Argive breast:
The soul of Ajax burn'd above the rest.
As by his side the groaning warrior fell,
At the fierce foe he launch'd his piercing steel;
The foe, reclining, shunn'd the flying death;
But fate, Archilochus, demands thy breath:
Thy lofty birth no succour could impart,
The wings of death o'ertook thee on the dart;
Swift to perform heaven's fatal will, it fled
Full on the juncture of the neck and head,
And took the joint, and cut the nerves in twain:
The dropping head first tumbled on the plain.
So just the stroke, that yet the body stood
Erect, then roll'd along the sands in blood.

"Here, proud Polydamas, here turn thy eyes!
(The towering Ajax loud-insulting cries:)
Say, is this chief extended on the plain
A worthy vengeance for Prothoenor slain?
Mark well his port! his figure and his face
Nor speak him vulgar, nor of vulgar race;
Some lines, methinks, may make his lineage known,
Antenor's brother, or perhaps his son."

He spake, and smiled severe, for well he knew
The bleeding youth: Troy sadden'd at the view.
But furious Acamas avenged his cause;
As Promachus his slaughtered brother draws,
He pierced his heart—"Such fate attends you all,
Proud Argives! destined by our arms to fall.
Not Troy alone, but haughty Greece, shall share
The toils, the sorrows, and the wounds of war.
Behold your Promachus deprived of breath,
A victim owed to my brave brother's death.
Not unappeased he enters Pluto's gate,
Who leaves a brother to revenge his fate."

Heart-piercing anguish struck the Grecian host,
But touch'd the breast of bold Peneleus most;
At the proud boaster he directs his course;
The boaster flies, and shuns superior force.
But young Ilioneus received the spear;
Ilioneus, his father's only care:
(Phorbas the rich, of all the Trojan train
Whom Hermes loved, and taught the arts of gain:)
Full in his eye the weapon chanced to fall,
And from the fibres scoop'd the rooted ball,
Drove through the neck, and hurl'd him to the plain;
He lifts his miserable arms in vain!
Swift his broad falchion fierce Peneleus spread,
And from the spouting shoulders struck his head;
To earth at once the head and helmet fly;
The lance, yet sticking through the bleeding eye,
The victor seized; and, as aloft he shook
The gory visage, thus insulting spoke:

"Trojans! your great Ilioneus behold!
Haste, to his father let the tale be told:
Let his high roofs resound with frantic woe,
Such as the house of Promachus must know;
Let doleful tidings greet his mother's ear,
Such as to Promachus' sad spouse we bear,
When we victorious shall to Greece return,

And the pale matron in our triumphs mourn."

Dreadful he spoke, then toss'd the head on high;
The Trojans hear, they tremble, and they fly:
Aghast they gaze around the fleet and wall,
And dread the ruin that impends on all.

Daughters of Jove! that on Olympus shine,
Ye all-beholding, all-recording nine!
O say, when Neptune made proud Ilion yield,
What chief, what hero first embrued the field?
Of all the Grecians what immortal name,
And whose bless'd trophies, will ye raise to fame?

Thou first, great Ajax! on the unsanguined plain
Laid Hyrtius, leader of the Mysian train.
Phalces and Mermer, Nestor's son o'erthrew,
Bold Merion, Morys and Hippotion slew.
Strong Periphaetes and Prothoon bled,
By Teucer's arrows mingled with the dead,
Pierced in the flank by Menelaus' steel,
His people's pastor, Hyperenor fell;
Eternal darkness wrapp'd the warrior round,
And the fierce soul came rushing through the wound.
But stretch'd in heaps before Oileus' son,
Fall mighty numbers, mighty numbers run;
Ajax the less, of all the Grecian race
Skill'd in pursuit, and swiftest in the chase.

BOOK XV

ARGUMENT

THE FIFTH BATTLE AT THE SHIPS; AND THE ACTS OF AJAX

Jupiter, awaking, sees the Trojans repulsed from the trenches, Hector in a swoon, and Neptune at the head of the Greeks: he is highly incensed at the artifice of Juno, who appeases him by her submissions; she is then sent to Iris and Apollo. Juno, repairing to the assembly of the gods, attempts, with extraordinary address, to incense them against Jupiter; in particular she touches Mars with a violent resentment; he is ready to take arms, but is prevented by Minerva. Iris and Apollo obey the orders of Jupiter; Iris commands Neptune to leave the battle, to which, after much reluctance and passion, he consents. Apollo reinspires Hector with vigour, brings him back to the battle, marches before him with his aegis, and turns the fortune of the fight. He breaks down great part of the Grecian wall: the Trojans rush in, and attempt to fire the first line of the fleet, but are, as yet, repelled by the greater Ajax with a prodigious slaughter.

Now in swift flight they pass the trench profound,
And many a chief lay gasping on the ground:
Then stopp'd and panted, where the chariots lie
Fear on their cheek, and horror in their eye.
Meanwhile, awaken'd from his dream of love,
On Ida's summit sat imperial Jove:
Round the wide fields he cast a careful view,
There saw the Trojans fly, the Greeks pursue;
These proud in arms, those scatter'd o'er the plain
And, 'midst the war, the monarch of the main.
Not far, great Hector on the dust he spies,
(His sad associates round with weeping eyes,)
Ejecting blood, and panting yet for breath,
His senses wandering to the verge of death.
The god beheld him with a pitying look,
And thus, incensed, to fraudful Juno spoke:

"O thou, still adverse to the eternal will,
For ever studious in promoting ill!
Thy arts have made the godlike Hector yield,
And driven his conquering squadrons from the field.
Canst thou, unhappy in thy wiles, withstand
Our power immense, and brave the almighty hand?
Hast thou forgot, when, bound and fix'd on high,
From the vast concave of the spangled sky,
I hung thee trembling in a golden chain,
And all the raging gods opposed in vain?
Headlong I hurl'd them from the Olympian hall,
Stunn'd in the whirl, and breathless with the fall.
For godlike Hercules these deeds were done,
Nor seem'd the vengeance worthy such a son:
When, by thy wiles induced, fierce Boreas toss'd
The shipwreck'd hero on the Coan coast,
Him through a thousand forms of death I bore,
And sent to Argos, and his native shore.
Hear this, remember, and our fury dread,
Nor pull the unwilling vengeance on thy head;
Lest arts and blandishments successless prove,
Thy soft deceits, and well-dissembled love."

The Thunderer spoke: imperial Juno mourn'd,
And, trembling, these submissive words return'd:

"By every oath that powers immortal ties,
The foodful earth and all-infolding skies;
By thy black waves, tremendous Styx! that flow
Through the drear realms of gliding ghosts below;

By the dread honours of thy sacred head,
And that unbroken vow, our virgin bed!
Not by my arts the ruler of the main
Steeps Troy in blood, and ranges round the plain:
By his own ardour, his own pity sway'd,
To help his Greeks, he fought and disobey'd:
Else had thy Juno better counsels given,
And taught submission to the sire of heaven."

"Think'st thou with me? fair empress of the skies!
(The immortal father with a smile replies;)
Then soon the haughty sea-god shall obey,
Nor dare to act but when we point the way.
If truth inspires thy tongue, proclaim our will
To yon bright synod on the Olympian hill;
Our high decree let various Iris know,
And call the god that bears the silver bow.
Let her descend, and from the embattled plain
Command the sea-god to his watery reign:
While Phoebus hastes great Hector to prepare
To rise afresh, and once more wake the war:
His labouring bosom re-inspires with breath,
And calls his senses from the verge of death.
Greece chased by Troy, even to Achilles' fleet,
Shall fall by thousands at the hero's feet.
He, not untouch'd with pity, to the plain
Shall send Patroclus, but shall send in vain.
What youths he slaughters under Ilion's walls!
Even my loved son, divine Sarpedon, falls!
Vanquish'd at last by Hector's lance he lies.
Then, nor till then, shall great Achilles rise:
And lo! that instant, godlike Hector dies.
From that great hour the war's whole fortune turns,
Pallas assists, and lofty Ilion burns.
Not till that day shall Jove relax his rage,
Nor one of all the heavenly host engage
In aid of Greece. The promise of a god
I gave, and seal'd it with the almighty nod,
Achilles' glory to the stars to raise;
Such was our word, and fate the word obeys."

The trembling queen (the almighty order given)
Swift from the Idaean summit shot to heaven.
As some wayfaring man, who wanders o'er
In thought a length of lands he trod before,
Sends forth his active mind from place to place,
Joins hill to dale, and measures space with space:
So swift flew Juno to the bless'd abodes,

If thought of man can match the speed of gods.
There sat the powers in awful synod placed;
They bow'd, and made obeisance as she pass'd
Through all the brazen dome: with goblets crown'd
They hail her queen; the nectar streams around.
Fair Themis first presents the golden bowl,
And anxious asks what cares disturb her soul?

To whom the white-arm'd goddess thus replies:
"Enough thou know'st the tyrant of the skies,
Severely bent his purpose to fulfil,
Unmoved his mind, and unrestrain'd his will.
Go thou, the feasts of heaven attend thy call;
Bid the crown'd nectar circle round the hall:
But Jove shall thunder through the ethereal dome
Such stern decrees, such threaten'd woes to come,
As soon shall freeze mankind with dire surprise,
And damp the eternal banquets of the skies."

The goddess said, and sullen took her place;
Black horror sadden'd each celestial face.
To see the gathering grudge in every breast,
Smiles on her lips a spleenful joy express'd;
While on her wrinkled front, and eyebrow bent,
Sat stedfast care, and lowering discontent.
Thus she proceeds—"Attend, ye powers above!
But know, 'tis madness to contest with Jove:
Supreme he sits; and sees, in pride of sway.
Your vassal godheads grudgingly obey:
Fierce in the majesty of power controls;
Shakes all the thrones of heaven, and bends the poles.
Submiss, immortals! all he wills, obey:
And thou, great Mars, begin and show the way.
Behold Ascalaphus! behold him die,
But dare not murmur, dare not vent a sigh;
Thy own loved boasted offspring lies o'erthrown,
If that loved boasted offspring be thy own."

Stern Mars, with anguish for his slaughter'd son,
Smote his rebelling breast, and fierce begun:
"Thus then, immortals! thus shall Mars obey;
Forgive me, gods, and yield my vengeance way:
Descending first to yon forbidden plain,
The god of battles dares avenge the slain;
Dares, though the thunder bursting o'er my head
Should hurl me blazing on those heaps of dead."

With that he gives command to Fear and Flight

To join his rapid coursers for the fight:
Then grim in arms, with hasty vengeance flies;
Arms that reflect a radiance through the skies.
And now had Jove, by bold rebellion driven,
Discharged his wrath on half the host of heaven;
But Pallas, springing through the bright abode,
Starts from her azure throne to calm the god.
Struck for the immortal race with timely fear,
From frantic Mars she snatch'd the shield and spear;
Then the huge helmet lifting from his head,
Thus to the impetuous homicide she said:

"By what wild passion, furious! art thou toss'd?
Striv'st thou with Jove? thou art already lost.
Shall not the Thunderer's dread command restrain,
And was imperial Juno heard in vain?
Back to the skies wouldst thou with shame be driven,
And in thy guilt involve the host of heaven?
Ilion and Greece no more should Jove engage,
The skies would yield an ampler scene of rage;
Guilty and guiltless find an equal fate
And one vast ruin whelm the Olympian state.
Cease then thy offspring's death unjust to call;
Heroes as great have died, and yet shall fall.
Why should heaven's law with foolish man comply
Exempted from the race ordain'd to die?"

This menace fix'd the warrior to his throne;
Sullen he sat, and curb'd the rising groan.
Then Juno call'd (Jove's orders to obey)
The winged Iris, and the god of day.
"Go wait the Thunderer's will (Saturnia cried)
On yon tall summit of the fountful Ide:
There in the father's awful presence stand,
Receive, and execute his dread command."

She said, and sat; the god that gilds the day,
And various Iris, wing their airy way.
Swift as the wind, to Ida's hills they came,
(Fair nurse of fountains, and of savage game)
There sat the eternal; he whose nod controls
The trembling world, and shakes the steady poles.
Veil'd in a mist of fragrance him they found,
With clouds of gold and purple circled round.
Well-pleased the Thunderer saw their earnest care,
And prompt obedience to the queen of air;
Then (while a smile serenes his awful brow)
Commands the goddess of the showery bow:

"Iris! descend, and what we here ordain,
Report to yon mad tyrant of the main.
Bid him from fight to his own deeps repair,
Or breathe from slaughter in the fields of air.
If he refuse, then let him timely weigh
Our elder birthright, and superior sway.
How shall his rashness stand the dire alarms,
If heaven's omnipotence descend in arms?
Strives he with me, by whom his power was given,
And is there equal to the lord of heaven?"

The all-mighty spoke; the goddess wing'd her flight
To sacred Ilion from the Idaean height.
Swift as the rattling hail, or fleecy snows,
Drive through the skies, when Boreas fiercely blows;
So from the clouds descending Iris falls,
And to blue Neptune thus the goddess calls:

"Attend the mandate of the sire above!
In me behold the messenger of Jove:
He bids thee from forbidden wars repair
To thine own deeps, or to the fields of air.
This if refused, he bids thee timely weigh
His elder birthright, and superior sway.
How shall thy rashness stand the dire alarms
If heaven's omnipotence descend in arms?
Striv'st thou with him by whom all power is given?
And art thou equal to the lord of heaven?"

"What means the haughty sovereign of the skies?
(The king of ocean thus, incensed, replies;)
Rule as he will his portion'd realms on high;
No vassal god, nor of his train, am I.
Three brother deities from Saturn came,
And ancient Rhea, earth's immortal dame:
Assign'd by lot, our triple rule we know;
Infernal Pluto sways the shades below;
O'er the wide clouds, and o'er the starry plain,
Ethereal Jove extends his high domain;
My court beneath the hoary waves I keep,
And hush the roarings of the sacred deep;
Olympus, and this earth, in common lie:
What claim has here the tyrant of the sky?
Far in the distant clouds let him control,
And awe the younger brothers of the pole;
There to his children his commands be given,
The trembling, servile, second race of heaven."

"And must I then (said she), O sire of floods!
Bear this fierce answer to the king of gods?
Correct it yet, and change thy rash intent;
A noble mind disdains not to repent.
To elder brothers guardian fiends are given,
To scourge the wretch insulting them and heaven."

"Great is the profit (thus the god rejoin'd)
When ministers are blest with prudent mind:
Warn'd by thy words, to powerful Jove I yield,
And quit, though angry, the contended field:
Not but his threats with justice I disclaim,
The same our honours, and our birth the same.
If yet, forgetful of his promise given
To Hermes, Pallas, and the queen of heaven,
To favour Ilion, that perfidious place,
He breaks his faith with half the ethereal race;
Give him to know, unless the Grecian train
Lay yon proud structures level with the plain,
Howe'er the offence by other gods be pass'd,
The wrath of Neptune shall for ever last."

Thus speaking, furious from the field he strode,
And plunged into the bosom of the flood.
The lord of thunders, from his lofty height
Beheld, and thus bespoke the source of light:

"Behold! the god whose liquid arms are hurl'd
Around the globe, whose earthquakes rock the world,
Desists at length his rebel-war to wage,
Seeks his own seas, and trembles at our rage;
Else had my wrath, heaven's thrones all shaking round,
Burn'd to the bottom of his seas profound;
And all the gods that round old Saturn dwell
Had heard the thunders to the deeps of hell.
Well was the crime, and well the vengeance spared;
Even power immense had found such battle hard.
Go thou, my son! the trembling Greeks alarm,
Shake my broad aegis on thy active arm,
Be godlike Hector thy peculiar care,
Swell his bold heart, and urge his strength to war:
Let Ilion conquer, till the Achaian train
Fly to their ships and Hellespont again:
Then Greece shall breathe from toils." The godhead said;
His will divine the son of Jove obey'd.
Not half so swift the sailing falcon flies,
That drives a turtle through the liquid skies,

As Phoebus, shooting from the Idaean brow,
Glides down the mountain to the plain below.
There Hector seated by the stream he sees,
His sense returning with the coming breeze;
Again his pulses beat, his spirits rise;
Again his loved companions meet his eyes;
Jove thinking of his pains, they pass'd away,
To whom the god who gives the golden day:

"Why sits great Hector from the field so far?
What grief, what wound, withholds thee from the war?"

The fainting hero, as the vision bright
Stood shining o'er him, half unseal'd his sight:

"What blest immortal, with commanding breath,
Thus wakens Hector from the sleep of death?
Has fame not told, how, while my trusty sword
Bathed Greece in slaughter, and her battle gored,
The mighty Ajax with a deadly blow
Had almost sunk me to the shades below?
Even yet, methinks, the gliding ghosts I spy,
And hell's black horrors swim before my eye."

To him Apollo: "Be no more dismay'd;
See, and be strong! the Thunderer sends thee aid.
Behold! thy Phoebus shall his arms employ,
Phoebus, propitious still to thee and Troy.
Inspire thy warriors then with manly force,
And to the ships impel thy rapid horse:
Even I will make thy fiery coursers way,
And drive the Grecians headlong to the sea."

Thus to bold Hector spoke the son of Jove,
And breathed immortal ardour from above.
As when the pamper'd steed, with reins unbound,
Breaks from his stall, and pours along the ground;
With ample strokes he rushes to the flood,
To bathe his sides, and cool his fiery blood;
His head, now freed, he tosses to the skies;
His mane dishevell'd o'er his shoulders flies:
He snuffs the females in the well-known plain,
And springs, exulting, to his fields again:
Urged by the voice divine, thus Hector flew,
Full of the god; and all his hosts pursue.
As when the force of men and dogs combined
Invade the mountain goat, or branching hind;
Far from the hunter's rage secure they lie

Close in the rock, (not fated yet to die)
When lo! a lion shoots across the way!
They fly: at once the chasers and the prey.
So Greece, that late in conquering troops pursued,
And mark'd their progress through the ranks in blood,
Soon as they see the furious chief appear,
Forget to vanquish, and consent to fear.

Thoas with grief observed his dreadful course,
Thoas, the bravest of the Ćtolian force;
Skill'd to direct the javelin's distant flight,
And bold to combat in the standing fight,
Not more in councils famed for solid sense,
Than winning words and heavenly eloquence.
"Gods! what portent (he cried) these eyes invades?
Lo! Hector rises from the Stygian shades!
We saw him, late, by thundering Ajax kill'd:
What god restores him to the frighted field;
And not content that half of Greece lie slain,
Pours new destruction on her sons again?
He comes not, Jove! without thy powerful will;
Lo! still he lives, pursues, and conquers still!
Yet hear my counsel, and his worst withstand:
The Greeks' main body to the fleet command;
But let the few whom brisker spirits warm,
Stand the first onset, and provoke the storm.
Thus point your arms; and when such foes appear,
Fierce as he is, let Hector learn to fear."

The warrior spoke; the listening Greeks obey,
Thickening their ranks, and form a deep array.

Each Ajax, Teucer, Merion gave command,
The valiant leader of the Cretan band;
And Mars-like Meges: these the chiefs excite,
Approach the foe, and meet the coming fight.
Behind, unnumber'd multitudes attend,
To flank the navy, and the shores defend.
Full on the front the pressing Trojans bear,
And Hector first came towering to the war.
Phoebus himself the rushing battle led;
A veil of clouds involved his radiant head:
High held before him, Jove's enormous shield
Portentous shone, and shaded all the field;
Vulcan to Jove the immortal gift consign'd,
To scatter hosts and terrify mankind,
The Greeks expect the shock, the clamours rise
From different parts, and mingle in the skies.

Dire was the hiss of darts, by heroes flung,
And arrows leaping from the bow-string sung;
These drink the life of generous warriors slain:
Those guiltless fall, and thirst for blood in vain.
As long as Phoebus bore unmoved the shield,
Sat doubtful conquest hovering o'er the field;
But when aloft he shakes it in the skies,
Shouts in their ears, and lightens in their eyes,
Deep horror seizes every Grecian breast,
Their force is humbled, and their fear confess'd.
So flies a herd of oxen, scatter'd wide,
No swain to guard them, and no day to guide,
When two fell lions from the mountain come,
And spread the carnage through the shady gloom.
Impending Phoebus pours around them fear,
And Troy and Hector thunder in the rear.
Heaps fall on heaps: the slaughter Hector leads,
First great Arcesilas, then Stichius bleeds;
One to the bold Boeotians ever dear,
And one Menestheus' friend and famed compeer.
Medon and Iasus, Ćneas sped;
This sprang from Phelus, and the Athenians led;
But hapless Medon from Oileus came;
Him Ajax honour'd with a brother's name,
Though born of lawless love: from home expell'd,
A banish'd man, in Phylace he dwell'd,
Press'd by the vengeance of an angry wife;
Troy ends at last his labours and his life.
Mecystes next Polydamas o'erthrew;
And thee, brave Clonius, great Agenor slew.
By Paris, Deiochus inglorious dies,
Pierced through the shoulder as he basely flies.
Polites' arm laid Echius on the plain;
Stretch'd on one heap, the victors spoil the slain.
The Greeks dismay'd, confused, disperse or fall,
Some seek the trench, some skulk behind the wall.
While these fly trembling, others pant for breath,
And o'er the slaughter stalks gigantic death.
On rush'd bold Hector, gloomy as the night;
Forbids to plunder, animates the fight,
Points to the fleet: "For, by the gods! who flies,
Who dares but linger, by this hand he dies;
No weeping sister his cold eye shall close,
No friendly hand his funeral pyre compose.
Who stops to plunder at this signal hour,
The birds shall tear him, and the dogs devour."
Furious he said; the smarting scourge resounds;
The coursers fly; the smoking chariot bounds;

The hosts rush on; loud clamours shake the shore;
The horses thunder, earth and ocean roar!
Apollo, planted at the trench's bound,
Push'd at the bank: down sank the enormous mound:
Roll'd in the ditch the heapy ruin lay;
A sudden road! a long and ample way.
O'er the dread fosse (a late impervious space)
Now steeds, and men, and cars tumultuous pass.
The wondering crowds the downward level trod;
Before them flamed the shield, and march'd the god.
Then with his hand he shook the mighty wall;
And lo! the turrets nod, the bulwarks fall:
Easy as when ashore an infant stands,
And draws imagined houses in the sands;
The sportive wanton, pleased with some new play,
Sweeps the slight works and fashion'd domes away:
Thus vanish'd at thy touch, the towers and walls;
The toil of thousands in a moment falls.

The Grecians gaze around with wild despair,
Confused, and weary all the powers with prayer:
Exhort their men, with praises, threats, commands;
And urge the gods, with voices, eyes, and hands.
Experienced Nestor chief obtests the skies,
And weeps his country with a father's eyes.

"O Jove! if ever, on his native shore,
One Greek enrich'd thy shrine with offer'd gore;
If e'er, in hope our country to behold,
We paid the fattest firstlings of the fold;
If e'er thou sign'st our wishes with thy nod:
Perform the promise of a gracious god!
This day preserve our navies from the flame,
And save the relics of the Grecian name."

Thus prayed the sage: the eternal gave consent,
And peals of thunder shook the firmament.
Presumptuous Troy mistook the accepting sign,
And catch'd new fury at the voice divine.
As, when black tempests mix the seas and skies,
The roaring deeps in watery mountains rise,
Above the sides of some tall ship ascend,
Its womb they deluge, and its ribs they rend:
Thus loudly roaring, and o'erpowering all,
Mount the thick Trojans up the Grecian wall;
Legions on legions from each side arise:
Thick sound the keels; the storm of arrows flies.
Fierce on the ships above, the cars below,

These wield the mace, and those the javelin throw.

While thus the thunder of the battle raged,
And labouring armies round the works engaged,
Still in the tent Patroclus sat to tend
The good Eurypylus, his wounded friend.
He sprinkles healing balms, to anguish kind,
And adds discourse, the medicine of the mind.
But when he saw, ascending up the fleet,
Victorious Troy; then, starting from his seat,
With bitter groans his sorrows he express'd,
He wrings his hands, he beats his manly breast.
"Though yet thy state require redress (he cries)
Depart I must: what horrors strike my eyes!
Charged with Achilles' high command I go,
A mournful witness of this scene of woe;
I haste to urge him by his country's care
To rise in arms, and shine again in war.
Perhaps some favouring god his soul may bend;
The voice is powerful of a faithful friend."

He spoke; and, speaking, swifter than the wind
Sprung from the tent, and left the war behind.
The embodied Greeks the fierce attack sustain,
But strive, though numerous, to repulse in vain:
Nor could the Trojans, through that firm array,
Force to the fleet and tents the impervious way.
As when a shipwright, with Palladian art,
Smooths the rough wood, and levels every part;
With equal hand he guides his whole design,
By the just rule, and the directing line:
The martial leaders, with like skill and care,
Preserved their line, and equal kept the war.
Brave deeds of arms through all the ranks were tried,
And every ship sustained an equal tide.
At one proud bark, high-towering o'er the fleet,
Ajax the great, and godlike Hector meet;
For one bright prize the matchless chiefs contend,
Nor this the ships can fire, nor that defend:
One kept the shore, and one the vessel trod;
That fix'd as fate, this acted by a god.
The son of Clytius in his daring hand,
The deck approaching, shakes a flaming brand;
But, pierced by Telamon's huge lance, expires:
Thundering he falls, and drops the extinguish'd fires.
Great Hector view'd him with a sad survey,
As stretch'd in dust before the stern he lay.
"Oh! all of Trojan, all of Lycian race!

Stand to your arms, maintain this arduous space:
Lo! where the son of royal Clytius lies;
Ah, save his arms, secure his obsequies!"

This said, his eager javelin sought the foe:
But Ajax shunn'd the meditated blow.
Not vainly yet the forceful lance was thrown;
It stretch'd in dust unhappy Lycophron:
An exile long, sustain'd at Ajax' board,
A faithful servant to a foreign lord;
In peace, and war, for ever at his side,
Near his loved master, as he lived, he died.
From the high poop he tumbles on the sand,
And lies a lifeless load along the land.
With anguish Ajax views the piercing sight,
And thus inflames his brother to the fight:

"Teucer, behold! extended on the shore
Our friend, our loved companion! now no more!
Dear as a parent, with a parent's care
To fight our wars he left his native air.
This death deplored, to Hector's rage we owe;
Revenge, revenge it on the cruel foe.
Where are those darts on which the fates attend?
And where the bow which Phoebus taught to bend?"

Impatient Teucer, hastening to his aid,
Before the chief his ample bow display'd;
The well-stored quiver on his shoulders hung:
Then hiss'd his arrow, and the bowstring sung.
Clytus, Pisenor's son, renown'd in fame,
(To thee, Polydamas! an honour'd name)
Drove through the thickest of the embattled plains
The startling steeds, and shook his eager reins.
As all on glory ran his ardent mind,
The pointed death arrests him from behind:
Through his fair neck the thrilling arrow flies;
In youth's first bloom reluctantly he dies.
Hurl'd from the lofty seat, at distance far,
The headlong coursers spurn his empty car;
Till sad Polydamas the steeds restrain'd,
And gave, Astynous, to thy careful hand;
Then, fired to vengeance, rush'd amidst the foe:
Rage edged his sword, and strengthen'd every blow.

Once more bold Teucer, in his country's cause,
At Hector's breast a chosen arrow draws:
And had the weapon found the destined way,

Thy fall, great Trojan! had renown'd that day.
But Hector was not doom'd to perish then:
The all-wise disposer of the fates of men
(Imperial Jove) his present death withstands;
Nor was such glory due to Teucer's hands.
At its full stretch as the tough string he drew,
Struck by an arm unseen, it burst in two;
Down dropp'd the bow: the shaft with brazen head
Fell innocent, and on the dust lay dead.
The astonish'd archer to great Ajax cries;
"Some god prevents our destined enterprise:
Some god, propitious to the Trojan foe,
Has, from my arm unfailing, struck the bow,
And broke the nerve my hands had twined with art,
Strong to impel the flight of many a dart."

"Since heaven commands it (Ajax made reply)
Dismiss the bow, and lay thy arrows by:
Thy arms no less suffice the lance to wield,
And quit the quiver for the ponderous shield.
In the first ranks indulge thy thirst of fame,
Thy brave example shall the rest inflame.
Fierce as they are, by long successes vain;
To force our fleet, or even a ship to gain,
Asks toil, and sweat, and blood: their utmost might
Shall find its match—No more: 'tis ours to fight."

Then Teucer laid his faithless bow aside;
The fourfold buckler o'er his shoulder tied;
On his brave head a crested helm he placed,
With nodding horse-hair formidably graced;
A dart, whose point with brass refulgent shines,
The warrior wields; and his great brother joins.

This Hector saw, and thus express'd his joy:
"Ye troops of Lycia, Dardanus, and Troy!
Be mindful of yourselves, your ancient fame,
And spread your glory with the navy's flame.
Jove is with us; I saw his hand, but now,
From the proud archer strike his vaunted bow:
Indulgent Jove! how plain thy favours shine,
When happy nations bear the marks divine!
How easy then, to see the sinking state
Of realms accursed, deserted, reprobate!
Such is the fate of Greece, and such is ours:
Behold, ye warriors, and exert your powers.
Death is the worst; a fate which all must try;
And for our country, 'tis a bliss to die.

The gallant man, though slain in fight he be,
Yet leaves his nation safe, his children free;
Entails a debt on all the grateful state;
His own brave friends shall glory in his fate;
His wife live honour'd, all his race succeed,
And late posterity enjoy the deed!"

This roused the soul in every Trojan breast:
The godlike Ajax next his Greeks address'd:

"How long, ye warriors of the Argive race,
(To generous Argos what a dire disgrace!)
How long on these cursed confines will ye lie,
Yet undetermined, or to live or die?
What hopes remain, what methods to retire,
If once your vessels catch the Trojan fire?
Make how the flames approach, how near they fall,
How Hector calls, and Troy obeys his call!
Not to the dance that dreadful voice invites,
It calls to death, and all the rage of fights.
'Tis now no time for wisdom or debates;
To your own hands are trusted all your fates;
And better far in one decisive strife,
One day should end our labour or our life,
Than keep this hard-got inch of barren sands,
Still press'd, and press'd by such inglorious hands."

The listening Grecians feel their leader's flame,
And every kindling bosom pants for fame.
Then mutual slaughters spread on either side;
By Hector here the Phocian Schedius died;
There, pierced by Ajax, sunk Laodamas,
Chief of the foot, of old Antenor's race.
Polydamas laid Otus on the sand,
The fierce commander of the Epeian band.
His lance bold Meges at the victor threw;
The victor, stooping, from the death withdrew;
(That valued life, O Phoebus! was thy care)
But Croesmus' bosom took the flying spear:
His corpse fell bleeding on the slippery shore;
His radiant arms triumphant Meges bore.
Dolops, the son of Lampus, rushes on,
Sprung from the race of old Laomedon,
And famed for prowess in a well-fought field,
He pierced the centre of his sounding shield:
But Meges, Phyleus' ample breastplate wore,
(Well-known in fight on Selle's winding shore;
For king Euphetes gave the golden mail,

Compact, and firm with many a jointed scale)
Which oft, in cities storm'd, and battles won,
Had saved the father, and now saves the son.
Full at the Trojan's head he urged his lance,
Where the high plumes above the helmet dance,
New ting'd with Tyrian dye: in dust below,
Shorn from the crest, the purple honours glow.
Meantime their fight the Spartan king survey'd,
And stood by Meges' side a sudden aid.
Through Dolops' shoulder urged his forceful dart,
Which held its passage through the panting heart,
And issued at his breast. With thundering sound
The warrior falls, extended on the ground.
In rush the conquering Greeks to spoil the slain:
But Hector's voice excites his kindred train;
The hero most, from Hicetaon sprung,
Fierce Melanippus, gallant, brave, and young.
He (ere to Troy the Grecians cross'd the main)
Fed his large oxen on Percote's plain;
But when oppress'd, his country claim'd his care,
Return'd to Ilion, and excell'd in war;
For this, in Priam's court, he held his place,
Beloved no less than Priam's royal race.
Him Hector singled, as his troops he led,
And thus inflamed him, pointing to the dead.

"Lo, Melanippus! lo, where Dolops lies;
And is it thus our royal kinsman dies?
O'ermatch'd he falls; to two at once a prey,
And lo! they bear the bloody arms away!
Come on—a distant war no longer wage,
But hand to hand thy country's foes engage:
Till Greece at once, and all her glory end;
Or Ilion from her towery height descend,
Heaved from the lowest stone; and bury all
In one sad sepulchre, one common fall."

Hector (this said) rush'd forward on the foes:
With equal ardour Melanippus glows:
Then Ajax thus—"O Greeks! respect your fame,
Respect yourselves, and learn an honest shame:
Let mutual reverence mutual warmth inspire,
And catch from breast to breast the noble fire,
On valour's side the odds of combat lie;
The brave live glorious, or lamented die;
The wretch that trembles in the field of fame,
Meets death, and worse than death, eternal shame."

His generous sense he not in vain imparts;
It sunk, and rooted in the Grecian hearts:
They join, they throng, they thicken at his call,
And flank the navy with a brazen wall;
Shields touching shields, in order blaze above,
And stop the Trojans, though impell'd by Jove.
The fiery Spartan first, with loud applause.
Warms the bold son of Nestor in his cause.
"Is there (he said) in arms a youth like you,
So strong to fight, so active to pursue?
Why stand you distant, nor attempt a deed?
Lift the bold lance, and make some Trojan bleed."

He said; and backward to the lines retired;
Forth rush'd the youth with martial fury fired,
Beyond the foremost ranks; his lance he threw,
And round the black battalions cast his view.
The troops of Troy recede with sudden fear,
While the swift javelin hiss'd along in air.
Advancing Melanippus met the dart
With his bold breast, and felt it in his heart:
Thundering he falls; his falling arms resound,
And his broad buckler rings against the ground.
The victor leaps upon his prostrate prize:
Thus on a roe the well-breath'd beagle flies,
And rends his side, fresh-bleeding with the dart
The distant hunter sent into his heart.
Observing Hector to the rescue flew;
Bold as he was, Antilochus withdrew.
So when a savage, ranging o'er the plain,
Has torn the shepherd's dog, or shepherd's swain,
While conscious of the deed, he glares around,
And hears the gathering multitude resound,
Timely he flies the yet-untasted food,
And gains the friendly shelter of the wood:
So fears the youth; all Troy with shouts pursue,
While stones and darts in mingled tempest flew;
But enter'd in the Grecian ranks, he turns
His manly breast, and with new fury burns.

Now on the fleet the tides of Trojans drove,
Fierce to fulfil the stern decrees of Jove:
The sire of gods, confirming Thetis' prayer,
The Grecian ardour quench'd in deep despair;
But lifts to glory Troy's prevailing bands,
Swells all their hearts, and strengthens all their hands.
On Ida's top he waits with longing eyes,
To view the navy blazing to the skies;

Then, nor till then, the scale of war shall turn,
The Trojans fly, and conquer'd Ilion burn.
These fates revolved in his almighty mind,
He raises Hector to the work design'd,
Bids him with more than mortal fury glow,
And drives him, like a lightning, on the foe.
So Mars, when human crimes for vengeance call,
Shakes his huge javelin, and whole armies fall.
Not with more rage a conflagration rolls,
Wraps the vast mountains, and involves the poles.
He foams with wrath; beneath his gloomy brow
Like fiery meteors his red eye-balls glow:
The radiant helmet on his temple burns,
Waves when he nods, and lightens as he turns:
For Jove his splendour round the chief had thrown,
And cast the blaze of both the hosts on one.
Unhappy glories! for his fate was near,
Due to stern Pallas, and Pelides' spear:
Yet Jove deferr'd the death he was to pay,
And gave what fate allow'd, the honours of a day!

Now all on fire for fame, his breast, his eyes
Burn at each foe, and single every prize;
Still at the closest ranks, the thickest fight,
He points his ardour, and exerts his might.
The Grecian phalanx, moveless as a tower,
On all sides batter'd, yet resists his power:
So some tall rock o'erhangs the hoary main,
By winds assail'd, by billows beat in vain,
Unmoved it hears, above, the tempest blow,
And sees the watery mountains break below.
Girt in surrounding flames, he seems to fall
Like fire from Jove, and bursts upon them all:
Bursts as a wave that from the cloud impends,
And, swell'd with tempests, on the ship descends;
White are the decks with foam; the winds aloud
Howl o'er the masts, and sing through every shroud:
Pale, trembling, tired, the sailors freeze with fears;
And instant death on every wave appears.
So pale the Greeks the eyes of Hector meet,
The chief so thunders, and so shakes the fleet.

As when a lion, rushing from his den,
Amidst the plain of some wide-water'd fen,
(Where numerous oxen, as at ease they feed,
At large expatiate o'er the ranker mead)
Leaps on the herds before the herdsman's eyes;
The trembling herdsman far to distance flies;

Some lordly bull (the rest dispersed and fled)
He singles out; arrests, and lays him dead.
Thus from the rage of Jove-like Hector flew
All Greece in heaps; but one he seized, and slew:
Mycenian Periphes, a mighty name,
In wisdom great, in arms well known to fame;
The minister of stern Eurystheus' ire
Against Alcides, Copreus was his sire:
The son redeem'd the honours of the race,
A son as generous as the sire was base;
O'er all his country's youth conspicuous far
In every virtue, or of peace or war:
But doom'd to Hector's stronger force to yield!
Against the margin of his ample shield
He struck his hasty foot: his heels up-sprung;
Supine he fell; his brazen helmet rung.
On the fallen chief the invading Trojan press'd,
And plunged the pointed javelin in his breast.
His circling friends, who strove to guard too late
The unhappy hero, fled, or shared his fate.

Chased from the foremost line, the Grecian train
Now man the next, receding toward the main:
Wedged in one body at the tents they stand,
Wall'd round with sterns, a gloomy, desperate band.
Now manly shame forbids the inglorious flight;
Now fear itself confines them to the fight:
Man courage breathes in man; but Nestor most
(The sage preserver of the Grecian host)
Exhorts, adjures, to guard these utmost shores;
And by their parents, by themselves implores.

"Oh friends! be men: your generous breasts inflame
With mutual honour, and with mutual shame!
Think of your hopes, your fortunes; all the care
Your wives, your infants, and your parents share:
Think of each living father's reverend head;
Think of each ancestor with glory dead;
Absent, by me they speak, by me they sue,
They ask their safety, and their fame, from you:
The gods their fates on this one action lay,
And all are lost, if you desert the day."

He spoke, and round him breathed heroic fires;
Minerva seconds what the sage inspires.
The mist of darkness Jove around them threw
She clear'd, restoring all the war to view;
A sudden ray shot beaming o'er the plain,

And show'd the shores, the navy, and the main:
Hector they saw, and all who fly, or fight,
The scene wide-opening to the blaze of light,
First of the field great Ajax strikes their eyes,
His port majestic, and his ample size:
A ponderous mace with studs of iron crown'd,
Full twenty cubits long, he swings around;
Nor fights, like others, fix'd to certain stands
But looks a moving tower above the bands;
High on the decks with vast gigantic stride,
The godlike hero stalks from side to side.
So when a horseman from the watery mead
(Skill'd in the manage of the bounding steed)
Drives four fair coursers, practised to obey,
To some great city through the public way;
Safe in his art, as side by side they run,
He shifts his seat, and vaults from one to one;
And now to this, and now to that he flies;
Admiring numbers follow with their eyes.

From ship to ship thus Ajax swiftly flew,
No less the wonder of the warring crew.
As furious, Hector thunder'd threats aloud,
And rush'd enraged before the Trojan crowd;
Then swift invades the ships, whose beaky prores
Lay rank'd contiguous on the bending shores;
So the strong eagle from his airy height,
Who marks the swans' or cranes' embodied flight,
Stoops down impetuous, while they light for food,
And, stooping, darkens with his wings the flood.
Jove leads him on with his almighty hand,
And breathes fierce spirits in his following band.
The warring nations meet, the battle roars,
Thick beats the combat on the sounding prores.
Thou wouldst have thought, so furious was their fire,
No force could tame them, and no toil could tire;
As if new vigour from new fights they won,
And the long battle was but then begun.
Greece, yet unconquer'd, kept alive the war,
Secure of death, confiding in despair:
Troy in proud hopes already view'd the main
Bright with the blaze, and red with heroes slain:
Like strength is felt from hope, and from despair,
And each contends, as his were all the war.

"Twas thou, bold Hector! whose resistless hand
First seized a ship on that contested strand;
The same which dead Protesilaus bore,

The first that touch'd the unhappy Trojan shore:
For this in arms the warring nations stood,
And bathed their generous breasts with mutual blood.
No room to poise the lance or bend the bow;
But hand to hand, and man to man, they grow:
Wounded, they wound; and seek each other's hearts
With falchions, axes, swords, and shorten'd darts.
The falchions ring, shields rattle, axes sound,
Swords flash in air, or glitter on the ground;
With streaming blood the slippery shores are dyed,
And slaughter'd heroes swell the dreadful tide.

Still raging, Hector with his ample hand
Grasps the high stern, and gives this loud command:

"Haste, bring the flames! that toil of ten long years
Is finished; and the day desired appears!
This happy day with acclamations greet,
Bright with destruction of yon hostile fleet.
The coward-counsels of a timorous throng
Of reverend dotards check'd our glory long:
Too long Jove lull'd us with lethargic charms,
But now in peals of thunder calls to arms:
In this great day he crowns our full desires,
Wakes all our force, and seconds all our fires."

He spoke—the warriors at his fierce command
Pour a new deluge on the Grecian band.
Even Ajax paused, (so thick the javelins fly,)
Stepp'd back, and doubted or to live or die.
Yet, where the oars are placed, he stands to wait
What chief approaching dares attempt his fate:
Even to the last his naval charge defends,
Now shakes his spear, now lifts, and now protends;
Even yet, the Greeks with piercing shouts inspires,
Amidst attacks, and deaths, and darts, and fires.

"O friends! O heroes! names for ever dear,
Once sons of Mars, and thunderbolts of war!
Ah! yet be mindful of your old renown,
Your great forefathers' virtues and your own.
What aids expect you in this utmost strait?
What bulwarks rising between you and fate?
No aids, no bulwarks your retreat attend,
No friends to help, no city to defend.
This spot is all you have, to lose or keep;
There stand the Trojans, and here rolls the deep.
'Tis hostile ground you tread; your native lands

Far, far from hence: your fates are in your hands."

Raging he spoke; nor further wastes his breath,
But turns his javelin to the work of death.
Whate'er bold Trojan arm'd his daring hands,
Against the sable ships, with flaming brands,
So well the chief his naval weapon sped,
The luckless warrior at his stern lay dead:
Full twelve, the boldest, in a moment fell,
Sent by great Ajax to the shades of hell.

BOOK XVI

ARGUMENT

THE SIXTH BATTLE, THE ACTS AND DEATH OF PATROCLUS

Patroclus (in pursuance of the request of Nestor in the eleventh book) entreats Achilles to suffer him to go to the assistance of the Greeks with Achilles' troops and armour. He agrees to it, but at the same time charges him to content himself with rescuing the fleet, without further pursuit of the enemy. The armour, horses, soldiers, and officers are described. Achilles offers a libation for the success of his friend, after which Patroclus leads the Myrmidons to battle. The Trojans, at the sight of Patroclus in Achilles' armour, taking him for that hero, are cast into the uttermost consternation; he beats them off from the vessels, Hector himself flies, Sarpedon is killed, though Jupiter was averse to his fate. Several other particulars of the battle are described; in the heat of which, Patroclus, neglecting the orders of Achilles, pursues the foe to the walls of Troy, where Apollo repulses and disarms him, Euphorbus wounds him, and Hector kills him, which concludes the book.

So warr'd both armies on the ensanguined shore,
While the black vessels smoked with human gore.
Meantime Patroclus to Achilles flies;
The streaming tears fall copious from his eyes
Not faster, trickling to the plains below,
From the tall rock the sable waters flow.
Divine Pelides, with compassion moved.
Thus spoke, indulgent, to his best beloved:

"Patroclus, say, what grief thy bosom bears,
That flows so fast in these unmanly tears?
No girl, no infant whom the mother keeps
From her loved breast, with fonder passion weeps;
Not more the mother's soul, that infant warms,
Clung to her knees, and reaching at her arms,
Than thou hast mine! Oh tell me, to what end
Thy melting sorrows thus pursue thy friend?

"Griev'st thou for me, or for, my martial band?
Or come sad tidings from our native land?
Our fathers live (our first, most tender care),
Thy good Menoetius breathes the vital air,
And hoary Peleus yet extends his days;
Pleased in their age to hear their children's praise.
Or may some meaner cause thy pity claim?
Perhaps yon relics of the Grecian name,
Doom'd in their ships to sink by fire and sword,
And pay the forfeit of their haughty lord?
Whate'er the cause, reveal thy secret care,
And speak those sorrows which a friend would share."
A sigh that instant from his bosom broke,
Another follow'd, and Patroclus spoke:

"Let Greece at length with pity touch thy breast,
Thyself a Greek; and, once, of Greeks the best!
Lo! every chief that might her fate prevent,
Lies pierced with wounds, and bleeding in his tent:
Eurypylus, Tydides, Atreus' son,
And wise Ulysses, at the navy groan,
More for their country's wounds than for their own.
Their pain soft arts of pharmacy can ease,
Thy breast alone no lenitives appease.
May never rage like thine my soul enslave,
O great in vain! unprofitably brave!
Thy country slighted in her last distress,
What friend, what man, from thee shall hope redress?
No—men unborn, and ages yet behind,
Shall curse that fierce, that unforgiving mind.

"O man unpitying! if of man thy race;
But sure thou spring'st not from a soft embrace,
Nor ever amorous hero caused thy birth,
Nor ever tender goddess brought thee forth:
Some rugged rock's hard entrails gave thee form,
And raging seas produced thee in a storm,
A soul well suiting that tempestuous kind,
So rough thy manners, so untamed thy mind.

"If some dire oracle thy breast alarm,
If aught from Jove, or Thetis, stop thy arm,
Some beam of comfort yet on Greece may shine,
If I but lead the Myrmidonian line:
Clad in thy dreadful arms if I appear,
Proud Troy shall tremble, and desert the war;
Without thy person Greece shall win the day,

And thy mere image chase her foes away.
Press'd by fresh forces, her o'erlabour'd train
Shall quit the ships, and Greece respire again."
Thus, blind to fate! with supplicating breath,
Thou begg'st his arms, and in his arms thy death.
Unfortunately good! a boding sigh
Thy friend return'd; and with it, this reply:
"Patroclus! thy Achilles knows no fears;
Nor words from Jove nor oracles he hears;
Nor aught a mother's caution can suggest;
The tyrant's pride lies rooted in my breast.
My wrongs, my wrongs, my constant thought engage,
Those, my sole oracles, inspire my rage:
I made him tyrant: gave him power to wrong
Even my: I felt it; and shall feel it long.
The maid, my black-eyed maid, he forced away,
Due to the toils of many a well-fought day;
Due to my conquest of her father's reign;
Due to the votes of all the Grecian train.
From me he forced her; me, the bold and brave,
Disgraced, dishonour'd, like the meanest slave.
But bear we this—the wrongs I grieve are past;
'Tis time our fury should relent at last:
I fix'd its date; the day I wish'd appears:
How Hector to my ships his battle bears,
The flames my eyes, the shouts invade my ears.
Go then, Patroclus! court fair honour's charms
In Troy's famed fields, and in Achilles' arms:
Lead forth my martial Myrmidons to fight,
Go save the fleets, and conquer in my right.
See the thin relics of their baffled band
At the last edge of yon deserted land!
Behold all Ilion on their ships descends;
How the cloud blackens, how the storm impends!
It was not thus, when, at my sight amazed,
Troy saw and trembled, as this helmet blazed:
Had not the injurious king our friendship lost,
Yon ample trench had buried half her host.
No camps, no bulwarks now the Trojans fear,
Those are not dreadful, no Achilles there;
No longer flames the lance of Tydeus' son;
No more your general calls his heroes on:
Hector, alone, I hear; his dreadful breath
Commands your slaughter, or proclaims your death.
Yet now, Patroclus, issue to the plain:
Now save the ships, the rising fires restrain,
And give the Greeks to visit Greece again.
But heed my words, and mark a friend's command,

Who trusts his fame and honours in thy hand,
And from thy deeds expects the Achaian host
Shall render back the beauteous maid he lost:
Rage uncontroll'd through all the hostile crew,
But touch not Hector, Hector is my due.
Though Jove in thunder should command the war,
Be just, consult my glory, and forbear.
The fleet once saved, desist from further chase,
Nor lead to Ilion's walls the Grecian race;
Some adverse god thy rashness may destroy;
Some god, like Phoebus, ever kind to Troy.
Let Greece, redeem'd from this destructive strait,
Do her own work; and leave the rest to fate.
O! would to all the immortal powers above,
Apollo, Pallas, and almighty Jove!
That not one Trojan might be left alive,
And not a Greek of all the race survive:
Might only we the vast destruction shun,
And only we destroy the accursed town!"
Such conference held the chiefs; while on the strand
Great Jove with conquest crown'd the Trojan band.
Ajax no more the sounding storm sustain'd,
So thick the darts an iron tempest rain'd:
On his tired arm the weighty buckler hung;
His hollow helm with falling javelins rung;
His breath, in quick short pantings, comes and goes;
And painful sweat from all his members flows.
Spent and o'erpower'd, he barely breathes at most;
Yet scarce an army stirs him from his post;
Dangers on dangers all around him glow,
And toil to toil, and woe succeeds to woe.

Say, Muses, throned above the starry frame,
How first the navy blazed with Trojan flame?

Stern Hector waved his sword, and standing near,
Where furious Ajax plied his ashen spear,
Full on the lance a stroke so justly sped,
That the broad falchion lopp'd its brazen head;
His pointless spear the warrior shakes in vain;
The brazen head falls sounding on the plain.
Great Ajax saw, and own'd the hand divine;
Confessing Jove, and trembling at the sign,
Warn'd he retreats. Then swift from all sides pour
The hissing brands; thick streams the fiery shower;
O'er the high stern the curling volumes rise,
And sheets of rolling smoke involve the skies.

Divine Achilles view'd the rising flames,
And smote his thigh, and thus aloud exclaims:
"Arm, arm, Patroclus! Lo, the blaze aspires!
The glowing ocean reddens with the fires.
Arm, ere our vessels catch the spreading flame;
Arm, ere the Grecians be no more a name;
I haste to bring the troops."—The hero said;
The friend with ardour and with joy obey'd.

He cased his limbs in brass; and first around
His manly legs, with silver buckles bound
The clasping greaves; then to his breast applies
The flaming cuirass of a thousand dyes;
Emblazed with studs of gold his falchion shone
In the rich belt, as in a starry zone:
Achilles' shield his ample shoulders spread,
Achilles' helmet nodded o'er his head:
Adorn'd in all his terrible array,
He flash'd around intolerable day.
Alone untouch'd, Pelides' javelin stands,
Not to be poised but by Pelides' hands:
From Pelion's shady brow the plant entire
Old Chiron rent, and shaped it for his sire;
Whose son's great arm alone the weapon wields,
The death of heroes, and the dread of fields.

The brave Automedon (an honour'd name,
The second to his lord in love and fame,
In peace his friend, and partner of the war)
The winged coursers harness'd to the car;
Xanthus and Balius, of immortal breed,
Sprung from the wind, and like the wind in speed.
Whom the wing'd harpy, swift Podarge, bore,
By Zephyr pregnant on the breezy shore:
Swift Pedasus was added to their side,
(Once great Aetion's, now Achilles' pride)
Who, like in strength, in swiftness, and in grace,
A mortal courser match'd the immortal race.

Achilles speeds from tent to tent, and warms
His hardy Myrmidons to blood and arms.
All breathing death, around the chief they stand,
A grim, terrific, formidable band:
Grim as voracious wolves, that seek the springs
When scalding thirst their burning bowels wrings;
When some tall stag, fresh-slaughtered in the wood,
Has drench'd their wide insatiate throats with blood,
To the black fount they rush, a hideous throng,

With paunch distended, and with lolling tongue,
Fire fills their eye, their black jaws belch the gore,
And gorged with slaughter still they thirst for more.
Like furious, rush'd the Myrmidonian crew,
Such their dread strength, and such their deathful view.

High in the midst the great Achilles stands,
Directs their order, and the war commands.
He, loved of Jove, had launch'd for Ilion's shores
Full fifty vessels, mann'd with fifty oars:
Five chosen leaders the fierce bands obey,
Himself supreme in valour, as in sway.

First march'd Menestheus, of celestial birth,
Derived from thee, whose waters wash the earth,
Divine Sperchius! Jove-descended flood!
A mortal mother mixing with a god.
Such was Menestheus, but miscall'd by fame
The son of Borus, that espoused the dame.

Eudorus next; whom Polymele the gay,
Famed in the graceful dance, produced to-day.
Her, sly Cellenius loved: on her would gaze,
As with swift step she form'd the running maze:
To her high chamber from Diana's quire,
The god pursued her, urged, and crown'd his fire.
The son confess'd his father's heavenly race,
And heir'd his mother's swiftness in the chase.
Strong Echecleus, bless'd in all those charms
That pleased a god, succeeded to her arms;
Not conscious of those loves, long hid from fame,
With gifts of price he sought and won the dame;
Her secret offspring to her sire she bare;
Her sire caress'd him with a parent's care.

Pisander follow'd; matchless in his art
To wing the spear, or aim the distant dart;
No hand so sure of all the Emathian line,
Or if a surer, great Patroclus! thine.

The fourth by Phoenix' grave command was graced,
Laerces' valiant offspring led the last.

Soon as Achilles with superior care
Had call'd the chiefs, and order'd all the war,
This stern remembrance to his troops he gave:
"Ye far-famed Myrmidons, ye fierce and brave!
Think with what threats you dared the Trojan throng,

Think what reproach these ears endured so long;
'Stern son of Peleus, (thus ye used to say,
While restless, raging, in your ships you lay)
Oh nursed with gall, unknowing how to yield;
Whose rage defrauds us of so famed a field:
If that dire fury must for ever burn,
What make we here? Return, ye chiefs, return!'
Such were your words—Now, warriors! grieve no more,
Lo there the Trojans; bathe your swords in gore!
This day shall give you all your soul demands,
Glut all your hearts, and weary all your hands!"

Thus while he roused the fire in every breast,
Close and more close the listening cohorts press'd;
Ranks wedged in ranks; of arms a steely ring
Still grows, and spreads, and thickens round the king.
As when a circling wall the builder forms,
Of strength defensive against wind and storms,
Compacted stones the thickening work compose,
And round him wide the rising structure grows:
So helm to helm, and crest to crest they throng,
Shield urged on shield, and man drove man along;
Thick, undistinguish'd plumes, together join'd,
Float in one sea, and wave before the wind.

Far o'er the rest in glittering pomp appear,
There bold Automedon, Patroclus here;
Brothers in arms, with equal fury fired;
Two friends, two bodies with one soul inspired.

But mindful of the gods, Achilles went
To the rich coffer in his shady tent;
There lay on heaps his various garments roll'd,
And costly furs, and carpets stiff with gold,
(The presents of the silver-footed dame)
From thence he took a bowl, of antique frame,
Which never man had stained with ruddy wine,
Nor raised in offerings to the power divine,
But Peleus' son; and Peleus' son to none
Had raised in offerings, but to Jove alone.
This tinged with sulphur, sacred first to flame,
He purged; and wash'd it in the running stream.
Then cleansed his hands; and fixing for a space
His eyes on heaven, his feet upon the place
Of sacrifice, the purple draught he pour'd
Forth in the midst; and thus the god implored:

"O thou supreme! high-throned all height above!

O great Pelasgic, Dodonaean Jove!
Who 'midst surrounding frosts, and vapours chill,
Presid'st on bleak Dodona's vocal hill:
(Whose groves the Selli, race austere! surround,
Their feet unwash'd, their slumbers on the ground;
Who hear, from rustling oaks, thy dark decrees;
And catch the fates, low-whispered in the breeze;)
Hear, as of old! Thou gav'st, at Thetis' prayer,
Glory to me, and to the Greeks despair.
Lo, to the dangers of the fighting field
The best, the dearest of my friends, I yield,
Though still determined, to my ships confined;
Patroclus gone, I stay but half behind.
Oh! be his guard thy providential care,
Confirm his heart, and string his arm to war:
Press'd by his single force let Hector see
His fame in arms not owing all to me.
But when the fleets are saved from foes and fire,
Let him with conquest and renown retire;
Preserve his arms, preserve his social train,
And safe return him to these eyes again!"

Great Jove consents to half the chief's request,
But heaven's eternal doom denies the rest;
To free the fleet was granted to his prayer;
His safe return, the winds dispersed in air.
Back to his tent the stern Achilles flies,
And waits the combat with impatient eyes.

Meanwhile the troops beneath Patroclus' care,
Invade the Trojans, and commence the war.
As wasps, provoked by children in their play,
Pour from their mansions by the broad highway,
In swarms the guiltless traveller engage,
Whet all their stings, and call forth all their rage:
All rise in arms, and, with a general cry,
Assert their waxen domes, and buzzing progeny.
Thus from the tents the fervent legion swarms,
So loud their clamours, and so keen their arms:
Their rising rage Patroclus' breath inspires,
Who thus inflames them with heroic fires:

"O warriors, partners of Achilles' praise!
Be mindful of your deeds in ancient days;
Your godlike master let your acts proclaim,
And add new glories to his mighty name.
Think your Achilles sees you fight: be brave,
And humble the proud monarch whom you save."

Joyful they heard, and kindling as he spoke,
Flew to the fleet, involved in fire and smoke.
From shore to shore the doubling shouts resound,
The hollow ships return a deeper sound.
The war stood still, and all around them gazed,
When great Achilles' shining armour blazed:
Troy saw, and thought the dread Achilles nigh,
At once they see, they tremble, and they fly.

Then first thy spear, divine Patroclus! flew,
Where the war raged, and where the tumult grew.
Close to the stern of that famed ship which bore
Unbless'd Protesilaus to Ilion's shore,
The great Paeonian, bold Pyrechmes stood;
(Who led his bands from Axius' winding flood;)
His shoulder-blade receives the fatal wound;
The groaning warrior pants upon the ground.
His troops, that see their country's glory slain,
Fly diverse, scatter'd o'er the distant plain.
Patroclus' arm forbids the spreading fires,
And from the half-burn'd ship proud Troy retires;
Clear'd from the smoke the joyful navy lies;
In heaps on heaps the foe tumultuous flies;
Triumphant Greece her rescued decks ascends,
And loud acclaim the starry region rends.
So when thick clouds enwrap the mountain's head,
O'er heaven's expanse like one black ceiling spread;
Sudden the Thunderer, with a flashing ray,
Bursts through the darkness, and lets down the day:
The hills shine out, the rocks in prospect rise,
And streams, and vales, and forests, strike the eyes;
The smiling scene wide opens to the sight,
And all the unmeasured ether flames with light.

But Troy repulsed, and scatter'd o'er the plains,
Forced from the navy, yet the fight maintains.
Now every Greek some hostile hero slew,
But still the foremost, bold Patroclus flew:
As Areilycus had turn'd him round,
Sharp in his thigh he felt the piercing wound;
The brazen-pointed spear, with vigour thrown,
The thigh transfix'd, and broke the brittle bone:
Headlong he fell. Next, Thoas was thy chance;
Thy breast, unarm'd, received the Spartan lance.
Phylides' dart (as Amphidus drew nigh)
His blow prevented, and transpierced his thigh,
Tore all the brawn, and rent the nerves away;

In darkness, and in death, the warrior lay.

In equal arms two sons of Nestor stand,
And two bold brothers of the Lycian band:
By great Antilochus, Atymnius dies,
Pierced in the flank, lamented youth! he lies,
Kind Maris, bleeding in his brother's wound,
Defends the breathless carcase on the ground;
Furious he flies, his murderer to engage:
But godlike Thrasimed prevents his rage,
Between his arm and shoulder aims a blow;
His arm falls spouting on the dust below:
He sinks, with endless darkness cover'd o'er:
And vents his soul, effused with gushing gore.

Slain by two brothers, thus two brothers bleed,
Sarpedon's friends, Amisodarus' seed;
Amisodarus, who, by Furies led,
The bane of men, abhorr'd Chimaera bred;
Skill'd in the dart in vain, his sons expire,
And pay the forfeit of their guilty sire.

Stopp'd in the tumult Cleobulus lies,
Beneath Oileus' arm, a living prize;
A living prize not long the Trojan stood;
The thirsty falchion drank his reeking blood:
Plunged in his throat the smoking weapon lies;
Black death, and fate unpitying, seal his eyes.

Amid the ranks, with mutual thirst of fame,
Lycon the brave, and fierce Peneleus came;
In vain their javelins at each other flew,
Now, met in arms, their eager swords they drew.
On the plumed crest of his Boeotian foe
The daring Lycon aim'd a noble blow;
The sword broke short; but his, Peneleus sped
Full on the juncture of the neck and head:
The head, divided by a stroke so just,
Hung by the skin; the body sunk to dust.

O'ertaken Neamas by Merion bleeds,
Pierced through the shoulder as he mounts his steeds;
Back from the car he tumbles to the ground:
His swimming eyes eternal shades surround.

Next Erymas was doom'd his fate to feel,
His open'd mouth received the Cretan steel:
Beneath the brain the point a passage tore,

Crash'd the thin bones, and drown'd the teeth in gore:
His mouth, his eyes, his nostrils, pour a flood;
He sobs his soul out in the gush of blood.

As when the flocks neglected by the swain,
Or kids, or lambs, lie scatter'd o'er the plain,
A troop of wolves the unguarded charge survey,
And rend the trembling, unresisting prey:
Thus on the foe the Greeks impetuous came;
Troy fled, unmindful of her former fame.

But still at Hector godlike Ajax aim'd,
Still, pointed at his breast, his javelin flamed.
The Trojan chief, experienced in the field,
O'er his broad shoulders spread the massy shield,
Observed the storm of darts the Grecians pour,
And on his buckler caught the ringing shower:
He sees for Greece the scale of conquest rise,
Yet stops, and turns, and saves his loved allies.

As when the hand of Jove a tempest forms,
And rolls the cloud to blacken heaven with storms,
Dark o'er the fields the ascending vapour flies,
And shades the sun, and blots the golden skies:
So from the ships, along the dusky plain,
Dire Flight and Terror drove the Trojan train.
Even Hector fled; through heads of disarray
The fiery coursers forced their lord away:
While far behind his Trojans fall confused;
Wedged in the trench, in one vast carnage bruised:
Chariots on chariots roll: the clashing spokes
Shock; while the madding steeds break short their yokes.
In vain they labour up the steepy mound;
Their charioteers lie foaming on the ground.
Fierce on the rear, with shouts Patroclus flies;
Tumultuous clamour fills the fields and skies;
Thick drifts of dust involve their rapid flight;
Clouds rise on clouds, and heaven is snatch'd from sight.
The affrighted steeds their dying lords cast down,
Scour o'er the fields, and stretch to reach the town.
Loud o'er the rout was heard the victor's cry,
Where the war bleeds, and where the thickest die,
Where horse and arms, and chariots he o'erthrown,
And bleeding heroes under axles groan.
No stop, no check, the steeds of Peleus knew:
From bank to bank the immortal coursers flew.
High-bounding o'er the fosse, the whirling car
Smokes through the ranks, o'ertakes the flying war,

And thunders after Hector; Hector flies,
Patroclus shakes his lance; but fate denies.
Not with less noise, with less impetuous force,
The tide of Trojans urge their desperate course,
Than when in autumn Jove his fury pours,
And earth is loaden with incessant showers;
(When guilty mortals break the eternal laws,
Or judges, bribed, betray the righteous cause;)
From their deep beds he bids the rivers rise,
And opens all the flood-gates of the skies:
The impetuous torrents from their hills obey,
Whole fields are drown'd, and mountains swept away;
Loud roars the deluge till it meets the main;
And trembling man sees all his labours vain!

And now the chief (the foremost troops repell'd)
Back to the ships his destined progress held,
Bore down half Troy in his resistless way,
And forced the routed ranks to stand the day.
Between the space where silver Simois flows,
Where lay the fleets, and where the rampires rose,
All grim in dust and blood Patroclus stands,
And turns the slaughter on the conquering bands.
First Pronous died beneath his fiery dart,
Which pierced below the shield his valiant heart.
Thestor was next, who saw the chief appear,
And fell the victim of his coward fear;
Shrunk up he sat, with wild and haggard eye,
Nor stood to combat, nor had force to fly;
Patroclus mark'd him as he shunn'd the war,
And with unmanly tremblings shook the car,
And dropp'd the flowing reins. Him 'twixt the jaws,
The javelin sticks, and from the chariot draws.
As on a rock that overhangs the main,
An angler, studious of the line and cane,
Some mighty fish draws panting to the shore:
Not with less ease the barbed javelin bore
The gaping dastard; as the spear was shook,
He fell, and life his heartless breast forsook.

Next on Eryalus he flies; a stone,
Large as a rock, was by his fury thrown:
Full on his crown the ponderous fragment flew,
And burst the helm, and cleft the head in two:
Prone to the ground the breathless warrior fell,
And death involved him with the shades of hell.
Then low in dust Epaltes, Echius, lie;
Ipheas, Evippus, Polymelus, die;

Amphoterus and Erymas succeed;
And last Tlepolemus and Pyres bleed.
Where'er he moves, the growing slaughters spread
In heaps on heaps a monument of dead.

When now Sarpedon his brave friends beheld
Grovelling in dust, and gasping on the field,
With this reproach his flying host he warms:
"Oh stain to honour! oh disgrace to arms!
Forsake, inglorious, the contended plain;
This hand unaided shall the war sustain:
The task be mine this hero's strength to try,
Who mows whole troops, and makes an army fly."

He spake: and, speaking, leaps from off the car:
Patroclus lights, and sternly waits the war.
As when two vultures on the mountain's height
Stoop with resounding pinions to the fight;
They cuff, they tear, they raise a screaming cry;
The desert echoes, and the rocks reply:
The warriors thus opposed in arms, engage
With equal clamours, and with equal rage.

Jove view'd the combat: whose event foreseen,
He thus bespoke his sister and his queen:
"The hour draws on; the destinies ordain,
My godlike son shall press the Phrygian plain:
Already on the verge of death he stands,
His life is owed to fierce Patroclus' hands,
What passions in a parent's breast debate!
Say, shall I snatch him from impending fate,
And send him safe to Lycia, distant far
From all the dangers and the toils of war;
Or to his doom my bravest offspring yield,
And fatten, with celestial blood, the field?"

Then thus the goddess with the radiant eyes:
"What words are these, O sovereign of the skies!
Short is the date prescribed to mortal man;
Shall Jove for one extend the narrow span,
Whose bounds were fix'd before his race began?
How many sons of gods, foredoom'd to death,
Before proud Ilion must resign their breath!
Were thine exempt, debate would rise above,
And murmuring powers condemn their partial Jove.
Give the bold chief a glorious fate in fight;
And when the ascending soul has wing'd her flight,
Let Sleep and Death convey, by thy command,

The breathless body to his native land.
His friends and people, to his future praise,
A marble tomb and pyramid shall raise,
And lasting honours to his ashes give;
His fame ('tis all the dead can have) shall live."

She said: the cloud-compeller, overcome,
Assents to fate, and ratifies the doom.
Then touch'd with grief, the weeping heavens distill'd
A shower of blood o'er all the fatal field:
The god, his eyes averting from the plain,
Laments his son, predestined to be slain,
Far from the Lycian shores, his happy native reign.
Now met in arms, the combatants appear;
Each heaved the shield, and poised the lifted spear;
From strong Patroclus' hand the javelin fled,
And pass'd the groin of valiant Thrasymed;
The nerves unbraced no more his bulk sustain,
He falls, and falling bites the bloody plain.
Two sounding darts the Lycian leader threw:
The first aloof with erring fury flew,
The next transpierced Achilles' mortal steed,
The generous Pedasus of Theban breed:
Fix'd in the shoulder's joint, he reel'd around,
Roll'd in the bloody dust, and paw'd the slippery ground.
His sudden fall the entangled harness broke;
Each axle crackled, and the chariot shook:
When bold Automedon, to disengage
The starting coursers, and restrain their rage,
Divides the traces with his sword, and freed
The encumbered chariot from the dying steed:
The rest move on, obedient to the rein:
The car rolls slowly o'er the dusty plain.

The towering chiefs to fiercer fight advance:
And first Sarpedon whirl'd his weighty lance,
Which o'er the warrior's shoulder took its course,
And spent in empty air its dying force.
Not so Patroclus' never-erring dart;
Aim'd at his breast it pierced a mortal part,
Where the strong fibres bind the solid heart.
Then as the mountain oak, or poplar tall,
Or pine (fit mast for some great admiral)
Nods to the axe, till with a groaning sound
It sinks, and spreads its honours on the ground,
Thus fell the king; and laid on earth supine,
Before his chariot stretch'd his form divine:
He grasp'd the dust distain'd with streaming gore,

And, pale in death, lay groaning on the shore.
So lies a bull beneath the lion's paws,
While the grim savage grinds with foamy jaws
The trembling limbs, and sucks the smoking blood;
Deep groans, and hollow roars, rebellow through the wood.

Then to the leader of the Lycian band
The dying chief address'd his last command;
"Glaucus, be bold; thy task be first to dare
The glorious dangers of destructive war,
To lead my troops, to combat at their head,
Incite the living, and supply the dead.
Tell them, I charged them with my latest breath
Not unrevenged to bear Sarpedon's death.
What grief, what shame, must Glaucus undergo,
If these spoil'd arms adorn a Grecian foe!
Then as a friend, and as a warrior fight;
Defend my body, conquer in my right:
That, taught by great examples, all may try
Like thee to vanquish, or like me to die."
He ceased; the Fates suppress'd his labouring breath,
And his eyes darken'd with the shades of death.
The insulting victor with disdain bestrode
The prostrate prince, and on his bosom trod;
Then drew the weapon from his panting heart,
The reeking fibres clinging to the dart;
From the wide wound gush'd out a stream of blood,
And the soul issued in the purple flood.
His flying steeds the Myrmidons detain,
Unguided now, their mighty master slain.
All-impotent of aid, transfix'd with grief,
Unhappy Glaucus heard the dying chief:
His painful arm, yet useless with the smart
Inflicted late by Teucer's deadly dart,
Supported on his better hand he stay'd:
To Phoebus then ('twas all he could) he pray'd:

"All-seeing monarch! whether Lycia's coast,
Or sacred Ilion, thy bright presence boast,
Powerful alike to ease the wretch's smart;
O hear me! god of every healing art!
Lo! stiff with clotted blood, and pierced with pain,
That thrills my arm, and shoots through every vein,
I stand unable to sustain the spear,
And sigh, at distance from the glorious war.
Low in the dust is great Sarpedon laid,
Nor Jove vouchsafed his hapless offspring aid;
But thou, O god of health! thy succour lend,

To guard the relics of my slaughter'd friend:
For thou, though distant, canst restore my might,
To head my Lycians, and support the fight."

Apollo heard; and, suppliant as he stood,
His heavenly hand restrain'd the flux of blood;
He drew the dolours from the wounded part,
And breathed a spirit in his rising heart.
Renew'd by art divine, the hero stands,
And owns the assistance of immortal hands.
First to the fight his native troops he warms,
Then loudly calls on Troy's vindictive arms;
With ample strides he stalks from place to place;
Now fires Agenor, now Polydamas:
Ćneas next, and Hector he accosts;
Inflaming thus the rage of all their hosts.

"What thoughts, regardless chief! thy breast employ?
Oh too forgetful of the friends of Troy!
Those generous friends, who, from their country far,
Breathe their brave souls out in another's war.
See! where in dust the great Sarpedon lies,
In action valiant, and in council wise,
Who guarded right, and kept his people free;
To all his Lycians lost, and lost to thee!
Stretch'd by Patroclus' arm on yonder plains,
O save from hostile rage his loved remains!
Ah let not Greece his conquer'd trophies boast,
Nor on his corse revenge her heroes lost!"

He spoke: each leader in his grief partook:
Troy, at the loss, through all her legions shook.
Transfix'd with deep regret, they view o'erthrown
At once his country's pillar, and their own;
A chief, who led to Troy's beleaguer'd wall
A host of heroes, and outshined them all.
Fired, they rush on; first Hector seeks the foes,
And with superior vengeance greatly glows.

But o'er the dead the fierce Patroclus stands,
And rousing Ajax, roused the listening bands:

"Heroes, be men; be what you were before;
Or weigh the great occasion, and be more.
The chief who taught our lofty walls to yield,
Lies pale in death, extended on the field.
To guard his body Troy in numbers flies;
Tis half the glory to maintain our prize.

Haste, strip his arms, the slaughter round him spread,
And send the living Lycians to the dead."

The heroes kindle at his fierce command;
The martial squadrons close on either hand:
Here Troy and Lycia charge with loud alarms,
Thessalia there, and Greece, oppose their arms.
With horrid shouts they circle round the slain;
The clash of armour rings o'er all the plain.
Great Jove, to swell the horrors of the fight,
O'er the fierce armies pours pernicious night,
And round his son confounds the warring hosts,
His fate ennobling with a crowd of ghosts.

Now Greece gives way, and great Epigeus falls;
Agacleus' son, from Budium's lofty walls;
Who chased for murder thence a suppliant came
To Peleus, and the silver-footed dame;
Now sent to Troy, Achilles' arms to aid,
He pays due vengeance to his kinsman's shade.
Soon as his luckless hand had touch'd the dead,
A rock's large fragment thunder'd on his head;
Hurl'd by Hectorean force it cleft in twain
His shatter'd helm, and stretch'd him o'er the slain.

Fierce to the van of fight Patroclus came,
And, like an eagle darting at his game,
Sprung on the Trojan and the Lycian band.
What grief thy heart, what fury urged thy hand,
O generous Greek! when with full vigour thrown,
At Sthenelaus flew the weighty stone,
Which sunk him to the dead: when Troy, too near
That arm, drew back; and Hector learn'd to fear.
Far as an able hand a lance can throw,
Or at the lists, or at the fighting foe;
So far the Trojans from their lines retired;
Till Glaucus, turning, all the rest inspired.
Then Bathyclaeus fell beneath his rage,
The only hope of Chalcon's trembling age;
Wide o'er the land was stretch'd his large domain,
With stately seats, and riches blest in vain:
Him, bold with youth, and eager to pursue
The flying Lycians, Glaucus met and slew;
Pierced through the bosom with a sudden wound,
He fell, and falling made the fields resound.
The Achaians sorrow for their heroes slain;
With conquering shouts the Trojans shake the plain,
And crowd to spoil the dead: the Greeks oppose;

An iron circle round the carcase grows.

Then brave Laogonus resign'd his breath,
Despatch'd by Merion to the shades of death:
On Ida's holy hill he made abode,
The priest of Jove, and honour'd like his god.
Between the jaw and ear the javelin went;
The soul, exhaling, issued at the vent.
His spear Aeneas at the victor threw,
Who stooping forward from the death withdrew;
The lance hiss'd harmless o'er his covering shield,
And trembling struck, and rooted in the field;
There yet scarce spent, it quivers on the plain,
Sent by the great Aeneas' arm in vain.
"Swift as thou art (the raging hero cries)
And skill'd in dancing to dispute the prize,
My spear, the destined passage had it found,
Had fix'd thy active vigour to the ground."

"O valiant leader of the Dardan host!
(Insulted Merion thus retorts the boast)
Strong as you are, 'tis mortal force you trust,
An arm as strong may stretch thee in the dust.
And if to this my lance thy fate be given,
Vain are thy vaunts; success is still from heaven:
This, instant, sends thee down to Pluto's coast;
Mine is the glory, his thy parting ghost."

"O friend (Menoetius' son this answer gave)
With words to combat, ill befits the brave;
Not empty boasts the sons of Troy repel,
Your swords must plunge them to the shades of hell.
To speak, beseems the council; but to dare
In glorious action, is the task of war."

This said, Patroclus to the battle flies;
Great Merion follows, and new shouts arise:
Shields, helmets rattle, as the warriors close;
And thick and heavy sounds the storm of blows.
As through the shrilling vale, or mountain ground,
The labours of the woodman's axe resound;
Blows following blows are heard re-echoing wide,
While crackling forests fall on every side:
Thus echoed all the fields with loud alarms,
So fell the warriors, and so rung their arms.

Now great Sarpedon on the sandy shore,
His heavenly form defaced with dust and gore,

And stuck with darts by warring heroes shed,
Lies undistinguish'd from the vulgar dead.
His long-disputed corse the chiefs enclose,
On every side the busy combat grows;
Thick as beneath some shepherd's thatch'd abode
(The pails high foaming with a milky flood)
The buzzing flies, a persevering train,
Incessant swarm, and chased return again.

Jove view'd the combat with a stern survey,
And eyes that flash'd intolerable day.
Fix'd on the field his sight, his breast debates
The vengeance due, and meditates the fates:
Whether to urge their prompt effect, and call
The force of Hector to Patroclus' fall,
This instant see his short-lived trophies won,
And stretch him breathless on his slaughter'd son;
Or yet, with many a soul's untimely flight,
Augment the fame and horror of the fight.
To crown Achilles' valiant friend with praise
At length he dooms; and, that his last of days
Shall set in glory, bids him drive the foe;
Nor unattended see the shades below.
Then Hector's mind he fills with dire dismay;
He mounts his car, and calls his hosts away;
Sunk with Troy's heavy fates, he sees decline
The scales of Jove, and pants with awe divine.

Then, nor before, the hardy Lycians fled,
And left their monarch with the common dead:
Around, in heaps on heaps, a dreadful wall
Of carnage rises, as the heroes fall.
(So Jove decreed!) At length the Greeks obtain
The prize contested, and despoil the slain.
The radiant arms are by Patroclus borne;
Patroclus' ships the glorious spoils adorn.

Then thus to Phoebus, in the realms above,
Spoke from his throne the cloud-compelling Jove:
"Descend, my Phoebus! on the Phrygian plain,
And from the fight convey Sarpedon slain;
Then bathe his body in the crystal flood,
With dust dishonour'd, and deform'd with blood;
O'er all his limbs ambrosial odours shed,
And with celestial robes adorn the dead.
Those rites discharged, his sacred corse bequeath
To the soft arms of silent Sleep and Death.
They to his friends the immortal charge shall bear;

His friends a tomb and pyramid shall rear:
What honour mortals after death receive,
Those unavailing honours we may give!"

Apollo bows, and from mount Ida's height,
Swift to the field precipitates his flight;
Thence from the war the breathless hero bore,
Veil'd in a cloud, to silver Simois' shore;
There bathed his honourable wounds, and dress'd
His manly members in the immortal vest;
And with perfumes of sweet ambrosial dews
Restores his freshness, and his form renews.
Then Sleep and Death, two twins of winged race,
Of matchless swiftness, but of silent pace,
Received Sarpedon, at the god's command,
And in a moment reach'd the Lycian land;
The corse amidst his weeping friends they laid,
Where endless honours wait the sacred shade.

Meanwhile Patroclus pours along the plains,
With foaming coursers, and with loosen'd reins.
Fierce on the Trojan and the Lycian crew,
Ah blind to fate! thy headlong fury flew
Against what fate and powerful Jove ordain,
Vain was thy friend's command, thy courage vain.
For he, the god, whose counsels uncontroll'd
Dismay the mighty, and confound the bold;
The god who gives, resumes, and orders all,
He urged thee on, and urged thee on to fall.

Who first, brave hero! by that arm was slain,
Who last beneath thy vengeance press'd the plain;
When heaven itself thy fatal fury led,
And call'd to fill the number of the dead?
Adrestus first; Autonous then succeeds;
Echeclus follows; next young Megas bleeds,
Epistor, Melanippus, bite the ground;
The slaughter, Elasus and Mulius crown'd:
Then sunk Pylartes to eternal night;
The rest, dispersing, trust their fates to flight.

Now Troy had stoop'd beneath his matchless power,
But flaming Phoebus kept the sacred tower
Thrice at the battlements Patroclus strook;
His blazing aegis thrice Apollo shook;
He tried the fourth; when, bursting from the cloud,
A more than mortal voice was heard aloud.

"Patroclus! cease; this heaven-defended wall
Defies thy lance; not fated yet to fall;
Thy friend, thy greater far, it shall withstand,
Troy shall not stoop even to Achilles' hand."

So spoke the god who darts celestial fires;
The Greek obeys him, and with awe retires.
While Hector, checking at the Scaean gates
His panting coursers, in his breast debates,
Or in the field his forces to employ,
Or draw the troops within the walls of Troy.
Thus while he thought, beside him Phoebus stood,
In Asius' shape, who reigned by Sangar's flood;
(Thy brother, Hecuba! from Dymas sprung,
A valiant warrior, haughty, bold, and young;)
Thus he accosts him. "What a shameful sight!
God! is it Hector that forbears the fight?
Were thine my vigour this successful spear
Should soon convince thee of so false a fear.
Turn thee, ah turn thee to the field of fame,
And in Patroclus' blood efface thy shame.
Perhaps Apollo shall thy arms succeed,
And heaven ordains him by thy lance to bleed."

So spoke the inspiring god; then took his flight,
And plunged amidst the tumult of the fight.
He bids Cebrion drive the rapid car;
The lash resounds, the coursers rush to war.
The god the Grecians' sinking souls depress'd,
And pour'd swift spirits through each Trojan breast.
Patroclus lights, impatient for the fight;
A spear his left, a stone employs his right:
With all his nerves he drives it at the foe.
Pointed above, and rough and gross below:
The falling ruin crush'd Cebrion's head,
The lawless offspring of king Priam's bed;
His front, brows, eyes, one undistinguish'd wound:
The bursting balls drop sightless to the ground.
The charioteer, while yet he held the rein,
Struck from the car, falls headlong on the plain.
To the dark shades the soul unwilling glides,
While the proud victor thus his fall derides.

"Good heaven! what active feats yon artist shows!
What skilful divers are our Phrygian foes!
Mark with what ease they sink into the sand!
Pity that all their practice is by land!"

Then rushing sudden on his prostrate prize,
To spoil the carcase fierce Patroclus flies:
Swift as a lion, terrible and bold,
That sweeps the field, depopulates the fold;
Pierced through the dauntless heart, then tumbles slain,
And from his fatal courage finds his bane.
At once bold Hector leaping from his car,
Defends the body, and provokes the war.
Thus for some slaughter'd hind, with equal rage,
Two lordly rulers of the wood engage;
Stung with fierce hunger, each the prey invades,
And echoing roars rebellow through the shades.
Stern Hector fastens on the warrior's head,
And by the foot Patroclus drags the dead:
While all around, confusion, rage, and fright,
Mix the contending hosts in mortal fight.
So pent by hills, the wild winds roar aloud
In the deep bosom of some gloomy wood;
Leaves, arms, and trees, aloft in air are blown,
The broad oaks crackle, and the Sylvans groan;
This way and that, the rattling thicket bends,
And the whole forest in one crash descends.
Not with less noise, with less tumultuous rage,
In dreadful shock the mingled hosts engage.
Darts shower'd on darts, now round the carcase ring;
Now flights of arrows bounding from the string:
Stones follow stones; some clatter on the fields,
Some hard, and heavy, shake the sounding shields.
But where the rising whirlwind clouds the plains,
Sunk in soft dust the mighty chief remains,
And, stretch'd in death, forgets the guiding reins!

Now flaming from the zenith, Sol had driven
His fervid orb through half the vault of heaven;
While on each host with equal tempests fell
The showering darts, and numbers sank to hell.
But when his evening wheels o'erhung the main,
Glad conquest rested on the Grecian train.
Then from amidst the tumult and alarms,
They draw the conquer'd corse and radiant arms.
Then rash Patroclus with new fury glows,
And breathing slaughter, pours amid the foes.
Thrice on the press like Mars himself he flew,
And thrice three heroes at each onset slew.
There ends thy glory! there the Fates untwine
The last, black remnant of so bright a line:
Apollo dreadful stops thy middle way;
Death calls, and heaven allows no longer day!

For lo! the god in dusky clouds enshrined,
Approaching dealt a staggering blow behind.
The weighty shock his neck and shoulders feel;
His eyes flash sparkles, his stunn'd senses reel
In giddy darkness; far to distance flung,
His bounding helmet on the champaign rung.
Achilles' plume is stain'd with dust and gore;
That plume which never stoop'd to earth before;
Long used, untouch'd, in fighting fields to shine,
And shade the temples of the mad divine.
Jove dooms it now on Hector's helm to nod;
Not long—for fate pursues him, and the god.

His spear in shivers falls; his ample shield
Drops from his arm: his baldric strows the field:
The corslet his astonish'd breast forsakes:
Loose is each joint; each nerve with horror shakes;
Stupid he stares, and all-assistless stands:
Such is the force of more than mortal hands!

A Dardan youth there was, well known to fame,
From Panthus sprung, Euphorbus was his name;
Famed for the manage of the foaming horse,
Skill'd in the dart, and matchless in the course:
Full twenty knights he tumbled from the car,
While yet he learn'd his rudiments of war.
His venturous spear first drew the hero's gore;
He struck, he wounded, but he durst no more.
Nor, though disarm'd, Patroclus' fury stood:
But swift withdrew the long-protended wood.
And turn'd him short, and herded in the crowd.
Thus, by an arm divine, and mortal spear,
Wounded, at once, Patroclus yields to fear,
Retires for succour to his social train,
And flies the fate, which heaven decreed, in vain.
Stern Hector, as the bleeding chief he views,
Breaks through the ranks, and his retreat pursues:
The lance arrests him with a mortal wound;
He falls, earth thunders, and his arms resound.
With him all Greece was sunk; that moment all
Her yet-surviving heroes seem'd to fall.
So, scorch'd with heat, along the desert score,
The roaming lion meets a bristly boar,
Fast by the spring; they both dispute the flood,
With flaming eyes, and jaws besmear'd with blood;
At length the sovereign savage wins the strife;
And the torn boar resigns his thirst and life.

Patroclus thus, so many chiefs o'erthrown,
So many lives effused, expires his own.
As dying now at Hector's feet he lies,
He sternly views him, and triumphant cries:

"Lie there, Patroclus! and with thee, the joy
Thy pride once promised, of subverting Troy;
The fancied scenes of Ilion wrapt in flames,
And thy soft pleasures served with captive dames.
Unthinking man! I fought those towers to free,
And guard that beauteous race from lords like thee:
But thou a prey to vultures shalt be made;
Thy own Achilles cannot lend thee aid;
Though much at parting that great chief might say,
And much enjoin thee, this important day.

'Return not, my brave friend (perhaps he said),
Without the bloody arms of Hector dead.'
He spoke, Patroclus march'd, and thus he sped."

Supine, and wildly gazing on the skies,
With faint, expiring breath, the chief replies:

"Vain boaster! cease, and know the powers divine!
Jove's and Apollo's is this deed, not thine;
To heaven is owed whate'er your own you call,
And heaven itself disarm'd me ere my fall.
Had twenty mortals, each thy match in might,
Opposed me fairly, they had sunk in fight:
By fate and Phoebus was I first o'erthrown,
Euphorbus next; the third mean part thy own.
But thou, imperious! hear my latest breath;
The gods inspire it, and it sounds thy death:
Insulting man, thou shalt be soon as I;
Black fate o'erhangs thee, and thy hour draws nigh;
Even now on life's last verge I see thee stand,
I see thee fall, and by Achilles' hand."

He faints: the soul unwilling wings her way,
(The beauteous body left a load of clay)
Flits to the lone, uncomfortable coast;
A naked, wandering, melancholy ghost!

Then Hector pausing, as his eyes he fed
On the pale carcase, thus address'd the dead:

"From whence this boding speech, the stern decree
Of death denounced, or why denounced to me?

Why not as well Achilles' fate be given
To Hector's lance? Who knows the will of heaven?"

Pensive he said; then pressing as he lay
His breathless bosom, tore the lance away;
And upwards cast the corse: the reeking spear
He shakes, and charges the bold charioteer.
But swift Automedon with loosen'd reins
Rapt in the chariot o'er the distant plains,
Far from his rage the immortal coursers drove;
The immortal coursers were the gift of Jove.

BOOK XVII

ARGUMENT

THE SEVENTH BATTLE, FOR THE BODY OF PATROCLUS.—THE ACTS OF MENELAUS

Menelaus, upon the death of Patroclus, defends his body from the enemy: Euphorbus, who attempts it, is slain. Hector advancing, Menelaus retires; but soon returns with Ajax, and drives him off. This, Glaucus objects to Hector as a flight, who thereupon puts on the armour he had won from Patroclus, and renews the battle. The Greeks give way, till Ajax rallies them: Aeneas sustains the Trojans. Aeneas and Hector Attempt the chariot of Achilles, which is borne off by Automedon. The horses of Achilles deplore the loss of Patroclus: Jupiter covers his body with a thick darkness: the noble prayer of Ajax on that occasion. Menelaus sends Antilochus to Achilles, with the news of Patroclus' death: then returns to the fight, where, though attacked with the utmost fury, he and Meriones, assisted by the Ajaces, bear off the body to the ships.

The time is the evening of the eight-and-twentieth day. The scene lies in the fields before Troy.

On the cold earth divine Patroclus spread,
Lies pierced with wounds among the vulgar dead.
Great Menelaus, touch'd with generous woe,
Springs to the front, and guards him from the foe.
Thus round her new-fallen young the heifer moves,
Fruit of her throes, and first-born of her loves;
And anxious (helpless as he lies, and bare)
Turns, and re-turns her, with a mother's care,
Opposed to each that near the carcase came,
His broad shield glimmers, and his lances flame.

The son of Panthus, skill'd the dart to send,
Eyes the dead hero, and insults the friend.
"This hand, Atrides, laid Patroclus low;
Warrior! desist, nor tempt an equal blow:

To me the spoils my prowess won, resign:
Depart with life, and leave the glory mine"

The Trojan thus: the Spartan monarch burn'd
With generous anguish, and in scorn return'd:
"Laugh'st thou not, Jove! from thy superior throne,
When mortals boast of prowess not their own?
Not thus the lion glories in his might,
Nor panther braves his spotted foe in fight,
Nor thus the boar (those terrors of the plain;)
Man only vaunts his force, and vaunts in vain.
But far the vainest of the boastful kind,
These sons of Panthus vent their haughty mind.
Yet 'twas but late, beneath my conquering steel
This boaster's brother, Hyperenor, fell;
Against our arm which rashly he defied,
Vain was his vigour, and as vain his pride.
These eyes beheld him on the dust expire,
No more to cheer his spouse, or glad his sire.
Presumptuous youth! like his shall be thy doom,
Go, wait thy brother to the Stygian gloom;
Or, while thou may'st, avoid the threaten'd fate;
Fools stay to feel it, and are wise too late."

Unmoved, Euphorbus thus: "That action known,
Come, for my brother's blood repay thy own.
His weeping father claims thy destined head,
And spouse, a widow in her bridal bed.
On these thy conquer'd spoils I shall bestow,
To soothe a consort's and a parent's woe.
No longer then defer the glorious strife,
Let heaven decide our fortune, fame, and life."

Swift as the word the missile lance he flings;
The well-aim'd weapon on the buckler rings,
But blunted by the brass, innoxious falls.
On Jove the father great Atrides calls,
Nor flies the javelin from his arm in vain,
It pierced his throat, and bent him to the plain;
Wide through the neck appears the grisly wound,
Prone sinks the warrior, and his arms resound.
The shining circlets of his golden hair,
Which even the Graces might be proud to wear,
Instarr'd with gems and gold, bestrew the shore,
With dust dishonour'd, and deform'd with gore.

As the young olive, in some sylvan scene,
Crown'd by fresh fountains with eternal green,

Lifts the gay head, in snowy flowerets fair,
And plays and dances to the gentle air;
When lo! a whirlwind from high heaven invades
The tender plant, and withers all its shades;
It lies uprooted from its genial bed,
A lovely ruin now defaced and dead:
Thus young, thus beautiful, Euphorbus lay,
While the fierce Spartan tore his arms away.
Proud of his deed, and glorious in the prize,
Affrighted Troy the towering victor flies:
Flies, as before some mountain lion's ire
The village curs and trembling swains retire,
When o'er the slaughter'd bull they hear him roar,
And see his jaws distil with smoking gore:
All pale with fear, at distance scatter'd round,
They shout incessant, and the vales resound.

Meanwhile Apollo view'd with envious eyes,
And urged great Hector to dispute the prize;
(In Mentes' shape, beneath whose martial care
The rough Ciconians learn'd the trade of war;)
"Forbear (he cried) with fruitless speed to chase
Achilles' coursers, of ethereal race;
They stoop not, these, to mortal man's command,
Or stoop to none but great Achilles' hand.
Too long amused with a pursuit so vain,
Turn, and behold the brave Euphorbus slain;
By Sparta slain! for ever now suppress'd
The fire which burn'd in that undaunted breast!"

Thus having spoke, Apollo wing'd his flight,
And mix'd with mortals in the toils of fight:
His words infix'd unutterable care
Deep in great Hector's soul: through all the war
He darts his anxious eye; and, instant, view'd
The breathless hero in his blood imbued,
(Forth welling from the wound, as prone he lay)
And in the victor's hands the shining prey.
Sheath'd in bright arms, through cleaving ranks he flies,
And sends his voice in thunder to the skies:
Fierce as a flood of flame by Vulcan sent,
It flew, and fired the nations as it went.
Atrides from the voice the storm divined,
And thus explored his own unconquer'd mind:

"Then shall I quit Patroclus on the plain,
Slain in my cause, and for my honour slain!
Desert the arms, the relics, of my friend?

Or singly, Hector and his troops attend?
Sure where such partial favour heaven bestow'd,
To brave the hero were to brave the god:
Forgive me, Greece, if once I quit the field;
'Tis not to Hector, but to heaven I yield.
Yet, nor the god, nor heaven, should give me fear,
Did but the voice of Ajax reach my ear:
Still would we turn, still battle on the plains,
And give Achilles all that yet remains
Of his and our Patroclus—" This, no more
The time allow'd: Troy thicken'd on the shore.
A sable scene! The terrors Hector led.
Slow he recedes, and sighing quits the dead.

So from the fold the unwilling lion parts,
Forced by loud clamours, and a storm of darts;
He flies indeed, but threatens as he flies,
With heart indignant and retorted eyes.
Now enter'd in the Spartan ranks, he turn'd
His manly breast, and with new fury burn'd;
O'er all the black battalions sent his view,
And through the cloud the godlike Ajax knew;
Where labouring on the left the warrior stood,
All grim in arms, and cover'd o'er with blood;
There breathing courage, where the god of day
Had sunk each heart with terror and dismay.

To him the king: "Oh Ajax, oh my friend!
Haste, and Patroclus' loved remains defend:
The body to Achilles to restore
Demands our care; alas, we can no more!
For naked now, despoiled of arms, he lies;
And Hector glories in the dazzling prize."
He said, and touch'd his heart. The raging pair
Pierced the thick battle, and provoke the war.
Already had stern Hector seized his head,
And doom'd to Trojan gods the unhappy dead;
But soon as Ajax rear'd his tower-like shield,
Sprung to his car, and measured back the field,
His train to Troy the radiant armour bear,
To stand a trophy of his fame in war.

Meanwhile great Ajax (his broad shield display'd)
Guards the dead hero with the dreadful shade;
And now before, and now behind he stood:
Thus in the centre of some gloomy wood,
With many a step, the lioness surrounds
Her tawny young, beset by men and hounds;

Elate her heart, and rousing all her powers,
Dark o'er the fiery balls each hanging eyebrow lours.
Fast by his side the generous Spartan glows
With great revenge, and feeds his inward woes.

But Glaucus, leader of the Lycian aids,
On Hector frowning, thus his flight upbraids:

"Where now in Hector shall we Hector find?
A manly form, without a manly mind.
Is this, O chief! a hero's boasted fame?
How vain, without the merit, is the name!
Since battle is renounced, thy thoughts employ
What other methods may preserve thy Troy:
'Tis time to try if Ilion's state can stand
By thee alone, nor ask a foreign hand:
Mean, empty boast! but shall the Lycians stake
Their lives for you? those Lycians you forsake?
What from thy thankless arms can we expect?
Thy friend Sarpedon proves thy base neglect;
Say, shall our slaughter'd bodies guard your walls,
While unreveng'd the great Sarpedon falls?
Even where he died for Troy, you left him there,
A feast for dogs, and all the fowls of air.
On my command if any Lycian wait,
Hence let him march, and give up Troy to fate.
Did such a spirit as the gods impart
Impel one Trojan hand or Trojan heart,
(Such as should burn in every soul that draws
The sword for glory, and his country's cause)
Even yet our mutual arms we might employ,
And drag yon carcase to the walls of Troy.
Oh! were Patroclus ours, we might obtain
Sarpedon's arms and honour'd corse again!
Greece with Achilles' friend should be repaid,
And thus due honours purchased to his shade.
But words are vain—Let Ajax once appear,
And Hector trembles and recedes with fear;
Thou dar'st not meet the terrors of his eye;
And lo! already thou prepar'st to fly."

The Trojan chief with fix'd resentment eyed
The Lycian leader, and sedate replied:

"Say, is it just, my friend, that Hector's ear
From such a warrior such a speech should hear?
I deem'd thee once the wisest of thy kind,
But ill this insult suits a prudent mind.

I shun great Ajax? I desert my train?
'Tis mine to prove the rash assertion vain;
I joy to mingle where the battle bleeds,
And hear the thunder of the sounding steeds.
But Jove's high will is ever uncontroll'd,
The strong he withers, and confounds the bold;
Now crowns with fame the mighty man, and now
Strikes the fresh garland from the victor's brow!
Come, through yon squadrons let us hew the way,
And thou be witness, if I fear to-day;
If yet a Greek the sight of Hector dread,
Or yet their hero dare defend the dead."

Then turning to the martial hosts, he cries:
"Ye Trojans, Dardans, Lycians, and allies!
Be men, my friends, in action as in name,
And yet be mindful of your ancient fame.
Hector in proud Achilles' arms shall shine,
Torn from his friend, by right of conquest mine."

He strode along the field, as thus he said:
(The sable plumage nodded o'er his head:)
Swift through the spacious plain he sent a look;
One instant saw, one instant overtook
The distant band, that on the sandy shore
The radiant spoils to sacred Ilion bore.
There his own mail unbraced the field bestrow'd;
His train to Troy convey'd the massy load.
Now blazing in the immortal arms he stands;
The work and present of celestial hands;
By aged Peleus to Achilles given,
As first to Peleus by the court of heaven:
His father's arms not long Achilles wears,
Forbid by fate to reach his father's years.

Him, proud in triumph, glittering from afar,
The god whose thunder rends the troubled air
Beheld with pity; as apart he sat,
And, conscious, look'd through all the scene of fate.
He shook the sacred honours of his head;
Olympus trembled, and the godhead said;
"Ah, wretched man! unmindful of thy end!
A moment's glory; and what fates attend!
In heavenly panoply divinely bright
Thou stand'st, and armies tremble at thy sight,
As at Achilles' self! beneath thy dart
Lies slain the great Achilles' dearer part.
Thou from the mighty dead those arms hast torn,

Which once the greatest of mankind had worn.
Yet live! I give thee one illustrious day,
A blaze of glory ere thou fad'st away.
For ah! no more Andromache shall come
With joyful tears to welcome Hector home;
No more officious, with endearing charms,
From thy tired limbs unbrace Pelides' arms!"

Then with his sable brow he gave the nod
That seals his word; the sanction of the god.
The stubborn arms (by Jove's command disposed)
Conform'd spontaneous, and around him closed:
Fill'd with the god, enlarged his members grew,
Through all his veins a sudden vigour flew,
The blood in brisker tides began to roll,
And Mars himself came rushing on his soul.
Exhorting loud through all the field he strode,
And look'd, and moved, Achilles, or a god.
Now Mesthles, Glaucus, Medon, he inspires,
Now Phorcys, Chromius, and Hippothous fires;
The great Thersilochus like fury found,
Asteropaeus kindled at the sound,
And Ennomus, in augury renown'd.

"Hear, all ye hosts, and hear, unnumber'd bands
Of neighbouring nations, or of distant lands!
'Twas not for state we summon'd you so far,
To boast our numbers, and the pomp of war:
Ye came to fight; a valiant foe to chase,
To save our present, and our future race.
Tor this, our wealth, our products, you enjoy,
And glean the relics of exhausted Troy.
Now then, to conquer or to die prepare;
To die or conquer are the terms of war.
Whatever hand shall win Patroclus slain,
Whoe'er shall drag him to the Trojan train,
With Hector's self shall equal honours claim;
With Hector part the spoil, and share the fame."

Fired by his words, the troops dismiss their fears,
They join, they thicken, they protend their spears;
Full on the Greeks they drive in firm array,
And each from Ajax hopes the glorious prey:
Vain hope! what numbers shall the field o'erspread,
What victims perish round the mighty dead!

Great Ajax mark'd the growing storm from far,
And thus bespoke his brother of the war:

"Our fatal day, alas! is come, my friend;
And all our wars and glories at an end!
'Tis not this corse alone we guard in vain,
Condemn'd to vultures on the Trojan plain;
We too must yield: the same sad fate must fall
On thee, on me, perhaps, my friend, on all.
See what a tempest direful Hector spreads,
And lo! it bursts, it thunders on our heads!
Call on our Greeks, if any hear the call,
The bravest Greeks: this hour demands them all."

The warrior raised his voice, and wide around
The field re-echoed the distressful sound.
"O chiefs! O princes, to whose hand is given
The rule of men; whose glory is from heaven!
Whom with due honours both Atrides grace:
Ye guides and guardians of our Argive race!
All, whom this well-known voice shall reach from far,
All, whom I see not through this cloud of war;
Come all! let generous rage your arms employ,
And save Patroclus from the dogs of Troy."

Oilean Ajax first the voice obey'd,
Swift was his pace, and ready was his aid:
Next him Idomeneus, more slow with age,
And Merion, burning with a hero's rage.
The long-succeeding numbers who can name?
But all were Greeks, and eager all for fame.
Fierce to the charge great Hector led the throng;
Whole Troy embodied rush'd with shouts along.
Thus, when a mountain billow foams and raves,
Where some swoln river disembogues his waves,
Full in the mouth is stopp'd the rushing tide,
The boiling ocean works from side to side,
The river trembles to his utmost shore,
And distant rocks re-bellow to the roar.

Nor less resolved, the firm Achaian band
With brazen shields in horrid circle stand.
Jove, pouring darkness o'er the mingled fight,
Conceals the warriors' shining helms in night:
To him, the chief for whom the hosts contend
Had lived not hateful, for he lived a friend:
Dead he protects him with superior care.
Nor dooms his carcase to the birds of air.

The first attack the Grecians scarce sustain,
Repulsed, they yield; the Trojans seize the slain.

Then fierce they rally, to revenge led on
By the swift rage of Ajax Telamon.
(Ajax to Peleus' son the second name,
In graceful stature next, and next in fame)
With headlong force the foremost ranks he tore;
So through the thicket bursts the mountain boar,
And rudely scatters, for a distance round,
The frighted hunter and the baying hound.
The son of Lethus, brave Pelasgus' heir,
Hippothous, dragg'd the carcase through the war;
The sinewy ankles bored, the feet he bound
With thongs inserted through the double wound:
Inevitable fate o'ertakes the deed;
Doom'd by great Ajax' vengeful lance to bleed:
It cleft the helmet's brazen cheeks in twain;
The shatter'd crest and horse-hair strow the plain:
With nerves relax'd he tumbles to the ground:
The brain comes gushing through the ghastly wound:
He drops Patroclus' foot, and o'er him spread,
Now lies a sad companion of the dead:
Far from Larissa lies, his native air,
And ill requites his parents' tender care.
Lamented youth! in life's first bloom he fell,
Sent by great Ajax to the shades of hell.

Once more at Ajax Hector's javelin flies;
The Grecian marking, as it cut the skies,
Shunn'd the descending death; which hissing on,
Stretch'd in the dust the great Iphytus' son,
Schedius the brave, of all the Phocian kind
The boldest warrior and the noblest mind:
In little Panope, for strength renown'd,
He held his seat, and ruled the realms around.
Plunged in his throat, the weapon drank his blood,
And deep transpiercing through the shoulder stood;
In clanging arms the hero fell and all
The fields resounded with his weighty fall.

Phorcys, as slain Hippothous he defends,
The Telamonian lance his belly rends;
The hollow armour burst before the stroke,
And through the wound the rushing entrails broke:
In strong convulsions panting on the sands
He lies, and grasps the dust with dying hands.

Struck at the sight, recede the Trojan train:
The shouting Argives strip the heroes slain.
And now had Troy, by Greece compell'd to yield,

Fled to her ramparts, and resign'd the field;
Greece, in her native fortitude elate,
With Jove averse, had turn'd the scale of fate:
But Phoebus urged Ćneas to the fight;
He seem'd like aged Periphas to sight:
(A herald in Anchises' love grown old,
Revered for prudence, and with prudence bold.)

Thus he—"What methods yet, O chief! remain,
To save your Troy, though heaven its fall ordain?
There have been heroes, who, by virtuous care,
By valour, numbers, and by arts of war,
Have forced the powers to spare a sinking state,
And gain'd at length the glorious odds of fate:
But you, when fortune smiles, when Jove declares
His partial favour, and assists your wars,
Your shameful efforts 'gainst yourselves employ,
And force the unwilling god to ruin Troy."

Ćneas through the form assumed descries
The power conceal'd, and thus to Hector cries:
"Oh lasting shame! to our own fears a prey,
We seek our ramparts, and desert the day.
A god, nor is he less, my bosom warms,
And tells me, Jove asserts the Trojan arms."

He spoke, and foremost to the combat flew:
The bold example all his hosts pursue.
Then, first, Leocritus beneath him bled,
In vain beloved by valiant Lycomede;
Who view'd his fall, and, grieving at the chance,
Swift to revenge it sent his angry lance;
The whirling lance, with vigorous force address'd,
Descends, and pants in Apisaon's breast;
From rich Paeonia's vales the warrior came,
Next thee, Asteropeus! in place and fame.
Asteropeus with grief beheld the slain,
And rush'd to combat, but he rush'd in vain:
Indissolubly firm, around the dead,
Rank within rank, on buckler buckler spread,
And hemm'd with bristled spears, the Grecians stood,
A brazen bulwark, and an iron wood.
Great Ajax eyes them with incessant care,
And in an orb contracts the crowded war,
Close in their ranks commands to fight or fall,
And stands the centre and the soul of all:
Fix'd on the spot they war, and wounded, wound
A sanguine torrent steeps the reeking ground:

On heaps the Greeks, on heaps the Trojans bled,
And, thickening round them, rise the hills of dead.

Greece, in close order, and collected might,
Yet suffers least, and sways the wavering fight;
Fierce as conflicting fires the combat burns,
And now it rises, now it sinks by turns.
In one thick darkness all the fight was lost;
The sun, the moon, and all the ethereal host
Seem'd as extinct: day ravish'd from their eyes,
And all heaven's splendours blotted from the skies.
Such o'er Patroclus' body hung the night,
The rest in sunshine fought, and open light;
Unclouded there, the aerial azure spread,
No vapour rested on the mountain's head,
The golden sun pour'd forth a stronger ray,
And all the broad expansion flamed with day.
Dispersed around the plain, by fits they fight,
And here and there their scatter'd arrows light:
But death and darkness o'er the carcase spread,
There burn'd the war, and there the mighty bled.

Meanwhile the sons of Nestor, in the rear,
(Their fellows routed,) toss the distant spear,
And skirmish wide: so Nestor gave command,
When from the ships he sent the Pylian band.
The youthful brothers thus for fame contend,
Nor knew the fortune of Achilles' friend;
In thought they view'd him still, with martial joy,
Glorious in arms, and dealing death to Troy.

But round the corse the heroes pant for breath,
And thick and heavy grows the work of death:
O'erlabour'd now, with dust, and sweat, and gore,
Their knees, their legs, their feet, are covered o'er;
Drops follow drops, the clouds on clouds arise,
And carnage clogs their hands, and darkness fills their eyes.
As when a slaughter'd bull's yet reeking hide,
Strain'd with full force, and tugg'd from side to side,
The brawny curriers stretch; and labour o'er
The extended surface, drunk with fat and gore:
So tugging round the corse both armies stood;
The mangled body bathed in sweat and blood;
While Greeks and Ilians equal strength employ,
Now to the ships to force it, now to Troy.
Not Pallas' self, her breast when fury warms,
Nor he whose anger sets the world in arms,
Could blame this scene; such rage, such horror reign'd;

Such, Jove to honour the great dead ordain'd.

Achilles in his ships at distance lay,
Nor knew the fatal fortune of the day;
He, yet unconscious of Patroclus' fall,
In dust extended under Ilion's wall,
Expects him glorious from the conquered plain,
And for his wish'd return prepares in vain;
Though well he knew, to make proud Ilion bend
Was more than heaven had destined to his friend.
Perhaps to him: this Thetis had reveal'd;
The rest, in pity to her son, conceal'd.

Still raged the conflict round the hero dead,
And heaps on heaps by mutual wounds they bled.
"Cursed be the man (even private Greeks would say)
Who dares desert this well-disputed day!
First may the cleaving earth before our eyes
Gape wide, and drink our blood for sacrifice;
First perish all, ere haughty Troy shall boast
We lost Patroclus, and our glory lost!"

Thus they: while with one voice the Trojans said,
"Grant this day, Jove! or heap us on the dead!"

Then clash their sounding arms; the clangours rise,
And shake the brazen concave of the skies.

Meantime, at distance from the scene of blood,
The pensive steeds of great Achilles stood:
Their godlike master slain before their eyes,
They wept, and shared in human miseries.
In vain Automedon now shakes the rein,
Now plies the lash, and soothes and threats in vain;
Nor to the fight nor Hellespont they go,
Restive they stood, and obstinate in woe:
Still as a tombstone, never to be moved,
On some good man or woman unreproved
Lays its eternal weight; or fix'd, as stands
A marble courser by the sculptor's hands,
Placed on the hero's grave. Along their face
The big round drops coursed down with silent pace,
Conglobing on the dust. Their manes, that late
Circled their arched necks, and waved in state,
Trail'd on the dust beneath the yoke were spread,
And prone to earth was hung their languid head:
Nor Jove disdain'd to cast a pitying look,
While thus relenting to the steeds he spoke:

"Unhappy coursers of immortal strain,
Exempt from age, and deathless, now in vain;
Did we your race on mortal man bestow,
Only, alas! to share in mortal woe?
For ah! what is there of inferior birth,
That breathes or creeps upon the dust of earth;
What wretched creature of what wretched kind,
Than man more weak, calamitous, and blind?
A miserable race! but cease to mourn:
For not by you shall Priam's son be borne
High on the splendid car: one glorious prize
He rashly boasts: the rest our will denies.
Ourself will swiftness to your nerves impart,
Ourself with rising spirits swell your heart.
Automedon your rapid flight shall bear
Safe to the navy through the storm of war.
For yet 'tis given to Troy to ravage o'er
The field, and spread her slaughters to the shore;
The sun shall see her conquer, till his fall
With sacred darkness shades the face of all."

He said; and breathing in the immortal horse
Excessive spirit, urged them to the course;
From their high manes they shake the dust, and bear
The kindling chariot through the parted war:
So flies a vulture through the clamorous train
Of geese, that scream, and scatter round the plain.
From danger now with swiftest speed they flew,
And now to conquest with like speed pursue;
Sole in the seat the charioteer remains,
Now plies the javelin, now directs the reins:
Him brave Alcimedon beheld distress'd,
Approach'd the chariot, and the chief address'd:

"What god provokes thee rashly thus to dare,
Alone, unaided, in the thickest war?
Alas! thy friend is slain, and Hector wields
Achilles' arms triumphant in the fields."

"In happy time (the charioteer replies)
The bold Alcimedon now greets my eyes;
No Greek like him the heavenly steeds restrains,
Or holds their fury in suspended reins:
Patroclus, while he lived, their rage could tame,
But now Patroclus is an empty name!
To thee I yield the seat, to thee resign
The ruling charge: the task of fight be mine."

He said. Alcimedon, with active heat,
Snatches the reins, and vaults into the seat.
His friend descends. The chief of Troy descried,
And call'd Æneas fighting near his side.

"Lo, to my sight, beyond our hope restored,
Achilles' car, deserted of its lord!
The glorious steeds our ready arms invite,
Scarce their weak drivers guide them through the fight.
Can such opponents stand when we assail?
Unite thy force, my friend, and we prevail."

The son of Venus to the counsel yields;
Then o'er their backs they spread their solid shields:
With brass refulgent the broad surface shined,
And thick bull-hides the spacious concave lined.
Them Chromius follows, Aretus succeeds;
Each hopes the conquest of the lofty steeds:
In vain, brave youths, with glorious hopes ye burn,
In vain advance! not fated to return.

Unmov'd, Automedon attends the fight,
Implores the Eternal, and collects his might.
Then turning to his friend, with dauntless mind:
"Oh keep the foaming coursers close behind!
Full on my shoulders let their nostrils blow,
For hard the fight, determined is the foe;
'Tis Hector comes: and when he seeks the prize,
War knows no mean; he wins it or he dies."

Then through the field he sends his voice aloud,
And calls the Ajaces from the warring crowd,
With great Atrides. "Hither turn, (he said,)
Turn where distress demands immediate aid;
The dead, encircled by his friends, forego,
And save the living from a fiercer foe.
Unhelp'd we stand, unequal to engage
The force of Hector, and Æneas' rage:
Yet mighty as they are, my force to prove
Is only mine: the event belongs to Jove."

He spoke, and high the sounding javelin flung,
Which pass'd the shield of Aretus the young:
It pierced his belt, emboss'd with curious art,
Then in the lower belly struck the dart.
As when a ponderous axe, descending full,
Cleaves the broad forehead of some brawny bull:

Struck 'twixt the horns, he springs with many a bound,
Then tumbling rolls enormous on the ground:
Thus fell the youth; the air his soul received,
And the spear trembled as his entrails heaved.

Now at Automedon the Trojan foe
Discharged his lance; the meditated blow,
Stooping, he shunn'd; the javelin idly fled,
And hiss'd innoxious o'er the hero's head;
Deep rooted in the ground, the forceful spear
In long vibrations spent its fury there.
With clashing falchions now the chiefs had closed,
But each brave Ajax heard, and interposed;
Nor longer Hector with his Trojans stood,
But left their slain companion in his blood:
His arms Automedon divests, and cries,
"Accept, Patroclus, this mean sacrifice:
Thus have I soothed my griefs, and thus have paid,
Poor as it is, some offering to thy shade."

So looks the lion o'er a mangled boar,
All grim with rage, and horrible with gore;
High on the chariot at one bound he sprung,
And o'er his seat the bloody trophies hung.

And now Minerva from the realms of air
Descends impetuous, and renews the war;
For, pleased at length the Grecian arms to aid,
The lord of thunders sent the blue-eyed maid.
As when high Jove denouncing future woe,
O'er the dark clouds extends his purple bow,
(In sign of tempests from the troubled air,
Or from the rage of man, destructive war,)
The drooping cattle dread the impending skies,
And from his half-till'd field the labourer flies:
In such a form the goddess round her drew
A livid cloud, and to the battle flew.
Assuming Phoenix' shape on earth she falls,
And in his well-known voice to Sparta calls:
"And lies Achilles' friend, beloved by all,
A prey to dogs beneath the Trojan wall?
What shame 'o Greece for future times to tell,
To thee the greatest in whose cause he fell!"
"O chief, O father! (Atreus' son replies)
O full of days! by long experience wise!
What more desires my soul, than here unmoved
To guard the body of the man I loved?
Ah, would Minerva send me strength to rear

This wearied arm, and ward the storm of war!
But Hector, like the rage of fire, we dread,
And Jove's own glories blaze around his head!"

Pleased to be first of all the powers address'd,
She breathes new vigour in her hero's breast,
And fills with keen revenge, with fell despite,
Desire of blood, and rage, and lust of fight.
So burns the vengeful hornet (soul all o'er),
Repulsed in vain, and thirsty still of gore;
(Bold son of air and heat) on angry wings
Untamed, untired, he turns, attacks, and stings.
Fired with like ardour fierce Atrides flew,
And sent his soul with every lance he threw.

There stood a Trojan, not unknown to fame,
Aetion's son, and Podes was his name:
With riches honour'd, and with courage bless'd,
By Hector loved, his comrade, and his guest;
Through his broad belt the spear a passage found,
And, ponderous as he falls, his arms resound.
Sudden at Hector's side Apollo stood,
Like Phaenops, Asius' son, appear'd the god;
(Asius the great, who held his wealthy reign
In fair Abydos, by the rolling main.)

"Oh prince! (he cried) Oh foremost once in fame!
What Grecian now shall tremble at thy name?
Dost thou at length to Menelaus yield,
A chief once thought no terror of the field?
Yet singly, now, the long-disputed prize
He bears victorious, while our army flies:
By the same arm illustrious Podes bled;
The friend of Hector, unrevenged, is dead!"
This heard, o'er Hector spreads a cloud of woe,
Rage lifts his lance, and drives him on the foe.

But now the Eternal shook his sable shield,
That shaded Ide and all the subject field
Beneath its ample verge. A rolling cloud
Involved the mount; the thunder roar'd aloud;
The affrighted hills from their foundations nod,
And blaze beneath the lightnings of the god:
At one regard of his all-seeing eye
The vanquish'd triumph, and the victors fly.

Then trembled Greece: the flight Peneleus led;
For as the brave Boeotian turn'd his head

To face the foe, Polydamas drew near,
And razed his shoulder with a shorten'd spear:
By Hector wounded, Leitus quits the plain,
Pierced through the wrist; and raging with the pain,
Grasps his once formidable lance in vain.

As Hector follow'd, Idomen address'd
The flaming javelin to his manly breast;
The brittle point before his corslet yields;
Exulting Troy with clamour fills the fields:
High on his chariots the Cretan stood,
The son of Priam whirl'd the massive wood.
But erring from its aim, the impetuous spear
Struck to the dust the squire and charioteer
Of martial Merion: Coeranus his name,
Who left fair Lyctus for the fields of fame.
On foot bold Merion fought; and now laid low,
Had graced the triumphs of his Trojan foe,
But the brave squire the ready coursers brought,
And with his life his master's safety bought.
Between his cheek and ear the weapon went,
The teeth it shatter'd, and the tongue it rent.
Prone from the seat he tumbles to the plain;
His dying hand forgets the falling rein:
This Merion reaches, bending from the car,
And urges to desert the hopeless war:
Idomeneus consents; the lash applies;
And the swift chariot to the navy flies.

Not Ajax less the will of heaven descried,
And conquest shifting to the Trojan side,
Turn'd by the hand of Jove. Then thus begun,
To Atreus's seed, the godlike Telamon:

"Alas! who sees not Jove's almighty hand
Transfers the glory to the Trojan band?
Whether the weak or strong discharge the dart,
He guides each arrow to a Grecian heart:
Not so our spears; incessant though they rain,
He suffers every lance to fall in vain.
Deserted of the god, yet let us try
What human strength and prudence can supply;
If yet this honour'd corse, in triumph borne,
May glad the fleets that hope not our return,
Who tremble yet, scarce rescued from their fates,
And still hear Hector thundering at their gates.
Some hero too must be despatch'd to bear
The mournful message to Pelides' ear;

For sure he knows not, distant on the shore,
His friend, his loved Patroclus, is no more.
But such a chief I spy not through the host:
The men, the steeds, the armies, all are lost
In general darkness—Lord of earth and air!
Oh king! Oh father! hear my humble prayer:
Dispel this cloud, the light of heaven restore;
Give me to see, and Ajax asks no more:
If Greece must perish, we thy will obey,
But let us perish in the face of day!"

With tears the hero spoke, and at his prayer
The god relenting clear'd the clouded air;
Forth burst the sun with all-enlightening ray;
The blaze of armour flash'd against the day.
"Now, now, Atrides! cast around thy sight;
If yet Antilochus survives the fight,
Let him to great Achilles' ear convey
The fatal news"—Atrides hastes away.

So turns the lion from the nightly fold,
Though high in courage, and with hunger bold,
Long gall'd by herdsmen, and long vex'd by hounds,
Stiff with fatigue, and fretted sore with wounds;
The darts fly round him from a hundred hands,
And the red terrors of the blazing brands:
Till late, reluctant, at the dawn of day
Sour he departs, and quits the untasted prey,
So moved Atrides from his dangerous place
With weary limbs, but with unwilling pace;
The foe, he fear'd, might yet Patroclus gain,
And much admonish'd, much adjured his train:

"O guard these relics to your charge consign'd,
And bear the merits of the dead in mind;
How skill'd he was in each obliging art;
The mildest manners, and the gentlest heart:
He was, alas! but fate decreed his end,
In death a hero, as in life a friend!"

So parts the chief; from rank to rank he flew,
And round on all sides sent his piercing view.
As the bold bird, endued with sharpest eye
Of all that wings the mid aerial sky,
The sacred eagle, from his walks above
Looks down, and sees the distant thicket move;
Then stoops, and sousing on the quivering hare,
Snatches his life amid the clouds of air.

Not with less quickness, his exerted sight
Pass'd this and that way, through the ranks of fight:
Till on the left the chief he sought, he found,
Cheering his men, and spreading deaths around:

To him the king: "Beloved of Jove! draw near,
For sadder tidings never touch'd thy ear;
Thy eyes have witness'd what a fatal turn!
How Ilion triumphs, and the Achaians mourn.
This is not all: Patroclus, on the shore
Now pale and dead, shall succour Greece no more.
Fly to the fleet, this instant fly, and tell
The sad Achilles, how his loved-one fell:
He too may haste the naked corse to gain:
The arms are Hector's, who despoil'd the slain."

The youthful warrior heard with silent woe,
From his fair eyes the tears began to flow:
Big with the mighty grief, he strove to say
What sorrow dictates, but no word found way.
To brave Laodocus his arms he flung,
Who, near him wheeling, drove his steeds along;
Then ran the mournful message to impart,
With tearful eyes, and with dejected heart.

Swift fled the youth: nor Menelaus stands
(Though sore distress'd) to aid the Pylian bands;
But bids bold Thrasymede those troops sustain;
Himself returns to his Patroclus slain.
"Gone is Antilochus (the hero said);
But hope not, warriors, for Achilles' aid:
Though fierce his rage, unbounded be his woe,
Unarm'd, he fights not with the Trojan foe.
'Tis in our hands alone our hopes remain,
'Tis our own vigour must the dead regain,
And save ourselves, while with impetuous hate
Troy pours along, and this way rolls our fate."

"'Tis well (said Ajax), be it then thy care,
With Merion's aid, the weighty corse to rear;
Myself, and my bold brother will sustain
The shock of Hector and his charging train:
Nor fear we armies, fighting side by side;
What Troy can dare, we have already tried,
Have tried it, and have stood." The hero said.
High from the ground the warriors heave the dead.
A general clamour rises at the sight:
Loud shout the Trojans, and renew the fight.

Not fiercer rush along the gloomy wood,
With rage insatiate, and with thirst of blood,
Voracious hounds, that many a length before
Their furious hunters, drive the wounded boar;
But if the savage turns his glaring eye,
They howl aloof, and round the forest fly.
Thus on retreating Greece the Trojans pour,
Wave their thick falchions, and their javelins shower:
But Ajax turning, to their fears they yield,
All pale they tremble and forsake the field.

While thus aloft the hero's corse they bear,
Behind them rages all the storm of war:
Confusion, tumult, horror, o'er the throng
Of men, steeds, chariots, urged the rout along:
Less fierce the winds with rising flames conspire
To whelm some city under waves of fire;
Now sink in gloomy clouds the proud abodes,
Now crack the blazing temples of the gods;
The rumbling torrent through the ruin rolls,
And sheets of smoke mount heavy to the poles.
The heroes sweat beneath their honour'd load:
As when two mules, along the rugged road,
From the steep mountain with exerted strength
Drag some vast beam, or mast's unwieldy length;
Inly they groan, big drops of sweat distil,
The enormous timber lumbering down the hill:
So these—Behind, the bulk of Ajax stands,
And breaks the torrent of the rushing bands.
Thus when a river swell'd with sudden rains
Spreads his broad waters o'er the level plains,
Some interposing hill the stream divides.
And breaks its force, and turns the winding tides.
Still close they follow, close the rear engage;
Aeneas storms, and Hector foams with rage:
While Greece a heavy, thick retreat maintains,
Wedged in one body, like a flight of cranes,
That shriek incessant, while the falcon, hung
High on poised pinions, threats their callow young.
So from the Trojan chiefs the Grecians fly,
Such the wild terror, and the mingled cry:
Within, without the trench, and all the way,
Strow'd in bright heaps, their arms and armour lay;
Such horror Jove impress'd! yet still proceeds
The work of death, and still the battle bleeds.

BOOK XVIII

ARGUMENT

THE GRIEF OF ACHILLES, AND NEW ARMOUR MADE HIM BY VULCAN

The news of the death of Patroclus is brought to Achilles by Antilochus. Thetis, hearing his lamentations, comes with all her sea- nymphs to comfort him. The speeches of the mother and son on this occasion. Iris appears to Achilles by the command of Juno, and orders him to show himself at the head of the intrenchments. The sight of him turns the fortunes of the day, and the body of Patroclus is carried off by the Greeks. The Trojans call a council, where Hector and Polydamas disagree in their opinions: but the advice of the former prevails, to remain encamped in the field. The grief of Achilles over the body of Patroclus.

Thetis goes to the palace of Vulcan to obtain new arms for her son. The description of the wonderful works of Vulcan: and, lastly, that noble one of the shield of Achilles.

The latter part of the nine-and-twentieth day, and the night ensuing, take up this book: the scene is at Achilles' tent on the sea-shore, from whence it changes to the palace of Vulcan.

Thus like the rage of fire the combat burns,
And now it rises, now it sinks by turns.
Meanwhile, where Hellespont's broad waters flow,
Stood Nestor's son, the messenger of woe:
There sat Achilles, shaded by his sails,
On hoisted yards extended to the gales;
Pensive he sat; for all that fate design'd
Rose in sad prospect to his boding mind.
Thus to his soul he said: "Ah! what constrains
The Greeks, late victors, now to quit the plains?
Is this the day, which heaven so long ago
Ordain'd, to sink me with the weight of woe?
(So Thetis warn'd;) when by a Trojan hand
The bravest of the Myrmidonian band
Should lose the light! Fulfilled is that decree;
Fallen is the warrior, and Patroclus he!
In vain I charged him soon to quit the plain,
And warn'd to shun Hectorean force in vain!"

Thus while he thinks, Antilochus appears,
And tells the melancholy tale with tears.
"Sad tidings, son of Peleus! thou must hear;
And wretched I, the unwilling messenger!
Dead is Patroclus! For his corse they fight;
His naked corse: his arms are Hector's right."

A sudden horror shot through all the chief,

And wrapp'd his senses in the cloud of grief;
Cast on the ground, with furious hands he spread
The scorching ashes o'er his graceful head;
His purple garments, and his golden hairs,
Those he deforms with dust, and these he tears;
On the hard soil his groaning breast he threw,
And roll'd and grovell'd, as to earth he grew.
The virgin captives, with disorder'd charms,
(Won by his own, or by Patroclus' arms,)
Rush'd from their tents with cries; and gathering round,
Beat their white breasts, and fainted on the ground:
While Nestor's son sustains a manlier part,
And mourns the warrior with a warrior's heart;
Hangs on his arms, amidst his frantic woe,
And oft prevents the meditated blow.

Far in the deep abysses of the main,
With hoary Nereus, and the watery train,
The mother-goddess from her crystal throne
Heard his loud cries, and answer'd groan for groan.
The circling Nereids with their mistress weep,
And all the sea-green sisters of the deep.
Thalia, Glauce (every watery name),
Nesaea mild, and silver Spio came:
Cymothoe and Cymodoce were nigh,
And the blue languish of soft Alia's eye.
Their locks Actaea and Limnoria rear,
Then Proto, Doris, Panope appear,
Thoa, Pherusa, Doto, Melita;
Agave gentle, and Amphithoe gay:
Next Callianira, Callianassa show
Their sister looks; Dexamene the slow,
And swift Dynamene, now cut the tides:
Iaera now the verdant wave divides:
Nemertes with Apseudes lifts the head,
Bright Galatea quits her pearly bed;
These Orythia, Clymene, attend,
Maera, Amphinome, the train extend;
And black Janira, and Janassa fair,
And Amatheia with her amber hair.
All these, and all that deep in ocean held
Their sacred seats, the glimmering grotto fill'd;
Each beat her ivory breast with silent woe,
Till Thetis' sorrows thus began to flow:

"Hear me, and judge, ye sisters of the main!
How just a cause has Thetis to complain!
How wretched, were I mortal, were my fate!

How more than wretched in the immortal state!
Sprung from my bed a godlike hero came,
The bravest far that ever bore the name;
Like some fair olive, by my careful hand
He grew, he flourish'd and adorn'd the land
To Troy I sent him: but the fates ordain
He never, never must return again.
So short a space the light of heaven to view,
So short, alas! and fill'd with anguish too!
Hear how his sorrows echo through the shore!
I cannot ease them, but I must deplore;
I go at least to bear a tender part,
And mourn my loved-one with a mother's heart."

She said, and left the caverns of the main,
All bathed in tears; the melancholy train
Attend her way. Wide-opening part the tides,
While the long pomp the silver wave divides.
Approaching now, they touch'd the Trojan land;
Then, two by two, ascended up the strand.
The immortal mother, standing close beside
Her mournful offspring, to his sighs replied;
Along the coast their mingled clamours ran,
And thus the silver-footed dame began:

"Why mourns my son? thy late preferr'd request
The god has granted, and the Greeks distress'd:
Why mourns my son? thy anguish let me share,
Reveal the cause, and trust a parent's care."

He, deeply groaning—"To this cureless grief,
Not even the Thunderer's favour brings relief.
Patroclus—Ah!—say, goddess, can I boast
A pleasure now? revenge itself is lost;
Patroclus, loved of all my martial train,
Beyond mankind, beyond myself is slain!
Lost are those arms the gods themselves bestow'd
On Peleus; Hector bears the glorious load.
Cursed be that day, when all the powers above
Thy charms submitted to a mortal love:
O hadst thou still, a sister of the main,
Pursued the pleasures of the watery reign:
And happier Peleus, less ambitious, led
A mortal beauty to his equal bed!
Ere the sad fruit of thy unhappy womb
Had caused such sorrows past, and woes to come.
For soon, alas! that wretched offspring slain,
New woes, new sorrows, shall create again.

'Tis not in fate the alternate now to give;
Patroclus dead, Achilles hates to live.
Let me revenge it on proud Hector's heart,
Let his last spirit smoke upon my dart;
On these conditions will I breathe: till then,
I blush to walk among the race of men."

A flood of tears, at this, the goddess shed:
"Ah then, I see thee dying, see thee dead!
When Hector falls, thou diest."—"Let Hector die,
And let me fall! (Achilles made reply)
Far lies Patroclus from his native plain!
He fell, and falling, wish'd my aid in vain.
Ah then, since from this miserable day
I cast all hope of my return away;
Since, unrevenged, a hundred ghosts demand
The fate of Hector from Achilles' hand;
Since here, for brutal courage far renown'd,
I live an idle burden to the ground,
(Others in council famed for nobler skill,
More useful to preserve, than I to kill,)
Let me—But oh! ye gracious powers above!
Wrath and revenge from men and gods remove:
Far, far too dear to every mortal breast,
Sweet to the soul, as honey to the taste:
Gathering like vapours of a noxious kind
From fiery blood, and darkening all the mind.
Me Agamemnon urged to deadly hate;
'Tis past—I quell it; I resign to fate.
Yes—I will meet the murderer of my friend;
Or (if the gods ordain it) meet my end.
The stroke of fate the strongest cannot shun:
The great Alcides, Jove's unequall'd son,
To Juno's hate, at length resign'd his breath,
And sunk the victim of all-conquering death.
So shall Achilles fall! stretch'd pale and dead,
No more the Grecian hope, or Trojan dread!
Let me, this instant, rush into the fields,
And reap what glory life's short harvest yields.
Shall I not force some widow'd dame to tear
With frantic hands her long dishevell'd hair?
Shall I not force her breast to heave with sighs,
And the soft tears to trickle from her eyes?
Yes, I shall give the fair those mournful charms—
In vain you hold me—Hence! my arms! my arms!—
Soon shall the sanguine torrent spread so wide,
That all shall know Achilles swells the tide."

"My son (coerulean Thetis made reply,
To fate submitting with a secret sigh,)
The host to succour, and thy friends to save,
Is worthy thee; the duty of the brave.
But canst thou, naked, issue to the plains?
Thy radiant arms the Trojan foe detains.
Insulting Hector bears the spoils on high,
But vainly glories, for his fate is nigh.
Yet, yet awhile thy generous ardour stay;
Assured, I meet thee at the dawn of day,
Charged with refulgent arms (a glorious load),
Vulcanian arms, the labour of a god."

Then turning to the daughters of the main,
The goddess thus dismiss'd her azure train:

"Ye sister Nereids! to your deeps descend;
Haste, and our father's sacred seat attend;
I go to find the architect divine,
Where vast Olympus' starry summits shine:
So tell our hoary sire"—This charge she gave:
The sea-green sisters plunge beneath the wave:
Thetis once more ascends the bless'd abodes,
And treads the brazen threshold of the gods.

And now the Greeks from furious Hector's force,
Urge to broad Hellespont their headlong course;
Nor yet their chiefs Patroclus' body bore
Safe through the tempest to the tented shore.
The horse, the foot, with equal fury join'd,
Pour'd on the rear, and thunder'd close behind:
And like a flame through fields of ripen'd corn,
The rage of Hector o'er the ranks was borne.
Thrice the slain hero by the foot he drew;
Thrice to the skies the Trojan clamours flew:
As oft the Ajaces his assault sustain;
But check'd, he turns; repuls'd, attacks again.
With fiercer shouts his lingering troops he fires,
Nor yields a step, nor from his post retires:
So watchful shepherds strive to force, in vain,
The hungry lion from a carcase slain.
Even yet Patroclus had he borne away,
And all the glories of the extended day,
Had not high Juno from the realms of air,
Secret, despatch'd her trusty messenger.
The various goddess of the showery bow,
Shot in a whirlwind to the shore below;
To great Achilles at his ships she came,

And thus began the many-colour'd dame:

"Rise, son of Peleus! rise, divinely brave!
Assist the combat, and Patroclus save:
For him the slaughter to the fleet they spread,
And fall by mutual wounds around the dead.
To drag him back to Troy the foe contends:
Nor with his death the rage of Hector ends:
A prey to dogs he dooms the corse to lie,
And marks the place to fix his head on high.
Rise, and prevent (if yet you think of fame)
Thy friend's disgrace, thy own eternal shame!"

"Who sends thee, goddess, from the ethereal skies?"
Achilles thus. And Iris thus replies:

"I come, Pelides! from the queen of Jove,
The immortal empress of the realms above;
Unknown to him who sits remote on high,
Unknown to all the synod of the sky."
"Thou comest in vain (he cries, with fury warm'd);
Arms I have none, and can I fight unarm'd?
Unwilling as I am, of force I stay,
Till Thetis bring me at the dawn of day
Vulcanian arms: what other can I wield,
Except the mighty Telamonian shield?
That, in my friend's defence, has Ajax spread,
While his strong lance around him heaps the dead:
The gallant chief defends Menoetius' son,
And does what his Achilles should have done."

"Thy want of arms (said Iris) well we know;
But though unarm'd, yet clad in terrors, go!
Let but Achilles o'er yon trench appear,
Proud Troy shall tremble, and consent to fear;
Greece from one glance of that tremendous eye
Shall take new courage, and disdain to fly."

She spoke, and pass'd in air. The hero rose:
Her aegis Pallas o'er his shoulder throws;
Around his brows a golden cloud she spread;
A stream of glory flamed above his head.
As when from some beleaguer'd town arise
The smokes, high curling to the shaded skies;
(Seen from some island, o'er the main afar,
When men distress'd hang out the sign of war;)
Soon as the sun in ocean hides his rays,
Thick on the hills the flaming beacons blaze;

With long-projected beams the seas are bright,
And heaven's high arch reflects the ruddy light:
So from Achilles' head the splendours rise,
Reflecting blaze on blaze against the skies.
Forth march'd the chief, and distant from the crowd,
High on the rampart raised his voice aloud;
With her own shout Minerva swells the sound;
Troy starts astonish'd, and the shores rebound.
As the loud trumpet's brazen mouth from far
With shrilling clangour sounds the alarm of war,
Struck from the walls, the echoes float on high,
And the round bulwarks and thick towers reply;
So high his brazen voice the hero rear'd:
Hosts dropp'd their arms, and trembled as they heard:
And back the chariots roll, and coursers bound,
And steeds and men lie mingled on the ground.
Aghast they see the living lightnings play,
And turn their eyeballs from the flashing ray.
Thrice from the trench his dreadful voice he raised,
And thrice they fled, confounded and amazed.
Twelve in the tumult wedged, untimely rush'd
On their own spears, by their own chariots crush'd:
While, shielded from the darts, the Greeks obtain
The long-contended carcase of the slain.

A lofty bier the breathless warrior bears:
Around, his sad companions melt in tears.
But chief Achilles, bending down his head,
Pours unavailing sorrows o'er the dead,
Whom late triumphant, with his steeds and car,
He sent refulgent to the field of war;
(Unhappy change!) now senseless, pale, he found,
Stretch'd forth, and gash'd with many a gaping wound.

Meantime, unwearied with his heavenly way,
In ocean's waves the unwilling light of day
Quench'd his red orb, at Juno's high command,
And from their labours eased the Achaian band.
The frighted Trojans (panting from the war,
Their steeds unharness'd from the weary car)
A sudden council call'd: each chief appear'd
In haste, and standing; for to sit they fear'd.
'Twas now no season for prolong'd debate;
They saw Achilles, and in him their fate.
Silent they stood: Polydamas at last,
Skill'd to discern the future by the past,
The son of Panthus, thus express'd his fears
(The friend of Hector, and of equal years;

The self-same night to both a being gave,
One wise in council, one in action brave):

"In free debate, my friends, your sentence speak;
For me, I move, before the morning break,
To raise our camp: too dangerous here our post,
Far from Troy walls, and on a naked coast.
I deem'd not Greece so dreadful, while engaged
In mutual feuds her king and hero raged;
Then, while we hoped our armies might prevail
We boldly camp'd beside a thousand sail.
I dread Pelides now: his rage of mind
Not long continues to the shores confined,
Nor to the fields, where long in equal fray
Contending nations won and lost the day;
For Troy, for Troy, shall henceforth be the strife,
And the hard contest not for fame, but life.
Haste then to Ilion, while the favouring night
Detains these terrors, keeps that arm from fight.
If but the morrow's sun behold us here,
That arm, those terrors, we shall feel, not fear;
And hearts that now disdain, shall leap with joy,
If heaven permit them then to enter Troy.
Let not my fatal prophecy be true,
Nor what I tremble but to think, ensue.
Whatever be our fate, yet let us try
What force of thought and reason can supply;
Let us on counsel for our guard depend;
The town her gates and bulwarks shall defend.
When morning dawns, our well-appointed powers,
Array'd in arms, shall line the lofty towers.
Let the fierce hero, then, when fury calls,
Vent his mad vengeance on our rocky walls,
Or fetch a thousand circles round the plain,
Till his spent coursers seek the fleet again:
So may his rage be tired, and labour'd down!
And dogs shall tear him ere he sack the town."

"Return! (said Hector, fired with stern disdain)
What! coop whole armies in our walls again?
Was't not enough, ye valiant warriors, say,
Nine years imprison'd in those towers ye lay?
Wide o'er the world was Ilion famed of old
For brass exhaustless, and for mines of gold:
But while inglorious in her walls we stay'd,
Sunk were her treasures, and her stores decay'd;
The Phrygians now her scatter'd spoils enjoy,
And proud Maeonia wastes the fruits of Troy.

Great Jove at length my arms to conquest calls,
And shuts the Grecians in their wooden walls,
Darest thou dispirit whom the gods incite?
Flies any Trojan? I shall stop his flight.
To better counsel then attention lend;
Take due refreshment, and the watch attend.
If there be one whose riches cost him care,
Forth let him bring them for the troops to share;
'Tis better generously bestow'd on those,
Than left the plunder of our country's foes.
Soon as the morn the purple orient warms,
Fierce on yon navy will we pour our arms.
If great Achilles rise in all his might,
His be the danger: I shall stand the fight.
Honour, ye gods! or let me gain or give;
And live he glorious, whosoe'er shall live!
Mars is our common lord, alike to all;
And oft the victor triumphs, but to fall."

The shouting host in loud applauses join'd;
So Pallas robb'd the many of their mind;
To their own sense condemn'd, and left to choose
The worst advice, the better to refuse.

While the long night extends her sable reign,
Around Patroclus mourn'd the Grecian train.
Stern in superior grief Pelides stood;
Those slaughtering arms, so used to bathe in blood,
Now clasp his clay-cold limbs: then gushing start
The tears, and sighs burst from his swelling heart.
The lion thus, with dreadful anguish stung,
Roars through the desert, and demands his young;
When the grim savage, to his rifled den
Too late returning, snuffs the track of men,
And o'er the vales and o'er the forest bounds;
His clamorous grief the bellowing wood resounds.
So grieves Achilles; and, impetuous, vents
To all his Myrmidons his loud laments.

"In what vain promise, gods! did I engage,
When to console Menoetius' feeble age,
I vowed his much-loved offspring to restore,
Charged with rich spoils, to fair Opuntia's shore?
But mighty Jove cuts short, with just disdain,
The long, long views of poor designing man!
One fate the warrior and the friend shall strike,
And Troy's black sands must drink our blood alike:
Me too a wretched mother shall deplore,

An aged father never see me more!
Yet, my Patroclus! yet a space I stay,
Then swift pursue thee on the darksome way.
Ere thy dear relics in the grave are laid,
Shall Hector's head be offer'd to thy shade;
That, with his arms, shall hang before thy shrine;
And twelve, the noblest of the Trojan line,
Sacred to vengeance, by this hand expire;
Their lives effused around thy flaming pyre.
Thus let me lie till then! thus, closely press'd,
Bathe thy cold face, and sob upon thy breast!
While Trojan captives here thy mourners stay,
Weep all the night and murmur all the day:
Spoils of my arms, and thine; when, wasting wide,
Our swords kept time, and conquer'd side by side."

He spoke, and bade the sad attendants round
Cleanse the pale corse, and wash each honour'd wound.
A massy caldron of stupendous frame
They brought, and placed it o'er the rising flame:
Then heap'd the lighted wood; the flame divides
Beneath the vase, and climbs around the sides:
In its wide womb they pour the rushing stream;
The boiling water bubbles to the brim.
The body then they bathe with pious toil,
Embalm the wounds, anoint the limbs with oil,
High on a bed of state extended laid,
And decent cover'd with a linen shade;
Last o'er the dead the milk-white veil they threw;
That done, their sorrows and their sighs renew.

Meanwhile to Juno, in the realms above,
(His wife and sister,) spoke almighty Jove.
"At last thy will prevails: great Peleus' son
Rises in arms: such grace thy Greeks have won.
Say (for I know not), is their race divine,
And thou the mother of that martial line?"

"What words are these? (the imperial dame replies,
While anger flash'd from her majestic eyes)
Succour like this a mortal arm might lend,
And such success mere human wit attend:
And shall not I, the second power above,
Heaven's queen, and consort of the thundering Jove,
Say, shall not I one nation's fate command,
Not wreak my vengeance on one guilty land?"

So they. Meanwhile the silver-footed dame

Reach'd the Vulcanian dome, eternal frame!
High-eminent amid the works divine,
Where heaven's far-beaming brazen mansions shine.
There the lame architect the goddess found,
Obscure in smoke, his forges flaming round,
While bathed in sweat from fire to fire he flew;
And puffing loud, the roaring billows blew.
That day no common task his labour claim'd:
Full twenty tripods for his hall he framed,
That placed on living wheels of massy gold,
(Wondrous to tell,) instinct with spirit roll'd
From place to place, around the bless'd abodes
Self-moved, obedient to the beck of gods:
For their fair handles now, o'erwrought with flowers,
In moulds prepared, the glowing ore he pours.
Just as responsive to his thought the frame
Stood prompt to move, the azure goddess came:
Charis, his spouse, a grace divinely fair,
(With purple fillets round her braided hair,)
Observed her entering; her soft hand she press'd,
And, smiling, thus the watery queen address'd:

"What, goddess! this unusual favour draws?
All hail, and welcome! whatsoe'er the cause;
Till now a stranger, in a happy hour
Approach, and taste the dainties of the bower."

High on a throne, with stars of silver graced,
And various artifice, the queen she placed;
A footstool at her feet: then calling, said,
"Vulcan, draw near, 'tis Thetis asks your aid."
"Thetis (replied the god) our powers may claim,
An ever-dear, an ever-honour'd name!
When my proud mother hurl'd me from the sky,
(My awkward form, it seems, displeased her eye,)
She, and Eurynome, my griefs redress'd,
And soft received me on their silver breast.
Even then these arts employ'd my infant thought:
Chains, bracelets, pendants, all their toys, I wrought.
Nine years kept secret in the dark abode,
Secure I lay, conceal'd from man and god:
Deep in a cavern'd rock my days were led;
The rushing ocean murmur'd o'er my head.
Now, since her presence glads our mansion, say,
For such desert what service can I pay?
Vouchsafe, O Thetis! at our board to share
The genial rites, and hospitable fare;
While I the labours of the forge forego,

And bid the roaring bellows cease to blow."

Then from his anvil the lame artist rose;
Wide with distorted legs oblique he goes,
And stills the bellows, and (in order laid)
Locks in their chests his instruments of trade.
Then with a sponge the sooty workman dress'd
His brawny arms embrown'd, and hairy breast.
With his huge sceptre graced, and red attire,
Came halting forth the sovereign of the fire:
The monarch's steps two female forms uphold,
That moved and breathed in animated gold;
To whom was voice, and sense, and science given
Of works divine (such wonders are in heaven!)
On these supported, with unequal gait,
He reach'd the throne where pensive Thetis sate;
There placed beside her on the shining frame,
He thus address'd the silver-footed dame:

"Thee, welcome, goddess! what occasion calls
(So long a stranger) to these honour'd walls?
'Tis thine, fair Thetis, the command to lay,
And Vulcan's joy and duty to obey."

To whom the mournful mother thus replies:
(The crystal drops stood trembling in her eyes:)
"O Vulcan! say, was ever breast divine
So pierced with sorrows, so o'erwhelm'd as mine?
Of all the goddesses, did Jove prepare
For Thetis only such a weight of care?
I, only I, of all the watery race
By force subjected to a man's embrace,
Who, sinking now with age and sorrow, pays
The mighty fine imposed on length of days.
Sprung from my bed, a godlike hero came,
The bravest sure that ever bore the name;
Like some fair plant beneath my careful hand
He grew, he flourish'd, and he graced the land:
To Troy I sent him! but his native shore
Never, ah never, shall receive him more;
(Even while he lives, he wastes with secret woe;)
Nor I, a goddess, can retard the blow!
Robb'd of the prize the Grecian suffrage gave,
The king of nations forced his royal slave:
For this he grieved; and, till the Greeks oppress'd
Required his arm, he sorrow'd unredress'd.
Large gifts they promise, and their elders send;
In vain—he arms not, but permits his friend

His arms, his steeds, his forces to employ:
He marches, combats, almost conquers Troy:
Then slain by Phoebus (Hector had the name)
At once resigns his armour, life, and fame.
But thou, in pity, by my prayer be won:
Grace with immortal arms this short-lived son,
And to the field in martial pomp restore,
To shine with glory, till he shines no more!"

To her the artist-god: "Thy griefs resign,
Secure, what Vulcan can, is ever thine.
O could I hide him from the Fates, as well,
Or with these hands the cruel stroke repel,
As I shall forge most envied arms, the gaze
Of wondering ages, and the world's amaze!"

Thus having said, the father of the fires
To the black labours of his forge retires.
Soon as he bade them blow, the bellows turn'd
Their iron mouths; and where the furnace burn'd,
Resounding breathed: at once the blast expires,
And twenty forges catch at once the fires;
Just as the god directs, now loud, now low,
They raise a tempest, or they gently blow;
In hissing flames huge silver bars are roll'd,
And stubborn brass, and tin, and solid gold;
Before, deep fix'd, the eternal anvils stand;
The ponderous hammer loads his better hand,
His left with tongs turns the vex'd metal round,
And thick, strong strokes, the doubling vaults rebound.

Then first he form'd the immense and solid shield;
Rich various artifice emblazed the field;
Its utmost verge a threefold circle bound;
A silver chain suspends the massy round;
Five ample plates the broad expanse compose,
And godlike labours on the surface rose.
There shone the image of the master-mind:
There earth, there heaven, there ocean he design'd;
The unwearied sun, the moon completely round;
The starry lights that heaven's high convex crown'd;
The Pleiads, Hyads, with the northern team;
And great Orion's more refulgent beam;
To which, around the axle of the sky,
The Bear, revolving, points his golden eye,
Still shines exalted on the ethereal plain,
Nor bathes his blazing forehead in the main.

Two cities radiant on the shield appear,
The image one of peace, and one of war.
Here sacred pomp and genial feast delight,
And solemn dance, and hymeneal rite;
Along the street the new-made brides are led,
With torches flaming, to the nuptial bed:
The youthful dancers in a circle bound
To the soft flute, and cithern's silver sound:
Through the fair streets the matrons in a row
Stand in their porches, and enjoy the show.

There in the forum swarm a numerous train;
The subject of debate, a townsman slain:
One pleads the fine discharged, which one denied,
And bade the public and the laws decide:
The witness is produced on either hand:
For this, or that, the partial people stand:
The appointed heralds still the noisy bands,
And form a ring, with sceptres in their hands:
On seats of stone, within the sacred place,
The reverend elders nodded o'er the case;
Alternate, each the attesting sceptre took,
And rising solemn, each his sentence spoke
Two golden talents lay amidst, in sight,
The prize of him who best adjudged the right.

Another part (a prospect differing far)
Glow'd with refulgent arms, and horrid war.
Two mighty hosts a leaguer'd town embrace,
And one would pillage, one would burn the place.
Meantime the townsmen, arm'd with silent care,
A secret ambush on the foe prepare:
Their wives, their children, and the watchful band
Of trembling parents, on the turrets stand.
They march; by Pallas and by Mars made bold:
Gold were the gods, their radiant garments gold,
And gold their armour: these the squadron led,
August, divine, superior by the head!
A place for ambush fit they found, and stood,
Cover'd with shields, beside a silver flood.
Two spies at distance lurk, and watchful seem
If sheep or oxen seek the winding stream.
Soon the white flocks proceeded o'er the plains,
And steers slow-moving, and two shepherd swains;
Behind them piping on their reeds they go,
Nor fear an ambush, nor suspect a foe.
In arms the glittering squadron rising round
Rush sudden; hills of slaughter heap the ground;

Whole flocks and herds lie bleeding on the plains,
And, all amidst them, dead, the shepherd swains!
The bellowing oxen the besiegers hear;
They rise, take horse, approach, and meet the war,
They fight, they fall, beside the silver flood;
The waving silver seem'd to blush with blood.
There Tumult, there Contention stood confess'd;
One rear'd a dagger at a captive's breast;
One held a living foe, that freshly bled
With new-made wounds; another dragg'd a dead;
Now here, now there, the carcases they tore:
Fate stalk'd amidst them, grim with human gore.
And the whole war came out, and met the eye;
And each bold figure seem'd to live or die.

A field deep furrow'd next the god design'd,
The third time labour'd by the sweating hind;
The shining shares full many ploughmen guide,
And turn their crooked yokes on every side.
Still as at either end they wheel around,
The master meets them with his goblet crown'd;
The hearty draught rewards, renews their toil,
Then back the turning ploughshares cleave the soil:
Behind, the rising earth in ridges roll'd;
And sable look'd, though form'd of molten gold.

Another field rose high with waving grain;
With bended sickles stand the reaper train:
Here stretched in ranks the levell'd swarths are found,
Sheaves heap'd on sheaves here thicken up the ground.
With sweeping stroke the mowers strow the lands;
The gatherers follow, and collect in bands;
And last the children, in whose arms are borne
(Too short to gripe them) the brown sheaves of corn.
The rustic monarch of the field descries,
With silent glee, the heaps around him rise.
A ready banquet on the turf is laid,
Beneath an ample oak's expanded shade.
The victim ox the sturdy youth prepare;
The reaper's due repast, the woman's care.

Next, ripe in yellow gold, a vineyard shines,
Bent with the ponderous harvest of its vines;
A deeper dye the dangling clusters show,
And curl'd on silver props, in order glow:
A darker metal mix'd intrench'd the place;
And pales of glittering tin the inclosure grace.
To this, one pathway gently winding leads,

Where march a train with baskets on their heads,
(Fair maids and blooming youths,) that smiling bear
The purple product of the autumnal year.
To these a youth awakes the warbling strings,
Whose tender lay the fate of Linus sings;
In measured dance behind him move the train,
Tune soft the voice, and answer to the strain.

Here herds of oxen march, erect and bold,
Rear high their horns, and seem to low in gold,
And speed to meadows on whose sounding shores
A rapid torrent through the rushes roars:
Four golden herdsmen as their guardians stand,
And nine sour dogs complete the rustic band.
Two lions rushing from the wood appear'd;
And seized a bull, the master of the herd:
He roar'd: in vain the dogs, the men withstood;
They tore his flesh, and drank his sable blood.
The dogs (oft cheer'd in vain) desert the prey,
Dread the grim terrors, and at distance bay.

Next this, the eye the art of Vulcan leads
Deep through fair forests, and a length of meads,
And stalls, and folds, and scatter'd cots between;
And fleecy flocks, that whiten all the scene.

A figured dance succeeds; such once was seen
In lofty Gnossus for the Cretan queen,
Form'd by Daedalean art; a comely band
Of youths and maidens, bounding hand in hand.
The maids in soft simars of linen dress'd;
The youths all graceful in the glossy vest:
Of those the locks with flowery wreath inroll'd;
Of these the sides adorn'd with swords of gold,
That glittering gay, from silver belts depend.
Now all at once they rise, at once descend,
With well-taught feet: now shape in oblique ways,
Confusedly regular, the moving maze:
Now forth at once, too swift for sight, they spring,
And undistinguish'd blend the flying ring:
So whirls a wheel, in giddy circle toss'd,
And, rapid as it runs, the single spokes are lost.
The gazing multitudes admire around:
Two active tumblers in the centre bound;
Now high, now low, their pliant limbs they bend:
And general songs the sprightly revel end.

Thus the broad shield complete the artist crown'd

With his last hand, and pour'd the ocean round:
In living silver seem'd the waves to roll,
And beat the buckler's verge, and bound the whole.

This done, whate'er a warrior's use requires
He forged; the cuirass that outshone the fires,
The greaves of ductile tin, the helm impress'd
With various sculpture, and the golden crest.
At Thetis' feet the finished labour lay:
She, as a falcon cuts the aerial way,
Swift from Olympus' snowy summit flies,
And bears the blazing present through the skies.

BOOK XIX

ARGUMENT

THE RECONCILIATION OF ACHILLES AND AGAMEMNON

Thetis brings to her son the armour made by Vulcan. She preserves the body of his friend from corruption, and commands him to assemble the army, to declare his resentment at an end. Agamemnon and Achilles are solemnly reconciled: the speeches, presents, and ceremonies on that occasion. Achilles is with great difficulty persuaded to refrain from the battle till the troops have refreshed themselves by the advice of Ulysses. The presents are conveyed to the tent of Achilles, where Briseis laments over the body of Patroclus. The hero obstinately refuses all repast, and gives himself up to lamentations for his friend. Minerva descends to strengthen him, by the order of Jupiter. He arms for the fight: his appearance described. He addresses himself to his horses, and reproaches them with the death of Patroclus. One of them is miraculously endued with voice, and inspired to prophesy his fate: but the hero, not astonished by that prodigy, rushes with fury to the combat.

The thirteenth day. The scene is on the sea-shore.

Soon as Aurora heaved her Orient head
Above the waves, that blush'd with early red,
(With new-born day to gladden mortal sight,
And gild the courts of heaven with sacred light,)
The immortal arms the goddess-mother bears
Swift to her son: her son she finds in tears
Stretch'd o'er Patroclus' corse; while all the rest
Their sovereign's sorrows in their own express'd.
A ray divine her heavenly presence shed,
And thus, his hand soft touching, Thetis said:

"Suppress, my son, this rage of grief, and know
It was not man, but heaven, that gave the blow;

Behold what arms by Vulcan are bestow'd,
Arms worthy thee, or fit to grace a god."

Then drops the radiant burden on the ground;
Clang the strong arms, and ring the shores around;
Back shrink the Myrmidons with dread surprise,
And from the broad effulgence turn their eyes.
Unmoved the hero kindles at the show,
And feels with rage divine his bosom glow;
From his fierce eyeballs living flames expire,
And flash incessant like a stream of fire:
He turns the radiant gift: and feeds his mind
On all the immortal artist had design'd.

"Goddess! (he cried,) these glorious arms, that shine
With matchless art, confess the hand divine.
Now to the bloody battle let me bend:
But ah! the relics of my slaughter'd friend!
In those wide wounds through which his spirit fled,
Shall flies, and worms obscene, pollute the dead?"

"That unavailing care be laid aside,
(The azure goddess to her son replied,)
Whole years untouch'd, uninjured shall remain,
Fresh as in life, the carcase of the slain.
But go, Achilles, as affairs require,
Before the Grecian peers renounce thine ire:
Then uncontroll'd in boundless war engage,
And heaven with strength supply the mighty rage!"

Then in the nostrils of the slain she pour'd
Nectareous drops, and rich ambrosia shower'd
O'er all the corse. The flies forbid their prey,
Untouch'd it rests, and sacred from decay.
Achilles to the strand obedient went:
The shores resounded with the voice he sent.
The heroes heard, and all the naval train
That tend the ships, or guide them o'er the main,
Alarm'd, transported, at the well-known sound,
Frequent and full, the great assembly crown'd;
Studious to see the terror of the plain,
Long lost to battle, shine in arms again.
Tydides and Ulysses first appear,
Lame with their wounds, and leaning on the spear;
These on the sacred seats of council placed,
The king of men, Atrides, came the last:
He too sore wounded by Agenor's son.
Achilles (rising in the midst) begun:

"O monarch! better far had been the fate
Of thee, of me, of all the Grecian state,
If (ere the day when by mad passion sway'd,
Rash we contended for the black-eyed maid)
Preventing Dian had despatch'd her dart,
And shot the shining mischief to the heart!
Then many a hero had not press'd the shore,
Nor Troy's glad fields been fatten'd with our gore.
Long, long shall Greece the woes we caused bewail,
And sad posterity repeat the tale.
But this, no more the subject of debate,
Is past, forgotten, and resign'd to fate.
Why should, alas, a mortal man, as I,
Burn with a fury that can never die?
Here then my anger ends: let war succeed,
And even as Greece has bled, let Ilion bleed.
Now call the hosts, and try if in our sight
Troy yet shall dare to camp a second night!
I deem, their mightiest, when this arm he knows,
Shall 'scape with transport, and with joy repose."

He said: his finish'd wrath with loud acclaim
The Greeks accept, and shout Pelides' name.
When thus, not rising from his lofty throne,
In state unmoved, the king of men begun:

"Hear me, ye sons of Greece! with silence hear!
And grant your monarch an impartial ear:
Awhile your loud, untimely joy suspend,
And let your rash, injurious clamours end:
Unruly murmurs, or ill-timed applause,
Wrong the best speaker, and the justest cause.
Nor charge on me, ye Greeks, the dire debate:
Know, angry Jove, and all-compelling Fate,
With fell Erinnys, urged my wrath that day
When from Achilles' arms I forced the prey.
What then could I against the will of heaven?
Not by myself, but vengeful Ate driven;
She, Jove's dread daughter, fated to infest
The race of mortals, enter'd in my breast.
Not on the ground that haughty fury treads,
But prints her lofty footsteps on the heads
Of mighty men; inflicting as she goes
Long-festering wounds, inextricable woes!
Of old, she stalk'd amid the bright abodes;
And Jove himself, the sire of men and gods,
The world's great ruler, felt her venom'd dart;

Deceived by Juno's wiles, and female art:
For when Alcmena's nine long months were run,
And Jove expected his immortal son,
To gods and goddesses the unruly joy
He show'd, and vaunted of his matchless boy:
'From us, (he said) this day an infant springs,
Fated to rule, and born a king of kings.'
Saturnia ask'd an oath, to vouch the truth,
And fix dominion on the favour'd youth.
The Thunderer, unsuspicious of the fraud,
Pronounced those solemn words that bind a god.
The joyful goddess, from Olympus' height,
Swift to Achaian Argos bent her flight:
Scarce seven moons gone, lay Sthenelus's wife;
She push'd her lingering infant into life:
Her charms Alcmena's coming labours stay,
And stop the babe, just issuing to the day.
Then bids Saturnius bear his oath in mind;
'A youth (said she) of Jove's immortal kind
Is this day born: from Sthenelus he springs,
And claims thy promise to be king of kings.'
Grief seized the Thunderer, by his oath engaged;
Stung to the soul, he sorrow'd, and he raged.
From his ambrosial head, where perch'd she sate,
He snatch'd the fury-goddess of debate,
The dread, the irrevocable oath he swore,
The immortal seats should ne'er behold her more;
And whirl'd her headlong down, for ever driven
From bright Olympus and the starry heaven:
Thence on the nether world the fury fell;
Ordain'd with man's contentious race to dwell.
Full oft the god his son's hard toils bemoan'd,
Cursed the dire fury, and in secret groan'd.
Even thus, like Jove himself, was I misled,
While raging Hector heap'd our camps with dead.
What can the errors of my rage atone?
My martial troops, my treasures are thy own:
This instant from the navy shall be sent
Whate'er Ulysses promised at thy tent:
But thou! appeased, propitious to our prayer,
Resume thy arms, and shine again in war."

" O king of nations! whose superior sway
(Returns Achilles) all our hosts obey!
To keep or send the presents, be thy care;
To us, 'tis equal: all we ask is war.
While yet we talk, or but an instant shun
The fight, our glorious work remains undone.

Let every Greek, who sees my spear confound
The Trojan ranks, and deal destruction round,
With emulation, what I act survey,
And learn from thence the business of the day.

The son of Peleus thus; and thus replies
The great in councils, Ithacus the wise:
"Though, godlike, thou art by no toils oppress'd,
At least our armies claim repast and rest:
Long and laborious must the combat be,
When by the gods inspired, and led by thee.
Strength is derived from spirits and from blood,
And those augment by generous wine and food:
What boastful son of war, without that stay,
Can last a hero through a single day?
Courage may prompt; but, ebbing out his strength,
Mere unsupported man must yield at length;
Shrunk with dry famine, and with toils declined,
The drooping body will desert the mind:
But built anew with strength-conferring fare,
With limbs and soul untamed, he tires a war.
Dismiss the people, then, and give command.
With strong repast to hearten every band;
But let the presents to Achilles made,
In full assembly of all Greece be laid.
The king of men shall rise in public sight,
And solemn swear (observant of the rite)
That, spotless, as she came, the maid removes,
Pure from his arms, and guiltless of his loves.
That done, a sumptuous banquet shall be made,
And the full price of injured honour paid.
Stretch not henceforth, O prince.! thy sovereign might
Beyond the bounds of reason and of right;
'Tis the chief praise that e'er to kings belong'd,
To right with justice whom with power they wrong'd."

To him the monarch: "Just is thy decree,
Thy words give joy, and wisdom breathes in thee.
Each due atonement gladly I prepare;
And heaven regard me as I justly swear!
Here then awhile let Greece assembled stay,
Nor great Achilles grudge this short delay.
Till from the fleet our presents be convey'd,
And Jove attesting, the firm compact made.
A train of noble youths the charge shall bear;
These to select, Ulysses, be thy care:
In order rank'd let all our gifts appear,
And the fair train of captives close the rear:

Talthybius shall the victim boar convey,
Sacred to Jove, and yon bright orb of day."

"For this (the stern Ćacides replies)
Some less important season may suffice,
When the stern fury of the war is o'er,
And wrath, extinguish'd, burns my breast no more.
By Hector slain, their faces to the sky,
All grim with gaping wounds, our heroes lie:
Those call to war! and might my voice incite,
Now, now, this instant, shall commence the fight:
Then, when the day's complete, let generous bowls,
And copious banquets, glad your weary souls.
Let not my palate know the taste of food,
Till my insatiate rage be cloy'd with blood:
Pale lies my friend, with wounds disfigured o'er,
And his cold feet are pointed to the door.
Revenge is all my soul! no meaner care,
Interest, or thought, has room to harbour there;
Destruction be my feast, and mortal wounds,
And scenes of blood, and agonizing sounds."

"O first of Greeks, (Ulysses thus rejoin'd,)
The best and bravest of the warrior kind!
Thy praise it is in dreadful camps to shine,
But old experience and calm wisdom mine.
Then hear my counsel, and to reason yield,
The bravest soon are satiate of the field;
Though vast the heaps that strow the crimson plain,
The bloody harvest brings but little gain:
The scale of conquest ever wavering lies,
Great Jove but turns it, and the victor dies!
The great, the bold, by thousands daily fall,
And endless were the grief, to weep for all.
Eternal sorrows what avails to shed?
Greece honours not with solemn fasts the dead:
Enough, when death demands the brave, to pay
The tribute of a melancholy day.
One chief with patience to the grave resign'd,
Our care devolves on others left behind.
Let generous food supplies of strength produce,
Let rising spirits flow from sprightly juice,
Let their warm heads with scenes of battle glow,
And pour new furies on the feebler foe.
Yet a short interval, and none shall dare
Expect a second summons to the war;
Who waits for that, the dire effects shall find,
If trembling in the ships he lags behind.

Embodied, to the battle let us bend,
And all at once on haughty Troy descend."

And now the delegates Ulysses sent,
To bear the presents from the royal tent:
The sons of Nestor, Phyleus' valiant heir,
Thias and Merion, thunderbolts of war,
With Lycomedes of Creiontian strain,
And Melanippus, form'd the chosen train.
Swift as the word was given, the youths obey'd:
Twice ten bright vases in the midst they laid;
A row of six fair tripods then succeeds;
And twice the number of high-bounding steeds:
Seven captives next a lovely line compose;
The eighth Briseis, like the blooming rose,
Closed the bright band: great Ithacus, before,
First of the train, the golden talents bore:
The rest in public view the chiefs dispose,
A splendid scene! then Agamemnon rose:
The boar Talthybius held: the Grecian lord
Drew the broad cutlass sheath'd beside his sword:
The stubborn bristles from the victim's brow
He crops, and offering meditates his vow.
His hands uplifted to the attesting skies,
On heaven's broad marble roof were fixed his eyes.
The solemn words a deep attention draw,
And Greece around sat thrill'd with sacred awe.

"Witness thou first! thou greatest power above,
All-good, all-wise, and all-surveying Jove!
And mother-earth, and heaven's revolving light,
And ye, fell furies of the realms of night,
Who rule the dead, and horrid woes prepare
For perjured kings, and all who falsely swear!
The black-eyed maid inviolate removes,
Pure and unconscious of my manly loves.
If this be false, heaven all its vengeance shed,
And levell'd thunder strike my guilty head!"

With that, his weapon deep inflicts the wound;
The bleeding savage tumbles to the ground;
The sacred herald rolls the victim slain
(A feast for fish) into the foaming main.

Then thus Achilles: "Hear, ye Greeks! and know
Whate'er we feel, 'tis Jove inflicts the woe;
Not else Atrides could our rage inflame,
Nor from my arms, unwilling, force the dame.

'Twas Jove's high will alone, o'erruling all,
That doom'd our strife, and doom'd the Greeks to fall.
Go then, ye chiefs! indulge the genial rite;
Achilles waits ye, and expects the fight."

The speedy council at his word adjourn'd:
To their black vessels all the Greeks return'd.
Achilles sought his tent. His train before
March'd onward, bending with the gifts they bore.
Those in the tents the squires industrious spread:
The foaming coursers to the stalls they led;
To their new seats the female captives move
Briseis, radiant as the queen of love,
Slow as she pass'd, beheld with sad survey
Where, gash'd with cruel wounds, Patroclus lay.
Prone on the body fell the heavenly fair,
Beat her sad breast, and tore her golden hair;
All beautiful in grief, her humid eyes
Shining with tears she lifts, and thus she cries:

"Ah, youth for ever dear, for ever kind,
Once tender friend of my distracted mind!
I left thee fresh in life, in beauty gay;
Now find thee cold, inanimated clay!
What woes my wretched race of life attend!
Sorrows on sorrows, never doom'd to end!
The first loved consort of my virgin bed
Before these eyes in fatal battle bled:
My three brave brothers in one mournful day
All trod the dark, irremeable way:
Thy friendly hand uprear'd me from the plain,
And dried my sorrows for a husband slain;
Achilles' care you promised I should prove,
The first, the dearest partner of his love;
That rites divine should ratify the band,
And make me empress in his native land.
Accept these grateful tears! for thee they flow,
For thee, that ever felt another's woe!"

Her sister captives echoed groan for groan,
Nor mourn'd Patroclus' fortunes, but their own.
The leaders press'd the chief on every side;
Unmoved he heard them, and with sighs denied.

"If yet Achilles have a friend, whose care
Is bent to please him, this request forbear;
Till yonder sun descend, ah, let me pay
To grief and anguish one abstemious day."

He spoke, and from the warriors turn'd his face:
Yet still the brother-kings of Atreus' race,
Nestor, Idomeneus, Ulysses sage,
And Phoenix, strive to calm his grief and rage:
His rage they calm not, nor his grief control;
He groans, he raves, he sorrows from his soul.

"Thou too, Patroclus! (thus his heart he vents)
Once spread the inviting banquet in our tents:
Thy sweet society, thy winning care,
Once stay'd Achilles, rushing to the war.
But now, alas! to death's cold arms resign'd,
What banquet but revenge can glad my mind?
What greater sorrow could afflict my breast,
What more if hoary Peleus were deceased?
Who now, perhaps, in Phthia dreads to hear
His son's sad fate, and drops a tender tear.
What more, should Neoptolemus the brave,
My only offspring, sink into the grave?
If yet that offspring lives; (I distant far,
Of all neglectful, wage a hateful war.)
I could not this, this cruel stroke attend;
Fate claim'd Achilles, but might spare his friend.
I hoped Patroclus might survive, to rear
My tender orphan with a parent's care,
From Scyros' isle conduct him o'er the main,
And glad his eyes with his paternal reign,
The lofty palace, and the large domain.
For Peleus breathes no more the vital air;
Or drags a wretched life of age and care,
But till the news of my sad fate invades
His hastening soul, and sinks him to the shades."

Sighing he said: his grief the heroes join'd,
Each stole a tear for what he left behind.
Their mingled grief the sire of heaven survey'd,
And thus with pity to his blue-eyed maid:

"Is then Achilles now no more thy care,
And dost thou thus desert the great in war?
Lo, where yon sails their canvas wings extend,
All comfortless he sits, and wails his friend:
Ere thirst and want his forces have oppress'd,
Haste and infuse ambrosia in his breast."

He spoke; and sudden, at the word of Jove,
Shot the descending goddess from above.

So swift through ether the shrill harpy springs,
The wide air floating to her ample wings,
To great Achilles she her flight address'd,
And pour'd divine ambrosia in his breast,
With nectar sweet, (refection of the gods!)
Then, swift ascending, sought the bright abodes.

Now issued from the ships the warrior-train,
And like a deluge pour'd upon the plain.
As when the piercing blasts of Boreas blow,
And scatter o'er the fields the driving snow;
From dusky clouds the fleecy winter flies,
Whose dazzling lustre whitens all the skies:
So helms succeeding helms, so shields from shields,
Catch the quick beams, and brighten all the fields;
Broad glittering breastplates, spears with pointed rays,
Mix in one stream, reflecting blaze on blaze;
Thick beats the centre as the coursers bound;
With splendour flame the skies, and laugh the fields around,

Full in the midst, high-towering o'er the rest,
His limbs in arms divine Achilles dress'd;
Arms which the father of the fire bestow'd,
Forged on the eternal anvils of the god.
Grief and revenge his furious heart inspire,
His glowing eyeballs roll with living fire;
He grinds his teeth, and furious with delay
O'erlooks the embattled host, and hopes the bloody day.

The silver cuishes first his thighs infold;
Then o'er his breast was braced the hollow gold;
The brazen sword a various baldric tied,
That, starr'd with gems, hung glittering at his side;
And, like the moon, the broad refulgent shield
Blazed with long rays, and gleam'd athwart the field.

So to night-wandering sailors, pale with fears,
Wide o'er the watery waste, a light appears,
Which on the far-seen mountain blazing high,
Streams from some lonely watch-tower to the sky:
With mournful eyes they gaze, and gaze again;
Loud howls the storm, and drives them o'er the main.

Next, his high head the helmet graced; behind
The sweepy crest hung floating in the wind:
Like the red star, that from his flaming hair
Shakes down diseases, pestilence, and war;
So stream'd the golden honours from his head,

Trembled the sparkling plumes, and the loose glories shed.
The chief beholds himself with wondering eyes;
His arms he poises, and his motions tries;
Buoy'd by some inward force, he seems to swim,
And feels a pinion lifting every limb.

And now he shakes his great paternal spear,
Ponderous and huge, which not a Greek could rear,
From Pelion's cloudy top an ash entire
Old Chiron fell'd, and shaped it for his sire;
A spear which stern Achilles only wields,
The death of heroes, and the dread of fields.

Automedon and Alcimus prepare
The immortal coursers, and the radiant car;
(The silver traces sweeping at their side;)
Their fiery mouths resplendent bridles tied;
The ivory-studded reins, return'd behind,
Waved o'er their backs, and to the chariot join'd.
The charioteer then whirl'd the lash around,
And swift ascended at one active bound.
All bright in heavenly arms, above his squire
Achilles mounts, and sets the field on fire;
Not brighter Phoebus in the ethereal way
Flames from his chariot, and restores the day.
High o'er the host, all terrible he stands,
And thunders to his steeds these dread commands:

"Xanthus and Balius! of Podarges' strain,
(Unless ye boast that heavenly race in vain,)
Be swift, be mindful of the load ye bear,
And learn to make your master more your care:
Through falling squadrons bear my slaughtering sword,
Nor, as ye left Patroclus, leave your lord."

The generous Xanthus, as the words he said,
Seem'd sensible of woe, and droop'd his head:
Trembling he stood before the golden wain,
And bow'd to dust the honours of his mane.
When, strange to tell! (so Juno will'd) he broke
Eternal silence, and portentous spoke.
"Achilles! yes! this day at least we bear
Thy rage in safety through the files of war:
But come it will, the fatal time must come,
Not ours the fault, but God decrees thy doom.
Not through our crime, or slowness in the course,
Fell thy Patroclus, but by heavenly force;
The bright far-shooting god who gilds the day

(Confess'd we saw him) tore his arms way.
No—could our swiftness o'er the winds prevail,
Or beat the pinions of the western gale,
All were in vain—the Fates thy death demand,
Due to a mortal and immortal hand."

Then ceased for ever, by the Furies tied,
His fateful voice. The intrepid chief replied
With unabated rage—"So let it be!
Portents and prodigies are lost on me.
I know my fate: to die, to see no more
My much-loved parents, and my native shore—
Enough—when heaven ordains, I sink in night:
Now perish Troy!" He said, and rush'd to fight.

BOOK XX

ARGUMENT

THE BATTLE OF THE GODS, AND THE ACTS OF ACHILLES

Jupiter, upon Achilles' return to the battle, calls a council of the gods, and permits them to assist either party. The terrors of the combat described, when the deities are engaged. Apollo encourages Ćneas to meet Achilles. After a long conversation, these two heroes encounter; but Ćneas is preserved by the assistance of Neptune. Achilles falls upon the rest of the Trojans, and is upon the point of killing Hector, but Apollo conveys him away in a cloud. Achilles pursues the Trojans with a great slaughter.

The same day continues. The scene is in the field before Troy.

Thus round Pelides breathing war and blood
Greece, sheathed in arms, beside her vessels stood;
While near impending from a neighbouring height,
Troy's black battalions wait the shock of fight.
Then Jove to Themis gives command, to call
The gods to council in the starry hall:
Swift o'er Olympus' hundred hills she flies,
And summons all the senate of the skies.
These shining on, in long procession come
To Jove's eternal adamantine dome.
Not one was absent, not a rural power
That haunts the verdant gloom, or rosy bower;
Each fair-hair'd dryad of the shady wood,
Each azure sister of the silver flood;
All but old Ocean, hoary sire! who keeps
His ancient seat beneath the sacred deeps.

On marble thrones, with lucid columns crown'd,
(The work of Vulcan,) sat the powers around.
Even he whose trident sways the watery reign
Heard the loud summons, and forsook the main,
Assumed his throne amid the bright abodes,
And question'd thus the sire of men and gods:

"What moves the god who heaven and earth commands,
And grasps the thunder in his awful hands,
Thus to convene the whole ethereal state?
Is Greece and Troy the subject in debate?
Already met, the louring hosts appear,
And death stands ardent on the edge of war."

"'Tis true (the cloud-compelling power replies)
This day we call the council of the skies
In care of human race; even Jove's own eye
Sees with regret unhappy mortals die.
Far on Olympus' top in secret state
Ourself will sit, and see the hand of fate
Work out our will. Celestial powers! descend,
And as your minds direct, your succour lend
To either host. Troy soon must lie o'erthrown,
If uncontroll'd Achilles fights alone:
Their troops but lately durst not meet his eyes;
What can they now, if in his rage he rise?
Assist them, gods! or Ilion's sacred wall
May fall this day, though fate forbids the fall."

He said, and fired their heavenly breasts with rage.
On adverse parts the warring gods engage:
Heaven's awful queen; and he whose azure round
Girds the vast globe; the maid in arms renown'd;
Hermes, of profitable arts the sire;
And Vulcan, the black sovereign of the fire:
These to the fleet repair with instant flight;
The vessels tremble as the gods alight.
In aid of Troy, Latona, Phoebus came,
Mars fiery-helm'd, the laughter-loving dame,
Xanthus, whose streams in golden currents flow,
And the chaste huntress of the silver bow.
Ere yet the gods their various aid employ,
Each Argive bosom swell'd with manly joy,
While great Achilles (terror of the plain),
Long lost to battle, shone in arms again.
Dreadful he stood in front of all his host;
Pale Troy beheld, and seem'd already lost;
Her bravest heroes pant with inward fear,

And trembling see another god of war.

But when the powers descending swell'd the fight,
Then tumult rose: fierce rage and pale affright
Varied each face: then Discord sounds alarms,
Earth echoes, and the nations rush to arms.
Now through the trembling shores Minerva calls,
And now she thunders from the Grecian walls.
Mars hovering o'er his Troy, his terror shrouds
In gloomy tempests, and a night of clouds:
Now through each Trojan heart he fury pours
With voice divine, from Ilion's topmost towers:
Now shouts to Simois, from her beauteous hill;
The mountain shook, the rapid stream stood still.

Above, the sire of gods his thunder rolls,
And peals on peals redoubled rend the poles.
Beneath, stern Neptune shakes the solid ground;
The forests wave, the mountains nod around;
Through all their summits tremble Ida's woods,
And from their sources boil her hundred floods.
Troy's turrets totter on the rocking plain,
And the toss'd navies beat the heaving main.
Deep in the dismal regions of the dead,
The infernal monarch rear'd his horrid head,
Leap'd from his throne, lest Neptune's arm should lay
His dark dominions open to the day,
And pour in light on Pluto's drear abodes,
Abhorr'd by men, and dreadful even to gods.

Such war the immortals wage; such horrors rend
The world's vast concave, when the gods contend
First silver-shafted Phoebus took the plain
Against blue Neptune, monarch of the main.
The god of arms his giant bulk display'd,
Opposed to Pallas, war's triumphant maid.
Against Latona march'd the son of May.
The quiver'd Dian, sister of the day,
(Her golden arrows sounding at her side,)
Saturnia, majesty of heaven, defied.
With fiery Vulcan last in battle stands
The sacred flood that rolls on golden sands;
Xanthus his name with those of heavenly birth,
But called Scamander by the sons of earth.

While thus the gods in various league engage,
Achilles glow'd with more than mortal rage:
Hector he sought; in search of Hector turn'd

His eyes around, for Hector only burn'd;
And burst like lightning through the ranks, and vow'd
To glut the god of battles with his blood.

Æneas was the first who dared to stay;
Apollo wedged him in the warrior's way,
But swell'd his bosom with undaunted might,
Half-forced and half-persuaded to the fight.
Like young Lycaon, of the royal line,
In voice and aspect, seem'd the power divine;
And bade the chief reflect, how late with scorn
In distant threats he braved the goddess-born.

Then thus the hero of Anchises' strain:
"To meet Pelides you persuade in vain:
Already have I met, nor void of fear
Observed the fury of his flying spear;
From Ida's woods he chased us to the field,
Our force he scattered, and our herds he kill'd;
Lyrnessus, Pedasus in ashes lay;
But (Jove assisting) I survived the day:
Else had I sunk oppress'd in fatal fight
By fierce Achilles and Minerva's might.
Where'er he moved, the goddess shone before,
And bathed his brazen lance in hostile gore.
What mortal man Achilles can sustain?
The immortals guard him through the dreadful plain,
And suffer not his dart to fall in vain.
Were God my aid, this arm should check his power,
Though strong in battle as a brazen tower."

To whom the son of Jove: "That god implore,
And be what great Achilles was before.
From heavenly Venus thou deriv'st thy strain,
And he but from a sister of the main;
An aged sea-god father of his line;
But Jove himself the sacred source of thine.
Then lift thy weapon for a noble blow,
Nor fear the vaunting of a mortal foe."

This said, and spirit breathed into his breast,
Through the thick troops the embolden'd hero press'd:
His venturous act the white-arm'd queen survey'd,
And thus, assembling all the powers, she said:

"Behold an action, gods! that claims your care,
Lo great Æneas rushing to the war!
Against Pelides he directs his course,

Phoebus impels, and Phoebus gives him force.
Restrain his bold career; at least, to attend
Our favour'd hero, let some power descend.
To guard his life, and add to his renown,
We, the great armament of heaven, came down.
Hereafter let him fall, as Fates design,
That spun so short his life's illustrious line:
But lest some adverse god now cross his way,
Give him to know what powers assist this day:
For how shall mortal stand the dire alarms,
When heaven's refulgent host appear in arms?"

Thus she; and thus the god whose force can make
The solid globe's eternal basis shake:
"Against the might of man, so feeble known,
Why should celestial powers exert their own?
Suffice from yonder mount to view the scene,
And leave to war the fates of mortal men.
But if the armipotent, or god of light,
Obstruct Achilles, or commence the fight.
Thence on the gods of Troy we swift descend:
Full soon, I doubt not, shall the conflict end;
And these, in ruin and confusion hurl'd,
Yield to our conquering arms the lower world."

Thus having said, the tyrant of the sea,
Coerulean Neptune, rose, and led the way.
Advanced upon the field there stood a mound
Of earth congested, wall'd, and trench'd around;
In elder times to guard Alcides made,
(The work of Trojans, with Minerva's aid,)
What time a vengeful monster of the main
Swept the wide shore, and drove him to the plain.

Here Neptune and the gods of Greece repair,
With clouds encompass'd, and a veil of air:
The adverse powers, around Apollo laid,
Crown the fair hills that silver Simois shade.
In circle close each heavenly party sat,
Intent to form the future scheme of fate;
But mix not yet in fight, though Jove on high
Gives the loud signal, and the heavens reply.

Meanwhile the rushing armies hide the ground;
The trampled centre yields a hollow sound:
Steeds cased in mail, and chiefs in armour bright,
The gleaming champaign glows with brazen light.
Amid both hosts (a dreadful space) appear,

There great Achilles; bold Æneas, here.
With towering strides Aeneas first advanced;
The nodding plumage on his helmet danced:
Spread o'er his breast the fencing shield he bore,
And, so he moved, his javelin flamed before.
Not so Pelides; furious to engage,
He rush'd impetuous. Such the lion's rage,
Who viewing first his foes with scornful eyes,
Though all in arms the peopled city rise,
Stalks careless on, with unregarding pride;
Till at the length, by some brave youth defied,
To his bold spear the savage turns alone,
He murmurs fury with a hollow groan;
He grins, he foams, he rolls his eyes around
Lash'd by his tail his heaving sides resound;
He calls up all his rage; he grinds his teeth,
Resolved on vengeance, or resolved on death.
So fierce Achilles on Æneas flies;
So stands Æneas, and his force defies.
Ere yet the stern encounter join'd, begun
The seed of Thetis thus to Venus' son:

"Why comes Æneas through the ranks so far?
Seeks he to meet Achilles' arm in war,
In hope the realms of Priam to enjoy,
And prove his merits to the throne of Troy?
Grant that beneath thy lance Achilles dies,
The partial monarch may refuse the prize;
Sons he has many; those thy pride may quell:
And 'tis his fault to love those sons too well,
Or, in reward of thy victorious hand,
Has Troy proposed some spacious tract of land
An ample forest, or a fair domain,
Of hills for vines, and arable for grain?
Even this, perhaps, will hardly prove thy lot.
But can Achilles be so soon forgot?
Once (as I think) you saw this brandish'd spear
And then the great Æneas seem'd to fear:
With hearty haste from Ida's mount he fled,
Nor, till he reach'd Lyrnessus, turn'd his head.
Her lofty walls not long our progress stay'd;
Those, Pallas, Jove, and we, in ruins laid:
In Grecian chains her captive race were cast;
'Tis true, the great Aeneas fled too fast.
Defrauded of my conquest once before,
What then I lost, the gods this day restore.
Go; while thou may'st, avoid the threaten'd fate;
Fools stay to feel it, and are wise too late."

To this Anchises' son: "Such words employ
To one that fears thee, some unwarlike boy;
Such we disdain; the best may be defied
With mean reproaches, and unmanly pride;
Unworthy the high race from which we came
Proclaim'd so loudly by the voice of fame:
Each from illustrious fathers draws his line;
Each goddess-born; half human, half divine.
Thetis' this day, or Venus' offspring dies,
And tears shall trickle from celestial eyes:
For when two heroes, thus derived, contend,
'Tis not in words the glorious strife can end.
If yet thou further seek to learn my birth
(A tale resounded through the spacious earth)
Hear how the glorious origin we prove
From ancient Dardanus, the first from Jove:
Dardania's walls he raised; for Ilion, then,
(The city since of many-languaged men,)
Was not. The natives were content to till
The shady foot of Ida's fountful hill.
From Dardanus great Erichthonius springs,
The richest, once, of Asia's wealthy kings;
Three thousand mares his spacious pastures bred,
Three thousand foals beside their mothers fed.
Boreas, enamour'd of the sprightly train,
Conceal'd his godhead in a flowing mane,
With voice dissembled to his loves he neigh'd,
And coursed the dappled beauties o'er the mead:
Hence sprung twelve others of unrivall'd kind,
Swift as their mother mares, and father wind.
These lightly skimming, when they swept the plain,
Nor plied the grass, nor bent the tender grain;
And when along the level seas they flew,
Scarce on the surface curl'd the briny dew.
Such Erichthonius was: from him there came
The sacred Tros, of whom the Trojan name.
Three sons renown'd adorn'd his nuptial bed,
Ilus, Assaracus, and Ganymed:
The matchless Ganymed, divinely fair,
Whom heaven, enamour'd, snatch'd to upper air,
To bear the cup of Jove (ethereal guest,
The grace and glory of the ambrosial feast).
The two remaining sons the line divide:
First rose Laomedon from Ilus' side;
From him Tithonus, now in cares grown old,
And Priam, bless'd with Hector, brave and bold;
Clytius and Lampus, ever-honour'd pair;

And Hicetaon, thunderbolt of war.
From great Assaracus sprang Capys, he
Begat Anchises, and Anchises me.
Such is our race: 'tis fortune gives us birth,
But Jove alone endues the soul with worth:
He, source of power and might! with boundless sway,
All human courage gives, or takes away.
Long in the field of words we may contend,
Reproach is infinite, and knows no end,
Arm'd or with truth or falsehood, right or wrong;
So voluble a weapon is the tongue;
Wounded, we wound; and neither side can fail,
For every man has equal strength to rail:
Women alone, when in the streets they jar,
Perhaps excel us in this wordy war;
Like us they stand, encompass'd with the crowd,
And vent their anger impotent and loud.
Cease then—Our business in the field of fight
Is not to question, but to prove our might.
To all those insults thou hast offer'd here,
Receive this answer: 'tis my flying spear."

He spoke. With all his force the javelin flung,
Fix'd deep, and loudly in the buckler rung.
Far on his outstretch'd arm, Pelides held
(To meet the thundering lance) his dreadful shield,
That trembled as it stuck; nor void of fear
Saw, ere it fell, the immeasurable spear.
His fears were vain; impenetrable charms
Secured the temper of the ethereal arms.
Through two strong plates the point its passage held,
But stopp'd, and rested, by the third repell'd.
Five plates of various metal, various mould,
Composed the shield; of brass each outward fold,
Of tin each inward, and the middle gold:
There stuck the lance. Then rising ere he threw,
The forceful spear of great Achilles flew,
And pierced the Dardan shield's extremest bound,
Where the shrill brass return'd a sharper sound:
Through the thin verge the Pelean weapon glides,
And the slight covering of expanded hides.
Æneas his contracted body bends,
And o'er him high the riven targe extends,
Sees, through its parting plates, the upper air,
And at his back perceives the quivering spear:
A fate so near him, chills his soul with fright;
And swims before his eyes the many-colour'd light.
Achilles, rushing in with dreadful cries,

Draws his broad blade, and at Æneas flies:
Æneas rousing as the foe came on,
With force collected, heaves a mighty stone:
A mass enormous! which in modern days
No two of earth's degenerate sons could raise.
But ocean's god, whose earthquakes rock the ground.
Saw the distress, and moved the powers around:

"Lo! on the brink of fate Æneas stands,
An instant victim to Achilles' hands;
By Phoebus urged; but Phoebus has bestow'd
His aid in vain: the man o'erpowers the god.
And can ye see this righteous chief atone
With guiltless blood for vices not his own?
To all the gods his constant vows were paid;
Sure, though he wars for Troy, he claims our aid.
Fate wills not this; nor thus can Jove resign
The future father of the Dardan line:
The first great ancestor obtain'd his grace,
And still his love descends on all the race:
For Priam now, and Priam's faithless kind,
At length are odious to the all-seeing mind;
On great Æneas shall devolve the reign,
And sons succeeding sons the lasting line sustain."

The great earth-shaker thus: to whom replies
The imperial goddess with the radiant eyes:
"Good as he is, to immolate or spare
The Dardan prince, O Neptune! be thy care;
Pallas and I, by all that gods can bind,
Have sworn destruction to the Trojan kind;
Not even an instant to protract their fate,
Or save one member of the sinking state;
Till her last flame be quench'd with her last gore,
And even her crumbling ruins are no more."

The king of ocean to the fight descends,
Through all the whistling darts his course he bends,
Swift interposed between the warrior flies,
And casts thick darkness o'er Achilles' eyes.
From great Æneas' shield the spear he drew,
And at his master's feet the weapon threw.
That done, with force divine he snatch'd on high
The Dardan prince, and bore him through the sky,
Smooth-gliding without step, above the heads
Of warring heroes, and of bounding steeds:
Till at the battle's utmost verge they light,
Where the slow Caucans close the rear of fight.

The godhead there (his heavenly form confess'd)
With words like these the panting chief address'd:

"What power, O prince! with force inferior far,
Urged thee to meet Achilles' arm in war?
Henceforth beware, nor antedate thy doom,
Defrauding fate of all thy fame to come.
But when the day decreed (for come it must)
Shall lay this dreadful hero in the dust,
Let then the furies of that arm be known,
Secure no Grecian force transcends thy own."

With that, he left him wondering as he lay,
Then from Achilles chased the mist away:
Sudden, returning with a stream of light,
The scene of war came rushing on his sight.
Then thus, amazed; "What wonders strike my mind!
My spear, that parted on the wings of wind,
Laid here before me! and the Dardan lord,
That fell this instant, vanish'd from my sword!
I thought alone with mortals to contend,
But powers celestial sure this foe defend.
Great as he is, our arms he scarce will try,
Content for once, with all his gods, to fly.
Now then let others bleed." This said, aloud
He vents his fury and inflames the crowd:
"O Greeks! (he cries, and every rank alarms)
Join battle, man to man, and arms to arms!
'Tis not in me, though favour'd by the sky,
To mow whole troops, and make whole armies fly:
No god can singly such a host engage,
Not Mars himself, nor great Minerva's rage.
But whatsoe'er Achilles can inspire,
Whate'er of active force, or acting fire;
Whate'er this heart can prompt, or hand obey;
All, all Achilles, Greeks! is yours to-day.
Through yon wide host this arm shall scatter fear,
And thin the squadrons with my single spear."

He said: nor less elate with martial joy,
The godlike Hector warm'd the troops of Troy:
"Trojans, to war! Think, Hector leads you on;
Nor dread the vaunts of Peleus' haughty son.
Deeds must decide our fate. E'en these with words
Insult the brave, who tremble at their swords:
The weakest atheist-wretch all heaven defies,
But shrinks and shudders when the thunder flies.
Nor from yon boaster shall your chief retire,

Not though his heart were steel, his hands were fire;
That fire, that steel, your Hector should withstand,
And brave that vengeful heart, that dreadful hand."

Thus (breathing rage through all) the hero said;
A wood of lances rises round his head,
Clamours on clamours tempest all the air,
They join, they throng, they thicken to the war.
But Phoebus warns him from high heaven to shun
The single fight with Thetis' godlike son;
More safe to combat in the mingled band,
Nor tempt too near the terrors of his hand.
He hears, obedient to the god of light,
And, plunged within the ranks, awaits the fight.

Then fierce Achilles, shouting to the skies,
On Troy's whole force with boundless fury flies.
First falls Iphytion, at his army's head;
Brave was the chief, and brave the host he led;
From great Otrynteus he derived his blood,
His mother was a Nais, of the flood;
Beneath the shades of Tmolus, crown'd with snow,
From Hyde's walls he ruled the lands below.
Fierce as he springs, the sword his head divides:
The parted visage falls on equal sides:
With loud-resounding arms he strikes the plain;
While thus Achilles glories o'er the slain:

"Lie there, Otryntides! the Trojan earth
Receives thee dead, though Gygae boast thy birth;
Those beauteous fields where Hyllus' waves are roll'd,
And plenteous Hermus swells with tides of gold,
Are thine no more."—The insulting hero said,
And left him sleeping in eternal shade.
The rolling wheels of Greece the body tore,
And dash'd their axles with no vulgar gore.

Demoleon next, Antenor's offspring, laid
Breathless in dust, the price of rashness paid.
The impatient steel with full-descending sway
Forced through his brazen helm its furious way,
Resistless drove the batter'd skull before,
And dash'd and mingled all the brains with gore.
This sees Hippodamas, and seized with fright,
Deserts his chariot for a swifter flight:
The lance arrests him: an ignoble wound
The panting Trojan rivets to the ground.
He groans away his soul: not louder roars,

At Neptune's shrine on Helice's high shores,
The victim bull; the rocks re-bellow round,
And ocean listens to the grateful sound.
Then fell on Polydore his vengeful rage,
The youngest hope of Priam's stooping age:
(Whose feet for swiftness in the race surpass'd:)
Of all his sons, the dearest, and the last.
To the forbidden field he takes his flight,
In the first folly of a youthful knight,
To vaunt his swiftness wheels around the plain,
But vaunts not long, with all his swiftness slain:
Struck where the crossing belts unite behind,
And golden rings the double back-plate join'd
Forth through the navel burst the thrilling steel;
And on his knees with piercing shrieks he fell;
The rushing entrails pour'd upon the ground
His hands collect; and darkness wraps him round.
When Hector view'd, all ghastly in his gore,
Thus sadly slain the unhappy Polydore,
A cloud of sorrow overcast his sight,
His soul no longer brook'd the distant fight:
Full in Achilles' dreadful front he came,
And shook his javelin like a waving flame.
The son of Peleus sees, with joy possess'd,
His heart high-bounding in his rising breast.
"And, lo! the man on whom black fates attend;
The man, that slew Achilles, is his friend!
No more shall Hector's and Pelides' spear
Turn from each other in the walks of war."—
Then with revengeful eyes he scann'd him o'er:
"Come, and receive thy fate!" He spake no more.

Hector, undaunted, thus: "Such words employ
To one that dreads thee, some unwarlike boy:
Such we could give, defying and defied,
Mean intercourse of obloquy and pride!
I know thy force to mine superior far;
But heaven alone confers success in war:
Mean as I am, the gods may guide my dart,
And give it entrance in a braver heart."

Then parts the lance: but Pallas' heavenly breath
Far from Achilles wafts the winged death:
The bidden dart again to Hector flies,
And at the feet of its great master lies.
Achilles closes with his hated foe,
His heart and eyes with flaming fury glow:
But present to his aid, Apollo shrouds

The favour'd hero in a veil of clouds.
Thrice struck Pelides with indignant heart,
Thrice in impassive air he plunged the dart;
The spear a fourth time buried in the cloud.
He foams with fury, and exclaims aloud:

"Wretch! thou hast 'scaped again; once more thy flight
Has saved thee, and the partial god of light.
But long thou shalt not thy just fate withstand,
If any power assist Achilles' hand.
Fly then inglorious! but thy flight this day
Whole hecatombs of Trojan ghosts shall pay."

With that, he gluts his rage on numbers slain:
Then Dryops tumbled to the ensanguined plain,
Pierced through the neck: he left him panting there,
And stopp'd Demuchus, great Philetor's heir.
Gigantic chief! deep gash'd the enormous blade,
And for the soul an ample passage made.
Laoganus and Dardanus expire,
The valiant sons of an unhappy sire;
Both in one instant from the chariot hurl'd,
Sunk in one instant to the nether world:
This difference only their sad fates afford
That one the spear destroy'd, and one the sword.

Nor less unpitied, young Alastor bleeds;
In vain his youth, in vain his beauty pleads;
In vain he begs thee, with a suppliant's moan,
To spare a form, an age so like thy own!
Unhappy boy! no prayer, no moving art,
E'er bent that fierce, inexorable heart!
While yet he trembled at his knees, and cried,
The ruthless falchion oped his tender side;
The panting liver pours a flood of gore
That drowns his bosom till he pants no more.

Through Mulius' head then drove the impetuous spear:
The warrior falls, transfix'd from ear to ear.
Thy life, Echeclus! next the sword bereaves,
Deep though the front the ponderous falchion cleaves;
Warm'd in the brain the smoking weapon lies,
The purple death comes floating o'er his eyes.
Then brave Deucalion died: the dart was flung
Where the knit nerves the pliant elbow strung;
He dropp'd his arm, an unassisting weight,
And stood all impotent, expecting fate:
Full on his neck the falling falchion sped,

From his broad shoulders hew'd his crested head:
Forth from the bone the spinal marrow flies,
And, sunk in dust, the corpse extended lies.
Rhigmas, whose race from fruitful Thracia came,
(The son of Pierus, an illustrious name,)
Succeeds to fate: the spear his belly rends;
Prone from his car the thundering chief descends.
The squire, who saw expiring on the ground
His prostrate master, rein'd the steeds around;
His back, scarce turn'd, the Pelian javelin gored,
And stretch'd the servant o'er his dying lord.
As when a flame the winding valley fills,
And runs on crackling shrubs between the hills;
Then o'er the stubble up the mountain flies,
Fires the high woods, and blazes to the skies,
This way and that, the spreading torrent roars:
So sweeps the hero through the wasted shores;
Around him wide, immense destruction pours
And earth is deluged with the sanguine showers
As with autumnal harvests cover'd o'er,
And thick bestrewn, lies Ceres' sacred floor;
When round and round, with never-wearied pain,
The trampling steers beat out the unnumber'd grain:
So the fierce coursers, as the chariot rolls,
Tread down whole ranks, and crush out heroes' souls,
Dash'd from their hoofs while o'er the dead they fly,
Black, bloody drops the smoking chariot dye:
The spiky wheels through heaps of carnage tore;
And thick the groaning axles dropp'd with gore.
High o'er the scene of death Achilles stood,
All grim with dust, all horrible in blood:
Yet still insatiate, still with rage on flame;
Such is the lust of never-dying fame!

BOOK XXI

ARGUMENT

THE BATTLE IN THE RIVER SCAMANDER

The Trojans fly before Achilles, some towards the town, others to the river Scamander: he falls upon the latter with great slaughter: takes twelve captives alive, to sacrifice to the shade of Patroclus; and kills Lycaon and Asteropeus. Scamander attacks him with all his waves: Neptune and Pallas assist the hero: Simois joins Scamander: at length Vulcan, by the instigation of Juno, almost dries up the river. This Combat ended, the other gods engage each other. Meanwhile Achilles continues the slaughter, drives the rest into Troy: Agenor only makes a stand, and is conveyed away in a cloud by Apollo; who (to delude Achilles) takes upon him Agenor's shape, and while he pursues him in that disguise, gives the Trojans an opportunity of retiring into their city.

The same day continues. The scene is on the banks and in the stream of Scamander.

And now to Xanthus' gliding stream they drove,
Xanthus, immortal progeny of Jove.
The river here divides the flying train,
Part to the town fly diverse o'er the plain,
Where late their troops triumphant bore the fight,
Now chased, and trembling in ignoble flight:
(These with a gathered mist Saturnia shrouds,
And rolls behind the rout a heap of clouds:)
Part plunge into the stream: old Xanthus roars,
The flashing billows beat the whiten'd shores:
With cries promiscuous all the banks resound,
And here, and there, in eddies whirling round,
The flouncing steeds and shrieking warriors drown'd.
As the scorch'd locusts from their fields retire,
While fast behind them runs the blaze of fire;
Driven from the land before the smoky cloud,
The clustering legions rush into the flood:
So, plunged in Xanthus by Achilles' force,
Roars the resounding surge with men and horse.
His bloody lance the hero casts aside,
(Which spreading tamarisks on the margin hide,)
Then, like a god, the rapid billows braves,
Arm'd with his sword, high brandish'd o'er the waves:
Now down he plunges, now he whirls it round,
Deep groan'd the waters with the dying sound;
Repeated wounds the reddening river dyed,
And the warm purple circled on the tide.
Swift through the foamy flood the Trojans fly,
And close in rocks or winding caverns lie:
So the huge dolphin tempesting the main,
In shoals before him fly the scaly train,
Confusedly heap'd they seek their inmost caves,
Or pant and heave beneath the floating waves.
Now, tired with slaughter, from the Trojan band
Twelve chosen youths he drags alive to land;
With their rich belts their captive arms restrains
(Late their proud ornaments, but now their chains).
These his attendants to the ships convey'd,
Sad victims destined to Patroclus' shade;

Then, as once more he plunged amid the flood,
The young Lycaon in his passage stood;

The son of Priam; whom the hero's hand
But late made captive in his father's land
(As from a sycamore, his sounding steel
Lopp'd the green arms to spoke a chariot wheel)
To Lemnos' isle he sold the royal slave,
Where Jason's son the price demanded gave;
But kind Eetion, touching on the shore,
The ransom'd prince to fair Arisbe bore.
Ten days were past, since in his father's reign
He felt the sweets of liberty again;
The next, that god whom men in vain withstand
Gives the same youth to the same conquering hand
Now never to return! and doom'd to go
A sadder journey to the shades below.
His well-known face when great Achilles eyed,
(The helm and visor he had cast aside
With wild affright, and dropp'd upon the field
His useless lance and unavailing shield,)
As trembling, panting, from the stream he fled,
And knock'd his faltering knees, the hero said.
"Ye mighty gods! what wonders strike my view!
Is it in vain our conquering arms subdue?
Sure I shall see yon heaps of Trojans kill'd
Rise from the shades, and brave me on the field;
As now the captive, whom so late I bound
And sold to Lemnos, stalks on Trojan ground!
Not him the sea's unmeasured deeps detain,
That bar such numbers from their native plain;
Lo! he returns. Try, then, my flying spear!
Try, if the grave can hold the wanderer;
If earth, at length this active prince can seize,
Earth, whose strong grasp has held down Hercules."

Thus while he spoke, the Trojan pale with fears
Approach'd, and sought his knees with suppliant tears
Loth as he was to yield his youthful breath,
And his soul shivering at the approach of death.
Achilles raised the spear, prepared to wound;
He kiss'd his feet, extended on the ground:
And while, above, the spear suspended stood,
Longing to dip its thirsty point in blood,
One hand embraced them close, one stopp'd the dart,
While thus these melting words attempt his heart:

"Thy well-known captive, great Achilles! see,
Once more Lycaon trembles at thy knee.
Some pity to a suppliant's name afford,
Who shared the gifts of Ceres at thy board;

Whom late thy conquering arm to Lemnos bore,
Far from his father, friends, and native shore;
A hundred oxen were his price that day,
Now sums immense thy mercy shall repay.
Scarce respited from woes I yet appear,
And scarce twelve morning suns have seen me here;
Lo! Jove again submits me to thy hands,
Again, her victim cruel Fate demands!
I sprang from Priam, and Laothoe fair,
(Old Altes' daughter, and Lelegia's heir;
Who held in Pedasus his famed abode,
And ruled the fields where silver Satnio flow'd,)
Two sons (alas! unhappy sons) she bore;
For ah! one spear shall drink each brother's gore,
And I succeed to slaughter'd Polydore.
How from that arm of terror shall I fly?
Some demon urges! 'tis my doom to die!
If ever yet soft pity touch'd thy mind,
Ah! think not me too much of Hector's kind!
Not the same mother gave thy suppliant breath,
With his, who wrought thy loved Patroclus' death."

These words, attended with a shower of tears,
The youth address'd to unrelenting ears:
"Talk not of life, or ransom (he replies):
Patroclus dead, whoever meets me, dies:
In vain a single Trojan sues for grace;
But least, the sons of Priam's hateful race.
Die then, my friend! what boots it to deplore?
The great, the good Patroclus is no more!
He, far thy better, was foredoom'd to die,
And thou, dost thou bewail mortality?
Seest thou not me, whom nature's gifts adorn,
Sprung from a hero, from a goddess born?
The day shall come (which nothing can avert)
When by the spear, the arrow, or the dart,
By night, or day, by force, or by design,
Impending death and certain fate are mine!
Die then,"—He said; and as the word he spoke,
The fainting stripling sank before the stroke:
His hand forgot its grasp, and left the spear,
While all his trembling frame confess'd his fear:
Sudden, Achilles his broad sword display'd,
And buried in his neck the reeking blade.
Prone fell the youth; and panting on the land,
The gushing purple dyed the thirsty sand.
The victor to the stream the carcase gave,
And thus insults him, floating on the wave:

"Lie there, Lycaon! let the fish surround
Thy bloated corpse, and suck thy gory wound:
There no sad mother shall thy funerals weep,
But swift Scamander roll thee to the deep,
Whose every wave some watery monster brings,
To feast unpunish'd on the fat of kings.
So perish Troy, and all the Trojan line!
Such ruin theirs, and such compassion mine.
What boots ye now Scamander's worshipp'd stream,
His earthly honours, and immortal name?
In vain your immolated bulls are slain,
Your living coursers glut his gulfs in vain!
Thus he rewards you, with this bitter fate;
Thus, till the Grecian vengeance is complete:
Thus is atoned Patroclus' honour'd shade,
And the short absence of Achilles paid."

These boastful words provoked the raging god;
With fury swells the violated flood.
What means divine may yet the power employ
To check Achilles, and to rescue Troy?
Meanwhile the hero springs in arms, to dare
The great Asteropeus to mortal war;
The son of Pelagon, whose lofty line
Flows from the source of Axius, stream divine!
(Fair Peribaea's love the god had crown'd,
With all his refluent waters circled round:)
On him Achilles rush'd; he fearless stood,
And shook two spears, advancing from the flood;
The flood impell'd him, on Pelides' head
To avenge his waters choked with heaps of dead.
Near as they drew, Achilles thus began:

"What art thou, boldest of the race of man?
Who, or from whence? Unhappy is the sire
Whose son encounters our resistless ire."

"O son of Peleus! what avails to trace
(Replied the warrior) our illustrious race?
From rich Paeonia's valleys I command,
Arm'd with protended spears, my native band;
Now shines the tenth bright morning since I came
In aid of Ilion to the fields of fame:
Axius, who swells with all the neighbouring rills,
And wide around the floated region fills,
Begot my sire, whose spear much glory won:
Now lift thy arm, and try that hero's son!"

Threatening he said: the hostile chiefs advance;
At once Asteropeus discharged each lance,
(For both his dexterous hands the lance could wield,)
One struck, but pierced not, the Vulcanian shield;
One razed Achilles' hand; the spouting blood
Spun forth; in earth the fasten'd weapon stood.
Like lightning next the Pelean javelin flies:
Its erring fury hiss'd along the skies;
Deep in the swelling bank was driven the spear,
Even to the middle earth; and quiver'd there.
Then from his side the sword Pelides drew,
And on his foe with double fury flew.
The foe thrice tugg'd, and shook the rooted wood;
Repulsive of his might the weapon stood:
The fourth, he tries to break the spear in vain;
Bent as he stands, he tumbles to the plain;
His belly open'd with a ghastly wound,
The reeking entrails pour upon the ground.
Beneath the hero's feet he panting lies,
And his eye darkens, and his spirit flies;
While the proud victor thus triumphing said,
His radiant armour tearing from the dead:

"So ends thy glory! Such the fate they prove,
Who strive presumptuous with the sons of Jove!
Sprung from a river, didst thou boast thy line?
But great Saturnius is the source of mine.
How durst thou vaunt thy watery progeny?
Of Peleus, Ćacus, and Jove, am I.
The race of these superior far to those,
As he that thunders to the stream that flows.
What rivers can, Scamander might have shown;
But Jove he dreads, nor wars against his son.
Even Achelous might contend in vain,
And all the roaring billows of the main.
The eternal ocean, from whose fountains flow
The seas, the rivers, and the springs below,
The thundering voice of Jove abhors to hear,
And in his deep abysses shakes with fear."

He said: then from the bank his javelin tore,
And left the breathless warrior in his gore.
The floating tides the bloody carcase lave,
And beat against it, wave succeeding wave;
Till, roll'd between the banks, it lies the food
Of curling eels, and fishes of the flood.
All scatter'd round the stream (their mightiest slain)

The amazed Paeonians scour along the plain;
He vents his fury on the flying crew,
Thrasius, Astyplus, and Mnesus slew;
Mydon, Thersilochus, with Ćnius, fell;
And numbers more his lance had plunged to hell,
But from the bottom of his gulfs profound
Scamander spoke; the shores return'd the sound.

"O first of mortals! (for the gods are thine)
In valour matchless, and in force divine!
If Jove have given thee every Trojan head,
'Tis not on me thy rage should heap the dead.
See! my choked streams no more their course can keep,
Nor roll their wonted tribute to the deep.
Turn then, impetuous! from our injured flood;
Content, thy slaughters could amaze a god."

In human form, confess'd before his eyes,
The river thus; and thus the chief replies:
"O sacred stream! thy word we shall obey;
But not till Troy the destined vengeance pay,
Not till within her towers the perjured train
Shall pant, and tremble at our arms again;
Not till proud Hector, guardian of her wall,
Or stain this lance, or see Achilles fall."

He said; and drove with fury on the foe.
Then to the godhead of the silver bow
The yellow flood began: "O son of Jove!
Was not the mandate of the sire above
Full and express, that Phoebus should employ
His sacred arrows in defence of Troy,
And make her conquer, till Hyperion's fall
In awful darkness hide the face of all?"

He spoke in vain—The chief without dismay
Ploughs through the boiling surge his desperate way.
Then rising in his rage above the shores,
From all his deep the bellowing river roars,
Huge heaps of slain disgorges on the coast,
And round the banks the ghastly dead are toss'd.
While all before, the billows ranged on high,
(A watery bulwark,) screen the bands who fly.
Now bursting on his head with thundering sound,
The falling deluge whelms the hero round:
His loaded shield bends to the rushing tide;
His feet, upborne, scarce the strong flood divide,
Sliddering, and staggering. On the border stood

A spreading elm, that overhung the flood;
He seized a bending bough, his steps to stay;
The plant uprooted to his weight gave way.
Heaving the bank, and undermining all;
Loud flash the waters to the rushing fall
Of the thick foliage. The large trunk display'd
Bridged the rough flood across: the hero stay'd
On this his weight, and raised upon his hand,
Leap'd from the channel, and regain'd the land.
Then blacken'd the wild waves: the murmur rose:
The god pursues, a huger billow throws,
And bursts the bank, ambitious to destroy
The man whose fury is the fate of Troy.
He like the warlike eagle speeds his pace
(Swiftest and strongest of the aerial race);
Far as a spear can fly, Achilles springs;
At every bound his clanging armour rings:
Now here, now there, he turns on every side,
And winds his course before the following tide;
The waves flow after, wheresoe'er he wheels,
And gather fast, and murmur at his heels.
So when a peasant to his garden brings
Soft rills of water from the bubbling springs,
And calls the floods from high, to bless his bowers,
And feed with pregnant streams the plants and flowers:
Soon as he clears whate'er their passage stay'd,
And marks the future current with his spade,
Swift o'er the rolling pebbles, down the hills,
Louder and louder purl the falling rills;
Before him scattering, they prevent his pains,
And shine in mazy wanderings o'er the plains.

Still flies Achilles, but before his eyes
Still swift Scamander rolls where'er he flies:
Not all his speed escapes the rapid floods;
The first of men, but not a match for gods.
Oft as he turn'd the torrent to oppose,
And bravely try if all the powers were foes;
So oft the surge, in watery mountains spread,
Beats on his back, or bursts upon his head.
Yet dauntless still the adverse flood he braves,
And still indignant bounds above the waves.
Tired by the tides, his knees relax with toil;
Wash'd from beneath him slides the slimy soil;
When thus (his eyes on heaven's expansion thrown)
Forth bursts the hero with an angry groan:

"Is there no god Achilles to befriend,

No power to avert his miserable end?
Prevent, O Jove! this ignominious date,
And make my future life the sport of fate.
Of all heaven's oracles believed in vain,
But most of Thetis must her son complain;
By Phoebus' darts she prophesied my fall,
In glorious arms before the Trojan wall.
Oh! had I died in fields of battle warm,
Stretch'd like a hero, by a hero's arm!
Might Hector's spear this dauntless bosom rend,
And my swift soul o'ertake my slaughter'd friend.
Ah no! Achilles meets a shameful fate,
Oh how unworthy of the brave and great!
Like some vile swain, whom on a rainy day,
Crossing a ford, the torrent sweeps away,
An unregarded carcase to the sea."

Neptune and Pallas haste to his relief,
And thus in human form address'd the chief:
The power of ocean first: "Forbear thy fear,
O son of Peleus! Lo, thy gods appear!
Behold! from Jove descending to thy aid,
Propitious Neptune, and the blue-eyed maid.
Stay, and the furious flood shall cease to rave
'Tis not thy fate to glut his angry wave.
But thou, the counsel heaven suggests, attend!
Nor breathe from combat, nor thy sword suspend,
Till Troy receive her flying sons, till all
Her routed squadrons pant behind their wall:
Hector alone shall stand his fatal chance,
And Hector's blood shall smoke upon thy lance.
Thine is the glory doom'd." Thus spake the gods:
Then swift ascended to the bright abodes.

Stung with new ardour, thus by heaven impell'd,
He springs impetuous, and invades the field:
O'er all the expanded plain the waters spread;
Heaved on the bounding billows danced the dead,
Floating 'midst scatter'd arms; while casques of gold
And turn'd-up bucklers glitter'd as they roll'd.
High o'er the surging tide, by leaps and bounds,
He wades, and mounts; the parted wave resounds.
Not a whole river stops the hero's course,
While Pallas fills him with immortal force.
With equal rage, indignant Xanthus roars,
And lifts his billows, and o'erwhelms his shores.

Then thus to Simois! "Haste, my brother flood;

And check this mortal that controls a god;
Our bravest heroes else shall quit the fight,
And Ilion tumble from her towery height.
Call then thy subject streams, and bid them roar,
From all thy fountains swell thy watery store,
With broken rocks, and with a load of dead,
Charge the black surge, and pour it on his head.
Mark how resistless through the floods he goes,
And boldly bids the warring gods be foes!
But nor that force, nor form divine to sight,
Shall aught avail him, if our rage unite:
Whelm'd under our dark gulfs those arms shall lie,
That blaze so dreadful in each Trojan eye;
And deep beneath a sandy mountain hurl'd,
Immersed remain this terror of the world.
Such ponderous ruin shall confound the place,
No Greeks shall e'er his perish'd relics grace,
No hand his bones shall gather, or inhume;
These his cold rites, and this his watery tomb."

He said; and on the chief descends amain,
Increased with gore, and swelling with the slain.
Then, murmuring from his beds, he boils, he raves,
And a foam whitens on the purple waves:
At every step, before Achilles stood
The crimson surge, and deluged him with blood.
Fear touch'd the queen of heaven: she saw dismay'd,
She call'd aloud, and summon'd Vulcan's aid.

"Rise to the war! the insulting flood requires
Thy wasteful arm! assemble all thy fires!
While to their aid, by our command enjoin'd,
Rush the swift eastern and the western wind:
These from old ocean at my word shall blow,
Pour the red torrent on the watery foe,
Corses and arms to one bright ruin turn,
And hissing rivers to their bottoms burn.
Go, mighty in thy rage! display thy power,
Drink the whole flood, the crackling trees devour.
Scorch all the banks! and (till our voice reclaim)
Exert the unwearied furies of the flame!"

The power ignipotent her word obeys:
Wide o'er the plain he pours the boundless blaze;
At once consumes the dead, and dries the soil
And the shrunk waters in their channel boil.
As when autumnal Boreas sweeps the sky,
And instant blows the water'd gardens dry:

So look'd the field, so whiten'd was the ground,
While Vulcan breathed the fiery blast around.
Swift on the sedgy reeds the ruin preys;
Along the margin winds the running blaze:
The trees in flaming rows to ashes turn,
The flowering lotos and the tamarisk burn,
Broad elm, and cypress rising in a spire;
The watery willows hiss before the fire.
Now glow the waves, the fishes pant for breath,
The eels lie twisting in the pangs of death:
Now flounce aloft, now dive the scaly fry,
Or, gasping, turn their bellies to the sky.
At length the river rear'd his languid head,
And thus, short-panting, to the god he said:

"Oh Vulcan! oh! what power resists thy might?
I faint, I sink, unequal to the fight—
I yield—Let Ilion fall; if fate decree—
Ah—bend no more thy fiery arms on me!"

He ceased; wide conflagration blazing round;
The bubbling waters yield a hissing sound.
As when the flames beneath a cauldron rise,
To melt the fat of some rich sacrifice,
Amid the fierce embrace of circling fires
The waters foam, the heavy smoke aspires:
So boils the imprison'd flood, forbid to flow,
And choked with vapours feels his bottom glow.
To Juno then, imperial queen of air,
The burning river sends his earnest prayer:

"Ah why, Saturnia; must thy son engage
Me, only me, with all his wasteful rage?
On other gods his dreadful arm employ,
For mightier gods assert the cause of Troy.
Submissive I desist, if thou command;
But ah! withdraw this all-destroying hand.
Hear then my solemn oath, to yield to fate
Unaided Ilion, and her destined state,
Till Greece shall gird her with destructive flame,
And in one ruin sink the Trojan name."

His warm entreaty touch'd Saturnia's ear:
She bade the ignipotent his rage forbear,
Recall the flame, nor in a mortal cause
Infest a god: the obedient flame withdraws:
Again the branching streams begin to spread,
And soft remurmur in their wonted bed.

While these by Juno's will the strife resign,
The warring gods in fierce contention join:
Rekindling rage each heavenly breast alarms:
With horrid clangour shock the ethereal arms:
Heaven in loud thunder bids the trumpet sound;
And wide beneath them groans the rending ground.
Jove, as his sport, the dreadful scene descries,
And views contending gods with careless eyes.
The power of battles lifts his brazen spear,
And first assaults the radiant queen of war:

"What moved thy madness, thus to disunite
Ethereal minds, and mix all heaven in fight?
What wonder this, when in thy frantic mood
Thou drovest a mortal to insult a god?
Thy impious hand Tydides' javelin bore,
And madly bathed it in celestial gore."

He spoke, and smote the long-resounding shield,
Which bears Jove's thunder on its dreadful field:
The adamantine aegis of her sire,
That turns the glancing bolt and forked fire.

Then heaved the goddess in her mighty hand
A stone, the limit of the neighbouring land,
There fix'd from eldest times; black, craggy, vast;
This at the heavenly homicide she cast.
Thundering he falls, a mass of monstrous size:
And seven broad acres covers as he lies.
The stunning stroke his stubborn nerves unbound:
Loud o'er the fields his ringing arms resound:
The scornful dame her conquest views with smiles,
And, glorying, thus the prostrate god reviles:

"Hast thou not yet, insatiate fury! known
How far Minerva's force transcends thy own?
Juno, whom thou rebellious darest withstand,
Corrects thy folly thus by Pallas' hand;
Thus meets thy broken faith with just disgrace,
And partial aid to Troy's perfidious race."

The goddess spoke, and turn'd her eyes away,
That, beaming round, diffused celestial day.
Jove's Cyprian daughter, stooping on the land,
Lent to the wounded god her tender hand:
Slowly he rises, scarcely breathes with pain,
And, propp'd on her fair arm, forsakes the plain.

This the bright empress of the heavens survey'd,
And, scoffing, thus to war's victorious maid:

"Lo! what an aid on Mars's side is seen!
The smiles' and loves' unconquerable queen!
Mark with what insolence, in open view,
She moves: let Pallas, if she dares, pursue."

Minerva smiling heard, the pair o'ertook,
And slightly on her breast the wanton strook:
She, unresisting, fell (her spirits fled);
On earth together lay the lovers spread.
"And like these heroes be the fate of all
(Minerva cries) who guard the Trojan wall!
To Grecian gods such let the Phrygian be,
So dread, so fierce, as Venus is to me;
Then from the lowest stone shall Troy be moved."
Thus she, and Juno with a smile approved.

Meantime, to mix in more than mortal fight,
The god of ocean dares the god of light.
"What sloth has seized us, when the fields around
Ring with conflicting powers, and heaven returns the sound:
Shall, ignominious, we with shame retire,
No deed perform'd, to our Olympian sire?
Come, prove thy arm! for first the war to wage,
Suits not my greatness, or superior age:
Rash as thou art to prop the Trojan throne,
(Forgetful of my wrongs, and of thy own,)
And guard the race of proud Laomedon!
Hast thou forgot, how, at the monarch's prayer,
We shared the lengthen'd labours of a year?
Troy walls I raised (for such were Jove's commands),
And yon proud bulwarks grew beneath my hands:
Thy task it was to feed the bellowing droves
Along fair Ida's vales and pendant groves.
But when the circling seasons in their train
Brought back the grateful day that crown'd our pain,
With menace stern the fraudful king defied
Our latent godhead, and the prize denied:
Mad as he was, he threaten'd servile bands,
And doom'd us exiles far in barbarous lands.
Incensed, we heavenward fled with swiftest wing,
And destined vengeance on the perjured king.
Dost thou, for this, afford proud Ilion grace,
And not, like us, infest the faithless race;
Like us, their present, future sons destroy,
And from its deep foundations heave their Troy?"

Apollo thus: "To combat for mankind
Ill suits the wisdom of celestial mind;
For what is man? Calamitous by birth,
They owe their life and nourishment to earth;
Like yearly leaves, that now, with beauty crown'd,
Smile on the sun; now, wither on the ground.
To their own hands commit the frantic scene,
Nor mix immortals in a cause so mean."

Then turns his face, far-beaming heavenly fires,
And from the senior power submiss retires:
Him thus retreating, Artemis upbraids,
The quiver'd huntress of the sylvan shades:

"And is it thus the youthful Phoebus flies,
And yields to ocean's hoary sire the prize?
How vain that martial pomp, and dreadful show
Of pointed arrows and the silver bow!
Now boast no more in yon celestial bower,
Thy force can match the great earth-shaking power."

Silent he heard the queen of woods upbraid:
Not so Saturnia bore the vaunting maid:
But furious thus: "What insolence has driven
Thy pride to face the majesty of heaven?
What though by Jove the female plague design'd,
Fierce to the feeble race of womankind,
The wretched matron feels thy piercing dart;
Thy sex's tyrant, with a tiger's heart?
What though tremendous in the woodland chase
Thy certain arrows pierce the savage race?
How dares thy rashness on the powers divine
Employ those arms, or match thy force with mine?
Learn hence, no more unequal war to wage—"
She said, and seized her wrists with eager rage;
These in her left hand lock'd, her right untied
The bow, the quiver, and its plumy pride.
About her temples flies the busy bow;
Now here, now there, she winds her from the blow;
The scattering arrows, rattling from the case,
Drop round, and idly mark the dusty place.
Swift from the field the baffled huntress flies,
And scarce restrains the torrent in her eyes:
So, when the falcon wings her way above,
To the cleft cavern speeds the gentle dove;
(Not fated yet to die;) there safe retreats,
Yet still her heart against the marble beats.

To her Latona hastes with tender care;
Whom Hermes viewing, thus declines the war:
"How shall I face the dame, who gives delight
To him whose thunders blacken heaven with night?
Go, matchless goddess! triumph in the skies,
And boast my conquest, while I yield the prize."

He spoke; and pass'd: Latona, stooping low,
Collects the scatter'd shafts and fallen bow,
That, glittering on the dust, lay here and there
Dishonour'd relics of Diana's war:
Then swift pursued her to her blest abode,
Where, all confused, she sought the sovereign god;
Weeping, she grasp'd his knees: the ambrosial vest
Shook with her sighs, and panted on her breast.

The sire superior smiled, and bade her show
What heavenly hand had caused his daughter's woe?
Abash'd, she names his own imperial spouse;
And the pale crescent fades upon her brows.

Thus they above: while, swiftly gliding down,
Apollo enters Ilion's sacred town;
The guardian-god now trembled for her wall,
And fear'd the Greeks, though fate forbade her fall.
Back to Olympus, from the war's alarms,
Return the shining bands of gods in arms;
Some proud in triumph, some with rage on fire;
And take their thrones around the ethereal sire.

Through blood, through death, Achilles still proceeds,
O'er slaughter'd heroes, and o'er rolling steeds.
As when avenging flames with fury driven
On guilty towns exert the wrath of heaven;
The pale inhabitants, some fall, some fly;
And the red vapours purple all the sky:
So raged Achilles: death and dire dismay,
And toils, and terrors, fill'd the dreadful day.

High on a turret hoary Priam stands,
And marks the waste of his destructive hands;
Views, from his arm, the Trojans' scatter'd flight,
And the near hero rising on his sight!
No stop, no check, no aid! With feeble pace,
And settled sorrow on his aged face,
Fast as he could, he sighing quits the walls;
And thus descending, on the guards he calls:

"You to whose care our city-gates belong,
Set wide your portals to the flying throng:
For lo! he comes, with unresisted sway;
He comes, and desolation marks his way!
But when within the walls our troops take breath,
Lock fast the brazen bars, and shut out death."
Thus charged the reverend monarch: wide were flung
The opening folds; the sounding hinges rung.
Phoebus rush'd forth, the flying bands to meet;
Struck slaughter back, and cover'd the retreat,
On heaps the Trojans crowd to gain the gate,
And gladsome see their last escape from fate.
Thither, all parch'd with thirst, a heartless train,
Hoary with dust, they beat the hollow plain:
And gasping, panting, fainting, labour on
With heavier strides, that lengthen toward the town.
Enraged Achilles follows with his spear;
Wild with revenge, insatiable of war.

Then had the Greeks eternal praise acquired,
And Troy inglorious to her walls retired;
But he, the god who darts ethereal flame,
Shot down to save her, and redeem her fame:
To young Agenor force divine he gave;
(Antenor's offspring, haughty, bold, and brave;)
In aid of him, beside the beech he sate,
And wrapt in clouds, restrain'd the hand of fate.
When now the generous youth Achilles spies.
Thick beats his heart, the troubled motions rise.
(So, ere a storm, the waters heave and roll.)
He stops, and questions thus his mighty soul;

"What, shall I fly this terror of the plain!
Like others fly, and be like others slain?
Vain hope! to shun him by the self-same road
Yon line of slaughter'd Trojans lately trod.
No: with the common heap I scorn to fall—
What if they pass'd me to the Trojan wall,
While I decline to yonder path, that leads
To Ida's forests and surrounding shades?
So may I reach, conceal'd, the cooling flood,
From my tired body wash the dirt and blood,
As soon as night her dusky veil extends,
Return in safety to my Trojan friends.
What if?—But wherefore all this vain debate?
Stand I to doubt, within the reach of fate?
Even now perhaps, ere yet I turn the wall,

The fierce Achilles sees me, and I fall:
Such is his swiftness, 'tis in vain to fly,
And such his valour, that who stands must die.
Howe'er 'tis better, fighting for the state,
Here, and in public view, to meet my fate.
Yet sure he too is mortal; he may feel
(Like all the sons of earth) the force of steel.
One only soul informs that dreadful frame:
And Jove's sole favour gives him all his fame."

He said, and stood, collected, in his might;
And all his beating bosom claim'd the fight.
So from some deep-grown wood a panther starts,
Roused from his thicket by a storm of darts:
Untaught to fear or fly, he hears the sounds
Of shouting hunters, and of clamorous hounds;
Though struck, though wounded, scarce perceives the pain;
And the barb'd javelin stings his breast in vain:
On their whole war, untamed, the savage flies;
And tears his hunter, or beneath him dies.
Not less resolved, Antenor's valiant heir
Confronts Achilles, and awaits the war,
Disdainful of retreat: high held before,
His shield (a broad circumference) he bore;
Then graceful as he stood, in act to throw
The lifted javelin, thus bespoke the foe:

"How proud Achilles glories in his fame!
And hopes this day to sink the Trojan name
Beneath her ruins! Know, that hope is vain;
A thousand woes, a thousand toils remain.
Parents and children our just arms employ,
And strong and many are the sons of Troy.
Great as thou art, even thou may'st stain with gore
These Phrygian fields, and press a foreign shore."

He said: with matchless force the javelin flung
Smote on his knee; the hollow cuishes rung
Beneath the pointed steel; but safe from harms
He stands impassive in the ethereal arms.
Then fiercely rushing on the daring foe,
His lifted arm prepares the fatal blow:
But, jealous of his fame, Apollo shrouds
The god-like Trojan in a veil of clouds.
Safe from pursuit, and shut from mortal view,
Dismiss'd with fame, the favoured youth withdrew.
Meanwhile the god, to cover their escape,
Assumes Agenor's habit, voice and shape,

Flies from the furious chief in this disguise;
The furious chief still follows where he flies.
Now o'er the fields they stretch with lengthen'd strides,
Now urge the course where swift Scamander glides:
The god, now distant scarce a stride before,
Tempts his pursuit, and wheels about the shore;
While all the flying troops their speed employ,
And pour on heaps into the walls of Troy:
No stop, no stay; no thought to ask, or tell,
Who 'scaped by flight, or who by battle fell.
'Twas tumult all, and violence of flight;
And sudden joy confused, and mix'd affright.
Pale Troy against Achilles shuts her gate:
And nations breathe, deliver'd from their fate.

BOOK XXII

ARGUMENT

THE DEATH OF HECTOR

The Trojans being safe within the walls, Hector only stays to oppose Achilles. Priam is struck at his approach, and tries to persuade his son to re-enter the town. Hecuba joins her entreaties, but in vain. Hector consults within himself what measures to take; but at the advance of Achilles, his resolution fails him, and he flies. Achilles pursues him thrice round the walls of Troy. The gods debate concerning the fate of Hector; at length Minerva descends to the aid of Achilles. She deludes Hector in the shape of Deiphobus; he stands the combat, and is slain. Achilles drags the dead body at his chariot in the sight of Priam and Hecuba. Their lamentations, tears, and despair. Their cries reach the ears of Andromache, who, ignorant of this, was retired into the inner part of the palace: she mounts up to the walls, and beholds her dead husband. She swoons at the spectacle. Her excess of grief and lamentation.

The thirtieth day still continues. The scene lies under the walls, and on the battlements of Troy.

Thus to their bulwarks, smit with panic fear,
The herded Ilians rush like driven deer:
There safe they wipe the briny drops away,
And drown in bowls the labours of the day.
Close to the walls, advancing o'er the fields
Beneath one roof of well-compacted shields,
March, bending on, the Greeks' embodied powers,
Far stretching in the shade of Trojan towers.
Great Hector singly stay'd: chain'd down by fate
There fix'd he stood before the Scaean gate;
Still his bold arms determined to employ,
The guardian still of long-defended Troy.

Apollo now to tired Achilles turns:
(The power confess'd in all his glory burns:)
"And what (he cries) has Peleus' son in view,
With mortal speed a godhead to pursue?
For not to thee to know the gods is given,
Unskill'd to trace the latent marks of heaven.
What boots thee now, that Troy forsook the plain?
Vain thy past labour, and thy present vain:
Safe in their walls are now her troops bestow'd,
While here thy frantic rage attacks a god."

The chief incensed—"Too partial god of day!
To check my conquests in the middle way:
How few in Ilion else had refuge found!
What gasping numbers now had bit the ground!
Thou robb'st me of a glory justly mine,
Powerful of godhead, and of fraud divine:
Mean fame, alas! for one of heavenly strain,
To cheat a mortal who repines in vain."

Then to the city, terrible and strong,
With high and haughty steps he tower'd along,
So the proud courser, victor of the prize,
To the near goal with double ardour flies.
Him, as he blazing shot across the field,
The careful eyes of Priam first beheld.
Not half so dreadful rises to the sight,
Through the thick gloom of some tempestuous night,
Orion's dog (the year when autumn weighs),
And o'er the feebler stars exerts his rays;
Terrific glory! for his burning breath
Taints the red air with fevers, plagues, and death.
So flamed his fiery mail. Then wept the sage:
He strikes his reverend head, now white with age;
He lifts his wither'd arms; obtests the skies;
He calls his much-loved son with feeble cries:
The son, resolved Achilles' force to dare,
Full at the Scaean gates expects the war;
While the sad father on the rampart stands,
And thus adjures him with extended hands:

"Ah stay not, stay not! guardless and alone;
Hector! my loved, my dearest, bravest son!
Methinks already I behold thee slain,
And stretch'd beneath that fury of the plain.
Implacable Achilles! might'st thou be
To all the gods no dearer than to me!

Thee, vultures wild should scatter round the shore.
And bloody dogs grow fiercer from thy gore.
How many valiant sons I late enjoy'd,
Valiant in vain! by thy cursed arm destroy'd:
Or, worse than slaughtered, sold in distant isles
To shameful bondage, and unworthy toils.
Two, while I speak, my eyes in vain explore,
Two from one mother sprung, my Polydore,
And loved Lycaon; now perhaps no more!
Oh! if in yonder hostile camp they live,
What heaps of gold, what treasures would I give!
(Their grandsire's wealth, by right of birth their own,
Consign'd his daughter with Lelegia's throne:)
But if (which Heaven forbid) already lost,
All pale they wander on the Stygian coast;
What sorrows then must their sad mother know,
What anguish I? unutterable woe!
Yet less that anguish, less to her, to me,
Less to all Troy, if not deprived of thee.
Yet shun Achilles! enter yet the wall;
And spare thyself, thy father, spare us all!
Save thy dear life; or, if a soul so brave
Neglect that thought, thy dearer glory save.
Pity, while yet I live, these silver hairs;
While yet thy father feels the woes he bears,
Yet cursed with sense! a wretch, whom in his rage
(All trembling on the verge of helpless age)
Great Jove has placed, sad spectacle of pain!
The bitter dregs of fortune's cup to drain:
To fill with scenes of death his closing eyes,
And number all his days by miseries!
My heroes slain, my bridal bed o'erturn'd,
My daughters ravish'd, and my city burn'd,
My bleeding infants dash'd against the floor;
These I have yet to see, perhaps yet more!
Perhaps even I, reserved by angry fate,
The last sad relic of my ruin'd state,
(Dire pomp of sovereign wretchedness!) must fall,
And stain the pavement of my regal hall;
Where famish'd dogs, late guardians of my door,
Shall lick their mangled master's spatter'd gore.
Yet for my sons I thank ye, gods! 'tis well;
Well have they perish'd, for in fight they fell.
Who dies in youth and vigour, dies the best,
Struck through with wounds, all honest on the breast.
But when the fates, in fulness of their rage,
Spurn the hoar head of unresisting age,
In dust the reverend lineaments deform,

And pour to dogs the life-blood scarcely warm:
This, this is misery! the last, the worse,
That man can feel! man, fated to be cursed!"

He said, and acting what no words could say,
Rent from his head the silver locks away.
With him the mournful mother bears a part;
Yet all her sorrows turn not Hector's heart.
The zone unbraced, her bosom she display'd;
And thus, fast-falling the salt tears, she said:

"Have mercy on me, O my son! revere
The words of age; attend a parent's prayer!
If ever thee in these fond arms I press'd,
Or still'd thy infant clamours at this breast;
Ah do not thus our helpless years forego,
But, by our walls secured, repel the foe.
Against his rage if singly thou proceed,
Should'st thou, (but Heaven avert it!) should'st thou bleed,
Nor must thy corse lie honour'd on the bier,
Nor spouse, nor mother, grace thee with a tear!
Far from our pious rites those dear remains
Must feast the vultures on the naked plains."

So they, while down their cheeks the torrents roll;
But fix'd remains the purpose of his soul;
Resolved he stands, and with a fiery glance
Expects the hero's terrible advance.
So, roll'd up in his den, the swelling snake
Beholds the traveller approach the brake;
When fed with noxious herbs his turgid veins
Have gather'd half the poisons of the plains;
He burns, he stiffens with collected ire,
And his red eyeballs glare with living fire.
Beneath a turret, on his shield reclined,
He stood, and question'd thus his mighty mind:

"Where lies my way? to enter in the wall?
Honour and shame the ungenerous thought recall:
Shall proud Polydamas before the gate
Proclaim, his counsels are obey'd too late,
Which timely follow'd but the former night,
What numbers had been saved by Hector's flight?
That wise advice rejected with disdain,
I feel my folly in my people slain.
Methinks my suffering country's voice I hear,
But most her worthless sons insult my ear,
On my rash courage charge the chance of war,

And blame those virtues which they cannot share.
No—if I e'er return, return I must
Glorious, my country's terror laid in dust:
Or if I perish, let her see me fall
In field at least, and fighting for her wall.
And yet suppose these measures I forego,
Approach unarm'd, and parley with the foe,
The warrior-shield, the helm, and lance, lay down.
And treat on terms of peace to save the town:
The wife withheld, the treasure ill-detain'd
(Cause of the war, and grievance of the land)
With honourable justice to restore:
And add half Ilion's yet remaining store,
Which Troy shall, sworn, produce; that injured Greece
May share our wealth, and leave our walls in peace.
But why this thought? Unarm'd if I should go,
What hope of mercy from this vengeful foe,
But woman-like to fall, and fall without a blow?
We greet not here, as man conversing man,
Met at an oak, or journeying o'er a plain;
No season now for calm familiar talk,
Like youths and maidens in an evening walk:
War is our business, but to whom is given
To die, or triumph, that, determine Heaven!"

Thus pondering, like a god the Greek drew nigh;
His dreadful plumage nodded from on high;
The Pelian javelin, in his better hand,
Shot trembling rays that glitter'd o'er the land;
And on his breast the beamy splendour shone,
Like Jove's own lightning, or the rising sun.
As Hector sees, unusual terrors rise,
Struck by some god, he fears, recedes, and flies.
He leaves the gates, he leaves the wall behind:
Achilles follows like the winged wind.
Thus at the panting dove a falcon flies
(The swiftest racer of the liquid skies),
Just when he holds, or thinks he holds his prey,
Obliquely wheeling through the aerial way,
With open beak and shrilling cries he springs,
And aims his claws, and shoots upon his wings:
No less fore-right the rapid chase they held,
One urged by fury, one by fear impell'd:
Now circling round the walls their course maintain,
Where the high watch-tower overlooks the plain;
Now where the fig-trees spread their umbrage broad,
(A wider compass,) smoke along the road.
Next by Scamander's double source they bound,

Where two famed fountains burst the parted ground;
This hot through scorching clefts is seen to rise,
With exhalations steaming to the skies;
That the green banks in summer's heat o'erflows,
Like crystal clear, and cold as winter snows:
Each gushing fount a marble cistern fills,
Whose polish'd bed receives the falling rills;
Where Trojan dames (ere yet alarm'd by Greece)
Wash'd their fair garments in the days of peace.
By these they pass'd, one chasing, one in flight:
(The mighty fled, pursued by stronger might:)
Swift was the course; no vulgar prize they play,
No vulgar victim must reward the day:
(Such as in races crown the speedy strife:)
The prize contended was great Hector's life.
As when some hero's funerals are decreed
In grateful honour of the mighty dead;
Where high rewards the vigorous youth inflame
(Some golden tripod, or some lovely dame)
The panting coursers swiftly turn the goal,
And with them turns the raised spectator's soul:
Thus three times round the Trojan wall they fly.
The gazing gods lean forward from the sky;
To whom, while eager on the chase they look,
The sire of mortals and immortals spoke:

"Unworthy sight! the man beloved of heaven,
Behold, inglorious round yon city driven!
My heart partakes the generous Hector's pain;
Hector, whose zeal whole hecatombs has slain,
Whose grateful fumes the gods received with joy,
From Ida's summits, and the towers of Troy:
Now see him flying; to his fears resign'd,
And fate, and fierce Achilles, close behind.
Consult, ye powers! ('tis worthy your debate)
Whether to snatch him from impending fate,
Or let him bear, by stern Pelides slain,
(Good as he is) the lot imposed on man."

Then Pallas thus: "Shall he whose vengeance forms
The forky bolt, and blackens heaven with storms,
Shall he prolong one Trojan's forfeit breath?
A man, a mortal, pre-ordain'd to death!
And will no murmurs fill the courts above?
No gods indignant blame their partial Jove?"

"Go then (return'd the sire) without delay,
Exert thy will: I give the Fates their way.

Swift at the mandate pleased Tritonia flies,
And stoops impetuous from the cleaving skies.

As through the forest, o'er the vale and lawn,
The well-breath'd beagle drives the flying fawn,
In vain he tries the covert of the brakes,
Or deep beneath the trembling thicket shakes;
Sure of the vapour in the tainted dews,
The certain hound his various maze pursues.
Thus step by step, where'er the Trojan wheel'd,
There swift Achilles compass'd round the field.
Oft as to reach the Dardan gates he bends,
And hopes the assistance of his pitying friends,
(Whose showering arrows, as he coursed below,
From the high turrets might oppress the foe,)
So oft Achilles turns him to the plain:
He eyes the city, but he eyes in vain.
As men in slumbers seem with speedy pace,
One to pursue, and one to lead the chase,
Their sinking limbs the fancied course forsake,
Nor this can fly, nor that can overtake:
No less the labouring heroes pant and strain:
While that but flies, and this pursues in vain.

What god, O muse, assisted Hector's force
With fate itself so long to hold the course?
Phoebus it was; who, in his latest hour,
Endued his knees with strength, his nerves with power:
And great Achilles, lest some Greek's advance
Should snatch the glory from his lifted lance,
Sign'd to the troops to yield his foe the way,
And leave untouch'd the honours of the day.

Jove lifts the golden balances, that show
The fates of mortal men, and things below:
Here each contending hero's lot he tries,
And weighs, with equal hand, their destinies.
Low sinks the scale surcharged with Hector's fate;
Heavy with death it sinks, and hell receives the weight.

Then Phoebus left him. Fierce Minerva flies
To stern Pelides, and triumphing, cries:
"O loved of Jove! this day our labours cease,
And conquest blazes with full beams on Greece.
Great Hector falls; that Hector famed so far,
Drunk with renown, insatiable of war,
Falls by thy hand, and mine! nor force, nor flight,
Shall more avail him, nor his god of light.

See, where in vain he supplicates above,
Roll'd at the feet of unrelenting Jove;
Rest here: myself will lead the Trojan on,
And urge to meet the fate he cannot shun."

Her voice divine the chief with joyful mind
Obey'd; and rested, on his lance reclined
While like Deiphobus the martial dame
(Her face, her gesture, and her arms the same),
In show an aid, by hapless Hector's side
Approach'd, and greets him thus with voice belied:

"Too long, O Hector! have I borne the sight
Of this distress, and sorrow'd in thy flight:
It fits us now a noble stand to make,
And here, as brothers, equal fates partake."

Then he: "O prince! allied in blood and fame,
Dearer than all that own a brother's name;
Of all that Hecuba to Priam bore,
Long tried, long loved: much loved, but honoured more!
Since you, of all our numerous race alone
Defend my life, regardless of your own."

Again the goddess: "Much my father's prayer,
And much my mother's, press'd me to forbear:
My friends embraced my knees, adjured my stay,
But stronger love impell'd, and I obey.
Come then, the glorious conflict let us try,
Let the steel sparkle, and the javelin fly;
Or let us stretch Achilles on the field,
Or to his arm our bloody trophies yield."

Fraudful she said; then swiftly march'd before:
The Dardan hero shuns his foe no more.
Sternly they met. The silence Hector broke:
His dreadful plumage nodded as he spoke:

"Enough, O son of Peleus! Troy has view'd
Her walls thrice circled, and her chief pursued.
But now some god within me bids me try
Thine, or my fate: I kill thee, or I die.
Yet on the verge of battle let us stay,
And for a moment's space suspend the day;
Let Heaven's high powers be call'd to arbitrate
The just conditions of this stern debate,
(Eternal witnesses of all below,
And faithful guardians of the treasured vow!)

To them I swear; if, victor in the strife,
Jove by these hands shall shed thy noble life,
No vile dishonour shall thy corse pursue;
Stripp'd of its arms alone (the conqueror's due)
The rest to Greece uninjured I'll restore:
Now plight thy mutual oath, I ask no more."

"Talk not of oaths (the dreadful chief replies,
While anger flash'd from his disdainful eyes),
Detested as thou art, and ought to be,
Nor oath nor pact Achilles plights with thee:
Such pacts as lambs and rabid wolves combine,
Such leagues as men and furious lions join,
To such I call the gods! one constant state
Of lasting rancour and eternal hate:
No thought but rage, and never-ceasing strife,
Till death extinguish rage, and thought, and life.
Rouse then thy forces this important hour,
Collect thy soul, and call forth all thy power.
No further subterfuge, no further chance;
'Tis Pallas, Pallas gives thee to my lance.
Each Grecian ghost, by thee deprived of breath,
Now hovers round, and calls thee to thy death."

He spoke, and launch'd his javelin at the foe;
But Hector shunn'd the meditated blow:
He stoop'd, while o'er his head the flying spear
Sang innocent, and spent its force in air.
Minerva watch'd it falling on the land,
Then drew, and gave to great Achilles' hand,
Unseen of Hector, who, elate with joy,
Now shakes his lance, and braves the dread of Troy.

"The life you boasted to that javelin given,
Prince! you have miss'd. My fate depends on Heaven,
To thee, presumptuous as thou art, unknown,
Or what must prove my fortune, or thy own.
Boasting is but an art, our fears to blind,
And with false terrors sink another's mind.
But know, whatever fate I am to try,
By no dishonest wound shall Hector die.
I shall not fall a fugitive at least,
My soul shall bravely issue from my breast.
But first, try thou my arm; and may this dart
End all my country's woes, deep buried in thy heart."

The weapon flew, its course unerring held,
Unerring, but the heavenly shield repell'd

The mortal dart; resulting with a bound
From off the ringing orb, it struck the ground.
Hector beheld his javelin fall in vain,
Nor other lance, nor other hope remain;
He calls Deiphobus, demands a spear—
In vain, for no Deiphobus was there.
All comfortless he stands: then, with a sigh;
"'Tis so—Heaven wills it, and my hour is nigh!
I deem'd Deiphobus had heard my call,
But he secure lies guarded in the wall.
A god deceived me; Pallas, 'twas thy deed,
Death and black fate approach! 'tis I must bleed.
No refuge now, no succour from above,
Great Jove deserts me, and the son of Jove,
Propitious once, and kind! Then welcome fate!
'Tis true I perish, yet I perish great:
Yet in a mighty deed I shall expire,
Let future ages hear it, and admire!"

Fierce, at the word, his weighty sword he drew,
And, all collected, on Achilles flew.
So Jove's bold bird, high balanced in the air,
Stoops from the clouds to truss the quivering hare.
Nor less Achilles his fierce soul prepares:
Before his breast the flaming shield he bears,
Refulgent orb! above his fourfold cone
The gilded horse-hair sparkled in the sun.
Nodding at every step: (Vulcanian frame!)
And as he moved, his figure seem'd on flame.
As radiant Hesper shines with keener light,
Far-beaming o'er the silver host of night,
When all the starry train emblaze the sphere:
So shone the point of great Achilles' spear.
In his right hand he waves the weapon round,
Eyes the whole man, and meditates the wound;
But the rich mail Patroclus lately wore
Securely cased the warrior's body o'er.
One space at length he spies, to let in fate,
Where 'twixt the neck and throat the jointed plate
Gave entrance: through that penetrable part
Furious he drove the well-directed dart:
Nor pierced the windpipe yet, nor took the power
Of speech, unhappy! from thy dying hour.
Prone on the field the bleeding warrior lies,
While, thus triumphing, stern Achilles cries:

"At last is Hector stretch'd upon the plain,
Who fear'd no vengeance for Patroclus slain:

Then, prince! you should have fear'd, what now you feel;
Achilles absent was Achilles still:
Yet a short space the great avenger stayed,
Then low in dust thy strength and glory laid.
Peaceful he sleeps, with all our rites adorn'd,
For ever honour'd, and for ever mourn'd:
While cast to all the rage of hostile power,
Thee birds shall mangle, and the gods devour."

Then Hector, fainting at the approach of death:
"By thy own soul! by those who gave thee breath!
By all the sacred prevalence of prayer;
Ah, leave me not for Grecian dogs to tear!
The common rites of sepulture bestow,
To soothe a father's and a mother's woe:
Let their large gifts procure an urn at least,
And Hector's ashes in his country rest."

"No, wretch accursed! relentless he replies;
(Flames, as he spoke, shot flashing from his eyes;)
Not those who gave me breath should bid me spare,
Nor all the sacred prevalence of prayer.
Could I myself the bloody banquet join!
No—to the dogs that carcase I resign.
Should Troy, to bribe me, bring forth all her store,
And giving thousands, offer thousands more;
Should Dardan Priam, and his weeping dame,
Drain their whole realm to buy one funeral flame:
Their Hector on the pile they should not see,
Nor rob the vultures of one limb of thee."

Then thus the chief his dying accents drew:
"Thy rage, implacable! too well I knew:
The Furies that relentless breast have steel'd,
And cursed thee with a heart that cannot yield.
Yet think, a day will come, when fate's decree
And angry gods shall wreak this wrong on thee;
Phoebus and Paris shall avenge my fate,
And stretch thee here before the Scaean gate."

He ceased. The Fates suppress'd his labouring breath,
And his eyes stiffen'd at the hand of death;
To the dark realm the spirit wings its way,
(The manly body left a load of clay,)
And plaintive glides along the dreary coast,
A naked, wandering, melancholy ghost!

Achilles, musing as he roll'd his eyes

O'er the dead hero, thus unheard, replies:
"Die thou the first! When Jove and heaven ordain,
I follow thee"—He said, and stripp'd the slain.
Then forcing backward from the gaping wound
The reeking javelin, cast it on the ground.
The thronging Greeks behold with wondering eyes
His manly beauty and superior size;
While some, ignobler, the great dead deface
With wounds ungenerous, or with taunts disgrace:

"How changed that Hector, who like Jove of late
Sent lightning on our fleets, and scatter'd fate!"

High o'er the slain the great Achilles stands,
Begirt with heroes and surrounding bands;
And thus aloud, while all the host attends:
"Princes and leaders! countrymen and friends!
Since now at length the powerful will of heaven
The dire destroyer to our arm has given,
Is not Troy fallen already? Haste, ye powers!
See, if already their deserted towers
Are left unmann'd; or if they yet retain
The souls of heroes, their great Hector slain.
But what is Troy, or glory what to me?
Or why reflects my mind on aught but thee,
Divine Patroclus! Death hath seal'd his eyes;
Unwept, unhonour'd, uninterr'd he lies!
Can his dear image from my soul depart,
Long as the vital spirit moves my heart?
If in the melancholy shades below,
The flames of friends and lovers cease to glow,
Yet mine shall sacred last; mine, undecay'd,
Burn on through death, and animate my shade.
Meanwhile, ye sons of Greece, in triumph bring
The corpse of Hector, and your paeans sing.
Be this the song, slow-moving toward the shore,
"Hector is dead, and Ilion is no more."

Then his fell soul a thought of vengeance bred;
(Unworthy of himself, and of the dead;)
The nervous ancles bored, his feet he bound
With thongs inserted through the double wound;
These fix'd up high behind the rolling wain,
His graceful head was trail'd along the plain.
Proud on his car the insulting victor stood,
And bore aloft his arms, distilling blood.
He smites the steeds; the rapid chariot flies;
The sudden clouds of circling dust arise.

Now lost is all that formidable air;
The face divine, and long-descending hair,
Purple the ground, and streak the sable sand;
Deform'd, dishonour'd, in his native land,
Given to the rage of an insulting throng,
And, in his parents' sight, now dragg'd along!

The mother first beheld with sad survey;
She rent her tresses, venerable grey,
And cast, far off, the regal veils away.
With piercing shrieks his bitter fate she moans,
While the sad father answers groans with groans
Tears after tears his mournful cheeks o'erflow,
And the whole city wears one face of woe:
No less than if the rage of hostile fires.
From her foundations curling to her spires,
O'er the proud citadel at length should rise,
And the last blaze send Ilion to the skies.
The wretched monarch of the falling state,
Distracted, presses to the Dardan gate.
Scarce the whole people stop his desperate course,
While strong affliction gives the feeble force:
Grief tears his heart, and drives him to and fro,
In all the raging impotence of woe.
At length he roll'd in dust, and thus begun,
Imploring all, and naming one by one:
"Ah! let me, let me go where sorrow calls;
I, only I, will issue from your walls
(Guide or companion, friends! I ask ye none),
And bow before the murderer of my son.
My grief perhaps his pity may engage;
Perhaps at least he may respect my age.
He has a father too; a man like me;
One, not exempt from age and misery
(Vigorous no more, as when his young embrace
Begot this pest of me, and all my race).
How many valiant sons, in early bloom,
Has that cursed hand send headlong to the tomb!
Thee, Hector! last: thy loss (divinely brave)
Sinks my sad soul with sorrow to the grave.
O had thy gentle spirit pass'd in peace,
The son expiring in the sire's embrace,
While both thy parents wept the fatal hour,
And, bending o'er thee, mix'd the tender shower!
Some comfort that had been, some sad relief,
To melt in full satiety of grief!"

Thus wail'd the father, grovelling on the ground,

And all the eyes of Ilion stream'd around.

Amidst her matrons Hecuba appears:
(A mourning princess, and a train in tears;)
"Ah why has Heaven prolong'd this hated breath,
Patient of horrors, to behold thy death?
O Hector! late thy parents' pride and joy,
The boast of nations! the defence of Troy!
To whom her safety and her fame she owed;
Her chief, her hero, and almost her god!
O fatal change! become in one sad day
A senseless corse! inanimated clay!"

But not as yet the fatal news had spread
To fair Andromache, of Hector dead;
As yet no messenger had told his fate,
Not e'en his stay without the Scaean gate.
Far in the close recesses of the dome,
Pensive she plied the melancholy loom;
A growing work employ'd her secret hours,
Confusedly gay with intermingled flowers.
Her fair-haired handmaids heat the brazen urn,
The bath preparing for her lord's return
In vain; alas! her lord returns no more;
Unbathed he lies, and bleeds along the shore!
Now from the walls the clamours reach her ear,
And all her members shake with sudden fear:
Forth from her ivory hand the shuttle falls,
And thus, astonish'd, to her maids she calls:

"Ah follow me! (she cried) what plaintive noise
Invades my ear? 'Tis sure my mother's voice.
My faltering knees their trembling frame desert,
A pulse unusual flutters at my heart;
Some strange disaster, some reverse of fate
(Ye gods avert it!) threats the Trojan state.
Far be the omen which my thoughts suggest!
But much I fear my Hector's dauntless breast
Confronts Achilles; chased along the plain,
Shut from our walls! I fear, I fear him slain!
Safe in the crowd he ever scorn'd to wait,
And sought for glory in the jaws of fate:
Perhaps that noble heat has cost his breath,
Now quench'd for ever in the arms of death."

She spoke: and furious, with distracted pace,
Fears in her heart, and anguish in her face,
Flies through the dome (the maids her steps pursue),

And mounts the walls, and sends around her view.
Too soon her eyes the killing object found,
The godlike Hector dragg'd along the ground.
A sudden darkness shades her swimming eyes:
She faints, she falls; her breath, her colour flies.
Her hair's fair ornaments, the braids that bound,
The net that held them, and the wreath that crown'd,
The veil and diadem flew far away
(The gift of Venus on her bridal day).
Around a train of weeping sisters stands,
To raise her sinking with assistant hands.
Scarce from the verge of death recall'd, again
She faints, or but recovers to complain.

"O wretched husband of a wretched wife!
Born with one fate, to one unhappy life!
For sure one star its baneful beam display'd
On Priam's roof, and Hippoplacia's shade.
From different parents, different climes we came.
At different periods, yet our fate the same!
Why was my birth to great Aetion owed,
And why was all that tender care bestow'd?
Would I had never been!—O thou, the ghost
Of my dead husband! miserably lost!
Thou to the dismal realms for ever gone!
And I abandon'd, desolate, alone!
An only child, once comfort of my pains,
Sad product now of hapless love, remains!
No more to smile upon his sire; no friend
To help him now! no father to defend!
For should he 'scape the sword, the common doom,
What wrongs attend him, and what griefs to come!
Even from his own paternal roof expell'd,
Some stranger ploughs his patrimonial field.
The day, that to the shades the father sends,
Robs the sad orphan of his father's friends:
He, wretched outcast of mankind! appears
For ever sad, for ever bathed in tears;
Amongst the happy, unregarded, he
Hangs on the robe, or trembles at the knee,
While those his father's former bounty fed
Nor reach the goblet, nor divide the bread:
The kindest but his present wants allay,
To leave him wretched the succeeding day.
Frugal compassion! Heedless, they who boast
Both parents still, nor feel what he has lost,
Shall cry, 'Begone! thy father feasts not here:'
The wretch obeys, retiring with a tear.

Thus wretched, thus retiring all in tears,
To my sad soul Astyanax appears!
Forced by repeated insults to return,
And to his widow'd mother vainly mourn:
He, who, with tender delicacy bred,
With princes sported, and on dainties fed,
And when still evening gave him up to rest,
Sunk soft in down upon the nurse's breast,
Must—ah what must he not? Whom Ilion calls
Astyanax, from her well-guarded walls,
Is now that name no more, unhappy boy!
Since now no more thy father guards his Troy.
But thou, my Hector, liest exposed in air,
Far from thy parents' and thy consort's care;
Whose hand in vain, directed by her love,
The martial scarf and robe of triumph wove.
Now to devouring flames be these a prey,
Useless to thee, from this accursed day!
Yet let the sacrifice at least be paid,
An honour to the living, not the dead!"

So spake the mournful dame: her matrons hear,
Sigh back her sighs, and answer tear with tear.

BOOK XXIII

ARGUMENT

FUNERAL GAMES IN HONOUR OF PATROCLUS

Achilles and the Myrmidons do honours to the body of Patroclus. After the funeral feast he retires to the sea-shore, where, falling asleep, the ghost of his friend appears to him, and demands the rites of burial; the next morning the soldiers are sent with mules and waggons to fetch wood for the pyre. The funeral procession, and the offering their hair to the dead. Achilles sacrifices several animals, and lastly twelve Trojan captives, at the pile; then sets fire to it. He pays libations to the Winds, which (at the instance of Iris) rise, and raise the flames. When the pile has burned all night, they gather the bones, place them in an urn of gold, and raise the tomb. Achilles institutes the funeral games: the chariot-race, the fight of the caestus, the wrestling, the foot-race, the single combat, the discus, the shooting with arrows, the darting the javelin: the various descriptions of which, and the various success of the several antagonists, make the greatest part of the book.

In this book ends the thirtieth day. The night following, the ghost of Patroclus appears to Achilles: the one-and-thirtieth day is employed in felling the timber for the pile: the two-and-thirtieth in burning it; and the three-and-thirtieth in the games. The scene is generally on the sea-shore.

Thus humbled in the dust, the pensive train
Through the sad city mourn'd her hero slain.
The body soil'd with dust, and black with gore,
Lies on broad Hellespont's resounding shore.
The Grecians seek their ships, and clear the strand,
All, but the martial Myrmidonian band:
These yet assembled great Achilles holds,
And the stern purpose of his mind unfolds:

"Not yet, my brave companions of the war,
Release your smoking coursers from the car;
But, with his chariot each in order led,
Perform due honours to Patroclus dead.
Ere yet from rest or food we seek relief,
Some rites remain, to glut our rage of grief."

The troops obey'd; and thrice in order led
(Achilles first) their coursers round the dead;
And thrice their sorrows and laments renew;
Tears bathe their arms, and tears the sands bedew.
For such a warrior Thetis aids their woe,
Melts their strong hearts, and bids their eyes to flow.
But chief, Pelides: thick-succeeding sighs
Burst from his heart, and torrents from his eyes:
His slaughtering hands, yet red with blood, he laid
On his dead friend's cold breast, and thus he said:

"All hail, Patroclus! let thy honour'd ghost
Hear, and rejoice on Pluto's dreary coast;
Behold! Achilles' promise is complete;
The bloody Hector stretch'd before thy feet.
Lo! to the dogs his carcase I resign;
And twelve sad victims, of the Trojan line,
Sacred to vengeance, instant shall expire;
Their lives effused around thy funeral pyre."

Gloomy he said, and (horrible to view)
Before the bier the bleeding Hector threw,
Prone on the dust. The Myrmidons around
Unbraced their armour, and the steeds unbound.
All to Achilles' sable ship repair,
Frequent and full, the genial feast to share.
Now from the well-fed swine black smokes aspire,
The bristly victims hissing o'er the fire:
The huge ox bellowing falls; with feebler cries
Expires the goat; the sheep in silence dies.
Around the hero's prostrate body flow'd,
In one promiscuous stream, the reeking blood.

And now a band of Argive monarchs brings
The glorious victor to the king of kings.
From his dead friend the pensive warrior went,
With steps unwilling, to the regal tent.
The attending heralds, as by office bound,
With kindled flames the tripod-vase surround:
To cleanse his conquering hands from hostile gore,
They urged in vain; the chief refused, and swore:

"No drop shall touch me, by almighty Jove!
The first and greatest of the gods above!
Till on the pyre I place thee; till I rear
The grassy mound, and clip thy sacred hair.
Some ease at least those pious rites may give,
And soothe my sorrows, while I bear to live.
Howe'er, reluctant as I am, I stay
And share your feast; but with the dawn of day,
(O king of men!) it claims thy royal care,
That Greece the warrior's funeral pile prepare,
And bid the forests fall: (such rites are paid
To heroes slumbering in eternal shade:)
Then, when his earthly part shall mount in fire,
Let the leagued squadrons to their posts retire."

He spoke: they hear him, and the word obey;
The rage of hunger and of thirst allay,
Then ease in sleep the labours of the day.
But great Pelides, stretch'd along the shore,
Where, dash'd on rocks, the broken billows roar,
Lies inly groaning; while on either hand
The martial Myrmidons confusedly stand.
Along the grass his languid members fall,
Tired with his chase around the Trojan wall;
Hush'd by the murmurs of the rolling deep,
At length he sinks in the soft arms of sleep.
When lo! the shade, before his closing eyes,
Of sad Patroclus rose, or seem'd to rise:
In the same robe he living wore, he came:
In stature, voice, and pleasing look, the same.
The form familiar hover'd o'er his head,
"And sleeps Achilles? (thus the phantom said:)
Sleeps my Achilles, his Patroclus dead?
Living, I seem'd his dearest, tenderest care,
But now forgot, I wander in the air.
Let my pale corse the rites of burial know,
And give me entrance in the realms below:
Till then the spirit finds no resting-place,
But here and there the unbodied spectres chase

The vagrant dead around the dark abode,
Forbid to cross the irremeable flood.
Now give thy hand; for to the farther shore
When once we pass, the soul returns no more:
When once the last funereal flames ascend,
No more shall meet Achilles and his friend;
No more our thoughts to those we loved make known;
Or quit the dearest, to converse alone.
Me fate has sever'd from the sons of earth,
The fate fore-doom'd that waited from my birth:
Thee too it waits; before the Trojan wall
Even great and godlike thou art doom'd to fall.
Hear then; and as in fate and love we join,
Ah suffer that my bones may rest with thine!
Together have we lived; together bred,
One house received us, and one table fed;
That golden urn, thy goddess-mother gave,
May mix our ashes in one common grave."

"And is it thou? (he answers) To my sight
Once more return'st thou from the realms of night?
O more than brother! Think each office paid,
Whate'er can rest a discontented shade;
But grant one last embrace, unhappy boy!
Afford at least that melancholy joy."

He said, and with his longing arms essay'd
In vain to grasp the visionary shade!
Like a thin smoke he sees the spirit fly,
And hears a feeble, lamentable cry.
Confused he wakes; amazement breaks the bands
Of golden sleep, and starting from the sands,
Pensive he muses with uplifted hands:

"'Tis true, 'tis certain; man, though dead, retains
Part of himself; the immortal mind remains:
The form subsists without the body's aid,
Aerial semblance, and an empty shade!
This night my friend, so late in battle lost,
Stood at my side, a pensive, plaintive ghost:
Even now familiar, as in life, he came;
Alas! how different! yet how like the same!"

Thus while he spoke, each eye grew big with tears:
And now the rosy-finger'd morn appears,
Shows every mournful face with tears o'erspread,
And glares on the pale visage of the dead.
But Agamemnon, as the rites demand,

With mules and waggons sends a chosen band
To load the timber, and the pile to rear;
A charge consign'd to Merion's faithful care.
With proper instruments they take the road,
Axes to cut, and ropes to sling the load.
First march the heavy mules, securely slow,
O'er hills, o'er dales, o'er crags, o'er rocks they go:
Jumping, high o'er the shrubs of the rough ground,
Rattle the clattering cars, and the shock'd axles bound
But when arrived at Ida's spreading woods,
(Fair Ida, water'd with descending floods,)
Loud sounds the axe, redoubling strokes on strokes;
On all sides round the forest hurls her oaks
Headlong. Deep echoing groan the thickets brown;
Then rustling, crackling, crashing, thunder down.
The wood the Grecians cleave, prepared to burn;
And the slow mules the same rough road return
The sturdy woodmen equal burdens bore
(Such charge was given them) to the sandy shore;
There on the spot which great Achilles show'd,
They eased their shoulders, and disposed the load;
Circling around the place, where times to come
Shall view Patroclus' and Achilles' tomb.
The hero bids his martial troops appear
High on their cars in all the pomp of war;
Each in refulgent arms his limbs attires,
All mount their chariots, combatants and squires.
The chariots first proceed, a shining train;
Then clouds of foot that smoke along the plain;
Next these the melancholy band appear;
Amidst, lay dead Patroclus on the bier;
O'er all the corse their scattered locks they throw;
Achilles next, oppress'd with mighty woe,
Supporting with his hands the hero's head,
Bends o'er the extended body of the dead.
Patroclus decent on the appointed ground
They place, and heap the sylvan pile around.
But great Achilles stands apart in prayer,
And from his head divides the yellow hair;
Those curling locks which from his youth he vow'd,
And sacred grew, to Sperchius' honour'd flood:
Then sighing, to the deep his locks he cast,
And roll'd his eyes around the watery waste:

"Sperchius! whose waves in mazy errors lost
Delightful roll along my native coast!
To whom we vainly vow'd, at our return,
These locks to fall, and hecatombs to burn:

Full fifty rams to bleed in sacrifice,
Where to the day thy silver fountains rise,
And where in shade of consecrated bowers
Thy altars stand, perfumed with native flowers!
So vow'd my father, but he vow'd in vain;
No more Achilles sees his native plain;
In that vain hope these hairs no longer grow,
Patroclus bears them to the shades below."

Thus o'er Patroclus while the hero pray'd,
On his cold hand the sacred lock he laid.
Once more afresh the Grecian sorrows flow:
And now the sun had set upon their woe;
But to the king of men thus spoke the chief:
"Enough, Atrides! give the troops relief:
Permit the mourning legions to retire,
And let the chiefs alone attend the pyre;
The pious care be ours, the dead to burn—"
He said: the people to their ships return:
While those deputed to inter the slain
Heap with a rising pyramid the plain.
A hundred foot in length, a hundred wide,
The growing structure spreads on every side;
High on the top the manly corse they lay,
And well-fed sheep and sable oxen slay:
Achilles covered with their fat the dead,
And the piled victims round the body spread;
Then jars of honey, and of fragrant oil,
Suspends around, low-bending o'er the pile.
Four sprightly coursers, with a deadly groan
Pour forth their lives, and on the pyre are thrown.
Of nine large dogs, domestic at his board,
Fall two, selected to attend their lord,
Then last of all, and horrible to tell,
Sad sacrifice! twelve Trojan captives fell.
On these the rage of fire victorious preys,
Involves and joins them in one common blaze.
Smear'd with the bloody rites, he stands on high,
And calls the spirit with a dreadful cry:

"All hail, Patroclus! let thy vengeful ghost
Hear, and exult, on Pluto's dreary coast.
Behold Achilles' promise fully paid,
Twelve Trojan heroes offer'd to thy shade;
But heavier fates on Hector's corse attend,
Saved from the flames, for hungry dogs to rend."

So spake he, threatening: but the gods made vain

His threat, and guard inviolate the slain:
Celestial Venus hover'd o'er his head,
And roseate unguents, heavenly fragrance! shed:
She watch'd him all the night and all the day,
And drove the bloodhounds from their destined prey.
Nor sacred Phoebus less employ'd his care;
He pour'd around a veil of gather'd air,
And kept the nerves undried, the flesh entire,
Against the solar beam and Sirian fire.

Nor yet the pile, where dead Patroclus lies,
Smokes, nor as yet the sullen flames arise;
But, fast beside, Achilles stood in prayer,
Invoked the gods whose spirit moves the air,
And victims promised, and libations cast,
To gentle Zephyr and the Boreal blast:
He call'd the aerial powers, along the skies
To breathe, and whisper to the fires to rise.
The winged Iris heard the hero's call,
And instant hasten'd to their airy hall,
Where in old Zephyr's open courts on high,
Sat all the blustering brethren of the sky.
She shone amidst them, on her painted bow;
The rocky pavement glitter'd with the show.
All from the banquet rise, and each invites
The various goddess to partake the rites.
"Not so (the dame replied), I haste to go
To sacred Ocean, and the floods below:
Even now our solemn hecatombs attend,
And heaven is feasting on the world's green end
With righteous Ethiops (uncorrupted train!)
Far on the extremest limits of the main.
But Peleus' son entreats, with sacrifice,
The western spirit, and the north, to rise!
Let on Patroclus' pile your blast be driven,
And bear the blazing honours high to heaven."

Swift as the word she vanish'd from their view;
Swift as the word the winds tumultuous flew;
Forth burst the stormy band with thundering roar,
And heaps on heaps the clouds are toss'd before.
To the wide main then stooping from the skies,
The heaving deeps in watery mountains rise:
Troy feels the blast along her shaking walls,
Till on the pile the gather'd tempest falls.
The structure crackles in the roaring fires,
And all the night the plenteous flame aspires.
All night Achilles hails Patroclus' soul,

With large libations from the golden bowl.
As a poor father, helpless and undone,
Mourns o'er the ashes of an only son,
Takes a sad pleasure the last bones to burn,
And pours in tears, ere yet they close the urn:
So stay'd Achilles, circling round the shore,
So watch'd the flames, till now they flame no more.
'Twas when, emerging through the shades of night.
The morning planet told the approach of light;
And, fast behind, Aurora's warmer ray
O'er the broad ocean pour'd the golden day:
Then sank the blaze, the pile no longer burn'd,
And to their caves the whistling winds return'd:
Across the Thracian seas their course they bore;
The ruffled seas beneath their passage roar.

Then parting from the pile he ceased to weep,
And sank to quiet in the embrace of sleep,
Exhausted with his grief: meanwhile the crowd
Of thronging Grecians round Achilles stood;
The tumult waked him: from his eyes he shook
Unwilling slumber, and the chiefs bespoke:

"Ye kings and princes of the Achaian name!
First let us quench the yet remaining flame
With sable wine; then, as the rites direct,
The hero's bones with careful view select:
(Apart, and easy to be known they lie
Amidst the heap, and obvious to the eye:
The rest around the margin will be seen
Promiscuous, steeds and immolated men:)
These wrapp'd in double cauls of fat, prepare;
And in the golden vase dispose with care;
There let them rest with decent honour laid,
Till I shall follow to the infernal shade.
Meantime erect the tomb with pious hands,
A common structure on the humble sands:
Hereafter Greece some nobler work may raise,
And late posterity record our praise!"

The Greeks obey; where yet the embers glow,
Wide o'er the pile the sable wine they throw,
And deep subsides the ashy heap below.
Next the white bones his sad companions place,
With tears collected, in the golden vase.
The sacred relics to the tent they bore;
The urn a veil of linen covered o'er.
That done, they bid the sepulchre aspire,

And cast the deep foundations round the pyre;
High in the midst they heap the swelling bed
Of rising earth, memorial of the dead.

The swarming populace the chief detains,
And leads amidst a wide extent of plains;
There placed them round: then from the ships proceeds
A train of oxen, mules, and stately steeds,
Vases and tripods (for the funeral games),
Resplendent brass, and more resplendent dames.
First stood the prizes to reward the force
Of rapid racers in the dusty course:
A woman for the first, in beauty's bloom,
Skill'd in the needle, and the labouring loom;
And a large vase, where two bright handles rise,
Of twenty measures its capacious size.
The second victor claims a mare unbroke,
Big with a mule, unknowing of the yoke:
The third, a charger yet untouch'd by flame;
Four ample measures held the shining frame:
Two golden talents for the fourth were placed:
An ample double bowl contents the last.
These in fair order ranged upon the plain,
The hero, rising, thus address'd the train:

"Behold the prizes, valiant Greeks! decreed
To the brave rulers of the racing steed;
Prizes which none beside ourself could gain,
Should our immortal coursers take the plain;
(A race unrivall'd, which from ocean's god
Peleus received, and on his son bestow'd.)
But this no time our vigour to display;
Nor suit, with them, the games of this sad day:
Lost is Patroclus now, that wont to deck
Their flowing manes, and sleek their glossy neck.
Sad, as they shared in human grief, they stand,
And trail those graceful honours on the sand!
Let others for the noble task prepare,
Who trust the courser and the flying car."

Fired at his word the rival racers rise;
But far the first Eumelus hopes the prize,
Famed though Pieria for the fleetest breed,
And skill'd to manage the high-bounding steed.
With equal ardour bold Tydides swell'd,
The steeds of Tros beneath his yoke compell'd
(Which late obey'd the Dardan chiefs command,
When scarce a god redeem'd him from his hand).

Then Menelaus his Podargus brings,
And the famed courser of the king of kings:
Whom rich Echepolus (more rich than brave),
To 'scape the wars, to Agamemnon gave,
(Ćthe her name) at home to end his days;
Base wealth preferring to eternal praise.
Next him Antilochus demands the course
With beating heart, and cheers his Pylian horse.
Experienced Nestor gives his son the reins,
Directs his judgment, and his heat restrains;
Nor idly warns the hoary sire, nor hears
The prudent son with unattending ears.

"My son! though youthful ardour fire thy breast,
The gods have loved thee, and with arts have bless'd;
Neptune and Jove on thee conferr'd the skill
Swift round the goal to turn the flying wheel.
To guide thy conduct little precept needs;
But slow, and past their vigour, are my steeds.
Fear not thy rivals, though for swiftness known;
Compare those rivals' judgment and thy own:
It is not strength, but art, obtains the prize,
And to be swift is less than to be wise.
'Tis more by art than force of numerous strokes
The dexterous woodman shapes the stubborn oaks;
By art the pilot, through the boiling deep
And howling tempest, steers the fearless ship;
And 'tis the artist wins the glorious course;
Not those who trust in chariots and in horse.
In vain, unskilful to the goal they strive,
And short, or wide, the ungovern'd courser drive:
While with sure skill, though with inferior steeds,
The knowing racer to his end proceeds;
Fix'd on the goal his eye foreruns the course,
His hand unerring steers the steady horse,
And now contracts, or now extends the rein,
Observing still the foremost on the plain.
Mark then the goal, 'tis easy to be found;
Yon aged trunk, a cubit from the ground;
Of some once stately oak the last remains,
Or hardy fir, unperish'd with the rains:
Inclosed with stones, conspicuous from afar;
And round, a circle for the wheeling car.
(Some tomb perhaps of old, the dead to grace;
Or then, as now, the limit of a race.)
Bear close to this, and warily proceed,
A little bending to the left-hand steed;
But urge the right, and give him all the reins;

While thy strict hand his fellow's head restrains,
And turns him short; till, doubling as they roll,
The wheel's round naves appear to brush the goal.
Yet (not to break the car, or lame the horse)
Clear of the stony heap direct the course;
Lest through incaution failing, thou mayst be
A joy to others, a reproach to me.
So shalt thou pass the goal, secure of mind,
And leave unskilful swiftness far behind:
Though thy fierce rival drove the matchless steed
Which bore Adrastus, of celestial breed;
Or the famed race, through all the regions known,
That whirl'd the car of proud Laomedon."

Thus (nought unsaid) the much-advising sage
Concludes; then sat, stiff with unwieldy age.
Next bold Meriones was seen to rise,
The last, but not least ardent for the prize.
They mount their seats; the lots their place dispose
(Roll'd in his helmet, these Achilles throws).
Young Nestor leads the race: Eumelus then;
And next the brother of the king of men:
Thy lot, Meriones, the fourth was cast;
And, far the bravest, Diomed, was last.
They stand in order, an impatient train:
Pelides points the barrier on the plain,
And sends before old Phoenix to the place,
To mark the racers, and to judge the race.
At once the coursers from the barrier bound;
The lifted scourges all at once resound;
Their heart, their eyes, their voice, they send before;
And up the champaign thunder from the shore:
Thick, where they drive, the dusty clouds arise,
And the lost courser in the whirlwind flies;
Loose on their shoulders the long manes reclined,
Float in their speed, and dance upon the wind:
The smoking chariots, rapid as they bound,
Now seem to touch the sky, and now the ground.
While hot for fame, and conquest all their care,
(Each o'er his flying courser hung in air,)
Erect with ardour, poised upon the rein,
They pant, they stretch, they shout along the plain.
Now (the last compass fetch'd around the goal)
At the near prize each gathers all his soul,
Each burns with double hope, with double pain,
Tears up the shore, and thunders toward the main.
First flew Eumelus on Pheretian steeds;
With those of Tros bold Diomed succeeds:

Close on Eumelus' back they puff the wind,
And seem just mounting on his car behind;
Full on his neck he feels the sultry breeze,
And, hovering o'er, their stretching shadows sees.
Then had he lost, or left a doubtful prize;
But angry Phoebus to Tydides flies,
Strikes from his hand the scourge, and renders vain
His matchless horses' labour on the plain.
Rage fills his eye with anguish, to survey
Snatch'd from his hope the glories of the day.
The fraud celestial Pallas sees with pain,
Springs to her knight, and gives the scourge again,
And fills his steeds with vigour. At a stroke
She breaks his rival's chariot from the yoke:
No more their way the startled horses held;
The car reversed came rattling on the field;
Shot headlong from his seat, beside the wheel,
Prone on the dust the unhappy master fell;
His batter'd face and elbows strike the ground;
Nose, mouth, and front, one undistinguish'd wound:
Grief stops his voice, a torrent drowns his eyes:
Before him far the glad Tydides flies;
Minerva's spirit drives his matchless pace,
And crowns him victor of the labour'd race.

The next, though distant, Menelaus succeeds;
While thus young Nestor animates his steeds:
"Now, now, my generous pair, exert your force;
Not that we hope to match Tydides' horse,
Since great Minerva wings their rapid way,
And gives their lord the honours of the day;
But reach Atrides! shall his mare outgo
Your swiftness? vanquish'd by a female foe?
Through your neglect, if lagging on the plain
The last ignoble gift be all we gain,
No more shall Nestor's hand your food supply,
The old man's fury rises, and ye die.
Haste then: yon narrow road, before our sight,
Presents the occasion, could we use it right."

Thus he. The coursers at their master's threat
With quicker steps the sounding champaign beat.
And now Antilochus with nice survey
Observes the compass of the hollow way.
'Twas where, by force of wintry torrents torn,
Fast by the road a precipice was worn:
Here, where but one could pass, to shun the throng
The Spartan hero's chariot smoked along.

Close up the venturous youth resolves to keep,
Still edging near, and bears him toward the steep.
Atrides, trembling, casts his eye below,
And wonders at the rashness of his foe.
"Hold, stay your steeds—What madness thus to ride
This narrow way! take larger field (he cried),
Or both must fall."—Atrides cried in vain;
He flies more fast, and throws up all the rein.
Far as an able arm the disk can send,
When youthful rivals their full force extend,
So far, Antilochus! thy chariot flew
Before the king: he, cautious, backward drew
His horse compell'd; foreboding in his fears
The rattling ruin of the clashing cars,
The floundering coursers rolling on the plain,
And conquest lost through frantic haste to gain.
But thus upbraids his rival as he flies:
"Go, furious youth! ungenerous and unwise!
Go, but expect not I'll the prize resign;
Add perjury to fraud, and make it thine—"
Then to his steeds with all his force he cries,
"Be swift, be vigorous, and regain the prize!
Your rivals, destitute of youthful force,
With fainting knees shall labour in the course,
And yield the glory yours."—The steeds obey;
Already at their heels they wing their way,
And seem already to retrieve the day.

Meantime the Grecians in a ring beheld
The coursers bounding o'er the dusty field.
The first who mark'd them was the Cretan king;
High on a rising ground, above the ring,
The monarch sat: from whence with sure survey
He well observed the chief who led the way,
And heard from far his animating cries,
And saw the foremost steed with sharpen'd eyes;
On whose broad front a blaze of shining white,
Like the full moon, stood obvious to the sight.
He saw; and rising, to the Greeks begun:
"Are yonder horse discern'd by me alone?
Or can ye, all, another chief survey,
And other steeds than lately led the way?
Those, though the swiftest, by some god withheld,
Lie sure disabled in the middle field:
For, since the goal they doubled, round the plain
I search to find them, but I search in vain.
Perchance the reins forsook the driver's hand,
And, turn'd too short, he tumbled on the strand,

Shot from the chariot; while his coursers stray
With frantic fury from the destined way.
Rise then some other, and inform my sight,
For these dim eyes, perhaps, discern not right;
Yet sure he seems, to judge by shape and air,
The great Ćtolian chief, renown'd in war."

"Old man! (Oileus rashly thus replies)
Thy tongue too hastily confers the prize;
Of those who view the course, nor sharpest eyed,
Nor youngest, yet the readiest to decide.
Eumelus' steeds, high bounding in the chase,
Still, as at first, unrivall'd lead the race:
I well discern him, as he shakes the rein,
And hear his shouts victorious o'er the plain."

Thus he. Idomeneus, incensed, rejoin'd:
"Barbarous of words! and arrogant of mind!
Contentious prince, of all the Greeks beside
The last in merit, as the first in pride!
To vile reproach what answer can we make?
A goblet or a tripod let us stake,
And be the king the judge. The most unwise
Will learn their rashness, when they pay the price."

He said: and Ajax, by mad passion borne,
Stern had replied; fierce scorn enhancing scorn
To fell extremes. But Thetis' godlike son
Awful amidst them rose, and thus begun:

"Forbear, ye chiefs! reproachful to contend;
Much would ye blame, should others thus offend:
And lo! the approaching steeds your contest end."
No sooner had he spoke, but thundering near,
Drives, through a stream of dust, the charioteer.
High o'er his head the circling lash he wields:
His bounding horses scarcely touch the fields:
His car amidst the dusty whirlwind roll'd,
Bright with the mingled blaze of tin and gold,
Refulgent through the cloud: no eye could find
The track his flying wheels had left behind:
And the fierce coursers urged their rapid pace
So swift, it seem'd a flight, and not a race.
Now victor at the goal Tydides stands,
Quits his bright car, and springs upon the sands;
From the hot steeds the sweaty torrents stream;
The well-plied whip is hung athwart the beam:
With joy brave Sthenelus receives the prize,

The tripod-vase, and dame with radiant eyes:
These to the ships his train triumphant leads,
The chief himself unyokes the panting steeds.

Young Nestor follows (who by art, not force,
O'erpass'd Atrides) second in the course.
Behind, Atrides urged the race, more near
Than to the courser in his swift career
The following car, just touching with his heel
And brushing with his tail the whirling wheel:
Such, and so narrow now the space between
The rivals, late so distant on the green;
So soon swift Æthe her lost ground regain'd,
One length, one moment, had the race obtain'd.

Merion pursued, at greater distance still,
With tardier coursers, and inferior skill.
Last came, Admetus! thy unhappy son;
Slow dragged the steeds his batter'd chariot on:
Achilles saw, and pitying thus begun:

"Behold! the man whose matchless art surpass'd
The sons of Greece! the ablest, yet the last!
Fortune denies, but justice bids us pay
(Since great Tydides bears the first away)
To him the second honours of the day."

The Greeks consent with loud-applauding cries,
And then Eumelus had received the prize,
But youthful Nestor, jealous of his fame,
The award opposes, and asserts his claim.
"Think not (he cries) I tamely will resign,
O Peleus' son! the mare so justly mine.
What if the gods, the skilful to confound,
Have thrown the horse and horseman to the ground?
Perhaps he sought not heaven by sacrifice,
And vows omitted forfeited the prize.
If yet (distinction to thy friend to show,
And please a soul desirous to bestow)
Some gift must grace Eumelus, view thy store
Of beauteous handmaids, steeds, and shining ore;
An ample present let him thence receive,
And Greece shall praise thy generous thirst to give.
But this my prize I never shall forego;
This, who but touches, warriors! is my foe."

Thus spake the youth; nor did his words offend;
Pleased with the well-turn'd flattery of a friend,

Achilles smiled: "The gift proposed (he cried),
Antilochus! we shall ourself provide.
With plates of brass the corslet cover'd o'er,
(The same renown'd Asteropaeus wore,)
Whose glittering margins raised with silver shine,
(No vulgar gift,) Eumelus! shall be thine."

He said: Automedon at his command
The corslet brought, and gave it to his hand.
Distinguish'd by his friend, his bosom glows
With generous joy: then Menelaus rose;
The herald placed the sceptre in his hands,
And still'd the clamour of the shouting bands.
Not without cause incensed at Nestor's son,
And inly grieving, thus the king begun:

"The praise of wisdom, in thy youth obtain'd,
An act so rash, Antilochus! has stain'd.
Robb'd of my glory and my just reward,
To you, O Grecians! be my wrong declared:
So not a leader shall our conduct blame,
Or judge me envious of a rival's fame.
But shall not we, ourselves, the truth maintain?
What needs appealing in a fact so plain?
What Greek shall blame me, if I bid thee rise,
And vindicate by oath th' ill-gotten prize?
Rise if thou darest, before thy chariot stand,
The driving scourge high-lifted in thy hand;
And touch thy steeds, and swear thy whole intent
Was but to conquer, not to circumvent.
Swear by that god whose liquid arms surround
The globe, and whose dread earthquakes heave the ground!"

The prudent chief with calm attention heard;
Then mildly thus: "Excuse, if youth have err'd;
Superior as thou art, forgive the offence,
Nor I thy equal, or in years, or sense.
Thou know'st the errors of unripen'd age,
Weak are its counsels, headlong is its rage.
The prize I quit, if thou thy wrath resign;
The mare, or aught thou ask'st, be freely thine
Ere I become (from thy dear friendship torn)
Hateful to thee, and to the gods forsworn."

So spoke Antilochus; and at the word
The mare contested to the king restored.
Joy swells his soul: as when the vernal grain
Lifts the green ear above the springing plain,

The fields their vegetable life renew,
And laugh and glitter with the morning dew;
Such joy the Spartan's shining face o'erspread,
And lifted his gay heart, while thus he said:

"Still may our souls, O generous youth! agree
'Tis now Atrides' turn to yield to thee.
Rash heat perhaps a moment might control,
Not break, the settled temper of thy soul.
Not but (my friend) 'tis still the wiser way
To waive contention with superior sway;
For ah! how few, who should like thee offend,
Like thee, have talents to regain the friend!
To plead indulgence, and thy fault atone,
Suffice thy father's merit and thy own:
Generous alike, for me, the sire and son
Have greatly suffer'd, and have greatly done.
I yield; that all may know, my soul can bend,
Nor is my pride preferr'd before my friend."

He said; and pleased his passion to command,
Resign'd the courser to Noemon's hand,
Friend of the youthful chief: himself content,
The shining charger to his vessel sent.
The golden talents Merion next obtain'd;
The fifth reward, the double bowl, remain'd.
Achilles this to reverend Nestor bears.
And thus the purpose of his gift declares:
"Accept thou this, O sacred sire! (he said)
In dear memorial of Patroclus dead;
Dead and for ever lost Patroclus lies,
For ever snatch'd from our desiring eyes!
Take thou this token of a grateful heart,
Though 'tis not thine to hurl the distant dart,
The quoit to toss, the ponderous mace to wield,
Or urge the race, or wrestle on the field:
Thy pristine vigour age has overthrown,
But left the glory of the past thy own."

He said, and placed the goblet at his side;
With joy the venerable king replied:

"Wisely and well, my son, thy words have proved
A senior honour'd, and a friend beloved!
Too true it is, deserted of my strength,
These wither'd arms and limbs have fail'd at length.
Oh! had I now that force I felt of yore,
Known through Buprasium and the Pylian shore!

Victorious then in every solemn game,
Ordain'd to Amarynces' mighty name;
The brave Epeians gave my glory way,
Ćtolians, Pylians, all resign'd the day.
I quell'd Clytomedes in fights of hand,
And backward hurl'd Ancaeus on the sand,
Surpass'd Iphyclus in the swift career,
Phyleus and Polydorus with the spear.
The sons of Actor won the prize of horse,
But won by numbers, not by art or force:
For the famed twins, impatient to survey
Prize after prize by Nestor borne away,
Sprung to their car; and with united pains
One lash'd the coursers, while one ruled the reins.
Such once I was! Now to these tasks succeeds
A younger race, that emulate our deeds:
I yield, alas! (to age who must not yield?)
Though once the foremost hero of the field.
Go thou, my son! by generous friendship led,
With martial honours decorate the dead:
While pleased I take the gift thy hands present,
(Pledge of benevolence, and kind intent,)
Rejoiced, of all the numerous Greeks, to see
Not one but honours sacred age and me:
Those due distinctions thou so well canst pay,
May the just gods return another day!"

Proud of the gift, thus spake the full of days:
Achilles heard him, prouder of the praise.

The prizes next are order'd to the field,
For the bold champions who the caestus wield.
A stately mule, as yet by toils unbroke,
Of six years' age, unconscious of the yoke,
Is to the circus led, and firmly bound;
Next stands a goblet, massy, large, and round.
Achilles rising, thus: "Let Greece excite
Two heroes equal to this hardy fight;
Who dare the foe with lifted arms provoke,
And rush beneath the long-descending stroke.
On whom Apollo shall the palm bestow,
And whom the Greeks supreme by conquest know,
This mule his dauntless labours shall repay,
The vanquish'd bear the massy bowl away."

This dreadful combat great Epeus chose;
High o'er the crowd, enormous bulk! he rose,
And seized the beast, and thus began to say:

"Stand forth some man, to bear the bowl away!
(Price of his ruin: for who dares deny
This mule my right; the undoubted victor I)
Others, 'tis own'd, in fields of battle shine,
But the first honours of this fight are mine;
For who excels in all? Then let my foe
Draw near, but first his certain fortune know;
Secure this hand shall his whole frame confound,
Mash all his bones, and all his body pound:
So let his friends be nigh, a needful train,
To heave the batter'd carcase off the plain."

The giant spoke; and in a stupid gaze
The host beheld him, silent with amaze!
'Twas thou, Euryalus! who durst aspire
To meet his might, and emulate thy sire,
The great Mecistheus; who in days of yore
In Theban games the noblest trophy bore,
(The games ordain'd dead OEdipus to grace,)
And singly vanquish the Cadmean race.
Him great Tydides urges to contend,
Warm with the hopes of conquest for his friend;
Officious with the cincture girds him round;
And to his wrist the gloves of death are bound.
Amid the circle now each champion stands,
And poises high in air his iron hands;
With clashing gauntlets now they fiercely close,
Their crackling jaws re-echo to the blows,
And painful sweat from all their members flows.
At length Epeus dealt a weighty blow
Full on the cheek of his unwary foe;
Beneath that ponderous arm's resistless sway
Down dropp'd he, nerveless, and extended lay.
As a large fish, when winds and waters roar,
By some huge billow dash'd against the shore,
Lies panting; not less batter'd with his wound,
The bleeding hero pants upon the ground.
To rear his fallen foe, the victor lends,
Scornful, his hand; and gives him to his friends;
Whose arms support him, reeling through the throng,
And dragging his disabled legs along;
Nodding, his head hangs down his shoulder o'er;
His mouth and nostrils pour the clotted gore;
Wrapp'd round in mists he lies, and lost to thought;
His friends receive the bowl, too dearly bought.

The third bold game Achilles next demands,
And calls the wrestlers to the level sands:

A massy tripod for the victor lies,
Of twice six oxen its reputed price;
And next, the loser's spirits to restore,
A female captive, valued but at four.
Scarce did the chief the vigorous strife prop
When tower-like Ajax and Ulysses rose.
Amid the ring each nervous rival stands,
Embracing rigid with implicit hands.
Close lock'd above, their heads and arms are mix'd:
Below, their planted feet at distance fix'd;
Like two strong rafters which the builder forms,
Proof to the wintry winds and howling storms,
Their tops connected, but at wider space
Fix'd on the centre stands their solid base.
Now to the grasp each manly body bends;
The humid sweat from every pore descends;
Their bones resound with blows: sides, shoulders, thighs
Swell to each gripe, and bloody tumours rise.
Nor could Ulysses, for his art renown'd,
O'erturn the strength of Ajax on the ground;
Nor could the strength of Ajax overthrow
The watchful caution of his artful foe.
While the long strife even tired the lookers on,
Thus to Ulysses spoke great Telamon:
"Or let me lift thee, chief, or lift thou me:
Prove we our force, and Jove the rest decree."

He said; and, straining, heaved him off the ground
With matchless strength; that time Ulysses found
The strength to evade, and where the nerves combine
His ankle struck: the giant fell supine;
Ulysses, following, on his bosom lies;
Shouts of applause run rattling through the skies.
Ajax to lift Ulysses next essays;
He barely stirr'd him, but he could not raise:
His knee lock'd fast, the foe's attempt denied;
And grappling close, they tumbled side by side.
Defiled with honourable dust they roll,
Still breathing strife, and unsubdued of soul:
Again they rage, again to combat rise;
When great Achilles thus divides the prize:

"Your noble vigour, O my friends, restrain;
Nor weary out your generous strength in vain.
Ye both have won: let others who excel,
Now prove that prowess you have proved so well."

The hero's words the willing chiefs obey,

From their tired bodies wipe the dust away,
And, clothed anew, the following games survey.

And now succeed the gifts ordain'd to grace
The youths contending in the rapid race:
A silver urn that full six measures held,
By none in weight or workmanship excell'd:
Sidonian artists taught the frame to shine,
Elaborate, with artifice divine;
Whence Tyrian sailors did the prize transport,
And gave to Thoas at the Lemnian port:
From him descended, good Eunaeus heir'd
The glorious gift; and, for Lycaon spared,
To brave Patroclus gave the rich reward:
Now, the same hero's funeral rites to grace,
It stands the prize of swiftness in the race.
A well-fed ox was for the second placed;
And half a talent must content the last.
Achilles rising then bespoke the train:
"Who hope the palm of swiftness to obtain,
Stand forth, and bear these prizes from the plain."

The hero said, and starting from his place,
Oilean Ajax rises to the race;
Ulysses next; and he whose speed surpass'd
His youthful equals, Nestor's son, the last.
Ranged in a line the ready racers stand;
Pelides points the barrier with his hand;
All start at once; Oileus led the race;
The next Ulysses, measuring pace with pace;
Behind him, diligently close, he sped,
As closely following as the running thread
The spindle follows, and displays the charms
Of the fair spinster's breast and moving arms:
Graceful in motion thus, his foe he plies,
And treads each footstep ere the dust can rise;
His glowing breath upon his shoulders plays:
The admiring Greeks loud acclamations raise:
To him they give their wishes, hearts, and eyes,
And send their souls before him as he flies.
Now three times turn'd in prospect of the goal,
The panting chief to Pallas lifts his soul:
"Assist, O goddess!" thus in thought he pray'd!
And present at his thought descends the maid.
Buoy'd by her heavenly force, he seems to swim,
And feels a pinion lifting every limb.
All fierce, and ready now the prize to gain,
Unhappy Ajax stumbles on the plain

(O'erturn'd by Pallas), where the slippery shore
Was clogg'd with slimy dung and mingled gore.
(The self-same place beside Patroclus' pyre,
Where late the slaughter'd victims fed the fire.)
Besmear'd with filth, and blotted o'er with clay,
Obscene to sight, the rueful racer lay;
The well-fed bull (the second prize) he shared,
And left the urn Ulysses' rich reward.
Then, grasping by the horn the mighty beast,
The baffled hero thus the Greeks address'd:

"Accursed fate! the conquest I forego;
A mortal I, a goddess was my foe;
She urged her favourite on the rapid way,
And Pallas, not Ulysses, won the day."

Thus sourly wail'd he, sputtering dirt and gore;
A burst of laughter echoed through the shore.
Antilochus, more humorous than the rest,
Takes the last prize, and takes it with a jest:

"Why with our wiser elders should we strive?
The gods still love them, and they always thrive.
Ye see, to Ajax I must yield the prize:
He to Ulysses, still more aged and wise;
(A green old age unconscious of decays,
That proves the hero born in better days!)
Behold his vigour in this active race!
Achilles only boasts a swifter pace:
For who can match Achilles? He who can,
Must yet be more than hero, more than man."

The effect succeeds the speech. Pelides cries,
"Thy artful praise deserves a better prize.
Nor Greece in vain shall hear thy friend extoll'd;
Receive a talent of the purest gold."
The youth departs content. The host admire
The son of Nestor, worthy of his sire.

Next these a buckler, spear, and helm, he brings;
Cast on the plain, the brazen burden rings:
Arms which of late divine Sarpedon wore,
And great Patroclus in short triumph bore.
"Stand forth the bravest of our host! (he cries)
Whoever dares deserve so rich a prize,
Now grace the lists before our army's sight,
And sheathed in steel, provoke his foe to fight.
Who first the jointed armour shall explore,

And stain his rival's mail with issuing gore,
The sword Asteropaeus possess'd of old,
(A Thracian blade, distinct with studs of gold,)
Shall pay the stroke, and grace the striker's side:
These arms in common let the chiefs divide:
For each brave champion, when the combat ends,
A sumptuous banquet at our tents attends."

Fierce at the word uprose great Tydeus' son,
And the huge bulk of Ajax Telamon.
Clad in refulgent steel, on either hand,
The dreadful chiefs amid the circle stand;
Louring they meet, tremendous to the sight;
Each Argive bosom beats with fierce delight.
Opposed in arms not long they idly stood,
But thrice they closed, and thrice the charge renew'd.
A furious pass the spear of Ajax made
Through the broad shield, but at the corslet stay'd.
Not thus the foe: his javelin aim'd above
The buckler's margin, at the neck he drove.
But Greece, now trembling for her hero's life,
Bade share the honours, and surcease the strife.
Yet still the victor's due Tydides gains,
With him the sword and studded belt remains.

Then hurl'd the hero, thundering on the ground,
A mass of iron (an enormous round),
Whose weight and size the circling Greeks admire,
Rude from the furnace, and but shaped by fire.
This mighty quoit Aetion wont to rear,
And from his whirling arm dismiss in air;
The giant by Achilles slain, he stow'd
Among his spoils this memorable load.
For this, he bids those nervous artists vie,
That teach the disk to sound along the sky.
"Let him, whose might can hurl this bowl, arise;
Who farthest hurls it, take it as his prize;
If he be one enrich'd with large domain
Of downs for flocks, and arable for grain,
Small stock of iron needs that man provide;
His hinds and swains whole years shall be supplied
From hence; nor ask the neighbouring city's aid
For ploughshares, wheels, and all the rural trade."

Stern Polypoetes stepp'd before the throng,
And great Leonteus, more than mortal strong;
Whose force with rival forces to oppose,
Uprose great Ajax; up Epeus rose.

Each stood in order: first Epeus threw;
High o'er the wondering crowds the whirling circle flew.
Leonteus next a little space surpass'd;
And third, the strength of godlike Ajax cast.
O'er both their marks it flew; till fiercely flung
From Polypoetes' arm the discus sung:
Far as a swain his whirling sheephook throws,
That distant falls among the grazing cows,
So past them all the rapid circle flies:
His friends, while loud applauses shake the skies,
With force conjoin'd heave off the weighty prize.

Those, who in skilful archery contend,
He next invites the twanging bow to bend;
And twice ten axes casts amidst the round,
Ten double-edged, and ten that singly wound
The mast, which late a first-rate galley bore,
The hero fixes in the sandy shore;
To the tall top a milk-white dove they tie,
The trembling mark at which their arrows fly.

"Whose weapon strikes yon fluttering bird, shall bear
These two-edged axes, terrible in war;
The single, he whose shaft divides the cord."
He said: experienced Merion took the word;
And skilful Teucer: in the helm they threw
Their lots inscribed, and forth the latter flew.
Swift from the string the sounding arrow flies;
But flies unbless'd! No grateful sacrifice,
No firstling lambs, unheedful! didst thou vow
To Phoebus, patron of the shaft and bow.
For this, thy well-aim'd arrow turn'd aside,
Err'd from the dove, yet cut the cord that tied:
Adown the mainmast fell the parted string,
And the free bird to heaven displays her wing:
Sea, shores, and skies, with loud applause resound,
And Merion eager meditates the wound:
He takes the bow, directs the shaft above,
And following with his eye the soaring dove,
Implores the god to speed it through the skies,
With vows of firstling lambs, and grateful sacrific
The dove, in airy circles as she wheels,
Amid the clouds the piercing arrow feels;
Quite through and through the point its passage found,
And at his feet fell bloody to the ground.
The wounded bird, ere yet she breathed her last,
With flagging wings alighted on the mast,
A moment hung, and spread her pinions there,

Then sudden dropp'd, and left her life in air.
From the pleased crowd new peals of thunder rise,
And to the ships brave Merion bears the prize.

To close the funeral games, Achilles last
A massy spear amid the circle placed,
And ample charger of unsullied frame,
With flowers high-wrought, not blacken'd yet by flame.
For these he bids the heroes prove their art,
Whose dexterous skill directs the flying dart.
Here too great Merion hopes the noble prize;
Nor here disdain'd the king of men to rise.
With joy Pelides saw the honour paid,
Rose to the monarch, and respectful said:

"Thee first in virtue, as in power supreme,
O king of nations! all thy Greeks proclaim;
In every martial game thy worth attest,
And know thee both their greatest and their best.
Take then the prize, but let brave Merion bear
This beamy javelin in thy brother's war."

Pleased from the hero's lips his praise to hear,
The king to Merion gives the brazen spear:
But, set apart for sacred use, commands
The glittering charger to Talthybius' hands.

BOOK XXIV

ARGUMENT

THE REDEMPTION OF THE BODY OF HECTOR

The gods deliberate about the redemption of Hector's body. Jupiter sends Thetis to Achilles, to dispose him for the restoring it, and Iris to Priam, to encourage him to go in person and treat for it. The old king, notwithstanding the remonstrances of his queen, makes ready for the journey, to which he is encouraged by an omen from Jupiter. He sets forth in his chariot, with a waggon loaded with presents, under the charge of Idaeus the herald. Mercury descends in the shape of a young man, and conducts him to the pavilion of Achilles. Their conversation on the way. Priam finds Achilles at his table, casts himself at his feet, and begs for the body of his son: Achilles, moved with compassion, grants his request, detains him one night in his tent, and the next morning sends him home with the body: the Trojans run out to meet him. The lamentations of Andromache, Hecuba, and Helen, with the solemnities of the funeral.

The time of twelve days is employed in this book, while the body of Hector lies in the tent of Achilles; and as many more are spent in the truce allowed for his interment. The scene is partly in Achilles' camp, and partly in Troy.

Now from the finish'd games the Grecian band
Seek their black ships, and clear the crowded strand,
All stretch'd at ease the genial banquet share,
And pleasing slumbers quiet all their care.
Not so Achilles: he, to grief resign'd,
His friend's dear image present to his mind,
Takes his sad couch, more unobserved to weep;
Nor tastes the gifts of all-composing sleep.
Restless he roll'd around his weary bed,
And all his soul on his Patroclus fed:
The form so pleasing, and the heart so kind,
That youthful vigour, and that manly mind,
What toils they shared, what martial works they wrought,
What seas they measured, and what fields they fought;
All pass'd before him in remembrance dear,
Thought follows thought, and tear succeeds to tear.
And now supine, now prone, the hero lay,
Now shifts his side, impatient for the day:
Then starting up, disconsolate he goes
Wide on the lonely beach to vent his woes.
There as the solitary mourner raves,
The ruddy morning rises o'er the waves:
Soon as it rose, his furious steeds he join'd!
The chariot flies, and Hector trails behind.
And thrice, Patroclus! round thy monument
Was Hector dragg'd, then hurried to the tent.
There sleep at last o'ercomes the hero's eyes;
While foul in dust the unhonour'd carcase lies,
But not deserted by the pitying skies:
For Phoebus watch'd it with superior care,
Preserved from gaping wounds and tainting air;
And, ignominious as it swept the field,
Spread o'er the sacred corse his golden shield.
All heaven was moved, and Hermes will'd to go
By stealth to snatch him from the insulting foe:
But Neptune this, and Pallas this denies,
And th' unrelenting empress of the skies,
E'er since that day implacable to Troy,
What time young Paris, simple shepherd boy,
Won by destructive lust (reward obscene),
Their charms rejected for the Cyprian queen.
But when the tenth celestial morning broke,
To heaven assembled, thus Apollo spoke:

"Unpitying powers! how oft each holy fane
Has Hector tinged with blood of victims slain?
And can ye still his cold remains pursue?
Still grudge his body to the Trojans' view?
Deny to consort, mother, son, and sire,
The last sad honours of a funeral fire?
Is then the dire Achilles all your care?
That iron heart, inflexibly severe;
A lion, not a man, who slaughters wide,
In strength of rage, and impotence of pride;
Who hastes to murder with a savage joy,
Invades around, and breathes but to destroy!
Shame is not of his soul; nor understood,
The greatest evil and the greatest good.
Still for one loss he rages unresign'd,
Repugnant to the lot of all mankind;
To lose a friend, a brother, or a son,
Heaven dooms each mortal, and its will is done:
Awhile they sorrow, then dismiss their care;
Fate gives the wound, and man is born to bear.
But this insatiate, the commission given
By fate exceeds, and tempts the wrath of heaven:
Lo, how his rage dishonest drags along
Hector's dead earth, insensible of wrong!
Brave though he be, yet by no reason awed,
He violates the laws of man and god."

"If equal honours by the partial skies
Are doom'd both heroes, (Juno thus replies,)
If Thetis' son must no distinction know,
Then hear, ye gods! the patron of the bow.
But Hector only boasts a mortal claim,
His birth deriving from a mortal dame:
Achilles, of your own ethereal race,
Springs from a goddess by a man's embrace
(A goddess by ourself to Peleus given,
A man divine, and chosen friend of heaven)
To grace those nuptials, from the bright abode
Yourselves were present; where this minstrel-god,
Well pleased to share the feast, amid the quire
Stood proud to hymn, and tune his youthful lyre."

Then thus the Thunderer checks the imperial dame:
"Let not thy wrath the court of heaven inflame;
Their merits, nor their honours, are the same.
But mine, and every god's peculiar grace
Hector deserves, of all the Trojan race:
Still on our shrines his grateful offerings lay,

(The only honours men to gods can pay,)
Nor ever from our smoking altar ceased
The pure libation, and the holy feast:
Howe'er by stealth to snatch the corse away,
We will not: Thetis guards it night and day.
But haste, and summon to our courts above
The azure queen; let her persuasion move
Her furious son from Priam to receive
The proffer'd ransom, and the corse to leave."

He added not: and Iris from the skies,
Swift as a whirlwind, on the message flies,
Meteorous the face of ocean sweeps,
Refulgent gliding o'er the sable deeps.
Between where Samos wide his forests spreads,
And rocky Imbrus lifts its pointed heads,
Down plunged the maid; (the parted waves resound;)
She plunged and instant shot the dark profound.
As bearing death in the fallacious bait,
From the bent angle sinks the leaden weight;
So pass'd the goddess through the closing wave,
Where Thetis sorrow'd in her secret cave:
There placed amidst her melancholy train
(The blue-hair'd sisters of the sacred main)
Pensive she sat, revolving fates to come,
And wept her godlike son's approaching doom.
Then thus the goddess of the painted bow:
"Arise, O Thetis! from thy seats below,
'Tis Jove that calls."—"And why (the dame replies)
Calls Jove his Thetis to the hated skies?
Sad object as I am for heavenly sight!
Ah may my sorrows ever shun the light!
Howe'er, be heaven's almighty sire obey'd—"
She spake, and veil'd her head in sable shade,
Which, flowing long, her graceful person clad;
And forth she paced, majestically sad.

Then through the world of waters they repair
(The way fair Iris led) to upper air.
The deeps dividing, o'er the coast they rise,
And touch with momentary flight the skies.
There in the lightning's blaze the sire they found,
And all the gods in shining synod round.
Thetis approach'd with anguish in her face,
(Minerva rising, gave the mourner place,)
Even Juno sought her sorrows to console,
And offer'd from her hand the nectar-bowl:
She tasted, and resign'd it: then began

The sacred sire of gods and mortal man:

"Thou comest, fair Thetis, but with grief o'ercast;
Maternal sorrows; long, ah, long to last!
Suffice, we know and we partake thy cares;
But yield to fate, and hear what Jove declares
Nine days are past since all the court above
In Hector's cause have moved the ear of Jove;
'Twas voted, Hermes from his godlike foe
By stealth should bear him, but we will'd not so:
We will, thy son himself the corse restore,
And to his conquest add this glory more.
Then hie thee to him, and our mandate bear:
Tell him he tempts the wrath of heaven too far;
Nor let him more (our anger if he dread)
Vent his mad vengeance on the sacred dead;
But yield to ransom and the father's prayer;
The mournful father, Iris shall prepare
With gifts to sue; and offer to his hands
Whate'er his honour asks, or heart demands."

His word the silver-footed queen attends,
And from Olympus' snowy tops descends.
Arrived, she heard the voice of loud lament,
And echoing groans that shook the lofty tent:
His friends prepare the victim, and dispose
Repast unheeded, while he vents his woes;
The goddess seats her by her pensive son,
She press'd his hand, and tender thus begun:

"How long, unhappy! shall thy sorrows flow,
And thy heart waste with life-consuming woe:
Mindless of food, or love, whose pleasing reign
Soothes weary life, and softens human pain?
O snatch the moments yet within thy power;
Not long to live, indulge the amorous hour!
Lo! Jove himself (for Jove's command I bear)
Forbids to tempt the wrath of heaven too far.
No longer then (his fury if thou dread)
Detain the relics of great Hector dead;
Nor vent on senseless earth thy vengeance vain,
But yield to ransom, and restore the slain."

To whom Achilles: "Be the ransom given,
And we submit, since such the will of heaven."

While thus they communed, from the Olympian bowers
Jove orders Iris to the Trojan towers:

"Haste, winged goddess! to the sacred town,
And urge her monarch to redeem his son.
Alone the Ilian ramparts let him leave,
And bear what stern Achilles may receive:
Alone, for so we will; no Trojan near
Except, to place the dead with decent care,
Some aged herald, who with gentle hand
May the slow mules and funeral car command.
Nor let him death, nor let him danger dread,
Safe through the foe by our protection led:
Him Hermes to Achilles shall convey,
Guard of his life, and partner of his way.
Fierce as he is, Achilles' self shall spare
His age, nor touch one venerable hair:
Some thought there must be in a soul so brave,
Some sense of duty, some desire to save."

Then down her bow the winged Iris drives,
And swift at Priam's mournful court arrives:
Where the sad sons beside their father's throne
Sat bathed in tears, and answer'd groan with groan.
And all amidst them lay the hoary sire,
(Sad scene of woe!) his face his wrapp'd attire
Conceal'd from sight; with frantic hands he spread
A shower of ashes o'er his neck and head.
From room to room his pensive daughters roam;
Whose shrieks and clamours fill the vaulted dome;
Mindful of those, who late their pride and joy,
Lie pale and breathless round the fields of Troy!
Before the king Jove's messenger appears,
And thus in whispers greets his trembling ears:

"Fear not, O father! no ill news I bear;
From Jove I come, Jove makes thee still his care;
For Hector's sake these walls he bids thee leave,
And bear what stern Achilles may receive;
Alone, for so he wills; no Trojan near,
Except, to place the dead with decent care,
Some aged herald, who with gentle hand
May the slow mules and funeral car command.
Nor shalt thou death, nor shall thou danger dread:
Safe through the foe by his protection led:
Thee Hermes to Pelides shall convey,
Guard of thy life, and partner of thy way.
Fierce as he is, Achilles' self shall spare
Thy age, nor touch one venerable hair;
Some thought there must be in a soul so brave,
Some sense of duty, some desire to save."

She spoke, and vanish'd. Priam bids prepare
His gentle mules and harness to the car;
There, for the gifts, a polish'd casket lay:
His pious sons the king's command obey.
Then pass'd the monarch to his bridal-room,
Where cedar-beams the lofty roofs perfume,
And where the treasures of his empire lay;
Then call'd his queen, and thus began to say:

"Unhappy consort of a king distress'd!
Partake the troubles of thy husband's breast:
I saw descend the messenger of Jove,
Who bids me try Achilles' mind to move;
Forsake these ramparts, and with gifts obtain
The corse of Hector, at yon navy slain.
Tell me thy thought: my heart impels to go
Through hostile camps, and bears me to the foe."

The hoary monarch thus. Her piercing cries
Sad Hecuba renews, and then replies:
"Ah! whither wanders thy distemper'd mind?
And where the prudence now that awed mankind?
Through Phrygia once and foreign regions known;
Now all confused, distracted, overthrown!
Singly to pass through hosts of foes! to face
(O heart of steel!) the murderer of thy race!
To view that deathful eye, and wander o'er
Those hands yet red with Hector's noble gore!
Alas! my lord! he knows not how to spare.
And what his mercy, thy slain sons declare;
So brave! so many fallen! To claim his rage
Vain were thy dignity, and vain thy age.
No—pent in this sad palace, let us give
To grief the wretched days we have to live.
Still, still for Hector let our sorrows flow,
Born to his own, and to his parents' woe!
Doom'd from the hour his luckless life begun,
To dogs, to vultures, and to Peleus' son!
Oh! in his dearest blood might I allay
My rage, and these barbarities repay!
For ah! could Hector merit thus, whose breath
Expired not meanly, in unactive death?
He poured his latest blood in manly fight,
And fell a hero in his country's right."

"Seek not to stay me, nor my soul affright
With words of omen, like a bird of night,

(Replied unmoved the venerable man;)
'Tis heaven commands me, and you urge in vain.
Had any mortal voice the injunction laid,
Nor augur, priest, nor seer, had been obey'd.
A present goddess brought the high command,
I saw, I heard her, and the word shall stand.
I go, ye gods! obedient to your call:
If in yon camp your powers have doom'd my fall,
Content—By the same hand let me expire!
Add to the slaughter'd son the wretched sire!
One cold embrace at least may be allow'd,
And my last tears flow mingled with his blood!"

From forth his open'd stores, this said, he drew
Twelve costly carpets of refulgent hue,
As many vests, as many mantles told,
And twelve fair veils, and garments stiff with gold,
Two tripods next, and twice two chargers shine,
With ten pure talents from the richest mine;
And last a large well-labour'd bowl had place,
(The pledge of treaties once with friendly Thrace:)
Seem'd all too mean the stores he could employ,
For one last look to buy him back to Troy!

Lo! the sad father, frantic with his pain,
Around him furious drives his menial train:
In vain each slave with duteous care attends,
Each office hurts him, and each face offends.
"What make ye here, officious crowds! (he cries).
Hence! nor obtrude your anguish on my eyes.
Have ye no griefs at home, to fix ye there:
Am I the only object of despair?
Am I become my people's common show,
Set up by Jove your spectacle of woe?
No, you must feel him too; yourselves must fall;
The same stern god to ruin gives you all:
Nor is great Hector lost by me alone;
Your sole defence, your guardian power is gone!
I see your blood the fields of Phrygia drown,
I see the ruins of your smoking town!
O send me, gods! ere that sad day shall come,
A willing ghost to Pluto's dreary dome!"

He said, and feebly drives his friends away:
The sorrowing friends his frantic rage obey.
Next on his sons his erring fury falls,
Polites, Paris, Agathon, he calls;
His threats Deiphobus and Dius hear,

Hippothous, Pammon, Helenes the seer,
And generous Antiphon: for yet these nine
Survived, sad relics of his numerous line.

"Inglorious sons of an unhappy sire!
Why did not all in Hector's cause expire?
Wretch that I am! my bravest offspring slain.
You, the disgrace of Priam's house, remain!
Mestor the brave, renown'd in ranks of war,
With Troilus, dreadful on his rushing car,
And last great Hector, more than man divine,
For sure he seem'd not of terrestrial line!
All those relentless Mars untimely slew,
And left me these, a soft and servile crew,
Whose days the feast and wanton dance employ,
Gluttons and flatterers, the contempt of Troy!
Why teach ye not my rapid wheels to run,
And speed my journey to redeem my son?"

The sons their father's wretched age revere,
Forgive his anger, and produce the car.
High on the seat the cabinet they bind:
The new-made car with solid beauty shined;
Box was the yoke, emboss'd with costly pains,
And hung with ringlets to receive the reins;
Nine cubits long, the traces swept the ground:
These to the chariot's polish'd pole they bound.
Then fix'd a ring the running reins to guide,
And close beneath the gather'd ends were tied.
Next with the gifts (the price of Hector slain)
The sad attendants load the groaning wain:
Last to the yoke the well-matched mules they bring,
(The gift of Mysia to the Trojan king.)
But the fair horses, long his darling care,
Himself received, and harness'd to his car:
Grieved as he was, he not this task denied;
The hoary herald help'd him, at his side.
While careful these the gentle coursers join'd,
Sad Hecuba approach'd with anxious mind;
A golden bowl that foam'd with fragrant wine,
(Libation destined to the power divine,)
Held in her right, before the steed she stands,
And thus consigns it to the monarch's hands:

"Take this, and pour to Jove; that safe from harms
His grace restore thee to our roof and arms.
Since victor of thy fears, and slighting mine,
Heaven, or thy soul, inspires this bold design;

Pray to that god, who high on Ida's brow
Surveys thy desolated realms below,
His winged messenger to send from high,
And lead thy way with heavenly augury:
Let the strong sovereign of the plumy race
Tower on the right of yon ethereal space.
That sign beheld, and strengthen'd from above,
Boldly pursue the journey mark'd by Jove:
But if the god his augury denies,
Suppress thy impulse, nor reject advice."

"'Tis just (said Priam) to the sire above
To raise our hands; for who so good as Jove?"
He spoke, and bade the attendant handmaid bring
The purest water of the living spring:
(Her ready hands the ewer and bason held:)
Then took the golden cup his queen had fill'd;
On the mid pavement pours the rosy wine,
Uplifts his eyes, and calls the power divine:

"O first and greatest! heaven's imperial lord!
On lofty Ida's holy hill adored!
To stern Achilles now direct my ways,
And teach him mercy when a father prays.
If such thy will, despatch from yonder sky
Thy sacred bird, celestial augury!
Let the strong sovereign of the plumy race
Tower on the right of yon ethereal space;
So shall thy suppliant, strengthen'd from above,
Fearless pursue the journey mark'd by Jove."

Jove heard his prayer, and from the throne on high,
Despatch'd his bird, celestial augury!
The swift-wing'd chaser of the feather'd game,
And known to gods by Percnos' lofty name.
Wide as appears some palace-gate display'd.
So broad, his pinions stretch'd their ample shade,
As stooping dexter with resounding wings
The imperial bird descends in airy rings.
A dawn of joy in every face appears:
The mourning matron dries her timorous tears:
Swift on his car the impatient monarch sprung;
The brazen portal in his passage rung;
The mules preceding draw the loaded wain,
Charged with the gifts: Idaeus holds the rein:
The king himself his gentle steeds controls,
And through surrounding friends the chariot rolls.
On his slow wheels the following people wait,

Mourn at each step, and give him up to fate;
With hands uplifted eye him as he pass'd,
And gaze upon him as they gazed their last.
Now forward fares the father on his way,
Through the lone fields, and back to Ilion they.
Great Jove beheld him as he cross'd the plain,
And felt the woes of miserable man.
Then thus to Hermes: "Thou whose constant cares
Still succour mortals, and attend their prayers;
Behold an object to thy charge consign'd:
If ever pity touch'd thee for mankind,
Go, guard the sire: the observing foe prevent,
And safe conduct him to Achilles' tent."

The god obeys, his golden pinions binds,
And mounts incumbent on the wings of winds,
That high, through fields of air, his flight sustain,
O'er the wide earth, and o'er the boundless main;
Then grasps the wand that causes sleep to fly,
Or in soft slumbers seals the wakeful eye:
Thus arm'd, swift Hermes steers his airy way,
And stoops on Hellespont's resounding sea.
A beauteous youth, majestic and divine,
He seem'd; fair offspring of some princely line!
Now twilight veil'd the glaring face of day,
And clad the dusky fields in sober grey;
What time the herald and the hoary king
(Their chariots stopping at the silver spring,
That circling Ilus' ancient marble flows)
Allow'd their mules and steeds a short repose,
Through the dim shade the herald first espies
A man's approach, and thus to Priam cries:
"I mark some foe's advance: O king! beware;
This hard adventure claims thy utmost care!
For much I fear destruction hovers nigh:
Our state asks counsel; is it best to fly?
Or old and helpless, at his feet to fall,
Two wretched suppliants, and for mercy call?"

The afflicted monarch shiver'd with despair;
Pale grew his face, and upright stood his hair;
Sunk was his heart; his colour went and came;
A sudden trembling shook his aged frame:
When Hermes, greeting, touch'd his royal hand,
And, gentle, thus accosts with kind demand:

"Say whither, father! when each mortal sight
Is seal'd in sleep, thou wanderest through the night?

Why roam thy mules and steeds the plains along,
Through Grecian foes, so numerous and so strong?
What couldst thou hope, should these thy treasures view;
These, who with endless hate thy race pursue?
For what defence, alas! could'st thou provide;
Thyself not young, a weak old man thy guide?
Yet suffer not thy soul to sink with dread;
From me no harm shall touch thy reverend head;
From Greece I'll guard thee too; for in those lines
The living image of my father shines."

"Thy words, that speak benevolence of mind,
Are true, my son! (the godlike sire rejoin'd:)
Great are my hazards; but the gods survey
My steps, and send thee, guardian of my way.
Hail, and be bless'd! For scarce of mortal kind
Appear thy form, thy feature, and thy mind."

"Nor true are all thy words, nor erring wide;
(The sacred messenger of heaven replied;)
But say, convey'st thou through the lonely plains
What yet most precious of thy store remains,
To lodge in safety with some friendly hand:
Prepared, perchance, to leave thy native land?
Or fliest thou now?—What hopes can Troy retain,
Thy matchless son, her guard and glory, slain?"

The king, alarm'd: "Say what, and whence thou art
Who search the sorrows of a parent's heart,
And know so well how godlike Hector died?"
Thus Priam spoke, and Hermes thus replied:

"You tempt me, father, and with pity touch:
On this sad subject you inquire too much.
Oft have these eyes that godlike Hector view'd
In glorious fight, with Grecian blood embrued:
I saw him when, like Jove, his flames he toss'd
On thousand ships, and wither'd half a host:
I saw, but help'd not: stern Achilles' ire
Forbade assistance, and enjoy'd the fire.
For him I serve, of Myrmidonian race;
One ship convey'd us from our native place;
Polyctor is my sire, an honour'd name,
Old like thyself, and not unknown to fame;
Of seven his sons, by whom the lot was cast
To serve our prince, it fell on me, the last.
To watch this quarter, my adventure falls:
For with the morn the Greeks attack your walls;

Sleepless they sit, impatient to engage,
And scarce their rulers check their martial rage."

"If then thou art of stern Pelides' train,
(The mournful monarch thus rejoin'd again,)
Ah tell me truly, where, oh! where are laid
My son's dear relics? what befals him dead?
Have dogs dismember'd (on the naked plains),
Or yet unmangled rest, his cold remains?"

"O favour'd of the skies! (thus answered then
The power that mediates between god and men)
Nor dogs nor vultures have thy Hector rent,
But whole he lies, neglected in the tent:
This the twelfth evening since he rested there,
Untouch'd by worms, untainted by the air.
Still as Aurora's ruddy beam is spread,
Round his friend's tomb Achilles drags the dead:
Yet undisfigured, or in limb or face,
All fresh he lies, with every living grace,
Majestical in death! No stains are found
O'er all the corse, and closed is every wound,
Though many a wound they gave. Some heavenly care,
Some hand divine, preserves him ever fair:
Or all the host of heaven, to whom he led
A life so grateful, still regard him dead."

Thus spoke to Priam the celestial guide,
And joyful thus the royal sire replied:
"Blest is the man who pays the gods above
The constant tribute of respect and love!
Those who inhabit the Olympian bower
My son forgot not, in exalted power;
And heaven, that every virtue bears in mind,
Even to the ashes of the just is kind.
But thou, O generous youth! this goblet take,
A pledge of gratitude for Hector's sake;
And while the favouring gods our steps survey,
Safe to Pelides' tent conduct my way."

To whom the latent god: "O king, forbear
To tempt my youth, for apt is youth to err.
But can I, absent from my prince's sight,
Take gifts in secret, that must shun the light?
What from our master's interest thus we draw,
Is but a licensed theft that 'scapes the law.
Respecting him, my soul abjures the offence;
And as the crime, I dread the consequence.

Thee, far as Argos, pleased I could convey;
Guard of thy life, and partner of thy way:
On thee attend, thy safety to maintain,
O'er pathless forests, or the roaring main."

He said, then took the chariot at a bound,
And snatch'd the reins, and whirl'd the lash around:
Before the inspiring god that urged them on,
The coursers fly with spirit not their own.
And now they reach'd the naval walls, and found
The guards repasting, while the bowls go round;
On these the virtue of his wand he tries,
And pours deep slumber on their watchful eyes:
Then heaved the massy gates, removed the bars,
And o'er the trenches led the rolling cars.
Unseen, through all the hostile camp they went,
And now approach'd Pelides' lofty tent.
On firs the roof was raised, and cover'd o'er
With reeds collected from the marshy shore;
And, fenced with palisades, a hall of state,
(The work of soldiers,) where the hero sat.
Large was the door, whose well-compacted strength
A solid pine-tree barr'd of wondrous length:
Scarce three strong Greeks could lift its mighty weight,
But great Achilles singly closed the gate.
This Hermes (such the power of gods) set wide;
Then swift alighted the celestial guide,
And thus reveal'd—"Hear, prince! and understand
Thou ow'st thy guidance to no mortal hand:
Hermes I am, descended from above,
The king of arts, the messenger of Jove,
Farewell: to shun Achilles' sight I fly;
Uncommon are such favours of the sky,
Nor stand confess'd to frail mortality.
Now fearless enter, and prefer thy prayers;
Adjure him by his father's silver hairs,
His son, his mother! urge him to bestow
Whatever pity that stern heart can know."

Thus having said, he vanish'd from his eyes,
And in a moment shot into the skies:
The king, confirm'd from heaven, alighted there,
And left his aged herald on the car,
With solemn pace through various rooms he went,
And found Achilles in his inner tent:
There sat the hero: Alcimus the brave,
And great Automedon, attendance gave:
These served his person at the royal feast;

Around, at awful distance, stood the rest.

Unseen by these, the king his entry made:
And, prostrate now before Achilles laid,
Sudden (a venerable sight!) appears;
Embraced his knees, and bathed his hands in tears;
Those direful hands his kisses press'd, embrued
Even with the best, the dearest of his blood!

As when a wretch (who, conscious of his crime,
Pursued for murder, flies his native clime)
Just gains some frontier, breathless, pale, amazed,
All gaze, all wonder: thus Achilles gazed:
Thus stood the attendants stupid with surprise:
All mute, yet seem'd to question with their eyes:
Each look'd on other, none the silence broke,
Till thus at last the kingly suppliant spoke:

"Ah think, thou favour'd of the powers divine!
Think of thy father's age, and pity mine!
In me that father's reverend image trace,
Those silver hairs, that venerable face;
His trembling limbs, his helpless person, see!
In all my equal, but in misery!
Yet now, perhaps, some turn of human fate
Expels him helpless from his peaceful state;
Think, from some powerful foe thou seest him fly,
And beg protection with a feeble cry.
Yet still one comfort in his soul may rise;
He hears his son still lives to glad his eyes,
And, hearing, still may hope a better day
May send him thee, to chase that foe away.
No comfort to my griefs, no hopes remain,
The best, the bravest, of my sons are slain!
Yet what a race! ere Greece to Ilion came,
The pledge of many a loved and loving dame:
Nineteen one mother bore—Dead, all are dead!
How oft, alas! has wretched Priam bled!
Still one was left their loss to recompense;
His father's hope, his country's last defence.
Him too thy rage has slain! beneath thy steel,
Unhappy in his country's cause he fell!

"For him through hostile camps I bent my way,
For him thus prostrate at thy feet I lay;
Large gifts proportion'd to thy wrath I bear;
O hear the wretched, and the gods revere!

"Think of thy father, and this face behold!
See him in me, as helpless and as old!
Though not so wretched: there he yields to me,
The first of men in sovereign misery!
Thus forced to kneel, thus grovelling to embrace
The scourge and ruin of my realm and race;
Suppliant my children's murderer to implore,
And kiss those hands yet reeking with their gore!"

These words soft pity in the chief inspire,
Touch'd with the dear remembrance of his sire.
Then with his hand (as prostrate still he lay)
The old man's cheek he gently turn'd away.
Now each by turns indulged the gush of woe;
And now the mingled tides together flow:
This low on earth, that gently bending o'er;
A father one, and one a son deplore:
But great Achilles different passions rend,
And now his sire he mourns, and now his friend.
The infectious softness through the heroes ran;
One universal solemn shower began;
They bore as heroes, but they felt as man.

Satiate at length with unavailing woes,
From the high throne divine Achilles rose;
The reverend monarch by the hand he raised;
On his white beard and form majestic gazed,
Not unrelenting; then serene began
With words to soothe the miserable man:

"Alas, what weight of anguish hast thou known,
Unhappy prince! thus guardless and alone
Two pass through foes, and thus undaunted face
The man whose fury has destroy'd thy race!
Heaven sure has arm'd thee with a heart of steel,
A strength proportion'd to the woes you feel.
Rise, then: let reason mitigate your care:
To mourn avails not: man is born to bear.
Such is, alas! the gods' severe decree:
They, only they are blest, and only free.
Two urns by Jove's high throne have ever stood,
The source of evil one, and one of good;
From thence the cup of mortal man he fills,
Blessings to these, to those distributes ill;
To most he mingles both: the wretch decreed
To taste the bad unmix'd, is cursed indeed;
Pursued by wrongs, by meagre famine driven,
He wanders, outcast both of earth and heaven.

The happiest taste not happiness sincere;
But find the cordial draught is dash'd with care.
Who more than Peleus shone in wealth and power
What stars concurring bless'd his natal hour!
A realm, a goddess, to his wishes given;
Graced by the gods with all the gifts of heaven.
One evil yet o'ertakes his latest day:
No race succeeding to imperial sway;
An only son; and he, alas! ordain'd
To fall untimely in a foreign land.
See him, in Troy, the pious care decline
Of his weak age, to live the curse of thine!
Thou too, old man, hast happier days beheld;
In riches once, in children once excell'd;
Extended Phrygia own'd thy ample reign,
And all fair Lesbos' blissful seats contain,
And all wide Hellespont's unmeasured main.
But since the god his hand has pleased to turn,
And fill thy measure from his bitter urn,
What sees the sun, but hapless heroes' falls?
War, and the blood of men, surround thy walls!
What must be, must be. Bear thy lot, nor shed
These unavailing sorrows o'er the dead;
Thou canst not call him from the Stygian shore,
But thou, alas! may'st live to suffer more!"

To whom the king: "O favour'd of the skies!
Here let me grow to earth! since Hector lies
On the bare beach deprived of obsequies.
O give me Hector! to my eyes restore
His corse, and take the gifts: I ask no more.
Thou, as thou may'st, these boundless stores enjoy;
Safe may'st thou sail, and turn thy wrath from Troy;
So shall thy pity and forbearance give
A weak old man to see the light and live!"

"Move me no more, (Achilles thus replies,
While kindling anger sparkled in his eyes,)
Nor seek by tears my steady soul to bend:
To yield thy Hector I myself intend:
For know, from Jove my goddess-mother came,
(Old Ocean's daughter, silver-footed dame,)
Nor comest thou but by heaven; nor comest alone,
Some god impels with courage not thy own:
No human hand the weighty gates unbarr'd,
Nor could the boldest of our youth have dared
To pass our outworks, or elude the guard.
Cease; lest, neglectful of high Jove's command,

I show thee, king! thou tread'st on hostile land;
Release my knees, thy suppliant arts give o'er,
And shake the purpose of my soul no more."

The sire obey'd him, trembling and o'eraw'd.
Achilles, like a lion, rush'd abroad:
Automedon and Alcimus attend,
(Whom most he honour'd, since he lost his friend,)
These to unyoke the mules and horses went,
And led the hoary herald to the tent;
Next, heap'd on high, the numerous presents bear,
(Great Hector's ransom,) from the polish'd car.
Two splendid mantles, and a carpet spread,
They leave: to cover and enwrap the dead.
Then call the handmaids, with assistant toil
To wash the body and anoint with oil,
Apart from Priam: lest the unhappy sire,
Provoked to passion, once more rouse to ire
The stern Pelides; and nor sacred age,
Nor Jove's command, should check the rising rage.
This done, the garments o'er the corse they spread;
Achilles lifts it to the funeral bed:
Then, while the body on the car they laid,
He groans, and calls on loved Patroclus' shade:

"If, in that gloom which never light must know,
The deeds of mortals touch the ghosts below,
O friend! forgive me, that I thus fulfil
(Restoring Hector) heaven's unquestion'd will.
The gifts the father gave, be ever thine,
To grace thy manes, and adorn thy shrine."

He said, and, entering, took his seat of state;
Where full before him reverend Priam sate;
To whom, composed, the godlike chief begun:
"Lo! to thy prayer restored, thy breathless son;
Extended on the funeral couch he lies;
And soon as morning paints the eastern skies,
The sight is granted to thy longing eyes:
But now the peaceful hours of sacred night
Demand reflection, and to rest invite:
Nor thou, O father! thus consumed with woe,
The common cares that nourish life forego.
Not thus did Niobe, of form divine,
A parent once, whose sorrows equall'd thine:
Six youthful sons, as many blooming maids,
In one sad day beheld the Stygian shades;
Those by Apollo's silver bow were slain,

These, Cynthia's arrows stretch'd upon the plain:
So was her pride chastised by wrath divine,
Who match'd her own with bright Latona's line;
But two the goddess, twelve the queen enjoy'd;
Those boasted twelve, the avenging two destroy'd.
Steep'd in their blood, and in the dust outspread,
Nine days, neglected, lay exposed the dead;
None by to weep them, to inhume them none;
(For Jove had turn'd the nation all to stone.)
The gods themselves, at length relenting gave
The unhappy race the honours of a grave.
Herself a rock (for such was heaven's high will)
Through deserts wild now pours a weeping rill;
Where round the bed whence Achelous springs,
The watery fairies dance in mazy rings;
There high on Sipylus's shaggy brow,
She stands, her own sad monument of woe;
The rock for ever lasts, the tears for ever flow.

"Such griefs, O king! have other parents known;
Remember theirs, and mitigate thy own.
The care of heaven thy Hector has appear'd,
Nor shall he lie unwept, and uninterr'd;
Soon may thy aged cheeks in tears be drown'd,
And all the eyes of Ilion stream around."

He said, and, rising, chose the victim ewe
With silver fleece, which his attendants slew.
The limbs they sever from the reeking hide,
With skill prepare them, and in parts divide:
Each on the coals the separate morsels lays,
And, hasty, snatches from the rising blaze.
With bread the glittering canisters they load,
Which round the board Automedon bestow'd.
The chief himself to each his portion placed,
And each indulging shared in sweet repast.
When now the rage of hunger was repress'd,
The wondering hero eyes his royal guest:
No less the royal guest the hero eyes,
His godlike aspect and majestic size;
Here, youthful grace and noble fire engage;
And there, the mild benevolence of age.
Thus gazing long, the silence neither broke,
(A solemn scene!) at length the father spoke:

"Permit me now, beloved of Jove! to steep
My careful temples in the dew of sleep:
For, since the day that number'd with the dead

My hapless son, the dust has been my bed;
Soft sleep a stranger to my weeping eyes;
My only food, my sorrows and my sighs!
Till now, encouraged by the grace you give,
I share thy banquet, and consent to live."

With that, Achilles bade prepare the bed,
With purple soft and shaggy carpets spread;
Forth, by the flaming lights, they bend their way,
And place the couches, and the coverings lay.
Then he: "Now, father, sleep, but sleep not here;
Consult thy safety, and forgive my fear,
Lest any Argive, at this hour awake,
To ask our counsel, or our orders take,
Approaching sudden to our open'd tent,
Perchance behold thee, and our grace prevent.
Should such report thy honour'd person here,
The king of men the ransom might defer;
But say with speed, if aught of thy desire
Remains unask'd; what time the rites require
To inter thy Hector? For, so long we stay
Our slaughtering arm, and bid the hosts obey."

"If then thy will permit (the monarch said)
To finish all due honours to the dead,
This of thy grace accord: to thee are known
The fears of Ilion, closed within her town;
And at what distance from our walls aspire
The hills of Ide, and forests for the fire.
Nine days to vent our sorrows I request,
The tenth shall see the funeral and the feast;
The next, to raise his monument be given;
The twelfth we war, if war be doom'd by heaven!"

"This thy request (replied the chief) enjoy:
Till then our arms suspend the fall of Troy."

Then gave his hand at parting, to prevent
The old man's fears, and turn'd within the tent;
Where fair Briseis, bright in blooming charms,
Expects her hero with desiring arms.
But in the porch the king and herald rest;
Sad dreams of care yet wandering in their breast.
Now gods and men the gifts of sleep partake;
Industrious Hermes only was awake,
The king's return revolving in his mind,
To pass the ramparts, and the watch to blind.
The power descending hover'd o'er his head:

"And sleep'st thou, father! (thus the vision said:)
Now dost thou sleep, when Hector is restored?
Nor fear the Grecian foes, or Grecian lord?
Thy presence here should stern Atrides see,
Thy still surviving sons may sue for thee;
May offer all thy treasures yet contain,
To spare thy age; and offer all in vain."

Waked with the word the trembling sire arose,
And raised his friend: the god before him goes:
He joins the mules, directs them with his hand,
And moves in silence through the hostile land.
When now to Xanthus' yellow stream they drove,
(Xanthus, immortal progeny of Jove,)
The winged deity forsook their view,
And in a moment to Olympus flew.
Now shed Aurora round her saffron ray,
Sprang through the gates of light, and gave the day:
Charged with the mournful load, to Ilion go
The sage and king, majestically slow.
Cassandra first beholds, from Ilion's spire,
The sad procession of her hoary sire;
Then, as the pensive pomp advanced more near,
(Her breathless brother stretched upon the bier,)
A shower of tears o'erflows her beauteous eyes,
Alarming thus all Ilion with her cries:

"Turn here your steps, and here your eyes employ,
Ye wretched daughters, and ye sons of Troy!
If e'er ye rush'd in crowds, with vast delight,
To hail your hero glorious from the fight,
Now meet him dead, and let your sorrows flow;
Your common triumph, and your common woe."

In thronging crowds they issue to the plains;
Nor man nor woman in the walls remains;
In every face the self-same grief is shown;
And Troy sends forth one universal groan.
At Scaea's gates they meet the mourning wain,
Hang on the wheels, and grovel round the slain.
The wife and mother, frantic with despair,
Kiss his pale cheek, and rend their scatter'd hair:
Thus wildly wailing, at the gates they lay;
And there had sigh'd and sorrow'd out the day;
But godlike Priam from the chariot rose:
"Forbear (he cried) this violence of woes;
First to the palace let the car proceed,
Then pour your boundless sorrows o'er the dead."

The waves of people at his word divide,
Slow rolls the chariot through the following tide;
Even to the palace the sad pomp they wait:
They weep, and place him on the bed of state.
A melancholy choir attend around,
With plaintive sighs, and music's solemn sound:
Alternately they sing, alternate flow
The obedient tears, melodious in their woe.
While deeper sorrows groan from each full heart,
And nature speaks at every pause of art.

First to the corse the weeping consort flew;
Around his neck her milk-white arms she threw,
"And oh, my Hector! Oh, my lord! (she cries)
Snatch'd in thy bloom from these desiring eyes!
Thou to the dismal realms for ever gone!
And I abandon'd, desolate, alone!
An only son, once comfort of our pains,
Sad product now of hapless love, remains!
Never to manly age that son shall rise,
Or with increasing graces glad my eyes:
For Ilion now (her great defender slain)
Shall sink a smoking ruin on the plain.
Who now protects her wives with guardian care?
Who saves her infants from the rage of war?
Now hostile fleets must waft those infants o'er
(Those wives must wait them) to a foreign shore:
Thou too, my son, to barbarous climes shall go,
The sad companion of thy mother's woe;
Driven hence a slave before the victor's sword
Condemn'd to toil for some inhuman lord:
Or else some Greek whose father press'd the plain,
Or son, or brother, by great Hector slain,
In Hector's blood his vengeance shall enjoy,
And hurl thee headlong from the towers of Troy.
For thy stern father never spared a foe:
Thence all these tears, and all this scene of woe!
Thence many evils his sad parents bore,
His parents many, but his consort more.
Why gav'st thou not to me thy dying hand?
And why received not I thy last command?
Some word thou would'st have spoke, which, sadly dear,
My soul might keep, or utter with a tear;
Which never, never could be lost in air,
Fix'd in my heart, and oft repeated there!"

Thus to her weeping maids she makes her moan,

Her weeping handmaids echo groan for groan.

The mournful mother next sustains her part:
"O thou, the best, the dearest to my heart!
Of all my race thou most by heaven approved,
And by the immortals even in death beloved!
While all my other sons in barbarous bands
Achilles bound, and sold to foreign lands,
This felt no chains, but went a glorious ghost,
Free, and a hero, to the Stygian coast.
Sentenced, 'tis true, by his inhuman doom,
Thy noble corse was dragg'd around the tomb;
(The tomb of him thy warlike arm had slain;)
Ungenerous insult, impotent and vain!
Yet glow'st thou fresh with every living grace;
No mark of pain, or violence of face:
Rosy and fair! as Phoebus' silver bow
Dismiss'd thee gently to the shades below."

Thus spoke the dame, and melted into tears.
Sad Helen next in pomp of grief appears;
Fast from the shining sluices of her eyes
Fall the round crystal drops, while thus she cries.

"Ah, dearest friend! in whom the gods had join'd
Tne mildest manners with the bravest mind,
Now twice ten years (unhappy years) are o'er
Since Paris brought me to the Trojan shore,
(O had I perish'd, ere that form divine
Seduced this soft, this easy heart of mine!)
Yet was it ne'er my fate, from thee to find
A deed ungentle, or a word unkind.
When others cursed the authoress of their woe,
Thy pity check'd my sorrows in their flow.
If some proud brother eyed me with disdain,
Or scornful sister with her sweeping train,
Thy gentle accents soften'd all my pain.
For thee I mourn, and mourn myself in thee,
The wretched source of all this misery.
The fate I caused, for ever I bemoan;
Sad Helen has no friend, now thou art gone!
Through Troy's wide streets abandon'd shall I roam!
In Troy deserted, as abhorr'd at home!"

So spoke the fair, with sorrow-streaming eye.
Distressful beauty melts each stander-by.
On all around the infectious sorrow grows;
But Priam check'd the torrent as it rose:

"Perform, ye Trojans! what the rites require,
And fell the forests for a funeral pyre;
Twelve days, nor foes nor secret ambush dread;
Achilles grants these honours to the dead."

He spoke, and, at his word, the Trojan train
Their mules and oxen harness to the wain,
Pour through the gates, and fell'd from Ida's crown,
Roll back the gather'd forests to the town.
These toils continue nine succeeding days,
And high in air a sylvan structure raise.
But when the tenth fair morn began to shine,
Forth to the pile was borne the man divine,
And placed aloft; while all, with streaming eyes,
Beheld the flames and rolling smokes arise.
Soon as Aurora, daughter of the dawn,
With rosy lustre streak'd the dewy lawn,
Again the mournful crowds surround the pyre,
And quench with wine the yet remaining fire.
The snowy bones his friends and brothers place
(With tears collected) in a golden vase;
The golden vase in purple palls they roll'd,
Of softest texture, and inwrought with gold.
Last o'er the urn the sacred earth they spread,
And raised the tomb, memorial of the dead.
(Strong guards and spies, till all the rites were done,
Watch'd from the rising to the setting sun.)
All Troy then moves to Priam's court again,
A solemn, silent, melancholy train:
Assembled there, from pious toil they rest,
And sadly shared the last sepulchral feast.
Such honours Ilion to her hero paid,
And peaceful slept the mighty Hector's shade.

CONCLUDING NOTE

We have now passed through the Iliad, and seen the anger of Achilles, and the terrible effects of it, at an end, as that only was the subject of the poem, and the nature of epic poetry would not permit our author to proceed to the event of the war, it perhaps may be acceptable to the common reader to give a short account of what happened to Troy and the chief actors in this poem after the conclusion of it.

I need not mention that Troy was taken soon after the death of Hector by the stratagem of the wooden horse, the particulars of which are described by Virgil in the second book of the Éneid.

Achilles fell before Troy, by the hand of Paris, by the shot of an arrow in his heel, as Hector had prophesied at his death, lib. xxii.

The unfortunate Priam was killed by Pyrrhus, the son of Achilles.

Ajax, after the death of Achilles, had a contest with Ulysses for the armour of Vulcan, but being defeated in his aim, he slew himself through indignation.

Helen, after the death of Paris, married Deiphobus his brother, and at the taking of Troy betrayed him, in order to reconcile herself to Menelaus her first husband, who received her again into favour.

Agamemnon at his return was barbarously murdered by Ćgysthus, at the instigation of Clytemnestra his wife, who in his absence had dishonoured his bed with Ćgysthus.

Diomed, after the fall of Troy, was expelled his own country, and scarce escaped with his life from his adulterous wife Ćgiale; but at last was received by Daunus in Apulia, and shared his kingdom; it is uncertain how he died.

Nestor lived in peace with his children, in Pylos, his native country.

Ulysses also, after innumerable troubles by sea and land, at last returned in safety to Ithaca, which is the subject of Homer's Odyssey.

For what remains, I beg to be excused from the ceremonies of taking leave at the end of my work, and from embarrassing myself, or others, with any defences or apologies about it. But instead of endeavouring to raise a vain monument to myself, of the merits or difficulties of it (which must be left to the world, to truth, and to posterity), let me leave behind me a memorial of my friendship with one of the most valuable of men, as well as finest writers, of my age and country, one who has tried, and knows by his own experience, how hard an undertaking it is to do justice to Homer, and one whom (I am sure) sincerely rejoices with me at the period of my labours. To him, therefore, having brought this long work to a conclusion, I desire to dedicate it, and to have the honour and satisfaction of placing together, in this manner, the names of Mr. CONGREVE, and of
March 25, 1720

ALEXANDER POPE

Alexander Pope – A Short Biography

Alexander Pope was born in Lombard Street, London, on the 21st of May 1688—the year of the Revolution. His father was a linen-merchant, in thriving circumstances, and said to have noble blood in his veins. His mother was Edith or Editha Turner, daughter of William Turner, Esq., of York. Mr Carruthers, in his excellent Life of the Poet, mentions that there was an Alexander Pope, a clergyman, in the remote parish of Reay, in Caithness, who rode all the way to Twickenham to pay his great namesake a visit, and was presented by him with a copy of the subscription edition of the "Odyssey," in five volumes quarto, which is still preserved by his descendants. Pope's father had made about £10,000 by trade; but being a Roman Catholic, and fond of a country life, he retired from business shortly after the Revolution, at the early age of forty-six. He resided first at Kensington, and then in Binfield, in the neighbourhood of Windsor Forest. He is said to have put his money in a strong box, and to have lived on the principal. His great delight was in his garden; and both he and his wife seem to have cherished the warmest interest in their son, who was very delicate in health, and their only child. Pope's study is still preserved in Binfield; and on the lawn, a cypress-tree which he is said to have planted, is pointed out.

Pope was a premature and precocious child. His figure was deformed—his back humped—his stature short (four feet six inches)—his legs and arms disproportionably long. He was sometimes compared to a spider, and sometimes to a windmill. The only mark of genius lay in his bright and piercing eye. He was sickly in constitution, and required and received great tenderness and care. Once, when three years old, he narrowly escaped from an angry cow, but was wounded in the throat. He was remarkable as a child for his amiable temper; and from the sweetness of his voice, received the name of the Little Nightingale. His aunt gave him his first lessons in reading, and he soon became an enthusiastic lover of books; and by copying printed characters, taught himself to write. When eight years old, he was placed under the care of the family priest, one Bannister, who taught him the Latin and Greek grammars together. He was next removed to a Catholic seminary at Twyford, near Winchester; and while there, read Ogilby's "Homer" and Sandys's "Ovid" with great delight. He had not been long at this school till he wrote a severe lampoon, of two hundred lines' length, on his master—so truly was the "boy the father of the man"—for which demi-Dunciad he was severely flogged. His father, offended at this, removed him to a London school, kept by a Mr Deane. This man taught the poet nothing; but his residence in London gave him the opportunity of attending the theatres. With these he was so captivated, that he wrote a kind of play, which was acted by his schoolfellows, consisting of speeches from Ogilby's "Iliad," tacked together with verses of his own. He became acquainted with Dryden's works, and went to Wills's coffee-house to see him. He says, "Virgilium tantum vidi." Such transient meetings of literary orbs are among the most interesting passages in biography. Thus met Galileo with Milton, Milton with Dryden, Dryden with Pope, and Burns with Scott. Carruthers strikingly remarks, "Considering the perils and uncertainties of a literary life—its precarious rewards, feverish anxieties, mortifications, and disappointments, joined to the tyranny of the Tonsons and Lintots, and the malice and envy of dunces, all of which Dryden had long and bitterly experienced—the aged poet could hardly have looked at the delicate and deformed boy, whose preternatural acuteness and sensibility were seen in his dark eyes, without a feeling approaching to grief, had he known that he was to fight a battle like that under which he was himself then sinking, even though the Temple of Fame should at length open to receive him." At twelve, he wrote the "Ode to Solitude;" and shortly after, his satirical piece on Elkanah Settle, and some of his translations and imitations. His next period, he says, was in Windsor Forest, where for several years he did nothing but read the classics and indite poetry. He wrote a tragedy, a comedy, and four books of an Epic called "Alexander," all of which afterwards he committed to the flames. He translated also a portion of Statius, and Cicero "De Senectute," and "thought himself the greatest genius that ever was." His father encouraged him in his studies, and when his verses did not please him, sent him back to "new turn" them, saying, "These are not good rhymes." His principal favourites were Virgil's "Eclogues," in Latin; and in English, Spencer, Waller, and Dryden—admiring Spencer, we presume, for his luxuriant fancy, Waller for his smooth versification, and Dryden for his vigorous sense and vivid sarcasm. In the Forest, he became acquainted with Sir William Trumbull, the retired secretary of state, a man of general accomplishments, who read, rode, conversed with the youthful poet; introduced him to old Wycherley, the dramatist; and was of material service to his views. With Wycherley, who was old, doted, and excessively vain, Pope did not continue long intimate. A coldness, springing from some criticisms which the youth ventured to make on the veteran's poetry, crept in between them. Walsh of Abberley, in Worcestershire, a man of good sense and taste, became, after a perusal of the "Pastorals" in MS., a warm friend and kind adviser of Pope's, who has immortalised him in more than one of his poems. Walsh told Pope that there had never hitherto appeared in Britain a poet who was at once great and correct, and exhorted him to aim at accuracy and elegance.

When fifteen, he visited London, in order to acquire a more thorough knowledge of French and Italian. At sixteen, he wrote the "Pastorals," and a portion of "Windsor Forest," although they were not published for some time afterwards. By his incessant exertions, he now began to feel his constitution injured. He imagined himself dying, and sent farewell letters to all his friends, including the Abbé Southcot. This gentleman communicated Pope's case to Dr Ratcliffe, who gave him some medical directions; by following which, the poet recovered. He was advised to relax in his studies, and to ride daily; and he prudently followed the advice. Many years afterwards, he repaid the benevolent Abbé by procuring for him, through Sir Robert Walpole, the nomination to an abbey in Avignon. This is only one of many proofs that, notwithstanding his waspish temper, and his no small share of malice as well as vanity, there was a warm heart in our poet.

In 1707, Pope became acquainted with Michael Blount of Maple, Durham, near Reading; whose two sisters, Martha and Teresa, he has commemorated in various verses. On his connexion with these ladies, some mystery rests. Bowles has strongly and plausibly urged that it was not of the purest or most creditable order. Others have contended that it did not go further than the manners of the age sanctioned; and they say, "a much greater license in conversation and in epistolary correspondence was permitted between the sexes than in our decorous age!" We are not careful to try and settle such a delicate question—only we are inclined to suspect, that when common decency quits the words of male and female parties in their mutual communications, it is a very ample charity that can suppose it to adhere to their actions. And nowhere do we find grosser language than in some of Pope's prose epistles to the Blounts.

His "Pastorals," after having been handed about in MS., and shewn to such reputed judges as Lord Halifax, Lord Somers, Garth, Congreve, &c., were at last, in 1709, printed in the sixth volume of Tonson's "Miscellanies." Like all well-finished commonplaces, they were received with instant and universal applause. It is humiliating to contrast the reception of these empty echoes of inspiration, these agreeable centos, with that of such genuine, although faulty poems, as Keat's "Endymion," Shelley's "Queen Mab," and Wordsworth's "Lyrical Ballads." Two years later, (in 1711), a far better and more characteristic production from his pen was ushered anonymously into the world. This was the "Essay on Criticism," a work which he had first written in prose, and which discovers a ripeness of judgment, a clearness of thought, a condensation of style, and a command over the information he possesses, worthy of any age in life, and almost of any mind in time. It serves, indeed, to shew what Pope's true forte was. That lay not so much in poetry, as in the knowledge of its principles and laws, not so much in creation, as in criticism. He was no Homer or Shakspeare; but he might have been nearly as acute a judge of poetry as Aristotle, and nearly as eloquent an expounder of the rules of art and the glories of genius as Longinus.

In the same year, Pope printed "The Rape of the Lock," in a volume of Miscellanies. Lord Petre had, much in the way described by the poet, stolen a lock of Miss Belle Fermor's hair, a feat which led to an estrangement between the families. Pope set himself to reconcile them by this beautiful poem, a poem which has embalmed at once the quarrel and the reconciliation to all future time. In its first version, the machinery was awanting, the "lock" was a desert, the "rape" a natural event, the small infantry of sylphs and gnomes were slumbering uncreated in the poet's mind; but in the next edition he contrived to introduce them in a manner so easy and so exquisite, as to remind you of the variations which occur in dreams, where one wonder seems softly to slide into the bosom of another, and where beautiful and fantastic fancies grow suddenly out of realities, like the bud from the bough, or the fairy-seeming wing of the summer-cloud from the stern azure of the heavens.

A little after this, Pope became acquainted with a far greater, better, and truer man than himself, Joseph Addison. Warburton, and others, have sadly misrepresented the connexion between these two famous wits, as well as their relative intellectual positions. Addison was a more amiable and childlike person than Pope. He had much more, too, of the Christian. He was not so elaborately polished and furbished as the author of "The Rape of the Lock;" but he had, naturally, a finer and richer genius. Pope found early occasion for imagining Addison his disguised enemy. He gave him a hint of his intention to introduce the machinery into "The Rape of the Lock." Of this, Addison disapproved, and said it was a delicious little thing already—merum sal. This, Pope, and some of his friends, have attributed to jealousy; but it is obvious that Addison could not foresee the success with which the machinery was to be managed, and did foresee the difficulties connected with tinkering such an exquisite production. We may allude here to the circumstances which, at a later date, produced an estrangement between these celebrated men. When Tickell, Addison's friend, published the first book of the "Iliad," in opposition to Pope's version, Addison gave it the preference. This moved Pope's indignation, and led him to assert that it was Addison's own composition. In this conjecture he was supported by Edward Young, who had known Tickell long and intimately, and had never heard of him having written at college, as was averred, this translation. It is now, however, we believe, certain, from the MS. which still exists, that Tickell was the real author. A coldness, from this date, began between Pope and Addison. An attempt to reconcile them only made matters worse; and at last the breach was rendered irremediable by Pope's writing the famous character of his rival, afterwards inserted in the Prologue to the Satires, a portrait drawn with the perfection of polished malice and bitter sarcasm, but which seems more a caricature than a likeness. Whatever Addison's faults, his conduct to Pope did not deserve such a return. The whole passage is only one of those painful incidents which disgrace the history of letters, and prove how much spleen, ingratitude, and baseness often co-exist with the highest parts. The words of Pope are as true now as ever they were—"the life of a wit is a warfare upon earth;" and a warfare in which poisoned missiles and every variety of falsehood are still common. We may also here mention, that while the friendship of Pope and Addison lasted, the former contributed the well-known prologue to the latter's "Cato."

One of Pope's most intimate friends in his early days was Henry Cromwell—a distant relative of the great Oliver—a gentleman of fortune, gallantry, and literary taste, who became his agreeable and fascinating, but somewhat dangerous, companion. He is supposed to have initiated Pope into some of the fashionable follies of the town. At this time, Pope's popularity roused one of his most formidable foes against him. This was that Cobbett of criticism, old John Dennis, a man of strong natural powers, much learning, and a rich, coarse vein of humour; but irascible, vindictive, vain, and capricious. Pope had provoked him by an attack in his "Essay on Criticism," and the savage old man revenged himself by a running fire of fierce diatribes against that "Essay" and "The Rape of the Lock." Pope waited till Dennis had committed himself by a powerful but furious assault on Addison's "Cato" (most of which Johnson has preserved in his Life of Pope); and then, partly to court Addison, and partly to indulge his spleen at the critic, wrote a prose satire, entitled, "The Narrative of Dr Robert Norris on the Frenzy of J.D." In this, however, he overshot the mark; and Addison signified to him that he was displeased with the spirit of his narrative, an intimation which Pope keenly resented. This scornful dog would not eat the dirty pudding that was graciously flung to him; and Pope found that, without having conciliated Addison, he had made Dennis's furnace of hate against himself seven times hotter than before.

In 1712 appeared "The Messiah," "The Dying Christian to his Soul," "The Temple of Fame," and the "Elegy on the Memory of an Unfortunate Lady." Her story is still involved in mystery. Her name is said to have been Wainsbury. She was attached to a lover above her degree, some say to the Duke of Berry, whom she had met in her early youth in France. In despair of obtaining her desire, she hanged herself. It is curious, if true, that she was as deformed in person as Pope himself. Her family seems to have been noble. In 1713, he published "Windsor Forest," an "Ode on St Cecilia's Day," and several papers in the Guardian—one of them being an exquisitely ironical paper, comparing Phillip's pastorals with his own, and affecting to give them the preference—the extracts being so selected as to damage his rival's claims. This year, also, he wrote, although he did not publish, his fine epistle to Jervas, the painter. Pope was passionately fond of the art of painting, and practised it a good deal under Jervas's instructions, although he did not reach great proficiency. The prodigy has yet to be born who combines the characters of a great painter and a great poet.

About this time, Pope commenced preparations for the great work of translating Homer; and subscription-papers, accordingly, were issued. Dean Swift was now in England, and took a deep interest in the success of this undertaking, recommending it in coffee-houses, and introducing the subject and Pope's name to the leading Tories. Pope met the Dean for the first time in Berkshire, where, in one of his fits of savage disgust at the conflicting parties of the period, he had retired to the house of a clergyman, and an intimacy commenced which was only terminated by death. We have often regretted that Pope had not selected some author more suitable to his genius than Homer. Horace or Lucretius, or even Ovid, would have been more congenial. His imitations of Horace shew us what he might have made of a complete translation. What a brilliant thing a version of Lucretius, in the style of the "Essay on Man," would have been! And his "Rape of the Lock" proves that he had considerable sympathy with the elaborate fancy, although not with the meretricious graces of Ovid. But with Homer, the severely grand, the simple, the warlike, the lover and painter of all Nature's old original forms—the ocean, the mountains, and the stars—what thorough sympathy could a man have who never saw a real mountain or a battle, and whose enthusiasm for scenery was confined to purling brooks, trim gardens, artificial grottos, and the shades of Windsor Forest? Accordingly, his Homer, although a beautiful and sparkling poem, is not a satisfactory translation of the "Iliad," and still less of the "Odyssey." He has trailed along the naked lances of the Homeric lines so many flowers and leaves that you can hardly recognise them, and feel that their point is deadened and their power gone. This at least is our opinion; although many to this day continue to admire these translations, and have even said that if they are not Homer, they are something better.

The "Iliad" took him six years, and was a work which cost him much anxiety as well as labour, the more as his scholarship was far from profound. He was assisted in the undertaking by Parnell (who wrote the Life of Homer), by Broome, Jortin, and others. The first volume appeared in June 1715, and the other volumes followed at irregular intervals. He began it in 1712, his twenty-fifth year, and finished it in 1718, his thirtieth year. Previous to its appearance, his remuneration for his poems had been small, and his circumstances were embarrassed; but the result of the subscription, which amounted to £5320, 4s., rendered him independent for life.

While at Binfield, he had often visited London; and there, in the society of Howe, Garth, Parnell, and the rest, used to indulge in occasional excesses, which did his feeble constitution no good; and once, according to Colley Cibber, he narrowly escaped a serious scrape in a house of a certain description, Colley, by his own account, "helping out the tomtit for the sake of Homer!" This statement, indeed, Pope has denied; but his veracity was by no means his strongest point. After writing a "Farewell to London," he retired, in 1715, to Twickenham, along with his parents; and remained there, cultivating his garden, digging his grottos, and diversifying his walks, till the end of his days.

Some years before, he had become acquainted with Lady Mary Wortley Montague, the most brilliant woman of her age—witty, fascinating, beautiful, and accomplished—full of enterprise and spirit, too, although decidedly French in her tastes, manners, and character. Pope fell violently in love with her, and had her undoubtedly in his eye when writing "Eloisa and Abelard," which he did at Oxford in 1716, shortly after her going abroad, and which appeared the next year. His passion was not requited, nay, was treated with contempt and ridicule; and he became in after years a bitter enemy and foul-mouthed detractor of the lady, although after her return, in 1718, she resided near him at Twickenham, and they seemed outwardly on good terms.

In 1717, and the succeeding year, Pope lost successively his father, Parnell, Garth, and Rowe, and bitterly felt their loss. He finished, as we have seen, the "Iliad" in 1718; but the fifth and sixth volumes, which were the last, did not appear till 1720. Its success, which at the time was triumphant, roused against him the whole host of envy and detraction. Dennis, and all Grub Street with him, were moved to assail him. Pamphlets after pamphlets were published, all of which, after reading with writhing anguish, Pope had the resolution to bind up into volumes—a great collection of calumny, which he preserved, probably, for purposes of future revenge. His own friends, on the other hand, hailed his work with applause, Gay writing a most graceful and elegant poem, in ottava rima, entitled, "Mr Pope's Welcome Home from Greece," in which his different friends are pictured as receiving him home on the shores of Britain, after an absence of six years. Bentley, that stern old Grecian, avoided the extremes of a howling Grub Street on the one hand, and a flattering aristocracy on the other, and expressed what is, we think, the just opinion when he said, "It is a pretty poem, but it is not Homer."

In 1721, he issued a selection from the poems of Parnell, and prefixed a very beautiful dedication to the Earl of Oxford, commencing with—

"Such were the notes thy once-loved poet sung,
Till death untimely stopp'd his tuneful tongue.
Oh, just beheld and lost, admired and mourn'd,
With softest manners, gentlest arts adorn'd!"

In 1722, he engaged to translate the "Odyssey." He employed Broome and Fenton as his assistants in the work; and the portions translated by them were thought as good as his. He remunerated them very handsomely. Of this work, the first three quarto volumes appeared in 1725; and the fourth and fifth, which completed the work, the following year. Pope sold the copyright to Lintot for £600.

He was busy at this time, too, with an edition of Shakspeare, not quite worthy of either poet. It appeared in six volumes, quarto, in 1725. His preface was good, but he was deficient in antiquarian lore; and his mortification was extreme when Theobald, destined to figure in "The Dunciad," a mere plodding hack, not only in his "Shakspeare Restored," exposed many blunders in Pope's edition; but issued, some years afterwards, an edition of his own, which was much better received by the public.

In 1726, there was a great gathering of the Tory wits at Twickenham. Swift had come from Ireland, and resided for some time with Pope. Bolingbroke came over occasionally from Dawley; and Gay was often there to laugh with, and be laughed at by, the rest. Swift had "Gulliver's Travels"—the most ingenious and elaborate libel against man and God ever written—in his pocket, nearly ready for publication; and we may conceive the grim, sardonic smile with which he read it to his friends, and their tumultuous mirth. Gay was projecting his "Beggars' Opera," and Pope preparing some of his witty "Miscellanies." At the end of two months, the Dean was hurried home by the tidings of Stella's illness. He left the "Travels" behind him, for the copyright of which Pope procured £300, a sum counted then very large, and which Swift generously handed over to Pope.

In September this year, when returning in Lord Bolingbroke's coach from Dawley, the poet was overturned in a little rivulet near Twickenhan, and nearly drowned. The unfortunate little man! One is reminded of Gulliver's accident in the Brobdignagian cream-pot. In trying to break the glasses of the coach, which were down, he severely cut his right hand, and lost the use of two of his fingers, an addition to his other deformities not very desirable; and we suspect that Pope thought Voltaire (who had met him at Bolingbroke's) but a miserable comforter, when, in a letter of pretended condolence, he asked—"Is it possible that those fingers which have written 'The Rape of the Lock,' and dressed Homer so becomingly in an English coat, should have been so barbarously treated? Let the hand of Dennis or of your poetasters be cut off; yours is sacred." It was perhaps in keeping that those mutilated fingers were soon to be employed in attacking Dennis, and that the embittered poet was about, with the half of his hand, but with the whole of his heart, to write "The Dunciad."

In the end of April 1727, we find Swift again in Twickenham, where his irritation at the continued ascendancy of Sir Robert Walpole served to infuse more venom into the "Miscellanies" concocted between him and Pope, two volumes of which appeared in June this year. Gay, also, and the ingenious and admirable Dr Arbuthnot, contributed their quota to these volumes. Swift speedily fell ill with that giddiness and deafness which were the avant-couriers of his final malady; and in August he left Twickenham, and in October, London and England, for ever.

In these "Miscellanies" there appeared the famous "Memoirs of Martinus Scriblerus," written chiefly by Pope, in which he lashed the various proficients in the bathos, under the names of flying fishes, swallows, parrots, frogs, eels, &c., and appended the initials of well-known authors to each head. This roused Grub Street, whose malice had nearly fallen asleep, into fresh fury, and he was bitterly assailed in every possible form. Like Hyder Ali, he now—to travesty Burke—"in the recesses of a mind capacious of such things, determined to leave all Duncedom an everlasting monument of vengeance, and became at length so confident of his force, so collected in his might, that he made no secret whatever of his dreadful resolution, but, compounding all the materials of fun, sarcasm, irony, and invective, into one black cloud, he hung for a while on the declivities of Richmond Hill; and whilst the authors were idly and stupidly gazing on this menacing meteor which blackened all their horizon, it suddenly burst and poured down the whole of its contents on the garrets of Grub Street. Then issued a scene of (ludicrous) woe, the like of which no eye had seen, no heart conceived, and which no tongue can adequately tell. All the horrors of literary war before known or heard of—(MacFlecknoe, the Rehearsal, &c.)—were mercy to the new tempest of havoc which burst from the brain of this remorseless poet. A storm of universal laughter filled every bookseller's shop, and penetrated into the remotest attics. The miserable dunces, in part, were stricken mad with rage—in part, dumb with consternation. Some fled for refuge to ale, and others to ink; while not a few fell, or feared to fall, into the 'jaws of famine.'" This singular poem was written in 1727. It was first printed surreptitiously (i.e., with the connivance of the author) in Dublin, and then reprinted in London. The first perfect edition, however, did not appear in London till 1729. On the day of its publication, according to Pope, a crowd of authors besieged the publisher's shop; and by entreaties, threats, nay, cries of treason, tried to hinder its appearance. What a scene it must have been—of teeth gnashing above ragged coats, and eyes glaring through old periwigs—of faces livid with famine and ferocity; while, to complete the confusion, hawkers, booksellers, and even lords, were mixed with the crowd, clamouring for its issue! And as, says Pope, "there is no stopping a torrent with a finger, out it came." The consequence he had foreseen. A universal howl of rage and pain burst from the aggrieved dunces, on whose naked sides the hot pitch had fallen. They pushed their rejoinders beyond the limits of civilised literary warfare; and although Pope had been coarse in his language, they were coarser far, and their blackguardism was not redeemed by wit or genius. Pope felt, or seemed to feel, entire indifference as to these assaults. On some of them, indeed, he could afford to look down with contempt, on account of their obvious animus and gross language. Others, again, were neutralised by the fact, that their authors had provoked reprisals by their previous insults or ingratitude to Pope. Many, however, were too obscure for his notice; and some, such as Aaron Hill and Bentley, did not deserve to be classed with the Theobalds and Ralphs. To Hill, he, after some finessing, was compelled to make an apology. Altogether, although this production increased Pope's fame, and the conception of his power, it did not tend to shew him in the most amiable light, or perhaps to promote his own comfort or peace of mind. After having emptied out his bile in "The Dunciad," he ought to have become mellower in temper, and resigned satire for ever. He continued, on the contrary, as ill-natured as before; and although he afterwards flew at higher game, the iron had entered into his soul, and he remained a satirist, and therefore an unhappy man, for life.

In 1731 appeared an "Epistle on Taste," which was very favourably received; only his enemies accused him of having satirised the Duke of Chandos in it, a man who had befriended Pope, and had lent him money. Pope denied the charge, although it is very possible, both from his own temperament, and from the frequent occurrence of similar cases of baseness in literary life, that it may have been true. Nothing is more common than for those who have been most liberally helped, to become first the secret, and then the open, enemies of their benefactors. In 1732 appeared his epistle on "The Use of Riches," addressed to Lord Bathurst. These two epistles were afterwards incorporated in his "Moral Essays."

As far back as 1725, Pope had been revolving the subject of the "Essay on Man;" and, indeed, some of its couplets remind you of "pebbles which had long been rolled over and polished in the ocean of his mind." It has been asserted, but not proved, that Lord Bolingbroke gave him the outline of this essay in prose. It is unquestionable, indeed, that Bolingbroke exercised influence over Pope's mind, and may have suggested some of the thoughts in the Essay; but it is not probable that a man like Pope would have set himself on such a subject simply to translate from another's mind. He published the first epistle of the Essay, in 1732, anonymously, as an experiment, and had the satisfaction to see it successful. It was received with rapture, and passed through several editions ere the author was known; although we must say that the value of this reception is considerably lessened, when we remember that the critics could not have been very acute who did not detect Pope's "fine Roman hand" in every sentence of this brilliant but most unsatisfactory and shallow performance.

In the same year died dear, simple-minded Gay, who found in Pope a sincere mourner, and an elegant elegiast; and on the 7th of June 1733, expired good old Mrs Pope, at the age of ninety-four. Pope, who had always been a dutiful son, erected an obelisk in his own grounds to her memory, with a simple but striking inscription in Latin. During this year, he published the third part of the "Essay on Man," an epistle to Lord Cobham, On the Knowledge and Characters of Man, and an Imitation of the First Satire of the Second Book of Horace. In this last, he attacks, in the most brutal style, his former love Lady Mary W. Montague, who replied in a piece of coarse cleverness, entitled, "Verses to the Imitator of the First Satire of the Second Book of Horace,"—verses in which she was assisted by Lord Harvey, another of Pope's victims. He wrote, but was prudent enough to suppress, an ironical reply.

In 1734 appeared his very clever and highly-finished epistle to Dr Arbuthnot (now entitled the "Prologue to the Satires"), who was then languishing toward death. Arbuthnot, from his deathbed, solemnly advised Pope to regulate his satire, and seems to have been afraid of his personal safety from his numerous foes. Pope replied in a manly but self-defensive style. He is said about this time to have in his walks carried arms, and had a large dog as his protector; but none of the dunces had courage enough to assail him. Dennis, who was no dunce, might have ventured on it—but he had become miserably infirm, poor, and blind; and Pope had heaped coals of fire on his head, by contributing a Prologue to a play which was acted for his behoof.

Our author's life becomes now little else than a record of multiplying labours and increasing infirmities. In 1734 appeared the fourth part of the "Essay on Man," and the Second Satire of the Second Book of Horace. In 1735 were issued his "Characters of Women: An Epistle to a Lady" (Martha Blount). In this appears his famous character of Atossa—the Duchess of Marlborough. It is said—we fear too truly—that these lines being shewn to her Grace, as a character of the Duchess of Buckingham, she recognised in them her own likeness, and bribed Pope with a thousand pounds to suppress it. He did so religiously—as long as she was alive—and then published it! In the same year he printed a second volume of his "Miscellaneous Works," in folio and quarto, uniform with the "Iliad" and "Odyssey," including a versification of the Satires of Donne; also, anonymously, a production disgraceful to his memory, entitled, "Sober Advice from Horace to the Young Gentlemen about Town," in which he commits many gross indecorums of language, and annexes the name of the great Bentley to several indecent notes. It is said that Bentley, when he read the pamphlet, cried, "'Tis an impudent dog, but I talked against his Homer, and the portentous cub never forgives."

The "Essay on Man" and the "Moral Epistles" were designed to be parts of a great system of ethics, which Pope had long revolved in his mind, and wished to incarnate in poetry. At this time occurred the strange, mysterious circumstances connected with the publication of his letters. It seems that, in 1729, Pope had recalled from his correspondents the letters he had written them, of many of which he had kept no copies. He was induced to this by the fact, that after Henry Cromwell's death, his mistress, Mrs Thomas, who was in indigent circumstances, had sold the letters which had passed between Pope and her keeper, to Curll the bookseller, who had published them without scruple. When Pope obtained his correspondence, he, according to his own statement, burned a great many and laid past the others, after having had a copy of them taken, and deposited in Lord Oxford's library. And his charge against Curll was, that he obtained surreptitiously some of these letters, and published them without Pope's consent. But, ere we come to the circumstances of the publication, several other things require to be noticed. In 1733, Curll, anxious to publish a Life of Pope, advertised for information; and, in consequence, one P.T., who professed to be an old friend of Pope's and his father's, wrote Curll a letter, giving an account of Pope's ancestry, which tallied exactly with what Pope himself, in a note to one of his poems, furnished the following year. P.T., in a second letter, offered to the publisher a large collection of Pope's letters, and inclosed a copy of an advertisement he had drawn out to be published by Curll. Strange as it seems, Curll took no notice of the proposal till 1735, when, having accidentally turned up a copy of P.T.'s advertisement, he sent it to Pope, with a letter requesting an interview, and mentioning that he had some papers of P.T.'s in reference to his family history, which he would shew him. Pope replied by three advertisements in the papers, denying all knowledge of P.T. or his collection of letters or MSS. P.T. then wrote Curll that he had printed the letters at his own expense, seeking a sum of money for them, and appointing an interview at a tavern to shew him the sheets. This was countermanded the next day, P.T. professing to be afraid of Pope and his "bravoes," although how Pope was to know of this meeting was, according to Curll, "the cream of the jest."

Soon after, a round, fat man, with a clergyman's gown and a barrister's band, called on Curll, at ten o'clock at night. He said his name was Smith, that he was a cousin of P.T.'s, and shewed the book in sheets, along with about a dozen of the original letters. After a good deal of negotiation with this personage, Curll obtained fifty copies of P.T.'s printed copies, and issued a flaming advertisement announcing the publication of Pope's letters for thirty years, and stating that the original MSS. were lying at his shop, and might be seen by any who chose, although not a single MS. seems to have been delivered. Smith, the day that the advertisement appeared, handed over, for a sum of money, about three hundred volumes to Curll. But as in the advertisement it was stated that various letters of lords were included, and as there is a law amongst regulations of the Upper House that no peer's letters can be published without his consent, at the instance of the Earl of Jersey, and in consequence, too, of an advertisement of Pope's, the books were seized, and Curll, and the printer of the paper where the advertisement appeared, were ordered to appear at the bar for breach of privilege. P.T. wrote Curll to tell him to conceal all that passed between him and the publisher, and promising him more valuable letters still. Curll, however, told the whole story; and as, when the books were examined, not a single lord's letter was found among them, Curll was acquitted, his books restored to him, the lords saying that they had been made the tools of Pope; and he proceeded to advertise the correspondence, in terms most insulting to Pope, who now felt himself compelled (!) to print, by subscription, his genuine letters, which, when printed, turned out, strange to tell, to be identical with those published by the rapacious bookseller! On viewing the whole transaction, we incline with Johnson, Warton, Bowles, Macaulay, and Carruthers, to look upon it as one of Pope's ape-like stratagems—to believe that P.T. was himself, Smith his agent, and that his objects were partly to outwit Curll, to mystify the public, to gratify that strange love of manoeuvring which dwelt as strongly in him as in any match-making mamma, and to attract interest and attention to the genuine correspondence when it should appear. Pope, it was said, could not "drink tea without a stratagem," and far less publish his correspondence without a series of contemptible tricks—tricks, however, in which he was true to his nature—that being a curious compound of the woman and the wit, the monkey and the genius.

In 1737, four of his Imitations of Horace were published, and in the next year appeared two Dialogues, each entitled "1738," which now form the Epilogue to the Satires. One of them was issued on the same day with Johnson's "London." In that year, too, he published his "Universal Prayer,"—a singular specimen of latitudinarian thought, expressed in a loose simplicity of language, quite unusual with its author. The next year he had intended to signalise by a third Dialogue, which he commenced in a vigorous style, but which he did not finish, owing to the dread of a prosecution before the Lords; and with the exception of letters (one of them interesting, as his last to Swift), his pen was altogether idle. In 1740, he did nothing but edit an edition of select Italian Poets. This year, Crousaz, a Swiss professor of note, having attacked (we think most justly) the "Essay on Man" as a mere Pagan prolusion—a thin philosophical smile cast on the Gordian knot of the mystery of the universe, instead of a sword cutting, or trying to cut, it in sunder—Warburton, a man of much talent and learning, but of more astuteness and anxiety to exalt himself, came forward to the rescue, and, with a mixture of casuistical cunning and real ingenuity, tried, as some one has it, "to make Pope a Christian," although, even in Warburton's hands, like the dying Donald Bane in "Waverley," he "makes but a queer Christian after all;" and his system, essentially Pantheistic, contrives to ignore the grand Scripture principles of a Fall, of a Divine Redeemer, of a Future World, and the glorious light or darkness which these and other Christian doctrines cast upon the Mystery of Man. If, however, Warburton, with all his scholastic subtlety, failed to make Pope a Christian, he made him a warm friend; Allen, Pope's acquaintance, a rich father-in-law; and himself, by and by, the Bishop of Gloucester. Sophistry has seldom, although sometimes, been thus richly rewarded.

The last scene of Pope's tiny and tortured existence was now at hand. But ere it closed, it must close like Dryden's, characteristically, with an author's quarrel. Colley Cibber had long been a favourite of Pope's ire, and had as often retorted scorn, till at last, by laughing upon the stage at Pope's play (partly Gay's), entitled, "Three Hours After Marriage," he roused the bard almost to frenzy; and Pope set to work to remodel "The Dunciad;" and, dethroning Theobald, set up Cibber as the lawful King of the Dull, a most unfortunate substitution, since, while Theobald was the ideal of stolid, solemn stupidity, Cibber was gay, light, pert, and clever; full of pluck, too, and who overflowed in reply, with pamphlets which gave Pope both a headache and a heartache whenever he perused them.

Pope had never been strong, and for many years the variety and multitude of his frailties had been increasing. He had habitually all his life been tormented with headaches, for which he found the steam of strong coffee the chief remedy. He had hurt his stomach, too, by indulging in excess of stimulating viands, such as potted lampreys, and in copious and frequent drams. He was assailed at last by dropsy and asthma; and on the 30th of May 1744, he breathed his last, fifty-six years of age. He had long, he said, "been tired of the world," and died with philosophic composure and serenity. He took the sacrament according to the form of the Roman Catholic Church; but merely, he said, because it "looked right." A little before his death, he called for his desk, and began an essay on the immortality of the soul, and on those material things which tend to weaken or to strengthen it for immortality, enumerating generous wines as among the latter influences, and spirituous liquors among the former! His last words were, "There is nothing that is meritorious but virtue and friendship; and, indeed, friendship itself is only a part of virtue." Thus, "motionless and moanless," without a word about Christ—the slightest syllable of repentance—and with a scrap of heathen morality in his mouth, died the brilliant Alexander Pope. Who is ready to say, "May my last end be like his"? His favourite Martha Blount behaved, according to some accounts, with disgusting unconcern on the occasion. So true it is, "there is no friendship among the wicked," even although the heartless Bolingbroke, too, was by, and seems to have succeeded in squeezing out some crocodile tears, as he bent over the dying poet, and said, "O God! what is man?" His remains were, according to his wish, deposited in Twickenham church, near his parents, where the single letter P on the stone alone distinguishes the spot.

Pope's character, apart from his poetry, which we intend criticising in our next volume, was not specially interesting or elevated. He was a spoiled child, a small self-tormentor, full to bursting with petty spites, mean animosities, and unfounded jealousies. While he sought, with the fury of a pampered slave, to trample on those authors that were beneath him in rank or in popularity, he could on all occasions fawn with the sycophancy of a eunuch upon the noble, the rich, and the powerful. Hazlitt speaks of Moore as a "pug-dog barking from the lap of a lady of quality at inferior passengers." The description is far more applicable to Pope. We have much allowance to make for the influence exerted on his mind by his singularly crooked frame and sickly habit of body, by his position as belonging to a proscribed faith, and by his want of training in a public school; but after all these deductions, we cannot but deplore the spectacle of one of the finest, clearest, and sharpest minds that England ever produced, so frequently reminding you of a bright sting set in the body, and steeped in the venom, of a wasp. And yet, withal, he possessed many virtues, which endeared him to a multitude of friends. He was a kind son. He was a faithful and devoted friend. He loved, if not man, yet many men with deep tenderness. A keen politician he was not; but, so far as he went along with his party, he was true to the common cause. In morals, he was greatly superior, in point of external decorum, to most of the wits of the time; but in falsehood, finesse, treachery, and envy, he stood at the bottom of the list, without that plea of poverty, or wretchedness, or despair, which so many of them might have urged. Uneasy, indeed, he always, and unhappy he often, was; but very much of his uneasiness and unhappiness sprung from his own fault. He attacked others, and could not bear to be attacked in return. He was a bully and a coward. He threw himself into a thorn-hedge, and was amazed that he came out covered with scratches and blood. While he shone in satirising many kinds of vice, he laid himself open to retort by his own want of delicacy. He, as well as Swift, was fond of alluding in his verse to polluted and forbidden things. There, and there alone, his taste deserted him; and there is something disgusting and unnatural in the combination of the elegant and the obscene—the coarse in sentiment and the polished in style. And whatever may be said for many of the amiable traits of the Man, there is very little to be said for the general tendency—so far as healthy morality and Christian principle are concerned—of the writings of the Poet.

Alexander Pope – A Concise Bibliography

The Major works
Pastorals (1709)
An Essay on Criticism (1711)
Messiah (1712)
The Rape of the Lock (1712 and enlarged in 1714)
Windsor Forest (1713)
Translation of the Iliad (1715-1720)
Eloisa to Abelard (1717)
Three Hours After Marriage, with others (1717)
Elegy to the Memory of an Unfortunate Lady (1717)
The Works of Shakespear, in Six Volumes (1723-1725)
Translation of the Odyssey (1725-1726)
Peri Bathous, Or the Art of Sinking in Poetry (1727)
The Dunciad (1728)
Essay on Man (1733-1734)
The Prologue to the Satires (1735)

www.ingramcontent.com/pod-product-compliance
Lightning Source LLC
Chambersburg PA
CBHW071618170426
43195CB00038B/1345